Not For Tourists Guide™ to **NEW YORK CITY**

W9-AFY-742

2007

Not For Tourists, Inc

published and designed by:
Not For Tourists, Inc
NFT™—Not For Tourists™ Guide to New York City 2007
www.notfortourists.com

Publisher
Jane Pirone

Information Design
Jane Pirone
Rob Tallia
Scot Covey
Ben Bray

Managing Editor
Rob Tallia

Database Manager
Ben Bray

City Editors
Nicole Baker
Krikor Daglian
Sarah Liston

Writing and Editing
Nicole Baker
Jake Bauman
Kristen Ball

Lauren Blankstein
Joshua Daniel Cochran
Dave Crish
Krikor Daglian
Michael Dale
V. Leslie Hendrickson
Katie Liederman
Sarah Liston
W. Scott Lyon
Liz Moran
Heather Quinlan
Jennifer Keeney Sendrow
Susan Shay
Marti Trgovich

Contributors
Ellen Diamond
Annie Holt
Judith-Noëlle Lamb
Steven McGhee
Will Meyer
Andreas Sugar
Sabina Wolfson

Research
Michael Dale
Ray Downs
Manny Rodriguez
Sho Spaeth

**Graphic Design/
Production**
Chesley Andrews
Scot Covey
Jeanette Rodriguez

Research Interns
Maggie Barron
Lily Chu

Graphic Design Intern
Lisette de Orbegoso

Proofing
Jack Schieffer

NFT would like to thank **Diana Pizzari**
for her hard work and dedication over
the past five years—best of luck!

All rights reserved. No portion of this book may be reproduced without written permission
from the publisher.

Printed in China
ISBN#0-9778031-1-2 $14.95
Copyright © 2006 by Not For Tourists, Inc.

Every effort has been made to ensure that the information in this book is as up-to-date as
possible at press time. However, many details are liable to change—as we have learned. The
publishers cannot accept responsibility for any consequences arising from the use of this
book.

Not For Tourists does not solicit individuals, organizations, or businesses for listings inclusion
in our guides, nor do we accept payment for inclusion into the editorial portion of our
book; the advertising sections, however, are exempt from this policy. We always welcome
communications from anyone regarding ANYTHING having to do with our books; please visit
us on our website at www.notfortourists.com for appropriate contact information.

Dear NFT User,

One of the best perks of being a New Yorker is being able to pull out a killer restaurant suggestion or realizing which hardware store carries the good shower hooks. Something about finding the bodega with the ripest fruit ups the ante for the jackpot for which we all strive: knowing the city inside and out. A notch in one's belt, if you will. The degree to which you morph from a transplant into a full-blown resident. The multi-weathered hat that looks so damn good.

Just as designers gravitate towards muses, and apprentices study under mentors, you, City Slicker, need a guide. Chances are, you've already gone mission impossible on the whole venture and have built a special pocket inside the double-lining of your coat to house your laminated and monogrammed NFT. The one that you have the bookstore put on hold for you every January. And if that's the case, then you'll be eager to unwrap each piece of luscious editorial candy we've added to the 2007 edition: scales to all the maps, so that you won't be confused by the bird's eye view; cross-streets for each listing; closing times for all restaurant kitchens (as your prime feasting continues to edge closer to midnight); self-storage and van/truck rental locations (for all those shoot-me moving adventures); and entirely new pages for Riverside Park, Hudson River Park, the Museum of Natural History, and the United Nations.

As you start piecemealing your way through this nifty black book, know that mighty words of talented souls fill your wandering eye. The contributors and the mighty NFT staff continue to draw expertise and energy from this city and cities across the country. Without them and their passions, we'd just be a bunch of mismatched socks left in the dryer. Our sincere appreciation goes out to them. And to all of you who use this book and have no problem reminding us we missed your fave bar, talk to us at www. notfortourists.com.

Here's to knowing this city inside and out,

Jane, Rob, Krikor, Nicole & Sarah

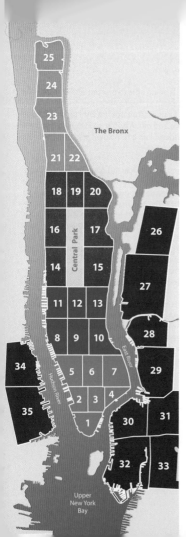

Subbook Map/Bus Map
foldout, last page

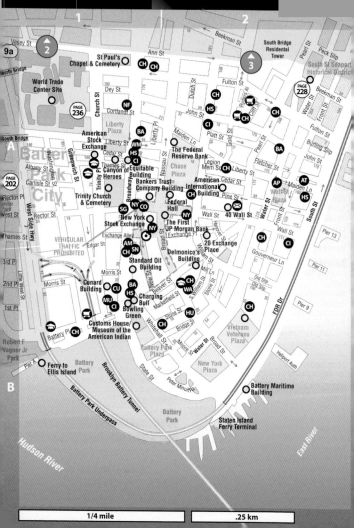

Okay, so here's where Gotham City got its name. Take away the concrete slabs, the looming skyscrapers, and the eerie sense of quiet cash, and you're left with history, tradition, and young, hungry VIPs. One-up 'em, Clark Kent. You know where the true ROIs are hidden downtown.

Bagels

• **Champs** • 70 Exchange Pl [New]

Banks

AM • Amalgamated • 52 Broadway [Exchange Pl]
AP • Apple • Wall St Plz [Maiden Ln]
AT • Atlantic • 15 Maiden Ln [Liberty Pl]
AT • Atlantic (ATM) • 71 South End Ave
BA • Bank of America • 150 Broadway [Liberty]
BA • Bank of America • 29 Broadway [Morris]
BA • Bank of America (ATM) • 175 Water St [John]
NY • Bank of New York • 1 Wall St [B'way]
NY • Bank of New York • 20 Broad St [Exchange Pl]
NY • Bank of New York • 45 Wall St [William]
CH • Chase • 1 Chase Plz [Pine]
CH • Chase • 214 Broadway [Fulton]
CH • Chase • 42 Broadway [Morris]
CH • Chase • 55 Water St [Hanover Sq]
CH • Chase (ATM) • Duane Reade • 1 Whitehall [Stone]
CH • Chase (ATM) • Duane Reade • 130 William [Fulton]
CH • Chase (ATM) • Duane Reade • 147 Fulton [B'way]
CH • Chase (ATM) • Duane Reade • 17 Battery Pl [Wash]
CH • Chase (ATM) • Duane Reade • 40 Fulton St [Pearl]
CH • Chase (ATM) • Duane Reade • 45 Pine St [William]
CH • Chase (ATM) • Duane Reade • 67 Broad St [Marketfield]
CH • Chase (ATM) • Duane Reade • 80 Maiden [Gold]
CH • Chase (ATM) • Duane Reade • 95 Wall St [Water]
CH • Chase (ATM) • Duane Reade • 99 John St [Cliff]
CI • Citibank • 1 Broadway [Battery Pl]
CI • Citibank • 111 Wall St [Front]
CI • Citibank • 120 Broadway [Cedar]
CI • Citibank (ATM) • 100 William St [Platt]
CO • Commerce • 2 Wall St [B'way]
HS • HSBC • 100 Maiden Ln [Pearl]
HS • HSBC • 110 William St [John]
HS • HSBC • 120 Broadway [Cedar]
HS • HSBC • 26 Broadway [Morris]
HU • Hudson United (ATM) • 90 Broad St [Stone]
CU • Municipal Credit Union (ATM) • 2 B'way [Stone]
NF • North Fork • 176 Broadway [Cortlandt]
SG • Signature • 71 Broadway [Rector]
SN • Sterling National • 42 Broadway [Morris]
WA • Wachovia (ATM) • 75 Broad St [S William]
WM • Washington Mutual • 140 Broadway [Liberty]

Landmarks

• **20 Exchange Place** • 20 Exchange Pl [William]
• **40 Wall St** • 40 Wall St [William]
• **American International Building** • 70 Pine St [Pearl]
• **American Stock Exchange** • 86 Trinity Pl [Thames]
• **Bankers Trust Company Building** • 16 Wall St [Nassau]
• **Battery Maritime Building** • 10 South St [Broad]
• **Bowling Green** • Broadway & State St
• **Canyon of Heroes** • Broadway [b/w Bowling Green and City Hall]
• **Charging Bull** • Bowling Green Park
• **Cunard Building** • 25 Broadway [Morris]
• **Customs House/Museum of the American Indian** • 1 Bowling Green [State]
• **Delmonico's Building** • 56 Beaver St [S William]
• **Ellis Island**
• **Equitable Building** • 120 Broadway [Cedar]
• **Federal Hall** • 26 Wall St [Broad]
• **The Federal Reserve Bank** • 33 Liberty St [William]
• **The First JP Morgan Bank** • 23 Wall St [Broad]
• **New York Stock Exchange** • 20 Broad St [Exchange Pl]
• **South Street Seaport** • South St [Fulton]
• **St Paul's Chapel & Cemetery** • Broadway & Fulton St
• **Standard Oil Building** • 26 Broadway [Morris]
• **Trinity Church & Cemetery** • Broadway & Wall St
• **Vietnam Veterans Plaza** • Coenties Slip & Water St
• **World Trade Center Site** • Church St & Vesey St

Post Offices

• **Wall Street** • 73 Pine St [Pearl]

Schools

• **High School for Economics and Finance** • 100 Trinity Pl [Cedar]
• **High School for Leadership & Public Service** • 90 Trinity Pl [Thames]
• **John V Lindsay Wildcat Academy** • 17 Battery Pl [Wash]
• **Millennium High** • 75 Broad St [S William]

Supermarkets

• **The Amish Market** • 17 Battery Pl [West St]
• **Associated** • 77 Fulton St [Front]
• **Jubilee Marketplace** • 99 John St [Cliff] ☮

Map

2 3 4

1

Let's be honest. Pinstripes and bumping bass don't go hand in hand. But a stiff shot of morning espresso and an equally stiff shot of evening vodka never made a stiff suit wrinkle. It's the stuff of Wall Street champs. Plus, those stripes make you look like a million. Honestly.

Coffee

- **180 Broadway Café** · 180 Broadway [Cortlandt]
- **Andrew's Coffee Shop** · 116 John St [Pearl]
- **Ashby's** · 120 Broadway [Cedar]
- **Au Bon Pain** · 1 State St Plz [Whitehall]
- **Au Bon Pain** · 222 Broadway [Ann]
- **Au Bon Pain** · 60 Broad St [Beaver]
- **Au Bon Pain** · 80 Pine St [Pearl]
- **Cosi** · 54 Pine St [William]
- **Cosi** · 55 Broad St [Beaver]
- **Dunkin' Donuts** · 139 Fulton St [Nassau]
- **Dunkin' Donuts** · 196 Broadway [John]
- **Dunkin' Donuts** · New York Stock Exchange Cafeteria · 20 Broad St [Exchange Pl]
- **Dunkin' Donuts** · 29 Broadway [Morris]
- **Dunkin' Donuts** · 40 Broad St [Exchange Pl]
- **Dunkin' Donuts** · 48 New St [Exchange Pl]
- **Dunkin' Donuts** · 50 Fulton St [Cliff]
- **Klatch** · 9 Maiden Ln [B'way]
- **Lane Café** · 75 Maiden Ln [William]
- **Leonidas** · 74 Trinity Pl [Thames]
- **Roxy Coffee Shop** · 20 John St [Nassau]
- **Seaport Café** · 89 South St [Beekman]
- **Seattle Coffee Roasters** · 110 William St [John]
- **Starbucks** · 1 Battery Park Plz [B'way]
- **Starbucks** · 100 Wall St [Water]
- **Starbucks** · 100 William St [Platt]
- **Starbucks** · 115 Broadway [Thames]
- **Starbucks** · 165 Broadway [Cortlandt]
- **Starbucks** · 195 Broadway [Dey]
- **Starbucks** · 2 Broadway [Beaver]
- **Starbucks** · 3 New York Plz [Broad]
- **Starbucks** · 45 Wall St [William]
- **Starbucks** · 55 Broad St [Beaver]
- **Starbucks** · 55 Liberty St [Nassau]
- **Starbucks** · 80 Pine St [Pearl]

Copy Shops

- **Acro Photo Printing** · 90 Maiden Ln [Gold] ♿
- **Administrative Resources** · 60 Broad St, 25th Fl [Beaver] ♿
- **Big Apple Copy and Printing Center** · 115 Broadway [Thames]
- **FedEx Kinko's** · 110 William St [John]
- **Hard Copy Printing** · 111 John St [Cliff]
- **Kinko's** · 100 Wall St [Water]
- **National Reprographics** · 160 Broadway [Liberty]
- **Perfect Copy Center** · 11 Broadway [Morris]
- **Quality Duplicating Services** · 111 Nassau St [Ann]
- **Sol Speedy** · 26 Water St [Morris]
- **Staples** · 200 Water St [Fulton]
- **The UPS Store** · 118A Fulton St [Dutch]
- **The UPS Store** · 5 Hanover Sq [Pearl]

Farmer's Markets

- **Bowling Green Greenmarket (Tues & Thurs 8am-5pm, Year Round)** · Battery Park Pl & Broadway
- **Downtown PATH (Tues 8am-6pm Apr-Dec, Thurs 8am-6pm Jun-Dec)** · Vesey St & Church St
- **South Street Seaport (Tues 8am-5pm June-Nov)** · Fulton b/w Water & Pearl

Gyms

- **Crunch Fitness** · 25 Broadway [Morris]
- **Curves (Women only)** · 118 Water St [Wall]
- **Equinox Fitness Club** · 14 Wall St [Nassau]
- **Heartworks Health & Fitness Center** · 180 Maiden Ln [Front]
- **John Street Fitness** · 80 John St [Gold]
- **Lucille Roberts Health Club (Women only)** · 143 Fulton St [Nassau]
- **New York Health & Racquet Club** · 39 Whitehall St [Pearl]
- **New York Sports Clubs** · 160 Water St [Fletcher]
- **New York Sports Clubs** · 30 Wall St [Broad]

Hardware Stores

- **Apple Specialties** · 19 Rector St [Wash]
- **Dick's Hardware** · 205 Pearl St [Fletcher]
- **Fulton Supply & Hardware** · 74 Fulton St [Edens Aly]
- **Whitehall Hardware** · 88 Greenwich St [Rector]
- **Wolff Hardware** · 75 Maiden Ln [William]

Liquor Stores

- **Famous Wines & Spirits** · 40 Exchange Pl [William]
- **Fulton Wines & Spirits** · 110 Fulton St [Dutch]
- **Maiden Lane Wines & Liquors** · 6 Maiden Ln [B'way]
- **New York Wine Exchange** · 9 Broadway [Morris]
- **Water Street Wine & Spirit** · 79 Pine St [Pearl]
- **West Street Wine & Spirits** · 56 West St [Rector]

Nightlife

- **John Street Bar & Grill** · 17 John St [Nassau]
- **Kilarney Rose** · 180 Beaver St [Pearl]
- **Liquid Assets** · Millennium Hilton Hotel · 55 Church St [Fulton]
- **Papoos** · 55 Broadway [Exchange Aly]
- **Remy Lounge** · 104 Greenwich St [Carlisle]
- **Ryan Maguire's Ale House** · 28 Cliff St [Fulton]
- **Ryan's Sports Bar & Restaurant** · 46 Gold St [Fulton]
- **Ulysses** · 95 Pearl St [Hanover Sq]
- **White Horse Tavern** · 25 Bridge St [Whitehall]

Restaurants

- **The 14 Wall St Restaurant** · 14 Wall St [Nassau]
- **Battery Gardens** · Battery Park, across from 17 State St [Pearl]
- **Bayards** · 1 Hanover Sq [Pearl]
- **Burritoville** · 36 Water St [Coenties Aly]
- **Carmela's** · 30 Water St [Broad]
- **Cassis on Stone** · 52 Stone St [Mill Ln]
- **Cosi Sandwich Bar** · 54 Pine St [William]
- **Cosi Sandwich Bar** · 55 Broad St [Beaver]
- **Daily Soup** · 41 John St [Nassau]
- **Financier Patisserie** · 62 Stone St [Mill]
- **Giovanni's Atrium** · 100 Washington St [Rector]
- **Heartland Brewery** · 93 South St [Fulton]
- **Lemongrass Grill** · 84 William St [Maiden Ln]
- **Les Halles** · 15 John St [B'way]
- **MJ Grill** · 110 John St [Cliff]
- **Papoos** · 55 Broadway [Exchange Aly]
- **Red** · 19 Fulton St [South]
- **Romi** · 19 Rector St [Wash]
- **Rosario's** · 38 Pearl St [Moore]
- **Roy's New York** · 130 Washington St [Albany]
- **Sam's Falafel (street cart)** · Liberty Plz [B'way]
- **Sophie's** · 73 New St [Beaver]
- **St Maggie's Café** · 120 Wall St [Front]
- **The Grotto** · 69 New St [Beaver]
- **Zaitzeff** · 72 Nassau St [John]
- **Zeytuna** · 59 Maiden Ln [William]

Shopping

- **Barclay Rex** · 75 Broad St [S William]
- **Century 21** · 22 Cortlandt St [B'way]
- **Christopher Norman Chocolates** · 60 New St [Exchange Pl]
- **Flowers of the World** · 80 Pine St [Pearl]
- **Godiva Chocolatier** · 33 Maiden Ln [Nassau]
- **Modell's** · 200 Broadway [John]
- **Radio Shack** · 114 Fulton St [Dutch]
- **Radio Shack** · 9 Broadway [Morris]
- **South Street Seaport** · 19 Fulton St [South]
- **The World of Golf** · 189 Broadway [John]
- **Yankees Clubhouse Shop** · 8 Fulton St [South]

Video Rental

- **Ann Street Entertainment** · 21 Ann St [Theatre Aly]

9

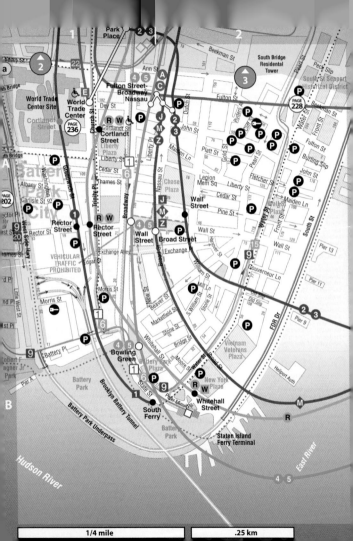

Attempting to drive---or park---during the day down here can be maddening, but you can check out the lots underneath the FDR if you really must drive. Subways are usually your best bet. We're psyched for the Calatrava station.

Subways

1 .... Rector St
1 .... South Ferry
2 **3** .... Wall St
4 **5** .... Bowling Green
4 **5** .... Wall St
2 **3** **4** **5** **A** **C** **J** **M** **Z**
.... Fulton St-Broadway-Nassau St
E .... World Trade Center
J **M** **Z** .... Broad St
R **W** .... Cortlandt St
R **W** .... Rector St
R **W** .... Whitehall St-South Ferry

PATH

• **World Trade Center Site**

Bus Lines

1 .... Fifth/Madison Aves
15 .... First/Second Aves
20 ..... Riverdale/246th St via Henry Hudson Pky
22 .... Madison/Chambers St
6 .... Seventh Ave/Broadway/Sixth Ave
9 .... Ave B/East Broadway

Bike Lanes

• • • • Recommended Route
• • • • Greenway

Car Rental

• **Enterprise** • 56 Fulton St [Front]
• **Hertz** • 20 Morris St [Wash]

Parking

Two luxuries most New Yorkers lack make the Triangle-Below-Canal sing: lofts and families. While you're waiting for your record to go platinum and The Right Person to divvy out a series of lifetime one-liners, roll by, stay, and gawk. You'll find your own luxurious tune someday, rockstar.

💲 Banks

BA • Bank of America • 100 Church St [Park Pl]
BA • Bank of America (ATM) • 57 Worth St [Church]
CH • Chase • 423 Canal St [Varick]
CH • Chase • 65 Worth St [Church]
CI • Citibank • 127 Hudson St [Beach]
CO • Commerce • 25 Hudson St [Duane]
EM • Emigrant • 110 Church St [Park Pl]
HS • HSBC • 110 West Broadway [Reade]
IC • Independence Community • 108 Hudson St [Franklin]
CU • Municipal Credit Union (ATM) • 40 Worth St [Church]
NF • North Fork • 90 West Broadway [Chambers]
CU• Skyline Federal Credit Union • 32 Sixth [Beach]

📍 Landmarks

• **The Dream House •** 275 Church St [White]
• **Duane Park •** Duane St & Hudson St
• *Ghostbusters* **Firehouse •** 14 N Moore St [Varick]
• **Harrison Street Row Houses •** Harrison St & Greenwich St
• **Washington Market Park •** Greenwich St [Chambers]

🚓 Police

• **1st Precinct •** 16 Ericsson Pl [Varick]

✉ Post Offices

• **Canal Street •** 350 Canal St [Church]
• **Church Street •** 90 Church St [Barclay]

🎓 Schools

• **Adelphi University •** 75 Varick St [Grand]
• **The Art Institute of New York City •** 75 Varick St [Grand]
• **Borough of Manhattan Community College •** 199 Chambers St [West St]
• **College of New Rochelle DC-37 Campus •** 125 Barclay St [Wash]
• **IS 289 •** 201 Warren St [Chambers]
• **Metropolitan College of New York •** 75 Varick St [Grand]
• **Montessori •** 53 Beach St [Collister]
• **New York Academy of Art •** 111 Franklin St [Church]
• **New York Law •** 57 Worth St [Church]
• **PS 150 Tribeca Learning Center •** 334 Greenwich St [Jay]
• **PS 234 Independence •** 292 Greenwich St [Chambers]
• **St John's University •** 101 Murray St [Greenwich St]
• **Unity High •** 121 Sixth Ave [Broome]
• **Washington Market •** 55 Hudson St [Jay]

🛒 Supermarkets

• **Amish Market •** 53 Park Pl [W B'way]
• **Bell Bates Natural Foods •** 97 Reade St [Church]
• **Food Emporium •** 316 Greenwich St [Duane]
• **Jin Market •** 111 Hudson St [N Moore] ⚙
• **Morgan's Market •** 13 Hudson St [Reade]

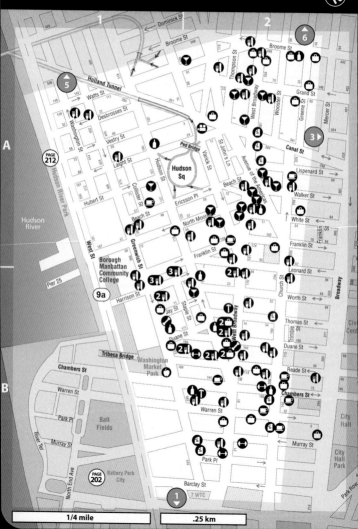

For arts, TriBeCa rocks---the film festival every year, the Knitting Factory (Map 3), the MELA Foundation's "Dream House, several galleries, and experimental music at Roulette. Stalwart bars such as Puffy's and Walker's can effectively wet your whistle while you're waiting to win the lotto so you can eat at Nobu.

2 3
1
Ma

Coffee

- **Dunkin' Donuts** • 100 Chambers St [Church]
- **Dunkin' Donuts** • 130 Church St [Murray]
- **Pecan** • 130 Franklin St [W B'way]
- **Starbucks** • 100 Church St [Park Pl]
- **Starbucks** • 125 Chambers St [W B'way]
- **Westside Coffee Shop II** • 323 Church St [Lispenard]
- **Zoie's Coffee Shop** • 49 Beach St [Collister]

Copy Shops

- **21 Laminating & Binding Center** • 130 Church St [Murray]
- **Bestype Imaging** • 285 West Broadway [Canal]
- **City Copies** • 158 Church St [Chambers]
- **Jean Paul Duplicating Center** • 275 Greenwich St [Murray]
- **Mail Boxes Etc** • 295 Greenwich St
- **PrintFacility** • 200 Church St [Thomas]
- **Shield Press** • 9 Lispenard St [6th Av]
- **The UPS Store** • 305 West Broadway [Canal]

Farmer's Markets

- **Tribeca (Wed and Sat 8am-3pm, Year Round)** • Greenwich St-Chambers & Duane

Gyms

- **24/7 Fitness** • 107 Chambers St [Church]
- **Equinox Fitness** • 54 Murray St [W B'way]
- **NYSC** • 151 Reade St [Hudson]

Hardware Stores

- **Ace Hardware** • 160 West Broadway [Worth]
- **Tribeca Hardware** • 154 Chambers St [W B'way]

Liquor Stores

- **Brite Buy Wines & Spirits** • 11 Sixth Ave [White]
- **Chambers Street Wines** • 160 Chambers St [Greenwich]
- **City Hall Wines & Spirits** • 108 Chambers St [Church]
- **Downtown Liquor Store** • 90 Hudson St [Leonard]
- **Hudson Wine & Spirits** • 165 Hudson St [Laight]
- **Tribeca Wine Merchants (Wine only)** • 40 Hudson St [Duane]
- **Tribeca Wines** • 327 Greenwich St [Duane]
- **Vintage New York (Wine only)** • 482 Broome St [Wooster]

Pet Shops

- **Dudley's Paw** • 327 Greenwich St [Duane]
- **Pet Bar South** • 117 West Broadway [Reade]

Movie Theaters

- **Tribeca Cinemas** • 54 Varick St [Laight]

Nightlife

- **46 Grand** • 46 Grand St [W B'way]
- **Anotheroom** • 249 West Broadway [Beach]
- **Brandy Library** • 25 North Moore St [W B'way]
- **Bubble Lounge** • 228 West Broadway [White]
- **Buster's Garage** • 180 West Broadway [Leonard]
- **Church Lounge** • Tribeca Grand Hotel- 25 Walker St [Church]
- **Circa Tabac** • 32 Watts St [Sullivan]
- **Lucky Strike** • 59 Grand St [W B'way]
- **Naked Lunch** • 17 Thompson St [Grand]
- **Nancy Whisky Pub** • 1 Lispenard St [W B'way]
- **Puffy's Tavern** • 81 Hudson St [Harrison]
- **Roulette** • 228 W Broadway [White]
- **Soho Grand Hotel** • 310 West Broadway [Canal]
- **Tribeca Tavern** • 247 West Broadway [Beach]
- **Walker's** • 16 N Moore St [W B'way]

Restaurants

- **66** • 241 Church St [Leonard]
- **A&M Roadhouse** • 57 Murray St [W B'way]
- **Azafran** • 77 Warren St [W B'way]
- **Bouley** • 120 W Broadway [Duane]
- **Bread Tribeca** • 301 Church St [Walker]
- **Bubby's** • 120 Hudson St [N Moore]
- **Café Noir** • 32 Grand St [Thompson]
- **Capsouto Frères** • 451 Washington St [Watts]
- **Centrico** • 211 West Broadway [Franklin]
- **Chanterelle** • 2 Harrison St [Hudson]
- **Church Lounge, Tribeca Grand Hotel** • 2 Ave of the Americas [White]
- **City Hall** • 131 Duane St [Church]
- **Columbine** • 229 West Broadway [White]
- **Cupping Room Café** • 359 West Broadway [Broome]
- **Danube** • 30 Hudson St [Duane]
- **Dekk** • 134 Reade St [Hudson]
- **Della Rovere** • 250 West Broadway [Beach]
- **Duane Park Café** • 157 Duane St [Hudson]
- **Dylan Prime** • 62 Laight St [Greenwich St]
- **Edward's** • 136 West Broadway [Duane]
- **Elixir Juice Bar** • 95 West Broadway [Chambers]
- **Félix** • 340 West Broadway [Grand]
- **Flor de Sol** • 361 Greenwich St [Harrison]
- **fresh** • 105 Reade St [W B'way]
- **The Harrison** • 355 Greenwich St [Harrison]
- **Il Giglio** • 81 Warren St [Greenwich St]
- **Ivy's Bistro** • 385 Greenwich St [N Moore]

- **Karahi** • 508 Broome St [W B'way]
- **Kitchenette** • 80 West Broadway [Warren]
- **Kori** • 253 Church St [Leonard]
- **Landmarc** • 179 West Broadway [Leonard]
- **Lucky Strike** • 59 Grand St [W B'way]
- **Lupe's East LA Kitchen** • 110 Sixth Ave [Sullivan]
- **Montrachet** • 239 West Broadway [White]
- **Nobu** • 105 Hudson St [Franklin]
- **Nobu, Next Door** • 105 Hudson St [Franklin]
- **Odeon** • 145 West Broadway [Thomas]
- **Pakistan Tea House** • 176 Church St [Reade]
- **Palacinka** • 28 Grand St [Thompson]
- **Petite Abeille** • 134 West Broadway
- **Roc** • 190 Duane St [Greenwich St]
- **Salaam Bombay** • 317 Greenwich St [Duane]
- **Sosa Borella** • 460 Greenwich St [Watts]
- **Spaghetti Western** • 58 Reade St [B'way]
- **Square Diner** • 33 Leonard St [W B'way]
- **Thalassa** • 179 Franklin St [Hudson]
- **Tribeca Grill** • 375 Greenwich St [Franklin]
- **Viet Café** • 345 Greenwich St [Jay]
- **Walker's** • 16 N Moore St [W B'way]
- **wichcraft** • 397 Greenwich St [Beach]
- **Yaffa's** • 353 Greenwich St [Harrison]
- **Zutto** • 77 Hudson St [Harrison]

Shopping

- **Assets London** • 152 Franklin St [Hudson]
- **Babylicious** • 51 Hudson St [Thomas]
- **Balloon Saloon** • 133 West Broadway [Duane]
- **Bazzini** • 339 Greenwich St [Jay]
- **Bell Bates Natural Food** • 97 Reade St [Church]
- **Boffi SoHo** • 31 1/2 Greene St [Grand]
- **Canal Street Bicycles** • 417 Canal St [6th]
- **Duane Park Patisserie** • 179 Duane St [Staple]
- **Gotham Bikes** • 112 West Broadway [Duane]
- **Issey Miyake** • 119 Hudson St [N Moore]
- **Jack Spade** • 56 Greene St [Broome]
- **Janovic** • 136 Church St [Warren]
- **Kings Pharmacy** • 5 Hudson St [Chambers]
- **Korin Japanese Trading** • 57 Warren St [W B'way]
- **Let There Be Neon** • 38 White St [Church]
- **Lucky Brand Dungarees** • 38 Greene St [Grand]
- **MarieBelle's Fine Treats & Chocolates** • 484 Broome St [Wooster]
- **New York Nautical** • 158 Duane [Hudson]
- **Oliver Peoples** • 366 West Broadway [Watts]
- **Shoofly** • 42 Hudson St [Thomas]
- **Steven Alan** • 103 Franklin St [Church]
- **Urban Archaeology** • 143 Franklin St [W B'way]
- **We Are Nuts About Nuts** • 165 Church St [Chambers]
- **What Comes Around Goes Around** • 351 W Broadway [Broome]
- **Willner Chemists** • 253 Broadway [Murray]

Map 2 · TriBeCa

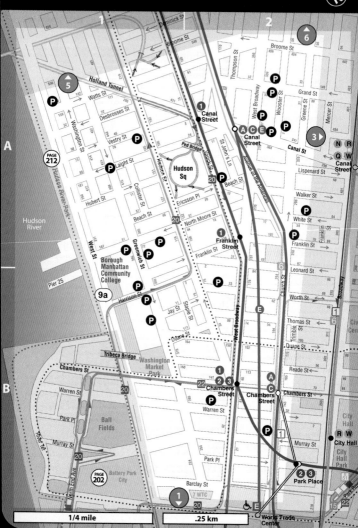

Moving around and parking in TriBeCa, especially in its northwest corner, isn't too bad, but the closer you get to City Hall and the WTC site, the more of a pain it is to find anything, especially during the week. Still, it's a lot better than many other NYC neighborhoods.

2 3 4

1

Ma

Subways

2 3 .... Park Pl
1 2 3 .... Chambers St
1 .... Canal St
1 ....Franklin St
A C .... Chambers St
A C E .... Canal St
R W............................. City Hall

Bus Lines

1 .... Broadway
20 .... Abingdon Sq
22 .... Seventh Ave/Sixth Ave/Broadway
6 .... Seventh Ave/Broadway/Sixth Ave

Bike Lanes

- • • • Recommended Route
- • • • Greenway

 Parking

The post office on Doyers Street always has a hellish line—it's worth going somewhere else. The area's great civic architecture includes the Municipal Building, the Surrogate's Court, Foley Square, and City Hall Park. Canal Street is the major tourist area, but it's where we buy our $10 knock-offs.

💲 Banks

- **AB • Abacus** • 181 Canal St [Mott]
- **AB • Abacus** • 6 Bowery [Doyers]
- **BA • Bank of America** • 260 Canal St [Lafayette]
- **BA • Bank of America** • 261 Broadway [Warren]
- **BA • Bank of America** • 50 Bayard St [Elizabeth]
- **BA • Bank of New York** • 233 Broadway [Park Pl]
- **CY • Cathay** • 129 Lafayette St [Howard]
- **CY • Cathay** • 45 East Broadway [Market]
- **CH • Chase** • 180 Canal St [Mott]
- **CH • Chase** • 2 Bowery [Doyers]
- **CH • Chase** • 231 Grand St [Bowery]
- **CH • Chase** • 280 Broadway [Reade]
- **CH • Chase (ATM)** • Duane Reade• 305 Broadway [Duane]
- **CH • Chase (ATM)** • 407 Broadway [Lispenard]
- **CH • Chase (ATM)** • 50 Bowery [Canal]
- **CT • Chinatrust** • 208 Canal St [Mulberry]
- **CA • Chinese American** • 245 Canal St [Lafayette]
- **CA • Chinese American** • 77 Bowery [Canal]
- **CI • Citibank** • 164 Canal St [Elizabeth]
- **CI • Citibank** • 2 Mott St [Chatham Sq]
- **CI • Citibank** • 250 Broadway [Murray]
- **CI • Citibank (ATM)** • 396 Broadway [Walker]
- **CO • Commerce** • 155 Canal St [Bowery]
- **EM • Emigrant** • 261 Broadway [Chambers]
- **GE • Great Eastern** • 16 E Broadway [Catherine St]
- **HS • HSBC** • 11 East Broadway [Catherine St]
- **HS • HSBC** • 254 Canal St [Lafayette]
- **HS • HSBC** • 265 Broadway [Lispenard]
- **HS • HSBC** • 58 Bowery [Canal]
- **CU • Municipal Credit Union** • 2 Lafayette St [Reade]
- **NF • North Fork** • 116 Bowery [Grand]
- **NF • North Fork** • 200 Lafayette St [Broome]
- **UO • United Orient** • 185 Canal St [Mott]
- **CU • US Courthouse Federal Credit Union** • 40 Foley Sq [Pearl]
- **VN • Valley National** • 434 Broadway [Howard]
- **VN • Valley National** • 93 Canal St [Eldridge]
- **WA • Washington Mutual** • 221 Canal St [Baxter]
- **WA • Washington Mutual** • 270 Broadway [Chambers]

✴ Community Gardens

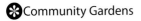

➕ Emergency Rooms

- **NYU Downtown** • 170 William St [Ann] ♿

⭕ Landmarks

- **African Burial Ground** • Duane St & Broadway
- **Bridge Café** • 279 Water St [Dover]
- **Brooklyn Bridge** • Chambers St & Centre St
- **Chinatown Ice Cream Factory** • 65 Bayard St [Mott]
- **Chinatown Visitors Kiosk** • Canal, Baxter, & Walker
- **City Hall** • Park Row & Broadway
- **Criminal Courthouse** • 100 Centre St [Leonard]
- **Doyers Street (Bloody Angle)** • Doyers St [Chatham Sq]
- **Eastern States Buddhist Temple** • 64 Mott St [Bayard]
- **Hall of Records/Surrogate's Court** • Chambers St & Park Row
- **Municipal Building** • Chambers St & Park Row
- **Not For Tourists** • 2 East Broadway [Chatham Sq]
- **Old Police Headquarters** • 240 Centre St [Grand]
- **Shearith Israel Cemetery** • 55 St James Pl [James]
- **Tweed Courthouse** • Chambers St & Broadway
- **Woolworth Building** • 233 Broadway [Park Pl]

📖 Libraries

- **Chatham Square** • 33 East Broadway [Catherine St]
- **New Amsterdam** • 9 Murray St [B'way]
- **NYC Municipal Archives** • 31 Chambers St [Elk]

⭕ Police

- **5th Precinct** • 19 Elizabeth St [Canal]

✉ Post Offices

- **Chinatown** • 6 Doyers St [Bowery]
- **Peck Slip** • 1 Peck Slip [Pearl]

🎓 Schools

- **French Culinary Institute** • 462 Broadway [Grand]
- **IS 131 Dr Sun Yat Sen** • 100 Hester St [Eldridge]
- **M298 Pace High** • 100 Hester St [Eldridge]
- **Murray Bergtraum High** • 411 Pearl St [St James Pl]
- **New York Career Institute** • 11 Park Pl [B'way]
- **Pace University** • 1 Pace Plz [Spruce]
- **PS 001 Alfred E Smith** • 8 Henry St [Catherine St]
- **PS 124 Yung Wing** • 40 Division St [Market]
- **PS 130 Hernando DeSoto** • 143 Baxter St [Hester]
- **St James** • 37 St James Pl [James]
- **St Joseph** • 1 Monroe St [Catherine St]
- **Transfiguration** • 29 Mott St [Mosco]

🛒 Supermarkets

- **C-Town** • 5 St James Pl [Pearl]
- **Dom's Fine Foods** • 202 Lafayette St [Kenmare]
- **Gourmet Garage** • 453 Broome St [Mercer]
- **Italian Food Center** • 186 Grand St [Mulberry]

Map 3 • **City Hall** / Chinatown

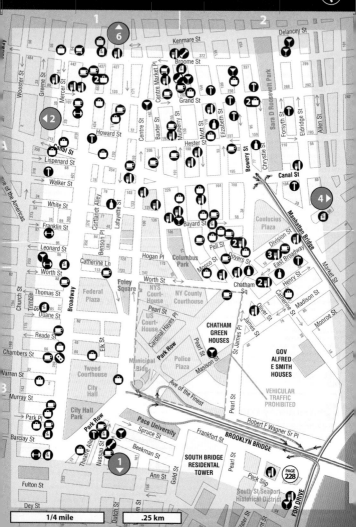

If you haven't had the crab soup dumplings at Joe's Shanghai on Pell Street, you should. For Vietnamese, Pho Viet Huong; Thai, Pongsri Thai; Italian, Il Palazzo. If you're not in the mood for Asian or Italian, you're screwed. The Bowery is still the epicenter for discount kitchen supplies and lighting fixtures.

Coffee

- **Blue Spoon Coffee** • 76 Chambers St [B'way]
- **Café Palermo** • 148 Mulberry St [Grand]
- **Caffe Del Arte** • 143 Mulberry St [Grand]
- **Dunkin' Donuts** • 132 Nassau St [Beekman]
- **Dunkin' Donuts** • 250 Broadway [Murray]
- **Dunkin' Donuts** • 321 Broadway [Thomas]
- **Ferrara Café** • 195 Grand St [Mulberry]
- **Green Tea Café** • 45 Mott St [Bayard]
- **Hip Cup Café** • 225 Park Row [Pearl]
- **Ho Wong Coffee House** • 146 Hester St [Elizabeth]
- **Kam Hing Coffee Shop** • 119 Baxter St [Hester]
- **Los Punito Café** • 117 Mulberry St [Hester]
- **Maria's Bakery** • 42 Mott St [Pell]
- **Mee Sum Coffee Shop** • 26 Pell St [Doyers]
- **Mei Lai Wah Coffee House** • 64 Bayard St [Mott]
- **Miro Café Corp** • 474 Broadway [Grand]
- **Nom Wah Tea Parlor** • 13 Doyers St [Chatham Sq]
- **Qq Café** • 50 E Broadway [Market]
- **Sambuca's Café & Desserts** • 105 Mulberry St [Canal]
- **Starbucks** • 111 Worth St [Lafayette]
- **Starbucks** • 233 Broadway [Park Pl]
- **Starbucks** • 241 Canal St [Centre]
- **Starbucks** • 291 Broadway [Reade]
- **Starbucks** • 38 Park Row [Beekman]
- **Starbucks** • 471 Broadway [Grand]

Copy Shops

- **Eastern Photo Lab** • 88 E Broadway [Forsyth]
- **Kinko's** • 105 Duane St [Trimble Pl]
- **Nassau Photo Lab** • 145 Nassau St [Spruce]
- **Print Facility** • 225 Broadway [Barclay]
- **Soho Reprographics** • 381 Broome St [Mulberry]
- **Staples** • 217 Broadway [Ann]
- **Staples** • 488 Broadway [Broome]
- **The UPS Store** • 342 Broadway [Catherine]
- **Visual Arts & Photo** • 63E Bayard St [Elizabeth]

Gyms

- **Eastern Athletic** • 80 Leonard St [Church]
- **Five Points Fitness** • 444 Broadway [Howard]
- **New York Sports Clubs** • 217 Broadway [Ann]
- **Tribeca Gym** • 79 Worth St [Church]

Hardware Stores

- **Carl Martinez Hardware** • 88 Canal St [Eldridge]
- **Design Source** • 115 Bowery [Grand]
- **East Broadway Appliance Hardware** • 59 East Broadway [Market]

- **Eastern Tool & Supply** • 428 Broadway [Howard]
- **Kessler Hardware & MFG** • 229 Grand St [Bowery]
- **OK Hardware** • 438 Broome St [B'way]
- **T&Y Hardware** • 101 Chrystie St [Grand]
- **Walker Supply** • 61 Walker St [B'way]
- **Weinstein & Holtzman** • 29 Park Row [Beekman]
- **World Construction** • 78 Forsyth St [Grand]

Liquor Stores

- **Chez Choi Liquor & Wine** • 49 Chrystie St [Hester]
- **Elizabeth Street Wine & Liquor** • 86 Elizabeth St [Grand]
- **Sun Wai Liquor Store** • 17 East Broadway [Catherine St]
- **Walker Liquors** • 101 Lafayette St [Walker]
- **Wine No Liquor Discount** • 12 Chatham Sq [B'way]

Pet Shops

- **Aqua Star Pet Shop (Fish)** • 172 Mulberry St [Broome]
- **Petland Discounts** • 132 Nassau St [Beekman]
- **Win Tropical Aquariums** • 169 Mott St [Broome]

Nightlife

- **The Beekman Pub** • 15 Beekman St [Nassau]
- **Capitale** • 130 Bowery [Grand]
- **Double Happiness** • 173 Mott St [Broome]
- **Experimental Intermedia** • 224 Centre St [Grand]
- **Happy Ending** • 302 Broome St [Forsyth]
- **Knitting Factory** • 74 Leonard St [Church]
- **Metropolitan Improvement Company** • 3 Madison St [Ave of the Finest]
- **Milk & Honey** • 134 Eldridge St [Broome]
- **The Paris Café** • 119 South St [Peck Slip]
- **Winnie's** • 104 Bayard St [Mulberry]

Restaurants

- **Bridge Café** • 279 Water St [Dover]
- **Canton** • 45 Division St [Market]
- **Cendrillon** • 45 Mercer St [Grand]
- **Cup & Saucer** • 89 Canal St [Eldridge]
- **Dim Sum Go Go** • 5 East Broadway [Catherine]
- **Excellent Dumpling House** • 111 Lafayette St [Canal]
- **Ferrara** • 195 Grand St [Mulberry]
- **Fuleen Seafood** • 11 Division St [Catherine St]
- **Golden Unicorn** • 18 E Broadway [Catherine St]
- **Goodies** • 1 East Broadway [Chatham Sq]
- **Il Palazzo** • 151 Mulberry St [Grand]
- **Joe's Shanghai** • 9 Pell St [Bowery]
- **L'Ecole** • 462 Broadway [Grand]
- **L'Orange Bleue** • 430 Broome St [Crosby]

- **Le Pain Quotidien** • 100 Grand St [Mercer]
- **Lily's** • 31 Oliver St [Henry]
- **Mandarin Court** • 61 Mott St [Bayard]
- **Mark Joseph Steakhouse** • 261 Water St [Peck Slip]
- **New York Noodle Town** • 28 Bowery [Bayard]
- **Nha Trang** • 148 Center St [Walker]
- **Nha Trang** • 87 Baxter St [White]
- **The Paris Café** • 119 South St [Peck Slip]
- **Pho Viet Huong** • 73 Mulberry St [Bayard]
- **Ping's** • 22 Mott St [Mosco]
- **Pongsri Thai** • 106 Bayard St [Mulberry]
- **Positano** • 122 Mulberry St [Hester]
- **Quartino** • 21 Peck Slip [Water]
- **Triple Eight Palace** • 88 East Broadway [Forsyth]
- **Umberto's Clam House** • 178 Mulberry St [Broome]
- **Wo Hop** • 17 Mott St [Mosco] ♿

Shopping

- **Aji Ichiban** • 167 Hester St [Mott]
- **Bangkok Center Grocery** • 104 Mosco St [Mulberry]
- **Bloomingdale's** • 504 Broadway [Broome]
- **Bowery Lighting** • 132 Bowery [Grand]
- **Catherine Street Meat Market** • 21 Catherine St [Henry]
- **Chinatown Ice Cream Factory** • 65 Bayard St [Elizabeth]
- **Dipalo Dairy** • 200 Grand St [Mott]
- **Fay Da Bakery** • 83 Mott St [Canal]
- **Fountain Pen Hospital** • 10 Warren St [B'way]
- **GS Food Market** • 250 Grand St
- **Hong Keung Seafood & Meat Market** • 75 Mulberry St [Bayard]
- **Industrial Plastic Supply** • 309 Canal St [Mercer]
- **J&R Music & Computer World** • 33 Park Row [Beekman]
- **Kate Spade** • 454 Broome St [Mercer]
- **Lung Moon Bakery** • 83 Mulberry St [Canal]
- **Mitchell's Place** • 15 Park Pl [B'way]
- **Modell's** • 55 Chambers St [B'way]
- **New Age Designer** • 38 Mott St [Pell]
- **The New York City Store** • 1 Centre St [Chambers]
- **Pearl Paint** • 308 Canal St [Mercer]
- **Pearl River Mart** • 477 Broadway [Broome]
- **Radio Shack** • 280 Broadway [Reade]
- **SoHo Art Materials** • 127 Grand St [Crosby]
- **Tan My My Market** • 253 Grand St [Chrystie]
- **Tent & Trails** • 21 Park Pl [Church]
- **Ting's Gift Shop** • 18 Doyers St [Bayard]
- **Unimax** • 269 Canal St [Cortlandt Aly]
- **Vespa** • 13 Crosby St [Grand]
- **Yellow Rat Bastard** • 478 Broadway [Broome]

Video Rental

- **Movie Bank USA** • Broadway & Chambers St ♿

21

Map 3 • City Hall / C

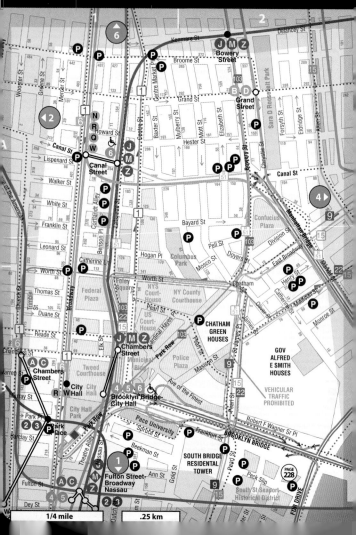

The Brooklyn Bridge is best approached from Pearl Street. Be careful about driving east on Canal Street—you have to make a right on Bowery or else you'll drive over the Manhattan Bridge. (Canal Street is one-way going west between Bowery and Chrystie.) Forget about street parking during the day.

Subways

2 3 .... Park Pl
4 5 6 J M Z ..... Brooklyn Bridge-City Hall-Chambers St
B D .... Grand St
6 J M Z N Q R W .... Canal St
R W .... City Hall
J M Z .... Bowery St
A C .... Chambers St
J M Z .... Fulton St/Broadway

Bus Lines

1 .... Broadway/Centre St
103 ....Bowery/Park Row
15 .... East Broadway/Park Row
22 .... Chambers/Madison St
6 .... Church St/Broadway
9 .... Park Row
⬛ .... Lafayette/Canal Sts

Bike Lanes

- • • • Marked Bike Lane
- • • • Recommended Route
- • • • Greenway

 Parking

Map 4 • Lower East Side

Kossar's Bialys—a top-five reason to be in New York. Culturally, Asians, Polish, Midwesterners—the Lower East Side is a mélange of immigrants and those who believe that if they can make it here, they can make it anywhere. Plus, the Pathmark has a parking lot!

2 | 3 | 4
1
Ma

24-Hour Pharmacies
• **Rite Aid** • 408 Grand St [Clinton] ♿

Bagels
• **Kossar's Bialys** • 367 Grand St [Essex]

Banks
BA • **Bank of America** • 318 Grand St [Orchard]
CH • **Chase (ATM)** • Duane Reade• 98 Delancey St [Ludlow]
CI • **Citibank** • 411 Grand St [Clinton]
EM • **Emigrant** • 465 Grand St [Dickstein Plz]
HS • **HSBC** • 307 Grand St [Allen]
CB • **New York Community** • 227 Cherry [Rutgers Slip]
WM • **Washington Mutual** • 104 Delancey St [Ludlow]

Community Gardens

Landmarks
• **Bialystoker Synagogue** • 7 Bialystoker Pl [Grand]
• **Eldridge Street Synagogue** • 12 Eldridge St [Division]
• **Essex Street Market** • 120 Essex St [Rivington]
• **Gouverneur Hospital** • Gouverneur Slip & Water St
• **Lower East Side Tenement Museum** • 90 Orchard St [Broome]

Libraries
• **Seward Park** • 192 East Broadway [Jefferson]

Police
• **7th Precinct** • 19 1/2 Pitt St [Broome]

Post Offices
• **Knickerbocker** • 128 East Broadway [Pike]
• **Pitt Station** • 185 Clinton St [Grand]

Schools
• **Beth Jacob Parochial** • 142 Broome St [Ridge]
• **Dual Language & Asian Studies High** • 350 Grand St [Essex]
• **Henry Street School for International Studies (M292)** • 220 Henry St [Clinton]
• **High School for History and Communication** • 350 Grand St [Essex]
• **JHS 056 Corlears** • 220 Henry St [Clinton]
• **Lower Manhattan Arts Academy** • 350 Grand St [Essex]
• **Mesivta Tifereth Jerusalem** • 145 East Broadway [Rutgers]
• **New Design High** • 350 Grand St [Essex]
• **PS 002 Meyer London** • 122 Henry St [Rutgers]
• **PS 042 Benjamin Altman** • 71 Hester St [Ludlow]
• **PS 110 Florence Nightingale** • 285 Delancey St [Columbia]
• **PS 126 Jacob Riis** • 80 Catherine St [Monroe]
• **PS 134 Henrietta Szold** • 293 East Broadway [Montgomery]
• **PS 137 John L Bernstein** • 327 Cherry St [Clinton]
• **PS 184M Shuang Wen** • 293 East Broadway [Montgomery]
• **Seward Park High** • 350 Grand St [Essex]
• **University Neighborhood High** • 200 Monroe St [Pike]
• **University Neighborhood Middle** • 220 Henry St [Clinton]
• **The Urban Assembly Academy of Government and Law** • 350 Grand St [Essex]

Supermarkets
• **Fine Fare** • 175 Clinton St [Grand]
• **Fine Fare** • 545 Grand St
• **Pathmark** • 227 Cherry St [Rutgers Slip]

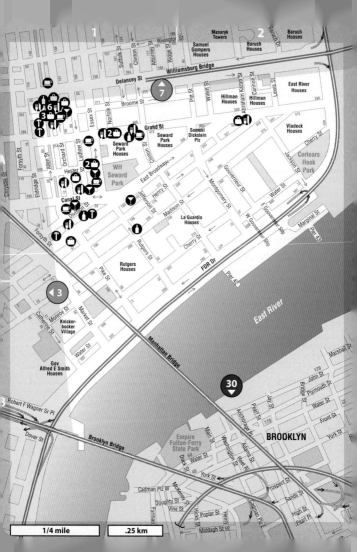

One key destination on the Lower East Side is Good World, a fabulous bar with excellent Scandinavian food. For great Jewish staples such as chocolate babka, check out Gertel's Bake Shop. For something more upscale, try Les Enfants Terribles.

Coffee

- **88 Orchard** • 88 Orchard St [Broome]
- **Flowers Café** • 355 Grand St [Essex]
- **Full City Coffee** • 409 Grand St [Clinton]
- **Happy Café** • 8 Allen St [Canal]
- **Starbucks** • 80 Delancey St [Allen]
- **Sunshine Factory Café** • 11 Essex St [Canal]

Hardware Stores

- **International Electrical** • 77 Allen St [Grand]
- **Karlee Hardware** • 98 East Broadway [Forsyth]
- **New York Home Center** • 71 Allen St [Grand]
- **Tom's Hardware** • 154 East Broadway [Rutgers]

Liquor Stores

- **Madison Liquor** • 195 Madison St [Rutgers]
- **Seward Park Liquors** • 393 Grand St [Suffolk]
- **Wedding Banquet Liquor** • 135 Division St [Canal]
- **Wing Tak Liquor** • 101 Allen St [Delancey]

Nightlife

- **Bar 169** • 169 East Broadway [Rutgers]
- **Clandestino** • 35 Canal St [Ludlow]
- **Good World** • 3 Orchard St [Canal]
- **King Size** • 21 Essex St [Canal]
- **Lolita** • 266 Broome St [Allen]

Restaurants

- **88 Orchard** • 88 Orchard St [Broome]
- **Barrio Chino** • 253 Broome St [Orchard]
- **Broomedoggs** • 250 Broome St [Orchard]
- **Congee Village** • 100 Allen St [Delancey]
- **El Bocadito** • 79 Orchard St [Broome]
- **El Castillo de Jagua 2** • 521 Grand St [Columbia]
- **Good World Bar & Grill** • 3 Orchard St [Canal]
- **Il Laboratorio del Gelato** • 95 Orchard St [Broome]
- **Kossar's Bagels and Bialys** • 367 Grand St [Essex]
- **Les Enfants Terribles** • 37 Canal St [Ludlow]
- **Little Giant** • 85 Orchard St [Broome]
- **Noah's Arc** • 399 Grand St [Suffolk]
- **Pho Bang** • 3 Pike St [Division]

Shopping

- **Baby Cakes** • 248 Broome St [Ludlow]
- **Doughnut Plant** • 379 Grand St [Norfolk]
- **Gertel's Bake Shop** • 53 Hester St [Ludlow]
- **Guss' Lower East Side Pickles** • 85 Orchard St [Broome]
- **Hong Kong Supermarket** • 109 East Broadway [Pike]
- **Il Laboratorio del Gelato** • 95 Orchard St [Broome]
- **Joe's Fabric Warehouse** • 102 Orchard St [Delancey]
- **Kossar's Bagels and Bialys** • 367 Grand St [Essex]
- **Mendel Goldberg Fabrics** • 72 Hester St [Orchard]
- **Moishe's Kosher Bake Shop** • 504 Grand St [E B'way]
- **Pippin** • 72 Orchard St [Grand]
- **Sweet Life** • 63 Hester St [Ludlow]

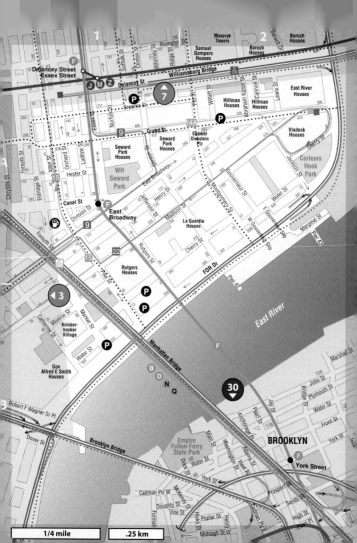

Plenty of opportunities exist for walking, biking, and blading. The Williamsburg and Manhattan bridges are both open to pedestrian traffic and provide incredible views that make you forget there's a way to get from Manhattan to Brooklyn underground. Parking isn't too bad, but it isn't great, either.

Subways

F .... East Broadway
F .... York St
F **J** **M** **Z** .... Delancey St-Essex St

Bus Lines

14 .... Grand St
15 .... Allen St
22 .... Madison St
9 .... East Broadway/Essex St
B 51 .... Forsyth St

Bike Lanes

- • • • Recommended Route
- • • • Greenway

Gas Stations

· **Mobil** · 2 Pike St [Division] ⊕

Parking

Let's all collectively thank our local deities for Jane Jacobs. If you don't know who she is, we can't help you—but you can ask at Chumley's, that literary speakeasy classic that makes the Village the Village. For bagels, Murray's is the place—but they don't toast, so don't even ask.

℞ 24-Hour Pharmacies

- **Duane Reade** • 378 Sixth Ave [Waverly]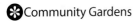

Bagels

- **Bagel Buffet** • 406 Sixth Ave [8th]
- **Bagels & Much More** • 70 Greenwich Ave [11th]
- **Bagels on the Square** • 7 Carmine St [6th Av]
- **Famous Bagels Buffet** • 510 Ave of the Americas [13th]
- **Hudson Bagels** • 502 Hudson St [Christopher]
- **Murray's Bagels** • 500 Sixth Ave [13th]

$ Banks

BA • **Bank of America (ATM)** • 390 Sixth Ave [8th]
CH • **Chase** • 158 W 14th St [7th Av]
CH • **Chase** • 204 W 4th St [Barrow]
CH • **Chase** • 302 W 12th St [8th Av]
CH • **Chase** • 345 Hudson St [Charlton]
CH • **Chase (ATM)** • Duane Reade • 378 Sixth Ave [Waverly]
CI • **Citibank (ATM)** • 75 Christopher St [4th]
EM • **Emigrant** • 375 Hudson St [Houston]
EM • **Emigrant** • 395 Sixth Ave [8th]
HS • **HSBC** • 101 W 14th St [6th Av]
HS • **HSBC** • 207 Varick St [Downing]
HS • **HSBC** • 80 Eighth Ave [14th]
NF • **North Fork** • 347 Sixth Ave [4th]
WM • **Washington Mutual** • 340 Sixth Ave [4th]

Community Gardens

Emergency Rooms

- **St Vincent's** • 153 W 11th St [7th Av]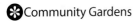

O Landmarks

- **The Cage (basketball court)** • 320 Sixth Ave at W 4th St
- **Chumley's** • 86 Bedford St [Barrow]
- **The Ear Inn** • Washington St & Spring St
- **Jefferson Market Courthouse** • 425 Sixth Ave [10th]
- **Old Homestead** • 56 Ninth Ave [14th]
- **Patchin Place** • W 10th St b/w Sixth Ave & Greenwich Ave
- **Stonewall Inn** • 53 Christopher St [7th Av]
- **Westbeth Building** • Washington St & Bethune St
- **White Horse Tavern** • 567 Hudson St [11th]

Libraries

- **Early Childhood Resource & Information Center** • 66 Leroy St [Hudson]
- **Hudson Park** • 66 Leroy St [Hudson]
- **Jefferson Market** • 425 Sixth Ave [10th]

Police

- **6th Precinct** • 233 W 10th St [Bleecker]

Post Offices

- **Village** • 201 Varick St [Houston]
- **West Village** • 527 Hudson St [Charles]

Schools

- **Chelsea Career and Technical Education High** • 131 Sixth Ave [Broome]
- **City as School** • 16 Clarkson St [Hudson]
- **City Country** • 146 W 13th St [6th Av]
- **Elisabeth Irwin High** • 40 Charlton St [Varick]
- **Empire State College–State University of New York** • 325 Hudson St [Vandam]
- **Greenwich House Music School** • 46 Barrow St [Bedford]
- **Greenwich Village** • 490 Hudson St [Grove St]
- **Joffrey Ballet** • 434 Sixth Ave [10th]
- **Little Red School House** • 272 Sixth Ave [Bleecker]
- **Merce Cunningham Studio** • 55 Bethune St [Wash]
- **The New School for Drama** • 151 Bank St [Wash]
- **Our Lady of Pompeii** • 240 Bleecker St [Carmine]
- **Pratt Institute** • 144 W 14th St [6th Av]
- **PS 3 The Charette** • 490 Hudson St [Grove St]
- **PS 41 Greenwich Village** • 116 W 11th St [6th Av]
- **PS 721 Manhattan Occupational Training** • 250 W Houston St [Varick]
- **St Joseph** • 111 Washington Pl [6th Av]
- **St Luke's** • 487 Hudson St [Christopher]
- **Village Community** • 272 W 10th St [Greenwich St]

Supermarkets

- **Associated** • 255 W 14th St [8th Av]
- **Balducci's** • 81 Eighth Ave [14th]
- **Citarella** • 424 Sixth Ave [9th]
- **D'Agostino** • 666 Greenwich St [Christopher]
- **D'Agostino** • 790 Greenwich St [Bethune]
- **Food Emporium** • 475 Sixth Ave [12th]
- **Gourmet Garage** • 117 Seventh Ave S [Christopher]
- **Gristede's** • 3 Sheridan Sq [Barrow]
- **Gristede's** • 585 Hudson St [Bank]
- **Western Beef** • 403 W 14th St [9th Av]

It may be a bit more difficult to navigate, but the West Village, with its beautiful town-homes on quaint tree-lined streets, is full of hidden gems. On a Sunday afternoon, stroll along the Hudson River Greenway, looking west at the river or east at all the posh new architecture. Lovely.

2 3 4
1

Ma

Coffee

- **Brewbar Coffee** • 327 W 11th St [Greenwich St]
- **Café 201** • 201 Varick St [Houston]
- **CC's Café** • 496 Hudson St [Christopher]
- **Chocolate Bar** • 48 Eighth Ave [4th]
- **Coffee Sweet Heart** • 69 Eighth Ave [13th]
- **Cosi** • 504 Sixth Ave [13th]
- **Doma** • 17 Perry St [Greenwich St]
- **Dunkin' Donuts** • 395 Hudson St [Clarkson]
- **Dunkin' Donuts** • 536 Sixth Ave [14th]
- **Dunkin' Donuts** • 75 Christopher St [4th]
- **The Grey Dog's Coffee** • 33 Carmine St [Bleecker]
- **Grounded** • 28 Jane St [4th]
- **Hudson Coffee Bar** • 350 Hudson St [Charlton]
- **Joe: The Art of Coffee** • 141 Waverly Pl [Gay]
- **Le Gamin Café** • 522 Hudson St [10th]
- **McNulty's Tea & Coffee Company** • 109 Christopher St [Bleecker]
- **Millers Tea Room** • 113 Christopher St [Bedford]
- **New World Coffee** • 488 Sixth Ave [12th]
- **Porto Rico Importing** • 201 Bleecker St [MacDougal]
- **Rocco's** • 243 Bleecker St [Leroy]
- **Sant Ambroeus** • 259 W 4th [Perry]
- **'sNice** • 45 Eighth Ave [4th]
- **Starbucks** • 150 Varick St [Vandam]
- **Starbucks** • 378 Sixth Ave [Waverly]
- **Starbucks** • 510 Sixth Ave [13th]
- **Starbucks** • 72 Grove St [4th]
- **Starbucks** • 93 Greenwich Ave [Bank]
- **Sucelt Coffee Shop** • 200 W 14th St [7th Av]
- **Sweet Life Café** • 147 Christopher St [Greenwich St]
- **Village Delight Café** • 323 Bleecker St [Christopher]

Copy Shops

- **Copy/Com** • 70A Greenwich Ave [11th]
- **Elite Copy Center** • 52 Carmine St [Bedford]
- **Mail Boxes Etc** • 302 W 12th St [8th Av]
- **Mail Boxes Etc** • 315 Bleecker St [Grove St]
- **Mail Boxes Etc** • 511 Sixth Ave [13th]
- **Village Copy Center** • 520 Hudson St [10th]

Farmer's Markets

- **Abingdon Square** (Sat 8 am–2 pm, year round) • W 12th St & Hudson St

Gyms

- **Crunch Fitness** • 152 Christopher St [Wash]
- **Curves (Women only)** • 345 W 14th St [8th Av]
- **Equinox Fitness Club** • 97 Greenwich Ave [12th]
- **Hanson Fitness** • 132 Perry St [Greenwich St]
- **New York Sports Clubs** • 125 Seventh Ave S [10th]♿
- **Printing House Fitness & Racquet Club** • 421 Hudson St [Leroy]
- **YMCA McBurney** • 125 W 14th St [6th Av]

Hardware Stores

- **Barney's Hardware** • 467 Sixth Ave [11th]
- **Blaustein Paint & Hardware** • 304 Bleecker St [Barrow]
- **Garber Hardware** • 710 Greenwich St [Charles]
- **Hardware Mart** • 140 W 14th St [6th Av]
- **Jonathan's Decorative Hardware** • 12 Perry St [7th Av]
- **Lock-It Hardware** • 59 Carmine St [Bedford]

Liquor Stores

- **Casa Oliveira Wines & Liquors** • 98 Seventh Ave S [Grove St]
- **Christopher Street Liquor Shoppe** • 45 Christopher St [Grove St]
- **Golden Rule Wine & Liquor** • 457 Hudson St [Barrow]
- **Imperial Liquors** • 579 Hudson St [Bank]
- **Manley's Liquor Store** • 35 Eighth Ave [4th]
- **North Village Liquors** • 254 W 14th St [7th Av]
- **Pop the Cork Wine Merchant** • 168 Seventh Ave S [Waverly]
- **Sea Grape Wine & Spirits** • 512 Hudson St [10th]
- **Spirits of Carmine** • 52 Carmine St [Bedford]
- **Village Vintner** • 448 Sixth Ave [10th]
- **Village Wine & Spirits** • 486 Sixth Ave [12th]
- **Vinvino Wine** • 56 King St [Varick]
- **Waverly Wine & Liquor** • 135 Waverly Pl [6th Av]
- **Wines by Com (Wine only)** • 23 Jones St [4th]

Pet Shops

- **Beasty Feast** • 630 Hudson St [Horatio]
- **Beasty Feast** • 680 Washington St [Charles]
- **Canine Styles Downtown** • 43 Greenwich Ave [Charles]
- **Groom-O-Rama** • 496 Sixth Ave [13th]
- **Parrots & Pups** • 45 Christopher St [Waverly]
- **Pet Central** • 237 Bleecker St [Leroy]
- **Pet Palace** • 109 W 10th St [6th Av]
- **Pet's Kitchen** • 116 Christopher St [Bedford]
- **Petland Discounts** • 389 Sixth Ave [Waverly]

Video Rental

- **Evergreen Video** • 37 Carmine St [Bedford]
- **Kim's Video** • 89 Christopher St [Bleecker]
- **World of Video** • 51 Greenwich Ave [Perry]

What can we say? Movies = Film Forum; Trendy = Spotted Pig; Burgers = Corner Bistro; Pizza = Joe's, John's; Burgers = Corner Bistro; Lobster Roll = Pearl Oyster Bar; Jazz = Village Vanguard; Speakeasy = Chumley's; Classic Bar = The Ear Inn. And we won't leave New York unless Florent does first.

2 | 3 | 4
1

Ma

🍸 Nightlife

- **2i's** • 248 W 14th St [7th Av]
- **APT** • 419 W 13th St [Wash]
- **Art Bar** • 52 Eighth Ave [4th]
- **Automatic Slims** • 733 Washington St [Bank]
- **Barrow's Pub** • 463 Hudson St [Barrow]
- **Chumley's** • 86 Bedford St [Barrow]
- **Cielo** • 18 Little W 12th St [9th Av]
- **Cornelia Street Café** • 29 Cornelia St [4th]
- **Culture Club** • 179 Varick St [Spring]
- **Daddy-O** • 44 Bedford St [Leroy]
- **Don Hill's** • 511 Greenwich St [Spring]
- **Duplex** • 61 Christopher St [7th Av]
- **The Ear Inn** • 326 Spring St [Greenwich]
- **Employees Only** • 510 Hudson St [10th]
- **Gaslight Lounge** • 400 W 14th St [9th Av]
- **Henrietta Hudson** • 438 Hudson St [Morton]
- **Hudson Bar and Books** • 636 Hudson St [Horatio]
- **Jazz Gallery** • 290 Hudson St [Spring]
- **Johnny's Bar** • 90 Greenwich Ave [12th]
- **Kettle of Fish** • 59 Christopher St [7th]
- **Little Branch** • 20 Seventh Ave S [12th]
- **Lotus** • 409 W 14th St [9th Av]
- **Luke and Leroy** • 21 Seventh Ave S [Leroy]
- **Smalls** • 183 W 10th St [4th]
- **SOB's** • 204 Varick St [Houston]
- **The Otheroom** • 143 Perry St [Wash]
- **Village Vanguard** • 178 Seventh Ave S [Perry]
- **Vol de Nuit** • 148 W 4th St [6th Av]
- **West** • 425 West St [11th]
- **White Horse Tavern** • 567 Hudson St [11th]
- **Wogie's** • 39 Greenwich Ave [Charles]

🍴 Restaurants

- **A Salt & Battery** • 112 Greenwich Ave [13th]
- **Agave** • 140 Seventh Ave S [Charles]
- **AOC** • 314 Bleecker St [Grove St]
- **Aquagrill** • 210 Spring St [Sullivan]
- **August** • 359 Bleecker St [Charles]
- **Benny's Burritos** • 113 Greenwich Ave [Jane]
- **Blue Ribbon Bakery** • 33 Downing St [Bedford]
- **Bonsignour** • 35 Jane St [8th Av]
- **Café Asean** • 117 W 10th St [Patchin Pl]
- **Caffe Torino** • 139 W 10th St [Greenwich Av]
- **Chez Brigitte** • 77 Greenwich Ave [7th]
- **Chumley's** • 86 Bedford St [Barrow]
- **Corner Bistro** • 331 W 4th St [Horatio]
- **Cowgirl** • 519 Hudson St [10th]
- **Day-O** • 103 Greenwich Ave [12th]
- **Diablo Royale** • 189 W 10th St [4th]
- **Do Hwa** • 55 Carmine St [Bedford]

- **Dragonfly** • 47 Seventh Ave [13th]
- **Employees Only** • 510 Hudson St [10th]
- **Fatty Crab** • 643 Hudson St [Gansevoort]
- **Florent** • 69 Gansevoort St [Wash] ♨
- **French Roast** • 78 W 11th St [6th Av]
- **Gonzo Restaurant** • 140 W 13th St [6th Av]
- **Gradisca** • 126 W 13th St [6th Av]
- **The Grey Dog's Coffee** • 33 Carmine St [Bedford]
- **Gusto** • 60 Greenwich Ave [7th Av]
- **Havana Alma de Cuba** • 94 Christopher St [Bleecker]
- **Home** • 20 Cornelia St [4th]
- **Hong Kong Noodle Bar** • 26 Carmine St [Bleecker]
- **Ivo & Lulu** • 558 Broome St [Varick]
- **Jefferson Grill** • 121 W 10th St [Greenwich Av]
- **Joe's Pizza** • 233 Bleecker St [Carmine]
- **John's Pizzeria** • 278 Bleecker St [Jones]
- **Jonez** • 41 Greenwich Ave [Charles]
- **La Palapa Rockola** • 359 Sixth Ave [Wash Pl]
- **Le Gamin** • 27 Bedford St [Downing]
- **MaMa Buddha** • 578 Hudson St [11th]
- **Mary's Fish Camp** • 64 Charles St [4th]
- **Mercadito** • 100 Seventh Ave S [Grove]
- **Mirchi** • 29 Seventh Ave S [Bedford]
- **Moustache** • 90 Bedford St [Grove St]
- **Old Homestead** • 56 Ninth Ave [14th]
- **One If By Land, TIBS** • 17 Barrow St [Bleecker]
- **Ony** • 357 Sixth Ave [Wash Pl]
- **Pastis** • 9 Ninth Ave [Little W 12th]
- **Pearl Oyster Bar** • 18 Cornelia St [4th]
- **Perry Street** • 176 Perry St [Wash]
- **Petite Abeille** • 466 Hudson St [Barrow]
- **Philip Marie** • 569 Hudson St [11th]
- **Pink Teacup** • 42 Grove St [Bleecker]
- **Po** • 31 Cornelia St [4th]
- **Risotteria** • 270 Bleecker St [Morton]
- **Sapore** • 55 Greenwich Ave [Perry]
- **Shopsin's** • 54 Carmine St [Bedford]
- **Snack Taverna** • 63 Bedford St [Morton]
- **'sNice** • 45 Eighth Ave [4th]
- **Souen** • 210 Sixth Ave [Prince]
- **Spice Market** • 403 W 13th St [9th Av]
- **Spotted Pig** • 314 W 11th St [Greenwich]
- **Tea & Sympathy** • 108 Greenwich Ave [13th]
- **Tortilla Flats** • 767 Washington St [12th]
- **Two Boots** • 201 W 11th St [Greenwich]
- **Voyage Restaurant** • 117 Perry St [Greenwich]
- **Yama** • 38 Carmine St [Bedford]

🎬 Movie Theaters

- **Film Forum** • 209 W Houston St [Varick]
- **IFC Center** • 323 Sixth Ave [3rd]
- **New York Public Library Jefferson Market Branch** • 425 Sixth Ave [10th]

🛍️ Shopping

- **Alexander McQueen** • 417 W 14th St [9th Av]
- **Alphabets** • 47 Greenwich Ave [Charles]
- **American Apparel** • 373 Sixth Ave [Waverly]
- **Bleecker Street Records** • 239 Bleecker St [Leroy]
- **Carry on Tea & Sympathy** • 110 Greenwich Ave [13th]
- **Cherry** • 19 Eighth Ave [Jane]
- **Cherry Men** • 17 Eighth Ave [Jane]
- **Chocolate Bar** • 48 Eighth Ave [4th]
- **CO Bigelow Chemists** • 414 Sixth Ave [9th]
- **Cynthia Rowley** • 376 Bleecker St [Perry]
- **Faicco's Pork Store** • 260 Bleecker St [Cornelia]
- **Flight 001** • 96 Greenwich Ave [Jane]
- **Geppetto's Toy Box** • 10 Christopher St [Gay]
- **Health & Harmony** • 470 Hudson St [Barrow]
- **Integral Yoga Natural Foods** • 229 W 13th St [7th Av]
- **Jacques Torres Chocolate Haven** • 350 Hudson St [Charlton]
- **Janovic** • 161 Sixth Ave [Spring]
- **Jeffrey** • 449 W 14th St [Wash]
- **The Leather Man** • 111 Christopher St [Bedford]
- **Little Pie Company** • 407 W 14th St [9th Av]
- **Magnolia Bakery** • 401 Bleecker St [11th]
- **Marc Jacobs** • 385 Bleecker St [Perry]
- **Matt Umanov Guitars** • 273 Bleecker St [Jones]
- **Murray's Cheese Shop** • 254 Bleecker St [Leroy]
- **Mxyplyzyk** • 125 Greenwich Ave [13th]
- **Myers of Keswick** • 634 Hudson St [Horatio]
- **O Ottomanelli's & Sons** • 285 Bleecker St [Jones]
- **Otte** • 121 Greenwich Ave [Jane]
- **The Porcelain Room** • 13 Christopher St [Gay]
- **Porto Rico Importing Company** • 201 Bleecker St [MacDougal]
- **Radio Shack** • 360 Sixth Ave [Wash Pl]
- **Radio Shack** • 49 Seventh Ave [13th]
- **Rebel Rebel Records** • 319 Bleecker St [Christopher]
- **Reserva Dominica Cigars** • 37A Seventh Ave [13th]
- **Scott Jordan Furniture** • 137 Varick St [Spring]
- **Stella McCartney** • 429 W 14th St [Greene]
- **Urban Outfitters** • 374 Sixth Ave [Waverly]
- **Vitra** • 29 Ninth Ave [13th]

35

Driving and parking are notoriously difficult here, except for Washington Street. Biking is a great alternative, with so many paths and the greenbelt on the Hudson. It's worth catching the subway at West 4th Street just to have an excuse to watch a basketball game at the Cage nearby.

Subways

①②③ⒻⓋ Ⓛ .... 14 St-6 Ave
① .... Christopher St-Sheridan Sq
① .... Houston St
ⒶⒸⒺⒻⓋ ⒷⒹ .... W 4 St
ⒶⒸⒺⓁ .... 14 St-8 Ave
ⒸⒺ .... Spring St

Bus Lines

11 .... Ninth Ave/Tenth Ave
14 .... 14th St Crosstown
20 .... Abingdon Sq
20 .... Seventh Ave/Eighth Ave/Central Park West
21 .... Houston St Crosstown
5 .... Fifth Ave/Sixth Ave/Riverside Dr
6 .... Seventh Ave/Sixth Ave/Broadway
8 .... 8th St/9th St Crosstown

Bike Lanes

- • • • Marked Bike Lane
- • • • Recommended Route
- • • • Greenway

PATH

- **14 St** • 14th St & Sixth Ave
- **9th St** • 9th St & Sixth Ave
- **Christopher St** • Christopher St & Hudson St

Car Rental

- **Big Apple Rent-A-Car** • 575 Washington St [Houston]
- **Dollar** • 99 Charles St [Bleecker]
- **Hertz** • 18 Morton St [7th Av]

Car Washes

- **Apple Management** • 332 W 11th St [Wash]
- **Lage Car Wash** • 124 Sixth Ave [Sullivan]
- **Village Car Wash & Lube** • 160 Leroy St [Wash]

Gas Stations

- **Lukoil** • 63 Eighth Ave [13th] ⊕
- **Mobil** • 140 Sixth Ave [Sullivan] ⊕
- **Mobil** • 290 West St [Canal] ⊕

Parking

Map 6 • Washington Sq / NYU / NoHo / Soho

Hints of bohemia still exist around Washington Square Park—thanks in part to scrappy preservationists working hard to keep developers and land-hungry NYU in line. The ultra-cool lofts of SoHo impress, even if the boring chain stores they house don't. Stroll along Washington Mews, a quaint cobblestone street.

24-Hour Pharmacies
- **Duane Reade** • 123 Third Ave [14th]
- **Duane Reade** • 24 E 14th St [University]
- **Duane Reade** • 598 Broadway [Houston]
- **Duane Reade** • 769 Broadway [9th]
- **Walgreen's** • 145 Fourth Ave [13th]

Bagels
- **Bagel Bob's** • 51 University Pl [10th]
- **The Bagel Café/Ray's Pizza** • 2 St Mark's Pl [3rd Av]
- **Giant Bagel Shop** • 120 University Pl [13th]

Banks
AP • **Apple** • 4 Irving Pl [14th]
AP • **Apple (ATM)** • Walgreen's• 145 Fourth Ave [13th]
AT • **Atlantic (ATM)** • Gristedes• 246 Mercer St [3rd]
AT • **Atlantic (ATM)** • Gristedes• 333 E 14th St [2nd Av]
BA • **Bank of America** • 589 Broadway [Houston]
BA • **Bank of America** • 72 2nd Ave [4th]
BA • **Bank of America (ATM** • 66 3rd Av [11]
BA • **Bank of America (ATM** • 742 Broadway [Astor Pl]
CH • **Chase** • 2 Astor Pl [Lafayette]
CH • **Chase** • 32 University Pl [9th]
CH • **Chase** • 525 Broadway [Spring]
CH • **Chase** • 623 Broadway [Houston]
CH • **Chase** • 785 Broadway [10th]
CH • **Chase** • 90 Fifth Ave [15th]
CH • **Chase (ATM)** • Duane Reade • 125 Third Ave [14th]
CH • **Chase (ATM)** • Duane Reade • 4 W 4th St [B'way]
CH • **Chase (ATM)** • Duane Reade • 598 Broadway [Houston]
CH • **Chase (ATM)** • Duane Reade • 636 Broadway [Bleecker]
CH • **Chase (ATM)** • Duane Reade • 761 Broadway [8th]
CI • **Citibank** • 555 LaGuardia Pl [3rd]
CO • **Commerce** • 666 Broadway [Bond]
CO • **Commerce** • 96 Fifth Ave [15th]
EM • **Emigrant** • 105 Second Ave [6th]
HS • **HSBC** • 1 E 8th St [5th Av]
HS • **HSBC** • 599 Broadway [Houston]
HS • **HSBC** • 799 Broadway [9th]
EC • **Independence Community** • 43 E 8th St [Greene]
NF • **North Fork** • 159 Second Ave [10th]
NF • **North Fork** • 594 Broadway [Houston]
SG • **Signature** • 65 Fifth Ave [13th]
WM • **Washington Mutual** • 130 Second Ave [St Marks]
WM • **Washington Mutual** • 57 Bond St
WM • **Washington Mutual** • 835 B'way [13]

Community Gardens

Emergency Rooms
- **New York Eye & Ear Infirmary** • 310 E 14th St [2nd Av]

Landmarks
- **11 Spring St** • Spring St & Elizabeth St
- **The Alamo (The Cube)** • Astor Pl & Fourth Ave
- **Asch Building (Brown Building)** • 23-29 Washington Pl [Greene]
- **Bayard-Condict Building** • 65 Bleecker St [Crosby]
- **CBGB & OMFUG** • 315 Bowery [Bleecker]
- **Colonnade Row** • 428 Lafayette St [Astor Pl]
- **Con Edison Building** • 145 E 14th St [Irving]
- **Cooper Union** • 30 Cooper Sq [Bowery]
- **Gem Spa** • 131 Second Ave [St Marks]
- **Grace Church** • 802 Broadway [11th]
- **Great Jones Fire House** • Great Jones St & Bowery
- **Joey Ramone Place** • Bowery & E 2nd St
- **Lombardi's** • 32 Spring St [Mott]
- **Mark Twain House** • 14 W 10th St [5th Av]
- **McSorley's** • 15 E 7th St [3rd Av]
- **Milano's** • 51 E Houston St [Mott]
- **New York Marble Cemetery** • 41 Second Ave [2nd]
- **Old Merchant's House** • 29 E 4th St [Lafayette]
- **The Public Theater** • 425 Lafayette St [Astor Pl]
- **Salmagundi Club** • 47 Fifth Ave [12th]
- **Singer Building** • 561 Broadway [Prince]
- **St Mark's-in-the-Bowery Church** • 131 E 10th St [3rd Av]
- **The Strand Bookstore** • 828 Broadway [12th St]
- **Wanamaker's** • Broadway & E 8th St
- **Washington Mews** • University Pl (entrance) [5th Av]
- **Washington Square Park** • Washington Sq [Wash Sq N]

Libraries
- **Ottendorfer** • 135 Second Ave [9th]

Post Offices
- **Cooper** • 93 Fourth Ave [11th]
- **Patchin** • 70 W 10th St [6th Av]
- **Prince** • 124 Greene St [Prince]

Schools
- **Alfred Adler Institute** • 594 Broadway [Houston]
- **Auxiliary Services** • 198 Forsyth St [Stanton]
- **Benjamin N Cardozo School of Law** • 55 Fifth Ave [12th]
- **Cascade HS Center For Multimedia Communications (M650)** • 198 Forsyth St [Stanton]

- **Cooper Union** • 30 Cooper Sq [4th Av]
- **Eugene Lang College** • 65 W 11th St [6th]
- **Gateway** • 236 Second Ave [14th]
- **Grace Church** • 86 Fourth Ave [11th]
- **Harvey Milk** • 2 Astor Pl [B'way]
- **Hebrew Union College** • 1 W 4th St [B'way]
- **Institute of Audio Research** • 64 University Pl [11th]
- **La Salle Academy** • 44 E 2nd St [2nd Av]
- **Legacy School for Intergrated Studies** • 33 W 13th St [5th Av]
- **Milano The New School for Management and Urban Policy** • 72 Fifth Ave [13th]
- **Nativity Mission** • 204 Forsyth St [Stanton]
- **New School for Social Research** • 66 W 12th St [6th Av]
- **New York Eye and Ear Institute** • 310 E 14th St [2nd Av]
- **New York University** • 22 Washington Sq N [MacDougal]
- **NYU Graduate School of Arts and Science** • 6 Washington Sq N [University]
- **NYU Leonard N Stern School of Business** • 44 W 4th St [Greene]
- **NYU School of Law** • 40 Washington Sq S [MacDougal]
- **NYU Shirley M Ehrenkranz School of Social Work** • 1 Washington Sq N [University]
- **NYU Steinhardt School of Education** • 82 Washington Sq E [Wash Pl]
- **NYU Wagner** • 295 Lafayette St [Jersey]
- **Parsons School of Design** • 66 Fifth Ave [13th]
- **PS 751 Career Development Center** • 113 E 4th St [1st Av]
- **Satellite Academy High** • 198 Forsyth St [Stanton]
- **St Anthony** • 60 MacDougal St [Houston]
- **St Patrick** • 233 Mott St [Prince]
- **The New School for Jazz and Contemporary Music** • 55 W 13th St [6th]
- **Third Street Music School Settlement** • 235 E 11th St [3rd Av]
- **Tisch School of Arts** • 721 Broadway [Waverly]
- **Tisch School of Arts–Dance** • 111 Second Ave [7th]

Supermarkets
- **Associated** • 130 Bleecker St [LaGuardia]
- **D'Agostino** • 64 University Pl [11th]
- **Dean & DeLuca** • 560 Broadway [Prince]
- **Garden of Eden Gourmet** • 7 E 14th St [5th Av]
- **Gristede's** • 113 Fourth Ave [12th]
- **Gristede's** • 246 Mercer St [3rd]
- **Gristede's** • 25 University Pl [8th]
- **Gristede's** • 333 E 14th St [2nd Av]
- **Gristede's** • 5 W 14th St [5th Av]
- **Met Food** • 107 Second Ave [6th]
- **Met Food** • 251 Mulberry St [Prince]
- **Trader Joe's** • 142 E 14th St [Irving]
- **Whole Foods Market** • 4 Union Sq S [University]

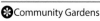

Map 8 · **Washington Sq / NYU / NoHo / SoHo**

If you can't find what you need here, it probably doesn't exist. Hardware stores are stocked with obscurities and so are local movie rental places (Kim's, TLA, Tower). Want a buzz? Check out the bargains at Warehouse Wines & Spirits or grab a coffee at Café Gitane's take out window.

Coffee

- **Anyway Café** • 34 E 2nd St [2nd Av]
- **Atlas Café** • 73 Second Ave [4th]
- **Au Bon Pain** • 58 E 8th St [Mercer]
- **Au Bon Pain** • 684 Broadway [3rd]
- **Café Angelique** • 68 Bleecker St [Crosby]
- **Café Gitane** • 242 Mott St [Prince]
- **Caffe Dante** • 79 MacDougal St [Bleecker]
- **Caffe Pane e Cioccolato** • 10 Waverly Pl [Mercer]
- **Caffe Reggio** • 119 MacDougal St [3rd]
- **Choux Factory** • 58 W 8th St [MacDougal]
- **Coffee Master** • 13 E 4th St [Lafayette]
- **Cosi** • 841 Broadway [13th]
- **Cremcaffe** • 65 Second Ave [4th]
- **Cuppa Cuppa** • 75 E 4th St [2nd Av]
- **Dean & DeLuca Café** • 560 Broadway [Prince]
- **Dean & DeLuca Café** • 75 University Pl [11th]
- **Dunkin' Donuts** • 166 Second Ave [11th]
- **Dunkin' Donuts** • 218 E 14th St [3rd Av]
- **Hiroko's** • 75 Thompson St [Spring]
- **Housing Works Used Book Café** • 126 Crosby St [Jersey]
- **J&B Express** • 123 3rd St [MacDougal]
- **Joe: The Art of Coffee** • 9 E 13th St [5th]
- **L'Angolo Café** • 108 W Houston St [Thompson]
- **La Lanterna** • 129 MacDougal St [3rd]
- **Le Petite Café** • 156 Spring St [W B'way]
- **Lulivo Café** • 184 Spring St [Thompson]
- **Mission Café** • 82 Second Ave [5th]
- **Mudspot** • 307 E 9th St [2nd Av]
- **Muffins & More** • 114 Fourth Ave [12th]
- **New World Coffee** • 412 W Broadway [Spring]
- **Once Upon A Tart** • 135 Sullivan St [Prince]
- **Open Pantry** • 184 Second Ave [12th]
- **Oren's Daily Roast** • 31 Waverly Pl [Greene]
- **Podunk** • 231 E 5th St [3rd Av]
- **Porto Rico** • 107 Thompson St [Prince]
- **Porto Rico** • 40 St Marks Pl [2nd Av]
- **Starbucks** • 13 Astor Pl [B'way]
- **Starbucks** • 145 Second Ave [9th]
- **Starbucks** • 21 E 8th St [University]
- **Starbucks** • 51 Astor Pl [4th Av]
- **Starbucks** • 665 Broadway [Bond]
- **Starbucks** • 72 Spring St [Lafayette]
- **Tea Spot** • 127 MacDougal St [3rd]
- **Thompson Café** • 68 Thompson St [Broome]
- **Veniero's** • 342 E 11th St [University]

Farmer's Markets

- **St Mark's Church** (Tues 8am-7pm May-Dec) • E 10th St & Second Ave

Copy Shops

- **Advanced Copy** • 552 LaGuardia Pl [3rd]
- **American Copy** • 201 E 10th St [2nd Av]
- **East Side Copy** • 15 E 13th St [5th Av]
- **FedEx Kinko's** • 21 Astor Pl [B'way]
- **First Prince Copy** • 22 Prince St [Elizabeth]
- **King Photocopy** • 45 E 7th St [2nd Av]
- **National Reprographics** • 594 Broadway [Houston]
- **New University Copy** • 11 Waverly Pl [Mercer]
- **NY Copy Center** • 204 E 11th St [3rd Av]
- **NY Copy Center** • 34 E 7th St [2nd Av]
- **Prince Street Copy Center** • 159 Prince St [Thompson]
- **Source Unlimited Printing** • 331 E 9th St [2nd Av]
- **Staples** • 5 Union Sq W [University]
- **Staples** • 769 Broadway [9th]
- **Village Copier** • 20 E 13th St [University]
- **Unique Copy Center** • 252 Greene St [Waverly]
- **The UPS Store** • 111 E 14th St [Irving]
- **The UPS Store** • 168 Second Ave [11th]
- **The UPS Store** • 319 Lafayette St [Houston]
- **The UPS Store** • 7 E 8th St [5th Av]

Gyms

- **24/7 Fitness Club** • 47 W 14th St [5th Av]
- **Clay** • 25 W 14th St [5th Av]
- **Crunch Fitness** • 404 Lafayette St [4th]
- **Crunch Fitness** • 54 E 13th St [B'way]
- **Crunch Fitness** • 623 Broadway [Houston]
- **Curves** (Women only) • 580 Broadway [Prince]
- **Dolphin Fitness** • 94 E 4th St [2nd Av]
- **Hanson Fitness** • 63 Greene St [Broome]
- **Hanson Fitness** • 826 Broadway [12th]
- **Lucille Roberts Health Club** • 80 Fifth Ave [14th]
- **NYHRC** • 24 E 13th St [University]
- **NYHRC** • 62 Cooper Sq [Astor Pl]
- **NY Sports Clubs** • 232 Mercer St [3rd]
- **NY Sports Clubs** • 34 W 14th St [5th Av]
- **NY Sports Clubs** • 503 Broadway [Broome]
- **Sol Goldman YM-YWHA** • 344 E 14th St [1st]
- **Synergy Fitness** • 227 Mulberry St [Spring]
- **The Union Square Sports Club** • 113 Fourth Ave [12th]

Movie Theaters

- **Angelika** • 18 W Houston St [Mercer]
- **Anthology Film Archives** • 32 Second Ave [2nd]
- **Cinema Village** • 22 E 12th St [University]
- **City Cinemas: Village East Cinemas** • 189 Second Ave [12th]
- **Landmark Sunshine Cinema** • 141 E Houston St [Eldridge]
- **Loews Cineplex Village VII** • 66 Third Ave [11th]
- **Metropol@Rififi** • 332 E 11th St [2nd]
- **NYU Cantor Film Center** • 36 E 8th St [Greene]
- **Quad Cinema** • 34 W 13th St [5th Av]
- **Regal Union Square Stadium 14** • 850 Broadway [14th]

Hardware Stores

- **10003 Hardware** • 90 University Pl [12th]
- **Ace Hardware** • 130 Fourth Ave [13th]
- **Allied Hardware** • 59 Second Ave [3rd]
- **Bowery Homes Supplies** • 55 Bond St [Bowery]
- **East Hardware** • 79 Third Ave [12th]
- **Home Locksmith** • 54 E 14th St [3rd Av]
- **Metropolitan Lumber & Hardware** • 175 Spring St [Thompson]
- **Mott Hardware** • 186 Mott St [Kenmare]
- **Shapiro** • 63 Bleecker St [Lafayette]
- **TS Hardware** • 52 E 8th St [Mercer]

Liquor Stores

- **Anthony Liquors** • 52 Spring St [Mulberry]
- **Astor Wines** • 12 Astor Pl [Lafayette]
- **B&S Zeeman** • 47 University Pl [9th]
- **Crossroads** • 55 W 14th St [5th Av]
- **Elizabeth & Vine** • 253 Elizabeth [Houston]
- **Miat Liquor Store** • 166 Second Ave [11th]
- **S&P Liquor & Wine** • 300 E 5th St [2nd Av]
- **Soho Wine & Spirits** • 461 West Broadway [Houston]
- **Spring Street Wine Shop** • 187 Spring St [Thompson]
- **Thompson Wine & Spirits** • 222 Thompson St [3rd]
- **Trader Joe's** • 138 E 14th St [Irving]
- **Warehouse Wines & Spirits** • 735 Broadway [Astor Pl]
- **Washington Square Wines** • 545 LaGuardia Pl [3rd]
- **Wine Therapy** (Wine only) • 171 Elizabeth St [Spring]

Pet Shops

- **Biscuits & Bath** • 41 W 13th St [5th Av]
- **Creature Features** • 21 E 3rd St [2nd Av]
- **Pacific Aquarium and Plant** (Fish) • 46 Delancey St [Eldridge]
- **Whiskers** • 235 E 9th St [Stuyvesant St]

Video Rental

- **Blockbuster** • 774 Broadway [9th]
- **Cinema Nolita** • 202B Elizabeth St [Prince]
- **Hollywood Video** • 46 Third Ave [10th]
- **Kim's Video** • 6 St Marks Pl [3rd Av]
- **Movie Bank USA** • 14th St & Fifth Ave ⊗
- **Movie Bank USA** • 14th St & Third Ave ⊗
- **Movie Bank USA** • 71 W Houston St [Wooster]
- **Movie Bank USA** • E 9th St & Broadway ⊗
- **TLA Video** • 52 W 8th St [MacDougal]
- **Tower Video** • 20 E 4th St [Lafayette]

Map 6 • Washington Sq / NYU / NoHo / SoHo

Pound for pound, still the most exciting place on the planet. Nightlife—try Bowery Ballroom, KGB, Joe's Pub, Milano's, and Mars Bar. Eats—Blue Ribbon, DeMarco's, Eight Mile, John's, Sammy's, the Strip House, and Angelica Kitchen. Shopping—MoMA, Moss, Paul Frank, Prada, Kiehl's, Kate's, the list goes on…

Nightlife

- **Ace of Clubs** • 9 Great Jones St [Lafayette]
- **Baggot Inn** • 82 W 3rd St [Thompson]
- **Bar Next Door** • 129 MacDougal St [3rd]
- **Bar Veloce** • 175 Second Ave [11th]
- **Beauty Bar** • 231 E 14th St [3rd Av]
- **Blue & Gold** • 79 E 7th St [1st Av]
- **Blue Note** • 131 W 3rd St [MacDougal]
- **Bowery Ballroom** • 6 Delancey [Bowery]
- **Bowery Poetry Club** • 308 Bowery [1st]
- **CBGB & OMFUG** • 315 Bowery [Bleecker]
- **Cedar Tavern** • 82 University Pl [11th]
- **Central Bar** • 109 E 9th St [4th Av]
- **Comedy Cellar** • 117 MacDougal [Minetta]
- **Continental** • 25 Third Ave [Stuyvesant]
- **Crash Mansion** • 199 Bowery [Spring]
- **Detour** • 328 Thompson St [3rd]
- **The Dove** • 228 Thompson St [3rd]
- **Fanelli's** • 94 Prince St [Mercer]
- **The Fish Bar** • 237 E 5th St [3rd Av]
- **Gibraltar Lounge** • 20 Prince St [Elizabeth]
- **Grassroots Tavern** • 20 St Marks Pl [2nd]
- **Holiday Lounge** • 75 St Marks Pl [1st]
- **Joe's Pub** • 425 Lafayette St [Astor Pl]
- **KGB** • 85 E 4th St [2nd Av]
- **Lit** • 93 Second Ave [5th]
- **Loreley** • 7 Rivington St [Bowery]
- **Mannahatta** • 316 Bowery [Bleecker]
- **Marion's** • 354 Bowery [Great Jones]
- **Mars Bar** • 25 E 1st St [2nd Av]
- **McSorley's** • 15 E 7th St [Shevchenko Pl]
- **Milady's** • 160 Prince St [Thompson]
- **Milano's** • 51 E Houston St [Mott]
- **Nevada Smith's** • 74 Third Ave [11th]
- **Peculier Pub** • 145 Bleecker St [LaGuardia]
- **Pravda** • 281 Lafayette St [Prince]
- **Red Bench** • 107 Sullivan St [Spring]
- **Riffi** • 332 E 11th St [2nd Av]
- **Sapphire Lounge** • 249 Eldridge St [Stanton]
- **Spring Street Lounge** • 48 Spring St [Mulberry]
- **Sweet & Vicious** • 5 Spring St [Bowery]
- **Terra Blues** • 149 Bleecker St [LaGuardia]
- **Urge Lounge** • 33 Second Ave [2nd]
- **Village Underground** • 130 W 3rd St [MacDougal]
- **Webster Hall** • 125 E 11th St [4th Av]

Restaurants

- **12 Chairs** • 56 MacDougal St [King]
- **A Salt & Battery** • 80 Second Ave [5th]
- **Acme Bar & Grill** • 9 Great Jones[Lafayette]
- **Angelica Kitchen** • 300 E 12th St [2nd Av]
- **Aroma** • 36 E 4th St [Bowery]
- **Around the Clock** • 8 Stuyvesant St [3rd]
- **Arturo's** • 106 W Houston St [Thompson]
- **Babbo** • 110 Waverly Pl [MacDougal]
- **Balthazar** • 80 Spring St [Crosby]
- **Bellavitae** • 21 Minetta Ln [Carmine St]
- **Ben's Pizza** • 177 Spring St [Thompson]
- **Blue 9 Burger** • 92 Third Ave [12th]
- **Blue Green Organic Juice Café** • 248 Mott St [Prince]
- **Blue Hill** • 75 Washington Pl [MacDougal]
- **Blue Ribbon** • 97 Sullivan St [Spring]
- **Blue Ribbon Sushi** • 119 Sullivan St [Prince]
- **Café Colonial** • 276 Elizabeth St [Houston]
- **Café Gitane** • 242 Mott St [Prince]
- **Café Habana** • 17 Prince St [Elizabeth]
- **Café Spice** • 72 University Pl [11th]
- **Cha An Tea House** • 230 E 9th St [Stuyvesant]
- **Chick-fil-A Express** • Weinstein Hall, 5 University Pl [Wash Sq N]
- **ChikaLicious** • 203 E 10th St [2nd Av]
- **Colors** • 417 Lafayette St [4th]
- **Cozy Soup & Burger** • 739 B'way [Astor Pl]
- **Cuba** • 222 Thompson St [3rd]
- **Cubana Café** • 110 Thompson St [Prince]
- **DeMarco's** • 146 West Houston [MacDougal]
- **Dojo East** • 24 St Marks Pl [2nd Av]
- **Dojo West** • 14 W 4th St [Mercer]
- **Eight Mile Creek** • 240 Mulberry St [Prince]
- **Five Points** • 31 Great Jones St [Lafayette]
- **Frank** • 88 Second Ave [5th]
- **Ghenet** • 284 Mulberry St [Houston]
- **Gotham Bar & Grill** • 12 E 12th St [5th Av]
- **Great Jones Café** • 54 Great Jones St [Bowery]
- **Hampton Chutney** • 68 Prince St [Crosby]
- **Holy Basil** • 149 Second Ave [9th]
- **Hummus Place** • 99 MacDougal [Bleecker]
- **Il Buco** • 47 Bond St [Bowery]
- **Il Mulino** • 86 W 3rd St [Thompson]
- **Indian Bread Co** • 194 Bleecker St [MacDougal]
- **Jack Rabbit Sports** • 42 w 14th St [5th av]
- **Jane** • 100 W Houston St [Thompson]
- **Jean Claude** • 137 Sullivan St [Prince]
- **Jeollado** • 116 E 4th St [1st Av]
- **John's of 12th Street** • 302 E 12th St [2nd]
- **Jules** • 65 St Marks Pl [1st Av]
- **Kelley & Ping** • 127 Greene St [Prince]
- **Khyber Pass** • 34 St Marks Pl [2nd Av]
- **Kittichai** • 60 Thompson St [Broome]
- **L'Ulivo Focacceria** • 184 Spring [Thompson]
- **La Esquina** • 106 Kenmare St [Cleveland]
- **Lombardi's** • 32 Spring St [Mott]
- **Mamoun's Falafel** • 119 MacDougal [3rd]
- **Mara's Homemade** • 342 E 6th St [2nd]
- **Melampo Imported Foods** • 105 Sullivan St [Spring]
- **Mercer Kitchen** • 99 Prince St [Mercer]
- **Mingala Burmese** • 21 E 7th St [Taras Shevchenko Pl]
- **Olive's** • 120 Prince St [Wooster]
- **Otto** • 1 Fifth Ave [Wash Mews]
- **Paul's Palace** • 131 Second Ave [St Marks]
- **Peanut Butter & Co** • 240 Sullivan St [3rd]
- **Peep** • 177 Prince St [Sullivan]
- **Penang** • 109 Spring St [Mercer]
- **Pepe Rosso** • 149 Sullivan St [Houston]
- **Pizza Box** • 176 Bleecker St [Sullivan]
- **Pommes Frites** • 123 Second Ave [7th]
- **Room 4 Dessert** • 17 Cleveland Pl [Kenmare]
- **Sala** • 344 Bowery [Great Jones]
- **Sammy's Roumanian** • 157 Chrystie St [Delancey]
- **Souen** • 28 E 13th St [University]
- **Spice** • 60 University Pl [10th]
- **Strip House** • 13 E 12th St [5th Av]
- **Temple** • 35 St Marks Pl [1st Av]
- **Tomoe Sushi** • 172 Thompson St [Houston]
- **Vegetarian's Paradise 2** • 144 W 4th St [6th]
- **Veselka** • 144 Second Ave [9th]
- **Yakitori Taisho** • 5 St Marks Pl [3rd Av]

Shopping

- **Academy Records** • 77 E 10th St [4th Av]
- **AG Adriano Goldschmied** • 111 Greene St [Prince]
- **Apple Store SoHo** • 103 Prince St [Greene]
- **Aveda** • 456 West Broadway [Prince]
- **BCBG by Max Azria** • 120 Wooster St [Prince]
- **Black Hound** • 170 Second Ave [11th]
- **Blades Board & Skate** • 659 B'way [Bond]
- **Block Drug Store** • 101 Second Ave [6th]
- **Chelsea Girl** • 63 Thompson St [Broome]
- **Circuit City** • 52 E 14th St [4th Av]
- **Crembebe** • 68 Second Ave [4th]
- **Daily 235** • 235 Elizabeth St [Prince]
- **DKNY** • 420 West Broadway [Spring]
- **Duncan Quinn** • 8 Spring St [Bowery]
- **East Village Cheese** • 40 Third Ave [10th]
- **East Village Music** • 85 E 4th St [2nd Av]
- **EDGE°ny NOHO** • 65 Bleecker [Lafayette]
- **EMS** • 591 Broadway [Houston]
- **Eye Candy** • 329 Lafayette St [Bleecker]
- **Fabulous Fanny's** • 335 E 9th St [2nd Av]
- **Global Table** • 107 Sullivan St [Spring]
- **Guitar Center** • 25 W 14th St [5th Av]
- **healthfully organic market** • 98 E 4th St [2]
- **Highway** • 238 Mott St [Prince]
- **Intermix** • 98 Prince St [Mercer]
- **Jam Paper & Envelope** • 135 Third Ave [15]
- **Kar'ikter** • 19 Prince St [Elizabeth]
- **Kate's Paperie** • 561 Broadway [Prince]
- **Kiehl's** • 109 Third Ave [13th]
- **Kim's Video** • 6 St Marks Pl [3rd Av]
- **Kinnu** • 43 Spring St [Mulberry]
- **Knit New York** • 307 E 14th St [2nd Av]
- **Leekan Designs** • 93 Mercer St [Spring]
- **Lighting by Gregory** • 158 Bowery [Delancey]
- **Lord Willy's** • 223 Mott St [Prince]
- **Lucky Wang** • 799 Broadway [11th]
- **The Market NYC** • 268 Mulberry St [Prince]
- **Meg** • 312 E 9th St [2nd Av]
- **Michael Anchin Glass** • 245 Elizabeth St [Prince]
- **Mixona** • 262 Mott St [Prince]
- **Mogu** • 258 Elizabeth St [Houston]
- **MoMA Design Store** • 81 Spring [Crosby]
- **Moss** • 146 Greene St [Prince]
- **Nancy Koltes** • 31 Spring St [Mott]
- **National Wholesale Liquidators** • 632 Broadway [Bleecker]
- **New York Adorned** • 47 Second Ave [3rd]
- **New York Central Art Supply** • 62 Third Ave [11th]
- **Other Music** • 15 E 4th St [Lafayette]
- **Otto Tootsi Plohound** • 273 Lafayette [Prince]
- **Otto Tootsi Plohound** • 413 W Broadway [Spring]
- **Paul Frank** • 195 Mulberry St [Kenmare]
- **Prada** • 575 Broadway [Prince]
- **Pylones** • 69 Spring St [Lafayette]
- **Radio Shack** • 781 Broadway [10th]
- **Raffeto's** • 144 W Houston St [MacDougal]
- **Resurrection Vintage** • 217 Mott St [Spring]
- **Saint Mark's Comics** • 11 St Marks Pl [3rd]
- **Screaming Mimi's** • 382 Lafayette St [4th]
- **Stereo Exchange** • 627 B'way [Bleecker]
- **The Stork Club** • 142 Sullivan St [Prince]
- **Stuart Moore** • 128 Prince St [Wooster]
- **Sullivan Street Bakery** • 73 Sullivan [Spring]
- **Surprise, Surprise** • 91 Third Ave [12th]
- **Tory by TRB** • 257 Elizabeth St [Houston]
- **Tower Records** • 692 Broadway [4th]
- **Trash & Vaudeville** • 4 St Marks Pl [3rd Av]
- **Uncle Sam's** • 37 W 8th St [5th Av]
- **Utrecht Art and Drafting Supplies** • 111 Fourth Ave [12th]
- **Veniero's** • 342 E 11th St [2nd Av]
- **Virgin Megastore** • 52 E 14th St [B'way]
- **White Trash** • 304 E 5th St [2nd Av]

43

Map 6 • Washington Sq / NYU / NoHo / SoHo

1/4 mile   .25 km

Considering how exciting and vibrant this section of the city is, parking should be way worse than it is. For biking, use Lafayette Street to go north and either Fifth Avenue or Second Avenue to go south. You can transfer to the BDFV subway from the 6 only going downtown—weird.

2 | 3 | 4
1

Ma

Subways

6	Astor Pl
6	Bleecker St
6	Spring St
F V	2 Ave
B D F V	Broadway-Lafayette St
J M Z	Bowery
L	3 Ave
4 5 6 L N Q R W	14 St-Union Sq
N R W	8 St-NYU
N R W	Prince St
C E	Spring St

Bus Lines

1	Fifth/Madison Aves
101	Third Ave/Lexington Ave/Amsterdam Ave
102	Third Ave/Lexington Ave/Malcolm X Blvd
103	Third Ave/Lexington Ave
14	14th St Crosstown
15	First/Second Aves
2	Fifth/Madison Aves/Powell Blvd
21	Houston St/Avenue C
3	Fifth/Madison Aves/St Nicholas Ave
5	Fifth Ave/Sixth Ave/Riverside Dr
7	Columbus Ave/Amsterdam Ave Lenox Ave/Sixth/Seventh Aves/Broadway
8	8th/9th Sts Crosstown
9	Ave B/East Broadway

Bike Lanes

- • • • Marked Bike Lane
- • • • Recommended Route

 Car Rental

- **Action Car Rental** · 741 Broadway [Astor Pl]
- **Avis** · 68 E 11th St [B'way]
- **Enterprise** · 221 Thompson St [Bleecker]
- **Hertz** · 12 E 13th St [5th Av]
- **Liberty Car Rental** · 220 E 9th St [Stuyvesant St]
- **National/Alamo** · 21 E 12th St [University]

Gas Stations

- **Exxon** · 24 Second Ave [1st] ☼

Parking

Map 7 East Village / Lower East Side

PAGE 208

Gazing north from Bridge Williamsburg's flow, Delancey delights---albeit crudely. A terse stroll away cooks Katz---legend of all delis---plating up its world-renowned corned beef. Near east, the airs of Tompkins Square, welcomingly crisp and required of those in need of a little breathing room...if you can afford it.

2 | 3 | 4
1

Ma

🅑 Bagels

- **535 Self** • 203 E Houston St [Ludlow]
- **Bagel Zone** • 50 Ave A [4th]
- **David's Bagels** • 228 First Ave [14th]
- **Houston's Bagel & Grill** • 283 E Houston St [Clinton]
- **New York Original Bagel** • 430 E 14th St [1st Av]

💲 Banks

- BP • **Banco Popular** • 134 Delancey St [Norfolk]
- BA • **Bank of America** • 126 Delancey St [Norfolk]
- CH • **Chase** • 109 Delancey St [Essex]
- CH • **Chase** • 255 First Ave [15th]
- CH • **Chase (ATM)** • Duane Reade • 194 E 2nd St [Av B]
- CH • **Chase (ATM)** • Duane Reade • 237 First Ave [14th]
- CI • **Citibank** • 50 Ave A [4th]
- HS • **HSBC** • 245 First Ave [15th]
- IC • **Independence Community** • 51 Ave A [4th]
- CU • **Lower East Side People's Federal Credit Union** • 134 Ave C [9th]
- CU • **Lower East Side People's Federal Credit Union** • 37 Ave B [3rd]
- WM • **Washington Mutual** • 20 Ave A [2nd]

❇ Community Gardens

⭕ Landmarks

- **Charlie Parker House** • 151 Ave B & Tompkins Sq Pk
- **General Slocum Monument** • Tompkins Sq Park [Av A]
- **Katz's Deli** • 205 E Houston St [Ludlow]
- **Nuyorican Poets Café** • 236 E 3rd St [Av C]
- **Pyramid Club** • Ave A b/w 6th & 7th Sts
- **Tompkins Square Park** • Ave A & E 9th St

📖 Libraries

- **Hamilton Fish Park** • 415 E Houston St [Columbia]
- **Tompkins Square** • 331 E 10th St [Av B]

⭕ Police

- **9th Precinct** • 130 Ave C [8th]

✉ Post Offices

- **Peter Stuyvesant** • 432 E 14th St [1st Av]
- **Tompkins Square** • 244 E 3rd St [Av C]

🎓 Schools

- **Bard High School Early College** • 525 E Houston St [Baruch Pl]
- **Children's Workshop (M361)** • 610 E 12th St [Av B]
- **CMSP - Marte Valle Secondary** • 145 Stanton St [Suffolk]
- **Comelia Connelly Center for Education** • 220 E 4th St [Av B]
- **East Side Community High** • 420 E 12th St [1st Av]
- **East Village Community** • 610 E 12th St [Av B]
- **Immaculate Conception** • 419 E 13th St [1st Av]
- **Lower East Side Prep** • 145 Stanton St [Suffolk]
- **Mary Help of Christians** • 435 E 11th St [1st Av]
- **NEST+M** • 111 Columbia St [Stanton]
- **Notre Dame** • 104 St Marks Pl [1st Av]
- **Our Lady of Sorrows** • 219 Stanton St [Pitt]
- **PS 015 Roberto Clemente** • 333 E 4th St [Av C]
- **PS 019 Asher Levy** • 185 First Ave [12th]
- **PS 020 Anna Silver** • 166 Essex St [Stanton]
- **PS 034 F D Roosevelt** • 730 E 12th St [Szold Pl]
- **PS 063 William McKinley** • 121 E 3rd St [1st Av]
- **PS 064 Robert Simon** • 600 E 6th St [Av B]
- **PS 140 Nathan Straus** • 123 Ridge St [Stanton]
- **PS 142 Amalia Castro** • 100 Attorney St [Rivington]
- **PS 188 The Island School** • 442 E Houston St [Baruch Dr]
- **PS 196 Umbrella** • 442 E Houston St [Baruch Dr]
- **PS 363 Neighborhood** • 121 E 3rd St [1st Av]
- **PS 364 Earth School** • 600 E 6th St [Av B]
- **PS 94M** • 442 E Houston St [Baruch Dr]
- **St Brigid** • 185 E 7th St [Av B]
- **Technology, Arts and Sciences Studio** • 185 First Ave [11th]
- **The Urban Assembly School of Business for Young Women** • 420 E 12th St [1st Av]
- **Tompkins Square Middle Extension** • 600 E 6th St [Av B]

🛒 Supermarkets

- **Associated** • 409 E 14th St [1st Av]
- **C-Town** • 188 Ave C [12th]
- **C-Town** • 71 Ave D [6th]
- **Key Food** • 43 Columbia St [Delancey]
- **Key Food** • 52 Ave A [4th]

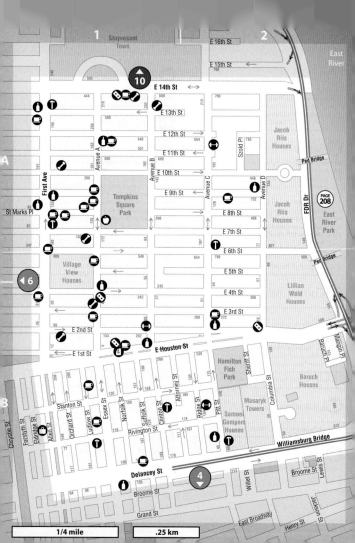

This quarter, indeed, is the isle's finest with regard to shades to espy and engage. The richest reach lays west of Avenue A, a pastiche of boutiques, cafés and slattern barrooms. Wander it all and define for yourself, for it's this very idea that makes *here* a thousand leagues from *there*.

Coffee

- **9th Street Espresso** • 700 E 9th St [Av C]
- **altcoffee** • 139 Ave A [9th St]
- **Borobudur Café** • 128 E 4th St [1st Av]
- **Café Pick Me Up** • 145 Ave A [9th St]
- **Ciao for Now** • 504 E 12th St [Av A]
- **City Market Café** • 131 Ave A [St Marks Pl]
- **Coffee Pot** • 41 Ave A [3rd]
- **Dunkin' Donuts** • 100 First Ave [6th]
- **Dunkin' Donuts** • 140 Delancey [Suffolk]
- **Dunkin' Donuts** • 215 First Ave [13th St]
- **Dunkin' Donuts** • 250 E Houston [Norfolk]
- **Dynasty Restaurant & Coffee Shop** • 600 E 14th St [Av B]
- **Kudo Beans** • 49 1/2 First Ave [3rd St]
- **Le Gamin Café** • 536 E 5th St [Av A]
- **Live Juice** • 85 Ave A [6th St]
- **Maria's Café** • 32 Ave C [3rd St]
- **Pink Pony Café** • 176 Ludlow St [Stanton]
- **Rush Hour** • 134 Ludlow St [Rivington]
- **Simone Espresso & Wine Bar** • 134 First Ave [St Marks]
- **Sympathy for the Kettle** • 109 St Marks Pl [1st Av]

Copy Shops

- **FedEx Kinko's** • 250 E Houston St [Norfolk]

Farmer's Markets

- **Tompkins Square Park (Sun 8 am–6 pm, year round)** • E 7th St & Ave A

Gyms

- **Curves (Women only)** • 114 Ridge St [Rivington]
- **Curves (Women only)** • 182 Ave C [11th St]
- **Dolphin Fitness Clubs** • 18 Ave B [2nd St]

Hardware Stores

- **Ace Hardware** • 55 First Ave [3rd St]
- **CHP Hardware** • 96 Ave C [6th St]
- **H&W Hardware** • 220 First Ave [13th St]
- **HH Hardware** • 111 Rivington St [Essex]
- **Rosa Hardware** • 85 Pitt St [Rivington]
- **Rothstein Hardware** • 56 Clinton St [Rivington]
- **Saifee Hardware** • 114 First Ave [7th St]

Liquor Stores

- **6 Avenue B Liquors** • 6 Ave B [2nd st]
- **Avenue A Wine & Liquor** • 196 Ave A [12th St]
- **East Village Wines** • 138 First Ave [St Marks Pl]
- **Gary's Liquor** • 141 Essex St [Rivington]
- **Jade Fountain Liquor** • 123 Delancey St [Norfolk]
- **Loon Chun Liquor** • 47 Pitt St [Delancey]
- **Marty's Liquors** • 133 Ave D [9th]
- **Nizga Liquors** • 58 Ave A [4th St]
- **Sale Price Liquor** • 24 Ave C [3rd St]
- **Wines on 1st** • 224 First Ave [13th St]

Pet Shops

- **Alpha Pet City** • 249 E 10th St [1st Av]
- **Animal Cracker** • 103 E 2nd St [1st Av]
- **East Village Pet Grooming Salon** • 223 Ave B [13th St]
- **Mikey's Pet Shop** • 130 E 7th St [Av A]
- **Petland Discounts** • 530 E 14th St [Av A]
- **Poopah's Pet Boutique** • 47 Ave A [3rd St]

Video Rental

- **Blockbuster** • 250 E Houston St [Norfolk]
- **Bus Stop Video Shop** • 3 Ave D [2nd St]
- **Crossbay Video** • 502 E 14th St [Av A]
- **Two Boots** • 42 Ave A [3rd St]

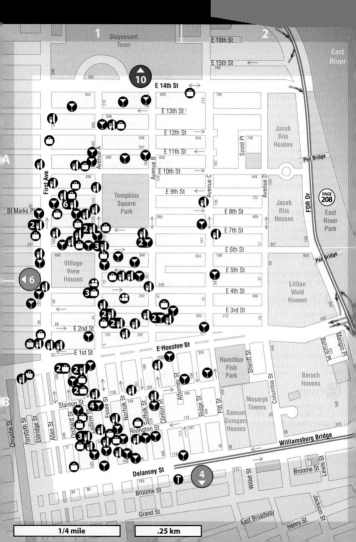

Once again, one of those unique places on the planet that you don't ever have to really leave——the bars are just so cool (2A, 7B, Bouche, Joe's), the live music even cooler (Lakeside, Tonic, Mercury Lounge). For food, Banjara rocks 6th Street and Mama's is an institution. Oh, and you can shop here, too.

🎬 Movie Theaters

- **Two Boots Pioneer Theater** • 155 E 3rd St [Av A]

🎵 Nightlife

- **11th Street Bar** • 510 E 11th St [Av A]
- **151** • 151 Rivington [Suffolk]
- **2A** • 25 Ave A [2nd St]
- **7B** • 108 Ave B [7th St]
- **Ace Bar** • 531 E 5th St [Av A]
- **Arlene Grocery** • 95 Stanton St [Ludlow]
- **Back Room** • 102 Norfolk St [Delancey]
- **Barramundi** • 67 Clinton St [Rivington]
- **Boss Tweed's Saloon** • 115 Essex St [Rivington]
- **Bouche Bar** • 540 E 5th St [Av A]
- **Bua** • 122 St Marks Pl [1st Av]
- **Cake Shop** • 152 Ludlow St [Stanton]
- **Cheap Shots** • 140 First Ave [St Marks]
- **Cherry Tavern** • 441 E 6th St [1st Av]
- **The Delancey** • 168 Delancey St [Clinton]
- **The Edge** • 95 E 3rd St [1st Av]
- **The Hanger** • 217 E 3rd St [Av B]
- **Hi-Fi** • 169 Ave A [11th St]
- **Joe's Bar** • 520 E 6th St [Av A]
- **Korova Milk Bar** • 200 Ave A [13th St]
- **Lakeside Lounge** • 162 Ave B [10th St]
- **Laugh Lounge NYC** • 151 Essex St [Stanton]
- **Living Room** • 154 Ludlow St [Stanton]
- **The Magician** • 118 Rivington St [Essex]
- **Manitoba's** • 99 Ave B [6th St]
- **Max Fish** • 178 Ludlow St [Stanton]
- **Mercury Lounge** • 217 E Houston [Essex]
- **Mona's** • 224 Ave B [13th St]
- **Motor City** • 127 Ludlow St [Rivington]
- **NuBlu** • 62 Ave C [5th St]
- **Nuyorican Poet's Café** • 236 E 3rd St [Av C]
- **Parkside Lounge** • 317 E Houston St [Attorney]
- **The Phoenix** • 447 E 13th St [1st Av]
- **Pianos** • 158 Ludlow St [Stanton]
- **The Porch** • 115 Ave C [8th St]
- **Rothko** • 116 Suffolk St [Rivington]
- **Scenic** • 25 Ave B [2nd St]
- **Sidewalk** • 94 Ave A [6th St]
- **Sin-e** • 150 Attorney St [Stanton]
- **Sophie's** • 507 E 5th St [Av A]
- **The Stone** • Ave C & E 2nd St [2nd]
- **Three of Cups Lounge** • 83 First Ave [5th St]
- **Tonic** • 107 Norfolk St [Delancey]
- **Welcome to the Johnsons** • 123 Rivington St [Essex]
- **Zum Schneider** • 107 Ave C [7th St]

🍴 Restaurants

- **1492** • 60 Clinton St [Rivington]
- **7A** • 109 Ave A [7th St] 🚇
- **Azul Bistro** • 152 Stanton St [Suffolk]
- **B3** • 33 Ave B [3rd St]
- **Banjara** • 97 First Ave [6th St]
- **Benny's Burritos** • 93 Ave A [6th St]
- **Bereket Turkish Kebab House** • 187 E Houston St [Orchard] 🚇
- **Boca Chica** • 13 First Ave [1st St]
- **Café Mogador** • 101 St Marks Pl [1st Av]
- **Caracas Arepa Bar** • 91 E 7th St [1st Av]
- **Clinton St Baking Company** • 4 Clinton St [Houston]
- **Dash Dogs** • 127 Rivington St [Norfolk]
- **David's Bagels** • 228 First Ave [14th St]
- **Dawgs on Park** • 178 E 7th St [Av B]
- **Dok Suni's** • 119 First Ave [7th St]
- **El Castillo de Jaqua** • 113 Rivington St [Essex]
- **El Sombrero** • 108 Stanton St [Ludlow]
- **Esashi** • 32 Ave A [3rd]
- **Essex Restaurant** • 120 Essex St [Rivington]
- **Flea Market Café** • 131 Ave A [St Marks]
- **Flor's Kitchen** • 149 First Ave [9th St]
- **Hummus Place** • 109 St Marks Pl [1st Av]
- **Il Bagatto** • 192 E 2nd St [Av B]
- **Il Posto Accanto** • 190 E 2nd St [Av B]
- **inoteca** • 98 Rivington St [Ludlow]
- **Kate's Joint** • 58 Ave B [4th St]
- **Katz's Delicatessen** • 205 E Houston St [Ludlow]
- **Kuma Inn** • 113 Ludlow St [Delancey]
- **Kura Sushi** • 67 First Ave [4th St]
- **La Caverna** • 122 Rivington St [Essex]
- **Lavagna** • 545 E 5th St [Av A]
- **Le French Diner** • 188 Orchard St [Stanton]
- **Le Gamin** • 536 E 5th St [Av A]
- **Le Pere Pinard** • 175 Ludlow St [Stanton]
- **Lil' Frankie's Pizza** • 19 First Ave [1st St]
- **The Lite Touch Restaurant** • 151 Ave A [10 St]
- **Mama's Food Shop** • 200 E 3rd St [Av B]
- **Mo Pitkin's House of Satisfaction** • 34 Ave A [3rd St]
- **Momofuku** • 163 First Ave [10th St]
- **Moustache** • 265 E 10th St [1st Av]
- **Nicky's Vietnamese Sandwiches** • 150 E 2nd St [Av A]
- **Odessa** • 119 Ave A [St Marks] 🚇
- **Old Devil Moon** • 511 E 12th St [Av A]
- **Panna II Indian Restaurant** • 93 First Ave [6th St]
- **Pylos** • 128 E 7th St [Av A]
- **Raga** • 433 E 6th St [1st Av]
- **Sapporo East** • 245 E 10th St [1st Av]
- **Schiller's** • 131 Rivington St [Norfolk]
- **Share** • 406 E 9th St [1st Av]
- **Sidewalk** • 94 Ave A [6th St]
- **St Dymphna's** • 118 St Marks Pl [1st Av]
- **The Sunburnt Cow** • 137 Ave C [9th St]
- **Supper** • 156 E 2nd St [Av A]
- **Takahachi** • 85 Ave A [6th St]
- **Tasting Room** • 72 E 1st St [1st Av]
- **Teany** • 90 Rivington St [Orchard]
- **Thor** • 107 Rivington St [Ludlow]
- **Two Boots** • 37 Ave A [3rd St]
- **Yaffa Café** • 97 St Marks Pl [1st Av]
- **Yonah Schimmel's Knishery** • 137 E Houston St [Forsyth]
- **Yuca Bar** • 111 Ave A [7th St]
- **Zum Schneider** • 107 Ave C [7th St]

🛍️ Shopping

- **A Cheng** • 443 E 9th St [1st Av]
- **A-One Record Shop** • 439 E 6th St [1st Av]
- **Alphabets** • 115 Ave A [7th St]
- **Altman Luggage** • 135 Orchard St [Rivington]
- **Amarcord Vintage Fashion** • 84 E 7th St [1st Av]
- **American Apparel** • 183 E Houston St [Orchard]
- **Babeland** • 94 Rivington St [Ludlow]
- **De La Vega** • 102 St Marks Pl [1st Av]
- **Dowel Quality Products** • 91 First Ave [6th St]
- **Earthmatters** • 177 Ludlow St [Stanton]
- **Economy Candy** • 108 Rivington St [Essex]
- **Essex Street Retail Market** • 120 Essex St [Rivington]
- **Etherea** • 66 Ave A [5th St]
- **Exit 9** • 64 Ave A [5th St]
- **First Flight Music** • 174 First Ave [11th St]
- **Frock** • 148 Orchard St [Rivington]
- **Gracefully** • 28 Ave A [2nd St]
- **Gringer & Sons** • 29 First Ave [2nd St]
- **The Hanger Bar & Boutique** • 217 E 3rd St [Av B]
- **Happy Happy Happy** • 157 Allen St [Rivington]
- **Lancelotti** • 66 Ave A [5th St]
- **Ludlow Guitars** • 164 Ludlow St [Stanton]
- **Masturbakers** • 511 E 12th St [Av A]
- **The Paris Apartment** • 70 E 1st St [1st Av]
- **Peggy Pardon** • 153 Ludlow St [Stanton]
- **R&S Strauss Auto Store** • 644 E 14th St [Av C]
- **Russ & Daughters** • 179 E Houston St [Orchard]
- **Tahir** • 412 E 9th St [1st Av]
- **TG170** • 170 Ludlow St [Stanton]
- **Tiny Living** • 125 E 7th St [Av A]
- **Yonah Schimmel's Knishery** • 137 E Houston St [Forsyth]

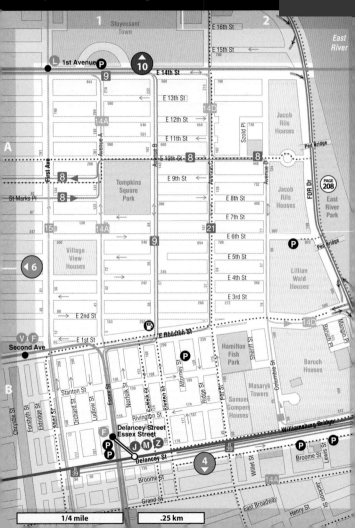

The subway lines, here, scant. Bordered northerly by the gray laser, L, southernmost by the choco-convolution, JMZ, and, of course, for better/worse, F l'orange. The clime teeming with vivid colors—yet often gray. Parking here is, well, parking here—the hippest 'hood this side of Williamsburg?

Subways

Ⓕ Ⓙ Ⓜ Ⓩ .... Delancey St-Essex St
Ⓛ .... First Ave
Ⓕ Ⓥ ....Second Ave

Bus Lines

14 .... 14th St/Ave A/Ave D
15 .... First Ave
21 .... First St/Ave C
8 .... 9th St/10th St
9 .... 14th St/Ave B
B 39 .... Delancey St

Bike Lanes

- • • • Marked Bike Lane
- • • • Recommended Route
- • • • Greenway

Gas Stations

• **Mobil** • 253 E 2nd St [Av C] ♨

Parking

Map 8 · **Chelsea**

Lincoln Tunnel
← to NJ

W 40th St

W 39th St

W 38th St

W 37th St

Dyer Ave

W 36th St

W 35th St

W 34th St

W 33rd St

J A Farley
Post Office

W 31st St

W 30th St

W 29th St

W 28th St

Chelsea Park

Penn

Hudson
River
Park

Jacob K Javits
Convention
Center

PAGE
214

High Line
Elevated
Railroad

PAGE
212

Starrett-Lehigh
Building

W 27th St

Station

South

Hudson River

West Side Hwy

Eleventh Ave

Tenth Ave

Ninth Ave

Eighth Ave

W 26th St

W 25th St

Houses

W 24th St

W 23rd St

W 22nd St

W 21st St

General
Theological
Seminary

W 20th St

W 19th St

W 18th St

W 17th St

W 16th St

W 15th St

W 14th St

Hudson
River
Park

Chelsea
Waterside
Park

W Chelsea Piers

PAGE
238

Penn
Station/
MSG

PAGE
279

PAGE
24

1/4 mile   .25 km

West of Eighth Avenue near extinct grasses 'til the sidewalk that is Hudson River Park. The district's glory, Javits, banal, and life's rudiments, while available, not as near or plentiful as in other city reaches, 'cept, of course, for ART. During weekends, a fine street bazaar off 39th west of Tenth Avenue.

24-Hour Pharmacies

• **Duane Reade** • 460 Eighth Ave [33rd] ♿

Bagels

• **Murray's Bagels** • 242 Eighth Ave [22nd]
• **Ruthy's** • Chelsea Market • 75 Ninth Ave [16th]

Banks

AT • **Atlantic (ATM)** • Gristedes • 225 Ninth Ave [24th]
AT • **Atlantic (ATM)** • Gristedes • 307 W 26th St [8th]
BA • **Bank of America (ATM)** • 312 W 34th St [8th]
BA • **Bank of America (ATM)** • 320 W 34th St [8th Av]
CH • **Chase** • 475 W 23rd St [10th Av]
CH • **Chase (ATM)** • 238 Eighth Ave [22nd]
CH • **Citibank** • 322 W 23rd St [8th Av]
CI • **Citibank (ATM)** • 111 Eighth Ave [16th]
CI • **Citibank (ATM)** • 88 Tenth Ave [16th]
MA • **Marathon Bank** • 250 Ninth Ave [25th]
NF • **North Fork** • 520 Eighth Ave [36th]
PN • **PNC (ATM)** • Tommy Hilfiger, 6th Flr • 601 W 26th St [11th Av]
WA • **Wachovia** • 66 Ninth Ave [15th]
WM • **Washington Mutual** • 111 Eighth Ave [16th]
WM • **Washington Mutual** • 601 Eighth Ave [39th]

Community Gardens

Landmarks

• **General Theological Seminary** • 175 Ninth Ave [20th]
• **High Line Elevated Railroad** • Gansevoort to 34th St, west of Tenth Ave
• **JA Farley Post Office** • 441 Eighth Ave [31st]
• **Jacob K Javits Convention Center** • 36th St & Eleventh Ave
• **Starrett-Lehigh Building** • 27th St & Eleventh Ave

Police

• **Mid-Town South** • 357 W 35th St [9th Av]

Post Offices

• **James A Farley** • 421 Eighth Ave [31st] ♿
• **London Terrace** • 234 Tenth Ave [24th]
• **Port Authority** • 76 Ninth Ave [16th]

Schools

• **Bayard Rustin Educational Complex** • 351 W 18th St [8th Av]
• **Corlears** • 324 W 15th St [8th Av]
• **General Theological Seminary** • 175 Ninth Ave [20th]
• **Guardian Angel** • 193 Tenth Ave [22nd]
• **Humanities Preparatory** • 351 W 18th St [8th Av]
• **The James Baldwin School** • 351 W 18th St [8th Av]
• **The Lorge School** • 353 W 17th St [9th Av]
• **MS 260 Clinton School for Writers & Artists** • 320 W 21st St [8th Av]
• **NYC Lab HS - Collaborative Studies** • 333 W 17th St [8th Av]
• **NYC Lab MS - Collaborative Studies** • 333 W 17th St [8th Av]
• **NYC Museum School** • 333 W 17th St [8th Av]
• **PS 11 William T Harris** • 320 W 21st St [8th Av]
• **PS 33 Chelsea** • 281 Ninth Ave [26th]
• **St Columba** • 331 W 25th St [8th Av]
• **St Michael Academy** • 425 W 33rd St [9th Av]
• **Technical Career Institute** • 320 W 31st St [8th Av]

Supermarkets

• **D'Agostino** • 257 W 17th St [8th Av]
• **D'Agostino** • 315 W 23rd St [8th Av]
• **Gristede's** • 221 Eighth Ave [21st]
• **Gristede's** • 225 Ninth Ave [24th]
• **Gristede's** • 307 W 26th St [8th Av]

On the cusp of downtown's demarcation, 14th, up Eighth go mad. Venture Ninth nearer the 40s for class confection and spartan saloons. Most nights on Eighth between 25th and 14th a veritable theater ado about manhood. For escap(ad)es—La Luncheonette, Empire Diner, and swerve of shore.

Coffee

- **254 Snack Shop Corp** • 254 Tenth Ave [25th]
- **Dunkin' Donuts** • 269 Eighth Ave [24th]
- **Dunkin' Donuts** • 525 Eighth Ave [36th]
- **From Earth To You Gourmet Café** • 252 Tenth Ave [25th]
- **Paradise Café & Muffins** • 139 Eighth Ave [17th]
- **Starbucks** • 124 Eighth Ave [16th]
- **Starbucks** • 177 Eighth Ave [19th]
- **Starbucks** • 255 Eighth Ave [23rd]
- **Starbucks** • 450 W 33rd St [10th Av]
- **Starbucks** • 494 Eighth Ave [35th]
- **Starbucks** • 655 W 34th St [11th Av]
- **Starbucks** • 76 Ninth Ave [16th]
- **The Sun Gourmet Deli** • 440 Ninth Ave [34th]

Copy Shops

- **Corporate Reproduction Center** • 460 W 34th St [10th Av]
- **Empire Graphic Service** • 347 W 36th St [8th Av]
- **Empire State Blue Print** • 555 Eighth Ave [38th]
- **FedEx Kinko's** • 655 W 34th St [11th Av]
- **Hart Reproduction Services** • 555 Eighth Ave [38th]
- **Mail Boxes Etc** • 245 Eighth Ave [22nd]
- **Printech Business Systems** • 519 Eighth Ave [36th]
- **Staples** • 500 Eighth Ave [35th]
- **The UPS Store** • 328 Eighth Ave [26th]

Gyms

- **Chelsea Piers Sports Center** • Chelsea Piers - Pier 60 [30th]
- **New York Sports Clubs** • 128 Eighth Ave [16th]
- **New York Sports Clubs** • 270 Eighth Ave [24th]

Hardware Stores

- **Diener Park** • 194 Eighth Ave [20th]
- **Hardware Depot** • 399 Eighth Ave [30th]
- **Mercer Sq Hardware** • 286 Eighth Ave [24th]
- **MJ Hardware & Electric** • 520 Eighth Ave [36th]
- **NF Hardware** • 219 Ninth Ave [24th]
- **Scheman & Grant** • 545 Eighth Ave [37th]
- **True Value Hardware** • 191 Ninth Ave [22nd]

Liquor Stores

- **34th Street Winery** • 460 W 34th St [10th Av]
- **Cambridge Wine & Liquor** • 594 Eighth Ave [39th]
- **Chelsea Liquor** • 114 Ninth Ave [17th]
- **Chelsea Wine Vault** • Chelsea Market • 75 Ninth Ave [16th]
- **Delauren Wines & Liquors** • 332 Eighth Ave [27th]
- **London Terrace Liquor** • 221 Ninth Ave [24th]
- **Philippe Wine & Liquor** • 312 W 23rd St [8th Av]
- **River Bend Vineyards (Wine only)** • 307 W 38th St [8th Av]
- **US Wine & Liquor** • 486 Ninth Ave [37th]

Movie Theaters

- **Clearview's Chelsea West** • 333 W 23rd St [8th Av]
- **Loews 34th Street** • 312 W 34th St [8th]

Nightlife

- **Billymark's West** • 332 Ninth Ave [29th]
- **Blarney Stone** • 340 Ninth Ave [29th]
- **Cajun** • 129 Eighth Ave [16th]
- **Chelsea Brewing Company** • Pier 59 [17th]
- **Copacabana** • 560 W 34th St [11th Av]
- **Crobar** • 530 W 28th St [10th Av]
- **Half King** • 505 W 23rd St [10th Av]
- **Hammerstein Ballroom** • 311 W 34th St [8th Av]
- **Molly Wee Pub** • 402 Eighth Ave [30th]
- **Red Rock West** • 457 W 17th St [10th Av]
- **Roxy** • 515 W 18th St [10th Av]
- **The Park** • 118 Tenth Ave [17th]
- **West Side Tavern** • 360 W 23rd St [9th Av]

Pet Shops

- **Barking Zoo** • 172 Ninth Ave [21st]
- **Petland Discounts** • 312 W 23rd St [8th]

Restaurants

- **202 Café** • Chelsea Market • 75 Ninth Ave [16th]
- **Better Burger Chelsea** • 178 Eighth Ave [19th]
- **Blue Moon Mexican Café** • 150 Eighth Ave [17th]
- **Bottino** • 246 Tenth Ave [24th]
- **Bright Food Shop** • 216 Eighth Ave [21st]
- **Buddakan** • Chelsea Market • 75 Ninth Ave [16th]
- **Burritoville** • 352 W 39th St [9th Av]
- **Chelsea Bistro & Bar** • 358 W 23rd St [9th Av]
- **Cheyenne Diner** • 411 Ninth Ave [33rd] ⊗
- **Cola's Italian** • 148 Eighth Ave [17th]
- **Cookshop** • 156 Tenth Ave [20th]
- **Cupcake Café** • 522 Ninth Ave [39th]
- **El Cid** • 322 W 15th St [8th Av]
- **Empire Diner** • 210 Tenth Ave [22nd] ⊗
- **Frank's Restaurant** • 410 W 16th St [9th Av]
- **Grand Sichuan Int'l** • 229 Ninth Ave [24th]
- **Havana Chelsea** • 190 Eighth Ave [20th]
- **La Luncheonette** • 130 Tenth Ave [18th]
- **La Taza de Oro** • 96 Eighth Ave [15th]
- **Le Gamin** • 183 Ninth Ave [21st]
- **Manganaro Foods** • 488 Ninth Ave [37th]
- **Matsuri, Maritime Hotel** • 369 W 16th St [9th Av]
- **Moonstruck Diner** • 400 W 23rd St [9th]
- **Morimoto** • 88 Tenth Ave [16th]
- **Pepe Giallo** • 253 Tenth Ave [25th]
- **The Red Cat** • 227 Tenth Ave [23rd]
- **Sandwich Planet** • 534 Ninth Ave [40th]
- **Skylight Diner** • 402 W 34th St [9th Av] ⊗
- **Soul Fixin's** • 371 W 34th St [9th Av]
- **Spice** • 199 Eighth Ave [20th]
- **Tick Tock Diner** • 481 Eighth Ave [34th] ⊗
- **Viceroy** • 160 Eighth Ave [18th]

Shopping

- **B&H Photo** • 420 Ninth Ave [33rd]
- **Buon Italia** • Chelsea Market • 75 Ninth Ave [16th]
- **Chelsea Garden Center** • 499 Tenth Ave [38th]
- **Chelsea Market Baskets** • Chelsea Market • 75 Ninth Ave [16th]
- **Chelsea Wholesale Flower Market** • Chelsea Market • 75 Ninth Ave [16th]
- **Eleni's** • Chelsea Market • 75 Ninth Ave [16th]
- **Fat Witch Bakery** • Chelsea Market • 75 Ninth Ave [16th]
- **Find Outlet** • 361 W 17th St [9th Av]
- **Kitchen Market** • 218 Eighth Ave [21st]
- **New Museum Store** • 556 W 22nd [11th Av]

Video Rental

- **Alan's Alley Video** • 207A Ninth Ave [23rd]
- **Blockbuster** • 300 W 20th St [8th Av]
- **Movie Bank USA** • W 34th St & Eighth Ave ⊗

Thankfully, for the zealous pedestrians, no train lines west of Eighth. Maybe someday. Beneath the hallowed Garden betwixt 31st and 33rd Streets rests Penn Station. However, 'less you trek to points outside the city, you'd better lace them 'kicks (or jump bus 34) to Javits.

Subways

A **C** **E**	34 St-Penn Station
A **C** **E**	14th St/Eighth Ave
C **E**	23rd St

Bus Lines

10 **20**	Seventh Ave/Eighth Ave/Central Park W
11	Ninth Ave/Tenth Ave
14	14th St Crosstown
16	34th St Crosstown
23	23rd St Crosstown
34	34th St Crosstown

Bike Lanes

- • • • Marked Bike Lanes
- • • • Recommended Route
- • • • Greenway

Car Rental

- **Chelsea Rental** • 549 W 26th St [10th Av]

Car Washes

- **Chelsea Car Wash** • 450 W 15th St [9th Av]
- **Steve's Detailing & Tires** • 516 W 27th St [10th Av]

Gas Stations

- **Exxon** • 110 Eighth Ave [15th]
- **Getty** • 239 Tenth Ave [24th]
- **Mobil** • 309 Eleventh Ave [30th]
- **Mobil** • 70 Tenth Ave [15th]

Parking

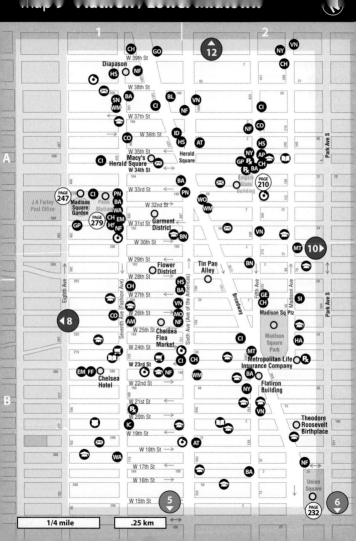

Flatiron / Lower Midtown is where you will spend a lot of time when your cousins from Iowa visit. Top-notch restaurants, Macy's, the Empire State Building, and curiosities like the infamous Chelsea Hotel make for some happy tourists. Lovely Madison Square Park is perfect for summer reading.

24-Hour Pharmacies

- **Duane Reade** • 180 W 20th St [7th Av]
- **Duane Reade** • 358 Fifth Ave [34th]
- **Walgreen's** • 33 E 23rd St [Madison]
- **Walgreen's** • 350 Fifth Ave [34th]

Bagels

- **23rd Street Bagel** • 170 W 23rd St [7th]
- **Bagel Maven** • 362 Seventh Ave [30th]
- **Bagels & Co** • 243 W 38th St [7th Av]
- **Brooklyn Bagels** • 319 Fifth Ave [32nd]
- **Empire City Bagels** • 729 Sixth [24th]
- **New York City Bagel** • 601 Sixth Ave [17th]

Banks

- **AM** • **Amalgamated** • 15 Union Sq W [15th]
- **AM** • **Amalgamated** • 275 Seventh [26th]
- **AP** • **Apple (ATM)** • 350 Fifth Ave [34th]
- **AT** • **Atlantic** • 960 Sixth Ave [35th]
- **AT** • **Atlantic (ATM)** • Bed Bath & Beyond • 620 Sixth Ave [18th]
- **BL** • **Bank Leumi** • 1400 Broadway [38th]
- **BA** • **Bank of America** • 1 Penn Plz E [34th]
- **BA** • **Bank of America** • 116 Fifth [17th]
- **BA** • **Bank of America** • 1293 B'way [33rd]
- **BA** • **Bank of America** • 350 Fifth [34th]
- **BA** • **Bank of America** • 515 Seventh [38th]
- **BA** • **Bank of America** • 800 Sixth [27th]
- **BA** • **Bank of America** • 186 Fifth Ave [23rd]
- **BA** • **Bank of New York** • 162 Fifth [21st]
- **BA** • **Bank of New York** • 260 Madison
- **NY** • **Bank of New York** • Empire State Bldg• 350 Fifth Ave [34th]
- **BN** • **Broadway National** • 250 Fifth [28]
- **BN** • **Broadway National** • 855 Sixth Ave [30th]
- **CH** • **Chase** • 1411 Broadway [39th]
- **CH** • **Chase** • 2 Penn Plz [31st]
- **CH** • **Chase** • 225 Fifth Ave [27th]
- **CH** • **Chase** • 260 Madison Ave [39th]
- **CH** • **Chase** • 305 Seventh Ave [27th]
- **CH** • **Chase** • 349 Fifth Ave [34th]
- **CH** • **Chase** • 71 W 23rd St [6th Av]
- **CI** • **Citibank** • 1107 Broadway [24th]
- **CI** • **Citibank** • 201 W 34th St [7th Av]
- **CI** • **Citibank** • 411 Fifth Ave [38th]
- **CI** • **Citibank** • 717 Sixth Ave [23rd]
- **CI** • **Citibank** • 79 Fifth Ave [16th]
- **CI** • **Citibank (ATM)** • 1384 Broadway [37th]
- **CO** • **Commerce** • 200 W 26th St [7th Av]
- **CO** • **Commerce** • 401 Fifth Ave [37th]
- **CO** • **Commerce** • 469 Seventh Ave [35th]
- **EM** • **Emigrant** • 250 W 23rd St [7th Av]
- **EM** • **Emigrant** • 371 Seventh Ave [30th]
- **FF** • **Fourth Federal Savings** • 242 W 23rd St [7th Av]
- **GO** • **Gotham Bank of New York** • 1412 Broadway [39th]
- **GE** • **Great Eastern** • 235 Fifth Ave [27th]
- **HA** • **Habib American** • 99 Madison Ave [29th]
- **HS** • **HSBC** • 1350 Broadway [36th]
- **HS** • **HSBC** • 5 Penn Plz [34th]
- **HS** • **HSBC** • 550 Seventh Ave [40th]
- **HS** • **HSBC** • 800 Sixth Ave [27th]
- **ID** • **IDB** • 1350 Broadway [36th]
- **IC** • **Independence Community** • 169 Seventh Ave [24th]
- **MT** • **M&T** • 95 Madison Ave [29th]
- **MT** • **M&T (ATM)** • 200 Fifth Ave [24th]
- **CU** • **Montauk Credit Union** • 111 W 26th St [6th Av]
- **NF** • **North Fork** • 1 Penn Plz [34th]
- **NF** • **North Fork** • 10 E 34th St [5th Av]
- **NF** • **North Fork** • 100 W 26th St [6th Av]
- **NF** • **North Fork** • 1001 Sixth [37th]
- **NF** • **North Fork** • 120 W 23rd St [6th Av]
- **NF** • **North Fork** • 1407 Broadway [38th]
- **NF** • **North Fork** • 31 E 17th [Union Sq W]
- **NF** • **North Fork** • 370 Seventh Ave [30th]
- **NF** • **North Fork** • 404 Fifth Ave [37th]
- **PN** • **PNC (ATM)** • Penn Station, Amtrack
- **PN** • **PNC (ATM)** • Manhattan Mall • Sixth Ave & W 33rd St
- **SG** • **Signature** • 61 Madison Ave [27th]
- **SN** • **Sterling National** • 512 Seventh [38]
- **VN** • **Valley National** • 1040 Sixth [39th]
- **VN** • **Valley National** • 145 Fifth Ave [21st]
- **VN** • **Valley National** • 275 Madison [40th]
- **VN** • **Valley National** • 295 Fifth Ave [31st]
- **VN** • **Valley National** • 776 Sixth [26th]
- **WA** • **Wachovia** • 120 Seventh Ave [17th]
- **WA** • **Wachovia (ATM)** • 1 Penn Plz [34th]
- **WA** • **Wachovia** • 390 Seventh [32nd]
- **WM** • **Washington Mutual** • 1260 B'way [32nd]
- **WM** • **Washington Mutual** • 498 Seventh Ave [37th]
- **WM** • **Washington Mutual** • 700 Sixth [22nd]
- **WO** • **Woori America** • 1250 Broadway [32nd]

Landmarks

- **Chelsea Hotel** • 23rd St b/w Seventh & Eighth Aves
- **Chelsea Flea Market** • 112 W 25th St [6th Av]
- **Diaspon** • Seventh Ave b/w 38th & 39th Sts
- **Empire State Building** • 34th St & Fifth Ave
- **Flatiron Building** • 175 Fifth Ave [22nd]
- **Flower District** • 28th St b/w Sixth & Seventh Aves
- **Garment District** • West 30s south of Herald Sq
- **Macy's Herald Square** • 151 W 34th St [7th Av]
- **Madison Square Garden** • 4 Penn Plz [31st]
- **Madison Square Park** • 23rd St & Broadway
- **Metropolitan Life Insurance Co** • 1 Madison Ave [23rd]
- **Penn Station** • 31st St & Eighth Ave
- **Theodore Roosevelt Birthplace** • 28 E 20th St [B'way]

- **Tin Pan Alley** • W 28th St b/w Sixth Ave & Broadway
- **Union Square** • 14th St-Union Sq

Libraries

- **Andrew Heiskell Library for the Blind** • 40 W 20th St [5th Av]
- **Muhlenberg** • 209 W 23rd St [7th Av]
- **Science, Industry, and Business Library** • 188 Madison St [34th]

Police

- **10th Precinct** • 230 W 20th St [7th Av]

Post Offices

- **Empire State** • 19 W 33rd St [5th Av]
- **Greeley Square** • 39 W 31st St [B'way]
- **Midtown** • 223 W 38th St [7th Av]
- **Old Chelsea** • 217 W 18th St [7th Av]
- **Station 138 (Macy's)** • 151 W 34th St [7th Av]

Schools

- **American Academy of Dramatic Arts** • 120 Madison Ave [30th]
- **Apex Technical** • 635 Sixth Ave [19th]
- **Ballet Tech / NYC PS for Dance** • 890 Broadway [19th]
- **The Chubb Institute** • 498 Seventh Ave [37th]
- **Community High** • 40 E 29th St [Madison]
- **Fashion Institute of Technology** • 227 W 27th St [7th Av]
- **The Graduate Center (CUNY)** • 365 Fifth Ave [35th]
- **High School for Fashion Industries** • 225 W 24th St [7th Av]
- **Institute for Culinary Education** • 50 W 23rd St [5th Av]
- **John A Coleman** • 590 Sixth Ave [17th]
- **Liberty High** • 250 W 18th St [7th Av]
- **Manhattan Village Academy** • 43 W 22nd St [5th Av]
- **NYU School of Continuing and Professional Studies** • 145 Fifth Ave [21st]
- **Phillips Beth Israel School of Nursing** • 776 Sixth Ave [26th]
- **Physical City High** • 55 E 25th St [Park]
- **Satellite Academy High** • 120 W 30th St [6th Av]
- **The School of Film And Television** • 39 W 19th St [5th Av]
- **Touro College** • 27 W 23rd St [5th Av]
- **Xavier High** • 30 W 16th St [5th Av]

Supermarkets

- **Garden of Eden Gourmet** • 162 W 23rd St [7th Av]
- **Whole Foods Market** • 250 Seventh Ave [24th]

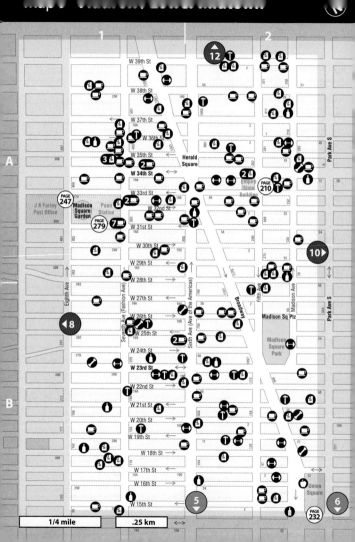

This area contains two of New York's most famous business districts, the Garment District and the Flower District (see the "Essentials" map). The big box retailers and chains have invaded Sixth Avenue (including Best Buy, Outback Steakhouse, the Olive Garden, and Home Depot). Whoopee!

8 9 10
5 6 7

Ma

Coffee

- **Aleem's Coffee Shop** • 46 W 21st St [5th Av]
- **Andrew's Coffee Shop** • 246 W 38th St [7th Av]
- **Andrew's Coffee Shop** • 463 Seventh Ave [35th]
- **Anesis Café** • 42 W 35th St [5th Av]
- **Antique Café** • 234 W 27th St [7th Av]
- **Antique Café** • 55 W 26th St [5th Av]
- **Au Bon Pain** • 151 W 34th St [7th Av]
- **Au Bon Pain** • 420 Fifth Ave [38th]
- **Au Bon Pain** • 73 Fifth Ave [15th]
- **The Bread Factory Café** • 470 Seventh Ave [35th]
- **Café 34** • 250 W 34th St [7th Av]
- **Café Beyond** • 620 Sixth Ave [18th]
- **Café Bonjour** • 20 E 39th St [Madison]
- **Café Bonjour Too** • 2 E 39th St [5th Av]
- **Café Express** • 138 W 32nd St [6th Av]
- **Café Muse** • 43 W 32nd St [B'way]
- **Café Pom Pom** • 169 W 32nd St [7th Av]
- **Caffe Rafaella** • 134 Seventh Ave S [10th]
- **Coco Moka Café** • 2 Penn Plz [31st]
- **Cosi** • 498 Seventh Ave [37th]
- **Cosi** • 700 Sixth Ave [22nd]
- **Dunkin' Donuts** • 1 Penn Plz [34th]
- **Dunkin' Donuts** • 1286 Broadway [33rd]
- **Dunkin' Donuts** • 150 W 30th St [6th Av]
- **Dunkin' Donuts** • 2 Penn Plz [31st]
- **Dunkin' Donuts** • 24 E 23rd St [Madison]
- **Dunkin' Donuts** • 289 Seventh Ave [26th]
- **Dunkin' Donuts** • 302 Fifth Ave [31st]
- **Dunkin' Donuts** • 401 Seventh Ave [32nd]
- **Dunkin' Donuts** • 51 E 34th St [Madison]
- **Dunkin' Donuts** • Madison Ave [28th]
- **Elemental Foods** • 235 Park Ave S [19th]
- **Guy & Gallard** • 1001 Sixth Ave [37th]
- **Guy & Gallard** • 180 Madison Ave [34th]
- **Guy & Gallard** • 245 W 38th St [7th Av]
- **Guy & Gallard** • 469 Seventh Ave [35th]
- **Guy & Gallard** • 475 Park Ave S [31st]
- **Guy & Gallard IV** • 339 Seventh Ave [29th]
- **Harrie's Coffee Shop** • 1407 Broadway [38th]
- **Jamie's** • 164 Madison Ave [33rd]
- **Java Shop** • 30 W 35th St [5th Av]
- **Kavehaz** • 37 W 26th St [B'way]
- **Keko Café** • 121 Madison Ave [30th]
- **Le Café Catering Deli Bread And Bakery** • 1 Penn Plz [34th]
- **Le Gamin Café** • 258 W 15th St [8th Av]
- **M Café** • 901 Sixth Ave [32nd]
- **News Bar** • 2 W 19th St [5th Av]
- **Primo Cappachino** • Penn Station LIRR
- **Seattle Coffee Roasters** • 202 W 34th St [7th Av]
- **Starbucks** • 1 Penn Plz [34th]
- **Starbucks** • 1 Penn Plz (Concourse level) [34th]
- **Starbucks** • 1372 Broadway [37th]
- **Starbucks** • 151 W 34th St [7th Av]
- **Starbucks** • 200 Madison Ave [35th]
- **Starbucks** • 261 Fifth Ave [29th]
- **Starbucks** • 334 Fifth Ave [33rd]
- **Starbucks** • 370 Seventh Ave [30th]
- **Starbucks** • 41 Union Sq W [16th]
- **Starbucks** • 450 Seventh Ave [35th]
- **Starbucks** • 462 Seventh Ave [35th]
- **Starbucks** • 525 Seventh Ave [38th]
- **Starbucks** • 684 Sixth Ave [21st]
- **Starbucks** • 750 Sixth Ave [25th]
- **Starbucks** • 750 Seventh Ave [26th]
- **Starbucks** • 875 Sixth Ave [31st]
- **T Salon Emporium** • 11 E 20th St [B'way]
- **Takken America** • 38 W 38th St [5th Av]
- **West Front Store** • 411 Fifth Ave [37th]

Copy Shops

- **A Esteban & Co** • 132 W 36th St [B'way]
- **A-A-D United Reprographic Services** • 40 W 25th St [B'way]
- **AAA Wonder Copy & Printing** • 174 Fifth Ave [22nd]
- **Acu-Copy** • 26 W 39th St [5th Av]
- **Advanced Printing NYC** • 263 W 38th St [8th Av]
- **Alphagraphics** • 2363 Fifth Ave [28th]
- **Bernie's Copy Center / Penn Graphics** • 242 W 30th St [7th Av]
- **Beyond Printing** • 450 Seventh Ave [35th]
- **Carr & Dash** • 470 Seventh Ave [35th]
- **Century Copy Center** • 70 Seventh Ave [15th]
- **Comzone** • 21 E 15th St [5th Av]
- **Copy Door Corp** • 1011 Sixth Ave [38th]
- **Copy Specialists** • 48 W 21st St [B'way]
- **Copy Specialists** • 71 W 23rd St [6th Av]
- **Digital Data Solutions** • 1133 Broadway [26th]
- **Digitech Printers** • 150 W 30th St [6th Av]
- **Esteban** • 31 W 27th St [B'way]
- **Exact** • 1 W 34th St [5th Av] ⓦ
- **FedEx Kinko's** • 191 Madison Ave [34th] ⓦ
- **FedEx Kinko's** • Empire State Bldg • 350 Fifth Ave [34th] ⓦ
- **FedEx Kinko's** • 500 Seventh Ave [37th]
- **Five Star** • 242 W 36th St [7th Av]
- **Flynns** • 827 Ave of the Americas [29th]
- **Iron Copy Center** • 25 E 20th St [B'way]
- **Kinko's** • 245 Seventh Ave [24th]
- **Kinko's** • 650 Sixth Ave [20th]
- **Kwik Kopy Printing** • 7 E 15th St [5th Av]
- **Lightning Copy** • 54 W 39th St [6th Av]
- **Lithomatic Business Forms** • 233 W 18th St [7th Av]
- **Longacre Copy Center** • 1385 Broadway [37th]
- **Mail Boxes Etc** • 244 Madison Ave [38th]
- **McNair Duplicating** • 14 E 38th St [Madison]
- **Metropolitan Duplicating & Imaging** • 216 W 18th St [7th Av] ⓦ
- **National Reproductions** • 229 W 28th St [7th Av]
- **National Reprographics** • 44 W 18th St [5th Av]
- **Oak Hill Graphics** • 18 E 39th St [Madison]
- **Pims USA** • 245 W 17th St [7th Av]
- **Quorum** • 450 Seventh Ave [35th]
- **Rainbow Photo Lab II** • 120 W 33rd St [6th Av]
- **Showbran Photo** • 1410 Broadway [39th]
- **Sir Speedy** • 234 W 35th St [7th Av]
- **Speedway Copy & Printing** • 62 W 36th St [6th Av]
- **Staples** • 1293 Broadway [33rd]
- **Staples** • 16 E 34th St [5th Av]
- **Staples** • 699 Sixth Ave [22nd]
- **Staples** • Penn Station
- **Swift Copy Printing** • 10 E 36th St [Madison]
- **The UPS Store** • 101 W 23rd St [6th Av]
- **The UPS Store** • 130 Seventh Ave [18th]
- **The UPS Store** • 1357 Broadway [36th]
- **The UPS Store** • 243 Fifth Ave [28th]
- **Village Copier** • 12 E 39th St [5th Av] ⓦ
- **Wholesale Copies** • 1 E 28th St Fl 4 [5th]

Farmer's Markets

- **Union Square Greenmarket (Mon, Wed, Fri & Sat 8am-6pm Year Round)** • E 17th St & Broadway

Gyms

- **19th Street Gym** • 22 W 19th St [5th Av]
- **Bally Total Fitness** • 139 W 32nd St [6th]
- **Bally Total Fitness** • 641 Sixth Ave [20th]
- **Crunch Fitness** • 144 W 38th St [B'way]
- **Curves** • 36 W 34th St [5th Av]
- **David Barton Gym** • 215 W 23rd St [7th Av]
- **Equinox Fitness Club** • 897 Broadway [20]
- **The Fitness Club** • 11 Madison Ave [24th]
- **New York Health & Racquet Club** • 60 W 23rd St [6th Av]
- **NYSC** • 1372 Broadway [37th]
- **NYSC** • 200 Madison Ave [35th]
- **NYSC** • 50 W 34th St [5th Av]
- **Peak Performance Sport & Fitness Center** • 54 W 21st St [6th Av]
- **Steel Gym** • 146 W 23rd St [6th Av]

Hardware Stores

- **727 Hardware** • 727 Sixth Ave [24th]
- **Adco Hardware** • 23 W 35th St [5th Av]
- **Admore Hardware & Lock** • 11 E 33rd St [5th Av]
- **B&N Hardware** • 12 W 19th St [5th Av]
- **Central Hardware & Electric** • 55 W 39th St [5th Av]
- **Elm Electric & Hardware** • 884 Sixth Ave [32nd]
- **Halmor Hardware and Supply** • 43 W 20th St [5th Av]
- **Harris Hardware** • 151 W 19th St [7th Av]
- **Home Depot** • 40 W 23rd St [5th Av]
- **J&M Hardware & Locksmiths** • 19 E 21st St [B'way]
- **KDM Hardware** • 147 W 26th St [6th Av]
- **Kove Brothers Hardware** • 189 Seventh Ave [21st]
- **Spacesaver Hardware** • 132 W 23rd St [6th Av]
- **Whitey's Hardware** • 244 Fifth Ave [28th]

Liquor Stores

- **A&J Kessler Liquors** • 23 E 28th St [Madison]
- **Chelsea Wine Cellar** • 200 W 21st St [7th Av]
- **Harry's Liquors** • 270 W 36th St [8th Av]
- **House of Cheers** • 261 W 18th St [8th Av]
- **Landmark Wine & Spirit** • 167 W 23rd St [7th Av]
- **Lewis-Kaye Wines & Liquors** • 60 E 34th St [Madison]
- **Madison Avenue Liquors** • 244 Madison Ave [38th]
- **Manor House Liquor Store** • 61 W 23rd St [6th Av]
- **Old Chelsea Wine & Liquor Store** • 86 Seventh Ave [15th]
- **Sonest Liquors** • 878 Sixth Ave [31st]
- **Union Square Wine & Spirits** • 33 Union Sq W [16th]
- **Wine Gallery** • 576 Sixth Ave [16th]

Pet Shops

- **Doggone Purrrty** • 151 W 25th St [7th Av]
- **Pet Central** • 193 Madison Ave [35th]
- **Pet Central** • 754 Sixth Ave [26th]
- **Pet Central Corp** • 247 W 23rd St [7th Av]
- **Petco** • 860 Broadway [17th]
- **Trixie & Peanut** • 23 E 20th St [B'way]

63

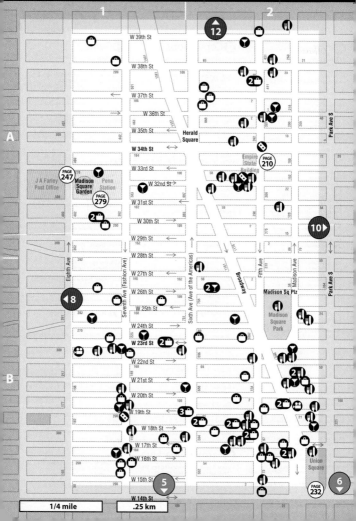

A lackluster bar scene drives Midtown suits south after work. Forgo Union Square for spirits at Old Town Bar & Restaurant or Silver Swan. Just west, Cafeteria dishes out comfort food 24/7. If you plan to dine at Craft or Eleven Madison Park, bring a week's pay.

 Movie Theaters

- **Clearview's Chelsea** • 260 W 23rd St [8th Av]
- **Loews 19th Street East** • 890 Broadway [19th]

Nightlife

- **Avalon** • 660 Sixth Ave [20th]
- **Blarney Stone** • 106 W 32nd St [6th Av]
- **Club Shelter** • 20 W 39th St [5th Av]
- **Cutting Room** • 19 W 24th St [B'way]
- **Ginger Man** • 11 E 36th St [Madison]
- **Gotham Comedy Club** • 208 W 23rd St [7th Av]
- **Kavehaz** • 37 W 26th St [B'way]
- **Live Bait** • 14 E 23rd St [Madison]
- **Merchants** • 112 Seventh Ave [17th]
- **Old Town Bar & Restaurant** • 45 E 18th St [B'way]
- **Peter McManus** • 152 Seventh Ave [19th]
- **Satalla** • 37 W 26th St [B'way]
- **Sky Bar at La Quinta** • 17 west 32nd [5th Av]
- **Splash Bar** • 50 W 17th St [6th Av]
- **Suede** • 161 W 23rd St [7th Av]
- **Tir Na Nog** • 5 Penn Plz [34th]
- **Under The Volcano** • 12 E 36th St [Madison]

Restaurants

- **Basta Pasta** • 37 W 17th St [5th Av]
- **Blaggard's Pub** • 8 W 38th St [5th Av]
- **BLT Fish** • 21 W 17th St [5th Av]
- **Blue Water Grill** • 31 Union Sq W [16th]
- **Bolo** • 23 E 22nd St [B'way]
- **Burritoville** • 264 W 23rd St [8th Av]
- **Butterfield 8** • 5 E 38th St [5th Av]
- **Cafeteria** • 119 Seventh Ave [17th] 🌙
- **Chat 'n Chew** • 10 E 16th St [5th Av]
- **City Bakery** • 3 W 18th St [5th Av]
- **Coffee Shop** • 29 Union Sq W [16th]
- **Craft** • 43 E 19th St [B'way]
- **Eisenberg's Sandwich Shop** • 174 Fifth Ave [22nd]
- **Eleven Madison Park** • 11 Madison Ave [24th]
- **Elmo** • 156 Seventh Ave [19th]
- **Evergreen Shang HAI Restaurant** • 10 E 38th St [5th Av]
- **Francisco's Centro Vasco** • 159 W 23rd [7th Av]
- **Giorgio's of Gramercy** • 27 E 21st St [B'way]
- **Gramercy Tavern** • 42 E 20th St [B'way]
- **Hangawi** • 12 E 32nd St [5th Av]
- **Kang Suh** • 1250 Broadway [32nd] 🌙
- **Koryodang** • 31 W 32nd St [6th Av]
- **Kum Gang San** • 49 W 32nd St [B'way] 🌙
- **Kunjip** • 9 W 32nd [5th Av] 🌙
- **La Fenice** • 120 W 23rd St [6th Av]
- **Le Pain Quotidien** • 38 E 19th St [B'way]
- **Le Zie 2000** • 172 Seventh Ave [20th]
- **Luna Park** • 50 E 17th St [Union Sq W]
- **Mayrose** • 920 Broadway [21st]
- **Mesa Grill** • 102 Fifth Ave [15th]
- **Minado** • 6 E 32nd St [5th Av]
- **Periyali** • 35 W 20th St [5th Av]
- **Petite Abeille** • 107 W 18th St [6th Av]
- **Republic** • 37 Union Sq W [16th]
- **RUB BBQ** • 208 W 23rd St [7th Av]
- **Salute** • 270 Madison Ave [40th]
- **Shake Shack** • Madison Sq Park
- **Silver Swan** • 41 E 20th St [B'way]
- **Tabla** • 11 Madison Ave [24th]
- **Tamarind** • 41 E 22nd St [B'way]
- **Toledo** • 6 E 36th St [5th Av]
- **Tocqueville** • 1 E 15th St [5th Av]
- **Uncle Moe's** • 14 W 19th St [5th AV]
- **Union Square Café** • 21 E 16th St [5th Av]
- **Waldy's Wood Fired Pizza** • 800 Sixth Ave [27th]
- **Woo Chon** • 8 W 36th St [5th Av] 🌙

Shopping

- **17 at 17 Thrift Shop** • 17 W 17th St [5th Av]
- **30th Street Guitars** • 236 W 30th St [7th Av]
- **ABC Carpet & Home** • 888 Broadway [19th]
- **Abracadabra** • 19 W 21st St [5th Av]
- **Academy Records & CDs** • 12 W 18th St [5th Av]
- **Adorama Camera** • 42 W 18th St [5th Av]
- **Al Friedman** • 44 W 18th St [5th Av]
- **Angel Street Thrift Shop** • 118 W 17th St [6th Av]
- **Anthropologie** • 85 Fifth Ave [16th]
- **Ariston** • 69 Fifth Ave [14th]
- **Aveda Environmental Lifestyle Store** • 140 Fifth Ave [19th]
- **Bed Bath & Beyond** • 620 Sixth Ave [18th]
- **buybuy Baby** • 270 Seventh Ave [26th]
- **Capitol Fishing Tackle** • 218 W 23rd St [7th Av]
- **Chelsea Flea Market** • 112 W 25th St [6th Av]
- **The City Quilter** • 133 W 25th St [6th Av]
- **CompUSA** • 420 Fifth Ave [38th]
- **The Container Store** • 629 Sixth Ave [19th]
- **Cupcake Café** • 18 W 18th St [5th Av]
- **DataVision** • 445 Fifth Ave [39th]
- **The Family Jewels** • 130 W 23rd St [6th Av]
- **Fish's Eddy** • 889 Broadway [19th]
- **Housing Works Thrift Shop** • 143 W 17th St [6th Av]
- **Jam Paper & Envelope** • 611 Sixth Ave [18th]
- **Janovic** • 215 Seventh Ave [22nd]
- **Jazz Record Center** • 236 W 26th St [7th Av]
- **Jensen-Lewis** • 89 Seventh Ave [15th]
- **Jim Smiley Vintage** • 128 W 23rd St [6th Av]
- **Just Bulbs** • 5 E 16th St [5th Av]
- **Krups Kitchen and Bath** • 11 W 18th St [5th Av]
- **Loehmann's** • 101 Seventh Ave [16th]
- **Lord & Taylor** • 424 Fifth Ave [38th]
- **Lucky Wang** • 82 Seventh Ave [13th]
- **Lulu Guiness** • 260 W 39th St [8th Av]
- **M&J Trimmings** • 1008 Sixth Ave [38th]
- **Macy's** • 151 W 34th St [7th Av]
- **Mandler's, The Original Sausage Co** • 26 E 17th St [B'way]
- **Manhattan Drum Shop & Music Studio** • 203 W 38th St [7th Av]
- **Otto Tootsi Plohound** • 137 Fifth Ave [20th]
- **Paper Presentations** • 23 W 18th St [5th Av]
- **Paragon Sporting Goods** • 867 Broadway [18th]
- **Phoenix** • 64 W 37th St [6th Av]
- **Pleasure Chest** • 156 Seventh Ave [19th]
- **Radio Shack** • 36 E 23rd St [Madison]
- **Rogue Music** • 251 W 30th St [7th Av]
- **Sam Flax** • 12 W 20th St [5th Av]
- **Space Kiddets** • 46 E 21st St [B'way]
- **Sports Authority** • 636 Sixth Ave [19th]
- **Teksvero** • 119 W 23rd St [6th Av]
- **Toho Shoji** • 990 Sixth Ave [37th]

Video Rental

- **Koryo Video (Korean only)** • 7 W 32nd St [5th Av]
- **Movie Bank USA** • E 34th St & Fifth Ave 🌙
- **Movie Bank USA** • W 19th St & Seventh Ave 🌙

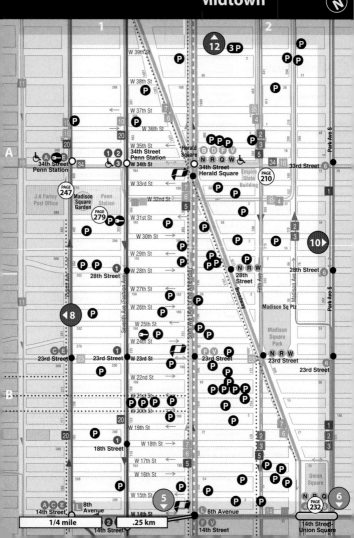

Parking during the day and on weekends is extremely difficult in this area, due to the number of business districts and commercial enterprises that are here. Driving isn't much better, since Lincoln Tunnel traffic has far-ranging repercussions. However, few areas boast better subway access.

Subways

1 **2** **3** . . . . 34 St-Penn Station
1 . . . . 18 St
1 . . . . 23 St
1 . . . . 28 St
B **D** **F** **V** **N** **Q** **R** **W** 34 St-Herald Sq
F **V** . . . . 23rd St
R **W** . . . . 23 St
R **W** . . . . 28 St

Bus Lines

10 **20** . . . . Seventh Ave/Eighth Ave
(Central Park West)/Frederick Douglass Blvd
16 . . . . 34th St Crosstown
2 **3** . . . . Fifth Ave/Madison Ave
23 . . . . 23rd St Crosstown
4 . . . . Fifth Ave/Madison Ave/Broadway
5 . . . . Fifth Ave/Sixth Ave/Riverdale Dr
6 . . . . Seventh Ave/Broadway/Sixth Ave
7 . . . . Columbus Ave/Amsterdam Ave/
Lenox Ave/Sixth Ave/Seventh Ave/Broadway
9 **32** . . . . Penn Station/Jackson Heights, Queens

Bike Lanes

• • • • Marked Bike Lanes
• • • • Recommended Route

PATH

• **23 St** • 23rd St & Sixth Ave
• **33 St** • 33rd St & Sixth Ave

Car Rental

• **Avis** • 220 W 31st St [7th Av]
• **Enterprise** • 106 W 24th St [6th Av]
• **Hertz** • 323 W 34th St [8th Av]

Parking

Map 10 · Murray F   ...amercy

This area is home to one of Manhattan's most pastoral and beautiful settings, Gramercy Park. It also contains two humongous and drab residential communities, Stuyvesant Town and Peter Cooper Village, plus huge Eastern Bloc-style apartment buildings like Kips Bay Towers. For juxtaposition, check out charming little Sniffen Court.

℞ 24-Hour Pharmacies

- **CVS Pharmacy** • 342 E 23rd St [2nd Av]
- **Duane Reade** • 155 E 34th St [Lex] ♿
- **Duane Reade** • 300 Park Ave S [23rd] ♿
- **Rite Aid** • 542 Second Ave [30th] ♿

◎ Bagels

- **Bagel du Jour** • 478 Third Ave [33rd]
- **Bagel & Schmear** • 116 E 28th St [Lex]
- **Bagelry** • 429 Third Ave [30th]
- **Bagels & More** • 331 Lexington Ave [39th]
- **Daniel's Bagels** • 569 Third Ave [38th]
- **David's Bagels** • 331 First Ave [19th]
- **Ess-A-Bagel** • 359 First Ave [21st]
- **Gramercy Bagels** • 246 Third Ave [20th]
- **La Bagel** • 263 First Ave [15th]
- **New York Bagel** • 587 First Ave [34th]
- **Pick-a-Bagel** • 297 Third Ave [22nd]

$ Banks

- **AM • Amalgamated** • 301 Third [23rd]
- **AT • Atlantic (ATM)** • Gristedes • 355 First Ave [21st]
- **AT • Atlantic (ATM)** • Gristedes • 460 Third Ave [32nd]
- **AT • Atlantic (ATM)** • Gristedes • 512 South Ave [37th]
- **BP • Banco Popular** • 441 Second [25th]
- **BA • Bank of America** • 345 Park Ave S [25th]
- **BA • Bank of America (ATM)** • 550 First Ave [33rd]
- **BA • Bank of America (ATM)** • 570 Second Ave [32nd]
- **BA • Bank of America (ATM)** • 90 Park Ave [40th]
- **CH • Chase** • 225 Park Ave S [18th]
- **CH • Chase** • 386 Park Ave S [27th]
- **CH • Chase** • 400 E 23rd St [1st Av]
- **CH • Chase** • 450 Third Ave [31st]
- **CH • Chase (ATM)** • 390 Park Ave S [27th]
- **CI • Citibank** • 1 Park Ave [33rd]
- **CI • Citibank** • 262 First Ave [15th]
- **CI • Citibank** • 90 Park Ave [40th]
- **CI • Citibank** • 25 Waterside Plz [26th]
- **CI • Citibank (ATM)** • 481 First Ave [28th]
- **CO • Commerce** • 260 Park Ave S [21st]
- **CO • Commerce** • 475 Park Ave S [31st]
- **DO • Doral** • 887 Park Ave [40th]
- **FS • Flushing Savings** • 33 Irving Pl [16th]
- **HS • HSBC** • 10 Union Sq E [15th]
- **HS • HSBC** • 2 Park Ave [33rd]
- **HS • HSBC** • 605 Third Ave [39th]
- **IC • Independence Community** • 250 Lexington Ave [35th]
- **IC • Independence Community** • 251 Park Ave S [20th]
- **MT • M&T** • 397 First Ave [23rd]
- **MA • Marathon Bank of New York** • 420 Park Ave S [29th]

- **MN • Metropolitan National** • 99 Park Ave [40th]
- **CU • Municipal Credit Union (ATM)** • 462 First Ave [27th]
- **NF • North Fork** • 245 E 34th St [2nd Av]
- **NF • North Fork** • 470 Park Ave S [31st]
- **WM • Washington Mutual** • 460 Park Ave S [31st]

✚ Emergency Rooms

- **Bellevue Hospital Center** • 462 First Ave [27th] ♿
- **Beth Israel Medical Center** • 281 First Ave [16th] ♿
- **Cabrini Medical Center** • 227 E 19th St [3rd Av] ♿
- **Hospital for Joint Diseases** • 301 E 17th St [2nd Av] ♿
- **NYU Medical Center: Tisch** • 560 First Ave [33rd] ♿
- **VA Hospital** • 423 E 23rd St [1st Av] ♿

◎ Landmarks

- **Gramercy Park** • Irving Pl & 20th St
- **National Arts Club** • 15 Gramercy Park S [20th]
- **Pete's Tavern** • 129 E 18th St [Irving]
- **The Players** • 16 Gramercy Park S [20th]
- **Sniffen Court** • 36th St & Third Ave
- **Tammany Hall/Union Sq Theater** • 100 E 17th St [Park]

◫ Libraries

- **Epiphany** • 228 E 23rd St [3rd Av]
- **Kips Bay** • 446 Third Ave [31st]

◎ Police

- **13th Precinct** • 230 E 21st St [3rd Av]

✉ Post Offices

- **Madison Square** • 149 E 23rd St [Lex]
- **Murray Hill** • 205 E 36th St [3rd Av]
- **Murray Hill Finance** • 115 E 34th St [Park]

◎ Schools

- **The American Sign Language & English Lower (M347)** • 225 E 23rd St [3rd Av]
- **The American Sign Language and English Dual Language High** • 225 E 23rd St [3rd Av]
- **Baruch College** • 151 E 25th St [Lex]
- **Baruch College Campus High** • 17 Lexington Ave [23rd]

- **Brooklyn Blue Feather Elementary** • 200 Park Ave S [17th]
- **The Child School** • 317 E 33rd St [2nd Av]
- **Churchill** • 301 E 29th St [2nd Av]
- **Epiphany Elementary** • 234 E 22nd St [3rd Av]
- **Friends Seminary** • 222 E 16th St
- **Health Prof & Human Svcs High** • 345 E 15th St [Perlman Pl]
- **HS 413 School of the Future** • 127 E 22nd St [Lex]
- **Institute for Collaborative Education** • 345 E 15th St [Perlman Pl]
- **Institute for Secondary Education** • 345 E 15th St [Perlman Pl]
- **JHS 104 Simon Baruch** • 330 E 21st St [2nd Av]
- **The Lee Strasberg Theater Institute** • 115 E 15th St [Irving]
- **Manhattan Night Comprehensive High** • 240 Second Ave [14th]
- **MS 255 Salk School of Science** • 319 E 19th St [2nd Av]
- **New York Film Academy** • 100 E 17th St [Union Sq E]
- **Norman Thomas High** • 111 E 33rd St [Park]
- **NYU Dental** • 345 E 24th St [1st Av]
- **NYU Medical Center** • 550 First Ave [33rd]
- **PS 040 Augustus St-Gaudens** • 319 E 19th St [2nd Av]
- **PS 116 Mary L Murray** • 210 E 33rd St [3rd Av]
- **PS 811 Bellevue Hospital** • 27th St & First Ave
- **School of Visual Arts** • 209 E 23rd St [3rd Av]
- **Stern College for Women of Yeshiva U** • 245 Lexington Ave [34th]
- **United Nations International** • 24 FDR Dr [25th]
- **Washington Irving High** • 40 Irving Pl [16th]

◎ Supermarkets

- **Associated** • 278 Park Ave S [22nd]
- **Associated** • 311 E 23rd St [2nd Av]
- **D'Agostino** • 341 Third Ave [25th]
- **D'Agostino** • 528 Third Ave [35th]
- **D'Agostino** • 578 Third Ave [38th]
- **Food Emporium** • 10 Union Sq E [15th]
- **Food Emporium** • 200 E 32nd St [3rd Av]
- **Gristede's** • 25 Waterside Plz [26th]
- **Gristede's** • 355 First Ave [21st]
- **Gristede's** • 460 Third Ave [32nd] ♿
- **Gristede's** • 512 Second Ave [37th]
- **Gristede's** • 549 Third Ave [36th]
- **Met Food** • 180 Third Ave [17th]

Map 70 Murray Hill Cemetery 13

2

East River

Queens Midtown Tunnel

Second Ave

Tunnel Approach St

Tunnel Exit St

E 39th St

E 38th St

E 37th St

Sniffen Ct

E 36th St

E 35th St

A

E 34th St **21**

E 33rd St

E 32nd St

Kips Bay Plaza

NYU Medical Center

E 31st St

Second Ave

First Ave

E 30th St

Park Ave S

Lexington Ave

Third Ave

E 29th St

E 28th St

E 27th St

Bellevue Hospital Center

Broadway Ay

E 26th St

Waterside Plaza

9

E 25th St

E 24th St

Vet Adm Medical Center

Asser Levy Pl

E 23rd St

E 22nd St

Marina & Skyport

E 21st St

FDR Dr

Marginal St

B

E 20th St

Gramercy Park

Peter Cooper Village

E 19th St

E 18th St

Irving Pl

E 17th St

Rutherford Pl

Stuyvesant Square

Nathan D Perlman Pl

E 16th St

Stuyvesant Town

E 16th St

Union Sq E

E 16th St **21**

PAGE 232

6

E 15th St

E 14th St

Avenue C

7

| 1/4 mile | .25 km |

The perfect balance of predictable (Dunkin' Donuts and Starbucks abound) and innovative (iPod deejay nights at Revival). Work up an endorphin rush at one of the ubiquitous New York Sports Clubs before cruising the meat market bars on First Avenue. Fortunately, there's Pete's Tavern, and all's again well.

Coffee

- **71 Irving** • 71 Irving Pl [19th]
- **Au Bon Pain** • 6 Union Sq E [14th]
- **Au Bon Pain** • 600 Third Ave [39th]
- **Cosi** • 257 Park Ave S [20th]
- **Cosi** • 461 Park Ave S [31st]
- **Delectica** • 564 Third Ave [37th]
- **Dip Café** • 416 Third Ave [29th]
- **Dunkin' Donuts** • 127 E 23rd St [Lex]
- **Dunkin' Donuts** • 152 W 34th St [7th Av]
- **Dunkin' Donuts** • 361 First Ave [21st]
- **Dunkin' Donuts** • 412 Third Ave [29th]
- **Dunkin' Donuts** • 476 Second Ave [27th]
- **Dunkin' Donuts** • 601 Second Ave [33rd]
- **Franchia Teahouse & Restaurant** • 12 Park Ave [35th]
- **Guy & Gallard** • 120 E 34th St [Lex]
- **Kabob Café** • 110 E 23rd St [Park]
- **Lady Mendl's Tea Salon** • 56 Irving Pl [17th]
- **Oren's Daily Roast** • 434 Third Ave [30th]
- **Plaza de Café** • 61 Lexington Ave [25th]
- **Push Café** • 294 Third Ave [22nd]
- **Starbucks** • 10 Union Sq E [15th]
- **Starbucks** • 145 Third Ave [15th]
- **Starbucks** • 286 First Ave [17th]
- **Starbucks** • 296 Third Ave [22nd]
- **Starbucks** • 3 Park Ave [33rd]
- **Starbucks** • 304 Park Ave S [23rd]
- **Starbucks** • 395 Third Ave [28th]
- **Starbucks** • 424 Park Ave S [29th]
- **Starbucks** • 585 Second Ave [32nd]
- **Starbucks** • 90 Park Ave [40th]
- **Sunburst** • 206 Third Ave [18th]
- **Trevi Coffee Shop** • 48 Union Sq E [16th]

Copy Shops

- **Columbia Enterprises** • 116 E 16th St [Irving]
- **Ever Ready Blue Print** • 200 Park Ave S [17th]
- **FedEx Kinko's** • 257 Park Ave S [20th]
- **Graphics Service Bureau** • 370 Park Ave S [26th]
- **Kinko's** • 600 Third Ave [39th]
- **Mail Boxes Etc** • 163 Third Ave [16th]
- **Mail Boxes Etc** • 350 Third Ave [26th]
- **On-Site Sourcing** • 443 Park Ave S Fl 3 [30th] ⊠
- **Pro-Print** • 424 Park Ave S [29th]
- **Staples** • 345 Park Ave S [25th]
- **Tower Copy East** • 427 Third Ave [30th]
- **The UPS Store** • 388 Second Ave [22nd]
- **The UPS Store** • 527 Third Ave [35th]

Gyms

- **Boom Fitness** • 4 Park Ave [34th]
- **Club 29** • 155 E 29th St [Lex]
- **Crunch Fitness** • 554 Second Ave [31st]
- **Curves (Women only)** • 139 E 23rd St [Lex]

- **Curves (Women only)** • 150 E 39th St [Lex]
- **New York Sports Clubs** • 10 Irving Pl [15th]
- **New York Sports Clubs** • 113 E 23rd St [Park] ⊠
- **New York Sports Clubs** • 131 E 31st St [Lex]
- **New York Sports Clubs** • 3 Park Ave [38th]
- **New York Sports Clubs** • 614 Second Ave [34th]
- **Park Avenue Executive Fitness** • 90 Park Ave [40th]
- **Rivergate Fitness Center** • 401 E 34th St [1st Av]
- **Synergy Fitness Clubs** • 321 E 22nd St [2nd Av]

Hardware Stores

- **Gurell Hardware** • 132 E 28th St [Lex]
- **HomeFront** • 202 E 29th St [3rd Av] ⊠
- **Lumber Boys** • 698 Second Ave [38th]
- **Lumberland Hardware** • 368 Third Ave [27th]
- **Simon's Hardware & Bath** • 421 Third Ave [29th]
- **Town & Village Hardware** • 337 First Ave [20th]
- **Vercesi Hardware** • 152 E 23rd St [Lex]
- **Warshaw Hardware & Electrical** • 248 Third Ave [20th]
- **Z Locksmith & Hardware** • 347 Third Ave [25th]

Pet Shops

- **Biscuits & Bath** • 701 Second Ave [38th]
- **Furry Paws** • 120 E 34th St [Lex]
- **Furry Paws 5** • 310 E 23rd St [2nd Av]
- **Natural Pet** • 238 Third Ave [20th]
- **New World Aquarium (Fish)** • 204 E 38th St [3rd Av]
- **Petco** • 550 Second Ave [30th]
- **Thirty-Third & Bird (Birds)** • 40 E 33rd St [Madison]

Liquor Stores

- **Buy Rite Discount Liquors** • 398 Third Ave [28th]
- **First Avenue Wine & Spirits Supermarket** • 383 First Ave [23rd]
- **Flynn Winfield Liquor** • 558 Third Ave [37th]
- **Frank's Liquor Shop** • 46 Union Sq E [16th]
- **Gramercy Park Wines & Spirits** • 104 E 23rd St [Park]
- **House of Wine & Liquor** • 250 E 34th St [2nd Av]
- **HS Wine & Liquor** • 161 Third Ave [16th]
- **Italian Wine Merchants** • 108 E 16th St [Union Sq E]
- **New Gramercy Liquors** • 279 Third Ave [21st]
- **Quality House** • 2 Park Ave [33rd]
- **Royal Wine Merchants** • 25 Waterside Plz [26th]
- **Stuyvesant Square Liquors** • 333 Second Ave [19th]
- **Vino** • 123 E 27th St [Lex]
- **Welcome Wine & Spirits Limited** • 424 Second Ave [24th]
- **Windsor Wine Shop** • 474 Third Ave [32nd]
- **Wine Shop** • 345 Lexington Ave [40th]
- **World Wine and Spirits** • 705 Second Ave [38th]
- **Zeichner Wine & Liquor** • 279 First Ave [16th]

Map 10 · Murray H

We can say at least one good thing for the "mall" at Kips Bay: nice multiplex. The meat market bars are at least balanced by Pete's Tavern and Waterfront Ale House, as well as a plethora of great eating choices---Pongal for great Indian dosas, Turkish Kitchen, Jaiya Thai, Les Halles, and top-end such as BLT Prime.

Movie Theaters

- **Loews Kips Bay** • 550 Second Ave [30th]
- **Scandinavia House** • 58 Park Ave [35th]

Nightlife

- **Bar 515** • 515 Third Ave [34th]
- **Belmont Lounge** • 117 E 15th St [Irving]
- **Irving Plaza** • 17 Irving Pl [15th]
- **The Jazz Standard** • 116 E 27th St [Lex]
- **Joshua Tree** • 513 Third Ave [34th]
- **Mercury Bar** • 493 Third Ave [33rd]
- **Molly's** • 287 Third Ave [22nd]
- **New York Comedy Club** • 241 E 24th St [3rd Av]
- **Paddy Reilly's Music Bar** • 519 Second Ave [29th]
- **Revival** • 129 E 15th St [Irving]
- **Rocky Sullivan's** • 129 Lexington Ave [29th]
- **Rodeo Bar & Grill** • 375 Third Ave [27th]
- **Waterfront Ale House** • 540 Second Ave [30th]

Restaurants

- **71 Irving** • 71 Irving Pl [19th]
- **Angelo & Maxie's** • 233 Park Ave S [19th]
- **AQ Café** • Scandinavia House • 58 Park Ave [38th]
- **Artisanal** • 2 Park Ave [33rd]
- **Bar Jamon** • 52 Irving Pl [17th]
- **Blockheads Burritos** • 499 Third Ave [34th]
- **BLT Prime** • 111 E 22nd St [Park]
- **Blue Smoke** • 116 E 27th St [Park]
- **Butai** • 115 E 18th St [Irving]
- **Candela** • 116 E 16th St [Union Sq E]
- **Coppola's** • 378 Third Ave [27th]
- **Curry Leaf** • 99 Lexington Ave [27th]
- **David's Bagels** • 331 First Ave [19th]
- **El Parador Café** • 325 E 34th St [2nd Av]
- **Ess-a-bagel** • 359 First Ave [21st]
- **Friend of a Farmer** • 77 Irving Pl [19th]
- **Gemini Diner** • 641 Second Ave [35th] ⏰
- **Gramercy Restaurant** • 184 Third Ave [17th] ⏰
- **Haandi** • 113 Lexington Ave [28th]
- **I Trulli** • 122 E 27th St [Lex]
- **Jackson Hole** • 521 Third Ave [35th]
- **Jaiya Thai** • 396 Third Ave [28th]
- **L'aanam** • 393 Third Ave [28th]
- **L'Express** • 249 Park Ave S [20th] ⏰
- **Les Halles** • 411 Park Ave S [29th]
- **Mexico Lindo** • 459 Second Ave [26th]
- **Paquitos** • 160 E 28th St [Lex]
- **Park Avenue Country Club** • 381 Park Ave S [27th]
- **Patsy's Pizzeria** • 509 Third Ave [34th]
- **Penelope** • 159 Lexington Ave [30th]
- **Pete's Tavern** • 129 E 18th St [Irving]
- **Pongal** • 110 Lexington Ave [28th]
- **Pongsri Thai** • 311 Second Ave [18th]
- **Posto** • 310 Second Ave [18th]
- **Pure Food and Wine** • 54 Irving Pl [17th]
- **Rare Bar & Grill** • Shelbourne Murray Hill Hotel • 303 Lexington Ave [37th]
- **Rice** • 115 Lexington Ave [28th]
- **Rodeo** • 375 Third Ave [27th]
- **Sarge's Deli** • 548 Third Ave [37th] ⏰
- **Totonno's Pizzeria Napolitano** • 462 Second Ave [26th]
- **Tracy J's Watering Hole** • 106 E 19th St [Park]
- **Turkish Kitchen** • 386 Third Ave [28th]
- **Via Emilia** • 240 Park Ave S [20th]
- **Water Club** • 500 E 30th St [FDR]
- **Yama** • 122 E 17th St [Irving]
- **Zen Palate** • 34 Union Sq E [16th]

Shopping

- **Alkit Pro Camera** • 222 Park Ave S [18th]
- **City Opera Thrift Shop** • 222 E 23rd St [3rd Av]
- **Foods of India** • 121 Lexington Ave [28th]
- **Housing Works Thrift Shop** • 157 E 23rd St [Lex]
- **Kalustyan's** • 123 Lexington Ave [28th]
- **Ligne Roset** • 250 Park Ave S [20th]
- **Nemo Tile Company** • 48 E 21st St [B'way]
- **Pastrami Factory** • 333 E 23rd St [2nd Av]
- **Pearl Paint** • 207 E 23rd St [3rd Av]
- **Poggenpohl US** • 230 Park Ave [45th]
- **Pookie & Sebastian** • 541 Third Ave [36th]
- **Quark Spy** • 240 E 29th St [3rd Av]
- **Urban Angler** • 206 Fifth Ave [25th]

Video Rental

- **Blockbuster** • 151 Third Ave [15th]
- **Blockbuster** • 155 E 34th St [Lex]
- **Blockbuster** • 312 First Ave [18th]
- **Blockbuster** • 344 Third Ave [25th]
- **Movie Bank USA** • 22nd St & Park Ave S ⏰
- **Movie Bank USA** • E 18th St & Third Ave ⏰
- **Video Stop** • 367 Third Ave [27th]

We've nearly given up on getting a Second Avenue subway line, especially after the transit strike. While waiting, we'll walk when the weather's nice. When it's a bit nasty? That Metro Card comes in handy on the many buses servicing the east side.

Subways

6	.... 23rd St
6	.... 28th St
6	.... 33rd St
4 **5** **6** **L** **N** **Q** **R** **W**	.... 14th St
L	.... First Ave
L	.... Third Ave

Bus Lines

1 **2** **3**	.... Fifth Ave/Madison Ave
101	.... Third Ave/Lexington Ave
102	.... Third Ave/Lexington Ave
103	.... Third Ave/Lexington Ave
9	.......................Avenue B/East Broadway
14	.... 14th St Crosstown
34	.... 34th St Crosstown
15	.... First Ave/Second Ave
16	.... 34th St Crosstown
21	.... Houston St Crosstown
23	.... 23rd St Crosstown
98	.... Third Ave/Lexington Ave

Bike Lanes

- • • • Marked Bike Lanes
- • • • Recommended Route
- • • • Greenway

Car Rental

- **Dollar** • 329 E 22nd St [2nd Av]
- **Hertz** • 150 E 24th St [Lex]
- **National/Alamo** • 142 E 31st St [Lex]

Gas Stations

- **Gulf** • E 23 St & FDR Dr

Parking

PAGE 216

PAGE 212

PAGE 282

PAGE 214

1

2

HENRY HUDSON PKWY

W 60th St

W 59th St

Time Warner Center

Columbus Circle

W 58th St

W 57th St

W 56th St

W 55th St

W 54th St

W 53rd St

W 52nd St

W 51st St

Dewitt Clinton Park

Hudson River

W 50th St

W 49th St

West Side Hwy

Hudson River Park

W 48th St

W 47th St

W 46th St

Eleventh Ave

Tenth Ave

Ninth Ave

Eighth Ave

Restaurant Row

W 45th St

Intrepid Sea, Air & Space Museum

W 44th St

W 43rd St

Theatre Row

W 42nd St

Dyer Ave

Port Authority Bus Terminal

W 41st St

W 40th St

Lincoln Tunnel

W 39th St

Jacob K Javits Convention Center

W 38th St

W 37th St

14

12

6

2

8

HS

CH

CI

CO

CH

HS

1/4 mile   .25 km

This neighborhood is really close to...well, everything. Within walking distance lie Central Park, Lincoln Center, Columbus Circle, Times Square, Theatre Row and Restaurant Row. A new bank opens every month, and the grocery options are plentiful above 49th. What it lacks in character, it makes up for in convenience.

24-Hour Pharmacies

- **CVS Pharmacy** • 400 W 58th St [9th Av] &

Bagels

- **H&H Bagels** • 639 W 46th St [11th Av]

Banks

CH • **Chase** • 471 W 42nd St [10th Av]
CI • **Chase** • 839 Ninth Ave [55th]
CI • **Citibank** • 401 W 42nd St [9th Av]
CO • **Commerce** • 582 Ninth Ave [42nd]
HS • **HSBC** • 330 W 42nd St [8th Av]
HS • **HSBC** • 601 W 57th St [11th Av]

Community Gardens

Emergency Rooms

- **St Luke's Roosevelt Hospital Center** • 1000 Tenth Ave [59th] &
- **St Vincent's Midtown** • 426 W 52nd St [9th Av] &

Landmarks

- **Intrepid Sea, Air & Space Museum** • Twelfth Ave & 45th St
- **Restaurant Row** • 46th St b/w Eighth & Ninth Aves
- **Theatre Row** • 42nd St b/w Ninth & Tenth Aves

Libraries

- **Columbus** • 742 Tenth Ave [51st]

Police

- **Mid-Town North** • 306 W 54th St [8th Av]

Post Offices

- **Radio City** • 322 W 52nd St [8th Av]
- **Times Square** • 340 W 42nd St [8th Av]

Schools

- **Alvin Ailey / Joan Weill Center for Dance** • 405 W 55th St [9th Av]
- **American Academy McAllister Institute** • 619 W 54th St [11th Av]
- **The Facing History School** • 525 W 50th St [10th Av]
- **Food and Finance High** • 525 W 50th St [10th Av]
- **High School for Environmental Studies** • 448 W 56th St [9th Av]
- **High School of Graphic Communication Arts** • 439 W 49th St [9th Av]
- **High School of Hospitality Management** • 525 W 50th St [10th Av]
- **Holy Cross** • 332 W 43rd St [8th Av]
- **Independence High (M544)** • 850 Tenth Ave [56th]
- **John Jay College** • 899 Tenth Ave [58th]
- **Manhattan Bridges High** • 525 W 50th St [10th Av]
- **Park West High** • 525 W 50th St [10th Av]
- **Professional Performing Arts High** • 328 W 48th St [8th Av]
- **PS 035** • 317 W 52nd St [8th Av]
- **PS 051 Elias Howe** • 520 W 45th St [10th Av]
- **PS 111 Adolph S Ochs** • 440 W 53rd St [9th Av]
- **PS 212 Midtown West** • 328 W 48th St [8th Av]
- **Sacred Heart of Jesus** • 456 W 52nd St [10th Av]
- **Urban Assembly School of Design & Construction** • 525 W 50th St [10th Av]

Supermarkets

- **Amish Market** • 731 Ninth Ave [50th]
- **D'Agostino** • 353 W 57th St [9th Av]
- **D'Agostino** • 815 Tenth Ave [54th]
- **Food Emporium** • 452 W 43rd St [10th Av]
- **Morton Williams** • 917 Ninth Ave [58th]

Whether you call it Hell's Kitchen or Clinton, this neighborhood's history has left Ninth Avenue packed with ethnic restaurants. It's New York's microcosmic answer to Epcot. For a latte and muffin---The Coffee Pot. If you're thirsty, Rudy's is it: red duct-taped booths, homemade bad-but-good lager, and a killer vibe.

Coffee

- **The Bread Factory Café** • 600 Ninth Ave [43rd]
- **Café Ole** • 453 W 54th St [10th Av]
- **The Coffee Pot** • 350 W 49th St [9th Av]
- **Dunkin' Donuts** • 580 Ninth Ave [42nd]
- **Dunkin' Donuts** • 815 Tenth Ave [54th]
- **Empire Coffee & Tea** • 568 Ninth Ave [41st]
- **Felix Coffee Shop** • 630 Tenth Ave [45th]
- **Flame Coffee House** • 893 Ninth Ave [58th]
- **Starbucks** • 322 W 57th St [8th Av]
- **Starbucks** • 325 W 49th St [8th Av]
- **Starbucks** • 555 W 42nd St [11th Av]
- **Starbucks** • 593 Ninth Ave [43rd]
- **Starbucks** • 682 Ninth Ave [47th]
- **Studio Coffee Shop** • 812 Tenth Ave [54th]

Copy Shops

- **C2 Media** • 423 W 55th St [9th Av]
- **Mail Boxes Etc** • 331 W 57th St [8th Av]
- **Mail Boxes Etc** • 676 Ninth Ave [47th]
- **Mega Copy Center** • 738 Tenth Ave [50th]
- **Sentinel Copy** • 333 W 52nd St [8th Av]
- **Xact** • 333 W 52nd St [8th Av]

Farmer's Markets

- **57th Street (Wed & Sat 8am-6pm, Year Round)** • W 57th St & Ninth Ave

Gyms

- **Bally Total Fitness** • 350 W 50th St [8th Av]
- **Crunch Fitness** • 555 W 42nd St [11th Av]
- **Curves (Women only)** • 314 W 53rd St [8th Av]
- **Manhattan Plaza Health Club** • 482 W 43rd St [10th Av]
- **New York Underground Fitness** • 440 W 57th St [9th Av]
- **Strand Health Club** • 500 W 43rd St [10th Av]

Hardware Stores

- **Columbus Hardware** • 852 Ninth Ave [56th]
- **Garden Hardware & Supply** • 701 Tenth Ave [48th]
- **HT Sales** • 718 Tenth Ave [49th]
- **Lopez Sentry Hardware** • 691 Ninth Ave [48th]
- **Metropolitan Lumber & Hardware** • 617 Eleventh Ave [46th]
- **Straight Hardware & Supply** • 613 Ninth Ave [44th]

Liquor Stores

- **54 Wine & Spirits** • 408 W 55th St [9th Av]
- **860 Ninth Liquors** • 860 Ninth Ave [56th]
- **B&G Wine & Liquor Store** • 507 W 42nd St [10th Av]
- **Manhattan Plaza Winery** • 589 Ninth Ave [42nd]
- **Ninth Avenue Vintner** • 669 Ninth Ave [46th]
- **Ninth Avenue Wine & Liquor** • 474 Ninth Ave [37th]
- **Ray & Frank Liquor Store** • 706 Ninth Ave [48th]
- **West 57th Street Wine & Spirit** • 340 W 57th St [8th Av]

Nightlife

- **Birdland** • 315 W 44th St [8th Av]
- **Bellevue Bar** • 538 Ninth Ave [40th]
- **Bull Moose Saloon** • 357 W 44th St [9th Av]
- **Don't Tell Mama** • 343 W 46th St [8th Av]
- **Hudson Hotel Library** • 356 W 58th St [9th Av]
- **Rudy's Bar & Grill** • 627 Ninth Ave [44th]
- **Siberia Bar** • 356 W 40th St [9th Av]
- **Vintage** • Chelsea Market• 753 Ninth Ave [51st]
- **Xth** • 642 Tenth Ave [45th]

Pet Shops

- **Canine Castle** • 410 W 56th St [9th Av]
- **Metropets** • 594 Ninth Ave [43rd]
- **Petland Discounts** • 734 Ninth Ave [50th]
- **Spoiled Brats** • 340 W 49th St [8th Av]

Restaurants

- **Afghan Kebab House** • 764 Ninth Ave [51st]
- **Ariana Afghan Kebab** • 787 Ninth Ave [52nd]
- **Burrito Box** • 885 Ninth Ave [57th]
- **Burritoville** • 625 Ninth Ave [44th]
- **Chipotle** • 620 Ninth Ave [44th]
- **Churruscaria Plataforma** • 316 W 49th St [8th Av]
- **Daisy May's BBQ USA** • 623 Eleventh Ave [46th]
- **Don Giovanni** • 358 W 44th St [9th Av]
- **Eatery** • 798 Ninth Ave [53rd]
- **Grand Sichuan Int'l** • 745 Ninth Ave [50th]
- **H&H Bagels** • 639 W 46th St [11th Av] ⓧ
- **Hallo Berlin** • 626 Tenth Ave [45th]
- **Hell's Kitchen** • 679 Ninth Ave [47th]
- **Hudson Cafeteria** • Hudson Hotel • 356 W 58th St [9th Av]
- **Island Burgers 'N Shakes** • 766 Ninth Ave [51st]
- **Jezebel** • 630 Ninth Ave [44th]
- **Joe Allen** • 326 W 46th St [8th Av]
- **Les Sans Culottes** • 347 W 46th St [8th Av]
- **Marseille** • 630 Ninth Ave [44th]
- **Meskerem** • 468 W 47th St [10th Av]
- **Morningstar** • 401 W 57th St [9th Av] ⓧ
- **The Nook** • 746 Ninth Ave [50th]
- **Old San Juan** • 765 Ninth Ave [51st]
- **Orso** • 322 W 46th St [8th Av]
- **Puttanesca** • 859 Ninth Ave [56th]
- **Ralph's** • 862 Ninth Ave [56th]
- **Taboon** • 773 Tenth Ave [52nd]
- **Tony Luke's** • 576 Ninth Ave [42nd]
- **Tout Va Bien** • 311 W 51st St [8th Av]
- **Turkish Cuisine** • 631 Ninth Ave [44th]
- **Uncle Nick's** • 747 Ninth Ave [50th]
- **Zen Palate** • 663 Ninth Ave [46th]

Shopping

- **Amy's Bread** • 672 Ninth Ave [47th]
- **Delphinium** • 358 W 47th St [9th Av]
- **Delphinium Home** • 653 Ninth Ave [46th]
- **Janovic** • 771 Ninth Ave [52nd]
- **Little Pie Company** • 424 W 43rd St [9th]
- **Metro Bicycles** • 360 W 47th St [9th Av]
- **Ninth Avenue International** • 543 Ninth Ave [40th]
- **Pan Aqua Diving** • 460 W 43rd St [10th]
- **Poseidon Bakery** • 629 Ninth Ave [44th]
- **Radio Shack** • 333 W 57th St [8th Av]
- **Sea Breeze** • 541 Ninth Ave [40th]

The avenues in this area are better than the highway. Try not to get caught on cross streets, and watch the potholes on Eleventh. At peak times there is no escaping the Lincoln Tunnel traffic, so just settle the f#*% down. The A-C-E is reliable during weekdays. At least something works.

Subways

Ⓒ Ⓔ .... 50th St

Ⓐ Ⓒ Ⓔ .... 42nd St/Port Authority Bus Terminal

Ⓐ Ⓒ Ⓑ Ⓓ ❶ .... 59th St/Columbus Cir

Bus Lines

11	.... Ninth Ave/Tenth Ave
16	.... 34th St Crosstown
27	.... 49th St/50th St Crosstown
31	.... 57th St Crosstown
42	.... 42nd St Crosstown
50	.... 49th St/50th St Crosstown
57	.... 57th St Crosstown
104	.... Broadway/42nd St

Bike Lanes

- • • • Marked Bike Lanes
- • • • Recommended Route
- • • • Greenway

Car Rental

- **All-State Auto Rental** • 540 W 44th St [10th Av]
- **Autorent Car Rental** • 415 W 45th St [9th Av]
- **Avis** • 515 W 43rd St [10th Av]
- **Courier Car Rental** • 537 Tenth Ave [40th]
- **Enterprise** • 667 Eleventh Ave [48th]
- **Hertz** • 346 W 40th St [8th Av]

Car Washes

- **JL Custom Car Cleaner (detailer)** • 349 W 54th St [8th Av]
- **New York Car Wash** • 625 Eleventh Ave [46th]

Gas Stations

- **Hess** • 502 W 45th St [10th Av]
- **Mobil** • 718 Eleventh Ave [51st] ☼

Parking

For many, Midtown = New York. Contrary to popular belief, Midtown is more than Times Square. "national headquarter" offices, and Rockefeller Center. Visit the original stuffed Winnie the Pooh at the Donnell Library, enjoy the music at Carnegie Hall, and don't be afraid to use the bathrooms in Bryant Park.

24-Hour Pharmacies

- **Duane Reade** • 100 W 57th St (6th Av)
- **Duane Reade** • 1627 Broadway (50th)
- **Duane Reade** • 224 W 57th St (B'way)
- **Duane Reade** • 4 Times Sq (43rd)
- **Duane Reade** • 625 Eighth Ave (40th)
- **Duane Reade** • 661 Eighth Ave (42nd)
- **Duane Reade** • 900 Eighth St (54th)
- **Rite Aid** • 301 W 50th St (8th Av)

Bagels

- **Bagel Café** • 850 Eighth Ave (51st)
- **Bagel Stix** • 814 Eighth Ave (53rd)
- **Bagel-N-Bean** • 828 Seventh Ave (53rd)
- **Bread Factory Café** • 935 Eighth Ave (55th)
- **Pick-a-Bagel** • 200 W 57th St (7th Av)
- **Times Square Bagels** • 200 W 44th St (7th Av)
- **Torino Deli** • 22 W 56th St (5th Av)

Banks

- **AM • Amalgamated** • 1745 Broadway (56th)
- **AP • Apple** • 1320 Sixth Ave (53rd)
- **AT • Atlantic** • 400 Madison Ave (48th)
- **BP • Banco Popular** • 7 W 51st St (5th Av)
- **BL • Bank Leumi** • 579 Fifth Ave (47th)
- **BA • Bank of America** • 1140 Sixth Ave (44th)
- **BA • Bank of America** • 1515 Broadway (44th)
- **BA • Bank of America** • 1680 Broadway (53rd)
- **BA • Bank of America** • 1775 Broadway (57th)
- **BA • Bank of America** • 25 W 51st St (Rockefeller Plz)
- **BA • Bank of America** • 335 Madison Ave (43)
- **BA • Bank of America** • 4 W 57th St (5th Av)
- **BA • Bank of America** • 56 E 42nd St (Madison)
- **BA • Bank of America** • 592 Fifth Ave (48th)
- **BA • Bank of America** • 625 Eighth Ave (40th)
- **BA • Bank of America (ATM)** • 1535 Broadway (45th)
- **BA • Bank of America (ATM)** • 247 W 42nd St (7th Av)
- **BA • Bank of America (ATM)** • 30 Rockefeller Plz (49th)
- **BA • Bank of America (ATM)** • 55 W 42nd St (6th Av)
- **BA • Bank of America (ATM)** • 77 W 55th St (6th Av)
- **NY • Bank of New York** • 51 W 51st St (Rockefeller Plz)
- **NY • Bank of New York** • 530 Fifth Ave (44th)
- **CH • Chase** • 11 W 51st St (Rockefeller Plz)
- **CH • Chase** • 1120 Sixth Ave (43rd)
- **CH • Chase** • 1251 Sixth Ave (50th)
- **CH • Chase** • 1370 Sixth Ave (56th)
- **CH • Chase** • 171 W 57th St (7th Av)
- **CH • Chase** • 250 W 57th St (B'way)
- **CH • Chase** • 3 Times Sq (42nd)
- **CH • Chase** • 401 Madison Ave (47th)
- **CH • Chase** • 510 Fifth Ave (43rd)
- **CH • Chase** • 600 Madison Ave (57th)
- **CH • Chase** • 810 Seventh Ave (53rd)
- **CL • Chiba Bank** • 1133 Sixth Ave (44th)
- **CI • Citibank** • 1 Rockefeller Plz (48th)
- **CI • Citibank** • 1345 Sixth Ave (54th)
- **CI • Citibank** • 1440 Broadway (41st)
- **CI • Citibank** • 1748 Broadway (56th)
- **CI • Citibank** • 330 Madison Ave (43rd)
- **CI • Citibank** • 640 Fifth Ave (51st)
- **CO • Commerce** • 1120 Sixth Ave (43rd)
- **CO • Commerce** • 1350 Sixth Ave (54th)
- **CO • Commerce** • 317 Madison Ave (42nd)
- **EM • Emigrant** • 5 E 42nd St (5th Av)
- **FR • First Republic** • 1230 Sixth Ave (49th)
- **HS • HSBC** • 1185 Sixth Ave (46th)
- **HS • HSBC** • 1271 Sixth Ave (51st)
- **HS • HSBC** • 1790 Broadway (58th)
- **HS • HSBC** • 415 Madison Ave (48th)
- **HS • HSBC** • 452 Fifth Ave (40th)
- **HS • HSBC** • 555 Madison Ave (55th)
- **HS • HSBC** • 666 Fifth Ave (53rd)
- **HU • Hudson United (ATM)** • 75 Rockefeller Plz (51st)
- **ID • IDB** • 511 Fifth Ave (43rd)
- **IC • Independence** • 550 Fifth Ave (45th)
- **IC • Independence** • 864 Eighth Ave (52nd)
- **MT • M&T** • 41 W 42nd St (6th Av)
- **MT • M&T** • 830 Eighth Ave (50th)
- **NF • North Fork** • 101 W 57th St (6th Av)
- **NF • North Fork** • 1166 Sixth Ave (45th)
- **NF • North Fork** • 1745 Broadway (56th)
- **NF • North Fork** • 424 Madison Ave (48th)
- **NF • North Fork** • 767 Fifth Ave (59th)
- **VN • Valley National** • 62 W 47th St (6th Av)
- **WA • Wachovia** • 1156 Sixth Ave (45th)
- **WA • Wachovia** • 1345 Sixth Ave (54th)
- **WA • Wachovia** • 1755 Broadway (56th)
- **WA • Wachovia** • 360 Madison Ave (45th)
- **WA • Wachovia** • 437 Madison Ave (49th)
- **WA • Wachovia** • 49 Rockefeller Plz (50th)
- **WA • Wachovia** • 540 Madison Ave (55th)
- **WA • Wachovia (ATM)** • 1100 Sixth Ave (42nd)
- **WA • Wachovia (ATM)** • 1568 Broadway (47th)
- **WM • Washington Mutual** • 1379 Sixth Ave (56th)
- **WM • Washington Mutual** • 1431 Broadway (40th)
- **WM • Washington Mutual** • 235 W 56th St (B'way)
- **WM • Washington Mutual** • 589 Fifth Ave (48th)
- **WM • Washington Mutual** • 787 Seventh Ave (51st)

Landmarks

- **Bryant Park** • 42nd St & 6th Ave
- **Carnegie Deli** • 854 Seventh Ave (55th)
- **Carnegie Hall** • 154 W 57th St (7th Av)
- **Dahesh Museum of Art** • 580 Madison Ave (56th)
- **The Debt Clock** • Sixth Ave & 44th St
- **Museum of Modern Art (MoMA)** • 11 W 53rd St (5th Av)
- **NY Public Library** • Fifth Ave & 42nd St
- **Plaza Hotel** • 768 Fifth Ave (58th)
- **RCA Building** • 30 Rockefeller Plz (49th)
- **Rockefeller Center** • 600 Fifth Ave (48th)
- **Royalton Hotel** • 44th St b/w Fifth Ave & Sixth Ave
- **St Patrick's Cathedral** • Fifth Ave & 50th St
- **Times Square** • 42nd St-Times Sq (7th Av)
- **Top of the Rock** • 600 Fifth Ave (48th)

Libraries

- **Donnell Library Center** • 20 W 53rd St (5th Av)
- **Humanities & Social Sciences Library** • 42nd St & Fifth Ave
- **Mid-Manhattan** • 455 Fifth Ave (40th)

Post Offices

- **Bryant** • 23 W 43rd St (5th Av)
- **Rockefeller Center** • 610 Fifth Ave (49th)

Schools

- **Berkeley College** • 3 E 43rd St (5th Av)
- **Circle in the Square Theater** • 1633 Broadway (50th)
- **Coalition School for Social Change** • 220 W 58th St (7th Av)
- **Daytop Village Secondary** • 54 W 40th St (6th Av)
- **Family School W St Luke Lutheran** • 308 W 46th St (8th Av)
- **Jacqueline Kennedy Onassis High** • 120 W 46th St (6th Av)
- **Katharine Gibbs** • 50 W 40th St (6th Av)
- **Laboratory Institute of Merchandising** • 12 E 53rd St (5th Av)
- **Landmark High** • 220 W 58th St (7th Av)
- **Lyceum Kennedy French** • 225 W 43rd St (7th Av)
- **Pace University** • 551 Fifth Ave (45th)
- **Practicing Law Institute** • 810 Seventh Ave (53rd)
- **Repertory Company High** • 123 W 43rd St (6th Av)
- **St Thomas Choir** • 202 W 58th St (7th Av)
- **SUNY College of Optometry** • 33 W 42nd St (5th Av)
- **Wood Tobe-Coburn** • 8 E 40th St (5th Av)

Supermarkets

- **Associated** • 225 W 57th St (B'way)
- **Citarella** • 1250 Sixth Ave (50th)
- **Food Emporium** • 810 Eighth Ave (49th)
- **Gristede's** • 907 Eighth Ave (54th)

People actually live here (not just the ones who never leave the office), so you can find just about anything within a short distance. This neighborhood doesn't shut down on weekends, but it is quieter than during the weekday rush so some joints are just M-F. Phone first.

8 9 10
5 6 7
Ma

Coffee

- **Au Bon Pain** • 1211 Sixth Ave [48th]
- **Au Bon Pain** • 125 W 55th St [6th Ave]
- **Au Bon Pain** • 1251 Sixth Ave [50th]
- **Au Bon Pain** • 16 E 44th St [Madison]
- **Au Bon Pain** • 444 Madison Ave [50th]
- **Au Bon Pain** • Port Authority • 625 Eighth Ave [41st]
- **Bistro New York International** • 1285 Ave of the Americas [51st]
- **The Bread Factory Café** • 672 Eighth Ave [43rd]
- **Café Metro** • 625 Eighth Ave [40th]
- **City Chow** • 1633 Broadway [50th]
- **Cosi** • 11 W 42nd St [5th Av]
- **Cosi** • 1633 Broadway [50th]
- **Cosi** • 61 W 48th St [6th Ave]
- **Cyber Café** • 250 W 49th St [B'way]
- **Dean & DeLuca Café** • 235 W 46th St
- **Dunkin' Donuts** • 30 Rockefeller Plz [49th]
- **Dunkin' Donuts** • 55 W 55th St [6th Av]
- **Dunkin' Donuts** • 761 Seventh Ave [50th]
- **Evergreen Coffee Shop Restaurant** • 145 W 47th St [6th Ave]
- **Fluffy's Café & Bakery** • 855 Seventh Ave [55th]
- **The Greeks Coffee Shop** • 347 Madison Ave [44th]
- **La Parisienne Coffee House** • 910 Seventh Ave [58th]
- **Lucky Star Café** • 250 W 43rd St [7th Av]
- **Oren's Daily Roast** • 33 E 58th St [Madison]
- **Red Flame Coffee Shop** • 67 W 44th St [6th Av]
- **Roy Bean** • 38 W 56th St [5th Ave]
- **Seattle Café** • 1634 Broadway [50th]
- **Sixth Avenue Café** • 1414 Ave of the Americas [58th]
- **Starbucks** • 1100 Sixth Ave [42nd]
- **Starbucks** • 1166 Sixth Ave [45th]
- **Starbucks** • 1185 Sixth Ave [46th]
- **Starbucks** • 120 W 56th St [6th Av]
- **Starbucks** • 1290 Sixth Ave [52nd]
- **Starbucks** • 1320 Sixth Ave [53rd]
- **Starbucks** • 1345 Sixth Ave [54th]
- **Starbucks** • 1380 Sixth Ave [56th]
- **Starbucks** • 142 W 57th St [6th Av]
- **Starbucks** • 1460 Broadway [42nd]
- **Starbucks** • 1500 Broadway [43rd]
- **Starbucks** • 1530 Broadway [45th]
- **Starbucks** • Marriott • 1535 Broadway [45]
- **Starbucks** • 156 W 52nd St [7th Av]
- **Starbucks** • 1585 Broadway [48th]
- **Starbucks** • 1656 Broadway [51st]
- **Starbucks** • 1675 Broadway [52nd]
- **Starbucks** • 1710 Broadway [54th]
- **Starbucks** • 251 W 42nd St [8th Av]
- **Starbucks** • 295 Madison Ave [41st]
- **Starbucks** • 30 Rockefeller Plz [49th]
- **Starbucks** • 30 Rockefeller Plz, Center Concourse [49th]
- **Starbucks** • 330 Madison Ave [43rd]
- **Starbucks** • 335 Madison Ave [43rd]
- **Starbucks** • 4 Columbus Cir [8th Av]
- **Starbucks** • 400 Madison Ave [48th]
- **Starbucks** • 45 E 51st St [Madison]
- **Starbucks** • 545 Fifth Ave [45th]
- **Starbucks** • 550 Madison Ave [55th]
- **Starbucks** • 575 Fifth Ave [47th]
- **Starbucks** • 600 Eighth Ave [39th]
- **Starbucks** • 684 Eighth Ave [43rd]
- **Starbucks** • Trump Tower• 725 Fifth Ave [56th]
- **Starbucks** • 750 Seventh Ave [50th]
- **Starbucks** • 770 Eighth Ave [47th]
- **Starbucks** • 825 Eighth Ave [50th]
- **Starbucks** • 870 Seventh Ave [56th]
- **Starbucks** • 871 Seventh Ave [52nd]
- **Teresa's Gourmet Coffee Bar** • 51 W 51st St [Rockefeller Plz]

Copy Shops

- **57th Street Copy Center** • 151 W 57th St [7th Av]
- **Accurate Copy Services** • 250 W 57th St [B'way]
- **Atlantic Blueprint** • 575 Madison Ave [56th]
- **BPI** • 295 Madison Ave [41st]
- **Commerce Photo-Print** • 16 W 46th St [5th Av]
- **The Complete Copy Center** • 1271 Sixth Ave [51st]
- **Deanco Press** • 767 Fifth Ave [59th]
- **Discovery Copy Services** • 45 W 45th St [5th Av] ⏰
- **Duplications Unlimited** • 149 W 55th St [6th Av]
- **Economy Blue Print** • McGraw-Hill Bldg • 1221 Sixth Ave [49th]
- **FedEx Kinko's** • 233 W 54th St [B'way]
- **Genie Instant Printing Center** • 37 W 43rd St [5th Av]
- **Hotel Copy Centers** • Hilton Hotel • 1335 Ave of the Americas [54th]
- **Kinko's** • 1211 Sixth Ave [48th] ⏰
- **Kinko's** • 16 E 52nd St [5th Av] ⏰
- **Kinko's** • 240 Central Park S [7th Av] ⏰
- **Kinko's** • 60 W 40th St [6th Av] ⏰
- **Kopy Kween** • 25 W 45th St [5th Av] ⏰
- **Natalia's Photo** • 3 W 46th St [5th Av]
- **Office Depot** • 1441 Broadway [41st]
- **Pip Printing** • 69 W 55th St [6th Av]
- **Pro-Print** • 18 W 45th St [5th Av]
- **Red Rose Legal Copy Centers** • 18 E 41st St [Madison]
- **Servco** • 1150 Sixth Ave [45th]
- **Skyline Duplication** • 151 W 46th St [6th] ⏰
- **Staples** • 1065 Sixth Ave [40th]
- **Staples** • 535 Fifth Ave [44th]
- **Staples** • 57 W 57th St [6th Av]
- **Staples** • 776 Eighth Ave [47th]
- **The UPS Store** • 1514 Broadway [44th]
- **The UPS Store** • 888C Eighth Ave [53rd]
- **The Village Copier** • 25 W 43rd St [5th Av]

Farmer's Markets

- **Rockefeller Center (Thur, Fri & Sat, 8 am–6 am, Jul–Aug)** • Rockefeller Plz & 50th St

Gyms

- **Athletic and Swim Club at Equitable Center** • 787 Seventh Ave [51st]
- **Bally Total Fitness** • 335 Madison Ave [43]
- **Bally Total Fitness** • 45 E 55th St [Madison]
- **Equinox Fitness Club** • 10 Columbus Cir [8th Av]
- **Equinox Fitness Club** • 1633 Broadway [50th]
- **Equinox Fitness Club** • 521 Fifth Ave [43]
- **Gold's Gym** • 250 W 54th St [B'way]
- **Gravity Fitness Center** • 119 W 56th St [6th Av]
- **Lucille Roberts Health Club (Women only)** • 300 W 40th St [8th Av]
- **Mid City Gym** • 244 W 49th St [B'way]
- **New York Athletic Club** • 180 Central Park S [7th Av]
- **New York Health & Racquet Club** • 110 W 56th St [6th Av]
- **New York Health & Racquet Club** • 20 E 50th St [Madison]
- **New York Sports Clubs** • 1221 Sixth Ave [48th]
- **New York Sports Clubs** • 1605 Broadway [49th]
- **New York Sports Clubs** • 1657 Broadway [52nd]
- **New York Sports Clubs** • 19 W 44th St [5th Av]
- **New York Sports Clubs** • 230 W 41st St [7th Av]
- **Sheraton New York & Manhattan Health Clubs** • 811 Seventh Ave [53rd]
- **Sports Club/LA** • 45 Rockefeller Plz [50th]

Hardware Stores

- **New Hippodrome Hardware** • 23 W 45th St [5th Av]

Liquor Stores

- **Athens Wine & Liquor** • 302 W 40th St [8th Av]
- **Carnegie Spirits & Wine** • 849 Seventh Ave [54th]
- **Columbus Circle Wine & Liquor** • 1780 Broadway [57th]
- **Fifty Fifth Street Liquor Shop** • 40 W 55th St [5th Av]
- **Morrell & Co Wine & Spirits** • 1 Rockefeller Plz [48th]
- **O'Ryan Package Store** • 1424 Sixth Ave [58th]
- **Park Avenue Liquor Shop** • 292 Madison Ave [41st]
- **Reidy Wine & Liquor** • 762 Eighth Ave [47th]
- **Westerly Liquors** • 921 Eighth Ave [55th]

Video Rental

- **Blockbuster** • 835 Eighth Ave [50th]
- **High Quality Video (Japanese only)** • 21 W 45th St [5th Av]
- **Movie Bank USA** • 4 Times Sq [43rd] ⏰
- **Movie Bank USA** • W 42nd St & Eighth Ave ⏰
- **Movie Bank USA** • W 53rd St & Sixth Ave ⏰
- **Movie Bank USA** • W 57th St & Broadway ⏰
- **Movie Bank USA** • W 57th St & Sixth Ave ⏰
- **Movie Bank USA** • W 58th St & Sixth Ave ⏰

Movies, music, theater, television...we have it all. Hit Virgil's for NFL-approved 'cue, check out the scene at the Russian Vodka Room, re-experience old TV episodes at the Museum of Television & Radio, catch a funky band at Roseland, or walk down the red carpet at the Ziegfeld.

😀 Movie Theaters

- **AMC Empire 25** • 234 W 42nd St [7th Av]
- **Bryant Park Summer Film Festival (outdoors)** • Bryant Park, b/w 40th & 42nd Sts
- **Clearview's Ziegfeld** • 141 W 54th St [6th Av]
- **Loews 42nd Street E Walk** • 247 W 42nd St [7th Av]
- **Loews State** • 1540 Broadway [45th]
- **MoMA** • 11 W 53rd St [5th Av]
- **Museum of TV and Radio** • 25 W 52nd St [5th Av]
- **New York Public Library-Donnell Library Center** • 20 W 53rd St [5th Av]
- **Paris Theatre** • 4 W 58th St [5th Av]

🍸 Nightlife

- **BB King Blues Club** • 237 W 42nd St [7th Av]
- **Blue Bar** • 59 W 44th St [6th Av]
- **Caroline's on Broadway** • 1626 Broadway [50th]
- **Chicago City Limits** • 318 W 53rd St [8th Av]
- **China Club** • 268 W 47th St [8th Av]
- **Flute** • 205 W 54th St [7th Av]
- **Heartland Brewery** • 127 W 43rd St [6th Av]
- **Heartland Brewery** • 1285 Sixth Ave [51st]
- **Iridium** • 1650 Broadway [51st]
- **Jimmy's Corner** • 140 W 44th St [B'way]
- **Paramount Bar** • 235 W 46th St [8th Av]
- **Roseland** • 239 W 52nd St [B'way]
- **The Royalton** • 44 W 44th St [6th Av]
- **Russian Vodka Room** • 265 W 52nd St [8th Av]
- **Show** • 135 W 41st St [8th Av]
- **St Andrews** • 120 W 44th St [6th Av]
- **Town Hall** • 123 W 43rd St [6th Av]

🐾 Pet Shops

- **Carangola New York Corporation** • 145 W 58th St [6th]

🍴 Restaurants

- **'21' Club** • 21 W 52nd St [5th Av]
- **Alain Ducasse** • 155 W 58th St [7th Av]
- **Aquavit** • 13 W 54th St [5th Av]
- **Baluchi's** • 240 W 56th St [B'way]
- **BG** • 754 Fifth Ave [57th]
- **Brasserie 8 1/2** • 9 W 57th St [5th Av]
- **Burger Joint** • Parker Meridien Hotel • 119 W 56th St [6th Av]
- **Carnegie Deli** • 854 Seventh Ave [55th]
- **Coldstone Creamery** • 253 W 42nd St [8th Av]
- **Cosi** • 11 W 42nd St [5th Av]
- **Cosi** • 1633 Broadway [50th]
- **Gallagher's Steak House** • 228 W 52nd St [B'way]
- **Haru** • 205 W 43rd St [7th Av]
- **Joe's Shanghai** • 24 W 56th St [5th Av]
- **La Bonne Soupe** • 48 W 55th St [5th Av]
- **Le Bernardin** • 155 W 51st St [7th Av]
- **Molyvos** • 871 Seventh Ave [56th]
- **Mont Blanc** • 306 W 48th St [8th Av]
- **Nation Restaurant & Bar** • 12 W 45th St [5th Av]
- **Nobu 57** • 40 W 57th St [5th Av]
- **Norma's** • Parker Meridien Hotel• 118 W 57th St [6th Av]
- **Per Se** • 10 Columbus Cir [58th]
- **Petrossian** • 182 W 58th St [7th Av]
- **Pongsri Thai** • 244 W 48th St [B'way]
- **Pret a Manger** • 135 W 50th St [5th Av]
- **Pret a Manger** • 1350 Sixth Ave [54th]
- **Primeburger** • 5 E 51st St [Madison]
- **Pump Energy Food** • 40 W 55th St [5th Av]
- **Redeye Grill** • 890 Seventh Ave [56th]
- **Seppi's** • 123 W 56th St [6th Av]
- **Shelly's New York** • 104 W 57th St [6th Av]
- **Spanky's BBQ** • 127 W 43rd St [6th Av]
- **Virgil's Real BBQ** • 152 W 44th St [6th Av]
- **wichcraft, Bryant Park** • Sixth Ave b/w 40th & 42nd St

🛍 Shopping

- **Alkit Pro Camera** • 830 Seventh Ave [53rd]
- **Baccarat** • 625 Madison Ave [59th]
- **Bergdorf Goodman** • 754 Fifth Ave [57th]
- **Brooks Brothers** • 346 Madison Ave [44th]
- **Burberry** • 9 E 57th St [5th Av]
- **Chanel** • 15 E 57th St [5th Av]
- **Colony Music** • 1619 Broadway [49th]
- **CompUSA** • 1775 Broadway [57th]
- **Crate & Barrel** • 650 Madison Ave [60th]
- **Drummer's World** • 151 W 46th St [6th Av]
- **Ermenegildo Zegna** • 663 Fifth Ave [52nd]
- **FAO Schwarz** • 767 Fifth Ave [59th]
- **Felissimo** • 10 W 56th St [5th Av]
- **Gucci** • 685 Fifth Ave [54th]
- **Henri Bendel** • 712 Fifth Ave [56th]
- **Joseph Patelson Music House** • 160 W 56th St [7th Av]
- **Kate's Paperie** • 140 W 57th St [6th Av]
- **Klavierhaus** • 211 W 58th St [7th Av]
- **Manny's Music** • 156 W 48th St [7th Av]
- **Mets Clubhouse Shop** • 11 W 42nd St [5th Av]
- **Mikimoto** • 730 Fifth Ave [57th]
- **Modell's** • 51 E 42nd St [Madison]
- **MoMA Design Store** • 44 W 53rd St [5th Av]
- **Museum of Arts and Design Shop** • 40 W 53rd St [5th]
- **NBA Store** • 666 Fifth Ave [53rd]
- **Niketown** • 6 E 57th St [5th Av]
- **Orvis Company** • 522 Fifth Ave [43rd]
- **Paul Stuart** • Madison Ave & 45th St
- **Petrossian Boutique** • 911 Seventh Ave [58th]
- **Radio Shack** • 50 E 42nd St [Madison]
- **Roberto's Woodwind Repair Shop** • 146 W 46th St [6th]
- **Saks Fifth Avenue** • 611 Fifth Ave [49th]
- **Sam Ash** • 160 W 48th St [7th Av]
- **Smythson of Bond Street** • 4 W 57th St [5th Av]
- **Steinway and Sons** • 109 W 57th St [6th Av]
- **Takashimaya** • 693 Fifth Ave [54th]
- **Tiffany & Co** • 727 Fifth Ave [56th]

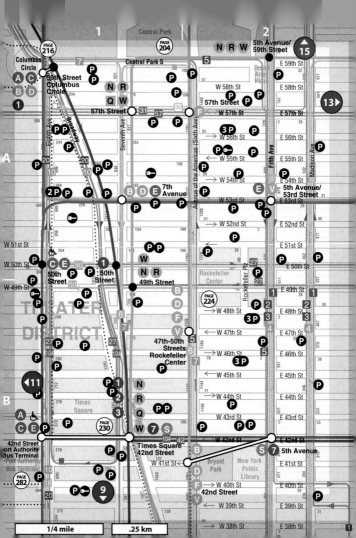

The best thing about Midtown is that almost every subway line has a couple of stops here. The worst thing about it is driving here. Avoid the hassle by leaving the car behind and making use of that shiny yellow MetroCard you are growing to love. It loves you back.

Subways

1 .... 50th St
1 **A** **C** **B** **D** .... 59th St-Columbus Cir
A **C** **E** .... 42nd St/Port Authority
B **D** **E** ....Seventh Ave
B **D** **F** **V** ... 47th St-50th St/Rockefeller Ctr
7 **B** **D** **F** **V** .... 42nd St/Fifth Ave
C **E** .... 50th St
E **V** ....Fifth Ave/53rd St
F .... 57th St
1 **2** **3** **7** **N** **Q** **R** **W** **S** ...... Times Sq/42nd St
N **R** **Q** **W** .... 57th St
N **R** **W** .... 49th St
N **R** **W** ....Fifth Ave/59th St

Bus Lines

1 **2** **3** **4** .... Fifth Ave/Madison Ave
10 **20** .... Seventh Ave/Eighth Ave (Central Park West)/Frederick Douglass Blvd
104 .... Broadway/42nd St
16 .... 34th St Crosstown
27 .... 49th St/50th St Crosstown
30 .... 57th St /72th St Crosstown
31 .... York Ave/57th St
42 .... 42nd St Crosstown
5 .... Fifth Ave/Sixth Ave/Riverside Dr
50 .... 49th St/50th St Crosstown
57 .... 57th St Crosstown
6 .... Seventh Ave/Broadway/Sixth Ave
7 .... Columbus Ave/Amsterdam Ave/ Lenox Ave/Sixth Ave/Seventh Ave/Broadway
Q32 .... Penn Station/Jackson Heights, Queens

Bike Lanes

- • • • Marked Bike Lanes
- • • • Recommended Route

Car Rental

- **Avis** • 153 W 54th St [6th Av]
- **Budget** • 304 W 49th St [8th Av]
- **Dollar** • 263 W 52nd St [B'way]
- **Hertz** • 126 W 55th St [6th Av]
- **National/Alamo** • 252 W 40th St [7th Av]

P Parking

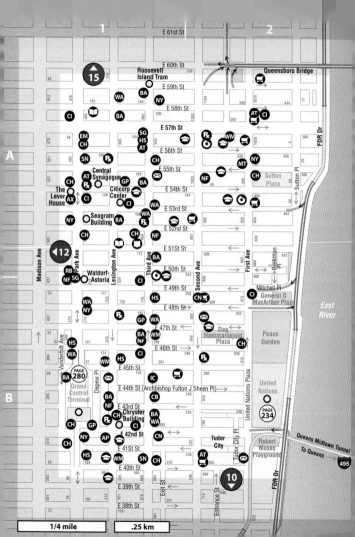

East Midtown is a lovely, quiet place despite international traffic to the consulates and the United Nations. Spend an afternoon admiring the architecture as you walk from Grand Central to the Queensboro Bridge, stopping off at the Chrysler Building, the gardens of Tudor City, and the townhouses of Sutton Place.

24-Hour Pharmacies

- **CVS Pharmacy** • 630 Lexington Ave [54th] ♿
- **Duane Reade** • 1076 Second Ave [57th] ♿
- **Duane Reade** • 401 Park Ave [54th] ♿
- **Duane Reade** • 485 Lexington Ave [46th] ♿
- **Duane Reade** • 852 Second Ave [45th] ♿
- **Duane Reade** • 866 Third Ave [53rd] ♿

Bagels

- **Ess-A-Bagel** • 831 Third Ave [51st]
- **Jumbo Bagels & Bialys** • 1070 Second Ave [56th]
- **Tal Bagels** • 977 First Ave [54th]

Banks

AX • AmEx Travel-Related Services • 374 Park Ave [53rd]
AP • Apple • 122 E 42nd St [Lex]
AT • Atlantic • 405 Park Ave [54th]
AT • Atlantic • 936 Third Ave [56th]
AT • Atlantic (ATM) • Gristedes • 1052 First Ave [57th]
AT • Atlantic (ATM) • Gristedes • 748 Second Ave [40th]
BA • Bank of America • 200 Park [45th]
BA • Bank of America • 425 Lexington Ave [43rd]
BA • Bank of America • 675 Third [43rd]
BA • Bank of America • 750 Third [47th]
BA • Bank of America • 900 Third [55th]
BA • Bank of America • 988 Third [59th]
BA • Bank of America (ATM) • 599 Lexington Ave [52nd]
BA • Bank of America (ATM) • 705 Lexington Ave [57th]
BA • Bank of America (ATM) • 825 Third [50th]
NY • Bank of NY • 100 E 42nd St [Park]
NY • Bank of NY • 1006 First Ave [55th]
NY • Bank of NY • 207 E 58th St [3rd Av]
NY • Bank of NY • 277 Park Ave [48th]
NY • Bank of NY • 360 Park Ave [52nd]
CH • Chase • 405 Lexington Ave [42nd]
CH • Chase • 410 Park Ave [55th]
CH • Chase • 445 Park Ave [56th]
CH • Chase • 60 E 42nd St [Madison]
CH • Chase • 633 Third Ave [41st]
CH • Chase • 825 United Nations Plz [46th]
CH • Chase • 850 Third Ave [52nd]
CH • Chase • 919 Third Ave [55th]
CH • Chase • 994 First Ave [55th]
CH • Chase (ATM) • 345 Park Ave [51st]
CH • Chase (ATM) • Duane Reade • 370 Lexington Ave [41st]
CH • Chase (ATM) • Grand Central Lobby • 89 E 42nd St [Vanderbilt]
CI • Citibank • 1044 First Ave [57th]
CI • Citibank • 145 E 42nd St [Lex]
CI • Citibank • 399 Park Ave [54th]
CI • Citibank • 460 Park Ave [57th]
CI • Citibank • 734 Third Ave [46th]
CI • Citibank • 800 Third Ave [49th]
CI • Citibank • 866 United Nations Plz [48th]
CI • Citibank (ATM) • 153 E 53rd St [Lex]
CO • Commerce • 685 Third Ave [43rd]
CN • Country Bank • 200 E 42nd St [3rd Av]
CN • Country Bank • 902 Second Ave [48th]
EM • Emigrant • 445 Park Ave [56th]
FR • First Republic • 320 Park Ave [50th]
HS • HSBC • 101 Park Ave [41st]
HS • HSBC • 250 Park Ave [47th]
HS • HSBC • 441 Lexington Ave [44th]
HS • HSBC • 777 Third Ave [48th]
HS • HSBC • 950 Third Ave [57th]
IC • Independence Community • 711 Third Ave [45th]
MT • M&T • 401 E 55th St [1st Av]
NF • North Fork • 1034 Second Ave [55th]
NF • North Fork • 109 E 42nd St [Park]
NF • North Fork • 320 Park Ave [50th]
NF • North Fork • 420 Lexington Ave [44th]
NF • North Fork • 643 Lexington Ave [54th]
NF • North Fork • 750 Third Ave [47th]
NF • North Fork • 770 Third Ave [48th]
NF • North Fork • 845 Third Ave [51st]
SG • Signature • 300 Park Ave [49th]
SG • Signature • 950 Third Ave [57th]
SN • Sterling National • 425 Park Ave [55th]
SN • Sterling National • 622 Third Ave [40th]
WA • Wachovia • 299 Park Ave [49th]
WA • Wachovia • 666 Third Ave [42nd]
WA • Wachovia • 731 Lexington Ave [59th]
WA • Wachovia • 757 Third Ave [47th]
WA • Wachovia • 866 Third Ave [53rd]
WA • Wachovia (ATM) • 230 Park [46th]
WM • Washington Mutual • 355 Lexington Ave [40th]
WM • Washington Mutual • 360 E 57th St [1st]
WM • Washington Mutual • 466 Lexington Ave [46th]
WM • Washington Mutual • 875 Third Ave [53rd]

Landmarks

- **Central Synagogue** • 123 E 55th St [Lex]
- **Chrysler Building** • 405 Lexington Ave [42nd]
- **Citicorp Center** • 153 E 53rd St [Lex]
- **Grand Central Terminal** • 42nd St
- **The Lever House** • 390 Park Ave [54th]
- **Roosevelt Island Tram** • E 59th St & Second Ave
- **Seagram Building** • 375 Park Ave [53rd]

- **United Nations** • First Ave b/w 42nd & 48th Sts
- **Waldorf-Astoria** • 301 Park Ave [49th]

Libraries

- **58th St** • 127 E 58th St [Lex]
- **Terence Cardinal Cooke-Cathedral** • 560 Lexington Ave [50th]

Police

- **17th Precinct** • 167 E 51st St [3rd Av]

Post Offices

- **Dag Hammarskjold** • 884 Second Ave [47th]
- **Franklin D Roosevelt** • 909 Third Ave [55th]
- **Grand Central Station** • 450 Lexington Ave [45th]
- **Tudor City** • 5 Tudor City Pl [41st]

Schools

- **Amity Language Institute** • 350 Lexington Ave [40th]
- **The Beekman School** • 220 E 50th St [3rd Av]
- **Cathedral High** • 350 E 56th St [1st Av]
- **Family School** • 323 E 47th St [2nd Av]
- **High School of Art & Design** • 1075 Second Ave [57th]
- **Montessori School of New York** • 347 E 55th St [2nd Av]
- **Neighborhood Playhouse** • 340 E 54th St [2nd Av]
- **NY Institute of Credit** • 380 Lexington Ave [41st]
- **PS 59 Beekman Hill** • 228 E 57th St [3rd Av]
- **Turtle Bay Music School** • 244 E 52nd St [3rd Av]

Supermarkets

- **Amish Market** • 240 E 45th St [3rd Av]
- **Associated** • 908 Second Ave [48th]
- **D'Agostino** • 1031 First Ave [57th]
- **D'Agostino** • 966 First Ave [53rd]
- **Food Emporium** • 405 E 59th St [1st Av]
- **Food Emporium** • 969 Second Ave [51st]
- **Gristede's** • 1052 First Ave [57th]
- **Gristede's** • 748 Second Ave [40th]

91

We've got your coffee fix covered here in East Midtown and, after you've pigged out at Grand Central Market, working out isn't a problem here either. It's also the unofficial area for your high-end kitchen—both to get it built and then to stock it.

8 9 10
5 6 7

Ma

Coffee

- **Ambrosia Café** • 158 E 45th St [3rd Av]
- **Andrew's Coffee Shop** • 138 E 43rd St [Lex]
- **Au Bon Pain** • 122 E 42nd St [Lex]
- **Au Bon Pain** • 600 Lexington Ave [52nd]
- **Au Bon Pain** • 875 Third Ave [53rd]
- **Bistro 300** • 49 E 49th St [Madison]
- **Buttercup Bake Shop** • 973 Second Ave [52nd]
- **Columbus Bakery** • 957 First Ave [53rd]
- **Cosi** • 38 E 45th St [Madison]
- **Cosi** • 60 E 56th St [Madison]
- **Cosi** • 685 Third Ave [43rd]
- **Dunkin' Donuts** • 1024 First Ave [56th]
- **Dunkin' Donuts** • 1093 Second Ave [58th]
- **Dunkin' Donuts** • 203 E 59th St [3rd Av]
- **Dunkin' Donuts** • 250 E 40th St [Tunnel Exit]
- **Dunkin' Donuts** • 47 E 42nd St [Madison]
- **Dunkin' Donuts** • 800 Second Ave [43rd]
- **Friars Coffee Shop** • 303 E 46th St [2nd Av]
- **Ing Direct** • 45 E 49th St [Madison]
- **Juan Valdez Café** • 140 E 57th St [Lex]
- **Mambi Lounge** • 933 Second Ave [50th]
- **Manhattan Espresso HD** • 146 E 49th St [Lex]
- **Morningstar Café** • 949 Second Ave [50th]
- **NY Luncheonette** • 135 E 50th St [Lex]
- **Oren's Daily Roast** • Grand Central Market • 105 E 42nd St [Park]
- **Palace Restaurant Coffee House** • 122 E 57th St [Lex]
- **Starbucks** • Grand Central • 107 E 43rd St [Lex]
- **Starbucks** • 116 E 57th St [Park]
- **Starbucks** • 125 Park Ave [41st]
- **Starbucks** • 135 E 57th St [Lex]
- **Starbucks** • 150 E 42nd St [Lex]
- **Starbucks** • 230 Park Ave [46th]
- **Starbucks** • 280 Park Ave [48th]
- **Starbucks** • Waldorf Astoria • 301 Park Ave [49th]
- **Starbucks** • 360 Lexington Ave [40th]
- **Starbucks** • 400 E 54th St [1st Av]
- **Starbucks** • 420 Lexington Ave [45th]
- **Starbucks** • 511 Lexington Ave [48th]
- **Starbucks** • 55 E 53rd St [Madison]
- **Starbucks** • 560 Lexington Ave [50th]
- **Starbucks** • 599 Lexington Ave [52nd]
- **Starbucks** • 630 Lexington Ave [54th]
- **Starbucks** • 639 Third Ave [41st]
- **Starbucks** • 685 Third Ave [43rd]
- **Starbucks** • 757 Third Ave [47th]
- **Starbucks** • 830 Third Ave [51st]
- **Starbucks** • 943 Second Ave [50th]
- **Starbucks** • Grand Central Station, Track 35

Copy Shops

- **Copy Cats** • 216 E 45th St [3rd Av]
- **Copy Right Reprographics** • 133 E 55th St [Lex]
- **Copy Room** • 850 Third Ave [52nd]
- **Digital Printing Innovations** • 805 Third Ave [49th]
- **Express Graphics** • Chrysler Building (arcade level) • 405 Lexington Ave [42nd]
- **EZCopying Corp** • 209 E 56th St [3rd Av]
- **Graphic Laboratory** • 228 E 45th St [3rd Av]
- **Kinko's** • 153 E 53rd St [Lex]
- **Kinko's** • 230 Park Ave [46th]
- **Kinko's** • 641 Lexington Ave [54th] ⌖
- **Kinko's** • 747 Third Ave [47th] ⌖
- **Lightning Copy Center** • 60 E 42nd St [Madison]
- **Mail Boxes Etc** • 1040 First Ave [57th]
- **Mail Boxes Etc** • 303 Park Ave [49th]
- **Mail Boxes Etc** • 847 Second Ave [45th]
- **Metro Copy and Duplicating** • 222 E 45th St [3rd Av]
- **Pro-Print** • 360 Lexington Ave [40th]
- **Staples** • 205 E 42nd St [3rd Av]
- **Staples** • 425 Park Ave [55th]
- **Staples** • 575 Lexington Ave [51st]
- **Staples** • 730 Third Ave [46th]
- **Statter** • 777 Third Ave [48th]
- **The UPS Store** • 132 E 43rd St [Lex]
- **The UPS Store** • 208 E 51st St [3rd Av]
- **The UPS Store** • 954 Third Ave [57th]

Farmer's Markets

- **Dag Hammarskjold Plaza** (Wed 8 am–6 pm, year round) • E 47th St & Second Ave

Gyms

- **Crunch Fitness** • 1109 Second Ave [59th]
- **Curves (Women only)** • 240 E 55th St [3rd Av]
- **Equinox Fitness Club** • 250 E 54th St [2nd Av]
- **Equinox Fitness Club** • 420 Lexington Ave [44th]
- **Excelsior Athletic Club** • 301 E 57th St [2nd Av]
- **Lift Gym** • 139 E 57th St [Lex]
- **New York Health & Racquet Club** • 115 E 57th St [Park]
- **New York Health & Racquet Club** • 132 E 45th St [Lex]
- **New York Sports Clubs** • 200 Park Ave [45th]
- **New York Sports Clubs** • 502 Park Ave [59th]
- **New York Sports Clubs** • 575 Lexington Ave [51st]
- **New York Sports Clubs** • 633 Third Ave [41st]
- **Strive Health and Fitness** • 330 E 59th St [2nd Av]
- **YMCA Vanderbilt** • 224 E 47th St [3rd Av]

Hardware Stores

- **55th Street Hardware** • 155 E 55th St [Lex]
- **Home Depot** • 980 Third Ave [59th]
- **Midtown Hardware** • 155 E 45th St [Lex]
- **Walbaum** • 881 First Ave [50th]

Liquor Stores

- **Ambassador Wines & Spirits** • 1020 Second Ave [54th]
- **American First Liquors** • 1059 First Ave [58th]
- **Beekman Liquors** • 500 Lexington Ave [47th]
- **Crush Wine & Spirits** • 153 E 57th St [Lex]
- **Diplomat Wine & Spirits** • 939 Second Ave [50th]
- **First Avenue Vintner** • 984 First Ave [54th]
- **Grand Harvest Wines** • Grand Central Terminal • 107 E 42nd St [Park]
- **Jeffrey Wine & Liquors** • 939 First Ave [52nd]
- **Midtown Wine & Liquor Shop** • 44 E 50th St [Madison]
- **Schumer's Wine & Liquors** • 59 E 54th St [Madison]
- **Sussex Wine & Spirits** • 300 E 42nd St [2nd Av]
- **Sutton Wine Shop** • 403 E 57th St [1st Av]
- **Turtle Bay Liquors** • 855 Second Ave [46th]
- **UN Liquor** • 885 First Ave [50th]
- **Viski Wines & Liquor** • 764 Third Ave [47th]

Video Rental

- **Blockbuster** • 1023 First Ave [56th]
- **Movie Bank USA** • E 57th St & Second Ave ⌖
- **New York Video** • 949 First Ave [52nd]

Pet Shops

- **Bird Camp (Birds)** • 300 E 53rd St [2nd Av]
- **Furry Paws** • 1036 First Ave [57th St]
- **Petland Discounts** • 976 Second Ave [52nd st]
- **Precious Pets** • 895 First Ave [50th]
- **Sherpa's Pet Trading** • 135 E 55th St [Lex]

There are endless possibilities for consumption. Restaurants and shops thrive here. (Check out Terence Conran under the bridge.) Second Avenue is most alive after dark when its many pubs crawl with locals and visitors alike. PJ Clarke's burgers 'n fries rule and Buttercup Bake Shop's cupcakes may become an addiction.

🎬 Movie Theaters

- **City Cinemas 1, 2, 3** • 1001 Third Ave [60th]
- **French Institute** • 55 E 59th St [Madison]
- **The ImaginAsian** • 239 E 59th St [3rd Av]
- **Instituto Cervantes** • 122 E 42nd St [Lex]
- **Japan Society** • 333 E 47th St [2nd Av]

🍸 Nightlife

- **Blarney Stone** • 710 Third Ave [45th]
- **The Campbell Apartment** • Grand Central Terminal
- **Fubar** • 305 E 50th St [2nd Av]
- **Kate Kearney's** • 251 E 50th St [3rd Av]
- **Metro 53** • 307 E 53rd St [2nd Av]
- **Sutton Place** • 1015 Second Ave [54th]

🍴 Restaurants

- **BLT Steak** • 106 E 57th St [Park]
- **Caffé Buon Gusto** • 1009 Second Ave [53rd]
- **Chola** • 232 E 58th St [3rd Av]
- **Cosi Sandwich Bar** • 60 E 56th St [Madison]
- **Dawat** • 210 E 58th St [3rd Av]
- **Docks Oyster Bar** • 633 Third Ave [41st]
- **Ess-A-Bagel** • 831 Third Ave [51st]
- **F&B** • 150 E 52nd St [Lex]
- **Felidia** • 243 E 58th St [3rd Av]
- **Four Seasons** • 99 E 52nd St [Park]
- **March** • 405 E 58th St [1st Av]
- **Menchanko-tei** • 131 E 45th St [Lex]
- **Metropolitan** • 959 First Ave [1st Av]
- **Nikki** • 151 E 50th St [Lex]
- **Oceana** • 55 E 54th St [Madison]
- **Organic Harvest Café** • 235 E 53rd St [3rd Av]
- **Oyster Bar** • Grand Central, Lower Level
- **Palm** • 837 Second Ave [45th]
- **Pershing Square** • 90 E 42nd St [Vanderbilt]
- **PJ Clarke's** • 915 Third Ave [55th]
- **Rosa Mexicano** • 1063 First Ave [58th]
- **Shun Lee Palace** • 155 E 55th St [Lex]
- **Sidecar** • 205 E 55th St [3rd Av]
- **Smith & Wollensky** • 797 Third Ave [49th]
- **Sparks Steak House** • 210 E 46th St [3rd Av]
- **Vong** • 200 E 54th St [3rd Av]
- **Zarela** • 953 Second Ave [51st]

🛍 Shopping

- **A&D Building** • 150 E 58th St [Lex]
- **Bridge Kitchenware** • 711 Third Ave [45th]
- **Buttercup Bake Shop** • 973 Second Ave [52nd]
- **Godiva Chocolatier** • 560 Lexington Ave [50th]
- **Ideal Cheese** • 942 First Ave [52nd]
- **Innovative Audio** • 150 E 58th St [Lex]
- **Mets Clubhouse Shop** • 143 E 54th St [Lex]
- **New York Transit Museum** • Grand Central, Main Concourse
- **New York Vintage Club** • 346 E 59th St [1st Av]
- **Pottery Barn** • 127 E 59th St [Lex]
- **Radio Shack** • 940 Third Ave [57th]
- **Sam Flax** • 900 Third Ave [55th]
- **Sports Authority** • 845 Third Ave [51st]
- **Terence Conran Shop** • 407 E 59th St [1st Av]
- **The World of Golf** • 147 E 47th St [Lex]
- **Yankee Clubhouse Shop** • 110 E 59th St [Park]
- **Zaro's Bread Basket** • 89 E 42nd St [Vanderbilt]

Once you get the hang of maneuvering the Queensboro Bridge you are golden, but it takes practice. Don't be surprised if multiple streets are closed on a (seemingly) random day—it just means that some dignitary, perhaps our President, is visiting the U.N. or staying at the Waldorf. Or both.

Ma

8 9 10
5 6 7

Subways

4 5 6 N R W ... Lexington Ave-59th St

6 E V .... 51st St-Lexington Ave-53rd St

4 5 6 7 S .... Grand Central-42nd St

Bus Lines

104 .... Broadway

15 .... First Ave/Second Ave

27 50 .... 49th St/50th St Crosstown

30 .... 72nd St/57th St Crosstown

31 .... York Ave/57th St

42 .... 42nd St Crosstown

57 .... 57th St Crosstown

57 .... Washington Heights/Midtown Limited

98 101 102 103 .... Third Ave/Lexington Ave

9 32 .... Queens-to-Midtown

Bike Lanes

- • • • Marked Bike Lanes
- • • • Recommended Route
- • • • Greenway

Car Rental

- **Avis** • 217 E 43rd St [3rd Av]
- **Avis** • 240 E 54th St [3rd Av]
- **Budget** • 225 E 43rd St [3rd Av]
- **Hertz** • 222 E 40th St [Tunnel Exit]
- **Hertz** • 310 E 48th St [2nd Av]
- **National/Alamo** • 138 E 50th St [Lex]
- **Prestige Car Rental** • 151 E 51st St [Lex]

P Parking

℞ 24-Hour Pharmacies

- **Duane Reade** • 2025 Broadway [69th] ♿
- **Duane Reade** • 253 W 72nd St [West End] ♿
- **Duane Reade** • 380 Amsterdam Ave [78th] ♿
- **Duane Reade** • 4 Amsterdam Ave [59th] ♿
- **Duane Reade** • 4 Columbus Cir [8th Av] ♿
- **Rite Aid** • 210 Amsterdam Ave [70th] ♿

◯ Bagels

- **72nd Street Bagel** • 130 W 72nd St [Columbus]
- **Bagel Talk** • 368 Amsterdam Ave [78th]
- **Bagels & Co** • 391 Amsterdam Ave [79th]
- **H&H Bagels** • 2239 Broadway [80th]

$ Banks

- **AP • Apple** • 2100 Broadway [73rd]
- **AP • Atlantic (ATM)** • Gristedes • 2109 Broadway [73rd]
- **AT • Atlantic (ATM)** • Gristedes • 504 Columbus Ave [84th]
- **AT • Atlantic (ATM)** • Gristedes • 80 West End Ave [63rd]
- **AT • Atlantic (ATM)** • Museum of Natural History • Central Park W & 79th St
- **BA • Bank of America (ATM)** • 192 Columbus Ave [69th]
- **BA • Bank of America (ATM)** • 1998 Broadway [68th]
- **BA • Bank of America (ATM)** • 2301 Broadway [83rd]
- **BA • Bank of America (ATM)** • 2310 Broadway [84th]
- **BA • Bank of America (ATM)** • 334 Amsterdam Ave [76th]
- **BA • Bank of New York** • 47 W 62nd St [B'way]
- **CH • Chase** • 1 Lincoln Plz [63rd]
- **CH • Chase** • 2099 Broadway [73rd]
- **CH • Chase** • 2219 Broadway [79th]
- **CH • Chase** • 260 Columbus Ave [72nd]
- **CI • Citibank** • 162 Amsterdam Ave [67th]
- **CI • Citibank** • 170 W 72nd St [Amsterdam]
- **CI • Citibank** • 4 Columbus Cir [8th Av]
- **CO • Commerce** • 1995 Broadway [68th]
- **CO • Commerce** • 2109 Broadway [73rd]
- **FR • First Republic** • 10 Columbus Cir
- **HS • HSBC** • 301 Columbus Ave [74th]
- **IC • Independence Community** • 2275 Broadway [82nd]
- **NF • North Fork** • 175 W 72nd [Amsterdam]
- **NF • North Fork** • 2025 Broadway [69th]
- **WA • Wachovia (ATM)** • 1841 B'way [60th]
- **WM • Washington Mutual** • 2139 B'way [75th]

❀ Community Gardens

◯ Landmarks

- **Ansonia Hotel** • 2109 Broadway [73rd]
- **The Dakota** • Central Park W & 72nd St
- **The Dorilton** • Broadway & 71st St
- **Lincoln Center** • Broadway & 64th St
- **The Majestic** • 115 Central Park W [71st]
- **Museum of Natural History** • Central Park W & 79th St
- **New York Historical Society** • 2 W 77th St [CPW]
- **Rotunda at 79th St Boat Basin** • W 79th St [Riverside Dr]
- **The San Remo** • Central Park W & 74th St

▥ Libraries

- **New York Public Library for the Performing Arts** • 40 Lincoln Center Plz [65th]
- **Riverside** • 127 Amsterdam Ave [65th]
- **St Agnes** • 444 Amsterdam Ave [81st]

◯ Police

- **20th Precinct** • 120 W 82nd St [Columbus]

✉ Post Offices

- **Ansonia** • 178 Columbus Ave [68th]
- **Columbus Circle** • 27 W 60th St [B'way]
- **Planetarium** • 127 W 83rd St [Columbus]

◉ Schools

- **American Musical and Dramatic Academy** • 2109 Broadway [73rd]
- **The Anderson School** • 100 W 84th St [Columbus]
- **Art and Technology High** • 122 Amsterdam Ave [65th]
- **Beacon High** • 227 W 61st St [Amsterdam]
- **Beit Rabban Day** • 8 W 70th St [CPW]
- **Blessed Sacrement** • 147 W 70th St [Columbus]
- **The Calhoun** • 433 West End Ave [81st]
- **The Calhoun Lower School** • 160 W 74th St [Amsterdam]
- **The Computer School (M245)** • 100 W 77th St [Columbus]
- **Collegiate** • 260 W 78th St [B'way]
- **Ethical Culture-Fieldston** • 33 Central Park W [63rd]
- **Fiorello H LaGuardia High** • 100 Amsterdam Ave [64th]
- **Fordham University** • 113 W 60th St [Columbus]
- **High School for Arts, Imagination & Inquiry** • 122 Amsterdam Ave [65th]
- **IS 044 William J O'Shea** • 100 W 77th St [Columbus]
- **Juilliard** • 60 Lincoln Ctr Plz [65th]

- **Law, Advocacy and Community Justice High** • 122 Amsterdam Ave [65th]
- **Louis D Brandeis High** • 145 W 84th St [Columbus]
- **Lucy Moses School For Music & Dance** • 129 W 67th St [B'way]
- **Manhattan Day** • 310 W 75th St [West End]
- **Manhattan Hunter HS of Science** • 122 Amsterdam Ave [65th]
- **Mannes College of Music** • 150 W 85th St [Columbus]
- **Martin Luther King High** • 122 Amsterdam Ave [65th]
- **Metropolitan Montessori** • 325 W 85th St [West End]
- **MS 244 Columbus Middle** • 100 W 77th St [Columbus]
- **New York Academy of Sciences** • 2 E 63rd St [5th Av]
- **New York Institute of Technology** • 1855 Broadway [61st]
- **Parkside** • 48 W 74th St [CPW]
- **Professional Children's School** • 132 W 60th St [Columbus]
- **PS 009 Sarah Anderson** • 100 W 84th St [Columbus]
- **PS 087 William Sherman** • 160 W 78th St [Amsterdam]
- **PS 191 Amsterdam** • 210 W 61st St [Amsterdam]
- **PS 199 Jesse Straus** • 270 W 70th St [West End]
- **PS 243 Center** • 270 W 70th St [West End]
- **PS 811** • 466 West End Ave [82nd]
- **PS 859 Special Music School of America** • 129 W 67th St [B'way]
- **Robert Louis Stevenson** • 24 W 74th St [CPW]
- **Rodeph Sholom** • 10 W 84th St [CPW]
- **Stephen Gaynor** • 22 W 74th St [Columbus]
- **Urban Assembly School for Media Studies** • 122 Amsterdam Ave [65th]
- **Winston Preparatory** • 4 W 76th St [CPW]
- **York Prep** • 40 W 68th St [CPW]

◯ Supermarkets

- **Balducci's** • 155 W 66th St [B'way]
- **Citarella** • 2135 Broadway [75th]
- **Fairway Market** • 2127 Broadway [74th]
- **Food Emporium** • 2008 Broadway [69th]
- **Gristede's** • 2109 Broadway [73rd]
- **Gristede's** • 25 Central Park W [63rd]
- **Gristede's** • 504 Columbus Ave [84th]
- **Gristede's** • 80 West End Ave [63rd]
- **Pioneer** • 289 Columbus Ave [73rd]
- **Western Beef** • 75 West End Ave [63rd]
- **Westside Market** • 2171 Broadway [77th] ♿
- **Whole Foods Market** • 59th St & Columbus Cir
- **Zabar's** • 2245 Broadway [80th]

99

Just moved in to the neighborhood? Hit Gracious Home—they really do have a bit of everything. Want to stay in for the evening? Hit Tower Records and lose yourself in a great audio-visual chain. As for everything else, from coffee shops to farmer's markets to hardware, liquor, and pet stores—it's here. And you can choose indies or chains. We love New York.

14 15
11 12 13

Ma

Coffee

- **Alice's Tea Cup** • 102 W 73rd St [Columbus]
- **Beard Papa** • 2167 Broadway [76th]
- **Columbus Bakery** • 474 Columbus Ave [83rd]
- **Cosi** • 2160 Broadway [76th]
- **Dean & DeLuca** • 10 Columbus Cir [B'way]
- **Edgar's Café** • 255 W 84th St [B'way]
- **Elixir Juice Bar** • 10 Columbus Cir [B'way]
- **International Café** • 5 W 63rd St [CPW]
- **Lenny's Café** • 302 Columbus Ave [74th]
- **New World Coffee** • 416 Columbus Ave [80th]
- **Sensuous Bean** • 66 W 70th St [Columbus]
- **Starbucks** • 152 Columbus Ave [67th]
- **Starbucks** • 1841 Broadway [60th]
- **Starbucks** • 2 Columbus Ave [59th]
- **Starbucks** • 2045 Broadway [70th]
- **Starbucks** • 2140 Broadway [75th]
- **Starbucks** • 2252 Broadway [81st]
- **Starbucks** • 267 Columbus Ave [72nd]
- **Starbucks** • 338 Columbus Ave [76th]
- **Starbucks** • 444 Columbus Ave [81st]

Copy Shops

- **Copy USA** • 210 W 83rd St [Amsterdam]
- **Gavin Printing** • 387 Amsterdam Ave [78th]
- **IBU Copy & Copy** • 517 Amsterdam Ave [85th]
- **Kinko's** • 221 W 72nd St [B'way] ✪
- **Mail Boxes Etc** • 163 Amsterdam Ave [67th]
- **Mail Boxes Etc** • 459 Columbus Ave [82nd]
- **Matrix Copy & Printing Services** • 140 W 72nd St [Columbus]
- **Panda Copy** • 2202 Broadway [78th]
- **Printing Express and Speed Copy Center** • 104 W 83rd St [Columbus]
- **Staples** • 2248 Broadway [80th]
- **Studio 305** • 313 Amsterdam Ave [75th]
- **The UPS Store** • 119 W 72nd St [Columbus]
- **The UPS Store** • 366 Amsterdam Ave [78th]
- **Upper Westside Copy Center** • 2054 Broadway [71st]

Farmer's Markets

- **77th Street (Sun, 10am-5pm, Year Round)** • W 77th St & Columbus Ave
- **Tucker Square (Thurs & Sat 8am-5pm, Year Round)** • W 66th St & Columbus Ave

Gyms

- **All Star Fitness Center** • 75 West End Ave [63rd]
- **Club 30** • 30 W 63rd St [B'way]
- **Crunch Fitness** • 162 W 83rd St [Amsterdam]
- **Curves (Women only)** • 76 W 85th St [Columbus]
- **Elysium Fitness Club** • 117 W 72nd St [Columbus]
- **Equinox Fitness Club** • 344 Amsterdam Ave [76th]
- **Fitness Express Manhattan (Women only)** • 142 W 72nd St [Columbus]
- **The JCC in Manhattan** • 334 Amsterdam Ave [76th]
- **New York Sports Clubs** • 2162 Broadway [77th]
- **New York Sports Clubs** • 23 W 73rd St [CPW]
- **New York Sports Clubs** • 248 W 80th St [B'way]
- **New York Sports Clubs** • 61 W 62nd St [B'way]
- **Reebok Sports Club NY** • 160 Columbus Ave [67th]
- **The Training Ground** • 118 W 72nd St [Columbus]
- **YMCA West Side** • 5 W 63rd St [CPW]

Hardware Stores

- **A&I Hardware** • 207 Columbus Ave [69th]
- **Amsterdam Hardware** • 147 Amsterdam Ave [66th]
- **Beacon Paint & Wallpaper** • 371 Amsterdam Ave [78th]
- **Ben Franklin Paints** • 2193 Broadway [78th]
- **Berg Hardware & Houseware** • 239 W 72nd St [B'way]
- **Gartner's Hardware** • 134 W 72nd St [Columbus]
- **Gracious Home** • 1992 Broadway [68th]
- **Klosty Hardware** • 471 Amsterdam Ave [83rd]
- **Supreme Hardware & Supply** • 65 W 73rd St [Columbus]

Liquor Stores

- **67 Wine & Spirits** • 179 Columbus Ave [68th]
- **79th Street Wine & Spirits** • 230 W 79th St [B'way]
- **Acker Merrall** • 160 W 72nd St [Amsterdam]
- **Bacchus Wine Made Simple (Wine only)** • 2056 Broadway [71st]
- **Beacon Wines & Spirits** • 2120 Broadway [74th]
- **Candlelight Wine** • 2315 Broadway [84th]
- **Central Wine & Liquor Store** • 227 Columbus Ave [70th]
- **Ehrlich Liquor Store** • 222 Amsterdam Ave [70th]
- **Nancy's Wines** • 313 Columbus Ave [75th]
- **Rose Wine & Liquor** • 449 Columbus Ave [81st]
- **West End Wine** • 204 West End Ave [70th]
- **West Side Wine & Spirits Shop** • 481 Columbus Ave [83rd]

Pet Shops

- **Doggie Kingdom** • 135 W 70th St [Columbus]
- **Furry Paws 4** • 141 Amsterdam Ave [66th]
- **Pet Health Store** • 440 Amsterdam Ave [81st]
- **Pet Market** • 210 W 72nd St [B'way]
- **Petland Discounts** • 137 W 72nd St [Columbus]

Video Rental

- **Blockbuster** • 197 Amsterdam Ave [69th]
- **Champagne Video** • 213 W 79th St [Amsterdam]
- **Flick's Video** • 175 W 72nd St [Amsterdam]
- **Movie Bank USA** • W 79th St & Amsterdam Ave ✪
- **Tower Records-Video-Books** • 1961 Broadway [66th]

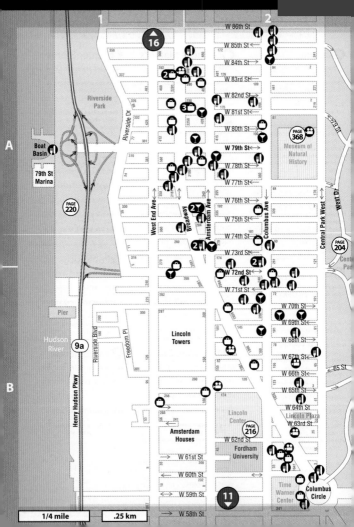

Bars here are either expensive or mundane or both, except for the cozy All-State Cafe. Yogi's is a cheap wannabe honky-tonk, and the Evelyn Lounge is about as close to a club as you'll find here. Restaurants abound, but are expensive and often inauthentic. Thank God for the recession special at Gray's Papaya.

Movie Theaters

- **American Museum of Natural History IMAX** • Central Park W & 79th St
- **Clearview's 62nd & Broadway** • 1871 Broadway [61st]
- **Lincoln Plaza Cinemas** • 30 Lincoln Plz [65th]
- **Loews 84th St** • 2310 Broadway [84th]
- **Loews Lincoln Square & IMAX Theatre** • 1992 Broadway [68th]
- **Makor** • 35 W 67th St [CPW]
- **Walter Reade Theater** • 70 Lincoln Plz [65th]

Nightlife

- **All-State Café** • 250 W 72nd St [B'way]
- **Beacon Theater** • 2124 Broadway [74th]
- **Bourbon Street** • 407 Amsterdam Ave [79th]
- **Café Des Artistes** • 1 W 67th St [CPW]
- **Dead Poet** • 450 Amsterdam Ave [82nd]
- **Dublin House** • 225 W 79th St [B'way]
- **Emerald Inn** • 205 Columbus Ave [69th]
- **The Evelyn Lounge** • 380 Columbus Ave [78th]
- **Jake's Dilemma** • 430 Amsterdam Ave [81st]
- **Makor** • 35 W 67th St [CPW]
- **P&G** • 279 Amsterdam Ave [73rd]
- **Prohibition** • 503 Columbus Ave [84th]
- **Stand-up NY** • 236 W 78th St [B'way]
- **Yogi's** • 2156 Broadway [76th]

Pet Shops

- **Doggie Kingdom** • 135 W 70th St [Columbus]
- **Furry Paws 4** • 141 Amsterdam Ave [66th]
- **Pet Health Store** • 440 Amsterdam Ave [81st]
- **Pet Market** • 210 W 72nd St [B'way]
- **Petland Discounts** • 137 W 72nd St [Columbus]

Restaurants

- **The 79th St Boat Basin Café (seasonal)** • W 79th St [Riverside Dr]
- **All-State Café** • 250 W 72nd St [B'way]
- **Asiate** • 80 Columbus Cir, 35th fl [B'way]
- **Baluchi's** • 283 Columbus Ave [73rd]
- **Big Nick's** • 2175 Broadway [77th] ⏰
- **Blondies** • 212 W 79th St [Amsterdam]
- **Café Des Artistes** • 1 W 67th St [CPW]
- **Café Lalo** • 201 W 83rd St [Amsterdam]
- **Café Luxembourg** • 200 W 70th St [Amsterdam]
- **China Fun** • 246 Columbus Ave [71st]
- **Crumbs** • 321 Amsterdam Ave [75th]
- **Edgar's Café** • 255 W 84th St [B'way]
- **EJ's Luncheonette** • 447 Amsterdam Ave [81st]
- **Epices du Traiteur** • 103 W 70th St [Columbus]
- **Fairway Café** • 2127 Broadway [74th]
- **The Firehouse** • 522 Columbus Ave [85th]
- **French Roast** • 2340 Broadway [85th] ⏰
- **Gabriel's** • 11 W 60th St [B'way]
- **Gari** • 370 Columbus Ave [78th]
- **Gray's Papaya** • 2090 Broadway [71st] ⏰
- **H&H Bagels** • 2239 Broadway [80th] ⏰
- **Harry's Burrito Junction** • 241 Columbus Ave [71st]
- **Hunan Park** • 235 Columbus Ave [71st]
- **Jackson Hole** • 517 Columbus Ave [85th]
- **Jean Georges** • 1 Central Park W [Columbus Cir]
- **Jean-Luc** • 507 Columbus Ave [84th]
- **Josie's** • 300 Amsterdam Ave [74th]
- **Kinoko** • 165 W 72nd St [Amsterdam]
- **La Caridad 78** • 2197 Broadway [78th]
- **Land Thai Kitchen** • 450 Amsterdam Ave [82nd]
- **Le Pain Quotidien** • 50 W 72nd St [CPW]
- **Lenge** • 200 Columbus Ave [69th]
- **Manhattan Diner** • 2180 Broadway [77th] ⏰
- **Penang** • 240 Columbus Ave [71st]
- **Picholine** • 35 W 64th St [CPW]
- **Planet Sushi** • 380 Amsterdam Ave [78th]
- **Rain** • 100 W 82nd St [Columbus]
- **Rosa Mexicano** • 61 Columbus Ave [62nd]
- **Ruby Foo's Dim Sum & Sushi Palace** • 2182 Broadway [77th]
- **Santa Fe** • 73 W 71st St [Columbus]
- **Sarabeth's** • 423 Amsterdam Ave [80th]
- **Taco Grill** • 146 W 72nd St [Columbus]
- **Vince and Eddie's** • 70 W 68th St [Columbus]
- **Vinnie's Pizza** • 285 Amsterdam Ave [73rd]
- **Whole Foods Café** • 10 Columbus Cir, downstairs [B'way]

Shopping

- **Allan & Suzi** • 416 Amsterdam Ave [80th]
- **Alphabets** • 2284 Broadway [82nd]
- **Balducci's** • 155 W 66th St [B'way]
- **Bed Bath & Beyond** • 1932 Broadway [65th]
- **Bonne Nuit** • 30 Lincoln Plz [65th]
- **Bruce Frank** • 215 W 83rd St [Amsterdam]
- **Bruno the King of Ravioli** • 2204 Broadway [78th]
- **Claire's Accessories** • 2267 Broadway [81st]
- **EMS** • 20 W 61st St [B'way]
- **Ethan Allen** • 103 West End Ave [64th]
- **Fish's Eddy** • 2176 Broadway [77th]
- **Godiva Chocolatier** • 245 Columbus Ave [71st]
- **Gracious Home** • 1992 Broadway [68th]
- **Harry's Shoes** • 2299 Broadway [83rd]
- **Housing Works Thrift Shop** • 306 Columbus Ave [74th]
- **Janovic** • 159 W 72nd St [Amsterdam]
- **Laytner's Linens** • 2270 Broadway [82nd]
- **Patagonia** • 426 Columbus Ave [81st]
- **Pookie & Sebastian** • 322 Columbus Ave [75th]
- **Tower Records/Video** • 1961 Broadway [66th]
- **Townshop** • 2273 Broadway [82nd]
- **Tumi** • 10 Columbus Cir [B'way]
- **West Side Records** • 233 W 72nd St [B'way]
- **Whole Foods Market** • 10 Columbus Cir [B'way]
- **Yarn Co** • 2274 Broadway [82nd]
- **Zabar's** • 2245 Broadway [80th]

Map 14 • Upper West Side (Lower)

Parking and driving are both actually doable in this area, with most of the available spots on or near Riverside Drive. We recommend the 79th Street Transverse for crossing Central Park. The Lincoln Center area is by far the messiest traffic problem here—you can avoid it by taking West End Avenue.

Subways

① ② ③ .... 72 St

① .... 66 St-Lincoln Center

① .... 79 St

Ⓑ Ⓓ Ⓐ Ⓒ .... 72 St

Ⓑ Ⓓ Ⓐ Ⓒ . 81 St-Museum of Natural History

Bus Lines

10 20 ... Seventh Ave/Eighth Ave/Douglass Blvd

104 .... Broadway/42nd St

11 .... Ninth Ave/Tenth Ave

5 ....Fifth Ave/Sixth Ave/Riverside Dr

57 .... 57th St Crosstown

66 .... 66th St/67th St Crosstown

7 ....Columbus Ave/Amsterdam Ave/
Lenox Ave/Sixth Ave/Broadway

72 ....72nd St Crosstown

79 .... 79th St Crosstown

Bike Lanes

• • • • Marked Bike Lanes
• • • • Recommended Route
• • • • Greenway

Car Rental

• **Avis** • 216 W 76th St [B'way]
• **Dollar** • 207 W 76th St [Amsterdam]
• **Enterprise** • 147 W 83rd St [Columbus]
• **Hertz** • 210 W 77th St [Amsterdam]
• **National/Alamo** • 219 W 77th St [B'way]

Ⓟ Parking

Map 6 Upper East Side (Lower)

E 86th St
E 85th St
The Jeffersons High-rise · Zion-St Mark's Evangelical Lutheran Church
E 84th St
E 83rd St
E 82nd St
Frank E Campbell Funeral Chapel
E 81st St
Lascoff Apothecary
E 80th St
New York Society Library
E 79th St
Butterfield Market
E 78th St
E 77th St
Cafe Carlyle · Bemelans Bar
E 76th St
Whitney Museum of American Art
E 75th St
E 74th St
E 73rd St
E 72nd St
Breakfast at Tiffany's Apartment Building
E 71st St
Frick Collection
Asia Society
E 70th St
E 69th St
E 68th St
E 67th St
The Manhattan House
E 66th St
Temple Emanu-El
E 65th St
E 64th St
E 63rd St
E 62nd St
E 61st St
E 60th St
E 59th St

Memorial Sloane Kettering Cancer Center
Cornell University Medical College
Rockefeller University
Mount Vernon Hotel Museum

Carl Schurz Park
East End Ave
John Jay Park
York Ave
First Ave
Second Ave
Third Ave
Lexington Ave
Park Ave
Madison Ave
Fifth Ave

Metropolitan Museum of Art

PAGE 366
PAGE 204

Central Park

FDR Dr
Bobby Wagner Walk

East River
Foot Bridge

Queensboro Bridge
To Queens

1/4 mile   .25 km

With nearly 20 supermarkets, at least half a dozen museums, numerous schools, and practically two banks on every corner, the southern half of the Upper East Side certainly doesn't lack for culture, education, or conveniences. One of its zip codes, 10021, is among the wealthiest in the country.

℞ 24-Hour Pharmacies

- **CVS Pharmacy** • 1396 Second Ave [72nd]
- **Duane Reade** • 1191 Second Ave [63rd] ♿
- **Duane Reade** • 1279 Third Ave [73rd] ♿
- **Duane Reade** • 1345 Third Ave [72nd] ♿
- **Duane Reade** • 1498 York Ave [79th] ♿
- **Duane Reade** • 773 Lexington Ave [60th] ♿
- **Walgreen's** • 1328 Second Ave [70th] ♿

Bagels

- **Bagel Mill Café** • 1461 Third Ave [82nd]
- **Bagel Shoppe** • 1421 Second Ave [74th]
- **Bagels & Co** • 1428 York Ave [76th]
- **Bagelworks** • 1229 First Ave [66th]
- **Eastside Bagel** • 1496 First Ave [78th]
- **H&H** • 1551 Second Ave [81st]
- **Hot & Tasty** • 1323 Second Ave [70th]
- **Monsieur Bagel** • 874 Lexington [66th]
- **NYC Bagels** • 1228 Second Ave [65th]
- **Pick A Bagel** • 1101 Lexington Ave [77th]
- **Pick A Bagel** • 1475 Second Ave [77th]
- **Tal Bagel** • 1228 Lexington Ave [83rd]

$ Banks

- **AP • Apple** • 1168 First Ave [64th]
- **AP • Apple** • 1555 First Ave [81st]
- **AT • Atlantic (ATM)** • 1180 Second Ave [62nd]
- **AT • Atlantic (ATM)** • 1208 First Ave [65th]
- **AT • Atlantic (ATM)** • 1365 Third Ave [78th]
- **AT • Atlantic (ATM)** • 1446 Second Ave [75th]
- **AT • Atlantic (ATM)** • 40 East 52nd Ave [81st]
- **AT • Atlantic (ATM)** • 410 E 61st St [1st Av]
- **BA • Bank of America** • 1066 Lexington
- **BA • Bank of America** • 1143 Lexington
- **BA • Bank of America (ATM)** • 1065 Third
- **NY • Bank of New York** • 706 Madison [63rd]
- **NY • Bank of New York** • 909 Madison [73rd]
- **CH • Chase** • 1003 Lexington Ave [72nd]
- **CH • Chase** • 1025 Madison Ave [79th]
- **CH • Chase** • 201 E 79th St [3rd Av]
- **CH • Chase** • 300 E 64th St [2nd Av]
- **CH • Chase** • 35 E 72nd St [Madison]
- **CH • Chase** • 360 E 72nd St [1st Av]
- **CH • Chase** • 501 E 79th St [York Av]
- **CH • Chase** • 770 Lexington Ave [60th]
- **CH • Chase** • 941 Lexington Ave [69th]
- **CH • Chase (ATM)** • 1000 Fifth Ave [81st]
- **CI • Citibank** • 1078 Third Ave [64th]
- **CI • Citibank** • 1285 First Ave [69th]
- **CI • Citibank** • 1512 First Ave [79th]
- **CI • Citibank** • 171 E 72nd St [3rd Av]
- **CI • Citibank** • 757 Madison Ave [65th]
- **CI • Citibank** • 785 Fifth Ave [59th]
- **CI • Citibank** • 976 Madison Ave [76th]
- **CI • Citibank (ATM)** • 1266 First Ave [68th]
- **CI • Citibank (ATM)** • 1275 York Ave [68th]
- **CI • Citibank (ATM)** • 510 E 62nd St [York Av]
- **CS • City and Suburban FSB** • 1404 Second Ave
- **CO • Commerce** • 1091 Third Ave [64th]
- **CO • Commerce** • 1470 Second Ave [77th]
- **CO • Commerce** • 1504 Third Ave [85th]
- **EM • Emigrant** • 812 Lexington Ave [63rd]
- **FF • Fourth Federal** • 1355 First Ave [73rd]
- **HS • HSBC** • 1002 Madison Ave [78th]
- **HS • HSBC** • 1165 Third Ave [68th]
- **HS • HSBC** • 1340 Third Ave [77th]
- **IC • Independence Community** • 1062 Third [63rd]
- **CU • Municipal Credit Union (ATM)** • NY 525 E 68th St [York Av]
- **NF • North Fork** • 1010 Third Ave [60th]
- **NF • North Fork** • 1011 Third Ave [60th]
- **NF • North Fork** • 1180 Third Ave [69th]
- **NF • North Fork** • 1295 Second Ave [68th]
- **NF • North Fork** • 1432 Second Ave [75th]
- **NF • North Fork** • 300 E 79th St [2nd Av]
- **VN • Valley National** • 1328 Second Ave [70th]
- **WA • Wachovia** • 1370 Third Ave [78th]
- **WM • Washington Mutual** • 1191 Third [69th]
- **WM • Washington Mutual** • 1308 First Ave
- **WM • Washington Mutual** • 1520 York Ave
- **WM • Washington Mutual** • 510 Park Ave

✚ Emergency Rooms

- **Lenox Hill** • 110 E 77th St [Park]
- **Manhattan Eye, Ear & Throat** • 210 E 64th St [3rd Av] ♿
- **New York Presbyterian-Weill Cornell Medical Center** • 525 E 68th St [York Av] ♿

O Landmarks

- **Asia Society** • 725 Park Av [71st]
- *Bemelman's Bar* • Carlyle Hotel • 35 E 76th St [Madison]
- *Breakfast at Tiffany's Apartment Building* • 169 E 71st St [Lex]
- **Butterfield Market** • 1114 Lexington [78th]
- **Café Carlyle** • 35 E 76th St [Madison]
- **Frank E Campbell Funeral Chapel** • 1076 Madison Ave [81st]
- **Frick Collection** • 1 E 70th St [5th Av]
- *The Jeffersons High-rise* • 185 E 85th St [3rd Av]
- **Lascoff Apothecary** • 1209 Lexington [82nd]
- **The Manhattan House** • 200 E 66th St [3rd Av]
- **Metropolitan Museum of Art** • 1000 Fifth Ave [81st]
- **Mount Vernon Hotel Museum** • 421 E 61st St [1st Av]
- **NY Society Library** • 53 E 79th [Madison]
- **Temple Emanu-El** • 1 E 65th St [5th Av]
- **Whitney Museum of American Art** • 945 Madison Ave [74th]
- **Zion-St Mark's Evangelical Lutheran Church** • 339 E 84th St [2nd Av]

Libraries

- **67th St** • 328 E 67th St [2nd Av]
- **NY Society Library** • 53 E 79th [Madison]
- **Webster** • 1465 York Ave [78th]
- **Yorkville** • 222 E 79th St [3rd Av]

Police

- **19th Precinct** • 153 E 67th St [Lex]

✉ Post Offices

- **Cherokee** • 1483 York Ave [79th]
- **Gracie** • 229 E 85th St [3rd Av]
- **Lenox Hill** • 217 E 70th St [3rd Av]

Schools

- **Abraham Lincoln** • 12 E 79th St [5th Av]
- **All Souls** • 1157 Lexington Ave [80th]
- **Allen-Stevenson** • 132 E 78th St [Lex]
- **Birch Wathen Lenox** • 210 E 77th St [3rd Av]
- **Brearly** • 610 E 83rd St [East End]
- **Browning** • 52 E 62nd St [Madison]
- **Buckley** • 113 E 73rd St [Park]
- **Caedmon** • 416 E 80th St [1st Av]
- **Cathedral** • 319 E 74th St [2nd Av]
- **Chapin** • 100 East End Ave [84th]
- **Cornell University Medical College** • 1300 York Ave [70th]
- **Dominican Academy** • 44 E 68th [Madison]
- **East Side Middle** • 1458 York Ave [78th]
- **Eleanor Roosevelt High** • 411 E 76th [1st]
- **Ella Baker** • 317 E 67th St [2nd Av]
- **Episcopal** • 35 E 69th St [Madison]
- **Geneva School** • 583 Park Ave [63rd]
- **Hewitt** • 45 E 75th St [Madison]
- **Hunter College** • 695 Park Ave [70th]
- **JHS 167 Robert Wagner** • 220 E 76th [3rd Av]
- **Loyola** • 980 Park Ave [83rd]
- **Lycée Francais de New York** • 505 E 75th St [York Av]
- **Manhattan High School for Girls** • 154 E 70th St [Lex]
- **Manhattan International High** • 317 E 67th St [2nd Av]
- **Martha Graham** • 316 E 63rd St [2nd Av]
- **Marymount** • 1026 Fifth Ave [84th]
- **Marymount Manhattan College** • 221 E 71st St [3rd Av]
- **New York School of Interior Design** • 170 E 70th St [Lex]
- **NYU Institute of Fine Arts** • 1 E 78th St [5th]
- **PS 006 Lillie D Blake** • 45 E 81st St [Madison]
- **PS 158 Bayard Taylor** • 1458 York [77th]
- **PS 183 R L Stevenson** • 419 E 66th [1st Av]
- **PS 290 Manhattan New School** • 311 E 82nd St [2nd Av]
- **Queen Sofia Spanish Institute** • 684 Park Ave [68th]
- **Rabbi Arthur Schneier Park East Day** • 164 E 68th St [Lex]
- **Ramaz Lower** • 125 E 85th St [Park]
- **Ramaz Middle** • 114 E 85th St [Madison]
- **Ramaz Upper** • 60 E 78th St [Madison]
- **Regis High** • 55 E 84th St [Madison]
- **Rockefeller University** • 1230 York Ave
- **Rudolf Steiner Lower** • 15 E 79th [5th Av]
- **Rudolf Steiner Upper** • 15 E 78th [5th Av]
- **The Smith School** • 1393 York Ave [74th]
- **Sotheby's Institute of Art** • 1334 York [71st]
- **St Ignatius Loyola** • 48 E 84th St [Madison]
- **St Jean Baptiste High** • 173 E 75th St [Lex]
- **St Stephan of Hungary** • 408 E 82nd [1st Av]
- **St Vincent Ferrer High** • 151 E 65th [Lex]
- **Talent Unlimited High** • 317 E 67th [2nd Av]
- **Town School** • 540 E 76th St [FDR]
- **Ukrainian Institute** • 2 E 79th St [5th Av]
- **Urban Academy Lab High** • 317 E 67th [2nd]
- **Vanguard High** • 317 E 67th St [2nd Av]

Supermarkets

- **Agata & Valentina** • 1505 First Ave [79th]
- **Associated** • 1565 First Ave [81st]
- **Citarella** • 1313 Third Ave [75th]
- **D'Agostino** • 1074 Lexington Ave [76th]
- **D'Agostino** • 1233 Lexington Ave [84th]
- **D'Agostino** • 1507 York Ave [80th]
- **Eli's Manhattan** • 1411 Third Ave [80th]
- **Food Emporium** • 1066 Third Ave [63rd]
- **Food Emporium** • 1175 Third Ave [68th]
- **Food Emporium** • 1331 First Ave [71st]
- **Food Emporium** • 1450 Third Ave [82nd]
- **Gourmet Garage East** • 301 E 64th St [2nd Av]
- **Grace's Marketplace** • 1237 Third Ave [71st]
- **Gristede's** • 1180 Second Ave [62nd]
- **Gristede's** • 1208 First Ave [65th]
- **Gristede's** • 1350 First Ave [72nd]
- **Gristede's** • 1365 Third Ave [78th]
- **Gristede's** • 1446 Second Ave [75th] ♿
- **Gristede's** • 40 East End Ave [81st]
- **Health Nuts** • 1208 Second Ave [63rd]

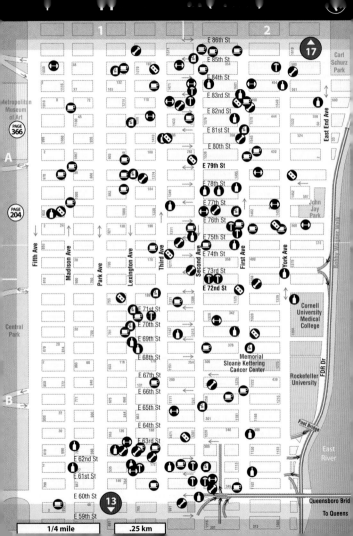

When it's time to dry-clean your silk peacock-feather-coated gown, you're in the right neighborhood. At least two of the city's haute couture dry cleaners reside here, Hallak Cleaners and Madame Paulette. When you O.D. on foie gras and pop a button, choose from millions of replacements at Tender Buttons.

Coffee

- **Anneliese's Pastries & Fine Foods** • 1516 First Ave [79th]
- **Beanocchio Café** • 1413 York Ave [75th]
- **The Bread Factory Café** • 785 Lexington Ave [61st]
- **Cafe Bacio** • 1223 Third Ave [71st]
- **City Chow Café** • 140 E 63rd St [Lex]
- **DT * UT** • 1626 Second Ave [84th]
- **Dunkin' Donuts** • 1225 First Ave [66th]
- **Dunkin' Donuts** • 1433 Second Ave [75th]
- **Dunkin' Donuts** • 1593 First Ave [83rd]
- **First Avenue Coffee Shop** • 1433 First Ave [75th]
- **Gene's Coffee Shop** • 26 E 60th St [Madison]
- **Gotham Coffee House** • 1298 Second Ave [68th]
- **Java Girl** • 348 E 66th St [2nd Av]
- **M Rohrs** • 303 E 85th St [2nd Av]
- **Nectar Coffee Shop** • 1022 Madison Ave [79th]
- **Nectar Coffee Shop** • 1090 Madison Ave [82nd]
- **Neil's Coffee Shop** • 961 Lexington Ave [70th]
- **New World Coffee** • 1046 Third Ave [62nd]
- **New World Coffee** • 1246 Lexington Ave [84th]
- **Oren's Daily Roast** • 1144 Lexington Ave [79th]
- **Oren's Daily Roast** • 1574 First Ave [82nd]
- **Oren's Daily Roast** • 985 Lexington Ave [71st]
- **Panini Da Roma** • 960 Lexington Ave [70th]
- **Starbucks** • 1102 First Ave [60th]
- **Starbucks** • 1117 Lexington Ave [78th]
- **Starbucks** • 1128 Third Ave [66th]
- **Starbucks** • 1290 Third Ave [74th]
- **Starbucks** • 1445 First Ave [75th]
- **Starbucks** • 1449 Second Ave [75th]
- **Starbucks** • 1488 Third Ave [84th]
- **Starbucks** • 1559 Second Ave [81st]
- **Starbucks** • 1631 First Ave [85th]
- **Starbucks** • 64 E 55th St [Madison]
- **Telegraphe Café** • 260 E 72nd St [2nd Av]
- **Tramway Coffee Shop** • 1143 Second Ave [59th]
- **Two Little Red Hens** • 1652 Second Ave [86th]
- **Viand Coffee Shop** • 1011 Madison Ave [78th]

Copy Shops

- **Copycats** • 1646 Second Ave [85th]
- **Copycats** • 968 Lexington Ave [70th]
- **Copyland Center** • 1597 Second Ave [83rd]
- **Copyland Center** • 335 E 65th St [2nd Av]
- **FedEx Kinko's** • 1122 Lexington Ave [78th]
- **Mail Boxes Etc** • 1202 Lexington Ave [82nd]
- **Mail Boxes Etc** • 1461 First Ave [76th]
- **Mail Boxes Etc** • 1173 Second Ave [62nd]
- **The UPS Store** • 1173 Second Ave [62nd]
- **The UPS Store** • 1275 First Ave [69th]
- **The UPS Store** • 1562 First Ave [81st]
- **Yorkville Copy Service** • 133 E 84th St [Lex]

Gyms

- **200 Club at Bristol Plaza** • 200 E 65th St [3rd Av]
- **Bio-Fitness** • 244 E 84th St [3rd Av]
- **Boom Fitness** • 1438 Third Ave [82nd]
- **Curves (Women only)** • 1460 Second Ave [76th]
- **David Barton Gym** • 30 E 85th St [Madison]
- **Elissa's Personal Best Gym** • 334 E 79th St [2nd Av]
- **Equinox Fitness Club** • 140 E 63rd St [Lex]
- **Equinox Fitness Club** • 205 E 85th St [3rd Av]
- **Lenox Hill Neighborhood House** • 331 E 70th St [1st Av]
- **New York Health & Racquet Club** • 1433 York Ave [76th]
- **New York Sports Clubs** • 349 E 76th St [2nd Av]
- **Promenade Health Club** • 530 E 76th St [FDR]
- **Sports Club/LA** • 330 E 61st St [1st Av]
- **Strathmore Swim & Health Club** • 400 E 84th St [1st Av]

Hardware Stores

- **72nd Street Hardware** • 1400 Second Ave [73rd]
- **ATB Locksmith & Hardware** • 1603 York Ave [85th]
- **Eastside Hardware** • 1175 Second Ave [62nd]
- **Gracious Home** • 1220 Third Ave [71st]
- **Home Plus** • 1400 Second Ave [73rd]
- **Kraft Hardware** • 315 E 62nd St [2nd Av]
- **Lexington Hardware & Electric** • 797 Lexington Ave [62nd]
- **New York Paint & Hardware** • 1593 Second Ave [83rd]
- **Queensboro Hardware** • 1157 Second Ave [61st]
- **Rainbow Ace Hardware** • 1449 First Ave [75th]
- **S&V General Supply** • 1450 First Ave [75th]
- **Thalco Maintenance Supply** • 1462 Second Ave [76th]

Liquor Stores

- **1375 First Liquors** • 1375 First Ave [73rd]
- **76 Liquors** • 1473 First Ave [77th]
- **Aulden Cellars** • 1334 York Ave [71st]
- **Big Apple Wine & Spirits** • 1408 Second Ave [73rd]
- **City Liquor** • 1145 Second Ave [60th]
- **Cork and Bottle Liquor Store** • 1158 First Ave [63rd]
- **Crown Wine & Liquor** • 1587 Second Ave [82nd]
- **Drink** • 235 E 69th St [2nd Av]
- **East River Liquors** • 1364 York Ave [73rd]
- **Eli's** • 1411 Third Ave [80th]

- **Embassy Liquors** • 796 Lexington Ave [62nd]
- **Garnet Wines & Liquors** • 929 Lexington Ave [68th]
- **Gracies Wine** • 1577 York Ave [84th]
- **Headington Wines & Liquors** • 1135 Lexington Ave [79th]
- **Lumers Fine Wines & Spirits** • 1479 Third Ave [83rd]
- **McCabe's Wines & Spirits** • 1347 Third Ave [77th]
- **Milli Liquors** • 1496 Second Ave [78th St]
- **Monro Wines & Liquors** • 68 East End Ave [82nd]
- **Morrell Wine Exchange** • 1035 Third Ave [62nd]
- **Rosenthal Wine Merchant (Wine only)** • 318 E 84th St [2nd Av]
- **Sherry-Lehman** • 679 Madison Ave [62nd]
- **Windsor Wine Shop** • 1103 First Ave [61st]
- **The Wine Shop** • 1585 First Ave [83rd]
- **Woody Liquor & Wine** • 1450 Second Ave [76th]
- **York Wines & Spirits** • 1291 First Ave [70th]

Pet Shops

- **American Kennels** • 798 Lexington Ave [62nd]
- **Animal Attractions** • 343 E 66th St [2nd Av]
- **Bark Place** • 415 E 72nd St [1st Av]
- **Biscuits & Bath** • 1535 First Ave [80th]
- **Calling All Pets** • 1590 York Ave [84th]
- **Calling All Pets** • 301 E 76th St [2nd Av]
- **Canine Styles** • 830 Lexington Ave [64th]
- **Canine Styles Uptown** • 1195 Lexington Ave [81st]
- **Dogs Cats & Co** • 208 E 82nd St [3rd Av]
- **Just Cats** • 244 E 60th St [3rd Av]
- **Le Chien Pet Salon** • 1044 Third Ave [62nd]
- **Pet Market** • 1400 Second Ave [73rd]
- **Pet Market** • 1570 First Ave [82nd]
- **Pet Necessities** • 236 E 75th St [3rd Av]
- **Pets on Lex** • 1275 Lexington Ave [86th]
- **Sutton Dog Parlour Kennel & Daycare Center** • 311 E 60th St [2nd Av]

Video Rental

- **Blockbuster** • 1270 First Ave [68th]
- **Champagne Video** • 1416 Third Ave [80th]
- **Champagne Video** • 1577 First Ave [82nd]
- **Fifth Dimension Video** • 1427 York Ave [76th]
- **Movie Bank USA** • 6 E 63rd St & Second Ave
- **Movie Bank USA** • E 72nd St & First Ave ⊠
- **Movie Bank USA** • E 74th St & Third Ave ⊠
- **Movie Bank USA** • E 79th St & Second Ave ⊠
- **Video Vogue** • 976 Lexington Ave [71st]
- **Videoroom** • 1487 Third Ave [84th]
- **York Video** • 1472 York Ave [78th]
- **Zitomer Department Store & Electronics** • 969 Madison Ave [76th]

Cool boutiques like Cantaloup, Scoop, and Pookie & Sebastian have made Second, Third, and Lexington Avenues hip shopping destinations. To stylishly accent newly purchased "downtown-style" duds, savvy shoppers also visit "Thrift Row," a string of East 70s and 80s thrift shops on (and near) Third Avenue. For drinking, it's the Subway

Movie Theaters

- **Asia Society** • 725 Park Ave [70th]
- **Clearview's Beekman One & Two** • 1271 Second Ave [67th]
- **Clearview's First & 62nd Street** • 400 E 62nd St [1st Av]
- **Czech Center** • 1109 Madison Ave [83rd]
- **Loews 72nd St East** • 1230 Third Ave [71]
- **Metropolitan Museum of Art** • 1000 Fifth Ave [81st]
- **UA East 85th Street** • 1629 First Ave [85]
- **UA Gemini** • 1210 Second Ave [64th]
- **Whitney Museum** • 945 Madison Ave [75]

Nightlife

- **Banshee Pub** • 1373 First Ave [74th]
- **The Bar at Etats-Unis** • 247 E 81st St [3rd]
- **Bemelman's Bar** • Carlyle Hotel • 35 E 76th St [Madison]
- **Brandy's Piano Bar** • 235 E 84th St [3rd]
- **Brother Jimmy's** • 1485 Second Ave [77th]
- **Café Carlyle** • Carlyle Hotel • 35 E 76th St
- **Club Macanudo** • 26 E 63rd St [Madison]
- **Comic Strip Live** • 1568 Second Ave [81st]
- **Dangerfield's** • 1118 First Ave [61st]
- **David Copperfield's** • 1394 York Ave [74th]
- **Feinstein's** • 540 Park Ave [61st]
- **Finnegan's Wake** • 1361 First Ave [73rd]
- **Fondue Lounge** • 303 E 80th St [2nd Av]
- **Lexington Bar & Books** • 1020 Lexington Ave [73rd]
- **Session 73** • 1359 First Ave [73rd]
- **Ship of Fools** • 1590 Second Ave [83rd]
- **Subway Inn** • 143 E 60th St [Lex]
- **Tin Lizzy** • 1647 Second Ave [85th]
- **Vudu** • 1487 First Ave [78th]

Restaurants

- **Afghan Kebab House II** • 1345 Second Ave [71st]
- **Atlantic Grill** • 1341 Third Ave [77th]
- **Aureole** • 34 E 61st St [Madison]
- **Baluchi's** • 1149 First Ave [63rd]
- **Baluchi's** • 1565 Second Ave [81st]
- **The Bar at Etats-Unis** • 247 E 81st St [3rd Av]
- **Barking Dog Luncheonette** • 1453 York Ave [77th]
- **Beyoglu** • 1431 Third Ave [81st]
- **Blue Green Organic Juice Café** • 203 E 74th St [3rd Av]
- **Brunelli** • 1409 York Ave [75th]
- **Burger Heaven** • 804 Lexington Ave [62nd]
- **Burke Café** • 1000 Third Ave [60th]
- **Burke in the Box at Bloomingdale's** • 1000 Third Ave [60th]
- **Café Boulud** • Surrey Hotel • 20 E 76th St [Madison]
- **Café Mingala** • 1393 Second Ave [72nd]
- **Café Sabarsky** • 1048 Fifth Ave [85th]
- **Candle 79** • 154 E 79th St [Lex]
- **Candle Café** • 1307 Third Ave [75th]
- **Canyon Road** • 1470 First Ave [77th]
- **Cilantro** • 1321 First Ave [71st]
- **Daniel** • 60 E 65th St [Park]
- **Davidburke & Donatella** • 133 E 61st St [Lex]
- **Dongun** • 309 E 83rd St [2nd Av]
- **EAT** • 1064 Madison Ave [81st]
- **Eat Here Now** • 839 Lexington Ave [64th]
- **EJ's Luncheonette** • 1271 Third Ave [73rd]
- **Elio's** • 1621 Second Ave [84th]
- **Etats-Unis** • 242 E 81st St [3rd Av]
- **Ethiopian Restaurant** • 1582 York Ave [83rd]
- **Haru** • 1329 Third Ave [76th]
- **Heidelberg** • 1648 Second Ave [86th]
- **Indian Tandoor Oven Restaurant** • 175 E 83rd St [3rd Av]
- **Jackson Hole** • 1611 Second Ave [84th]
- **Jackson Hole** • 232 E 64th St [3rd Av]
- **Jacque's Brasserie** • 204 E 85th St [3rd Av]
- **JG Melon** • 1291 Third Ave [74th]
- **John's Pizzeria** • 408 E 64th St [1st Av]
- **JoJo** • 160 E 64th St [Lex]
- **King's Carriage House** • 251 E 82nd St [2nd]
- **Le Pain Quotidien** • 1131 Madison Ave [84]
- **Le Pain Quotidien** • 1336 First Ave [72nd]
- **Le Pain Quotidien** • 833 Lexington Ave [64th]
- **Lexington Candy Shop/Luncheonette** • 1226 Lexington Ave [83rd]
- **Malaga** • 406 E 73rd St [1st Av]
- **Mary Ann's** • 1503 Second Ave [78th]
- **Maya** • 1191 First Ave [65th]
- **Mimi's Pizza & Restaurant** • 1248 Lexington Ave [84th]
- **Orsay** • 1057 Lexington Ave [75th]
- **Our Place** • 1444 Third Ave [82nd]
- **Park Avenue Café** • 100 E 63rd St [Park]
- **Payard Patisserie & Bistro** • 1032 Lexington Ave [74th]
- **Penang** • 1596 Second Ave [83rd]
- **Pintaile's Pizza** • 1443 York Ave [77th]
- **Pintaile's Pizza** • 1577 York Ave [84th]
- **Post House** • 28 E 63rd St [Madison]
- **River** • 345 Amsterdam Ave [76th]
- **Sarabeth's at the Whitney** • 945 Madison Ave [75th]
- **Serafina** • 29 E 61st St [Madison]
- **Serendipity 3** • 225 E 60th St [3rd Av]
- **Sette Mezzo** • 969 Lexington Ave [70th]
- **Slice, The Perfect Food** • 1413 Second Ave [74th]
- **Sushi of Gari** • 402 E 78th St [1st Av]
- **Totonno Pizzeria Napolitano** • 1544 Second Ave [80th]
- **Viand** • 1011 Madison Ave [78th]
- **Viand** • 673 Madison Ave [61st]

Shopping

- **A Bear's Place** • 789 Lexington Ave [61st]
- **American Apparel** • 1090 Third Ave [64th]
- **Anika Inez** • 243 E 78th St [3rd Av]
- **Arthritis Thrift Shop** • 1383 Third Ave [79]
- **Aveda Environmental Lifestyle Store** • 1122 Third Ave [66th]
- **Bang & Olufsen** • 952 Madison Ave [75th]
- **Barneys New York** • 660 Madison Ave [61]
- **Bed Bath & Beyond** • 410 E 61st St [1st]
- **Beneath** • 265 E 78th St [2nd Av]
- **Bis Designer Resale** • 1134 Madison Ave, 2nd Fl [84th]
- **Black Orchid Books** • 303 E 81st St [2nd]
- **Bloomingdale's** • 1000 Third Ave [60th]
- **Bra Smyth** • 905 Madison Ave [73rd]
- **Butterfield Market** • 1114 Lexington Ave [78th]
- **Cancer Care Thrift Shop** • 1480 Third Ave [84th]
- **Cantaloup** • 1036 Lexington Ave [74th]
- **Cantaloup Destination Denim** • 1359 Second Ave [72nd]
- **Caviarteria** • 1012 Lexington Ave [73rd]
- **Chuckies** • 1073 Third Ave [63rd]
- **Chuckies** • 1169 Madison Ave [86th]
- **CK Bradley** • 146 E 74th St [Lex]
- **Council Thrift Shop** • 246 E 84th St [2nd]
- **Designer Resale** • 324 E 81st St [2nd Av]
- **Designer Resale Too** • 311 E 81st St [2nd]
- **Diesel** • 770 Lexington Ave [61st]
- **DKNY** • 655 Madison Ave [60th]
- **Dolce & Gabbana** • 825 Madison Ave [69]
- **Donna Karan** • 819 Madison Ave [68th]
- **Dylan's Candy Bar** • 1011 Third Ave [60th]
- **EAT Gifts** • 1062 Madison Ave [80th]
- **Eli's Manhattan** • 1411 Third Ave [80th]
- **Elk Candy** • 1628 Second Ave [85th]
- **Encore** • 1132 Madison Ave, 2nd Fl [84th]
- **Fishs Eddy** • 1388 Third Ave [70th]
- **French Sole** • 985 Lexington Ave [71st]
- **Fresh** • 1367 Third Ave [78th]
- **Garnet Wines & Liquors** • 929 Lexington Ave [69th]
- **Gentlemen's Resale** • 322 E 81st St [2nd]
- **Giorgio Armani** • 760 Madison Ave [65th]
- **Gracious Home** • 1217 Third Ave [70th]
- **Health Nuts** • 1208 Second Ave [63rd]
- **Hermes** • 691 Madison Ave [62nd]
- **Housing Works Thrift Shop** • 202 E 77th St [3rd Av]
- **Janovic** • 1150 Third Ave [67th]
- **Jump** • 1210 Third Ave [70th]
- **Kate's Paperie** • 1282 Third Ave [74th]
- **La Maison du Chocolat** • 1018 Madison Ave [79th]
- **La Terrine** • 1024 Lexington Ave [73rd]
- **Lascoff Apothecary** • 1209 Lexington Ave [82nd]
- **Logos Bookstore** • 1575 York Ave [84th]
- **Lyric Hi-Fi** • 1221 Lexington Ave [83rd]
- **Marimekko** • 1262 Third Ave [73rd]
- **Martine's Chocolates too** • 400 E 82nd St [1st Av]
- **Memorial Sloan-Kettering Thrift Shop** • 1440 Third Ave [82nd]
- **Michael's The Consignment Shop for Women** • 1041 Madison Ave [80th]
- **Morgane Le Fay** • 746 Madison Ave [65th]
- **Myla** • 20 E 69th St [Madison]
- **Oldies, Goldies & Moldies** • 1609 Second Ave [84th]
- **Orwasher's** • 308 E 78th St [2nd Av]
- **Ottomanelli Brothers** • 1549 York Ave [82]
- **Pomegranate** • 201 E 74th St [3rd Av]
- **Pookie & Sebastian** • 1488 Second Ave [77]
- **Pookie & Sebastian** • 249 E 77th St [2nd]
- **Pylones** • 842 Lexington Ave [64th]
- **Radio Shack** • 1267 Lexington Ave [85th]
- **Radio Shack** • 1477 Third Ave [83rd]
- **Radio Shack** • 1462 Second Ave [76th]
- **Radio Shack** • 925 Lexington Ave [68th]
- **Ralph Lauren** • 888 Madison Ave [72nd]
- **Ropal Stationary** • 1504 Second Ave [78th]
- **Scoop** • 1275 Third Ave [73rd]
- **Sherry-Lehmann** • 679 Madison Ave [61]
- **The Shoe Box** • 1349 Third Ave [77th]
- **Spence-Chapin Thrift Shop** • 1473 Third Ave [83rd]
- **Steuben** • 667 Madison Ave [61st]
- **Sylvia Pines Uniquities** • 1102 Lexington Ave [77th]
- **Tender Buttons** • 143 E 62nd St [Lex]
- **The Woolgathering** • 318 E 84th St [2nd]
- **Venture Stationers** • 1156 Madison Ave [85th]
- **Vintage Collections** • 147 E 72nd St, 2nd Fl [Lex]
- **William Poll** • 1051 Lexington Ave [75th]
- **Yorkville Meat Emporium** • 1560 Second Ave [81st]
- **Yves St Laurent** • 855 Madison Ave [71st]
- **Zitomer** • 969 Madison Ave [76th]

Parking is extremely difficult during the day due to the number of schools in this area. It gets a bit better (but not much) at night, especially in the upper 70s and lower 80s near the FDR. (You'll never find legal street parking near Bloomingdale's, however.) Park Avenue is the best street to travel downtown during rush hour.

Subways

❶❷❸	96 St
❶	103 St
❶	86 St
Ⓑ Ⓒ	103 St
Ⓑ Ⓒ	86 St
Ⓑ Ⓒ	96 St

Bus Lines

10	Seventh Ave/Central Park W
104	Broadway
106	106th St Crosstown
11	Columbus Ave/Amsterdam Ave
116	116th St Crosstown
5	Fifth Ave/Sixth Ave/Riverside Dr
60	LaGuardia Airport
7	Columbus Ave/Amsterdam Ave
86	86th St Crosstown
96	96th St Crosstown

Bike Lanes

- • • • Marked Bike Lanes
- • • • Recommended Route
- • • • Greenway

Car Rental

- **Avis** • 310 E 64th St [2nd Av]
- **Dollar** • 160 E 87th St [Lex]
- **Enterprise** • 425 E 61st St [1st Av]
- **Hertz** • 327 E 64th St [2nd Av]
- **Hertz** • Carlyle Hotel • 355 E 76th St [1st Av]
- **National/Alamo** • 305 E 80th St [2nd Av]

Gas Stations

- **Mobil** • 1132 York Ave [61st] ☼

Parking

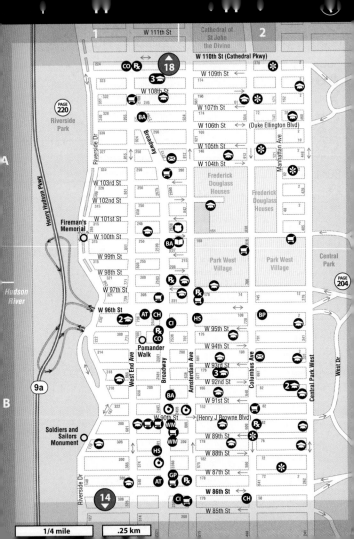

This residential neighborhood isn't hip, nor is it cheap. Central Park West, Riverside Drive, and West End Avenue are the most coveted addresses, but the numbered streets are better for peeping into other people's apartments. It also has great park access, with both Riverside and Central Parks bordering the area.

24-Hour Pharmacies

- **CVS Pharmacy** • 540 Amsterdam Ave [86th] 🖨
- **CVS Pharmacy** • 743 Amsterdam Ave [96th] 🖨
- **Duane Reade** • 2522 Broadway [94th] 🖨
- **Duane Reade** • 2589 Broadway [98th] 🖨
- **Duane Reade** • 609 Columbus Ave [89th] 🖨
- **Rite Aid** • 2833 Broadway [110th] 🖨

Bagels

- **Bagel Basket** • 618 Amsterdam Ave [90th]
- **Hot & Crusty Bagel Café** • 2387 Broadway [88th]
- **Tal Bagels** • 2446 Broadway [90th]

Banks

- AT • **Atlantic (ATM)** • Gristedes • 251 W 86th St [B'way]
- AT • **Atlantic (ATM)** • Gristedes • 262 W 96th St [B'way]
- BP • **Banco Popular** • 90 W 96th St [Columbus]
- BA • **Bank of America** • 2770 Broadway [107th]
- BA • **Bank of America (ATM)** • 2461 Broadway [91st]
- BA • **Bank of America (ATM)** • 2620 Broadway [99th]
- CH • **Chase** • 2551 Broadway [96th]
- CH • **Chase** • 59 W 86th St [Columbus]
- CI • **Citibank** • 2350 Broadway [85th]
- CI • **Citibank** • 2560 Broadway [96th]
- CO • **Commerce** • 2521 Broadway [94th]
- CO • **Commerce** • 2831 Broadway [110th]
- HS • **HSBC** • 2401 Broadway [88th]
- HS • **HSBC** • 739 Amsterdam Ave [96th]
- NF • **North Fork** • 2379 Broadway [85th]
- NF • **North Fork** • 2460 Broadway [91st]
- WM • **Washington Mutual** • 2438 Broadway [90th]
- WM • **Washington Mutual** • 2554 Broadway [96th]

Community Gardens

Landmarks

- **Fireman's Memorial** • W 100th St & Riverside Dr
- **Pomander Walk** • 261 W 94th St [B'way]
- **Soldiers and Sailors Monument** • Riverside Dr & 89th St

Libraries

- **Bloomingdale** • 150 W 100th St [Columbus]

Police

- **24th Precinct** • 151 W 100th St [Amsterdam]

Post Offices

- **Cathedral** • 215 W 104th St [Amsterdam]
- **Park West** • 693 Columbus Ave [94th]

Schools

- **Abraham Joshua Heschel** • 270 W 89th St [B'way]
- **Aichhorn** • 23 W 106th St [CPW]
- **Alexander Robertson** • 3 W 95th St [CPW]
- **Ascension** • 220 W 108th St [Amsterdam]
- **Columbia Grammar and Prepatory** • 5 W 93rd St [CPW]
- **De la Salle Academy** • 202 W 97th St [Amsterdam]
- **Dwight** • 291 Central Park W [89th]
- **Edward A Reynolds West Side High (M505)** • 140 W 102nd St [Amsterdam]
- **Holy Name of Jesus** • 202 W 97th St [Amsterdam]
- **JHS 54 Booker T Washington** • 103 W 107th St [Columbus]
- **Morningside Montessori** • 251 W 100th St [B'way]
- **Mott Hall II** • 234 W 109th St [Amsterdam]
- **MS 246 Crossroads** • 234 W 109th St [Amsterdam]
- **MS 247 Dual Language Middle** • 32 W 92nd St [CPW]
- **MS 250 Collaborative** • 735 West End Ave [96th]
- **MS 256 Academic and Athletic Excellence** • 154 W 93rd St [Amsterdam]
- **MS 258 Community Action** • 154 W 93rd St [Amsterdam]
- **PS 038 Roberto Clemente** • 232 E 103rd St [2nd Av]
- **PS 075 Emily Dickinson** • 735 West End Ave [96th]
- **PS 084 Lillian Weber** • 32 W 92nd St [CPW]
- **PS 145 Bloomingdale** • 150 W 105th St [Columbus]
- **PS 163 Alfred E Smith** • 163 W 97th St [Amsterdam]
- **PS 165 Robert E Simon** • 234 W 109th St [Amsterdam]
- **PS 166 Richard Rogers School of the Arts and Technology** • 132 W 89th St [Columbus]
- **PS 333 Manhattan School for Children** • 154 W 93rd St [Amsterdam]
- **Solomon Schechter High** • 1 W 91st St [CPW]
- **St Agnes Boys** • 555 West End Ave [87th]
- **St Gregory the Great** • 138 W 90th St [Columbus]
- **Studio Elementary** • 124 W 95th St [Columbus]
- **Trinity** • 139 W 91st St [Columbus]
- **Upper Trevor Day** • 1 W 88th St [CPW]
- **West Side Montessori** • 309 W 92nd St [West End]
- **Yeshiva Ketena of Manhattan** • 346 W 89th St [West End]

Supermarkets

- **Associated** • 13 W 100th St [CPW]
- **Associated** • 755 Amsterdam Ave [97th]
- **C-Town** • 818 Columbus Ave [100th]
- **D'Agostino** • 633 Columbus Ave [91st]
- **Food Emporium** • 2415 Broadway [89th]
- **Gourmet Garage West** • 2567 Broadway [96th]
- **Gristede's** • 251 W 86th St [B'way]
- **Gristede's** • 2704 Broadway [104th] 🖨
- **Gristede's** • 2780 Broadway [107th]
- **Gristede's Mega Store** • 262 W 96th St [B'way] 🖨
- **Kosher Marketplace** • 2442 Broadway [90th]
- **Met Food** • 530 Amsterdam Ave [86th]

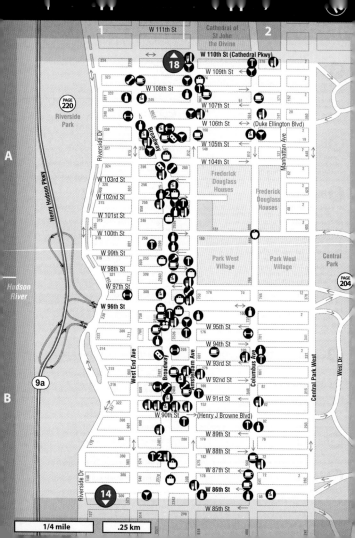

Watering holes in this area can be monotonous, but the Broadway Dive and The Ding Dong Lounge make things a little more interesting. Above 96th Street, there are less expensive bars and restaurants, including many thrifty Latin spots. Also, check out Symphony Space for music and readings.

Coffee

- 108 Mini Café • 196 W 108th St [Amsterdam]
- Columbus Café • 556 Columbus Ave [87th]
- Dunkin' Donuts • 2547 Broadway [95th]
- Dunkin' Donuts • 929 Amsterdam Ave [105th]
- Leafstorm Tea • 176 W 94th St [Amsterdam]
- Maxmile Café • 642 Amsterdam Ave [91st]
- Silver Moon Bakery • 2740 Broadway [105th]
- Sip • 998 Amsterdam Ave [109th]
- Starbucks • 2498 Broadway [93rd]
- Starbucks • 2521 Broadway [94th]
- Starbucks • 2600 Broadway [98th]
- Starbucks • 2681 Broadway [102nd]
- Starbucks • 540 Columbus Ave [86th]
- Three Star Coffee Shop • 541 Columbus Ave [86th]
- Westway Café • 2800 Broadway [108th]
- Zanny's Café • 975 Columbus Ave [108th]

Copy Shops

- Columbia Copy Center • 2790 Broadway [108th]
- Copy Concept • 216 W 103rd st [b'way]
- Copy Door • 70 W 86th St [Columbus]
- Copy Experts & Computer Center • 2440 Broadway [90th]
- Foxy Copy • 211 W 92nd St [Amsterdam]
- Global Copy • 2578 Broadway [97th]
- Mail Boxes Etc • 2444 Broadway [90th]
- Mail Boxes Etc • 2565 Broadway [96th]
- Riverside Printing & Copying • 924 Columbus Ave [105th]
- Riverside Resumes • 248 W 106th St [B'way]
- The UPS Store • 2753 Broadway [106th]

Farmer's Markets

- 97th Street (Fri, 8 am–2 pm, year round) • W 97th St & Columbus Ave

Gyms

- Body Strength Fitness • 250 W 106th St [B'way]
- Equinox Fitness Club • 2465 Broadway [91st]
- New York Sports Clubs • 2527 Broadway [94th]
- Paris Health Club • 752 West End Ave [97th]
- Synergy Fitness Clubs • 700 Columbus Ave [94th]

Hardware Stores

- Ace Hardware • 610 Columbus Ave [90th]
- Altman Hardware • 641 Amsterdam Ave [91st]
- Aquarius Hardware & Housewares • 601 Amsterdam Ave [89th]
- B Cohen & Son • 969 Amsterdam Ave [107th]
- Broadway Home Centers • 2672 Broadway [102nd]
- C&S Hardware • 788 Amsterdam Ave [98th]
- Columbus Distributors • 687 Columbus Ave [93rd]
- Garcia Hardware Store • 995 Columbus Ave [109th]
- Grand Metro Home Centers • 2554 Broadway [96th]
- Leo Hardware • 716 Amsterdam Ave [95th]
- Mike's Lumber Store • 254 W 88th St [B'way]
- World Houseware • 2617 Broadway [99th]

Liquor Stores

- 86th Corner Wine & Liquor • 536 Columbus Ave [86th]
- Best Liquor & Wine • 2648 Broadway [100th]
- Columbus Avenue Wine & Spirits • 730 Columbus Ave [96th]
- Gotham Wines And Liquors • 2517 Broadway [94th]
- H&H Broadway Wine Center • 2669 Broadway [102nd]
- Hong Liquor Store • 2616 Broadway [99th]
- Martin Brothers Liquor Store • 2781 Broadway [107th]
- Mitchell's Wine & Liquor Store • 200 W 86th St [Amsterdam]
- Polanco Liquor Store • 948 Amsterdam Ave [107th]
- Riverside Liquor • 2746 Broadway [106th]
- Roma Discount Wine & Liquor • 737 Amsterdam Ave [96th]
- Turin Wines & Liquors • 609 Columbus Ave [89th]
- Vintage New York (Wine only) • 2492 Broadway [93rd]
- Westlane Wines & Liquor • 689 Columbus Ave [93rd]
- Wine Place • 2406 Broadway [88th]

Movie Theaters

- Leonard Nimoy Thalia • 2537 Broadway [95th]

Nightlife

- Abbey Pub • 237 W 105th St [B'way]
- Broadway Dive • 2662 Broadway [101st]
- The Ding Dong Lounge • 929 Columbus Ave [105th]
- Dive Bar • 732 Amsterdam Ave [96th]
- La Negrita • 999 Columbus Ave [109th]
- Night Café • 938 Amsterdam Ave [106th]
- The Parlour • 250 W 86th St [B'way]
- Roadhouse • 988 Amsterdam Ave [109th]
- Sip • 998 Amsterdam Ave [109th]
- Smoke • 2751 Broadway [106th]

Pet Shops

- Little Creatures • 770 Amsterdam Ave [97]
- Pet Market • 2821 Broadway [109th]
- Pet Stop • 564 Columbus Ave [87th]
- Petco • 2475 Broadway [92nd]
- Petland Discounts • 2708 Broadway [104]
- Petqua Ny Aquatics & Pet Warehouse • 2604 Broadway [98th]

Restaurants

- A • 947 Columbus Ave [106th]
- AIX • 2398 Broadway [88th]
- Awash • 947 Amsterdam Ave [106th]
- Barney Greengrass • 541 Amsterdam Ave [105th]
- Bella Luna • 584 Columbus Ave [86th]
- Café Con Leche • 726 Amsterdam Ave [96th]
- Carmine's • 2450 Broadway [91st]
- City Diner • 2441 Broadway [90th]
- Docks Oyster Bar • 2427 Broadway [90th]
- Flor de Mayo • 2651 Broadway [101st]
- Gabriela's • 688 Columbus Ave [94th]
- Gennaro • 665 Amsterdam Ave [92nd]
- Henry's • 2745 Broadway [105th]
- Jerusalem Restaurant • 2715 Broadway [104th]
- Lemongrass Grill • 2534 Broadway [95th]
- Mary Ann's • 2452 Broadway [91st]
- Miss Mamie's Spoonbread Too • 366 W 110th St [Manhattan]
- Pampa • 768 Amsterdam Ave [98th]
- Popover Café • 551 Amsterdam Ave [87th]
- Restaurant Broadway • 2664 Broadway [101st]
- Saigon Grill • 620 Amsterdam Ave [90th]
- Talia's Steakhouse • 668 Amsterdam Ave [93rd]
- Trattoria Pesce & Pasta • 625 Columbus Ave [91st]

Shopping

- Ann Taylor • 2380 Broadway [87th]
- Banana Republic • 2360 Broadway [86th]
- Ben & Jerry's • 2360 Broadway [104th]
- Gothic Cabinet Craft • 2652 Broadway [101st]
- Gourmet Garage • 2567 Broadway [87th]
- Health Nuts • 2611 Broadway [99th]
- Janovic • 2680 Broadway [102nd]
- Joon's Fine Seafood • 774 Amsterdam Ave [98th]
- Metro Bicycles • 231 W 96th St [B'way]
- Mugi Pottery • 993 Amsterdam Ave [109th]
- New York Flowers & Plant Shed • 209 W 96th St [Amsterdam]
- Planet Kids • 2688 Broadway [103rd]

Video Rental

- Blockbuster • 2510 Broadway [94th]
- Blockbuster • 2689 Broadway [103rd]
- Movie Place • 237 W 105th St [B'way]

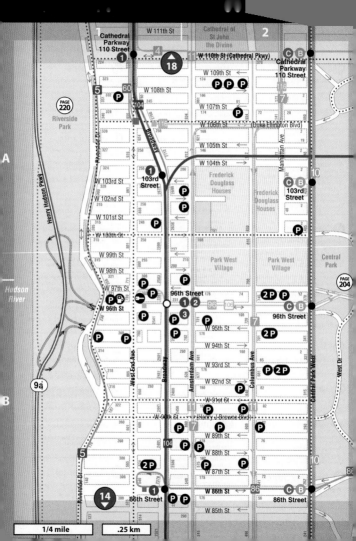

The 96th Street Transverse is by far the best way to cross Central Park. And isn't it nice that the Upper West Side has two separate subway lines?

14 15
11 12 13

Ma

Subways

1 2 3 .... 96 St
1 .... 103 St
1 .... 86 St
B C .... 103 St
B C .... 86 St
B C .... 96 St

Bus Lines

10 .... Seventh Ave/Central Park W
104 .... Broadway
106 .... 106th St Crosstown
11 .... Columbus Ave/Amsterdam Ave
116 .... 116th St Crosstown
5 .... Fifth Ave/Sixth Ave/Riverside Dr
60 .... LaGuardia Airport
7 .... Columbus Ave/Amsterdam Ave
86 .... 86th St Crosstown
96 .... 96th St Crosstown

Bike Lanes

- • • • Marked Bike Lanes
- • • • Recommended Route
- • • • Greenway

Car Rental

• **AAMCAR** • 303 W 96th St [West End]

Gas Stations

• **Exxon** • 303 W 96th St [West End] ⏱

Parking

Map 19 • Upper East Side / East Harlem

The northern Upper East Side, known as "Yorkville," has changed since German and Austro-Hungarian immigrants heavily populated it. Nowadays, it's home to a variety of folks, including recent college grads, seniors, young families, and Wall Streeters. Despite the continual sprout of residential high-rises, many relatively affordable walk-ups still remain.

24-Hour Pharmacies

- **CVS Pharmacy** • 1622 Third Ave [91st]
- **Duane Reade** • 1231 Madison Ave [88th]
- **Duane Reade** • 125 E 86th St [Park]
- **Duane Reade** • 1675 Third Ave [93rd]
- **Duane Reade** • 401 E 86th St [1st Av]
- **Rite Aid** • 146 E 86th St [Lex]

Bagels

- **Bagel Bob's** • 1638 York Ave [86th]
- **Bagel Express** • 1804 Second Ave [93rd]
- **Bagel Mill** • 1700 First Ave [88th]
- **Corner Bagel Market** • 1324 Lexington Ave [88th]
- **New York Hot Bagel** • 1585 Third Ave [89th]
- **Tal Bagels** • 3 86th St [2nd Av]

Banks

AT • Atlantic (ATM) • Gristedes • 1343 Lexington Ave [89th]
AT • Atlantic (ATM) • Gristedes • 205 E 96th St
AT • Atlantic (ATM) • Gristedes • 350 E 86th St [2nd Av]
BA • Bank of America (ATM) • 1276 Lexington Ave [86th]
BA • Bank of America (ATM) • 1538 Third Ave [86th]
CH • Chase • 12 E 86th St [5th Av]
CH • Chase • 126 E 86th St [Lex]
CH • Chase • 1641 Third St [3rd Av]
CH • Chase • 2065 Second Ave [106th]
CH • Chase • 255 E 86th St [2nd Av]
CH • Chase • 453 E 86th St [York Ave]
CI • Citibank • 123 E 86th St [Lex]
CI • Citibank • 1275 Madison Ave [91st]
CS • City and Suburban FSB • 345 E 86th St [2nd Av]
EM • Emigrant • 1270 Lexington Ave [86th]
FF • Fourth Federal Savings • 1751 Second Ave [91st]
HS • HSBC • 186 E 86th St [3rd Av]
HS • HSBC • 45 E 89th St [Madison]
CU • Municipal Credit Union (ATM) • Metropolitan Hospital • 1901 First Ave [97th]
NF • North Fork • 1536 Third Ave [86th]
WM • Washington Mutual • 1221 Madison Ave [86th]

Community Gardens

Emergency Rooms

- **Metropolitan** • 1901 First Ave [97th]
- **Mt Sinai Medical Center** • 1468 Madison Ave [101st]

Landmarks

- **Cooper-Hewitt Museum** • 2 E 91st St [5th]
- **Glaser's Bake Shop** • 1670 First Ave [87th]
- **Gracie Mansion** • Carl Schulz Park & 88th St

- **Henderson Place** • East End Ave & E 86th St
- **Jewish Museum** • 1109 Fifth Ave [92nd]
- **Museo del Barrio** • Fifth Ave & 104th St
- **Museum of the City of New York** • Fifth Ave & 103rd St
- **Old Municipal Asphalt Plant (Asphalt Green)** • 90th St & FDR Dr
- **Papaya King** • 179 E 86th St [3rd Av]
- **Schaller & Weber** • 1654 Second Ave [86th]
- **Solomon R Guggenheim Museum** • 1071 Fifth Ave [88th]
- **St Nicholas Russian Orthodox Cathedral** • 15 E 97th St [5th Av]

Libraries

- **96th Street** • 112 E 96th St [Park]
- **New York Academy of Medicine Library** • 1216 Fifth Ave [102nd]

Police

- **23rd Precinct** • 162 E 102nd St [3rd Av]

Post Offices

- **Yorkville** • 1617 Third Ave [91st]

Schools

- **Academy of Environmental Science Secondary High (M635)** • 410 E 100th St [1st Av]
- **Amber Charter** • 220 E 106th St [3rd Av]
- **The Bilingual Bicultural School (M182)** • 219 E 109th St [3rd Av]
- **Ballet Academy East** • 1651 Third Ave [92]
- **Brick Church** • 62 E 92nd St [Madison]
- **Central Park East I Elementary** • 1573 Madison Ave [106th]
- **Central Park East II (M964)** • 19 E 103rd St [5th Av]
- **Central Park East Secondary** • 1573 Madison Ave [106th]
- **Convent of the Sacred Heart** • 1 E 91st St [5th Av]
- **Dalton** • 108 E 89th St [Park]
- **East Harlem Block** • 1615 Madison Ave [108th]
- **East Harlem School at Exodus House** • 309 E 103rd St [2nd Av]
- **Harbor Science & Arts Charter** • 1 E 104th St [5th Av]
- **Heritage** • 1680 Lexington Ave [105th]
- **HS 580 Richard Green High School of Teaching** • 421 E 88th St [1st Av]
- **Hunter College Elementary** • 71 E 94th St [Madison]
- **Hunter College High** • 71 E 94th St [Madison]
- **JHS 013 Jackie Robinson** • 1573 Madison Ave [106th]
- **JHS 099 Julio De Burgos School & Environmental Science** • 410 E 100th St [1st Av]
- **La Scuola D'Italia Guglielmo M** • 12 E 96th St [5th Av]
- **Life Sciences Secondary** • 320 E 96th St [2nd Av]

- **Lower Trevor Day** • 11 E 89th St [5th Av]
- **Manhattan Country** • 7 E 96th St [5th Av]
- **Mount Sinai School of Medicine** • 1 Gustave Levy Pl [5th Av]
- **MS 224 Manhattan East Center for Arts & Academics** • 410 E 100th St [1st Av]
- **National Academy of Fine Arts** • 5 E 89th St [5th Av]
- **Nightingale-Bamford** • 20 E 92nd St [5th Av]
- **Our Lady of Good Counsel** • 323 E 91st St [2nd Av]
- **Park East High** • 230 E 105th St [3rd Av]
- **PS 050 Vito Marcantonio** • 433 E 100th St [1st Av]
- **PS 072** • 131 E 104th St [Park]
- **PS 077 Lower Lab** • 1700 Third Ave [95th]
- **PS 083 Luis Munoz Rivera** • 219 E 109th St [3rd Av]
- **PS 108 Angelo Del Toro** • 1615 Madison Ave [108th]
- **PS 109 Century** • 410 E 100th St [1st Av]
- **PS 146 Ann M Short** • 421 E 106th St [1st Av]
- **PS 169 Robert F Kennedy** • 110 E 88th St [Park]
- **PS 171 Patrick Henry** • 19 E 103rd St [5th Av]
- **PS 198 Isador and Ida Straus** • 1700 Third Ave [95th]
- **Reece** • 180 E 93rd St [3rd Av]
- **School of Cooperative Technical Education** • 321 E 96th St [2nd Av]
- **Solomon Schechter** • 50 E 87th St [Madison]
- **Spence** • 22 E 91st St [5th Av]
- **St Bernard's** • 4 E 98th St [5th Av]
- **St David's** • 12 E 89th St [5th Av]
- **St Francis de Sales** • 116 E 97th St [Park]
- **St Joseph Yorkville** • 420 E 87th St [1st Av]
- **St Lucy's Academy** • 340 E 104th St [2nd Av]
- **Tag Young Scholars JHS (M012)** • 240 E 109th St [3rd Av]
- **The Trevor Day School** • 11 E 89th St [5th Av]
- **Tito Puente Educational Complex (M117)** • 240 E 109th St [3rd Av]
- **Young Women's Leadership High** • 105 E 106th St [Park]

Supermarkets

- **Associated** • 1486 Lexington Ave [96th]
- **Associated** • 1635 Lexington Ave [103rd]
- **Associated** • 1968 Second Ave [101st]
- **C-Town** • 1721 First Ave [89th]
- **Food Emporium** • 1211 Madison Ave [87th]
- **Food Emporium** • 1660 Second Ave [86th]
- **Gourmet Garage** • 1245 Park Ave [96th]
- **Gristede's** • 1227 E 86th St [Park]
- **Gristede's** • 1343 Lexington Ave [90th]
- **Gristede's** • 1356 Lexington Ave [90th]
- **Gristede's** • 1637 York Ave [86th]
- **Gristede's** • 1644 York Ave [86th]
- **Gristede's** • 202 E 96th St [3rd Av]
- **Gristede's Mega Store** • 350 E 86th St [2nd Av]
- **Key Food** • 1769 Second Ave [92nd]
- **Met Food** • 235 E 106th St [3rd Av]
- **Pioneer** • 1407 Lexington Ave [92nd]
- **Pioneer** • 2076 First Ave [106th]

Map 19 · Upper East Side / East Harlem

Mistakenly perceived as a culinary wasteland, this area abounds with great eats, from cozy Italian (Pinocchio) to candlelit Brazilian (Zebu Grill). Although 86th Street resembles a suburban strip mall with ho-hum, omnipresent retailers like Best Buy and Banana Republic, there are plenty of independent shops scattered along the side streets.

Coffee

- **Dunkin' Donuts** • 1276 Lexington Ave [86th]
- **Dunkin' Donuts** • 1391 Madison Ave [97]
- **Dunkin' Donuts** • 1392 Lexington Ave [92]
- **Dunkin' Donuts** • 1630 Madison Ave [109]
- **Dunkin' Donuts** • 1760 Second Ave [92nd]
- **Dunkin' Donuts** • 1880 Third Ave [104th]
- **Dunkin' Donuts** • 345 E 93rd St [2nd Av]
- **Juliano Gourmet Coffee** • 1378 Lexington Ave [91st]
- **Just in Time Café** • 119 E 96th St [Park]
- **Starbucks** • 120 E 87th St [Park]
- **Starbucks** • 1378 Madison Ave [96th]
- **Starbucks** • 1642 Third Ave [92nd]
- **Starbucks** • 400 E 90th St [1st Av]
- **Viand Coffee Shop** • 300 E 86th St [2nd]

Copy Shops

- **Best Photo 96** • 1387 Madison Ave [96th]
- **Copy Quest** • 163 E 92nd St [Lex]
- **Desktop USA** • 1476 Lexington Ave [95th]
- **Mail Boxes Etc** • 1369 Madison Ave [96th]
- **Mail Boxes Etc** • 1710 First Ave [88th]
- **Orbis Brynmore Lithographers** • 1735 Second Ave [90th]
- **Staples** • 1280 Lexington Ave [86th]
- **The UPS Store** • 1324 Lexington Ave [88th]
- **The UPS Store** • 1636 Third Ave [92nd]
- **The UPS Store** • 217 E 86th St [3rd Av]

Gyms

- **92nd Street Y–May Center** • 1395 Lexington Ave [92nd]
- **Bally Total Fitness** • 144 E 86th St [Lex]
- **Bally Total Fitness** • 1915 Third Ave [106th]
- **Carnegie Park Swim & Health Club** • 200 E 94th St [3rd Av]
- **Curves (Women only)** • 1711 First Ave [89th]
- **Monterey Sports Club** • 175 E 96th St [Lex]
- **NYSC** • 151 E 86th St [Lex]
- **NYSC** • 1637 Third Ave [92nd]
- **Synergy Fitness Clubs** • 1781 Second Ave [92nd]

Hardware Stores

- **Century Lumber** • 1875 Second Ave [90th]
- **El Barrio Hardware** • 1876 Third Ave [104th]
- **Feldman's Housewares** • 1304 Madison Ave [92nd]
- **Johnny's Hardware** • 1708 Lexington Ave [107th]
- **K&G Hardware & Supply** • 401 E 90th St [1st Av]
- **Morales Brothers Hardware** • 1959 Third Ave [108th]
- **Service Hardware** • 1338 Lexington Ave [89th]
- **Wankel's Hardware & Paint** • 1573 Third [88th]

Liquor Stores

- **86th Street Wine & Liquor** • 306 E 86th St [2nd Av]
- **Best Cellars (Wine only)** • 1291 Lexington Ave [97th]
- **East 87th Street Wine Traders** • 1693 Second Ave [88th]
- **Edwin's Wines & Liquors** • 176 E 103rd St [3rd Av]
- **Explorers Wines & Liquors** • 1755 Lexington Ave [107th]
- **House of J&H** • 2073 Second Ave [106th]
- **K&D Wines & Spirits** • 1366 Madison Ave [96th]
- **Mercedes Liquor Store** • 102 E 103rd St [Park]
- **Mister Wright** • 1593 Third Ave [90th]
- **Normandie Wines (Wine only)** • 1834 Second Ave [95th]
- **Park East Liquors** • 1657 York Ave [87th]
- **Uptown Wine Shop (Wine only)** • 1361 Lexington Ave [90th]
- **West Coast Wine & Liquor** • 1440 Lexington Ave [94th]
- **Yorkshire Wines & Spirits** • 1646 First Ave [86th]

Movie Theaters

- **92nd Street Y** • Lexington Ave & 92nd St
- **City Cinemas: East 86th Street** • 210 E 86th St [3rd Av]
- **Loews Cineplex Orpheum** • 1538 Third Ave [87th]
- **Solomon R Guggenheim Museum** • 1071 Fifth Ave [88th]

Nightlife

- **Auction House** • 300 E 89th St [2nd Av]
- **Big Easy** • 1768 Second Ave [92nd]
- **Cavatappo Wine Bar** • 1728 Second Ave [90th]
- **Kinsale Tavern** • 1672 Third Ave [94th]
- **Marty O'Brien's** • 1696 Second Ave [88th]
- **Rathbones Pub** • 1702 Second Ave [88th]
- **Tool Box** • 1742 Second Ave [91st]

Pet Shops

- **Furry Paws** • 1705 Third Ave [96th]
- **Petco** • 147 E 86th St [Lex]
- **Petland Discounts** • 304 E 86th St [2nd]
- **Posh Paws Tall & Small** • 1758 First Ave [91st]
- **World Wide Kennel** • 1661 First Ave [86]

Restaurants

- **Barking Dog Luncheonette** • 1678 Third Ave [94th]
- **Bella Cucina** • 1293 Lexington Ave [87th]
- **Carino** • 1710 Second Ave [89th]
- **Chef Ho's Peking Duck Grill** • 1720 Second Ave [89th]
- **Choux Factory** • 1685 First Ave [87th]
- **Cilantro** • 1712 Second Ave [89th]
- **El Paso Taqueria** • 1642 Lexington Ave [104]
- **Elaine's** • 1703 Second Ave [88th]
- **Jackson Hole** • 1270 Madison Ave [91st]
- **Kebap G** • 1830 Second Ave [94th]
- **Knick's Lunch East** • 1732 Second Ave [90] ⊠
- **La Fonda Boricua** • 169 E 106th St [Lex]
- **Luca Restaurant** • 1712 First Ave [89th]
- **Nick's Restaurant & Pizzeria** • 1814 Second Ave [94th]
- **Nina's Argentinean Pizzeria** • 1750 Second Ave [91st]
- **Papaya King** • 179 E 86th St [3rd Av]
- **Pinocchio** • 1748 First Ave [91st]
- **Pintaile's Pizza** • 26 E 91st St [5th Av]
- **Sabora Mexico** • 1744 First Ave [90th]
- **Saigon Grill** • 1700 Second Ave [88th]
- **Sarabeth's** • 1295 Madison Ave [92nd]
- **Viand Grill** • 300 E 86th St [2nd Av]
- **York Grill** • 1690 York Ave [89th]
- **Yura & Company** • 1292 Madison Ave [92nd]
- **Yura & Company** • 1645 Third Ave [92nd]
- **Yura & Company** • 1659 Third Ave [93rd]
- **Zebu Grill** • 305 E 92nd St [2nd Av]

Shopping

- **Best Buy** • 1280 Lexington Ave [86th]
- **Blacker & Kooby** • 1204 Madison Ave [88th]
- **Blades Board & Skate** • 120 W 72nd St [Columbus]
- **Blue Tree** • 1283 Madison Ave [91st]
- **Capezio** • 1651 Third Ave [92nd]
- **The Children's General Store** • 168 E 91st St [Lex]
- **Ciao Bella Gelato** • 27 E 92nd St [Madison]
- **Cooper-Hewitt National Design Museum Shop** • 2 E 91st St [5th Av]
- **Coup de Coeur** • 1628 Third Ave [91st]
- **Doyle New York** • 175 E 87th St [3rd Av]
- **Eli's Vinegar Factory** • 431 E 91st St [1st]
- **Face Stockholm** • 1263 Madison Ave [90th]
- **Glaser's Bake Shop** • 1670 First Ave [87th]
- **Housing Works Thrift Shop** • 1730 Second Ave [90th]
- **Kessie & Co** • 163 E 87th St [Lex]
- **La Tropezienne** • 2131 First Ave [110th]
- **Laytner's Linens** • 237 E 86th St [3rd Av]
- **MAD Vintage Couture & Designer Resale** • 167 E 87th St [Lex]
- **Marsha DD** • 1574 Third Ave [88th]
- **Martha Frances Mississippi Cheesecake** • 1707 Second Ave [88th]
- **Nellie M Boutique** • 1309 Lexington Ave [88th]
- **New York Replacement Parts Corp** • 1456 Lexington Ave [94th]
- **Orva** • 155 E 86th St [Lex]
- **Pickles, Olives Etc** • 1647 First Ave [86th]
- **Schaller & Weber** • 1654 Second Ave [86]
- **Schatzie's Prime Meats** • 1200 Madison Ave [87th]
- **Seraphim's Ark** • 100 E 96th St [Park]
- **Service Hardware** • 1338 Lexington Ave [89th]
- **Shatzi The Shop** • 243 E 86th St [3rd Av]
- **Soccer Sport Supply** • 1745 First Ave [90th]
- **Spence-Chapin Thrift Shop** • 1850 Second Ave [96th]
- **Steve Madden** • 150 E 86th St [Lex]
- **Super Runners Shop** • 1337 Lexington Ave [89th]
- **Temptations** • 1737 York Ave [90th]
- **Two Little Red Hens** • 1652 Second Ave [86th]
- **Williams-Sonoma** • 1175 Madison Ave [86th]

Video Rental

- **Blockbuster** • 1646 First Ave [86th]
- **Blockbuster** • 1707 Third Ave [96th]
- **Blockbuster** • 1924 Third Ave [106th]
- **Movie Bank USA** • E 86th St & First Ave ⊠
- **We Deliver Videos** • 1716 First Ave [89th]

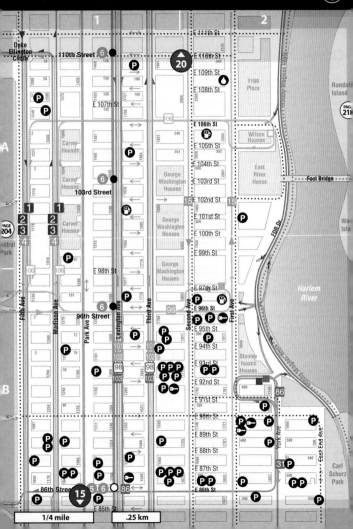

With the construction finally underway for the much-anticipated Second Avenue Subway, there is hope for a population that, for generations, has made the ceremonial schlep all the way to Lex just to sardine itself on the East Side's sole subway line—the Manhattan version of *March of the Penguins*.

Subways

4 5 6 .... 86 St
6 .... 96 St
6 .... 103 St

Bus Lines

1 2 3 .... Fifth Ave/Madison Ave
101 .... Third Ave/Lexington Ave
102 .... Third Ave/Lexington Ave
103 .... Third Ave/Lexington Ave
106 .... 96th St/106th St Crosstown
15 .... First Ave/Second Ave
31 .... York Ave/57th St
4 .... Fifth Ave/Madison Ave/Broadway
86 .... 86th St Crosstown
96 .... 96th St Crosstown
98 .... Washington Heights/Midtown

Bike Lanes

• • • Marked Bike Lanes
• • • Recommended Route
• • • Greenway

Car Rental

• **Avis** • 420 E 90th St [1st Av]
• **Budget** • 152 E 87th St [Lex]
• **Enterprise** • 1833 First Ave [95th]
• **Hertz** • 412 E 90th St [1st Av]

Car Washes

• **LMC Car Wash** • 334 E 109th St [2nd Av]

Gas Stations

• **Amoco** • 1599 Lexington Ave [101st]
• **BP** • 1855 First Ave [96th]
• **Getty** • 348 E 106th St [1st Av]

Parking

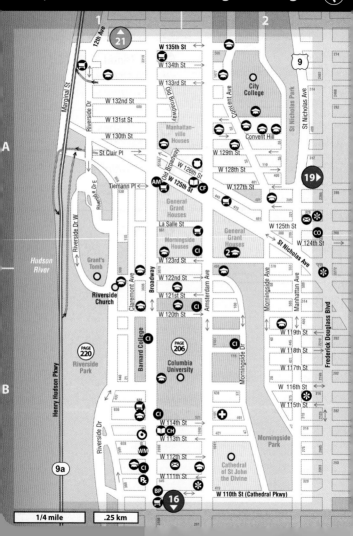

Map 18 • Columbia / Morningside Heights N

Columbia / Morningside Heights, like many of its student residents, is still trying to find itself: Is it edgy and diverse, or polished and posh? Recent gentrification suggests the latter, although some areas maintain their grittier facades. Don't miss the breathtaking Cathedral of St. John the Divine.

24-Hour Pharmacies

- **Duane Reade** • 2864 Broadway [111th] ☺

Bagels

- **Nussbaum & Wu** • 2897 Broadway [113th]

Banks

AM • **Amalgamated** • 564 W 125th St [Old B'way]
BP • **Banco Popular** • 2852 Broadway [111th]
CF • **Carver Federal Savings (ATM)** • 503 W 125th St [Amsterdam]
CH • **Chase** • 2824 Broadway [109th]
CI • **Citibank** • 1310 Amsterdam Ave [La Salle]
CI • **Citibank** • 2861 Broadway [111th]
CI • **Citibank (ATM)** • Teachers College Columbia University • 2922 Broadway [114th]
CI • **Citibank (ATM)** • Barnard College• 3009 Broadway [119th]
CI • **Citibank (ATM)** • 420 W 118th St [Morningside Dr]
CI • **Citibank (ATM)** • 525 W 120th St [Amsterdam]
CO • **Commerce** • 300 W 125th St [F Douglass]
WM • **Washington Mutual** • 2875 Broadway [112th]

Community Gardens

Emergency Rooms

- **St Luke's** • 1111 Amsterdam Ave [115th] ☺

Landmarks

- **Cathedral of St John the Divine** • 112th St & Amsterdam Ave
- **City College** • 138th St & Convent Ave
- **Columbia University** • 116th St & Broadway
- **Grant's Tomb** • 122nd St & Riverside Dr
- **Riverside Church** • 490 Riverside Dr [122nd]

Libraries

- **George Bruce** • 518 W 125th St [Amsterdam]
- **Morningside Heights Library** • 2900 Broadway [113th]

Police

- **26th Precinct** • 520 W 126th St [Amsterdam]

Post Offices

- **Columbia University** • 534 W 112th St [Amsterdam]
- **Manhattanville** • 365 W 125th St [Manhattan]

Schools

- **A Philip Randolph Campus High** • 443 W 135th St [Convent]
- **Annunciation** • 461 W 131st St [Amsterdam]
- **Bank Street College of Education** • 610 W 112th St [B'way]
- **Barnard College** • 3009 Broadway [119th]
- **Cathedral** • 1047 Amsterdam Ave [111th]
- **City College** • 138th Street and Convent Ave
- **Columbia University** • 2960 Broadway [116th]
- **The Cooke Center for Learning** • 475 Riverside Dr [120th]
- **Corpus Christi** • 535 W 121st St [Amsterdam]
- **IS 195 Roberto Clemente** • 625 W 133rd St [B'way]
- **IS 223 Mott Hall** • 71 Convent Ave [130th]
- **IS 286 Renaissance Military** • 509 W 129th St [Amsterdam]
- **Jewish Theological Seminary of America** • 3080 Broadway [122nd]
- **Kipp Starr College Preparatory (M726)** • 433 W 123rd St [Morningside Av]
- **Manhattan School of Music** • 120 Claremont Ave [122nd]
- **Powell MS for Law & Social Justice** • 509 W 129th St [Amsterdam]
- **PS 036 Margaret Douglas** • 123 Morningside Dr [121st]
- **PS 125 Ralph Bunche** • 425 W 123rd St [Morningside Av]
- **PS 129 John H Finley** • 425 W 130th St [St Nicholas Ter]
- **PS 161 Pedro A Campos** • 499 W 133rd St [Amsterdam]
- **PS 180 Hugo Newman** • 370 W 120th St [Manhattan]
- **St Hilda and Hugh** • 619 W 114th St [B'way]
- **St Joseph's School of the Holy Family** • 168 Morningside Ave [126th]
- **Teachers College, Columbia University** • 525 W 120th St [Amsterdam]
- **Thurgood Marshall Academy Lower** • 425 W 130th St [St Nicholas Ter]

Supermarkets

- **Associated** • 2943 Broadway [115th]
- **C-Town** • 3320 Broadway [134th]
- **C-Town** • 560 W 125th St [Old B'way]
- **Citarella** • 461 W 125th St [Amsterdam]
- **D'Ag Fresh Market** • 2828 Broadway [110th]
- **Fairway Market** • 2328 Twelfth Ave [133rd]
- **Met Food** • 1316 Amsterdam Ave [La Salle]

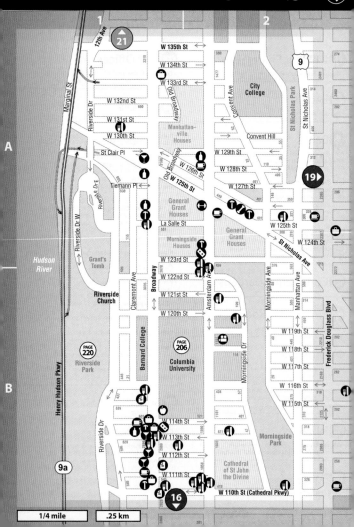

Map 18 • **Columbia / Morningside Heights** N

For coffee, toiletries, and such, it is quickest to shop Broadway south of 116th Street. Options thin out as you head north or east. For an outdoor brunch, savor an omelet at Le Monde. Cozy Saurin Parke provides free wi-fi, and chummy 1020 Bar offers darts and pool.

Coffee

- **Dunkin' Donuts** • 1342 Amsterdam Ave [125th]
- **Dunkin' Donuts** • 321 W 125th St [F Douglass]
- **Jimbo's Coffee Shop** • 1345 Amsterdam Ave [125th]
- **Oren's Daily Roast** • 2882 Broadway [112th]
- **Saurin Parke Café** • 301 W 110th St [F Douglass]
- **Starbucks** • 2853 Broadway [111th]
- **Starbucks** • 2929 Broadway [115th]

Copy Shops

- **Broadway Copy Center** • 3062 Broadway [121st]
- **The UPS Store** • 603 W 115th St [B'way]
- **The Village Copier** • 2872 Broadway [112th] ♿

Farmer's Markets

- **Columbia (8 am-6 pm year round, Sun 8am-6pm May-Dec)** • Broadway b/w 114 & 115th Sts

Gyms

- **Lucille Roberts Health Club (Women only)** • 505 W 125th St [Amsterdam]

Hardware Stores

- **Academy Hardware & Supply** • 2869 Broadway [112th]
- **Clinton Supply** • 1256 Amsterdam Ave [122nd]
- **Columbia Hardware** • 2905 Broadway [113th]
- **Philip Glick Supply** • 421 W 125th St [F Douglass]
- **TriBoro Hardware** • 433 W 125th St [Morningside Av]
- **University Houseware and Hardware** • 2901 Broadway [113th]

Liquor Stores

- **Amsterdam Liquor Mart** • 1356 Amsterdam Ave [126th]
- **Caro Wines & Liquor** • 3139 Broadway [La Salle]
- **International Wines and Spirits** • 2903 Broadway [113th]
- **Wine & Liquors Authority** • 574 W 125th St [B'way]

Movie Theaters

- **Italian Academy** • 1161 Amsterdam Ave [117th]

Nightlife

- **Cotton Club** • 656 W 125th St [St Clair Pl]
- **Heights Bar & Grill** • 2867 Broadway [112th st]
- **Nacho Mama's Kitchen Bar** • 2893 Broadway [113th]
- **West End** • 2911 Broadway [114th]

Pet Shops

- **NYC Pet Place** • 431 W 125th St [Manhattan]

Restaurants

- **Bistro Ten 18** • 1018 Amsterdam Ave [110th]
- **Dinosaur Bar-B-Que** • 646 W 131st St [B'way]
- **Hungarian Pastry Shop** • 1030 Amsterdam Ave [111th]
- **Kitchenette** • 1272 Amsterdam Ave [123rd]
- **Koronet Pizza** • 2848 Broadway [111th]
- **Le Monde** • 2885 Broadway [112th]
- **M&G Soul Food Diner** • 383 W 125th St [Morningside Av]
- **Massawa** • 1239 Amsterdam Ave [121st]
- **Max** • 1274 Amsterdam Ave [123rd]
- **Mill Korean** • 2895 Broadway [113th]
- **Ollie's** • 2957 Broadway [116th]
- **P + W Sandwich Shop** • 1030 Amsterdam Ave [111th]
- **Pisticci** • 125 La Salle St [B'way]
- **Sezz Medi** • 1260 Amsterdam Ave [122nd]
- **Symposium** • 544 W 113th St [Amsterdam]
- **Terrace in the Sky** • 400 W 119th St [Morningside Dr]
- **Toast** • 3157 Broadway [La Salle]
- **V&T Pizzeria** • 1024 Amsterdam Ave [110th]

Shopping

- **El Mundo** • 3300 Broadway [133rd]
- **JAS Mart** • 2847 Broadway [111th]
- **Kim's Mediapolis** • 2906 Broadway [114th]
- **Labyrinth Books** • 536 W 112th St [Amsterdam]
- **Mondel Chocolates** • 2913 Broadway [114th]

Video Rental

- **Blockbuster** • 1280 Amsterdam Ave [123rd]
- **Kim's Mediapolis** • 2906 Broadway [114th]

Map 18 • Columbia / Morningside Heights

Parking in Manhattan is never easy, but its not as tricky here. The same goes for driving, and Riverside Drive remains a smart alternative to a congested West Side Highway. The local 1 subway never keeps you waiting long, but the B and C only offer limited service.

Subways

1 .... 116th St Columbia University
1 .... 125th St
1 .... Cathedral Pkwy (110th St)
B **C** .... 135th St
A **C** **B** **D** .... 125th St

Bus Lines

100 .... 86th St Crosstown
101 .... 96th St Crosstown
104 .... 106th St Crosstown
11 .... Columbus Ave/Amsterdam Ave
18 .... Convent Ave
3 .... Fifth Ave/Madison Ave
4 .... Fifth Ave/Sixth Ave/Riverside Dr
5 .... Columbus Ave/Amsterdam Ave
Bx15 .... 116th St Crosstown

Bike Lanes

- • • • Marked Bike Lanes
- • • • Recommended Route
- • • • Greenway

Car Rental

• **U-Haul** • 3270 Broadway

Gas Stations

• **BP** • 3225 Broadway [129th]
• **Independent** • 619 W 125th St [129th] ⏰
• **Mobil** • 3260 Broadway [131st] ⏰

Parking

125th Street is the lifeline of this neighborhood, a street known for the Apollo, a zillion stores, and a place for players to strut their stuff. Working class and true Harlem, this is a solid nabe for New Yorkers who don't mind a little gruff, and possible run-ins with Bill Clinton.

 $ Banks

BP • Banco Popular • 231 W 125th St [7th Av]
BA • Bank of America • 215 W 125th St [7th Av]
BA • Bank of America (ATM) • 102 W 116th St [Lenox]
CF • Carver Federal Savings • 142 Lenox Ave [117th]
CF • Carver Federal Savings • 75 W 125th St [Lenox]
CH • Chase • 2218 Fifth Ave [135th]
CH • Chase • 300 W 135th St [F Douglass]
CH • Chase • 322 W 125th St [F Douglass]
CH • Chase • 55 W 125th St [Lenox]
CI • Citibank • 201 W 125th St [7th Av]
MT • M&T • 420 Lenox Ave [131st]
CU • Municipal Credit Union (ATM) • 2518 Frederick Douglass Blvd [134th]
NF • North Fork • 2310 Frederick Douglass Blvd [124th]
WM • Washington Mutual • 105 W 125th St [Lenox]

❊ Community Gardens

○ Landmarks

• **Alhambra Theatre and Ballroom •** 2116 Adam Clayton Powell Jr Blvd [121st]
• **Apollo Theater •** 253 W 125th St [F Douglass]
• **Duke Ellington Circle •** 110th St & Fifth Ave
• **Harlem YMCA •** 180 W 135th St [Lenox]
• **Langston Hughes Place •** 20 E 127th St [5th Av]
• **Marcus Garvey Park •** E 120-124th Sts & Madison Ave
• **Sylvia's •** 328 Lenox Ave [126th]

📖 Libraries

• **115th St (temporary location) •** 2011 Adam Clayton Powell Jr Blvd [121st]
• **115th Street (temporarily closed) •** 203 W 115th St [7th]
• **Harlem •** 9 W 124th St [5th Av]

🚓 Police

• **28th Precinct •** 2271 Frederick Douglass Blvd [122nd]
• **32nd Precinct •** 250 W 135th St [7th Av]

✉ Post Offices

• **Morningside •** 232 W 116th St [7th Av]

🏫 Schools

• **Christ Crusader Academy •** 302 W 124th St [F Douglass]
• **College of New Rochelle Rosa Parks Campus •** 144 W 125th St [Lenox]
• **Fellowship of Learning •** 70 W 126th St [Lenox]
• **Frederick Douglass Academy II •** 215 W 114th St [7th Av]
• **Harlem Children's Zone/Promise Academy Charter M284 •** 35 E 125th St [Madison]
• **Harlem Children's Zone/Promise Academy II Charter •** 220 W 121st St [7th Av]
• **Harlem Renaissance High •** 22 E 128th St [5th Av]
• **Helene Fuld School of Nursing North •** 26 E 120th St [Madison]
• **Henry Highland Garnet •** 175 W 134th St [7th Av]
• **IS 275 •** 175 W 134th St [7th Av]
• **JA Reisenbach Charter (M701) •** 257 W 117th St [F Douglass]
• **JHS 088 Wadleigh •** 215 W 114th St [7th Av]
• **Opportunity Charter •** 222 W 134th St [7th Av]
• **Pregnant and Parenting Students •** 22 E 128th St [5th Av]
• **PS 041 Family Academy •** 240 W 113th St [7th Av]
• **PS 076 A Philip Randolph •** 220 W 121st St [7th Av]
• **PS 092 Mary M Bethune Academy •** 222 W 134th St [7th Av]
• **PS 133 Fred R Moore •** 2121 Fifth Ave [130th]
• **PS 149 Sojourner Truth •** 41 W 117th St [Lenox]
• **PS 154 Harriet Tubman •** 250 W 127th St [7th Av]
• **PS 162 •** 34 W 118th St [5th Av]
• **PS 185 John M Langston •** 20 W 112th St [5th Av]
• **PS 208 Alain L Locke •** 21 W 111th St [5th Av]
• **PS 242M GP Brown Comp •** 134 W 122nd St [Lenox]
• **Rice High •** 74 W 124th St [Lenox]
• **Sister Clara Mohammed •** 102 W 116th St [Lenox]
• **Sisulu Children's Charter •** 125 W 115th St [Lenox]
• **St Aloysius •** 223 W 132nd St [7th Av]
• **Thurgood Marshall Academy •** 200 W 135th St [7th Av]
• **Wadleigh Arts High •** 215 W 114th St [7th Av]

🛒 Supermarkets

• **Associated •** 2170 Fifth Ave [132nd]
• **Associated •** 2296 Frederick Douglass Blvd [123rd]
• **Associated •** 448 Lenox Ave [132nd]
• **C-Town •** 2217 Adam Clayton Powell Jr Blvd [131st]
• **C-Town •** 24 W 135th St [Lenox]
• **Met Food •** 101 W 116th St [Lenox]
• **Met Food •** 238 W 116th St [7th Av]
• **Met Food •** 37 Lenox Ave [112th]
• **Pioneer •** 136 Lenox Ave [117th]

The Magic Johnson Multiplex is an awesome theater to attend for the added stimuli of audience interaction with the movie. For the best in Southern, down-home cooking, Amy Ruth's is the place to go. Try the pork chops, and order them swimming.

14 15
11 12 13

Ma

Coffee

- **Dunkin' Donuts** • 105 W 125th St [Lenox]
- **Dunkin' Donuts** • 53 W 116th St [Lenox]
- **Farafena Coffee Shop** • 219 W 116th St [Lenox]
- **Home Sweet Harlem Café** • 270 W 135th St [F Douglass]
- **Society Coffee & Juice** • 2104 Frederick Douglass Blvd [114th]
- **Starbucks** • 77 W 125th St [Lenox]

Copy Shops

- **Staples** • 105 W 125th St [Lenox]
- **The UPS Store** • 2216 Frederick Douglas Blvd [119th]
- **The UPS Store** • 55 W 116th St [Lenox]

Gyms

- **Curves (Women only)** • 2103 Frederick Douglass Blvd [114th]
- **New York Sports Clubs** • 2311 Frederick Douglass Blvd [124th]
- **YMCA Harlem** • 180 W 135th St [Lenox]

Hardware Stores

- **Citi General Hardware** • 100 St Nicholas Ave [115th]
- **Concordia Electrical & Plumbing** • 2297 Adam Clayton Powell Jr Blvd [135th]
- **Garcia Brothers Hardware** • 2258 Seventh Ave [133rd]
- **Harlem Locksmith** • 106 Lenox Ave [116th]
- **United Hardware** • 2160 Frederick Douglass Blvd [117th]
- **Virgo Houseware & Hardware** • 188 Lenox Ave [119th]

Liquor Stores

- **467 Lenox Liquors** • 467 Lenox Ave [133rd]
- **A&D Liquor** • 23 Lenox Ave [111th]
- **D&L Liquor** • 2178 Fifth Ave [132nd]
- **Fred's Wine & Liquors** • 77 Lenox Ave [114th]
- **Grand Liquors** • 2049 Frederick Douglass Blvd [111th]
- **Harlem Retail Wine & Liquor** • 1902 Adam Clayton Powell Jr Blvd [115th]
- **Harlem Vintage** • 2235 Frederick Douglass Blvd [121st]
- **Olympic Wine and Liquor** • 2391 Frederick Douglass Blvd [128th]
- **Palace Liquors** • 2215 Adam Clayton Powell Jr Blvd [131st]

Movie Theaters

- **Magic Johnson Harlem USA** • 300 W 125th St [F Douglass]

Nightlife

- **Apollo Theater** • 253 W 125th St [F Douglass]
- **Lenox Lounge** • 288 Lenox Ave [124th]

Pet Shops

- **Petland Discounts** • 56 W 117th St [Lenox]

Restaurants

- **African Kine Restaurant** • 256 W 116th St [F Douglass]
- **Amy Ruth's** • 113 W 116th St [Lenox]
- **Bayou** • 308 Lenox Ave [125th]
- **Ginger Restaurant** • 1400 Fifth Ave [115th]
- **Home Sweet Harlem Café** • 270 W 135th St [F Douglass]
- **IHOP** • 2294 Adam Clayton Powell Jr Blvd [135th] ♿
- **Keur Sokhna** • 225 W 116th St [7th Av]
- **Manna's Too** • 486 Lenox Ave [134th]
- **Native** • 101 W 118th St [Lenox]
- **Papaya King** • 121 W 125th St [Lenox]
- **Slice of Harlem** • 308 Lenox Ave [125th]
- **Sylvia's** • 328 Lenox Ave [126th]
- **Yvonne Yvonne** • 301 W 135th St [F Douglass]

Shopping

- **The Body Shop** • 1 E 125th St [5th Av]
- **Champs** • 208 W 125th St [7th Av]
- **Dr Jay's Harlem NYC** • 256 W 125th St [F Douglass]
- **H&M** • 125 W 125th St [Lenox]
- **Harlem Underground Clothing Co** • 2027 Fifth Ave [125th]
- **Harlemade** • 174 Lenox Ave [119th]
- **Jimmy Jazz** • 132 W 125th St [Lenox]
- **MAC Cosmetics** • 202 W 125th St [7th Av]
- **Malcolm Shabazz Harlem Market** • 58 W 116th St [Lenox]
- **Settepani** • 196 Lenox Ave [120th]
- **Studio Museum of Harlem Gift Shop** • 144 W 125th St [Lenox]
- **Wimp's Southern Style Bakery** • 29 W 125th St [5th Av]
- **Xukuma** • 183 Lenox Ave [119th]

Video Rental

- **Big Apple Video** • 1330 Fifth Ave [112th]
- **Blockbuster** • 121 W 125th St [Lenox]
- **Bus Stop Video** • 9 W 110th St [5th Av]
- **Movie Bank USA** • W 125th St & Frederick Douglas Blvd ♿

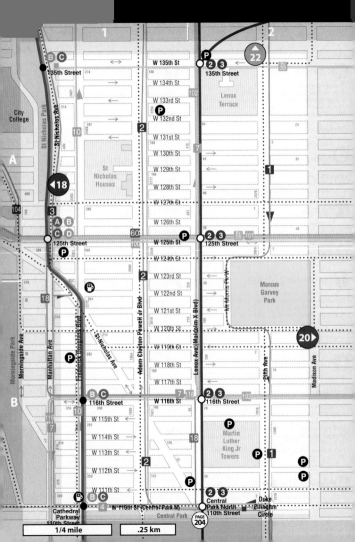

Do not use 125th as a crosstown route unless you like to sit in your car a lot and look at people moving faster than you. Use 135th or 110th instead. St. Nicholas Avenue has a nice bike path along its route.

14 15
11 12 13

Ma

Subways

2 **3** .... 116 St
2 **3** .... 125 St
2 **3** .... 135 St
2 **3** .... Central Park N (110 St)
B **C** .... 116 St
B **C** .... Cathedral Pkwy (110 St)

Bus Lines

1 .... Fifth Ave/Madison Ave
10 .... Seventh Ave/Eighth Ave/
Frederick Douglass Blvd
100 .... Amsterdam Ave/Broadway/125th St
101 ..... Third Ave/Lexington Ave/Amsterdam Ave
102 ..... Third Ave/Lexington Ave/Malcolm X Blvd
116 .... 116th St Crosstown
2 .... Fifth Ave/Madison Ave/Powell Blvd
4 .... Fifth Ave/Madison Ave/Broadway
60 .... LaGuardia Airport via 125th St
7 .... Columbus Ave/Amsterdam Ave/
Lenox Ave/Sixth Ave/Seventh Ave/Broadway
15 .... 125th St Crosstown
33 .... 135th St Crosstown

Bike Lanes

• • • Marked Bike Lanes
• • • Recommended Route

Gas Stations

• **Exxon** • 2040 Frederick Douglass Blvd [111th] ☼
• **Shell** • 235 St Nicholas Ave [122nd] ☼

P Parking

Rich and vibrant in history and culture, exploring El Barrio is highly recommended. Both Marcus Garvey and Jefferson Parks are excellent places to take a break, too.

Ma

$ Banks

AP • Apple • 124 E 125th St [Park]
BP • Banco Popular • 164 E 116th St [Lex]
BA • Bank of America • 157 E 125th St [Lex]
BA • Bank of America (ATM) • 2250 Third Ave [122nd]
CH • Chase • 160 E 125th St [Lex]
CI • Citibank • 2261 First Ave [116th]
WM • Washington Mutual • 103 E 125th St [Park]
WM • Washington Mutual • 179 E 116th St [3rd Av]

✺ Community Gardens

✚ Emergency Rooms

• **North General •** 1879 Madison Ave [122nd] ♿

○ Landmarks

• **Church of Our Lady of Mt Carmel •** 448 E 115th St [1st Av]
• **Harlem Courthouse •** 170 E 121st St [Lex]
• **Harlem Fire Watchtower •** Marcus Garvey Park
• **Keith Haring "Crack is Wack" Mural •** Second Ave & 127th St
• **Thomas Jefferson Swimming Pool •** 2180 First Ave [112th]

◲ Libraries

• **125th St •** 224 E 125th St [3rd Av]
• **Aguilar •** 174 E 110th St [Lex]

▣ Police

• **25th Precinct •** 120 E 119th St [Park]

✉ Post Offices

• **Oscar Garcia Rivera •** 153 E 110th St [Lex]
• **Triborough •** 167 E 124th St [Lex]

▤ Schools

• **All Saints •** 52 E 130th St [Madison]
• **Children's Storefront •** 70 E 129th St [Park]
• **The Choir Academy of Harlem •** 2005 Madison Ave [127th]
• **East Harlem Tech (M02P) •** 2351 First Ave [120th]
• **East Harlem Village Academy Charter (M709) •** 413 E 120th St [1st Av]
• **Harlem Day Charter •** 240 E 123rd St, 4th Fl [3rd Av]
• **Highway Christian Academy •** 132 E 111th St [Lex]
• **HS 435 Manhattan Center Math and Science •** 280 Pleasant Ave [115th]
• **Issac Newton JHS for Science & Math (M825) •** 260 Pleasant Ave [115th]
• **JHS 045 JC Roberts •** 2351 First Ave [120th]
• **Kappa II (M317) •** 144 E 128th St [Lex]
• **King's Academy •** 2341 Third Ave [127th]
• **Manhattan Center for Science & Math •** 260 Pleasant Ave [115th]
• **Mount Carmel-Holy Rosary •** 371 Pleasant Ave [119]
• **NY College of Podiatric Medicine •** 1800 Park Ave [125th]
• **Our Lady Queen of Angels •** 232 E 113th St [2nd Av]
• **PS 007 Samuel Stern •** 160 E 120th St [Lex]
• **PS 057 James W Johnson •** 176 E 115th St [3rd Av]
• **PS 079 Horan •** 55 E 120th St [Madison]
• **PS 096 Joseph Lanzetta •** 216 E 120th St [3rd Av]
• **PS 101 Draper •** 141 E 111th St [Lex]
• **PS 102 Jacques Cartier •** 315 E 113th St [2nd Av]
• **PS 112 Jose Celso Barbosa •** 535 E 119th St [Pleasant]
• **PS 030 Hernandez/Hughes •** 144 E 128th St [Lex]
• **PS 138 •** 144 E 128th St [Lex]
• **PS 155 William Paca •** 319 E 117th St [2nd Av]
• **PS 206 Jose Celso Barbosa •** 508 E 120th St [Pleasant]
• **River East (M037) •** 260 Pleasant Ave [115th]
• **St Ann •** 314 E 110th St [2nd Av]
• **St Paul •** 114 E 118th St [Park]
• **Urban Peace Academy (M695) •** 2351 First Ave [120th]

▤ Supermarkets

• **Associated •** 125 E 116th St [Park]
• **Associated •** 160 E 105th St [Lex]
• **Associated •** 2212 Third Ave [121st]
• **C-Town •** 309 E 115th St [2nd Av]
• **Pathmark •** 160 E 125th St [Lex]
• **Pioneer •** 1666 Madison Ave [111th]

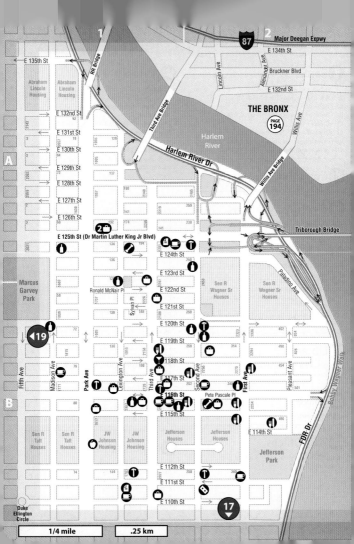

Patsy's Pizza really is the "original" New York thin-crust pizza, and Rao's is another New York landmark restaurant. El Barrio is also the unofficial "bakery" capital of New York.

☕ Coffee

- **Central Minimarket** • 2165 First Ave [112th]
- **Dunkin' Donuts** • 1773 Lexington Ave [110th]
- **Dunkin' Donuts** • 255 E 125th St [2nd Av]
- **The Harlem Tea Room** • 1793 Madison Ave [117th]
- **Juana's Luncheonette** • 242 E 116th St [3rd Av]
- **Kahlua's Café** • 2117 Third Ave [116th]
- **Treichville** • 339 E 118th St [2nd Av]

🖨 Copy Shops

- **Copykat Information & Business Center** • 1785 Lexington Ave [111th]
- **Patane Press** • 228 E 125th St [3rd Av]

🍊 Farmer's Markets

- **La Marqueta (Sat 8am-6pm July-Oct)** • E 115th St & Park Ave

🔨 Hardware Stores

- **B&B Supply & Hardware** • 2338 Second Ave [120th]
- **Brothers Hardware** • 218 E 125th St [3rd Av]
- **F&F Hardware** • 156 E 112th St [Madison]
- **N&J Locksmith & Hardware** • 1637 Park Ave [116th]
- **Right Line Hardware Supplies** • 2168 Second Ave [112th]
- **SM Hardware** • 2139 Third Ave [117th]

🍾 Liquor Stores

- **249 E 115th Liquor** • 249 E 115th St [2nd Av]
- **Harlem Liquor World** • 63 E 125th St [Madison]
- **IC Liquors** • 2255 First Ave [116th]
- **JM Liquor** • 1861 Lexington Ave [115th]
- **Lexington Wine and Liquor** • 2010 Lexington Ave [122nd]
- **RA Landrau Liquors & Wines** • 2334 Second Ave [120th]
- **Ramos Liquor Store** • 1814 Madison Ave [118th]
- **Third Avenue Liquors** • 2030 Third Ave [112th]

🍸 Nightlife

- **Café Creole** • 2167 Third Ave [118th]

🐾 Pet Shops

- **Ideal Pet Warehouse** • 356 E 116th St [1st Av]
- **Petland Discounts** • 167 E 125th St [Lex]

🍴 Restaurants

- **Camaradas** • 2241 First Ave [115th]
- **Creole** • 2167 Third Ave [118th]
- **La Hacienda** • 219 E 116th St [3rd Av]
- **Orbit East Harlem** • 2257 First Ave [116th]
- **Patsy's Pizzeria** • 2287 First Ave [118th]
- **Rao's** • 455 E 114th St [1st Av]
- **Sandy's Restaurant** • 2261 Second Ave [116th]

🛍 Shopping

- **Capri Bakery** • 186 E 116th St [3rd Av]
- **Casa Latina** • 151 E 116th St [Lex]
- **The Children's Place** • 163 E 125th St [Lex]
- **Don Paco Lopez Panaderia** • 2129 Third Ave [116th]
- **Gothic Cabinet Craft** • 2268 Third Ave [123rd]
- **La Marqueta** • Park Ave & 114th St
- **Morrone Bakery** • 324 E 116th St [2nd Av]
- **Motherhood Maternity** • 163 E 125th St [Lex]
- **Payless Shoe Source** • 2143 Third Ave [117th]
- **R&S Strauss Auto** • 2005 Third Ave [110th]
- **VIM** • 2239 Third Ave [122nd]

📹 Video Rental

- **First Run Video** • 1147 1/2 Second Ave [60th]

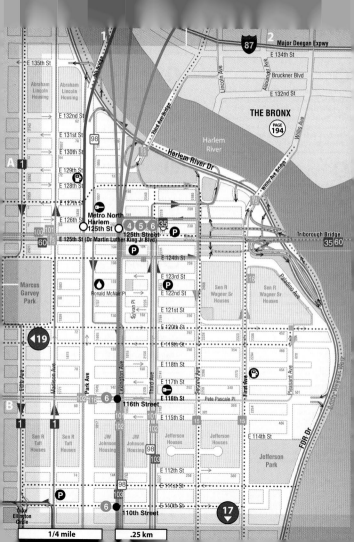

The best route to the Triborough is to go up Third Avenue and make a right on 124th Street, especially when the FDR is jammed. We feel for the folks who live over on Pleasant Avenue and have to hike five miles to the nearest subway (or worse yet, wait for the bus).

14 | 15
11 | 12 | 13

Ma

Subways

6 .... 110 St
6 .... 116 St
4 5 6 .... 125 St

Bus Lines

1 .... Fifth/Madison Aves
101 ..... Third Ave/Lexington Ave/Amsterdam Ave
102 ..... Third Ave/Lexington Ave/Malcolm X Blvd
103 .... Third/Lexington Aves
116 .... 116th St Crosstown
15 .... First Ave/Second Ave
35 .... Randall's Island/Ward Island
60 .... LaGuardia Airport
98 .... Washington Heights/Midtown
Bx 15 .... 125th St Crosstown

Bike Lanes

- • • • Marked Bike Lanes
- • • • Recommended Route
- • • • Greenway

Car Rental

- **A-Value Rent-A-Car** • 1851 Park Ave [126th]
- **Autorent Car Rental** • 220 E 117th St [3rd Av]

Car Washes

- **NY Car Spa** • 1771 Park Ave [123rd]

Gas Stations

- **Amoco** • 2276 First Ave [117th] ⏱
- **Gulf** • 1890 Park Ave [129th]

Parking

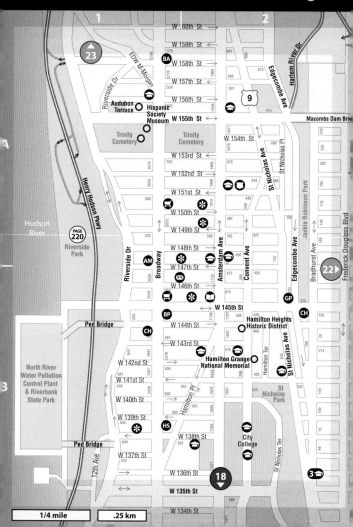

Map 21 • Manhattanville / Hamilton Heights

1/4 mile   .25 km

This neighborhood seems in the middle of an identity crisis, with the illustrious Hamilton Grange standing next to a vacant lot and the Trinity Cemetery overlooking an unimpressive section of Broadway. City College and the surrounding area, including Claremont Avenue, have interesting architecture and beautiful brownstones.

$ Banks

BP • Banco Popular • 3540 Broadway [145th]
BA • Bank of America (ATM) • 3579B Broadway [147th]
BA • Bank of America (ATM) • 3800 Broadway [158th]
CH • Chase • 330 W 145th St [Edgecombe]
CH • Chase • 3515 Broadway [144th]
HS • HSBC • 3418 Broadway [139th]
NF • North Fork • 700 St Nicholas Ave [145th]

Community Gardens

Landmarks

- **Audubon Terrace** • Broadway & W 155th St
- **Hamilton Grange National Memorial** • 287 Convent Ave [142nd]
- **Hamilton Heights Historic District** • W 141st b/w W 145th Sts & Convent Ave
- **Hispanic Society Museum** • 613 W 155th St [B'way]
- **Trinity Church Cemetery's Graveyard of Heroes** • 3699 Broadway [153rd]

Libraries

- **Hamilton Grange** • 503 W 145th St [Amsterdam]

Police

- **30th Precinct** • 451 W 151st St [Convent]

Post Offices

- **Hamilton Grange** • 521 W 146th St [Amsterdam]

Schools

- **Boricua College** • 3755 Broadway [156th]
- **Childs' Memorial Christian Academy** • 1763 Amsterdam Ave [147th]
- **City College** • 138th St & Convent Ave
- **Dance Theatre of Harlem** • 466 W 152nd St [Amsterdam]
- **Harlem School of the Arts** • 645 St Nicholas Ave [141st]
- **HS 685 Bread & Roses Integrated Arts High** • 6 Edgecombe Ave [135th]
- **Kappa IV (M302)** • 6 Edgecombe Ave [135th]
- **M283 Manhattan Theatre Lab** • 6 Edgecombe Ave [135th]
- **M304 Mott Hall High** • 6 Edgecombe Ave [135th]
- **M692 HS for Math, Science & Engineering at CCNY** • 138th St & Convent Ave
- **The Moore Learning Center** • 614 W 157th St [Morgan Pl]
- **Our Lady of Lourdes** • 468 W 143rd St [Amsterdam]
- **PS 028 Wright Brothers** • 475 W 155th St [Amsterdam]
- **PS 153 Adam C Powell** • 1750 Amsterdam Ave [147th]
- **PS 192 Jacob H Schiff** • 500 W 138th St [Amsterdam]

Supermarkets

- **C-Town** • 3550 Broadway [146th]
- **C-Town** • 3632 Broadway [149th]

Map 21 • Manhattanville / Hamilton Heights

There isn't a lot of variety in this neighborhood, but it's fantastic for cheap eats. New Caporal Fried Chicken is a neighborhood institution, but check out The Jyraffe for a fancier uptown bite. The Hide-A-Way is a great locals bar. For live jazz and African music, go to St. Nick's Pub.

Coffee

- **Astron Coffee Shop** • 3795 Broadway [158th]
- **Coffee Shop** • 398 W 145th St [Convent]
- **Dunkin' Donuts** • 3455 Broadway [141st]
- **Dunkin' Donuts** • 3600 Broadway [148th]
- **Java's Brewin'** • 1619 Amsterdam Ave [140th]

Copy Shops

- **Best Graphics Press** • 506 W 145th St [Amsterdam]

Gyms

- **NYC Fitness** • 3552 Broadway [146th]

Hardware Stores

- **Cohen & Cohen** • 1982 Amsterdam Ave [158th]
- **Felix Supply** • 3650 Broadway [150th]
- **O&J Hardware** • 3405 Broadway [138th]
- **Westside Home Center** • 3447 Broadway [141st]

Liquor Stores

- **2001 Liquor** • 3671 Broadway [152nd]
- **Brand's Liquor** • 550 W 145th St [Amsterdam]
- **JOCL Liquor Store** • 561 W 147th St [B'way]
- **Jumasol Liquors** • 1963 Amsterdam Ave [157th]
- **La Alta Gracia Liquor Store** • 3435 Broadway [140th]
- **Reliable Wine & Liquor Shop** • 3375 Broadway [137th]
- **Unity Liquors** • 708 St Nicholas Ave [146th]

Nightlife

- **St Nick's Pub** • 773 St Nicholas Ave [149th]
- **The Hide-A-Way** • 3578 Broadway [147th]

Pet Shops

- **Pet Ark** • 3450 Broadway [141st]

Restaurants

- **Copeland's** • 547 W 145th St [Amsterdam]
- **Devin's Fish & Chips** • 747 St Nicholas Ave [147th]
- **Jesus Taco** • 501 W 145th St [Amsterdam]
- **The Jyraffe** • 1940 Amsterdam Ave [156th]
- **New Caporal Fried Chicken** • 3772 Broadway [157th] ✚
- **Queen of Sheeba** • 317 W 141st St [F Douglass]
- **Raw Soul** • 348 W 145th St [Edgecombe]
- **Sunshine Jamaican Restaurant** • 695 St Nicholas Ave [145th]

Shopping

- **The Adventist Care Center** • 528 W 145th St [Amsterdam]
- **B-Jays USA** • 540 W 143rd St [Hamilton Pl]
- **El Mundo** • 3791 Broadway [158th]
- **Foot Locker** • 3549 Broadway [146th]
- **SOH-Straight Out of Harlem Creative Outlet** • 704 St Nicholas Ave [145th]
- **VIM** • 508 W 145th St [Amsterdam]

Video Rental

- **Santos Variety** • 3766 Broadway [156th]

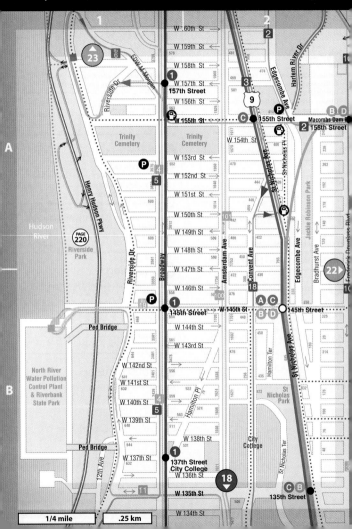

Map 21 • Manhattanville / Hamilton Heights

Despite the fact that the signs outside the 135th and 155th Street stations list the A and C trains, the A train stops at them only during late nights, when it runs local. Riverside Drive can be an intriguing alternative to traffic during rush hour as one moves closer to the George Washington Bridge.

Subways

1	137 St-City College
1	145 St
1	157 St
A **C** **B** **D**	145 St
C	155 St

Bus Lines

100	Amsterdam Ave/Broadway/125th St
101	Third Ave/Lexington Ave/Broadway/125th St
11	Ninth (Columbus)/Tenth (Amsterdam Ave)/Convent Ave
18	Convent Ave
2	Fifth Ave/Madison Ave/Powell Blvd
3	Fifth Ave/Madison Ave/St Nicholas Blvd
4	Fifth Ave/Madison Ave/Broadway
5	Fifth Ave/Sixth Ave/Riverside Dr
19	145th St Crosstown
6	E 161st St/E 163rd St

Bike Lanes

- • • • Marked Bike Lanes
- • • • Recommended Route
- • • • Greenway

Gas Stations

- **Getty** • 155 St Nicholas Ave [118th] ☼
- **Mobil** • 3740 Broadway [156th] ☼
- **Mobil** • 800 St Nicholas Ave [150th] ☼

Parking

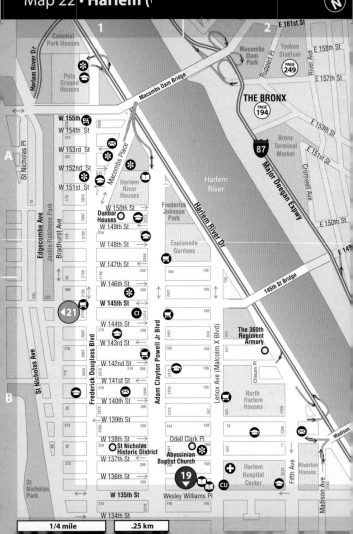

This part of New York is still pretty gritty, but don't let that working-class charm scare you away. There are many historic buildings to check out, and lots of atmosphere to breathe in. Plus, a number of new buildings are on the rise. The nabe is looking up.

Ma

💲Banks

CI • Citibank • 2481 Adam Clayton Powell Jr Blvd [144th]
CU • Municipal Credit Union (ATM) • Harlem Hospital • 506 Lenox Ave [135th]

✴️Community Gardens

➕Emergency Rooms

• **Harlem Hospital Center** • 506 Lenox Ave [135th] ♿

⭕Landmarks

• **The 369th Regiment Armory** • 2366 Fifth Ave [142nd]
• **Abyssinian Baptist Church** • 132 Odell Clark Pl [Lenox]
• **The Dunbar Houses** • Frederick Douglass Blvd & W 149th St
• **St Nicholas Historic District** • 202 W 138th St [7th Av]

📖Libraries

• **Countee Cullen** • 104 W 136th St [Lenox]
• **Macomb's Bridge** • 2650 Adam Clayton Powell Jr Blvd [152nd]
• **Schomburg Center for Research in Black Culture** • 515 Lenox Ave [136th]

✉️Post Offices

• **College Station** • 217 W 140th St [7th Av]
• **Colonial Park** • 99 Macombs Pl [154th]
• **Lincolnton** • 2266 Fifth Ave [138th]

🏫Schools

• **Frederick Douglass Academy** • Adam Clayton Powell Jr Blvd [149th]
• **PS 046 Tappan** • 2987 Frederick Douglass Blvd [145th]
• **PS 123 Mahalia Jackson** • 301 W 140th St [F Douglass]
• **PS 194 Countee Cullen** • 244 W 144th St [7th Av]
• **PS 197 John Russwurm** • 2230 Fifth Ave [136th]
• **PS 200 James Smith** • 2589 Adam Clayton Powell Jr Blvd [150th]
• **Resurrection** • 282 W 151st St [Macombs Pl]
• **St Charles Borromeo** • 214 W 142nd St [7th Av]
• **St Mark the Evangelist** • 55 W 138th St [Lenox]

🛒Supermarkets

• **Associated** • 2444 Seventh Ave [142nd]
• **Associated** • 2927 Frederick Douglass Blvd [155th]
• **Met Food** • 2541 Adam Clayton Powell Jr Blvd [147th]
• **Met Food** • 592 Lenox Ave [140th]
• **Pathmark** • 300 W 145th St [F Douglass]
• **Pioneer** • 2497 Adam Clayton Powell Jr Blvd [145th]

Map 22 • Harlem (U

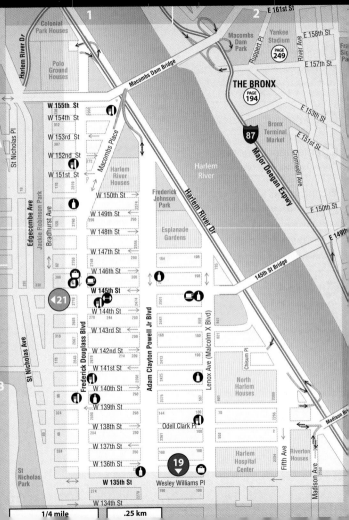

145th and Adam Clayton Powell serve as the main arteries for this area, and there are plenty of bodegas for everyone. Check out Miss Maude's on Lenox for some lunch or Charles' Southern-Style for classic fried chicken. For something a bit more upscale, try Londel's for supper.

Ma

Coffee

- **Dunkin' Donuts** • 110 W 145th St [Lenox]
- **Dunkin' Donuts** • 2730 Frederick Douglass Blvd [145th]

Copy Shops

- **Kev's Copy Center** • 2730 Frederick Douglass Blvd [145th]

Gyms

- **Curves (Women only)** • 274 W 145th St [F Douglass]

Liquor Stores

- **8th Avenue Liquor** • 2807 Frederick Douglass Blvd [149th]
- **All-Rite Liquors** • 2651 Frederick Douglass Blvd [142nd]
- **Friedland Wine & Liquor Store** • 605 Lenox Ave [141st]
- **Harlem Discount Liquors** • 2302 Adam Clayton Powell Jr Blvd [135th]
- **Luis Liquor** • 108 W 145th St [Lenox]
- **Sepia Liquor** • 2517 Adam Clayton Powell Jr Blvd [146th]

Restaurants

- **Charles' Southern-Style Chicken** • 2839 Frederick Douglass Blvd [151st]
- **Flash Inn** • 107 Macombs Pl [154th]
- **Londel's Supper Club** • 2620 Frederick Douglass Blvd [140th]
- **Margie's Red Rose** • 267 W 144th St [F Douglass]
- **Miss Maude's** • 547 Lenox Ave [138th]
- **Sugar Shack** • 2611 Frederick Douglass Blvd [139th]

Shopping

- **Baskin-Robbins** • 2730 Frederick Douglass Blvd [145th]
- **New York Public Library Shop** • Schomburg Ctr• 515 Lenox Ave [136th]

Map 22 · **Harlem (Upper)**

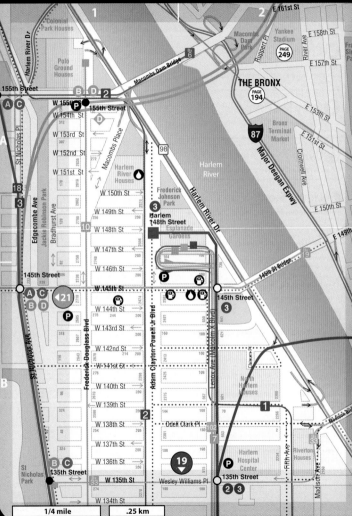

Driving is actually negotiable on all streets, and there's usually plenty of parking if you circle the block. With quick access to the FDR, and the 145th Bridge, it's a good place to pull off and explore.

Subways

3 .... 145 St
3 .... Harlem-148 St
B **D** .... 155 St

Bus Lines

1 .... Fifth Ave/Madison Ave
10 .... Seventh Ave/Eighth Ave
(Central Park West)/Frederick Douglass Blvd
102 ..... Third Ave/Lexington Ave/Malcolm X Blvd
2 .... Fifth Ave/Madison Ave/Powell Blvd
7 .... Columbus Ave/Amsterdam Ave/
Sixth Ave/Seventh Ave/Broadway
98 .... Washington Heights/Midtown
Bx 19 .... 145th St Crosstown
Bx 33 .... 135th St Crosstown
Bx 6 .... E 161st St/E 163rd St

Bike Lanes

- • • • Marked Bike Lanes
- • • • Recommended Route
- • • • Greenway

🌢 Car Washes

- **Harlem Hand Car Wash** • 2600 Adam Clayton
  Powell Jr Blvd [150th]
- **Los Amigos** • 119 W 145th St [Lenox]

⛽ Gas Stations

- **Amoco** • 232 W 145th St [7th Av] ⊗
- **Getty** • 119 W 145th St [Lenox]
- **Hess** • 128 W 145th St [Lenox] ⊗
- **Mobil** • 150 W 145th St [Lenox] ⊗

P Parking

Map 23 · **Washington Heights**

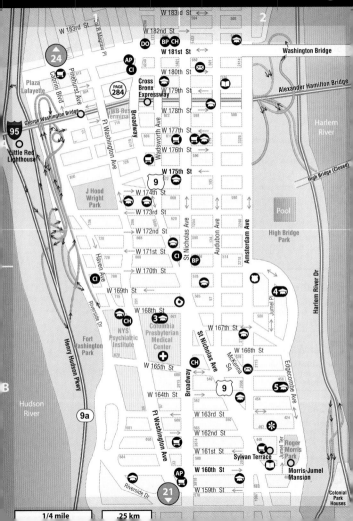

Washington Bridge

Alexander Hamilton Bridge

W 183rd St

W 182nd St

W 181st St

W 180th St

W 179th St

W 178th St

W 177th St

W 176th St

W 175th St

W 174th St

W 173rd St

W 172nd St

W 171st St

W 170th St

W 169th St

W 168th St

W 167th St

W 166th St

W 165th St

W 164th St

W 163rd St

W 162nd St

W 161st St

W 160th St

W 159th St

Cabrini Blvd

Pinehurst Ave

Fort Washington Ave

Haven Ave

Riverside Dr

Henry Hudson Pkwy

Broadway

Wadsworth Ave

St Nicholas Ave

Audubon Ave

Amsterdam Ave

Jumel Pl

Edgecombe Ave

Jumel Ter

Harlem River Dr

Plaza Lafayette

George Washington Bridge

Little Red Lighthouse

J Hood Wright Park

NYS Psychiatric Institute

Columbia Presbyterian Medical Center

Fort Washington Park

Hudson River

Cross Bronx Expressway

GWB Bus Terminal

Harlem River

High Bridge (Closed)

High Bridge Park

Pool

McKenna Sq

Sylvan Terrace

Roger Morris Park

Morris-Jumel Mansion

Colonial Park Houses

95

9

9

9a

24

21

PAGE 284

3

4

5

1/4 mile   .25 km

In this area, you'll see a street life unmatched anywhere else in the city. The Heights is lively, constantly moving, and somehow seems more vibrant with each passing year. Also check out Sylvan Terrace—the most un-Manhattan-looking place in Manhattan—it's way cool.

🥯 Bagels

• **Mike's Bagels** • 4003 Broadway [168th]

💲 Banks

AP • **Apple** • 3815 Broadway [159th]
AP • **Apple** • 706 W 181st St [B'way]
BP • **Banco Popular** • 1200 St Nicholas Ave [170th]
BP • **Banco Popular** • 615 W 181st St [St Nicholas]
CH • **Chase** • 1421 St Nicholas Ave [181st]
CH • **Chase** • 180 Ft Washington Ave [168th]
CH • **Chase** • 3940 Broadway [165th]
CI • **Citibank** • 4249 Broadway [180th]
CI • **Citibank (ATM)** • 4058 Broadway [171st]
CI • **Citibank (ATM)** • 60 Haven Ave [170th]
DO • **Doral** • 4246 Broadway [180th]

🌼 Community Gardens

➕ Emergency Rooms

• **Columbia-Presbyterian Medical Center** •
622 W 168th St [B'way] ♿

📍 Landmarks

• **Cross Bronx Expressway**
• **George Washington Bridge** • W 178th St [Henry Hudson]
• **Little Red Lighthouse** • under the George Washington Bridge [178th]
• **Morris-Jumel Mansion** • Edgecombe Ave & 161st St
• **Sylvan Terrace** • b/w Jumel Ter & St Nicholas Ave

📖 Libraries

• **Fort Washington** • 535 W 179th St [Audubon]
• **Washington Heights** • 1000 St Nicholas Ave [160th]

🚔 Police

• **33rd Precinct** • 2207 Amsterdam Ave [170th]

✉️ Post Offices

• **Audubon** • 511 W 165th St [Amsterdam]
• **Sergeant Riayan A Tejeda** • 555 W 180th St [Audubon]

🏫 Schools

• **Columbia University Medical Center** •
630 W 168th St [B'way]
• **Columbia University School of Dental and Oral Surgery** • 630 W 168th St [B'way]
• **Columbia University School of Nursing** •
630 W 168th St [B'way]
• **HS 552 Gregorio Luperon** • 516 W 181st St [Amsterdam]
• **Incarnation Elementary** • 570 W 175th St [Audubon]
• **Interboro** • 260 Audubon Ave [178th]
• **IS 164 Edward W Stitt** • 401 W 164th St [Edgecombe]
• **Mailman School of Public Health** •
722 W 168th St [Ft Wash]
• **Mirabel Sisters IS 90** • 21 Jumel Pl [168th]
• **MS 319 Minerva** • 21 Jumel Pl [168th]
• **MS 321 Maria Teresa** • 21 Jumel Pl [168th]
• **MS 326** • 401 W 164th St [Edgecombe]
• **MS 328** • 401 W 164th St [Edgecombe]
• **The Modern School** • 870 Riverside Dr [160th]
• **Patria (MS 324)** • 21 Jumel Pl [168th]
• **PS 004 Duke Ellington** • 500 W 160th St [Amsterdam]
• **PS 008 Luis Belliard** • 465 W 167th St [Jumel Pl]
• **PS 115 Humboldt** • 586 W 177th St [St Nicholas]
• **PS 128 Audubon** • 560 W 169th St [Audubon]
• **PS 173** • 306 Ft Washington Ave [173rd]
• **PS 210 21st Century Academy** • 4111 Broadway [174th]
• **St Rose of Lima** • 517 W 164th St [St Nicholas]
• **St Spyridon Parochial** • 120 Wadsworth Ave [179th]

🛒 Supermarkets

• **Associated** • 3871 Broadway [162nd]
• **Bravo Supermarket** • 1331 St Nicholas Ave [177th]
• **C-Town** • 1016 St Nicholas Ave [161st]
• **C-Town** • 1314 St Nicholas Ave [176th]
• **Gristede's** • 4037 Broadway [170th]
• **Karrot Cabrini** • 854 W 181st St [Cabrini]
• **Super Extra** • 3835 Broadway [160th]

Map 23 · **Washington Heights**

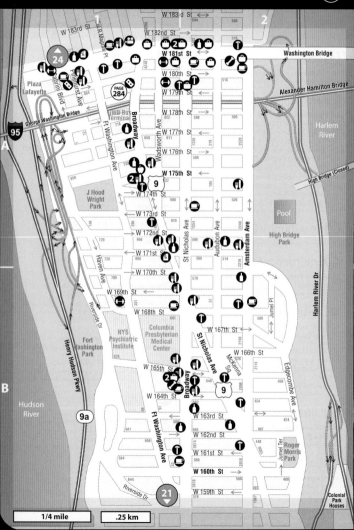

181st acts as a magnet for the entertainment in the area; all the big shops are there, and the street is a chaos of bodies. The restaurants are plentiful, with lots of Dominican options, but nothing you need to dress up for. Head to New Coliseum Theater for a Spanish-language flick.

Coffee

- **Chris Coffee Shop** • 500 W 168th St [Amsterdam]
- **Dunkin' Donuts** • 1266 St Nicholas Ave [173rd]
- **Dunkin' Donuts** • 1416 St Nicholas Ave [181st]
- **Dunkin' Donuts** • 2420 Amsterdam Ave [181st]
- **Dunkin' Donuts** • 3851 Broadway [161st]
- **Dunkin' Donuts** • 854 W 181st St [Col R Magaw]
- **Hathie's Coffee Shop** • 3915 Broadway [164th]
- **Jou Jou** • 603 W 168th St [B'way]
- **Starbucks** • 803 W 181st St [Ft Wash]
- **X Caffe** • 3952 Broadway [165th]

Copy Shops

- **The UPS Store** • 4049 Broadway [170th]
- **The UPS Store** • 809 W 181st St [Ft Wash]

Farmer's Markets

- **175th Street** (Thurs, 8am-6pm, June-Nov) • W 175th St & Broadway

Gyms

- **Big Gym** • 625 W 181st St [Wadsworth]
- **Curves** (Women only) • 216 Ft Washington Ave [169th]
- **Curves** (Women only) • 854 W 181st St [Cabrini]
- **Lucille Roberts Health Club** (Women only) • 1387 St Nicholas Ave [180th]

Hardware Stores

- **3841 Hardware** • 3841 Broadway [160th]
- **756 Hardware** • 756 W 181st St [Col R Magaw]
- **AHS Hardware** • 2416 Amsterdam Ave [180th]
- **AT Mini Hardware** • 1388 St Nicholas Ave [180th]
- **Chavin Hardware** • 1348 St Nicholas Ave [177th]
- **Cibao Hardware** • 1045 St Nicholas Ave [162nd]
- **E&T Hardware** • 4087 Broadway [172nd]
- **Ernesto's Hardware Store** • 2180 Amsterdam Ave [168th]
- **EZ Open Hardware** • 2304 Amsterdam Ave [174th]
- **Ferreteria Hardware** • 1087 St Nicholas Ave [164th]
- **Fort Washington Hardware** • 3918 Broadway [164th]
- **Nunez Hardware** • 4147 Broadway [175th]
- **Taveras Hardware** • 2029 Amsterdam Ave [161st]
- **Washington Heights Hardware** • 736 W 181st St [Col R Magaw]

Liquor Stores

- **Cabrina Wines & Liquors** • 831 W 181st St [Cabrini]
- **First KBJ** • 4189 Broadway [178th]
- **Galicia Liquors** • 3906 Broadway [158th]
- **Guadalupe Barbara** • 4084 Broadway [172nd]
- **Heights Liquor Supermarket** • 547 W 181st St [Audubon]
- **In Good Spirits** • 3879 Broadway [162nd]
- **McLiquor Store** • 2208 Amsterdam Ave [170th]
- **O&J Liquors** • 1045 St Nicholas Ave [162nd]
- **Vargas Liquor Store** • 114 Audubon Ave [171st]

Movie Theaters

- **New Coliseum Theatre** • 701 W 181st St [B'way]

Pet Shops

- **A&N Pet Place** • 3933 Broadway [165th]
- **Pet Place** • 518 W 181st St [Amsterdam]

Restaurants

- **Aqua Marina** • 4060 Broadway [171st]
- **Carrot Top Pastries** • 3931 Broadway [165th]
- **Coogan's** • 4015 Broadway [169th]
- **Dallas BBQ** • 3956 Broadway [166th]
- **El Conde Steak House** • 4139 Broadway [175th]
- **El Malecon** • 4141 Broadway [175th] ⏰
- **El Ranchito** • 4129 Broadway [175th]
- **Empire Szechuan** • 4041 Broadway [170th]
- **Hispaniola** • 839 W 181st St [Cabrini]
- **International Food House** • 4073 Broadway [172nd]
- **Jesse's Place** • 812 W 181st St [Pinehurst]
- **Jimmy Oro Restaurant** • 711 W 181st St [B'way]
- **Parrilla** • 3920 Broadway [164th]
- **Reme Restaurant** • 4021 Broadway [169th]
- **Restaurant Tenares** • 2306 Amsterdam Ave [161st]
- **Taino Restaurant** • 2228 Amsterdam Ave [171st]
- **Tipico Dominicano** • 4177 Broadway [177th] ⏰

Shopping

- **Baskin-Robbins** • 728 W 181st St [Col R Magaw]
- **Carrot Top Pastries** • 3931 Broadway [165th]
- **The Children's Place** • 600 W 181st St [St Nicholas]
- **Fever** • 1387 St Nicholas Ave [180th]
- **Foot co** • 599 W 181st St [St Nicholas]
- **Foot Locker** • 621 W 181st St [St Nicholas]
- **Goodwill Industries** • 512 W 181st St [Amsterdam]
- **Modell's** • 606 W 181st St [St Nicholas]
- **Payless Shoe Source** • 617 W 181st St [St Nicholas]
- **Planet Girls** • 3923 Broadway [164th]
- **Santana Banana** • 661 W 181st St [Wadsworth]
- **Tribeca** • 655 W 181st St [Wadsworth]
- **VIM** • 561 W 181st St [Audubon]

Video Rental

- **Blockbuster** • 4211 Broadway [180th]
- **Kappy's Record & Video World** • 91 Pinehurst Ave [181st]

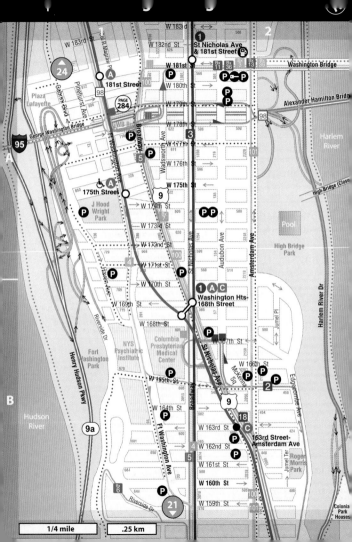

As you may note, this area acts as a hub for the GWB and the Cross Bronx Expressway. When on the main roads, just pay attention to where you're going. Use Amsterdam or St. Nick's for north-south travel. Once in the little streets, parking won't be too difficult.

Subways

1	181 St
A	175 St
A	181 St
1 A C	168 St-Washington Hts
C	163 St-Amsterdam Ave

Bus Lines

100	Amsterdam Ave/Broadway/125th St
101	Third and Lexington Aves/Malcolm X Blvd
18	Convent Ave
2	Fifth and Madison Aves/ Adam Clayton Powell Jr Blvd
3	Fifth and Madison Aves/St Nicholas Ave
4	Fifth and Madison Aves/Broadway
5	Fifth Ave/Sixth Ave/Riverside Dr
98	Washington Heights/Midtown
Bx 11	to Southern Blvd via 170th St
Bx 13	to Yankee Stadium via Ogden Ave
Bx 3	to Riverdale, 238th St-Broadway
Bx 35	to West Farms Rd via 167th St
Bx 36	to Olmstead Ave/Randall Ave via 180th St
Bx 7	Riverdale Ave/Broadway

Bike Lanes

- • • • Marked Bike Lanes
- • • • Recommended Route
- • • • Greenway

Car Rental

- **Uptown Car Rental** • 506 W 181st St [Amsterdam]

Gas Stations

- **Shell** • 2420 Amsterdam Ave [181st] ⏱

Parking

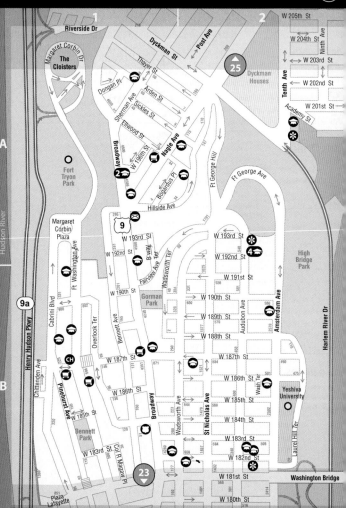

A great place for epic walks, this area is the only place on Manhattan Isle with decent inclines. The curvy streets in the center of the map are the best; steep as hell and winding. Fort Tryon Park and the Cloisters Museum should not be missed—great views from both.

$ Banks

CH • Chase • 596 Ft Washington Ave [187th]

✺ Community Gardens

○ Landmarks

- **Fort Tryon Park** • Ft Washington Ave
- **Yeshiva University Main Building (Zysman Hall)** • Amsterdam Ave & W 187th St

⬡ Police

- **34th Precinct** • 4295 Broadway [184th]

✉ Post Offices

- **Fort George** • 4558 Broadway [Hillside]

🎓 Schools

- **Business & Finance High** • 549 Audubon Ave [192nd]
- **City College Academy of the Arts** • 4600 Broadway [196th]
- **Health Careers & Sciences High** • 549 Audubon Ave [192nd]
- **IS 143 Eleanor Roosevelt** • 511 W 182nd St [Amsterdam]
- **IS 218 Salome Ukena** • 4600 Broadway [196th]
- **IS 528 Bea Fuller Rodgers** • 180 Wadsworth Ave [182nd]
- **Juan Bosch Public** • 12 Ellwood St [Hillside]
- **Law & Public Service High** • 549 Audubon Ave [192nd]
- **Media & Communications High** • 549 Audubon Ave [192nd]
- **Mesivta Rabbi Samson Raphael** • 8593 Bennett Ave [B'way]
- **Middle School 322** • 4600 Broadway [196th]
- **Mother Cabrini High** • 701 Ft Washington Ave [190th]
- **Our Lady Queen of Martyrs** • 71 Arden St [Sherman]
- **PS 005 Ellen Lurie** • 3703 Tenth Ave [Dyckman]
- **PS 048 PO Michael J Buczek** • 4360 Broadway [186th]
- **PS 132 Juan Pablo Duarte** • 185 Wadsworth Ave [182nd]
- **PS 152 Dyckman Valley** • 93 Nagle Ave [Sickles]
- **PS 187 Hudson Cliffs** • 349 Cabrini Blvd [190th]
- **PS 189** • 2580 Amsterdam Ave [188th]
- **Shabak Christian** • 362 Audubon Ave [183rd]
- **St Elizabeth** • 612 W 187th St [St Nicholas]
- **Yeshiva University** • 500 W 185th St [Amsterdam]
- **Yeshiva University High** • 2540 Amsterdam Ave [186th]

🛒 Supermarkets

- **Associated** • 592 Ft Washington Ave [187th]
- **Frank's Meat Market** • 807 W 187th St [Ft Wash]
- **Key Food** • 4365 Broadway [187th]
- **Pioneer** • 72 Nagle Ave [Ellwood]

Map 24 • **Fort George/Fort Tryon**

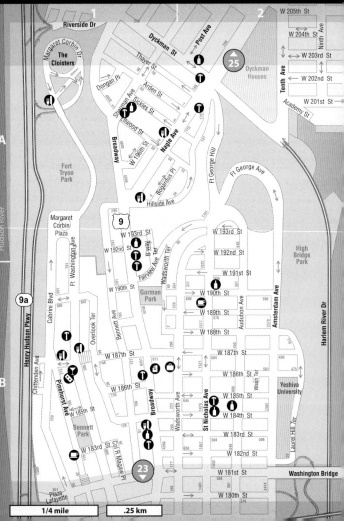

Sundries / Entertainment

Map 24

A cozy nightlife and lots of specialty restaurants here. There are a number of Irish bars to hop in north-wise, and 187th on the west is perfect to stop and grab a bite after humping all those hills. The east side of the nabe can be a bit sterile.

Coffee

- **Angela's Coffee Shop** • 805 W 187th St [Ft Wash]
- **The Archway** • 116 Pinehurst Ave [183rd]
- **Dunkin' Donuts** • 1599 St Nicholas Ave [190th]

Copy Shops

- **Staples** • 4320 Broadway [184th]

Hardware Stores

- **Apex Supply** • 4580 Broadway [196th]
- **Blue Bell Lumber** • 4309 Broadway [184th]
- **Century Hardware** • 4309 Broadway [184th]
- **Geomart Hardware** • 607 Ft Washington Ave [187th]
- **Nagle Hardware Store** • 145 Nagle Ave [Arden]
- **St Nicholas Hardware** • 1488 St Nicholas Ave [185th]
- **Supreme Hardware** • 106 Dyckman St [Nagle]
- **Victor Hardware Store** • 25 Sherman Ave [Sickles]
- **VNJ Hardware** • 4476 Broadway [192nd]

Liquor Stores

- **185th Street Liquor Store** • 4329 Broadway [184th]
- **Alex's Liquor Store** • 1598 St Nicholas Ave [190th]
- **Dyckman Liquors** • 121 Dyckman St [Post]
- **J&P Discount Liquors** • 377 Audubon Ave [184th]
- **Sanchez Liquors** • 4500 Broadway Bsmt [192nd]
- **Sherman Liquor** • 25 Sherman Ave [Sickles]
- **Yuan & Yuan Wine & Liquors** • 1492 St Nicholas Ave [185th]

Nightlife

- **The Monkey Room** • 589 Ft Washington Ave [187th]

Restaurants

- **107 West** • 811 W 187th St [Ft Wash]
- **Bleu Evolution** • 808 W 187th St [Ft Wash]
- **Caridad Restaurant** • 4311 Broadway [184th]
- **Frank's Pizzeria** • 94 Nagle Ave [Sickles]
- **New Leaf Café** • 1 Margaret Corbin Dr [Henry Hudson]
- **Rancho Jubilee** • 1 Nagle Ave [Hillside]

Video Rental

- **Ft Washington Video** • 805 W 187th St [Ft Wash]

Map 24 · Fort George/Fort Tryon

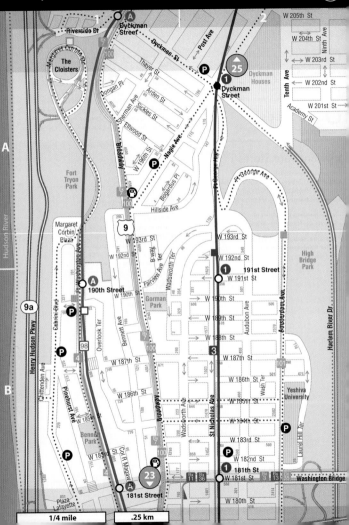

Subways

1 .... Dyckman St
1 .... 191 St
Ⓐ .... 190 St

Bus Lines

100 .... Broadway
100 .... Amsterdam Ave
3 .... St Nicholas Ave
4 .... Ft Washington Ave
98 .... Ft Washington Ave
Bx 7 .... Broadway

Bike Lanes

- • • • Marked Bike Lanes
- • • • Recommended Route
- • • • Greenway

Ⓟ Gas Stations

• **Rammco Service Station** • 4275 Broadway [182nd]

Ⓟ Parking

Map 25 • **Inwood**

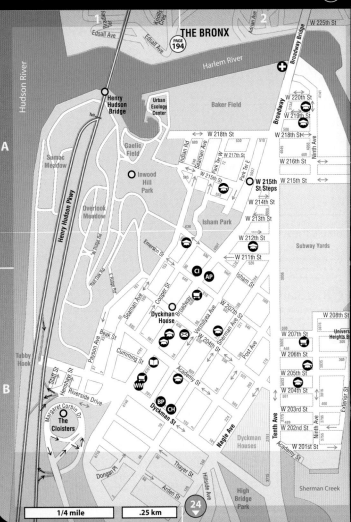

The greatest thing about this area is that so few people know about it. Inwood Hill Park is a magnificent place, with miles of paths winding up and down an actual old-growth forest. Lots of working families, starving musicians, and students tend to live here due to the still-reasonable rents.

21 22
18 19 20

Ma

💲Banks

AP • Apple • 4950 Broadway [207th]
BP • Banco Popular • 175 Dyckman St [Sherman]
CH • Chase • 161 Dyckman St [Sherman]
CI • Citibank • 4949 Broadway [207th]
WM • Washington Mutual • 211 Dyckman St [B'way]

➕Emergency Rooms

• **Columbia-Presbyterian Allen Pavilion •**
5141 Broadway [220th] ♿

⭕Landmarks

• **The Cloisters •** Ft Tryon Park
• **Dyckman House •** 4881 Broadway [204th]
• **Henry Hudson Bridge**
• **Inwood Hill Park**
• **West 215th St Steps•** W 215th St [Park Ter E]

📖Libraries

• **Inwood •** 4790 Broadway [Cumming]

✉️Post Offices

• **Inwood Post Office •** 90 Vermilyea Ave [204th]

🏫Schools

• **Amistad Dual Language •** 4862 Broadway [204th]
• **Good Shepherd •** 620 Isham St [Cooper]
• **IS 052 Inwood •** 650 Academy St [B'way]
• **Manhattan Christian Academy •** 401 W 205th St [9th Av]
• **Northeastern Academy •** 532 W 215th St [Park Ter E]
• **PS 018 •** 4124 Ninth Ave [220th]
• **PS 098 Shorac Kappock •** 512 W 212nd St [10th Av]
• **PS 176 •** 4862 Broadway [204th]
• **PS/IS 278 (M278) •** 407 W 219th St [9th Av]
• **St Jude •** 433 W 204th St [9th Av]
• **St Matthew Lutheran •** 200 Sherman Ave [204th]

🛒Supermarkets

• **C-Town •** 4918 Broadway [207th]
• **Fine Fare •** 4776 Broadway [Dyckman]
• **Pathmark •** 410 W 207th St [9th Av]

You'll find everything you'll ever need along Broadway, Dyckman or 207th. Plenty of eateries, pubs, and specialty shops. Get a taste of nature in the park, then get the best cheeseburger in the world at Piper's Kilt. And, of course, a bodega for everyone.

Coffee

- **Dunkin' Donuts** • 4932 Broadway [207th]

Copy Shops

- **The UPS Store** • 4768 Broadway [Dyckman]

Farmer's Markets

- **Inwood (Sat 8am-3pm, July-Nov)** • Isham St b/w Seaman Ave & Cooper St

Gyms

- **Curves (Women only)** • 5037 Broadway [215th]

Hardware Stores

- **Dick's Hardware** • 4947 Broadway [207th]
- **Inwood Paint & Hardware** • 165 Sherman Ave [204th]
- **J&A Hardware** • 132 Vermilyea Ave [207th]

Liquor Stores

- **PJ Liquor Warehouse** • 4898 Broadway [204th]
- **Q Royal** • 529 W 207th St [Sherman]

Nightlife

- **Keenan's Bar** • 4878 Broadway [204th]
- **Piper's Kilt** • 4944 Broadway [207th]

Pet Shops

- **Alberto's Pet Shop** • 8 Payson Ave [Riverside Dr]

Restaurants

- **Bobby's Fish and Seafood Market and Restaurant** • 3842 Ninth Ave [206th] ✪
- **Capitol Restaurant** • 4933 Broadway [207th]
- **Hoppin' Jalapenos Bar & Grill** • 597 W 207th St [B'way]
- **Tacos Puebla** • 5-22 W 207th St [Sherman]

Shopping

- **Carrot Top Pastries** • 5025 Broadway [214th]
- **The Cloisters** • Ft Tryon Park
- **Foot Locker** • 146 Dyckman St [Sherman]
- **K&R Florist** • 4955 Broadway [207th]
- **Payless Shoe Source** • 560 W 207th St [Vermilyea]
- **Radio Shack** • 180 Dyckman St [Vermilyea]
- **Radio Shack** • 576 W 207th St [Vermilyea]
- **Tread Bike Shop** • 225 Dyckman St [B'way]
- **VIM** • 565 W 207th St [Vermilyea]

Video Rental

- **Blockbuster** • 165 Dyckman St [Sherman]

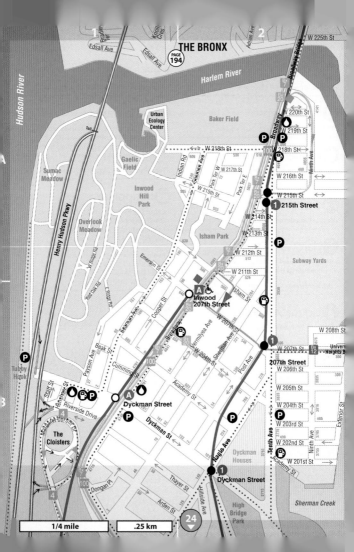

At the end of the A line and also served by the 1, Inwood is very accessible via public transportation. When driving, it's a short hop off the Hudson pre-toll; take the Dyckman exit. Parking is generally available in the side streets, and the traffic condition is typical---i.e. crazed.

Subways

1 .... 215 St
1 .... 207 St
A .... Dyckman St
A .... Inwood-207 St

Bus Lines

100 .... Amsterdam Ave/Broadway/125th St
4 .... Fifth/Madison Aves/Broadway
Bx 12 .... Riverdale/263rd St via Riverdale Ave
Bx 20 .... Riverdale/246th St via Henry Hudson Pky
Bx 7 .... Riverdale Ave/Broadway

Bike Lanes

- • • • Marked Bike Lanes
- • • • Recommended Route
- • • • Greenway

Car Washes

- **Broadway Bridge Car Wash** • 5134 Broadway [220th]
- **Broadway Hand Car Wash** • 4778 Broadway [Cumming]
- **Dyckman Car Wash** • 284 Dyckman St [Henshaw]

Gas Stations

- **BP** • 3936 Tenth Ave [Sherman] ✪
- **Getty** • 242 Dyckman St [Seaman] ✪
- **Getty** • 4880 Broadway [204th] ✪
- **Shell** • 3761 Tenth Ave [201st] ✪

Parking

What an Astoria address lacks in cachet, it makes up for in low rent and plentiful amenities. Astoria Park and Pool is a fine place to jog or swim by day, and join the crowds of kissing couples by night. Ditmars Boulevard, Broadway, 30th Avenue, and Steinway Street are lined with well-stocked groceries, assorted ethnic restaurants, small shops of every kind, and bars that range from dive bars to trendy lounges. The neighborhood's storied Greek/Cypriot population has largely drifted to the suburbs, but they left a few great restaurants like Agnanti, Aliada, Stamatis, and Zenon behind. Newer residents serve Middle Eastern and North African treats at Kabab Café, Laziza, or Jour et Nuit and proffer hearty Brazilian meals at Sabor Tropical and Churrascaria Girassol. Bohemian Hall is the city's last remaining beer garden with room for hundreds of drinkers in its backyard—just be sure to bring a book for the late-night subway ride home!

$ Banks

- **Astoria Federal** • 29-34 30th Ave [29th St]
- **Astoria Federal** • 31-24 Ditmars Blvd [31st St]
- **Astoria Federal** • 37-16 30th Ave [37th St]
- **Atlantic** • 28-07 Steinway St [28th Av]
- **Atlantic** • 29-10 Ditmars Blvd [29th St]
- **Atlantic** • 33-12 30th Ave [33rd St]
- **Atlantic** • 36-10 Broadway [36th St]
- **Bank of America** • 31-81 Steinway St [B'way]
- **Chase** • 21-21 Broadway [21st St]
- **Chase** • 22-45 31st St [Ditmars]
- **Chase** • 31-05 30th Ave [31st St]
- **Chase** • 38-18 Broadway [38th St]
- **Chase (ATM)** • 28-56 Steinway St [28th Av]
- **Citibank** • 22-16 31st St [Ditmars]
- **Citibank** • 25-91 Steinway St [28th Av]
- **Citibank (ATM)** • 25-10 30th Ave [27th St]
- **Commerce** • 31-04 Ditmars Blvd [31st St]
- **Commerce** • 31-90 Steinway St [B'way]
- **Doral** • 30-18 Steinway St [30th Av]
- **Flushing Savings** • 31-16 30th Ave [31st St]
- **Independence Community** • 22-59 31st St [23rd Av]
- **Independence Community** • 24-28 34th Ave [24th]
- **Independence Community** • 37-10 Broadway [37th]
- **Marathon** • 28-22 Steinway St [28th Av]
- **Marathon** • 31-01 Broadway [31st St]
- **Marathon** • 33-02 Ditmars Blvd [33rd St]
- **North Fork** • 22-04 31st St [Ditmars]
- **North Fork** • 30-98 Steinway St [31st Av]
- **North Fork** • 31-17 Broadway [31st St]
- **Ponce de Leon** • 34-05 Broadway [34th St]
- **Queens County Savings** • 30-75 Steinway St [31st]
- **Queens County Savings** • 31-09 Ditmars Blvd [31st]
- **Queens County Savings** • 31-42 Steinway St [31st]
- **Ridgewood Savings** • 43-14 Ditmars Blvd [43rd St]
- **Washington Mutual** • 22-30 31st St [Ditmars]
- **Washington Mutual** • 28-56 Steinway St [28th Av]

O Landmarks

- **American Museum of the Moving Image** • 36-01 35th Ave [36th St]
- **Astoria Park and Pool** • 19th St & 23rd Dr
- **Buzzer Thirty** • 38-01 23rd Ave [38th St]
- **Kaufman-Astoria Studios** • 34-12 36th St [34th St]
- **Socrates Sculpture Park** • Broadway & Vernon Blvd

🎬 Movie Theaters

- **Regal Entertainment Group** • 35-30 38th St [38th St]

🍸 Nightlife

- **The Albatross** • 36-19 24th Ave [36th St]
- **Bohemian Hall & Beer Garden** • 29-19 24th Ave [29th St]
- **Brick Café** • 30-95 33rd St [31st Av]
- **Café Bar** • 32-90 36th St [33rd St]
- **Cronin & Phelan** • 38-14 Broadway [38th St]
- **Fatty's Café** • 25-01 Ditmars Blvd [Crescent St]
- **Irish Rover** • 37-18 28th Ave [37th St]
- **Mary McGuire's** • 38-04 Broadway [38th St]
- **McCaffrey & Burke** • 28-54 31st St [Newtown]
- **McCann's Pub & Grill** • 36-15 Ditmars Blvd [36th St]
- **Rapture** • 34-27 28th Ave [34th St]
- **The Sparrow** • 24-01 29th St [24th Av]

🍴 Restaurants

- **Agnanti** • 19-06 Ditmars Blvd [19th St]
- **Aliada** • 29-19 Broadway [29th St]
- **Bel Aire Diner** • 31-91 21st St [B'way]
- **Bosna Express** • 31-29 12th St [31st Dr]
- **Christos Hasapo-Taverna** • 41-08 23rd Ave [41st St]
- **Churrascaria Girassol** • 33-18 28th Ave [33rd St]
- **Djardan** • 34-04 31st Ave [34th St]
- **Jour et Nuit** • 28-04 Steinway St [28th Av]
- **Kabab Café** • 25-12 Steinway St [25th Av]
- **Mombar** • 25-22 Steinway St [25th Av]
- **Neptune Diner** • 31-05 Astoria Blvd [31st St]
- **Roti Rani's** • 33-10 21st St [33rd Rd]
- **S'Agapo** • 34-21 34th St [34th Av]
- **Sabor Tropical** • 36-18 30th Ave [36th St]
- **Sal, Chris, and Charlie Deli** • 33-12 23rd Ave [33rd St]
- **Stamatis** • 29-12 23rd Ave [29th St]
- **Tokyo Japanese Restaurant** • 31-05 24th Ave [31st St]
- **Trattoria L'Incontro** • 21-76 31st St [Ditmars]
- **Watawa** • 33-10 Ditmars Blvd [33rd St]
- **Zenon** • 34-10 31st Ave [34th St]
- **Zlata Praha** • 28-48 31st St [Newtown]
- **Zygos Tavern** • 22-55 31st St [23rd Av]

🛍 Shopping

- **El Manara** • 25-95 Steinway St [28th St]
- **Emack & Boilio's** • 21-50 31st St [21st Av]
- **Jolson's Wines & Liquors** • 22-24 31st St [Ditmars]
- **Laziza of New York Pastries** • 25-78 Steinway St [28th Av]
- **Loveday 31** • 33-06 31st Ave [33rd St]
- **Martha's Country Bakery** • 36-21 Ditmars Blvd [36th St]
- **Mediterranean Foods** • 23-18 31st St [23rd Av]
- **Rose & Joe's Italian Bakery** • 22-40 31st St [Ditmars]
- **The Furniture Market** • 22-08 Astoria Blvd [Newtown]
- **The Second Best** • 30-07 Astoria Blvd [31st St]
- **Thessalikon Pastry Shop** • 33-21 31st Ave [33rd St]

Just minutes from Manhattan (with appropriately expansive skyline views), Long Island City's former industrial spaces are rapidly giving way to luxury residential units. The massive influx of affluent residents will certainly change the small-town feel of this waterfront enclave, but for now a pleasant mix of yuppies, artists, and blue-collar workers belly up to the bar in local standbys like P.J. Leahy's, Dominie's Hoek, and LIC Bar. It's worth a trip across the river for the affordable French bistro fare at Tournesol or the classic Italian cooking at Manducatis, ideally digested while relaxing in Gantry State Park. PS 1, the Noguchi, Socrates Sculpture Park, and the Fisher-Landau Center offer world-class art for a few dollars at most, but the unlimited screenings that a $65 membership to the American Museum of the Moving Image will get you might be the best deal around.

$ Banks

- **Bank of America** • 25-25 44th Dr [Crescent]
- **Bank of America** • 30-18 36th Ave [30th St]
- **Chase** • 10-51 Jackson Ave [Hunters Point]
- **Citibank** • One Court Sq [Jackson]
- **Citibank (ATM)** • 31-10 Thomson Ave [31st St]
- **Citibank (ATM)** • 32-02 Queens Blvd [Van Dam]
- **HSBC** • 22-15 43rd Ave [22nd St]
- **North Fork** • 44-04 21st St [44th Av]
- **State Bank** • 21-31 46th Ave [21st St]
- **Sterling National** • 30-00 47th Ave [30th St]

O Landmarks

- **5 Pointz/Crane Street Studios** • Jackson Ave & Crane St
- **Center for the Holographic Arts** • 45-10 Court Sq [Jackson]
- **The Chocolate Factory** • 5-49 49th Ave [5th St]
- **Citicorp Building** • 1 Court Sq [Jackson]
- **Fisher Landau Center for Art** • 38-27 30th Ave [38th]
- **Gantry State Park** • 50-50 Second St [51st Av]
- **Hunter's Point Historic District** • 45th Ave b/w 21st St & 23rd St
- **Local Project** • 21-36 44th Rd [21st St]
- **Long Island City Courthouse** • 25-10 Court Sq [Jackson]
- **The Noguchi Museum** • 9-01 33rd Rd [Vernon]
- **NY Center for Media Arts** • 45-12 Davis St [Jackson]
- **PS 1 Contemporary Art Center** • 22-25 Jackson Ave [46th Av]
- **SculptureCenter** • 44-19 Purves St [Jackson]
- **Silvercup Studios** • 42-22 22nd St [Queens Plz S]
- **The Space** • 42-16 West St [Jackson]

😃 Movie Theaters

- **Kaufman Studios Cinema 14** • 35-30 37th St [35th]

▼ Nightlife

- **The Cave** • 10-93 Jackson Ave [48th Av]
- **Dominie's Hoek** • 48-17 Vernon Blvd [48th Av]
- **LIC Bar** • 45-58 Vernon Blvd [46th Av]
- **McReilly's** • 46-42 Vernon Blvd [46th Rd]
- **PJ Leahy's** • 50-02 Vernon Blvd [50th Av]
- **Sunswick Limited** • 35-02 35th St [35th Av]
- **Water Taxi Beach** • Waterfront, 2nd St & Borden Ave

🍴 Restaurants

- **5 Stars Punjabi** • 13-15 43rd Ave [13th St]
- **Bella Via** • 47-46 Vernon Blvd [47th Rd]
- **Brooks 1890 Restaurant** • 24-28 Jackson Ave [Court Sq]
- **Café Henri** • 10-10 50th Ave [Vernon]
- **Court Square Diner** • 45-30 23rd St [45th Rd]
- **Cup Diner** • 35-01 36th St [35th Av]
- **Jackson Ave Steakhouse** • 12-23 Jackson Ave [48th Av]
- **Lil Bistro 33** • 33-04 36th Ave [33rd Av]
- **Lounge 47** • 347-10 Vernon Blvd [47th]
- **Manducatis** • 13-27 Jackson Ave [47th Av]
- **Masso** • 47-25 Vernon Blvd [47th Av]
- **Tournesol** • 50-12 Vernon Blvd [50th Av]
- **Tuk Tuk** • 49-06 Vernon Blvd [49th]
- **Water's Edge** • 44th Dr & East River

🛍 Shopping

- **Celtic Art** • 24-15 Jackson Ave [Pearson]
- **City Dog Lounge** • 49-02 Vernon Blvd [Hunters Pt]
- **Greenmarket** • 48th Ave b/w 5th St & Vernon Blvd
- **Next Level Floral Design** • 47-30 Vernon Blvd [47th Rd]
- **Slovak-Czech Varieties** • 10-59 Jackson Ave [Hunters Pt]
- **Subdivision** • 48-18 Vernon Blvd [48th Av]
- **Vine Wine** • 12-09 Jackson Ave [48th Av]

Pierogies and pastries abound in Greenpoint; kielbasas a-plenty hang in shop windows; and draft beers can be found dirt-cheap. While most of the necessary spots stretch up bustling Manhattan Ave, sneaking off for a quiet moment in McGolrick Park or a pint at the Pencil Factory is certainly as essential.

$ Banks

AP • Apple • 776 Manhattan Ave [Meserole]
CH • Chase • 798 Manhattan Ave [Calyer]
CI • Citibank • 836 Manhattan Ave [Noble]
DI • Dime • 814 Manhattan Ave [Calyer]
HS • HSBC • 896 Manhattan Ave [Greenpoint]
IC • Independence Community • 717 Manhattan Ave [Norman]
NF • North Fork • 807 Manhattan Ave [Calyer]

Nightlife

• **Enid's** • 560 Manhattan Ave [Driggs]
• **Europa** • 98 Meserole Ave [Lorimer]
• **Kingsland Tavern** • 244 Nassau Ave [Kingsland]
• **The Mark Bar** • 1025 Manhattan Ave [Green]
• **Matchless** • 557 Manhattan Ave [Driggs]
• **Pencil Factory** • 142 Franklin St [Greenpoint]
• **Tommy's Tavern** • 1041 Manhattan Ave [Freeman]
• **Warsaw** • 261 Driggs Ave [Eckford]

Restaurants

• **Acapulco Deli & Restaurant** • 1116 Manhattan Ave [Clay]
• **Amarin Café** • 617 Manhattan Ave [Nassau]
• **Baldo's Pizza** • 175 Nassau Ave [Diamond]
• **Bleu Drawes Café** • 97 Commercial St [Ash]
• **Casanova** • 338 McGuinness Blvd [Green]
• **Christina's** • 853 Manhattan Ave [Noble]
• **Dami's** • 931 Manhattan Ave [Kent St]
• **Divine Follie Café** • 929 Manhattan Ave [Kent St]
• **Enid's** • 560 Manhattan Ave [Driggs]
• **Erb** • 681 Manhattan Ave [Norman]
• **Lomzynianka** • 646 Manhattan Ave [Nassau]
• **Fresca Tortilla** • 620 Manhattan Ave [Nassau]
• **God Bless Deli** • 818 Manhattan Ave [Calyer]
• **Imperial Palace** • 748 Manhattan Ave [Meserole]
• **Johnny's Café** • 632 Manhattan Ave [Nassau]
• **Kam Loon** • 975 Manhattan Ave [India]
• **Lamb & Jaffey** • 1073 Manhattan Ave [Eagle]
• **Manhattan 3 Decker Restaurant** • 695 Manhattan Ave [Norman]
• **Monsignor's** • 905 Lorimer St [Nassau]
• **Moon Shadow** • 643 Manhattan Ave [Bedford]
• **Nassau Pizza** • 253 Nassau Ave [Kingsland]
• **Old Poland Restaurant** • 190 Nassau Ave [Humboldt]
• **OTT** • 970 Manhattan Ave [India]
• **Relax** • 68 Newell St [Nassau]
• **San Diego** • 999 Manhattan Ave [Huron]
• **Sapporo Haru** • 622 Manhattan Ave [Bedford]
• **SunView Luncheonette** • 221 Nassau Ave [N Henry]
• **Taco Bite** • 905 Lorimer St [Nassau]
• **Thai Café** • 925 Manhattan Ave [Kent St]
• **Valdiano** • 659 Manhattan Ave [Bedford]
• **Wasabi** • 638 Manhattan Ave [Bedford]

Shopping

• **Chopin Chemists** • 911 Manhattan Ave [Kent]
• **The City Mouse** • 1015 Manhattan Ave [Green]
• **Dee & Dee** • 777 Manhattan Ave [Meserole]
• **The Garden** • 921 Manhattan Ave [Kent]
• **Mini Me** • 123 Nassau Ave [Eckford]
• **Polam** • 952 Manhattan Ave [Java]
• **Pop's Popular Clothing** • 7 Franklin St [Meserole]
• **Syrena Bakery** • 207 Norman Ave [Humboldt]
• **The Thing** • 1001 Manhattan Ave [Huron]
• **Uncle Louie G's** • 172 Greenpoint Ave [Leonard]
• **The Vortex** • 1084 Manhattan Ave [Dupont]
• **Wizard Electroland** • 863 Manhattan Ave [Milton]

Williamsburg has a never-ending supply of cool nightspots like Galapagos, Northsix, and Bembe. Even spotty L train service can't stop folks from flooding in from Manhattan. Neighborhood fashion tip—stylish mullet optional.

$ Banks

- **AP • Apple** • 44 Lee Ave [Wilson St]
- **CH • Chase** • 225 Havemeyer St [B'way]
- **CC • Cross County Federal** • 175 Bedford Ave [N 7th]
- **DI • Dime** • 209 Havemeyer St [S 5th]
- **HS • HSBC** • 175 Broadway [Driggs]
- **NF • North Fork** • 185 Broadway [Driggs]
- **SI • Signature** • 84 Broadway [Berry]

O Landmarks

- **Brooklyn Brewery** • 79 N 11th St [Wythe]

Movie Theaters

- **Ocularis** • Galapagos Art Space • 70 N 6th St [Wythe]

Nightlife

- **The Abbey** • 536 Driggs Ave [N 8th]
- **Alligator Lounge** • 600 Metropolitan Ave [Lorimer]
- **Art Land** • 609 Grand St [Leonard]
- **Barcade** • 388 Union Ave [Ainslie]
- **Bembe** • 81 S 6th St [Berry]
- **Black Betty** • 366 Metropolitan Ave [Havemeyer]
- **Boogaloo** • 168 Marcy Ave [S 5th]
- **Brooklyn Ale House** • 103 Berry St [N 8th]
- **Brooklyn Brewery** • 79 N 11th St [Wythe]
- **Capone's** • 221 N 9th St [Roebling]
- **Charleston** • 174 Bedford Ave [N 7th]
- **Daddy's** • 437 Graham Ave [Frost]
- **East River Bar** • 97 S 6th St [Berry]
- **Galapagos** • 70 N 6th St [Wythe]
- **Greenpoint Tavern** • 188 Bedford Ave [N 7th]
- **Iona** • 180 Grand St [Bedford]
- **Laila Lounge** • 113 N 7th St [Berry]
- **Larry Lawrence** • 295 Grand St [Havemeyer]
- **Mugs Ale House** • 125 Bedford Ave [N 10th]
- **Northsix** • 66 N 6th St [Wythe]
- **Pete's Candy Store** • 709 Lorimer St [Richardson]
- **R Bar** • 451 Meeker Ave [Graham]
- **Red and Black** • 135 N 5th St [Bedford]
- **Royal Oak** • 594 Union Ave [Richardson]
- **Southside Lounge** • 41 Broadway [Wythe]
- **Spike Hill** • 184 Bedford Ave [N 7th]
- **Spuyten Duyvil** • 359 Metropolitan Ave [Havemeyer]
- **Supreme Trading** • 213 N 8th St [Roebling]
- **Surf Bar** • 139 N 6th St
- **Tainted Lady Lounge** • 318 Grand St [Havemeyer]
- **Trash** • 256 Grand St [Roebling]
- **Turkey's Nest** • 94 Bedford Ave [N 12th]
- **Union Pool** • 484 Union Ave [Rodney]

Restaurants

- **Acqua Santa** • 556 Driggs Ave [N 7th]
- **Allioli** • 291 Grand St [Havemeyer]
- **Anna Maria Pizza** • 179 Bedford Ave [N 7th]
- **Anytime** • 93 N 6th St [Wythe]
- **Aurora** • 70 Grand St [Wythe]
- **Bamonte's** • 32 Withers St [Union]
- **Bliss** • 191 Bedford Ave [N 6th]
- **Bonita** • 338 Bedford Ave [S 3rd]
- **Bozu** • 296 Grand St [Havemeyer]
- **Brick Oven Gallery** • 33 Havemeyer St [N 7th]
- **Buffalo Cantina** • 149 Havemeyer St [S 2nd]
- **Café Mexicano** • 513 Grand St [Union]
- **Diner** • 86 Broadway [Berry]
- **Du Mont** • 432 Union Ave [Devoe]
- **East 88** • 212 Bedford Ave [N 5th]
- **Fanny** • 425 Graham Ave [Withers]
- **Foodswings** • 295 Grand St [Havemeyer]
- **Gottlieb's Restaurant** • 352 Roebling St [Division]
- **Grand Café** • 167 Grand St [Bedford]
- **Kellogg's Diner** • 518 Metropolitan Ave [Union]
- **Lodge** • 318 Grand St [Havemeyer]
- **Lola's** • 454 Graham Ave [Richardson]
- **Miss Williamsburg Diner** • 206 Kent Ave [N 3rd]
- **My Moon** • 184 N 10th St [Driggs]
- **Park Luncheonette** • 334 Driggs Ave [Lorimer]
- **Peter Luger Steak House** • 178 Broadway [Driggs]
- **Planet Thailand** • 133 N 7th St [Berry]
- **Raymund's Place** • 124 Bedford Ave [N 10th]
- **Relish** • 225 Wythe St [N 3rd]
- **Roebling Tea Room** • 143 Roebling St [Metropolitan]
- **Sea** • 114 N 6th St [Berry]
- **Snacky** • 187 Grand St [Bedford]
- **Sparky's/Egg** • 135A N 5th St [Bedford]
- **Supercore Café** • 305 Bedford Ave [S 2nd]
- **Taco Chulo** • 318 Grand St [Havemeyer]
- **Teddy's Bar and Grill** • 96 Berry St [N 8th]
- **Uncle Mina** • 436 Union Ave [Devoe]
- **Union Picnic** • 577 Union Ave [Frost]
- **Vera Cruz** • 195 Bedford Ave [N 6th]
- **Williamsburgh Café** • 170 Wythe Ave [N 7th]
- [Roebling]
- **Yola's Café** • 542 Metropolitan Ave [Union]

Shopping

- **Amarcord Vintage Fashion** • 223 Bedford Ave [N 4th]
- **American Apparel** • 104 N 6th St [Berry]
- **Artist & Craftsman** • 761 Metropolitan Ave [Graham]
- **Beacon's Closet** • 88 N 11th St [Wythe]
- **Bedford Cheese Shop** • Mini Mall • 218 Bedford Ave [N 5th]
- **Brooklyn Industries** • 162 Bedford Ave [N 8th]
- **Buffalo Exchange** • 504 Driggs Ave [N 9th]
- **Catbird** • 390 Metropolitan Ave [Havemeyer]
- **Calliope** • 135 Grand St [Berry]
- **Domsey's Warehouse** • 431 Broadway [Hewes]
- **Earwax Records** • Mini Mall • 218 Bedford Ave [N 5th]
- **Emily's Pork Store** • 426 Graham Ave [Withers]
- **Flores Antiques Clothing** • 529 Driggs Ave [Lorimer]
- **Flowers By Marisol** • 568 Grand St [Lorimer]
- **Flying Squirrel** • 96 N 6th St [Wythe]
- **Golden Calf** • 86 N 6th St [Wythe]
- **Joe's Busy Corner** • 552 Driggs Ave [N 7th]
- **Mario and Sons Meat Market** • 662 Metropolitan Ave [Leonard]
- **Marlow and Sons** • 81 Broadway [Berry]
- **Matamoros Puebla Grocery** • 3193 Bedford Ave [N 6th]
- **Metropolitan Fish** • 635 Metropolitan Ave [Leonard]
- **Model T Meats** • 404 Graham Ave [Withers]
- **The Mini-Market** • Mini Mall • 218 Bedford Ave [N 5th]
- **Napoli Bakery** • 616 Metropolitan Ave [Leonard]
- **NY Design Room** • 339 Bedford Ave [S 3rd]
- **PS 9 Pet Supplies** • 169 N 9th St [Bedford]
- **Roulette** • 188 Havemeyer St [S 3rd]
- **Savino's** • 111 Conselyea St [Manhattan]
- **Spacial Etc** • 199 Bedford Ave [N 6th]
- **Spoonbill & Sugartown** • Mini Mall • 218 Bedford Ave [N 5th]
- **Tedone Dairy Products** • 597 Metropolitan Ave [Lorimer]
- **Two Jakes** • 320 Wythe Ave [Grand]
- **Yarn Tree** • 347 Bedford Ave [S 4th]

(**181**)

Map 30 • Brooklyn Heights / DUMBO / Downtown

Fans of the Brooklyn Heights Promenade have spilled into larger DUMBO lofts with equally stunning views. It's no surprise that shops and services resembling (and surpassing) those on Henry Street followed on Water and Front Streets. Neighborhood pastimes include spending an unbeatable afternoon by the water or hanging out at the Fulton Street Mall.

$ Banks

AT • Atlantic • Gristedes • 101 Clark St [Monroe Pl]
AT • Atlantic Liberty • 186 Montague St [Clinton]
BP • Banco Popular • 166 Livingston St [Smith]
BA • Bank of America • 205 Montague St [Clinton]
BA • Bank of America (ATM) • Marriott Hotel • 333 Adams St [Willoughby]
BF • Brooklyn Federal • 81 Court St [Livingston]
CH • Chase • 177 Montague St [Clinton]
CH • Chase • 4 MetroTech Ctr
CH • Chase (ATM) • 168 Myrtle Ave [Prince]
CH • Chase (ATM) • 386 Fulton St [Jay St]
CH • Chase (ATM) • 44 Court St [Joralemon]
CH • Chase (ATM) • 522 Fulton St [Hanover]
CI • Citibank • 181 Montague St [Clinton]
CI • Citibank (ATM) • LIU • 1 University Plz [Fleet Pl]
CC • Community Capital • 111 Livingston St [Adams]
FL • Fleet • 350 Fulton St [Pearl St]
HS • HSBC • 200 Montague St [Clinton]
HS • HSBC • 342 Fulton St [Red Hook]
IC • Independence • 195 Montague St [Clinton]
IC • Independence • 40 Washington St [Water]
NF • North Fork • 356 Fulton St [Red Hook]
NF • North Fork • 50 Court St [Joralemon]
WM • Washington Mutual • 66 Court St [Livingston]
WM • Washington Mutual • 9 DeKalb Ave [Albee]

○ Landmarks

• **Brooklyn Borough Hall** • 209 Joralemon St [Cadman Plz W]
• **Brooklyn Bridge** • Adams St & East River
• **Brooklyn Heights Promenade**
• **Brooklyn Historical Society** • 128 Pierrepont St [Clinton]
• **Brooklyn Ice Cream Factory** • Fulton Ferry Pier [Everit]
• **Brooklyn Navy Yard** • Waterfront [Cumberland]
• **Brooklyn Tabernacle** • 17 Smith St [Livingston]
• **Fulton Street Mall** • Fulton St b/w Flatbush Ave & Boerum Hall
• *Jetsons Building* • 110 York St [Jay St]
• *Junior's Restaurant* • 386 Flatbush Ave [DeKalb]
• **New York Transit Museum** • Boerum Pl & Schermerhorn St

😃 Movie Theaters

• **Pavilion Brooklyn Heights** • 70 Henry St [Orange]
• **Regal/UA Court Street** • 108 Court St [State]

🍸 Nightlife

• **68 Jay Street Bar** • 68 Jay St [Front St]
• **Dumba** • 57 Jay St [Water]
• **Henry St Ale House** • 62 Henry St [Cranberry]
• **Low Bar** • 81 Washington St [York]
• **St Ann's Warehouse** • 38 Water St
• **Water Street Bar** • 66 Water St [Main]

🍴 Restaurants

• **Bubby's** • 1 Main St [Plymouth]
• **Chipotle** • 185 Montague St [Clinton]
• **Curry Leaf** • 151 Remsen St [Clinton]
• **DUMBO General Store** • 111 Front St [Adams]
• **Fascati Pizzeria** • 80 Henry St [Orange]
• **Five Front** • 5 Front St [Old Fulton]
• **Grimaldi's** • 19 Old Fulton St [Doughty]
• **Hale & Hearty Soup** • 32 Court St [Remsen]
• **Heights Café** • 84 Montague St [Hicks]
• **Henry's End** • 44 Henry St [Middagh]
• **Miso** • 40 Main St [Front St]
• **Noodle Pudding** • 38 Henry St [Middagh]
• **Pete's Downtown** • 2 Water St [Old Fulton]
• **The Plant** • 25 Jay St [Plymouth]
• **Pig'n Out Barbeque** • 60 Henry St [Cranberry]
• **Rice** • 81 Washington St [York]
• **River Café** • 1 Water St [Old Fulton]
• **Siggy's Good Food** • 76 Henry St [Orange]
• **Superfine** • 126 Front St [Pearl St]
• **Sushi California** • 71 Clark St [Henry]
• **Taco Madre** • 118 Montague St [Henry]
• **Thai 101** • 101 Montague St [Hicks]
• **Toro Restaurant** • 1 Front St [Old Fulton]

🛍 Shopping

• **Almondine Bakery** • 85 Water St [Main]
• **City Barn Antiques** • 145 Front St [Pearl St]
• **Design Within Reach** • 76 Montague St [Hicks]
• **Halcyon** • 57 Pearl St [Water]
• **Half Pint** • 55 Washington St [Front St]
• **Heights Prime Meats** • 59 Clark St [Henry]
• **Jacques Torres Chocolate** • 66 Water St [Main]
• **Lassen & Hennigs** • 114 Montague St [Henry]
• **Recycle-A-Bicycle** • 55 Washington St [Front St]
• **Tapestry the Salon** • 107 Montague St [Hicks]
• **West Elm** • 75 Front St [Main]
• **Wonk** • 68 Jay St [Front St]

Since Fort Greene has officially exploded, we say: try thinking small. Seek basement dive bars, hole-in-the-wall Caribbean cuisine, and neighborhood discount liquor stores. Natives will appreciate such riches as a walk by the colossal Masonic Temple or a cultural field trip to BAM.

$ Banks

AP • Apple • 414 Flushing Ave [Skillman]
CF • Carver Federal • 4 Hanson Pl [Ashland]
CH • Chase • 20 Flatbush Ave [Nevins]
CH • Chase • 210 Flushing Ave [Wash Av]
CH • Chase • 975 Bedford Ave [DeKalb]
CI • Citibank • 430 Myrtle Ave [Clinton]
HS • HSBC • 118 Flatbush Ave [State]
IC • Independence Community • Pratt • 200 Willoughby Ave [Hall]

O Landmarks

• **Brooklyn Academy of Music •** 30 Lafayette Ave [Ashland]
• **Brooklyn Masonic Temple •** 317 Clermont Ave [Lafayette]
• **Fort Greene Park •** DeKalb Ave & Washington Park
• **Lafayette Avenue Presbyterian Church •** 85 S Oxford St [Lafayette]
• **Long Island Rail Road Station •** Hanson Pl & Flatbush Ave
• **Pratt Institute Power Plant •** 200 Willoughby Ave [Hall]
• **Steiner Studios •** 15 Washington Ave [Flushing]
• **Williamsburgh Savings Bank Building •** 1 Hanson Pl [Ashland]

Movie Theaters

• **BAM Rose Cinemas •** BAM • 30 Lafayette Ave [St Felix]

Nightlife

• **BAMcafé •** BAM • 30 Lafayette Ave [St Felix]
• **Frank's Lounge •** 660 Fulton St [S Elliott Pl]
• **Moe's •** 80 Lafayette Ave [S Portland]
• **Reign Bar & Lounge •** 46 Washington Ave [Flushing]
• **Rope •** 415 Myrtle Ave [Clinton]
• **Sputnik •** 262 Taaffe Pl [DeKalb]
• **Stonehome Wine Bar •** 87 Lafayette Ave [S Portland]

Restaurants

• **1 Greene Sushi and Sashimi •** 1 Greene Ave [Fulton]
• **Academy Restaurant •** 69 Lafayette Ave [S Elliott Pl]
• **BAMcafé •** BAM • 30 Lafayette Ave [Ashland]
• **Black Iris •** 228 DeKalb Ave [Clermont]
• **Boca Soul •** 919 Fulton St [Waverly]
• **Brooklyn Moon Café •** 745 Fulton St [S Portland]

• **Buff Patty •** 376 Myrtle Ave [Clermont]
• **Cake Man Raven •** 708 Fulton St [Hanson]
• **Cambodian Cuisine •** 87 S Elliot Pl [Lafayette]
• **Castro's Restaurant •** 511 Myrtle Ave [Grand]
• **Chez Oskar •** 211 DeKalb Ave [Adelphi]
• **Dakar Restaurant •** 285 Grand Ave [Clifton]
• **Farmer in the Deli •** 357 Myrtle Ave [Adelphi]
• **Gia •** 68 Lafayette Ave [S Elliott Pl]
• **Good Joy Chinese Takeout •** 216 DeKalb Ave [Adelphi]
• **Habana Outpost •** 755 Fulton St [S Portland]
• **Ici •** 246 DeKalb Ave [Vanderbilt]
• **Joloff Restaurant •** 930 Fulton St [St James]
• **Kush •** 17 Putnam Ave [Grand]
• **Locanda Vini & Olii •** 129 Gates Ave [Cambridge]
• **LouLou •** 222 DeKalb Ave [Clermont]
• **Luz •** 177 Vanderbilt Ave [Myrtle]
• **Madiba •** 195 DeKalb Ave [Carlton]
• **Maggie Brown •** 455 Myrtle Ave [Wash Av]
• **Mario's Pizzeria •** 224 DeKalb Ave [Clermont]
• **Mo-Bay •** 112 DeKalb Ave [Ashland]
• **Mojito Restaurant •** 82 Washington Ave [Park]
• **New Orleans •** 747 Fulton St [S Portland]
• **Night of the Cookers •** 767 Fulton St [S Oxford]
• **Olea •** 171 Lafayette Ave [Adelphi]
• **Pequena •** 86 S Portland Ave [Lafayette]
• **Pratt Coffee Shop •** 274 Hall St [DeKalb]
• **Rice •** 166 DeKalb Ave [Cumberland]
• **Ruthie's Restaurant •** 96 DeKalb Ave [Ashland]
• **Scopello •** 63 Lafayette Ave [S Elliott Pl]
• **Thai 101 •** 455 Myrtle Ave [Wash Av]
• **Thomas Beisl •** 25 Lafayette Ave [Ashland]
• **Veliis •** 773 Fulton St [S Oxford]

Shopping

• **Cake Man Raven Confectionary •** 708 Fulton St [Hanson]
• **Carol's Daughter •** 1 S Elliott Pl [DeKalb]
• **Frosted Moon •** 154 Vanderbilt Ave [Myrtle]
• **The Greene Grape •** 765 Fulton St [S Oxford]
• **Kiki's Pet Spa •** 239 DeKalb Ave [Vanderbilt]
• **L'Epicerie •** 270 Vanderbilt Ave [DeKalb]
• **Malchijah Hats •** 225 DeKalb Ave [Clermont]
• **The Midtown Greenhouse Garden Center •** 115 Flatbush Ave [Hanson]
• **My Little India •** 96 S Elliott Pl [Fulton]
• **Nubian Heritage •** 560 Fulton St [Rockwell]
• **Owa African Market •** 434 Myrtle Ave [Waverly]
• **Planet Pleasure •** 527 Myrtle Ave [Steuben]
• **Sodafine •** 246 DeKalb Ave [Vanderbilt]
• **Target •** Atlantic Terminal • 139 Flatbush Ave [Atlantic]
• **White Elephant Gallery •** 572 Myrtle Ave [Classon]
• **Yu Interiors •** 15 Greene Ave [Cumberland]

Map 32 • **BoCoCa**

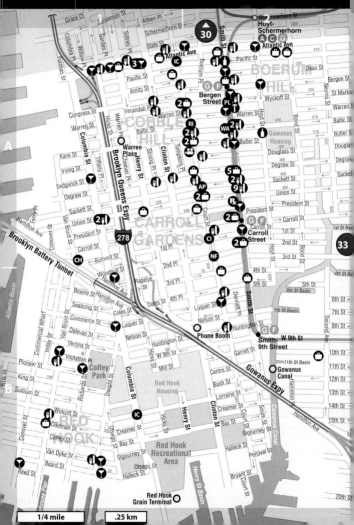

BOCOCA is one of the most convenient Brooklyn neighborhoods to live in because everything you need and want is on Court and Smith Streets. The former retains a traditional neighborhood feel, while the latter undergoes an upscale makeover. For a more adventurous stroll, check out Van Brunt Street in Red Hook.

Banks

- **AP • Apple •** 326 Court St [Sackett]
- **CH • Chase •** 79 Hamilton Ave [Summit]
- **CI • Citibank •** 375 Court St [Carroll]
- **IC • Independence Community •** 130 Court St [Atlantic]
- **IC • Independence Community •** 498 Columbia St [Lorraine]
- **NF • North Fork •** 420 Court St [1st Pl]
- **PL • Ponce de Leon •** 169 Smith St [Wyckoff]
- **RW • Ridgewood •** 244 Court St [Kane]
- **RS • Roosevelt Savings •** 1-37 12th St [3rd Av]
- **WM • Washington Mutual •** 192 Smith St [Warren St]

Landmarks

- **Gowanus Canal**
- **Phone Booth •** Huntington Street & Hamilton Ave
- **Red Hook Grain Terminal**
- **Warren Place •** Warren Pl [Warren St]

Movie Theaters

- **Cobble Hill Cinemas •** 265 Court St [Butler]

Nightlife

- **Boat •** 175 Smith St [Wyckoff]
- **Brazen Head •** 228 Atlantic Ave [Court St]
- **Brooklyn Inn •** 148 Hoyt St [Bergen]
- **Brooklyn Social •** 335 Smith St [Carroll]
- **Camp •** 179 Smith St [Wyckoff]
- **Floyd •** 131 Atlantic Ave [Henry]
- **Gowanus Yacht Club •** 323 Smith St [President]
- **The Hook •** 18 Commerce St [Columbia]
- **Kili •** 81 Hoyt St [State]
- **Last Exit •** 136 Atlantic Ave [Henry]
- **Liberty Heights Tap Room •** 34 Van Dyke St [Dwight]

- **Lillie's •** 46 Beard St [Dwight]
- **Magnetic Field •** 97 Atlantic Ave [Hicks]
- **Mini Bar •** 482 Court St [4th Pl]
- **Montero's •** 73 Atlantic Ave [Hicks]
- **Moonshine •** 317 Columbia St [Hicks]
- **Pioneer Bar-B-Q •** 318 Van Brunt St [Pioneer]
- **Red Hook Bait & Tackle •** 320 Van Brunt St [Pioneer]
- **Sugar Lounge •** 147A Columbia St [Kane]
- **Sunny's •** 253 Conover St [Reed]
- **Waterfront Ale House •** 155 Atlantic Ave [Clinton]

Restaurants

- **360 •** 360 Van Brunt St [Sullivan St]
- **Alma •** 187 Columbia St [Degraw]
- **Atlantic Chip Shop •** 129 Atlantic Ave [Henry]
- **Bar Tabac •** 128 Smith St [Dean]
- **Bouillabaisse 126 •** 126 Union St [Columbia]
- **Café Luluc •** 214 Smith St [Butler]
- **Café on Clinton •** 268 Clinton St [Verandah]
- **Chance •** 223 Smith St [Butler]
- **Chicory •** 243 DeGraw St [Clinton]
- **Cobble Grill •** 212 DeGraw St [Henry]
- **Cubana Café •** 272 Smith St [Degraw]
- **Cube 63 •** 234 Court St [Baltic]
- **Damascus Bread & Pastry Shop •** 195 Atlantic Ave [Court St]
- **Delicatessen •** 264 Clinton St [Verandah]
- **Donut House •** 314 Court St [Degraw]
- **El Portal •** 217 Smith St [Butler]
- **Faan •** 209 Smith St [Baltic]
- **Fatoosh •** 330 Hicks St [Atlantic]
- **Ferdinando's •** 151 Union St [Hicks]
- **Fragole •** 394 Court St [Carroll]
- **Frankie's 457 •** 457 Court St [Luquer]
- **The Grocery •** 288 Smith St [Sackett]
- **Gravy •** 100 Smith St [Atlantic]
- **Hill Diner •** 231 Court St [Warren St]
- **Hope & Anchor •** 347 Van Brunt St [Wolcott]
- **Joya •** 215 Court St [Warren St]
- **Le Petite Café •** 502 Court St [Nelson]
- **Liberty Heights Tap Room •** 34 Van Dyke St [Dwight]

- **Osaka •** 272 Court St [Butler]
- **Panino'teca 275 •** 275 Smith St [Sackett]
- **Patois •** 255 Smith St [Degraw]
- **Royal's Downtown •** 215 Union St [Henry]
- **Savoia •** 277 Smith St [Sackett]
- **Schnack •** 122 Union St [Columbia]
- **Sherwood Café/Robin des Bois •** 195 Smith St [Warren St]
- **Siam Garden •** 172 Court St [Amity]
- **Soul Spot •** 302 Atlantic Ave [Smith]
- **Tuk Tuk •** 204 Smith St [Baltic]
- **Zaytoons •** 283 Smith St [Sackett]

Shopping

- **American Apparel •** 112 Court St [State]
- **American Beer Distributors •** 256 Court St [Kane]
- **Baked •** 359 Van Brunt St [Dikeman]
- **Book Court •** 163 Court St [Dean]
- **Brooklyn Industries •** 100 Smith St [Atlantic]
- **Butter •** 389 Atlantic Ave [Bond]
- **Caputo's Fine Foods •** 460 Court St [3rd Pl]
- **D'Amico Foods •** 309 Court St [Degraw]
- **Environment337 •** 337 Smith St [Carroll]
- **Frida's Closet •** 296 Smith St [Union]
- **The Green Onion •** 274 Smith St [Sackett]
- **Hats & •** 266 President St [Court St]
- **Kimera •** 366 Atlantic Ave [Hoyt]
- **Lowe's •** 118 Second Ave [10th]
- **Marquet •** 221 Court St [Warren St]
- **Mazzola Bakery •** 192 Union St [Henry]
- **Nova Zembla •** 117 Atlantic Ave [Henry]
- **Refinery •** 254 Smith St [Douglass]
- **Rocketship •** 208 Smith St [Baltic]
- **Sahadi Importing Company •** 187 Atlantic Ave [Court St]
- **Staubitz Meat Market •** 222 Court St [Baltic]
- **Swallow •** 361 Smith St [2nd]
- **Sweet Melissa •** 276 Court St [Butler]
- **Tuller •** 199 Court St [Wyckoff]
- **Zipper •** 333 Smith St [President]

Park Slope / Prospect Heights / Windsor Ter

Map 33

Essentials / Sundries

Bucolic Park Slope features Cosby-esque brownstones, neighbors waving across flowerboxes, and children playing stickball. Really. Anything you need is here: world-class library, museum, park, and botanic gardens; convenient shopping and renowned public schools. Residents swear by the Park Slope Food Co-op (membership required), Community Book Store, and PS 321 Flea Market.

$ Banks

- **AF • Astoria Federal •** 110 Seventh Ave [President]
- **AF • Astoria Federal •** 459 Fifth Ave [10th]
- **BA • Bank of America (ATM) •** Atlantic Terminal • 139 Flatbush Ave [Atlantic]
- **CF • Carver Federal (ATM) •** Atlantic Terminal • 139 Flatbush Ave [Atlantic]
- **CH • Chase •** 127 Seventh Ave [Carroll]
- **CH • Chase •** 401 Flatbush Ave [8th Av]
- **CH • Chase •** 444 Fifth Ave [9th]
- **CI • Citibank •** 114 Seventh Ave [President]
- **DO • Doral •** 478 Fifth Ave [11th]
- **HS • HSBC •** 325 9th St [5th Av]
- **IC • Independence Community •** 234 Prospect Park W [Windsor]
- **MT • M&T •** 354 Flatbush Ave [St Johns]
- **NF • North Fork •** 516 Fifth Ave [13th]
- **NF • North Fork •** 856 Washington Ave [Lincoln]
- **RS • Roosevelt Savings •** Pathmark • 625 Atlantic Ave [5th Av]
- **WM • Washington Mutual •** 533 Fifth Ave

O Landmarks

- **Brooklyn Botanic Garden •** 900 Washington Ave [Crown]
- **Brooklyn Conservatory of Music •** 58 Seventh Ave [Lincoln]
- **Brooklyn Public Library (Central Branch) •** Grand Army Plz [Grand]
- **Grand Army Plaza •** Flatbush Ave & Plaza St
- **Park Slope Food Co-op •** 782 Union St [7th Av]

🎬 Movie Theaters

- **Pavilion Movie Theatres •** 188 Prospect Park W [Greenwood]

🎭 Nightlife

- **Bar Sepia •** 234 Underhill Ave [Lincoln]
- **Bar Toto •** 411 11th St [6th Av]
- **Barbes •** 376 9th St [6th Av]
- **Buttermilk •** 577 Fifth Ave [16th]
- **Cattyshack •** 249 Fourth Ave [President]
- **Excelsior •** 390 Fifth Ave [6th]
- **Farrell's •** 215 Prospect Park W [16th]
- **Freddy's •** 485 Dean St [6th Av]
- **The Gate •** 321 Fifth Ave [3rd St]
- **Ginger's •** 363 Fifth Ave [5th]
- **Great Lakes •** 284 Fifth Ave [1st St]
- **Half •** 626 Vanderbilt Ave [Park]
- **Hank's Saloon •** 46 Third Ave [Atlantic]
- **Lighthouse Tavern •** 243 Fifth Ave [Carroll]
- **Loki Lounge •** 304 Fifth Ave [2nd]
- **Lucky 13 Saloon •** 273 13th St [5th Av]
- **Mooney's Pub •** 353 Flatbush Ave [Park]
- **O'Connor's •** 39 Fifth Ave [Bergen]
- **Park Slope Ale House •** 356 Sixth Ave [5]
- **Patio Lounge •** 179 Fifth Ave [Berkeley]

- **Puppet's Jazz Bar •** 294 Fifth Ave [1st St]
- **Royale •** 506 Fifth Ave [12th]
- **Soda •** 629 Vanderbilt Ave [Prospect Pl]
- **Southpaw •** 125 Fifth Ave [Sterling]
- **Up Over Jazz Café •** 351 Flatbush Ave [Park]

🍴 Restaurants

- **12th Street Bar and Grill •** 1123 Eighth Ave [11th]
- **16th St Gourmet •** 212 Prospect Park W [16th]
- **2nd Street Café •** 189 Seventh Ave [2nd]
- **Al Di La Trattoria •** 248 Fifth Ave [Carroll]
- **Anthony's •** 426 Seventh Ave [14th]
- **Applewood •** 501 11th St [7th Av]
- **Beast •** 638 Bergen St [Vanderbilt]
- **Beet •** 344 Seventh Ave [10th]
- **Beso •** 210 Fifth Ave [Union]
- **Black Pearl •** 803 Union St [7th Av]
- **Blue Ribbon Brooklyn •** 280 Fifth Ave [1]
- **Bogota Latin Bistro •** 141 Fifth Ave [St Johns]
- **Bonnie's Grill •** 278 Fifth Ave [1st St]
- **Brooklyn Fish Camp •** 162 Fifth Ave [Douglass]
- **Café Steinhof •** 422 Seventh Ave [14th]
- **ChipShop •** 383 Fifth Ave [6th]
- **Christie's Jamaican Patties •** 334 Flatbush Ave [Sterling]
- **Coco Roco •** 392 Fifth Ave [6th]
- **Convivium Osteria •** 68 Fifth Ave [St Marks Pl]
- **Cousin John's Café and Bakery •** 70 Seventh Ave [Lincoln]
- **Dizzy's •** 511 Ninth St [8th Av]
- **Elora's •** 272 Prospect Park W [17th]
- **Franny's •** 295 Flatbush Ave [Prospect Pl]
- **Garden Café •** 620 Vanderbilt Ave [Prospect Pl]
- **Gourmet Grill •** 291 Fifth Ave [2nd]
- **Jack's •** 519 Fifth Ave [13th]
- **Java Indonesian Rijsttafel •** 455 Seventh Ave [16th]
- **Johnny Mack's •** 1114 Eighth Ave [11th]
- **Junior's Restaurant •** 386 Flatbush Ave [St Johns]
- **Kinara •** 473 Fifth Ave [11th]
- **La Taqueria •** 72 Seventh Ave [Berkeley]
- **Long Tan •** 196 Fifth Ave [Berkeley]
- **Los Pollitos II •** 148 Fifth Ave [St Johns]
- **Maria's Mexican Bistro •** 669 Union St [4th Av]
- **The Minnow •** 442 9th St [7th Av]
- **Mitchell's Soul Food •** 617 Vanderbilt Ave [St Marks Av]
- **Nana •** 155 Fifth Ave [Lincoln]
- **New Prospect Café •** 393 Flatbush Ave [Sterling]
- **Olive Vine Café •** 362 15th St [7th Av]
- **Olive Vine Café •** 54 Seventh Ave [St Johns]
- **Parkside Restaurant •** 355 Flatbush Ave [Park]
- **Red Hot •** 349 Seventh Ave [10th]
- **Rice •** 311 Seventh Ave [Eighth]
- **Rose Water •** 787 Union St [6th Av]
- **Santa Fe Grill •** 62 Seventh Ave [Lincoln]

- **Seventh Avenue Donut Shop •** 324 Seventh Ave [9th]
- **Sotto Voce •** 225 Seventh Ave [4th]
- **Stone Park Café •** 324 Fifth Ave [3rd St]
- **Sushi Tatsu •** 347 Flatbush Ave [Sterling]
- **Tom's •** 782 Washington Ave [Sterling]
- **Tost •** 427 Seventh Ave [14th]
- **Tutta Pasta •** 160 Seventh Ave [Garfield]
- **Two Boots •** 514 2nd St [32nd]
- **Windsor Café •** 220 Prospect Park W [16th]

🛍 Shopping

- **3R Living •** 276 Fifth Ave [Garfield]
- **Artesana Home •** 170 Seventh Ave [1st St]
- **Baby Bird •** 428 Seventh Ave [14th]
- **Barnes & Noble •** 267 Seventh Ave [6th]
- **Beacon's Closet •** 220 Fifth Ave [President]
- **Bird •** 430 Seventh Ave [14th]
- **Blue Apron Foods •** 812 Union St [7th Av]
- **Bob and Judi's Collectibles •** 217 Fifth Ave [President]
- **Boing Boing •** 204 Sixth Ave [Union]
- **Brooklyn Industries •** 206 Fifth Ave [Union]
- **Brooklyn Superhero Supply •** 372 Fifth Ave [5th]
- **Castor & Pollux •** 76 Sixth Ave [Flatbush]
- **Clay Pot •** 162 Seventh Ave [Garfield]
- **Cog and Pearl •** 190 Fifth Ave [Berkeley]
- **Community Book Store •** 143 Seventh Ave [Garfield]
- **Ecco Home Design •** 232 Seventh Ave [4th]
- **Eidolon •** 233 Fifth Ave [Carroll]
- **Fabrica •** 619 Vanderbilt Ave [Prospect Pl]
- **Fifth Avenue Record and Tape Center •** 439 Fifth Ave [9th]
- **Greenjeans •** 449 Seventh Ave [16th]
- **Hibiscus •** 564A Vandebilt Ave [Bergen]
- **Hooti Couture •** 321 Flatbush Ave [Prospect Pl]
- **JackRabbit Sports •** 151 Seventh Ave [Garfield]
- **Leaf and Bean •** 83 Seventh Ave [Berkeley]
- **Loom •** 115 Seventh Ave [President]
- **Mandee •** 509 Fifth Ave [13th]
- **Mostly Modern •** 383 Seventh Ave [12th]
- **Nancy Nancy •** 244 Fifth Ave [Carroll]
- **Orange Blossom •** 180 Lincoln Pl [7th Av]
- **Park Slope Food Co-op •** 782 Union St [7th Av]
- **Pieces •** 671 Vanderbilt Ave [Prospect Pl]
- **Premium Goods •** 347 Fifth Ave [4th]
- **PS 321 Flea Market •** Seventh Ave and First St
- **Rare Device •** 453 Seventh Ave [16th]
- **RedLipstick •** 560 Vanderbilt Ave [Dean]
- **Reverse •** 176 Fifth Ave [Lincoln]
- **Shoe Mine •** 463 Seventh Ave [16th]
- **Somethin' Else •** 294 Fifth Ave [1st St]
- **Sound Track •** 119 Seventh Ave [Carroll]
- **Stitch Therapy •** 176 Lincoln Pl [7th Av]
- **Traditions •** 465 Fifth Ave [10th]
- **Trailer Park •** 77 Sterling Pl [6th Av]
- **Uncle Louie G's •** 741 Union St [5th Av]

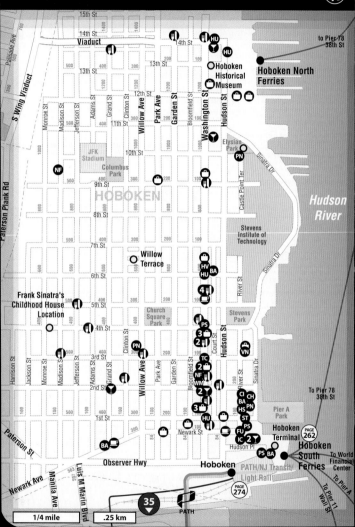

Map 34 · Hoboken

Just 9 minutes away from Manhattan by PATH train or 10 minutes by ferry, Hoboken is almost (but not quite) another borough of New York City. Luxury condos and a fancy chain-store strip mall now inhabit the perimeter of this once-gritty longshoreman town, but the center of Hoboken retains its small scale. At only about a mile square and in a grid system, the area lends itself nicely to a stroll. While wandering, you'll discover Hoboken's remaining mom-and-pop butchers, bakeries, and Italian specialty shops, as well as its members-only social clubs. At night, the town can take on a frat party vibe as recent grads pour in for pub-crawls and good-time college revelry.

$ Banks

BA • Bank of America • 1 Firehouse Plz [1st]
BA • Bank of America • 615 Washington St [6th]
BA • Bank of America (ATM) • New Jersey Transit • 1 Hudson Pl [Observer]
BA • Bank of America (ATM) • Hoboken Mall • 400 Newark Ave [Grand]
CH • Chase • 125 River St [1st]
CI • Citibank • 5 Marine View Plz [River St]
HS • Haven Savings • 621 Washington St [6th]
HS • HSBC • 5 Marine View Plz [River St]
HU • Hudson United • 101 Washington St [Dudley]
HU • Hudson United • 1325 Hudson St [13th]
HU • Hudson United • 60 14th St [Washington]
HU • Hudson United • 609 Washington St [6th]
IC • Independence Community • 86 River St [Newark]
NF • North Fork • 220 Washington St [2nd]
NF • North Fork • 301 Washington St [3rd]
NF • North Fork • 940 Madison St [9th]
PS • Pamrapo Savings • 401 Washington St [4th]
PN • PNC • 111 River St [1st]
PN • PNC (ATM) • Steven's Institute • 1 Castle Point Ter
PN • PNC (ATM) • St Mary Hospital • 308 Willow Ave [3rd]
PS • Provident Savings • 77 River St [Newark]
PS • Provident Savings (ATM) • P&I Building • 1 Hudson Pl [Observer]
ST • Sumitomo Trust • 111 River St [1st]
VN • Valley National • 305 River St [3rd]
WA • Wachovia • 95 River St [1st]
WM • Washington Mutual • 222 Washington St [2nd]

O Landmarks

• **Elysian Park**
• **Frank Sinatra's Childhood House Location** • 415 Monroe St [4th]
• **Hoboken Historical Museum** • 1301 Hudson St [13th]
• **Hoboken Terminal** • 1 Hudson Pl [River St]
• **Willow Terrace** • 6th & 7th St b/w Willow Ave & Clinton St

Y Nightlife

• **Black Bear** • 205 Washington St [2nd]
• **City Bistro** • 56 14th St [Washington]
• **Leo's Grandezvous** • 200 Grand St [2nd]

• **Maxwell's** • 1039 Washington St [10th]
• **Mile Square** • 221 Washington St [2nd]
• **Oddfellows** • 80 River St [Newark]
• **Texas Arizona** • 76 River St [Newark]

Restaurants

• **Amanda's** • 908 Washington St [9th]
• **Arthur's Tavern** • 237 Washington St [2nd]
• **Baja** • 104 14th St [Washington]
• **Bangkok City** • 335 Washington St [3rd]
• **Biggies Clam Bar** • 318 Madison St [3rd]
• **Brass Rail** • 135 Washington St [1st]
• **Cucharamama** • 233 Clinton St [2nd]
• **Delfino's** • 500 Jefferson St [5th]
• **East LA** • 508 Washington St [5th]
• **Far Side Bar & Grill** • 531 Washington St [5th]
• **Frankie & Johnnie's** • 163 14th St [Bloomfield]
• **Gaslight** • 400 Adams St [4th]
• **Hoboken Gourmet Company** • 423 Washington St [4th]
• **Karma Kafe** • 505 Washington St [5th]
• **La Isla** • 104 Washington St [1st]
• **La Tartuferia** • 1405 Grand St [14th]
• **Robongi** • 520 Washington St [5th]
• **Sushi Lounge** • 200 Hudson St [2nd]
• **Trattoria Saporito** • 328 Washington St [3rd]
• **Zafra** • 301 Willow Ave [3rd]

Shopping

• **Air Studio** • 55 2nd St [1st]
• **Basic Foods** • 204 Washington St [2nd]
• **Battaglia's** • 319 Washington St [3rd]
• **Big Fun Toys** • 602 Washington St [6th]
• **City Paint & Hardware** • 130 Washington St [1st]
• **Galatea** • 1224 Washington St [12th]
• **Hand Mad** • 86 Park Ave [Newark]
• **Hoboken Farmboy** • 127 Washington St [1st]
• **Kings Fresh Ideas** • 333 River Rd [3rd]
• **Kings Fresh Ideas** • 1212 Shipyard Ln [12th]
• **Lisa's Italian Deli** • 901 Park Ave [9th]
• **Makeovers** • 302 Washington St [3rd]
• **Peper** • 1028 Washington St [10th]
• **Sobsey's Produce** • 92 Bloomfield St [Newark]
• **Sparrow Wine and Liquor** • 1224 Shipyard Ln [12th]
• **Sparrow Wine and Liquor** • 126 Washington St [1st]
• **Tunes New & Used CDs** • 225 Washington St [2nd]
• **Yes I Do** • 312 Washington St [3rd]

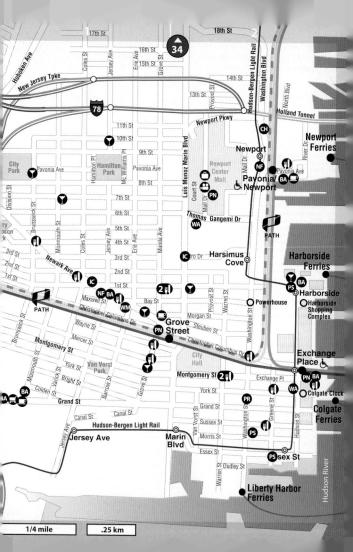

If you are taking the ferry from Manhattan, you will quickly notice that the entire waterfront of Jersey City is under construction. (You'll see at least ten new buildings going up.) Is Jersey City the "Sixth Borough" of New York? Not yet, but when all of the building is complete, it will be interesting to see what has evolved. With many fine restaurants and an increasing number of after-work hangouts popping up, especially near the Grove Street area, Jersey City is growing as a neighborhood that is well worth checking out. If you don't believe us, check out the area surrounding gorgeous Hamilton Park. On the downside—those two damned malls.

💲 Banks

- **BA • Bank of America** • 10 Exchange Pl [Hudson]
- **BA • Bank of America** • 123 Harborside Financial Ctr [Hudson]
- **BA • Bank of America** • 125 Pavonia Ave [Washington]
- **BA • Bank of America** • 186 Newark Ave [Jersey]
- **BA • Bank of America (ATM)** • 235 Monmouth St [Colden]
- **CH • Chase** • 575 Washington Blvd [Greene]
- **CH • Chase (ATM)** • 570 Washington Blvd, 1st Fl [Holland Tunnel]
- **IC • Independence** • 214 Newark Ave [1st]
- **IC • Independence** • 400 Marin Blvd [Metro Plz]
- **NF • North Fork** • 201 Newark Ave [Jersey]
- **NF • North Fork** • 525 Washington Blvd
- **PS • Pamrapo Savings (ATM)** • Liberty Wine & Deli • 200 Washington St [Morris]
- **PS • Pamrapo Savings (ATM)** • The Green Cow Deli • 34 Greene St [Essex]
- **PN • PNC** • 1 Exchange Pl [Hudson]
- **PN • PNC** • 95 Christopher Columbus Dr [Grove]
- **PN • PNC (ATM)** • Newport Centre • 30 Mall Dr W [Thomas Gangemi]
- **PS • Provident Savings** • 1 2nd St [Hudson]
- **PS • Provident Savings** • 239 Washington St [York]
- **PS • Provident Savings** • Goldman Sachs Tower • 30 Hudson St [Morris]
- **VN • Valley National** • 46 Essex St [Greene]
- **WA • Wachovia** • 101 Hudson St [York]
- **WA • Wachovia** • 145 Thomas Gangemi Dr [Mall Dr W]
- **WM • Washington Mutual** • 163 Newark Ave [Barrow]

🅾 Landmarks

- **Colgate Clock** • 105 Hudson St [York]
- **Powerhouse** • 344 Washington St [Bay]
- **Harborside Shopping Complex**

🎬 Movie Theaters

- **Loews Cineplex Newport Center 11** • 30 Mall Dr W [Thomas Gangemi]

🍸 Nightlife

- **Dennis and Maria's Bar** • 322 1/2 7th St [Monmouth]
- **Hamilton Park Ale House** • 708 Jersey Ave [10th]
- **Lamp Post Bar and Grille** • 382 2nd St [Bruswick]
- **LITM** • 140 Newark Ave [Grove]
- **Markers** • Harborside Financial Ctr, Plz II [Hudson]
- **The Merchant** • 279 Grove St [Montgomery]
- **PJ Ryan's** • 172 1st St [Luis Munoz Marin]
- **White Star** • 230 Brunswick St [Pavonia]

🍴 Restaurants

- **Amelia's Bistro** • 187 Warren St [Essex]
- **Casablanca Grill** • 354 Grove St [Bay]
- **Ibby's Falafel** • 303 Grove St [Wayne]
- **Iron Monkey** • 97 Greene St [York]
- **Kitchen Café** • 60 Sussex St [Greene]
- **Komegashi** • 103 Montgomery St [Warren]
- **Komegashi Too** • 99 Pavonia Ave [River Dr S]
- **Light Horse Tavern** • 199 Washington St [Morris]
- **Madame Claude** • 364 4th St [4th]
- **Marco and Pepe** • 289 Grove St [Mercer]
- **Miss Saigon** • 249 Newark Ave [Coles]
- **Oddfellows Restaurant** • 111 Montgomery St [Warren]
- **Presto's Restaurant** • 199 Warren St [Morris]
- **Pronto Cena** • 87 Sussex St [Washington St]
- **Rosie Radigans** • 10 Exchange Pl , Lobby [Hudson]
- **Saigon Café** • 188 Newark Ave [Jersey]
- **Tania's** • 348 Grove St [Bay]
- **Uno Chicago Bar & Grill** • 286 Washington St [Christopher Columbus]

🛍 Shopping

- **Harborside Shopping Complex**
- **Newport Center Mall** • 30 Mall Dr W [Thomas Gangemi]

Don't be afraid of the Boogie Down Bronx. Decades of entrenched poverty and poor urban planning once frayed many neighborhoods, but the borough today is no longer the burning wreck your parents warned you about years ago.

Communities

Belmont's Arthur Avenue **3** is still an authentic Little Italy even though many businesses now belong to Albanians. Woodlawn **9** is home to many Irish immigrants and it's got the pubs to prove it. With 15,372 units, towering Co-op City **13** is rightly called a city within the city; it even has its own mall! The Mott Haven **14** and Longwood **15** historic districts boast beautiful homes, but "The Hub" **16** features the grand architecture of the past conveniently filled with the discount shopping of today. For antiques, visit the cobblestone corridor of Bruckner Boulevard **17** at Alexander Avenue. Some of the city's grandest homes sit in the wooded environs of Riverdale **4**, while City Island **12** resembles nothing so much a New England fishing village crossed with a New Jersey suburb.

Culture

The New York Botanical Garden **8** and the Bronx Zoo **10** are justly famous, well worth whatever effort it may take to get there. For a beautiful view of the Hudson and the Palisades beyond, choose the botanical garden and historic estate Wave Hill **5** or the quirky Hall of Fame for Great Americans **2** featuring 98 bronze busts of notable citizens in a grand outdoor colonnade. Explore your inner Goth at historic Woodlawn Cemetery **7** or Poe Cottage **18**, the American poet's final home.

Sports

The House that Ruth Built needs no introduction. You simply can't call yourself a New Yorker until you've taken in an afternoon game at Yankee Stadium **1**. Van Cortlandt Park **6** offer playgrounds, ball fields, tennis and basketball courts, hiking trails, stables for horseback riding, and one of golf's classic golf courses, "Vanny."

Nature

The restoration of the Bronx River **19** coincides with the improvement of green spaces throughout the borough. Pelham Bay Park **11** is the city's largest at 2,764 acres, offering many recreational opportunities in addition to the Thomas Pell Wildlife Sanctuary, two nature centers, and immensely popular Orchard Beach.

Food

Belmont:
- Dominick's, 2335 Arthur Ave, 718-733-2807—Famous old-school Italian-American where there are no menus and no set prices.
- Pasquale Rigoletto Restaurant, 2311 Arthur Ave, 718-365-6644—Hearty meals served by friendly staff.

- Full Moon, 602 East 187th St, 718-584-3451—Wonderful pizza and calzones.
- Roberto Restaurant 603 Crescent Ave, 718-733-9503—Classic fare, rumored to be the best around.
- Arthur Avenue Retail Market, 2344 Arthur Ave—Get all the right ingredients for home-cooked Italian meals.

City Island:
- Johnny's Reef, 2 City Island Ave, 718-885-2090—Local favorite for fresh, inexpensive seafood.
- Le Refuge Inn, 620 City Island Ave, 718-885-2478—Excellent French prix fixe meals in a historic B&B.

Riverdale:
- Riverdale Garden, 4574 Manhattan College Pkwy, 718-884-5232—Upscale American and Continental food in a beautiful setting.
- Siam Square Thai Restaurant, 564 Kappock St, 718-432-8200—Well-prepared Thai standards, helpful staff.
- An Beal Bocht, 445 West 238th St, 718-884-7127—Café/bar/coffee shop hangout for the hip, young, and Irish.
- S&S Cheesecake, 222 West 238th St, 718-549-3888—Forget Junior's, this is the city's best.

The Hub:
- In God We Trust, 441 E 153rd St, 718-401-3595—A café within a dry goods shop serving authentic Ghanaian food.

University Heights:
- African-American Restaurant, 1987 University Ave, 718-731-8595—24-hour diner serving soul food alongside traditional Ghanaian specialties.
- Ebe Ye Yie, 2364 Jerome Ave, 718-563-6064—Hearty Ghanaian meals.

Concourse Village:
- The Feeding Tree, 892 Gerard Ave, 718-293-5025—Delicious Jamaican food close to Yankee Stadium.

Kingsbridge:
- El Economico, 5589 Broadway, 718-796-4851—Home-style Puerto Rican meals.

Pelham Bay:
- Louie & Ernie's, 1300 Crosby Ave, 718-829-6230—Their thin-crust pizza is the best in the borough.

Landmarks

1 Yankee Stadium
2 Hall of Fame for Great Americans
3 Arthur Avenue
4 Riverdale
5 Wave Hill
6 Van Cortlandt Park
7 Woodlawn Cemetery
8 New York Botanical Garden
9 Woodlawn
10 Bronx Zoo
11 Pelham Bay Park
12 City Island
13 Co-op City
14 Mott Haven
15 Longwood
16 The Hub
17 Bruckner Boulevard
18 Poe Cottage
19 Bronx River

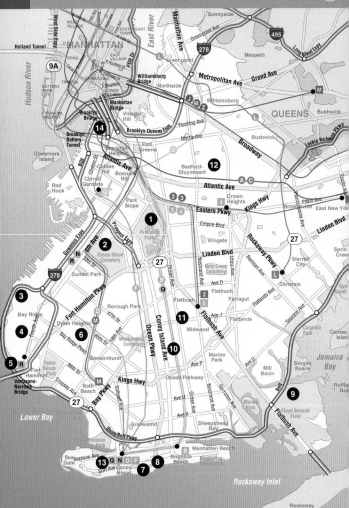

Until "The Great Mistake of 1898," Brooklyn was its own thriving city. Today, the Borough of Kings could still make a damn fine city all on its own. Although Manhattan will most likely overshadow Brooklyn for all of eternity, in recent years Brooklyn has begun to receive more than its fair share of attention. As Manhattan loses its neighborhood flavor while rents continue to soar, Brooklyn's popularity is at an all-time high. Scores of recent college grads, immigrants, ex-Manhattanites, and even celebs are increasingly calling Brooklyn home. Along with the residential boom, Brooklyn has bloomed into a cultural and entertainment mecca with top-notch restaurants, a thriving art and film scene, and plenty of unique shops. Throw in a bunch of cool bars, mind-blowing cultural diversity, and some of the city's best urban parks, and you get what may be the best place to live on the planet.

Communities

As the largest borough by population (over 2.5 million!), Brooklyn holds a special place as one of the nation's most important urban areas. Here you can find pretty much any type of community—for better or for worse. As gentrification marches deeper into Brooklyn, the borough is changing fast. Neighborhoods most likely to see their first baby boutiques open soon include Red Hook, East Williamsburg, Prospect-Lefferts Gardens, and Crown Heights.

The first thing you notice when looking at Brooklyn on a map is the sheer size of it. Yet much of Brooklyn is largely unknown to most New Yorkers. Yes, Brooklyn Heights, Williamsburg, and Park Slope are nice communities that are fun to explore. However, if you've never ventured out into Brooklyn than the obligatory trip to Coney Island, you're missing some fantastic neighborhoods. For instance, Bay Ridge **4** has beautiful single-family homes along its western edge, a killer view of the Verranzano Bridge, and a host of excellent shops and restaurants. Dyker Heights **6** is composed of almost all single-family homes, many of which go all-out with Christmas light displays during the holiday season. Brighton Beach **8** continues to be a haven for many Russian expatriates. The quiet, tree-lined streets of both Ocean Parkway **10** and Midwood **11** can make one forget all about the hustle and bustle of downtown Brooklyn, or downtown anywhere else for that matter. Finally, Bedford-Stuyvesant **12** has a host of cool public buildings, fun eateries, and beautiful brownstones.

Sports

No, the Dodgers are never coming back. This is still hard for many Brooklynites to accept and accounts for much of the nostalgia that is still associated with the borough. If you can get beyond the fact that Ebbets Fields is now a giant concrete housing complex, then you will enjoy spending a fine summer evening watching the Cyclones at Coney Island. If you can never let go, then join the Brooklyn Kickball League to relive the happier moments of your childhood.

Attractions

There are plenty of reasons to dislike Coney Island **7**, but they're simply not good enough when you stack them up against the Cyclone, the Wonder Wheel, Nathan's, Totonno's, the beach, the freaks, and The Warriors. Close by is the Aquarium **13**. Nature trails, parked blimps, views of the water, and scenic marinas all make historical Floyd Bennett Field **9** a worthwhile trip. For more beautiful views, you can check out Owl's Point Park **3** in Bay Ridge, or the parking lot underneath the Verrazano-Narrows Bridge **5** (located right off the Shore Parkway). The Verrazano might not be New York's most beautiful bridge, but it's hands-down the most awe-inspiring. Both Green-Wood Cemetery **2** and Prospect Park **1** provide enough greenery to keep you happy until you get to Yosemite. Finally, Brooklyn Heights **14** is the most beautiful residential neighborhood in all of New York. Don't believe us? Go stand on the corner of Willow and Orange Streets.

Food

Here are some restaurants in some of the outlying areas of Brooklyn: See pages 178 to 189 for other Brooklyn eateries.
Bay Ridge: Tuscany Grill, 8620 Third Ave, 718-921-5633—The gorgonzola steak is a must.
Coney Island: Totonno Pizzeria Napolitano, 1524 Neptune Ave, 718-372-8606—Paper-thin pizza. Bizarre hours.
Midwood: DiFara's Pizzeria, E 15th St & Ave J, 718-258-1367—Dirty, cheap, disgusting…awesome!
Sunset Park: Nyonya, 5223 Eighth Ave, 718-633-0808—Good quality Malaysian.
Sheepshead Bay: Randazzo's Clam Bar, 2017 Emmons Avenue, 718-615-0010—Essential summer dining.

Landmarks

1 Prospect Park	6 Dyker Heights	11 Midwood
2 Green-Wood Cemetery	7 Coney Island	12 Bedford-Stuyvesant
3 Owl's Point Park	8 Brighton Beach	13 New York Aquarium
4 Bay Ridge	9 Floyd Bennett Field	14 Brooklyn Heights
5 Verrazano-Narrows Bridge	10 Ocean Parkway	

If Brooklyn is the new Manhattan, is Queens the new Brooklyn? The most culturally diverse county in the country has a growing population of young, post-collegiate types drawn by lower rents, cheap drinks, and fantastic ethnic eats. Enjoy it while it lasts, friends.

Communities

From the stately Tudor homes of Forest Hills **28** Gardens to the hip-hop beat of Jamaica Avenue **11**, Queens has it all. Eastern Queens tends toward suburbia, while the communities along the borough's southern border often feature active industrial districts. All things Asian can be found in Flushing **20**, the city's largest Chinatown. Sunnyside **21** and Woodside **22** are home to Irish and Mexican immigrants alike, making it easy to find a proper pint and a fabulous taco on the same block. Jackson Heights' **6** 74th Street is Little India, while 82nd Street holds South and Central American businesses. Corona **23** blends old-school Italian-American delis with Latino salsa. Elmhurst **24** has attracted Asian, Southeast Asian, and South American immigrants to set up shop on its crowded streets. Island Broad Channel **12** feels like a sleepy village, while the gritty Rockaways **13** offer the only surfing beaches in the city.

Culture

Fans of contemporary art have long known P.S. 1 **4** is the place to be, especially during its summer weekend WarmUp parties. The Noguchi Museum **3**, dedicated to the work of the Japanese-American sculptor, and neighboring Socrates Sculpture Park **2**, a waterfront space with changing exhibitions, are less known. The Fischer Landau Center **25** is almost entirely unknown despite its world-class collection of modern art. Movie buffs should look for repertory screenings at the American Museum of the Moving Image **5**. The delightfully kitschy Louis Armstrong House **26** is a must-see. In Flushing Meadows-Corona Park, the New York Hall of Science **8** beckons the geeky kid in all of us with its hands-on exhibits while the Queens Museum of Art's **9** detailed scale model of the city will wow even the most jaded New Yorkers.

Sports

Head to Shea Stadium **10** when you're ready to "meet the Mets." Feel free to root for the visiting team if you like—Mets supporters are much more subdued than their Yankee rivals. The U.S. Open **7** takes place right across the street at the National Tennis Center. Get out of that cruddy OTB and see the ponies live at the Aqueduct Racetrack **14**. Hitch a ride to Rockaway Beach **13** for swimming and surfing or paddle out in a kayak on loan from the Long Island City Community Boathouse **27**. Astoria Pool **1** is the city's largest with room for 3,000 swimmers. For bowling, all-night Whitestone Lanes **18** is da place.

Nature

Gantry State Park's **29** spacious piers attract strollers and urban fishermen alike with its impressive panoramic views of the Manhattan skyline. The Jamaica Bay Wildlife Refuge **15** in Gateway National Recreation Area is internationally known for bird-watching. The Queens Zoo **19** is small but interesting, housing only animals native to North America. Flushing Meadows-Corona Park **7** is designed for active recreation, while Alley Pond Park **16** and Forest Park **17** have wooded trails perfect for wandering.

Food

As entire books have been written on where to eat in Queens, these are just a handful of suggestions:
Corona: Leo's Latticini (aka Mama's), 46-02 104th St, 718-898-6639—Insanely good Italian sandwiches that pair well with dessert from the Lemon Ice King, 52-02 108th Street, 718-699-5133, just a few blocks away.
Forest Hills: Nick's Pizza, 108-26 Ascan Ave, 718-263-1126—Queens' best pizza, hands-down.
Sunnyside: Tangra Masala, 39-23 Queens Blvd, 718-786-8181—Chinese-Indian fusion palace where you must order the Lollipop Chicken.
Bayside: Uncle Jack's, 39-40 Bell Blvd, 718-229-1100—Mayor Bloomberg's favorite steakhouse serves up fine flesh.
Flushing: Spicy and Tasty, 39-07 Prince Street, 718-359-1601—The name of this Sichuan place is entirely accurate.
Woodside:
- Spicy Mina, 64-23 Broadway, 718-205-2340—Authentic Bangladeshi food superior to the blander fare of 74th Street.
- Sripaphai, 64-13 39th Ave, 718-899-9599—Easily the best Thai food in the city.
- La Flor, 53-02 Roosevelt Ave, 718-426-8023—Fantastic neighborhood café with Mexican-inflected dishes.
Elmhurst: Minangasli, 86-10 Whitney Ave, 718-429-8207—Delicious, inexpensive Indonesian fare.

Landmarks

1	Astoria Pool	11	Jamaica	22	Woodside
2	Socrates Sculpture Park	12	Broad Channel	23	Corona
3	Noguchi Museum	13	The Rockaways	24	Elmhurst
4	PS 1 Art Museum	14	Aqueduct Racetrack	25	Fischer Landau Center
5	American Museum of the Moving Image	15	Jamaica Bay Wildlife Refuge	26	Louis Armstrong House
6	Jackson Heights	16	Alley Pond Park	27	Long Island City Community Boathouse
7	US Open/National Tennis Center	17	Forest Park	28	Forest Hills
8	Hall of Science	18	Whitestone Lanes	29	Gantry State Park
9	Queens Museum	19	Queens Zoo		
10	Shea Stadium	20	Flushing		
		21	Sunnyside		

Tell someone you're from Staten Island, and you're met with either pity or shock. That's because few ever visit, relying instead on word of mouth and an overactive imagination to keep them ensconced in another borough. Or even New Jersey. But it's time to get off that high horse and give Staten Island a look-see. As Italian as you' grandma Angelina, it has fantastic restaurants, museums, parks, and neighborhoods that make this part of the city feel more like *Our Town*. Stick to the highlights below, and you'll be glad you spent the day reaching out to the fifth borough. And who knows? Staten Island may always be overlooked, but the rents are reasonable.

Culture

1   **Snug Harbor Cultural Center**, 1000 Richmond Ter, 718-448-2500. Tired of the Met? Lines at MoMA too long? Then hang out with the Staten Island hoi-polloi at the Snug Harbor Cultural Center, an 83-acre space that features concerts, museums, musical, and exhibits. Its scenic waterside location also makes it ideal for weddings and parties.

2   **Jacques Marchais Museum of Tibetan Art**, 338 Lighthouse Ave, 718-987-3500. An impressive collection of Tibetan art, courtesy of former New York art collector Edna Coblentz, who had the surprising French pseudonym Jacques Marchais.

3   **Historic Richmondtown**, 441 Clark Ave, 718-351-1611. Staten Island loves its history and old-timey status, and shows it off beautifully in this 25-acre complex, with buildings dating back to the 17th century.

4   **Civic Center**, 10 Richmond Ter, 718-816-2000. Once Staten Island became part of New York City in 1898, plans were underway to build a civic center in St. George. The full plan was never entirely realized, but the resulting Borough Hall, Supreme Courthouse, and Family Courthouse are still an impressive collection of buildings in the French Renaissance style.

5   **Staten Island Village Hall**, 111 Canal St. Last remaining village hall building in Staten Island, a reminder of the borough's rural past.

6   **Alice Austen House**, 2 Hylan Blvd, 718-816-4506. Alice Austen was an early twentieth-century amateur photographer and a contemporary of Jacob Riis. Some of her 8,000 images are always on view at her house, which also provides a great view of lower New York Harbor.

Nature

7   **The Staten Island Greenbelt**, 200 Nevada Ave, 718-667-2165. Although this 2,500-acre swath of land (comprising several different parks) in the center of the island houses a golf course, a hospital, a scout camp, and several graveyards, plenty of woodsy areas remain relatively undeveloped and can be accessed only by walking trails. A good starting point is High Rock Park, accessible from Nevada Avenue. Great views abound.

8   **Blue Heron Nature Center**, 222 Poillon Ave, 718-967-3542. Accessible from Poillon Avenue in southwestern Staten Island, this quiet 147-acre park has a unique serenity to it. Good ponds, bird-watching, wetlands, streams, etc.

9   **Great Kills Park**, 718-987-6790. Part of the Gateway National Recreation Area, Great Kills Park is home to some excellent beaches, a marina, and a nature preserve. It's right off Hylan Boulevard.

10 **Wagner College**, 1 Campus Rd, 718-390-3100. Wagner's tranquil hilltop location rewards visitors with beautiful views of the serene surroundings. However, its best feature might be its planetarium. Accessible from Howard Avenue.

Other

11 **110/120 Longfellow Road**. Celebrate one of the greatest American films without having to schlep to Sicily. This address is where the Corleone family held court in *The Godfather*.

12 **Fresh Kills Landfill**, off Route 440. Don't call it a dump. Fresh Kills Landfill now has tours! But beware—the seagulls are more deadly than the germs.

13 **Ship Graveyard**, at Arthur Kill Rd and Rossville Ave. These ships of the damned make for great flickr photos.

14 **Staten Island Zoo**, 614 Broadway, 718-442-3100. Kids will go wild here, near the stunning Clove Lakes Park. Be sure to bring them to the vampire bat feedings.

Food

Snug Harbor:
RH Tugs, 1115 Richmond Ter, 718-447-6369.
Overlooks Kill Van Kull so there's a lot of tug and tanker action.

Rosebank:
Aesop's Tables, 1233 Bay St & Maryland Ave, 718-720-2005.
Seasonal dishes and a lush outdoor garden for the warmer months. Open for dinner, Tues-Sat.
Marina Café, 154 Mansion Ave, 718-967-3077.
Pricey seafood joint where the best feature is the view!

Richmondtown:
Parsonage, 74 Arthur Kill Rd & Clarke Ave, 718-351-7879.
A bit more upscale, the Parsonage offers lots of historical atmosphere alongside its risotto and pork chops.

West New Brighton:
Perking Latte, 840 Castleton Ave, 718-442-1534.
The perfect place to perk up, with brunch-y food and lots of coffee. Also has live music.

Driving In/ Through Staten Island

At certain times, the drive from Brooklyn to New Jersey via Staten Island is a quick trip. Take the Verrazano (but stop at an ATM first—it's $9) to the Staten Island Expressway (Route 278) to Route 440 to the Outerbridge Crossing, and you're almost halfway to Princeton or the Jersey shore. However...the Staten Island Expressway often gets jammed. Two scenic, though not really quicker, alternatives: one, take Hylan Boulevard all the way south to almost the southwest tip of Staten Island, and then cut up to the Outerbridge Crossing; two, take Richmond Terrace around the north shore and cross to New Jersey at the Goethals Bridge. Remember, neither is really faster, but at least you'll be moving.

General Information

Battery Park Parks Conservancy:
212-267-9700
Websites: www.batterypackcity.org
www.lowermanhattan.info
www.batteryparkcityonline.com
www.bpcparks.org
www.bpcdogs.org

Overview

The city within a city. Take that idea, watch *Pleasantville*, and add a good heap of OCD. Welcome to Battery Park City. Originally the brainchild of Nelson Rockefeller, this urban experiment transformed a WTC construction landfill into a 92-acre planned enclave on the southwestern tip of Manhattan. As your closet of an apartment will tell you, NY space is non-existent. That's why the idea of BPC requires a doubletake. It's about making public spaces (about 30% of those 92 acres) work within private entities. It's like taking Central Park, cutting it up, and saying, "Here, your neighborhood can have a chunk of it, and that street down there, and that street over there, too." Because, well, let's face it: Walking among private, commercial spaces day in and day out is rough on the claustrophobia (thank you, Financial District). In BPC you walk through spacious parks with weird statues and brick pavers all on your way to work, the grocery store, the gym, or the movie theater. Yeah, they've got it all, that city within a city.

As for actually living here: Do you have kids in tow? If not, venture elsewhere. Many NY families, roughly 25,000 people, hit the 40% of BPC that's dedicated residential space, including the future-forward "green" building, the Solaire. Outside: parks galore. Robert F. Wagner, Jr., South Cove, and Rector are all good choices. ,The Esplanade to walk along the Hudson; Nelson A. Rockefeller to play frisbee; North Cove to park your yacht. Amazing sculptures by Bourgeois, Otterness, Puryear, Dine, and Tolle. With enough architecture to keep the Roark in you alive: Stuyvesant High School, Siah Armajani's the Tribeca Bridge, Kevin

Roche's Museum of Jewish Heritage, Caesar Pelli's Winter Garden, and the World Financial Center. If you're into the whole "planned" neighborhood and "family" thing, this one's a keeper.

Bagels

- **Pick A Bagel** · Embassy Suites · 102 North End Ave [Vesey]

Banks

- **Bank of America (ATM)** · 4 World Financial Ctr [Vesey]
- **Chase** · 331 South End Ave [Albany]

Nightlife

- **Rise Bar @ the Ritz** · 2 West St

Schools

- **PS 89** · 201 Warren St [Clinton]
- **Stuyvesant High** · 345 Chambers St [North End]

Landmarks

- **Embassy Suites** · North End Ave [Vesey St]
- **The Irish Hunger Memorial** · Vesey St & North End Ave
- **Manhattan Sailing Club** · North Cove (Liberty St & North End Ave)
- **Mercantile Exchange** · 1 North End Ave [Vesey]
- **Museum of Jewish Heritage** · 36 Battery Pl [Little West]
- **Police Memorial** · Liberty St & South End Ave
- **The Real World Sculptures**
- **Ritz-Carlton** · Battery Pl [1st Pl]
- **Skyscraper Museum** · 39 Battery Pl [Little West]
- **Winter Garden** · 37 Vesey St [Church]

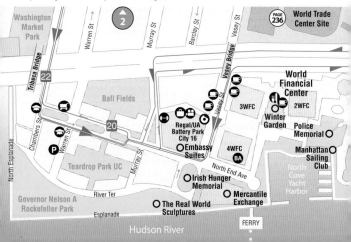

Parks & Places · **Battery Park City**

🛒 Supermarkets

- **Gourmet Heaven** • 450 North End Ave [Chambers]
- **Gristede's** • 315 South End Ave [Albany]
- **Gristede's** • 71 South End Ave [W Thames]

☕ Coffee

- **Au Bon Pain** • WFC • 200 Liberty St [West St]
- **Cosi** • 200 Vesey St [West St]
- **Financier Patisserie** • 220 Vesey St [W Side Hwy]
- **Starbucks** • 3 World Financial Ctr • 250 Vesey St [W Side Hwy]

🏋 Gyms

- **Battery Park Swim & Fitness Center** • Gateway Plz • 375 South End Ave [Liberty]
- **Liberty Club MCB** • 200 Rector Pl [South End]
- **New York Sports Clubs** • 102 North End Ave [Vesey]

🍾 Liquor Stores

- **Bulls & Bears Winery** • 309 South End Ave [Albany]

🎬 Movie Theaters

- **Regal Battery Park City 16** • Embassy Suites • 102 North End Ave [Vesey]

🍸 Nightlife

- **Rise Bar** • Ritz Carlton • 2 West St [Little West]

🐾 Pet Shops

- **Le Pet Spa** • 300 Rector Pl [South End]

🍴 Restaurants

- **Cove Restaurant** • 2 South End Ave [W Thames]
- **Foxhounds** • 320 South End Ave [Albany]
- **Gigino at Wagner Park** • 20 Battery Pl [Wash]
- **Grill Room** • WFC • 225 Liberty St [W Side Hwy]
- **Picasso Pizza** • 303 South End Ave [Albany]
- **PJ Clarke's** • 4 World Financial Ctr [Vesey]
- **Samantha's Fine Foods** • 235 South End Ave [Rector Pl]
- **Steamer's Landing** • 375 South End Ave [Liberty]
- **Wave Japanese Restaurant** • 21 South End Ave [W Thames]
- **Zen** • 311 South End Ave [Albany]

🛍 Shopping

- **DSW Shoe Warehouse** • 102 North End Ave [Vesey]

📹 Video Rental

- **Video Room** • 300 Rector Pl [South End]

🚗 Car Rental

- **Avis** • 345 South End Ave [Albany]

🅿 Parking

General Information

Website: www.centralparknyc.org
Central Park Conservancy: 212-310-6600
Shakespeare in the Park: 212-539-8750

Overview

In Central Park, you can leave car noise and concrete behind to find relative quiet and soft ground. Wandering aimlessly through the 843 acres, you'll discover many isolated corners and hiding places, despite the fact that 25 million people visit every year. On any given day, you'll see people disco roller-skating, juggling, walking their dogs, running, making out, meditating, playing softball, whining through soccer practice, and playing chess.

Designed by Frederick Law Olmsted and Calvert Vaux in the 1850s, Central Park has a diverse mix of attractions. Walking tours are offered by the Central Park Conservancy (www.centralparknyc.org), and you can always hail a horse-drawn carriage for a ride through the park.

Practicalities

Central Park is easily accessible by subway, since the Ⓐ Ⓒ Ⓑ Ⓓ Ⓝ Ⓡ Ⓠ Ⓦ ① ② ③ trains all circle the park. Parking along Central Park West is usually not difficult. Unless you're heading to the park for a big concert, a softball game, or Shakespeare in the Park, walking or hanging out (especially alone!) in the park at night is not recommended.

Nature

Bird-watching in Manhattan? Absolutely. More than 275 species of birds have been spotted in Central Park. The Ramble **27** is a good place to see them. There are an amazing number of both plant and animal species that inhabit the park, including the creatures housed in its two zoos **4** & **8**. A good source of information on all of the park's flora and fauna is schoolteacher Leslie Day's web site, www.nysite.com/nature/index.htm.

Architecture & Sculpture

Central Park was designed to thrill visitors at every turn. The Bethesda Fountain **11**, designed by Emma Stebbins, is one of the main attractions of the park. Don't miss the view of Turtle Pond from Belvedere Castle **16** (home of the Central Park Learning Center). The Arsenal **5** is a wonderful ivy-clad building that houses the Parks Department headquarters. Two of the most notable sculptures in the park are Alice in Wonderland **15** and the Obelisk **19**. Oh and one other tiny point of interest…the Metropolitan Museum of Art **24** also happens to be in the park.

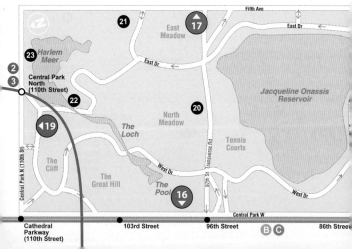

Open Spaces

New Yorkers covet space. Since they rarely get it in their apartments, they rely on large open areas such as Strawberry Fields **10**, the Great Lawn **26**, and Sheep's Meadow **28**. The Ramble **27** and the Cliff are still heavily forested, and are good for hiking around, but don't go near them after dark.

Performance

In warmer weather, Central Park is a microcosm of the great cultural attractions New York has to offer. The Delacorte Theater **18** is the home of Shakespeare in the Park, a New York tradition begun by famous director Joseph Papp. SummerStage **9** is now an extremely popular concert venue for all types of music, including the occasional killer rock concert. Opera companies and classical philharmonics also show up in the park frequently, as does the odd mega-star (Garth Brooks, Diana Ross, etc.).

Sports

Rollerblading and roller skating are very popular (not just at the Roller Skating Rink **7**—see www.centralparkskate. com, www.cpdsa.org, www.skatecity.com), as is jogging, especially around the reservoir (1.57 mi). The Great Lawn **26** boasts beautiful softball fields. Central Park has 30 tennis courts (if you make a reservation, you can walk right on to the court, 212-280-0205), fishing at Harlem Meer, gondola rides and boat rentals at the Loeb Boathouse **13**, model boat rentals at the Conservatory Water, chess and checkers at the Chess & Checkers House **25**, two ice-skating rinks **1** & **22**, croquet and lawn bowling just north of Sheep's Meadow **28**, and rock-climbing lessons at the North Meadow Rec Center **20**. You will also see volleyball, basketball, skateboarding, bicycling, and many pick-up soccer, frisbee, football, and kill-the-carrier games to join. If horseback riding is more your speed, you can rent a steed from Claremont Riding Academy (212-724-5100) on W 89th Street at Amsterdam Avenue and ride into the park. Finally, Central Park is where the NYC Marathon ends each year.

Landmarks

1 Wollman Rink
2 Carousel
3 The Dairy
4 Central Park Zoo
5 The Arsenal
6 Tavern on the Green
7 Roller Skating Rink
8 Children's Zoo
9 SummerStage

10 Strawberry Fields
11 Bethesda Fountain
12 Bow Bridge
13 Loeb Boathouse
14 Model Boat Racing
15 Alice in Wonderland
16 Belvedere Castle
17 Shakespeare Gardens
18 Delacorte Theater

19 The Obelisk
20 North Meadow Recreation Center
21 Conservatory Garden
22 Lasker Rink
23 Dana Discovery Center
24 Metropolitan Museum of Art

25 Chess & Checkers House
26 The Great Lawn
27 The Ramble
28 Sheep's Meadow

Police Precinct
86th St & Transverse Rd

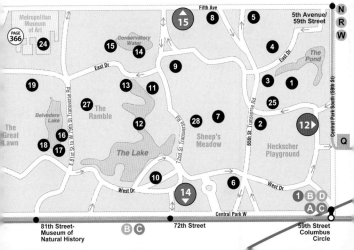

General Information

NFT Map:	18
Morningside Heights:	2960 Broadway & 116th St
Medical Center:	601 W 168th St
Phone:	212-854-1754
Website:	www.columbia.edu
Students Enrolled:	23,813
Endowment:	Market value as of June 30, 2004
	$4.493 billion

Overview

Columbia University's campus seems rather pastoral compared to other university campuses in New York. The main campus, located in Morningside Heights, spans six blocks between Broadway and Amsterdam Avenues. Most of the undergraduate classes are held here, along with several of the graduate schools. Other graduate schools, including the law school and School of International and Public Affairs, are close by on Amsterdam Avenue. The main libraries, Miller Theater, and St. Paul's Chapel are also located on the Morningside Heights campus. There are even a few halls for frisbee-throwing and pick-up soccer games.

Founded in 1754 as King's College, Columbia University is one of the country's most prestigious academic institutions. The university is well known for its core curriculum, a program of requirements that gives students an introduction to the most influential works in literature, philosophy, science, and other disciplines.

After residing in several downtown locations, Columbia moved to its present campus (designed by McKim, Mead, and White) in 1897. At the time, the surrounding area was sparsely populated, but during the more than 100 years since, the neighborhood of Morningside Heights has expanded considerably, and so has the university. Low Library is still the focal point of the campus, however, with the Alma Mater statue in front to greet visitors. Students line the stairs in front of the library on sunny days, eating lunch and chatting with classmates.

Town/gown relations in Morningside Heights are complicated. On the one hand, Columbia students, quick to part with their cash, help support local businesses. On the other hand, community members often oppose the school's policies, and there's resentment for what some perceive as heavy-handedness on Columbia's part. The most famous of these struggles came in response to Columbia's plans to build a gymnasium in Morningside Park. New plans to expand the university into Manhattanville are also being met with more resistance, but Columbia officials are trying a more collaborative approach this time.

Columbia's medical school was the first in the nation. The school is affiliated with the Columbia-Presbyterian Medical Center in Washington Heights and encompasses the graduate schools of medicine, dentistry, nursing, and public health. Columbia is the only Ivy League university with a journalism school, which was founded at the bequest of Joseph Pulitzer in 1912. (The prize is still administered there.) The school is also affiliated with Barnard College, Jewish Theological Seminary, Teachers College, and Union Theological Seminary.

Numerous movies have been filmed on or around the campus including *Ghostbusters*, *Hannah and Her Sisters*, and *Spiderman I* and *II*.

Notable alums and faculty include James Cagney, Art Garfunkel, Georgia O'Keeffe, Rodgers and Hammerstein, Paul Robeson, and Twyla Tharp; critic Lionel Trilling; baseball player Lou Gehrig; and writers Isaac Asimov, Joseph Heller, Carson McCullers, Eudora Welty, Zora Neale Hurston, and Herman Wouk. Business alumni include Warren Buffet, Alfred Knopf, Joseph Pulitzer, and Milton Friedman, while politicians Madeline Albright, Dwight Eisenhower, Alexander Hamilton, Robert Moses, Franklin Delano Roosevelt, and Teddy Roosevelt all graced the university's classrooms. In the field of law, Benjamin Cardozo, Ruth Bader Ginsburg, Charles Evans Hughes, and John Jay called Columbia home, and Stephen Jay Gould, Margaret Mead, and Benjamin Spock make the list of notable science alumni.

Tuition

Columbia undergraduate tuition and fees for the 2005-06 academic year were $33,246 plus $9,340 for room and board. Graduate school fees vary by college. We certainly hope father and mother are paying.

Sports

Columbia's football team, the Lions, was really, really bad back in the '80s. In fact, they almost set the record for straight losses by a major college football team when they dropped 44 consecutive games between 1983 and 1988. Not much has changed—their 2-10 record in 2005 was par for the course. The Lions play their mostly Ivy League opponents at Lawrence A. Wein Stadium (Baker Field), located way up at the top of Manhattan.

Columbia excels in other sports including crew, fencing, golf, tennis, and sailing. The university is represented by 29 men's and women's teams in the NCAA Division I. It also has the oldest wrestling team in the country.

Culture on Campus

Columbia features dance, film, music, theater, lectures, readings, and talks. Venues include: the Macy Gallery at the Teacher's College, which exhibits works by a variety of artists, including faculty and children's artwork; the fabulous Miller Theatre at 2960 Broadway, which primarily features musical performances and lectures; the student-run Postcrypt Art Gallery in the basement of St. Paul's Chapel; the Theatre of the Riverside Church for theatrical performances; and the Wallach Art Gallery on the 8th floor of Schermerhorn Hall, featuring art and architecture exhibits. Check the website for a calendar of events.

Phone Numbers

Morningside Campus	212-854-1754
Health Services Campus	212-854-2284
Visitors Center	212-854-4900
Public Affairs	212-854-5573
University Development and	877-854-ALUM(2586)
Alumni Relations	
Library Information	212-854-2271
Graduate School of Architecture, Planning,	212-854-3414
and Preservation	
School of the Arts	212-854-2134
Graduate School of Arts and Sciences	212-854-4737
School of Dental and Oral Surgery	212-305-6726
School of Engineering	212-854-2522
Graduate School of Engineering	212-854-2993
School of General Studies	212-854-2772
School of International and Public Affairs	212-854-5406
Graduate School of Journalism	212-854-8608
School of Law	212-854-2640
School of Nursing	212-305-5756
School of Public Health	212-305-3929
School of Social Work	212-851-2300

Overview

East River Park is a long, thin slice of land, sandwiched between the FDR Drive and the East River, and running from Montgomery Street up to 14th Street. It was built in the early 1940s as part of the FDR Drive; today, the park's recent refurbishments has made its sporting facilities some of the best Manhattan has to offer. The East River Esplanade, a walkway encircling many parts of the East Side, is a constant work-in-progress. The overall plan is to someday create one continuous green stretch from Maine to Florida, part of the highly ambitious East Coast Greenway project (greenway.org). But first we'll see if we can get East River Park to stretch as far as the UN. (Initial city plans are aiming to grow the park from Battery Park to 125th street.)

Attractions

No one would ever mistake East River Park for Battery Park. But to its credit, the city has made great improvements, cleaning and buffing it till it almost shines. The park comes alive in the summer and on weekends, when hundreds of families barbeque in the areas between the athletic fields, blaring music and eating to their hearts' content. Others

take leisurely strolls or jogs along the East River Esplanade, which offers dramatic views of the river and Brooklyn. Many have turned the park's unused areas into unofficial dog runs, places for pick-up games of ultimate frisbee or soccer, and sunbathing areas. And aside from bathing beauties, you'll also find fishermen waiting patiently for striped bass, if you can believe that! (Though shhh—not that we have to tell you, but nothing caught in the East River should be eaten—while the water quality has improved dramatically, it's still full of pollutants.)

Sports

The sports facilities at East River Park have undergone heavy reconstruction. The park now includes facilities for football, softball, basketball, soccer, tennis, and even cricket. Thankfully, many of the fields have been re-surfaced with a resilient synthetic turf—a smart move, given the amount of use the park gets by all the different sports leagues.

Facilities

There are three bathroom facilities located in the park—one at the tennis courts, one at the soccer/track field, and one up in the northern part of the park

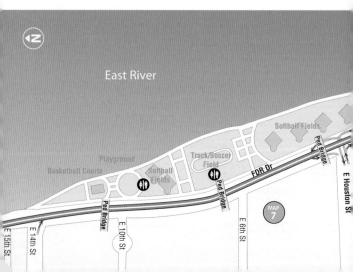

by the playground. The reconstruction has provided East River Park with new benches, game tables, a harbor seals spray sprinkler with animal art, and new water fountains. Aside from the occasional guy with a cart full of cold drinks, there aren't any food or drink facilities close by. Your best bet is to arrive at the park with any supplies you might need—if that's too difficult, try a bodega on Avenue D.

Safety

East River Park is relatively safe, especially during the daytime, but we would not recommend hanging out there—or in any other city park, for that matter—after dark, even if you're just passing through.

Esoterica

Built in 1941, the Corlears Hook Pavilion was the original home of Joseph Papp's Shakespeare in the Park. However, it closed in 1971, and has never quite returned to its glory days. Plans for the fancy $3.5 million amphitheater/restaurant that was to replace the sad-looking, abandoned, graffiti-covered Corlears Hook Pavilion band shell have been canned. A less ambitious reconstruction took place in 2001, however, and with new seating, a renovated band

shell, and a good scrubbing, the facility is currently open for use.

How to Get There

Two FDR Drive exits will get you very close to East River Park—the Houston Street exit and the Grand Street exit. Technically, cars are not allowed in the park. There is some parking available at the extreme south end of the park by Jackson Street off the access road, but it's hard to get to and poorly marked. Plan to find street parking just west of the FDR and cross over on a footbridge.

If you are taking the subway, you'd better have your hiking boots on—the fact that the closest subway (the Ⓕ train at Delancey/Essex Street) is so far away (at least four avenue blocks) is one of the reasons East River Park has stayed mainly a neighborhood park. Fortunately, if you're into buses, the 14 and the 18 get you pretty close. Regardless of the bus or subway lines, you will have to cross one of the five pedestrian bridges that traverse the FDR Drive, unless you approach via the East River Esplanade.

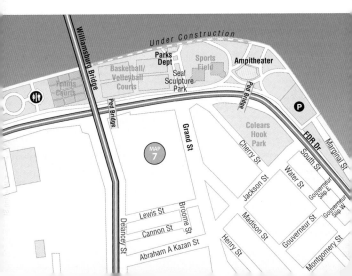

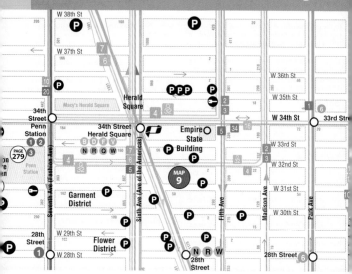

General Information

NFT Map: 9
Address: 350 Fifth Ave (& 34th St)
Phone: 212-736-3100
Website: www.esbnyc.com
Observatory Hours: 9:30 am to midnight, last
                      admission 11:15 pm.
Observatory Admission: $13 for adults, $12 for
children aged 12-17, seniors, military with ID, and $8
children aged 6-11. Toddlers (under 5) and military
personnel in uniform get in free.

Overview

Um, is this a trick question? If you don't already know
the Empire State Building, the jig is up, Mac. Put
down the NFT and back away slooowly. You're not a
true Manhattanite. So, folks, how did the giant end
up perching on our block? In 1930, at the hands of
raw men, raw material compounded day after day,
four-and-a-half stories per week. Those ravaged from
the Depression and eager to put their minds to work
built the 1,500-foot structure in just 14 months, way
ahead of schedule.

A year later, it served as an ambassador to visiting
dignitaries like Queen Elizabeth and years later,
your Aunt Elizabeth, as it has transformed into New
York City's famous national landmark. Movies have
been shot there. Big shots work there. And you can
take plenty of snapshots from the reason-you-go-
there-observation-deck on the 86th floor. No trick
questions asked.

The Lights

As far away as downtown and all the way uptown,
the lights of the Empire State Building soar above the
clouds, signifying an international holiday and/or an
interminable disease. On the 86th floor, a man with
binoculars and a direct line to the lighting engineers
waits. His reason du entonde? Close-flying flocks of
birds. One phone call, and the lights go out. Lest the
poor suckers smash their beaks and plunge to their
death from the mesmerizing lights. True story.

Lighting Schedule (for updates/changes, check www.esbnyc.com)

January · Martin Luther King, Jr Day
January · March of Dimes
January/Febuary · Lunar New Year
February 14 · Valentine's Day
February · President's Day
February · Westminster Kennel Club
February · Swisspeaks Festival for Switzerland
February · World Cup Archery Championship
March 17 · St Patrick's Day
March · Greek Independence Day
March · Equal Parents Day/Childrens' Rights
March · Wales/St David's Day
March · Oscar Week in NYC
March · Colon Cancer Awareness
March · Red Cross Month
March–April · Spring/Easter Week
April · Earth Day
April · Child Abuse Prevention
April · National Osteoporosis Society
April · Rain Forest Day
April · Israel Independence Day
April · Dutch Queen's Day
April · Tartan Day
May · Muscular Dystrophy
May · Armed Forces Day
May · Memorial Day
May · Police Memorial Day
May · Fire Department Memorial Day
May · Haitian Culture Awareness
June 14 · Flag Day
June · Portugal Day
June · NYC Triathlon
June · Stonewall Anniversary/Gay Pride
July 4 · Independence Day
July · Bahamas Independence Day
July · Bastille Day
July · Peru Independence

July · Columbia Heritage & Independence
August · US Open
August · Jamaica Independence Day
August · India Independence Day
August · Pakistan Independence Day
September · Mexico Independence Day
September · Labor Day
September · Brazil Independence Day
September · Pulaski Day
September · Race for the Cure
September · Switzerland admitted to the UN
September · Qatar Independence
September · Fleet Week/Support our Servicemen and Servicewomen/Memorial for 9/11
September · Feast of San Gennaro
October · Breast Cancer Awareness
October · German Reunification Day
October · Columbus Day
October 24 · United Nations Day
October · Big Apple Circus
October · Pennant/World Series win for the Yankees
October · Pennant/World Series win for the Mets [Ha!]
October · NY Knicks Opening Day
October–November · Autumn
October · Walk to End Domestic Violence
November · NYC Marathon
November · Veterans' Day
November · Alzheimer's Awareness
December · First night of Hannukah
December · "Day Without Art/Night Without Lights"/AIDS Awareness
December-January 7 (with interruptions) · Holiday Season

(211)

General Information

Hudson River Park Trust: 212-627-2020
Websites: www.hudsonriverpark.org
www.friendsofhudsonriverpark.org

Overview

West Side Highway trapeze artists? Hudson River Park may not ring a bell, but those high-flyers just may. They're part of the 550-acre and up-upcoming $330-million park development along the south and southwest coastline of Manhattan, from Battery Place to West 59th. Rivaling the 800 acres of public lawn in Midtown, Hudson River Park is quickly becoming downtown's Central Park. Just think length, not width. And think trapezes and half pipes, not zoos.

Born of the Hudson River Park Act in 1998, the Hudson River Park Trust focuses on preserving the natural, historical, and ecological environment, while alleviating dire sanitary conditions, expanding public access to the river, and promoting water-based recreation. Translated check-off list: Save the whales, er…um, American eel. Remember the sailors. Clean the water. Dredge the plastic baggies and random boots. Build pretty lookout areas. Give the people something more to do than look at water.

Also a mouthful: As part of the New York State Significant Coastal Fish and Wildlife Habitat, 400 acres of the total 550 thrive as estuarine sanctuary. This means the seventy fish species (There are fish in the Hudson?) and thirty bird species on the waterfront won't go belly up or beak down with all the marine preservation. Thanks to this effort, you'll be able to enjoy the winter flounder, white perch, owls, hawks, and songbirds for generations to come. (That's fantastic! Bob, tell them what else they've won…) What downtown, nature-loving, organic-eating savers of the planet have won is in what they've lost. As a mandate, office buildings, hotels, casino gambling boats, and manufacturing plants are prohibited from the HRP, as are residences (sorry, no water-front property next to your yacht) and jet skis (better to leave them in the Caymans).

Art

From exhibition to permanent collection, HRP takes its culture cue from the surrounding downtown art scene of TriBeCa, SoHo, and Chelsea. You were probably one of the thousands waiting in line to see *Ashes and Snow* in 2005. Gregory Colbert's rendition of the interactions between animals and humans took form in the temporary Nomadic Museum on Pier 54. Or maybe you checked out Malcolm Cochran's *Private Passage* on Clinton Cove (55th-57th St). Similar to your late night antics, you peered into a gigantic wine bottle. There, from portholes carved on the sides, you could see the interior of the stateroom of the Queen Mary. Or, hearkening back to an early time, the *Shadow of the Lusitania*. Justen Ladda recreated the shadow of the famous ship on the south side of Pier 54 (also home to reconstructed historic ships, not just their shadows), its original docking place with glass and planters. A more permanent piece in HRP: *Salinity Gradient* in TriBeCa. Paver stones spanning 2000 feet take the shape of Hudson marine creatures. Striped bass included. Not impressed? HRP Trust hired different designers for each segment of the park, with only the esplanade and waterfront railing as universal pieces. Check out the landscape design of each segment of the five-mile park. Or head to the Estuarium—a river education/research center at Pier 32. Or the Intrepid Sea-Air-Space Museum at Pier 86 (middle 40s) with vintage airplanes and sleek, modern jets. Nature centers are to be included in the sick repertoire of HRP art shortly.

Attractions

Season-specific events go on around HRP. Get back to fight-night basics on Pier 54 for Rumble on the River with live blood splattering with each KO. Sundays in the summer host Moon Dances on Pier 25 with free dance lessons before live New York bands play. Wednesday and Fridays in the summer boast River Flicks on Pier 54 and Pier 25 with throwback films like *The Goonies*. Pier of Fear is mainly a Halloween party for the kiddies, but if you're still down with dressing up as the *Scream* guy, hey, no one will stop you.

Sports

Think of sports in piers. You already know about ritzy Chelsea Piers, but soon enough "Pier plus a number" will become vernacular. And there are way more cooler and cheaper piers than CP. First and most useful for those athletic-minded souls, a five-mile running/biking/blading path that threads through the piers. It's a miniature divided highway—smooth, simple, and crowded during peak times (early evening). You'll find sunbathing lawns throughout (the most sport some will ever do). Pier 40: Three and a half ball fields. Area south of Houston: Three tennis courts. Mini-golf. Batting cages. Skateboard park. Beach volleyball. Trapeze lessons. Pier 40, CP, Pier 63, Pier 96: Free kayaking. Those are the highlights; for more that's up your own sports alley, check out the website.

How to Get There

Hmmm. How to get to the shoreline from more than 60 streets? The ❶ and Ⓐ Ⓒ Ⓔ will get you the closest. Any stop from Chambers to Christopher on the ❶ and any stop from Chambers to Columbus Circle on the Ⓐ Ⓒ Ⓔ . Go west 'til you hit water. You're there.

LEVEL ONE

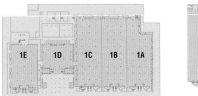

1E 1D 1C 1B 1A

LEVEL THREE

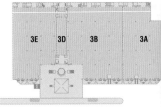

3E 3D 3B 3A

LEVEL TWO

South Concourse   North Concourse

North Pavilion

LEVEL FOUR

River Pavilion

Galleria

4E Terrace Lounge

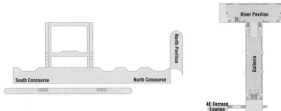

General Information

NFT Map: 8
Address: 655 W 34th St
Website: www.javitscenter.com
Phone Number: 212-216-2000
Fax Number: 212-216-2588

Overview

The Jacob K. Javits Center, designed by James Ingo Freed and completed in 1986, is a massive glass-and-steel behemoth of a convention hall next to the Hudson River between 34th and 40th Streets. It was built with the purpose of providing a place for big trade shows, conventions, and expositions, but its true purpose is clearly to annoy anyone who has to go there, since it's in the middle of nowhere with no subway link. Dissatisfaction with the convention center has brewed for a number of years, with complaints ranging from the aesthetic (big ugly box) to the practical (lack of space). Various plans have been proposed over the years to expand the center up or over the adjoining west side rail yards, and overhaul the building's facade. The Javits even got dragged into the Jets stadium fiasco, but seems to have emerged with some concrete progress towards a revamping: city and state planners have been accepting designs for expansions and renovations, and hopefully New York can have a more inviting, more integrated place for conventions soon.

ATMs

CH · Chase · Level One
CH · Chase · Level Three

Services

Coat/Luggage Check
Lost and Found
Concierge Services
Mailboxes Etc
First Aid
FedEx Kinko's Office and Print Center
Hudson News
Shoeshine
Information
Wi-Fi (hourly, daily and show plans available)

Food

The food at the Javits Center is, of course, rapaciously expensive, and, if you're exhibiting, usually sold out by 2:30 in the afternoon. Our suggestion is to look for people handing out Chinese food menus and have them deliver to your booth. (And yes, they take credit cards. And yes, it's bad Chinese food.)

Asian Star
The Bakery
Go Gourmet
The Grille
Boar's Head Deli
Market Fair/Korean Deli Buffet
Caliente Cab Company
Kosher Food and Sushi
Carvel Ice Cream Bakery
Nathan's
Cocktail Lounge
New York Pizza
Dai Kichi Sushi
Panini
The Dining Car
Villa Cucina Italiana
Feast of the Dragon
Villa Pizza
Gourmet Coffee Bar

How to Get There—Mass Transit

Until they extend that train, there's no direct subway access to the center. The closest subway stop is at 34th Street/Penn Station, but even that's a good 4- to 5-block hike away. You can also take the buses from the 42nd Street 42 and 34th Street 34 subway stops, which will both drop you off right outside the center.

There are also numerous shuttle buses that run to various participating hotels and other locales free of charge for convention goers. Schedules and routes vary for each convention, so ask at the information desk on the first floor.

From New Jersey, the NY Waterway operates a ferry from Weehawken, NJ that ships you across the Hudson River to 39th Street and Twelfth Avenue in 4 minutes, dropping you just one block from the Javits Center. The ferry leaves every 10-15 minutes during peak hours. Call 1-800-53-FERRY for a schedule and more information

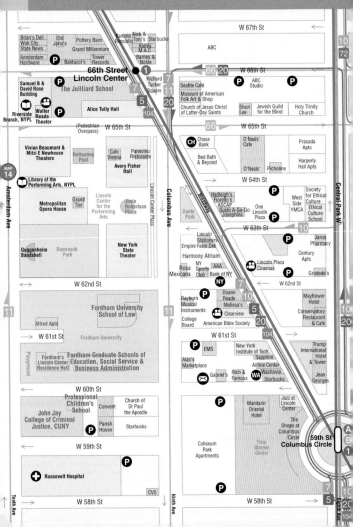

Lincoln Center / Columbus Circle

General Information

Website: ....www.lincolncenter.org
General Information: 212-546-2656 (212-LINCOLN)
Customer Service: 212-875-5456
Alice Tully Hall: 212-875-5050
Avery Fisher Hall: 212-875-5030
The Chamber Music Society: 212-875-5775
Film Society of Lincoln Center: 212-875-5600
Guided Tours: 212-875-5350
Jazz at Lincoln Center: 212-258-9800
The Julliard School: 212-799-5000
Lincoln Center Theater: 212-362-7600

The Metropolitan Opera House: 212-362-6000
New York City Ballet and Opera: 212-870-5570
New York Philharmonic: 212-875-5656
New York State Theater: 212-870-5500
Parking Garage: 212-874-9021
Walter Reade Theater: 212-875-5601

Ticket Purchase Phone Numbers
Alice Tully and Avery Fisher Halls: 212-721-6500
Film Society of Lincoln Center: 212-496-3809
MovieFone, Walter Reade Theater: 212-777-FILM
TeleCharge, Lincoln Center Theater: 212-239-6200
Ticketmaster, New York State Theater: 212-307-4100
Ticketmaster, Met & Ballet: 212-307-4100

Overview

Sometimes, the typical dinner-and-drinks can color only so many nights before you crave a more…let's say, cultured experience. Cue Lincoln Center. As one of Manhattan's most romantic spots, its stages have felt soft pirouettes of ballet slippers from the NYC Ballet, vibrations from sopranos in the Metropolitan Opera, and tap-tap-tap from the soles of trumpet-players. Culture indeed. This four-square-block area borders on cultural obscenity. Better leave dinner-and-drinks to the pre-show. However, visual aesthetic doesn't start and stop onstage. Lincoln Center also showcases some of the city's signature art and architectural gems: Henry Moore's "Reclining Figure" is the centerpiece of the reflecting pool and Mark Chagall's murals grace the foyer of the Metropolitan Opera House. Philip Johnson's Plaza Fountain anchors the entire center, creating an intimate space where New Yorkers can go to forget about their appallingly high rents and pretend they're in the scene from *Moonstruck* where Cher and Nicholas Cage meet to see *La Boheme*.

Who Lives Where

A mecca of tulle, tin, and strings, Lincoln Center houses companies, upon troupes, upon societies. Matching the performing group to the building means you won't end up watching *Swan Lake* when you should be listening to Mozart.. The most confusing part about Lincoln Center is that "Lincoln Center Theater" is two theaters—the Vivian Beaumont and the Mitzi E. Newhouse Theaters. Jazz at Lincoln Center moved into the Frederick P. Rose Hall in AOL/Time Warner Center.

American Ballet Theater — Metropolitan Opera House
Chamber Music Society — Samuel B. and David
   Rose Building
Film Society of Lincoln Center — Samuel B. and David
   Rose Building
Jazz at Lincoln Center — Frederick P. Rose Hall
Julliard Orchestra & Symphony — Alice Tully Hall
Metropolitan Opera Company — Metropolitan
   Opera House
Mitzi E. Newhouse Theater — Lincoln Center Theater
Mostly Mozart Festival — Avery Fisher Hall

New York City Ballet — New York State Theater
New York City Opera — New York State Theater
New York Philharmonic — Avery Fisher Hall
School of American Ballet — Samuel B. and David
   Rose Building
Stanley Kaplan Penthouse Performance Space —
   Samuel B. and David Rose Building
Vivian Beaumont Theater — Lincoln Center Theater
Walter Reade Theater — Samuel B. and David
   Rose Building

Columbus Circle

Okay, okay, the real reason you head to Columbus Circle is for Whole Foods. This mother ship, inside the closest thing to a shopping mall in NYC, anchors the Time Warner Center and the Mandarin Oriental Hotel, which by the way, has pillows on which your out-of-town guests will not sleep, unless they own a small kingdom. The Trump International Hotel and Tower soars nearby. Nougatine, of Jean-Georges fame, features as its premiere lunch spot… ahh…the other reason you go to Columbus Circle.

How to Get There

Lincoln Center is right off Broadway and only a few blocks north of Columbus Circle, which makes getting there easy. The closest subway is the 66th Street ❶ which has an exit right on the edge of the center. It's also an easy walk from the trains that roll into Columbus Circle. If you prefer above-ground transportation, the ❺ ❼ ❿ ⓫ ⅏ ⓥⓜ bus lines lines all stop within one block of Lincoln Center. There is also a parking lot underneath the complex for those bent on driving.

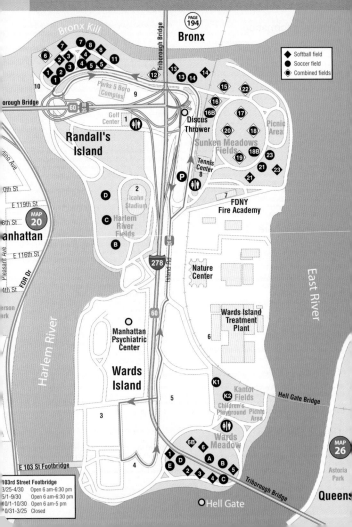

Bronx Kill

PAGE
194

Bronx

Triborough Bridge

◆ Softball field
● Soccer field
◉ Combined fields

Parks 5 Boro
Complex

10

...borough Bridge

60 M
35

Golf
Center

Discus
Thrower

**Randall's
Island**

9

Sunken Meadows
Fields

Picnic
Area

Tennis
Center

P

7

FDNY
Fire Academy

alno Ave

0th St

E 119th St

MAP
20

Icahn
Stadium

Harlem River
Fields

8th St

..anhattan

E 116th St

Pleasant Ave

FDR Dr

4th St

...rson
...rk

278

Nature
Center

35

60

Manhattan
Psychiatric
Center

**Wards
Island**

Wards Island
Treatment
Plant

6

East River

Harlem River

K1

K2

Kantor
Fields

Children's
Playground   Picnic
Area

5

**Wards
Meadow**

Hell Gate Bridge

MAP
26

3

4

E 103 St Footbridge

6B 6

1 D

A

B

E 2 3 4 C

5

Triborough Bridge

Astoria
Park

Queens

Hell Gate

103rd Street Footbridge
3/25-4/30   Open 6 am-6:30 pm
5/1-9/30   Open 6 am-6:30 pm
...0/1-10/30   Open 6 am-5 pm
...0/31-3/25   Closed

General Information

Randall's Island Sports Foundation: 212-830-7722; www.risf.org

Overview

Most New Yorkers associate Randall's Island solely with the Triborough Bridge, not realizing the island has 440 acres of parkland for public use. In fact, Randall's and Wards Islands, connected by landfill, contain some of Manhattan's best athletic fields and parks. Originally conceived of and built by the infamous Robert Moses, Randall's and Wards Island Park is now administered by the Randall's Island Sports Foundation. Their mission is to continue to improve and upgrade the park for the residents of New York City.

Phase I of their very big plan included replacing Downing Stadium with the recently completed, state-of-the-art Icahn Track & Field Stadium and the adjacent amphitheater for concerts. The Foundation is also improving all bike and pedestrian trails and renovating the soccer and softball fields. Future phases include adding a cricket field and ferry service, and there's even talk of a water park opening in 2006. Hopefully part of their plan will include some food facilities. As it is, the only food available is the snack bar in the golf center and the lunch trucks scattered around Icahn Stadium and the Fire Training Center.

Just south of Wards Island lies Hell Gate, a treacherous body of water where the Harlem and East Rivers meet. Many commercial and private vessels have come to grief in this stretch of water.

How to Get There

By Car: Take the Triborough Bridge, exit left to Randall's Island. There's a $4.50 toll to get on the island with your car. It's free to leave!

By Subway/Bus: From Manhattan: take the ❹ ❺ ❻ train to 125th Street, then transfer on the corner of 125th Street and Lexington Avenue for the ➌➎ bus to Randall's Island. There's a bus about every 40 minutes during the day. From Queens: take the Ⓜ from 61st Street-Woodside.

By Foot: A pedestrian footbridge at 103rd Street was built by Robert Moses in the '50s to provide Harlem residents access to the recreational facilities of the parks after then-City Council President Newbold Morris criticized the lack of facilities in Harlem. Today, the bridge is open only during summer daylight hours. See timetable on map.

1 **Randall's Island Golf Center** · 212-427-5689 · The golf center on Randall's Island has a driving range open year-round with 80 heated stalls, along with two 18-hole mini-golf courses, nine batting cages, and a snack bar. A weekend shuttle service is available every hour on the hour, 10 am–5 pm from Manhattan (86th Street and Third Avenue) and costs $10 round-trip. Summer hours are 6 am–11 pm Tuesday–Sunday and 11 am–11 pm on Mondays, with off-season hours from 8 am–8 pm Tuesday-Sunday and, 1 pm–8 pm on Mondays.

2 **Icahn Track & Field Stadium** · 212- 860-1899 x101· Named for financier Carl Icahn, the 10,000-seat stadium is the only state-of-the-art outdoor track and field venue in New York City with a 400-meter running track and a regulation-size soccer field.

3 **Supportive Employment Center** · 212-534-3866

4 **Charles H. Gay Shelter Care Center for Men** —Volunteers of America - Greater New York · 212-369-8900 · www.voa-gny.org

5 **Odyssey House Drug Rehab Center**—Mabon Building · 212-426-6677

6 **DEP Water Pollution Control Plant** · 718-595-6600 · www.ci.nyc.ny.us/html/dep/html/drainage.html

7 **Fire Department Training Center** · The NYC Fire Academy is located on 27 acres of landfill on the east side of Randall's Island. In an effort to keep the city's "bravest" in shape, the academy utilizes the easily accessible 68 acres of parkland for physical fitness programs. The ultra-cool training facility includes 11 Universal Studios-like buildings for simulations training, a 200,000 gallon water supply tank, gasoline and diesel fuel pumps, and a 300-car parking lot. In addition, the New York Transit Authority installed tracks and subway cars for learning and developing techniques to battle subway fires and other emergencies. It's really too bad they don't sell tickets and offer tours!

8 **Tennis Center** · 212- 427-6150 · 11 outdoor courts. Indoor courts heated for winter use.

9 **Robert Moses Building** · We're sure many an urban planning student has made a pilgrimage here.

10 **NYPD** · They launch cool-looking police boats from here.

General Information

Website: http://www.nycgovparks.org/sub_your_park/vt_riverside_park/vt_
                                           riverside_park.html or www.riversideparkfund.org
Riverside Park Administrator   (212) 408-0264
79th Street Boat Basin - Public Marina   (212) 496-2105

Overview

If Sally Struthers taught you anything about saving the world and still you cannot get to that darned third world country, your ticket to heaven awaits at Riverside Park. Pick a program and you're saved: Sponsor a Bench or Sponsor a Tree. Yes, apparently crabapple (or "crab apple" otherwise risking the tongue twister, "crap-abble") and London plane trees need your desperate help. For years, they've been subject to the cruelty of noxious gases from passing cars and dogs' territorial marks, but you, even you, cannot justify lovesick children carving hearts and initials in their bark. You may even remember those poor, diseased-looking trees, like cobras shedding their skins, bark peeling to reveal a lighter inner bark. Light bulb on yet? Those are London plane trees (no diseases involved). And don't forget those benches suffering the wrath of a million deadweights, as they stop to rest their walking feet. Surely, even Sally herself doesn't discriminate against the most deserving.

After you've sponsored your new friend, revel in the four miles of pure-parkalicious plain. Spanning from 72nd to 158th street, Riverside Park was designed in 1875 by Frederick Law Olmsted. It was expanded and adapted for active recreational use during the early 20th century without losing too much of its charm. In 1980, the New York City Landmarks Preservation Commission crowned Riverside Park between 72nd and 125th a "scenic landmark."

Things to do along 300 acres of green goodness: Walk. Run. Cycle. Skate. Kayak. Play ball, any ball. Throw in a couple dog walkers, and sure as sugar, you've got yourself a bone fide park (see Hudson River Park, Battery Park City, Central Park for reference).

Sights & Sounds

North waterfront between 147th and 152nd Streets. It's a looker. And forget about heading to Maine for your annual lighthouse tour. You'll find the Little Red Lighthouse in Washington Park, a staunch reminder of the shipping and sea-faring industries that helped transform the city you love into the city you love. To excite the secret Oscar slave in you, head to the Crabapple Grove at 91st for a self-guided tour of *You've Got Mail*, where Tom Hanks finally met Meg Ryan (as if they didn't know each other the whole time). While you're there, check out the Garden for All Seasons. You can take a guess at what kind of garden that is. Whistle not wet? Take a gander at the American elms that surreptitiously line Riverside Drive. Remember what it's like to have trees, real trees where you live. Or, if you're so over the tree thing, the Soldiers' and Sailors' Monument at 89th gives homage to Civil war heroes from New York and gives you +1 in preparing for that all-important tavern trivia game. Same goes for Grant's Tomb at 122nd, an intriguing monument, especially with Jazz Mobile (an off-shoot of T Mobile and Jazz at Lincoln Center…) strumming serious beats on a lazy summer day. Who knew the key to heaven's gates was in your backyard?

Swing a Ring

Located at Riverside Park's Hudson Beach (W 105th St), Swing a Ring is unique fitness apparatus that exists only in New York City (lucky us) and Santa Monica. There's a set for adults and a set for ankle-biters. It's free, permanent, open year-round, and virtually indestructible (read: won't be destroyed by wayward youth with too much spare time on their hands). Each May there's a "Swing a Ring Day" celebration featuring expert instruction for adults and youngsters. For more information about the rings and special events, visit www.swingaring.com. Once you try it, you'll never stop swinging! (Well, not until the big guy with the lycra bicycle shorts wants a turn.)

Practicalities

Take the ❶ ❷ ❸ to Riverside Park. Or just drive along Riverside Drive and park (no pun intended). And hey, be safe. Don't hang out there alone after dark.

1. Carlyle Court
2. Coral Towers
3. Thirteenth Street Residence Hall
4. 145 Fourth Avenue
5. Palladium Hall
6. 113 University Place
7. 838 Broadway
8. 7 E 12th Street
9. 7 E 12th Street
10. Casa Italiana Zerilli-Marimò
11. Third Avenue North Residence Hall
12. Rubin Residence Hall
13. Bronfman Center
14. Brittany Residence Hall
15. Lillian Vernon Center for International Affairs

16. Alumni Hall
17. Barney Building
18. 19 University Place
19. Cantor Film Center
20. 10 Astor Place
21. Deutches Haus
22. Glucksman Ireland House
23. Institute of French Studies/ La Maison Francaise
24. Weinstein Center for Student Living
25. Undergraduate Admissions
26. One-Half Fifth Avenue
27. 1-6 Washington Square North
    - School of Social Work
    - Graduate School of Arts and Science
28. Rufus D Smith Hall
29. Seventh Street Residence
30. 111, 113A Second Avenue

31. Silver Center Block
    - Silver Center for Arts and Science
    - Waverly Building
    - Brown Building
32. Kimball Block
    - Kimball Hall
    - Torch Club
    - Reprographic Services
    - 285 Mercer Street

33. Broadway Block
    - 715 Broadway
    - 719 Broadway
    - 721 Broadway
    - 1 Washington Place
    - 3 Washington Place
    - 5 Washington Place
34. NYU Health Center
35. 411 Lafayette Street

36. 48 Cooper Square
37. Hayden Residence Hall
38. Education Block
    - Pless Hall
    - Pless Annex
    - NYU Bookstore
    - East Building
    - Faye's @ the Square
    - Goddard Hall
39. Student Services Block
    - 25 West Fourth Street
    - Moses Center for Students with Disabilities
    - 242 Greene Street
    - 14A Washington Place
    - Carter Hall
    - 8 Washington Place
    - 269 Mercer Place
40. Meyer Block
    - Meyer Hall
    - Psychology Block
41. Provincetown Playhouse
    - Layering Program
42. Vanderbilt Hall
43. Judson Block
    - Kevorkian Center
    - Skirball Department
    - King Juan Carlos I Center
    - Furman Hall

44. Catholic Center at NYU
45. Kimmel Center for University Life
    - Skirball Center for the Performing Arts
46. Bobst Library
47. Schwartz Plaza
48. Shimkin Hall
    - Gould Welcome Center
49. Kaufman Management Center
50. Tisch Hall
51. Courant Institute
52. D'Agostino Hall
53. 561 La Guardia Place
54. 561 La Guardia Place
55. Mercer Street Residence

58. 530 La Guardia Place
59. Off-Campus Housing
60. Second Street Residence H.
61. University Plaza
62. Silver Towers
63. Coles Sports and Recreation Center
64. 194 Mercer Street
65. Puck Building
    - Wagner Graduate School of Public Service

General Information

NFT Map: 6
Phone: 212-998-1212
Website: www.nyu.edu
Enrollment: 50,917

Overview

Founded in 1831, the nation's largest private university sprawls throughout Manhattan, though its most recognizable buildings border Washington Square. Total enrollment is just over 50,000, about 20,000 of whom are undergraduates, and all of whom are more culturally savvy than any 10 other generic college students.

The expansion of NYU during recent years has not been seen by local residents as a positive development. Some Village folks blame NYU's sprawl for higher rents and diminished quirkiness. On the other hand, the students are a financial boon for businesses in the area, and many historical buildings (such as the row houses on Washington Square) are owned and kept in good condition by the university.

NYU comprises fifteen colleges, schools, and faculties, including the well-regarded Stern School of Business, the School of Law, and the Tisch School of Arts. It also has a school of Continuing and Professional Studies, with offerings in publishing, real estate and just about every other city-centric industry you could imagine. 33,721 people applied to NYU for undergraduate school last year; 10,015 were accepted. And listen up, boys, 61% of those enrolled last year were female.

It's also worth noting that the school holds a precious culinary pearl: the only Chick-fil-A location for miles (the closest is in Paramus, NJ). Located within the Weinstein Hall dining facility (5-11 University Pl), members of the general public are welcome to indulge in their delicious crispy chicken sandwiches complete with sweet, buttered buns and two tangy pickles and waffle fries. Perfection.

Tuition

Tuition costs roughly $16,000 per semester for undergrads (closer to $18,000 for Tisch), while graduate schools generally charge by points taken (except for Stern, which costs nearly $20,000 per semester). Check the NYU website for specific tuition information.

Sports

NYU isn't big on athletics. They don't have a football team. (Where would they play anyway?) It does have a number of other sports teams, though. The school competes in Division III and its mascot is the Bobcat.

Culture on Campus

The Grey Art Gallery usually has something cool (www.nyu.edu/greyart), and the new Skirball Center for the Performing Arts hosts live performances (www.skirballcenter.nyu.edu). NYU doesn't host nearly as many events as decent liberal arts schools in the middle of nowhere. Why should it? It's in Greenwich Village, surrounded by some of the world's best rock and jazz clubs, and on the same island as 700+ art galleries, thousands of restaurants, tons of revival and new cinema. This is both the blessing and the curse of NYU—no true "campus," but situated in the middle of the greatest cultural square mileage in the world.

Transportation

NYU runs its own campus transportation service for students, faculty, staff, and alumnus with school ID cards. They run 7 am to 2 am weekdays and 10 am to 2 am weekends.

Route A: 200 Water St (South Street Seaport) to 715 Broadway (near 4th St), stopping at the Lafayette and Broome Street dorms on the way.
Route B: Woolworth Building to 715 Broadway, passing through the same areas as Route A.
Route C: Ave C & 16th St loop to 715 Broadway, passing through SoHo, NoHo, and the East Village.
Route D: 715 Broadway loop through the West Village via the Greenwich Street dorm.
Route E: Midtown Center (SCPS near 42nd St and Fifth Ave) to 715 Broadway, stopping at the NYU Medical Center on the east side and passing the Gramercy Park area.

General Phone Numbers

Gould Welcome Center: 212-998-INFO (4636)
NYU Protection and Transportation Services:.. 212-998-2222
Undergraduate Admissions:................... 212-998-4500
Financial Aid:................................ 212-998-4444
University Registrar:......................... 212-998-4800
University Employment Office: 212-998-1250
Student Health Services: 212-443-1000
Kimmel Center for University Life:........... 212-998-4900
Bobst Library:.............................. 212-998-2500
Coles Sports Center:........................ 212-998-2020
NYU Card:.............................212-443-CARD (2273)

Academic Phone Numbers

All undergraduate programs:................. 212-998-4500
Summer Session:............................ 212-998-2292
Dental School: 212-998-9818
School of Education: 212-998-5030
Ehrenkranz School of Social Work:........... 212-998-5900
Gallatin School of Individualized Study:...... 212-998-7370
Graduate School of Arts & Science 212-998-8050
Graduate Computer Science................... 212-998-3063
Law School 212-998-6060
School of Medicine......................... 212-263-7300
School of Continuing and Professional 212-998-7200
   Studies Degree Program
School of Continuing and Professional 212-992-3300
   Studies Real Estate Institute
School of Continuing and Professional 212-998-7080
   Studies Non-Credit Program
Stern School of Business 212-998-0100
Tisch School of the Arts 212-998-1918
Wagner School of Public 212-998-7414
   Administration

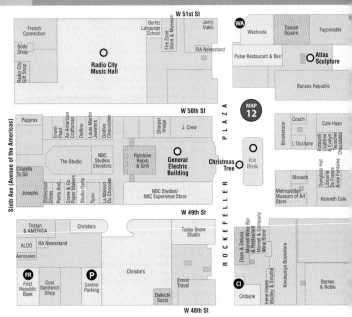

W 51st St

French Connection

Body Shop

Radio City Gift Shop

Berlitz Language School

Fire Zone Store & Museum

Jerry Vukic

RA Newstand

Radio City Music Hall

WA — Wachovia

Tuscan Square

Façonnable

Pulse Restaurant & Bar

Atlas Sculpture

Banana Republic

W 50th St

MAP 12

PLAZA

Papyrus

Erwin Pearl

An American Craftsman

Delfino

Louis Martin Jewelers

Godiva Chocolatier

Sharper Image

J. Crew

Citarella To Gp

The Studio

NBC Studios Elevators

Rainbow Room & Grill

General Electric Building

Christmas Tree

Ice Rink

Josephs

Statesman Shoes

Pants And...

Crane & Co Paper Makers

Studio Optix

Tumi

La Maison Du Chocolat

NBC Studios/ NBC Experience Store

Coach

Cole Haan

Brookstone

L'Occitane

Botticelli Crabtree & Evelyn Teuscher Chocolates

Movado

Sunglass Hut

Librairie De France Anne Fontaine

Metropolitan Museum of Art Store

Kenneth Cole

Sixth Ave (Avenue of the Americas)

ROCKEFELLER

W 49th St

Tristan & AMERICA

Christie's

Today Show Studio

ALDO

RA Newstand

Aerosoles

Dean & Deluca

Morrell Wine Bar & Restaurant

Morrell & Company Wine Store

Kinokuniya Bookstore

Barnes & Noble

FR — First Republic Bank

Cosi Sandwich Shop

P — Central Parking

Christie's

Exsus Travel

Daikichi Sushi

CI — Citibank

Irene Hayes Wadley & Smythe

W 48th St

STREET LEVEL

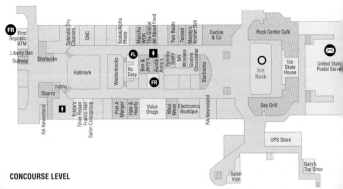

FR — First Republic ATM

Liberty Deli Subway

Splendid Dry Cleaners

GNC

Kodak/Alpha Photo

Manchu WOK

The Grill at All About Food

Two Boots

Tossed

Mandy's Kosher Deli

Cucina & Co

Rock Center Café

Starbucks

Hallmark

Waldenbooks

Its Easy

FL

Ben & Jerry's

Aunt Annie's

Yummy Sushi

NR Wireless

Godiva Chocolatier

Starbucks

Ice Rink

Ice Skate House

United States Postal Service

Dahlia

FR

Sbarro

RA Newstand

Eddie's Shoe Repair

Frabio Hair Salon Coturgroup

Pret A Manger

Hale & Hearty

Value Drugs

Maui Wowi

Electronics Boutique

RA Newstand

Sea Grill

UPS Store

Gary's Top Shoe

Salon Vijin

CONCOURSE LEVEL

General Information

NFT Map: 12
Phone: 212-632-3975
Website: www.rockefellercenter.com
Rink Phone: 212-332-7654
Rink Website: www.therinkatrockcenter.com
NBC Tour Phone: 212-664-3700

Overview

Perhaps you've been blinded five streets away by 25,000 Swarovski crystals. Or maybe you've glimpsed a gargantuan King Kong of a tree shooting seventy feet in the air and wondered how on earth such vegetation could grow in concrete. Regardless, you fall for antics, arrive in bewilderment at Rockefeller Center, and stay for the ice-skating rink, services at St. Patrick's, and the Rockettes at Radio City Music Hall.

When there's not a huge pine tree to distract you, you'll note that Rockefeller Center occupies three square blocks with a slew of retail, dining, and office facilities. Midtown corporate just ain't the same without its magic. Embodying the Art Deco architecture of the era, the center's legacy began during the Great Depression.

Today, the Associated Press, General Electric, and NBC call Rock their 9-5. (You've seen Dean & Deluca on TV during the *Today Show*'s outdoor broadcasts.) And "30 Rock" has *Saturday Night Live* and *Late Night with Conan O'Brien*. Not bad for a tree-hugger, huh?

Where to Eat

How hungry are you? Rock Center isn't a prime dining destination, but you won't starve if you find yourself in the area. For cheaper fare, try places down in the Concourse such as **Cosi**, **Pret A Manger**, or **Two Boots**. For fancier (read: overpriced) food, try the **Sea Grill** (overlooking the skating rink) or the **Rainbow Room** on the center's 65th floor. The food isn't straight out of *Restaurant Week*—you're paying for the view. **Tuscan Square**, 16 W 51st St, offers pretty decent Italian, though prices are a bit inflated here as well. Many restaurants in Rockefeller Center are open on Saturdays, but aside from the "nice" restaurants, only a few open their doors on Sundays.

Where to Shop

For all the mall-lovers out there, Rockefeller Center has its own underground version—heck, there's even a **Sharper Image** *and* a **Brookstone**! For original, non-commercialized goods, check out these stores in Rockefeller Center and the surrounding area:

FireZone Store and Museum · 50 Rockefeller Plaza · Official seller of FDNY merchandise.
Kinokuniya Bookstore · 10 W 49th St · Japanese language and Asian-themed English language books.
La Maison Du Chocolat · 30 Rockefeller Plaza · French chocolates.
Librairie De France · 610 Fifth Ave · Foreign bookseller, including French language texts, children's books, travel guides, and maps.
Teuscher Chocolates · 620 Fifth Ave · German chocolates.

And for the practical parts of your life: **Dahlia** (flowers), **Eddie's Shoe Repair**, **Kodak/Alpha Photo**, and **Splendid Dry Cleaners**. They're all located near the entrance to the Sixth Avenue subway (**B D F V**). **UPS** is in the area perpendicular to the **Sea Grill**. But it, like many of the stores in the Concourse, is closed on weekends. Unless you work in Rockefeller Center, it's not likely that you'll need to use them anyway.

The Rink

To practice your double loop: The rink opens Columbus Day weekend and closes early April to make way for the Rink Bar. Skating hours are 9 am–10:30 pm Monday-Thursday, 8:30 am–midnight Friday/Saturday, and 8:30 am–10 pm on Sundays. Skating prices range between $9 and $13 for adults, depending on the day you visit. (Weekends and holidays are the most expensive times to skate.) The skating rate for children ranges from $7 to $8 per session. Skate rental costs an additional $7 for all skaters. Lessons are available for $30 during the week and $32 during the weekend—call 212-332-7655 for more information. With hefty skating rates and a crowded rink, better to shoot for an early weekday morning or afternoon, or very early on the weekend.

Overview

Once upon a time, Roosevelt Island was populated by criminals, the sick, and the mentally ill, but that's all changed (no shortage in Manhattan, however). This slender tract of land between Manhattan and Queens has become prime real estate for families and UN officials.

The 147-acre island, formerly known as "Welfare Island" because of its population of outcasts and the poor, was re-named after Franklin D. Roosevelt in 1973, when the island began changing its image. The first residential housing complex opened in 1975. Visitors can check out some of the island's monuments, including the Smallpox Hospital and the Blackwell House (one of the oldest farmhouses in the city). Ironically, the Octagon Building, formerly a 19th-century mental hospital known for its deplorable conditions is being turned into luxury condos (so yes, you're still in New York). The lighthouse that stands on the island's northern tip was designed by James Renwick, Jr., of St. Patrick's Cathedral fame. The island's northern tip is also a popular destination for fishermen with iron gullets. The two rehab/convalescent hospitals on the island don't offer emergency services so if you're in need of medical attention right away you're out of luck. The island's main drag, Main Street (where did they come up with the name?), resembles a cement-block college campus circa 1968. Just south, closer to the tram, is a newly-developed stretch of condos that are fetching top dollar. Two of these buildings are residences for Memorial Sloane Kettering Cancer Center and Rockefeller and Cornell University employees.

Long time residents of Roosevelt Island take pride in their 30-year-old community, describing it as a place where people greet each other in the street and kids of all stripes play together. The housing situation on the island is becoming increasingly complicated, with many landlords looking to switch from rent-controlled status to market rates. Merchants have experienced problems too—lack of foot traffic, high rent, and high utility bills have forced some businesses to close. Those that survived are shabby and expensive. Residents flock to the Saturday morning green market under the parking garage but for the most part prefer to shop off the island. On a more positive note, Roosevelt Island is a quiet respite from the chaos of Manhattan. There's lots of green space and a long promenade where you can take in the dramatic views of midtown Manhattan (Hint: it is THE place to watch fireworks on July 4th.). Unless you live there, the superb view is really the only reason to stay after dark; Roosevelt Island's only bar closed in early 2005.

How to Get There

Roosevelt Island can be reached via the Ⓕ subway line, but its much more fun to take the tram. You can board it using a pay-per-ride (not an unlimited) Metrocard at 60th Street and Second Avenue in Manhattan—look for the big hulking mass drifting through the sky. It takes 4 minutes to cross and runs every 15 minutes (continuously during rush hour). To get there by car, take the Queensboro Bridge and follow signs for the 21st Street-North exit. Go north on 21st Street and make a left on 36th Avenue. Go west on 36th Avenue and cross over the red Roosevelt Island Bridge. The only legal parking is at Motorgate Plaza at the end of the bridge at Main Street.

$ Banks

- **Atlantic (ATM)** · Gristedes · 686 Main St [River Rd]

+ Hospitals

- **Coler Goldwater–Coler Campus (No ER)** · 900 Main St [West Rd]
- **Coler Goldwater–Goldwater Campus (No ER)** · 1 Main St [River Rd]

O Landmarks

- **Blackwell House** · 591 Main St
- **Blackwell's Lighthouse**
- **Chapel of the Good Shepherd**
- **Smallpox Hospital**
- **Tramway** · Tramway Plz [2nd Av]

Libraries

- **Roosevelt Island** · 524 Main St [East Rd]

Post Offices

- **Roosevelt Island** · 694 Main St [River Rd]

Schools

- **Lillie's International Christian** · 504 Main St [East Rd]
- **PS 217 Roosevelt Island** · 645 Main St

Supermarkets

- **Gristede's** · 686 N Main St [River Rd]

Restaurants

- **Trellis** · 549 Main St

Video Rental

- **KIO Enterprise** · 544 Main St [East Rd]
- **Movie Bank USA** · 559 Main St ⓐ

Subways

F ....Roosevelt Island

Bus Lines

Q 102 ....Main St / East and West Rds

P Parking

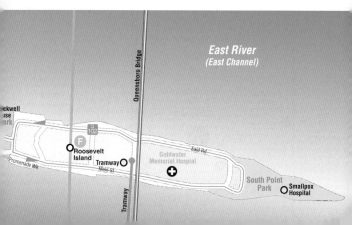

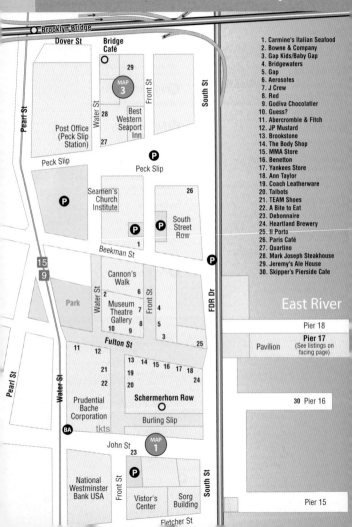

1. Carmine's Italian Seafood
2. Bowne & Company
3. Gap Kids/Baby Gap
4. Bridgewaters
5. Gap
6. Aerosoles
7. J Crew
8. Red
9. Godiva Chocolatier
10. Guess?
11. Abercrombie & Fitch
12. JP Mustard
13. Brookstone
14. The Body Shop
15. MMA Store
16. Benetton
17. Yankees Store
18. Ann Taylor
19. Coach Leatherware
20. Talbots
21. TEAM Shoes
22. A Bite to Eat
23. Debonnaire
24. Heartland Brewery
25. Il Porto
26. Paris Café
27. Quartino
28. Mark Joseph Steakhouse
29. Jeremy's Ale House
30. Skipper's Pierside Cafe

Parks & Places · **South Street Seaport**

Long before the Upper East Side was anything but a bunch of rich country estates, the South Street Seaport was alive as the center of activity in New York. The city sprouted because of its proximity to the sea and the ease of traveling in the never-frozen harbor. Although the Seaport is now more of a mini-mall than a center of maritime commerce, there are some gems hidden on these old shipping grounds.

South Street is the origin point of the world's first steamship, the first regularly scheduled transatlantic packet (the Black Ball Line), and America's first drydock. Sailors and landlubbers alike can celebrate the history of the Seaport by visiting the fantastic South Street Seaport Museum. Follow your trip to the museum by boarding one or more of the ships permanently moored in the harbor—the *Wavertree* (a full rigged ship from Southampton, England), the *Peking* (a four-masted barque from Hamburg, Germany), and the *Ambrose* (a 20th-century lightship). If you are a bit more adventurous, take a class on or charter one of the following: the *Pioneer* (a former Pennsylvania sloop re-rigged as a schooner), the *Lettie G. Howard* (a Massachusetts fishing schooner), or the *W.O. Decker* (a wooden tugboat built in Long Island City).

Walking around the beautifully preserved and renovated 19th-century buildings on the streets surrounding Pier 17 may lead to serious hunger. Forget the food court in the Pier buildings—this should be left to the teenagers that flock here—and head to the Heartland Brewery for pub food, Red for Mexican, Mark Joseph for steaks, The Paris Café for drinks, burgers, and seafood, or Quartino for organic pizzas, panini, and pasta plates.

For those who are looking to shop, you will see many of the same chain stores you find across the country. A few exceptions include the Yankee Clubhouse (fun for just about anyone but Red Sox fans) and Mariposa: The Butterfly Gallery. Mariposa displays Marshall Hill's lucite panels of butterflies from around the world.

The Brooklyn Bridge looms over the whole area—the back decks of the Pier 17 Pavilion have a great view, as does the East Side Promenade, which passes underneath it. Sadly, the most authentic part of the neighborhood, the Fulton Fish Market, has moved to the Bronx, leaving only the sweet stench of seafood from two centuries past lingering in the air. After all, what you see of the Seaport now is the result of a renovation that began in the 1960s and the Fish Market was the only thing going here for a while.

If you're downtown and looking for discounted theater tickets, the Seaport TKTS booth is at the northwest corner of Front and John Streets. Check the electronic board for show times and discounts, then go inside and book. At this location, matinee tickets are only sold the day before the performance. (A great way to get tickets to a hot show is by stopping here on Friday for a Saturday matinee.)

General Information

NFT Map: 1 & 3
Phone: 212-732-8257
Phone (museum): 212-748-8600
Museum:
   www.southstseaport.org
Retail:
   www.southstreetseaport.com
Landmarks:
   Schermerhorn Row
   Bridge Café
   Brooklyn Bridge

Banks

BA · Bank of America ·
175 Water St

Subways

② ③ ④ ⑤ Ⓙ Ⓜ Ⓩ
Fulton Street
Ⓐ Ⓒ ....Broadway-Nassau

Bus Lines

15 ....First and Second Aves
9 ....Ave B/East Broadway

Pier 17 Pavilion

9000 Perfumery Inc
ABCDE
Alamo Flags
American Eagle Outfitters
Art A La Carte
Bath & Body Works
Beyond The Wall
Broadway Beat
Christmas Dove
City Streets
Claire's Accessories
EB Games
Filmline Gallery
Footlocker
Jewelry Mine
Lids
Mariposa The Butterfly Gallery
Neighborhoodies
New York: A View of the World
The New York Shell Shop
The NY Yankees Clubhouse Shop
Nutcracker Sweets
Purple-icious
Sam Goody
Seaport News
Seaport Watch Co
The Sharper Image
Sunglass Hut & Watch Station
Teazeria
Victoria's Secret
Waxology

Food

Athenian Express
Bergin's Wine & Beer Garden
Cabana
Cajun Café
China Max
Cyber Cigar and Coffee Bar
Haagen Dazs
Harbour Lights
Little Tokyo
MacMenamin's Irish Pub
Murph's
Nathan's Famous
Pizza on the Pier
Salad Mania
Seaport Café
Sedutto Ice Cream
Sequoia
Simply Seafood
Subway
Taqueria Mexicali
Uno Chicago Grill
Yorkville Burgers

1 Broadway City
2 Olive Garden
3 Parsons School of Design
  Fashion Education Center
4 McDonald's

Theaters
Movie Theaters
Theme Restaurants/Stores

Hotels
Parkings
Other

Defined by the triangle created by 7th Ave's intersection with Broadway, Times Square—long ago known as Long Acre Square—today lays 'lectrically clear commercial blinding Disney theming restaurants as billboards shine. Foto touring pass entertaining, theaters glow and begging plainly. Scent of franks and espy dancing, prancing mesmerized by show. Summarily said, whatever one's heard or seen, hereto, a spectacle unprecedented in our incessantly volted existence. To an extreme, the realm telling. Often or seldom, see for oneself. Simply: wear sunglasses, especially at night.

Helpful Websites

www.timessquare.com
www.timessquarenyc.org

Transit

Take the ① ② ③ ⑦ **N R Q W** and ⑤ trains to get to the center of everything at the 42nd Street/Times Square stop.

ATMs

BA · Bank of America · 1515 Broadway
BA · Bank of America · 1523 Broadway
BA · Bank of America · 247 W 42nd St
CH · Chase · 3 Times Sq
CI · Citibank · 1155 Sixth Ave
CI · Citibank · 1440 Broadway
HS · HSBC · 1185 Sixth Ave
NF · North Fork · 1166 Sixth Ave
WM · Washington Mutual · 1431 Broadway
WA · Wachovia · 1568 Broadway

Hotels

Best Western President Hotel · 234 W 48th St
Best Western Ambassador · 132 W 45th St
Big Apple Hostel · 119 W 45th St
Broadway Inn · 264 W 46th St
Casablanca Hotel · 147 W 43rd St
Comfort Inn Midtown · 129 W 46th St
Doubletree Guest Suites · 1568 Broadway
Hilton Times Square · 234 W 42nd St
Hotel 41 · 206 W 41st St
Hotel Carter · 250 W 43rd St
Hotel St James · 109 W 45th St
Milford Plaza Hotel · 270 W 45th St
Millennium Broadway · 145 W 44th St
The Muse Hotel · 130 W 46th St
New York Marriott Marquis Hotel · 1535 Broadway
Paramount Hotel · 235 W 46th St
Portland Square Hotel · 132 W 47th St
Hotel Edison · 228 W 47th St
Quality Hotel Times Square · 157 W 47th St
Renaissance New York Hotel · 714 Seventh Ave
W New York Times Square · 1567 Broadway
Westin New York · 270 W 43rd St

Movie Theaters

AMC Empire 25 · 234 W 42nd St
Loews State · 1540 Broadway
Loews 42nd St E-Walk · 247 W 42nd St

Theaters

American Airlines Theater · 227 W 42nd St
Belasco Theatre · 111 W 44th St
Biltmore Theatre · 261 W 47th St
Booth Theatre · 222 W 45th St
Broadhurst Theatre · 235 W 44th St
Brooks Atkinson Theatre · 256 W 47th St
Cort Theatre · 138 W 48th St
Duffy Theatre · 1553 Broadway
Ethel Barrymore Theatre · 243 W 47th St
Ford Center for the Performing Arts · 213 W 42nd St
John Golden Theatre · 252 W 45th St
Harold & Miriam Steinberg Center for Theatre/ Laura Pets Theatre · 111 W 46th St
Helen Hayes Theatre · 240 W 44th St
Henry Miller Theatre · 124 W 43rd St
Imperial Theatre · 249 W 45th St
Longacre Theatre · 220 W 48th St
Lunt-Fontanne Theatre · 205 W 46th St
Lyceum Theatre · 149 W 45th St
Majestic Theatre · 274 W 44th St
Marquis Theatre · 1535 Broadway
Minskoff Theatre · 200 W 45th St
Music Box Theatre · 239 W 45th St
Nederlander Theatre · 208 W 41st St
New Amsterdam Theatre · 214 W 42nd St
New Victory Theatre · 209 W 42nd St
Palace Theatre · 1564 Broadway
Plymouth Theatre · 236 W 45th St
Richard Rodgers Theatre · 226 W 46th St
Royale Theatre · 242 W 45th St
Shubert Theatre · 225 W 44th St
St James Theatre · 246 W 44th St
Town Hall · 123 W 43rd St

* Here's a tip: You can win $20 *Rent* or *Avenue Q* tickets in the random drawing if you line up at the Nederlander by 6:30 pm, just in case that cousin wants to see "a show."

Theme Restaurants/ Stores

Applebee's · 234 W 42nd St
Pierre Au Tunnel · 250 W 47th St
BB King's Blues Club · 237 W 42nd St
Ben & Jerry's · 680 Eighth Ave
Blue Fin · 1567 Broadway
Broadway City · 241 W 42nd St
Bruegger's Bagels Bakery · 1115 Sixth Ave
Bubba Gump Shrimp Co · 1501 Broadway
Burger King · 561 Seventh Ave
Café Un Deux Trois · 123 W 44th St
Carmine's Restaurant · 200 W 44thSt
Center Stage Cafe · 1568 Broadway

Charley O's · 218 W 45th St
Chevy's Fresh Mex · 243 W 42nd St
The Children's Place · 1460 Broadway
China Club 268 W 47th St
Dallas BBQ · 132 W 43rd St
Dean & DeLuca · 235 W 46th St
District · 130 W 46th St
Drummers World · 151 W 46th St
Duane Reade Pharmacy · 115 W 42nd St
ESPN Sportszone · 4 Times Sq
Food Court · 234 W 42nd St
Foot Locker · 1530 Broadway
Hamburger Harry's · 145 W 45th St
Heartland Brewery · 127 W 43rd St
Howard Johnson's · 1551 Broadway
John's Brick Oven Pizzeria · 260 W 44th St
Jones New York · 119 W 40th St
Laura Belle · 120 W 43rd St
Le Marais · 150 W 46th St
Manhattan Chili Co · 1500 Broadway
McDonald's · 220 W 42nd St
McDonald's · 688 8th Ave
McDonald's · 1109 Sixth Ave
McDonald's · 1560 Broadway, 220 W 42nd St
Modell's · 234 W 42nd St
MTV · 1515 Broadway
MTV Store · 1515 Broadway
New Diamond Café · 224 W 47th St
Olive Garden · 2 Times Square
Planet Hollywood · 1540 Broadway
RAG · 1501 Broadway
Red Lobster · 5 Times Square
Rosie O'Grady's · 149 W 46th St
Sam Ash Music · 160 W 48th St
Sanrio · 233 W 42nd St
Sardi's · 234 W 44th St
Sbarro · 701 Seventh Ave
Staples · 1065 Sixth Ave
The Supper Club · 240 W 47th St
Swatch · 1528 Broadway
TGI Friday's · 1552 Broadway
Thomas Pink · 1155 Sixth Ave
Times Deli · 158 W 44th St
Times Square Deli · 211 W 43rd St
Toys 'R' Us · 1514-1560 Broadway
Virgil's Real Barbecue · 152 W 44th St
Virgin Megastore · 1540 Broadway
Viva Pancho · 156 W 44th St
Yankee Clubhouse Shop · 245 W 42nd St
Yum Thai Cuisine · 129 W 44th St

Other

Army Recruiting Office · Want to join the army? Opened in 1946, this Army Recruiting Office has turned more civilians into soldiers than any other recruiting station (43rd St & Broadway).
Fox News Channel Studios · 133 W 47th St
tkts · Discount theater tickets (47th & Broadway).

231

From 14th to 21st Streets, Sixth to Third Avenues, sits the nexus of downtown to mid, dear Union Square. Verdant environs once site for rally, burlesque, and debauchery. Today, tame place for smokes and turkey sandwich—and, of course, any protest opposing government that may, yawn, arise. Once a posh residential locale, evermore four-sided strip for retail, many of New York's finest restaurants sit off or near (Gotham Bar & Grill, Blue Water Grill, Gramercy Tavern, Union Square Cafe). For scholars and hermits, the live and legendary Strand Bookstore stakes its claim off Broadway at 12th.

Antebellum, this common once known as "The Forks" for its crossroad feel, was a site of some of the city's grandest domiciles. Fast-forward to the retail circus (known particularly as "The Ladies Mile"), now devolved to big-box scenes for the masses' needs. Today, may we say, Union Square is—both literally and figuratively—the page break dividing midtown's prose to downtown's verse.

From the stint between the floral sot that was the sixties and the early eighties, Union Square teemed with weed, a few needles, and, frankly, a more vital, yet perhaps more perilous, ambience. Today, having accorded mayoral ambitions, its sits Timesquared. Proof of surrounding life by, but, a few Marlboro boxes a'flit in winds and the odd mendicant yodeler. Generally, the society polite, half-romantic, the tourist-to-resident ratio balanced, polizei ubiquitous, the 25-digit clock over Virgin 31 minutes fast and the benches—in which there are miles—some of the city's most comfortable ('lest you sought to sleep upon. The tightly spaced rails infrangible.)

ATMs

AM · Amalgamated Bank of NY · 15 Union Sq
AP · Apple · 4 Irving Pl
AP · Apple · 145 Fourth Ave
CH · Chase · 225 Park Ave S
FS · Flushing Savings · 33 Irving Pl
HS · HSBC · 10 Union Sq E
WM · Washington Mutual · 835 Broadway

Hotels

Inn at Irving Place · 56 Irving Pl
W Hotel · 201 Park Avenue S

Stores/Restaurants

13 · 35 E 13th St
ABC Carpet & Home · 888 Broadway
Alkit Camera · 222 Park Ave S
American Eagle Outfitters · 19 Union Sq W
Andy's Deli · 873 Broadway
Angelo & Maxie's Steakhouse · 233 Park Ave S
Ann Sacks Tile & Stone · 37 E 18th St
Au Bon Pain · 6 Union Sq E
Babies R Us · 24 Union Sq E
Barnes & Noble · 33 E 17th St
Blue Water Grill · 31 Union Sq W
Caesar's Pizza · 861 Broadway
California Pizza · 122 University Pl
Candela · 116 E 16th St
Casa Mono · 52 Irving Pl
Chat 'n' Chew · 10 E 16th St
Cheap Jack's · 841 Broadway
The Children's Place · 36 Union Sq E
Cibar · 56 Irving Pl
Cingular Wireless · 31 E 17th St
Circuit City · 52-64 E 14th St
City Bakery · 3 W 18th St
City Crab & Seafood Co · 235 Park Ave S
Coffee Shop · 29 Union Sq W
Cosi · 841 Broadway
CVS · 215 Park Ave S (not 24 hours)
Diesel · 1 Union Sq W

Duane Reade · 873 Broadway
DSW · 40 E14th St, 3rd fl
EB Games · 107 E 14th St
FedEx · 4 Union Sq E
Filene's Basement · 4 Union Sq S
Food Emporium · 10 Union Sq E
Forbidden Planet · 840 Broadway
Forever 21 · 4 Union Sq S
Galaxy Global Eatery · 15 Irving Pl
Garden of Eden · 7 E 14th Street
GNC · 10 Union Sq E
Gotham Bar & Grill · 12 E 12th St
Gramery Tavern · 42 E 20th St
Haagen-Dazs · 117 E 14th St
Heartland Brewery · 35 Union Sq W
Illuminations · 873 Broadway
Link Bar & Lounge · 120 E 15th St
Los Dos Molinos · 119 E 18th St
Luna Park · 29 Union Sq W
Mandler's The Original Sausage Co · 26 E 17th St
McDonald's · 39 Union Sq W
Mesa Grill · 102 Fifth Ave
Oasis Day Spa · 108 E 16th St
Old Town Bar & Grill · 45 E 18th St
Paragon Sports · 867 Broadway
Park Avalon · 225 Park Ave S
Paul & Jimmy's · 123 E 18th St
PC Richard & Son · 120 E 14th St
Petco · 860 Broadway
Pete's Tavern · 129 E 18th St
Radio Shack · 866 Broadway
Republic · 37 Union Sq W
Rothman's · 200 Park Ave S
Sal Anthony's Restaurant · 55 Irving Pl
ShoeMania · 853 Broadway
Shija Day Spa · 37 Union Sq W
Sephora · 200 Park Ave S
Sleepy's · 874 Broadway
Staples · 5-9 Union Sq W
Starbucks · 10 Union Sq E
Starbucks · 41 Union Sq W
The Strand · 828 Broadway
Strawberry's · 38 E 14th St
Toasties Juice Bar · 25 Union Sq W
Union Bar · 204 Park Ave S
Union Square Café · 21 E 16th St
Union Square Wines & Spirits · 33 Union Sq W
University Locksmith & Hardware · 121 University Pl

Verbena Restaurant · 54 Irving Pl
Verizon Wireless · 859 Broadway
Virgin Megastore · 52 E 14th St
The Vitamin Shoppe · 25-30 Union Sq E
Whole Foods · 4 Union Sq S
Wiz · 17 Union Sq W
Yama · 122 E 17th St
Zen Palate · 34 Union Sq E

Entertainment

Century Center for the Performing Arts · 111 E 15th St
Classic Stage Company · 136 East 13th St
Darryl Roth Theatre/DR2 · 20 Union Sq E
Djoniba Dance and Drum Centre · 37 E 18th St
Irving Plaza · 17 Irving Pl
Lee Strasberg Theatre Institute · 115 E 15th St
Union Square Theatre · 100 E 17th St
Regal Union Square Stadium14 · 850 Broadway
Vineyard Theatre · 108 E 15th St

24 Hour Services

Duane Reade · 24 E 14th Street
Walgreens · 145 Fourth Ave

Other

Amalgamated Bank of New York · 11 Union Sq W
Beth Israel Phillips Ambulatory Center · 10 Union Sq E
Bowlmor Lanes · 110 University Pl
Carlyle Court · 25 Union Sq W
Con Edison · 4 Irving Pl
Crunch · 54 E 13th St
New York Sports Clubs · 10 Irving Pl
NY Film Academy · 100 E 17th St
The Palladium · 140 E 14th St
Peridance Center · 132 Fourth Ave
Zurich · 105 E 17th St

General D MacArthur Plaza

FDR Dr

E 48th Street

873

First Ave

352

Japan Society

Memorial to the Fallen

E 47th Street

Dag Hammarskjold Plaza

Venezuela

Peace Garden

E 46th Street

Turkey

Peace Statue

E 45th Street

2nd UN Plaza

Uganda

Visitors Entrance

Visitors Plaza

Kuwait

First UN Plaza

General Assembly

Rose Garden

East River

Promenade

E 44th Street

United Nations Plaza

MAP 13

International Women's Center

Conference Building

E 43rd Street

Ford Foundation

Tudor Park

Japanese Peace Bell Garden

Secretariat Building

FDR Dr

TUDOR CITY

Tudor City Pl

Fountain

E 42nd Street

Dag Hammarskjold Library

Queens Midtown Tunnel

Robert Moses Playground

To Queens

E 41st Street

495

General Information

Address:	First Ave b/w 42nd Street & 48th Street
Phone:	212-963-TOUR(8687)
Website:	http://www.un.org/Pubs/CyberSchoolBus/untour/subunh.htm
Guided Tour Hours:	9:30 am-4:45 pm except Thanksgiving Day, Christmas Day, New Year's Day, and weekends during January and February.
Guided Tour Admission:	$11.50 for adults, $8.50 for seniors, $7.50 for high school and college students, and $6.50 for students grades 1-8.

Overview

The United Nations Headquarters building, that giant domino teetering on the bank of the East River, opened its doors in 1951. It's here that the 191 member countries of the United Nations meet to fulfill the UN's mandate of maintaining international peace, developing friendly relations among nations, promoting development and human rights, and getting all the free f*#%ing parking they want. The UN is divided into bodies: the General Assembly, the Security Council, the Economic and Social Council, The Trusteeship Council, the Secretariat, and the International Court of Justice (located in the Hague). Specialized agencies like the World Health Organization (located in Geneva) and the UN Children's Fund (UNICEF) (located in New York) are part of the UN family.

The United Nations was founded at the end of World War II by world powers intending to create a body that would prevent war by fostering an ideal of collective security. New York was chosen to be home base when John D. Rockefeller Jr. donated $8.5 million to purchase the 18 acres the complex spans. The UN is responsible for a lot of good—its staff and agencies have been awarded nine Nobel Peace Prizes over the years. However, the sad truth is the United Nations hasn't completely lived up to the goals and objectives of its 1945 charter. (This situation isn't helped by the bloated US doing all it can to undermine many initiatives.) In 2004 and 2005, allegations of mismanagement and corruption surrounding the Oil-for-Food Programme for Iraq under Saddam Hussein led to renewed calls for reform.

Still, this is a place worth visiting. The UN Headquarters complex is an international zone complete with its own security force, fire department and post office (which issues UN stamps). It consists of four buildings: the Secretariat building (the 39-story tower), the General Assembly building, the Conference building, and the Dag Hammarskjöld Library. Once you clear what feels like airport security, you'll find yourself in the visitors' lobby where there are shops, a restaurant, and a scattering of topical small exhibits that come and go. The guided tour is your ticket out of the lobby and into important rooms like the Security Council Chambers and the impressive General Assembly Hall. Sometimes tour groups are allowed to briefly sit in on meetings, but don't expect to spy Kofi or his successor roaming the halls. Take a stroll through the Peace Bell Garden (off limits to the public, but it can be seen from the inside during the guided tour). The bell, a gift from Japan in 1954, was cast from coins collected by children from 60 different countries. A bronze statue by Henry Moore, "Reclining Figure: Hand," is located north of the Secretariat Building. The UN grounds are especially impressive when the 500 prize-winning rose bushes and 140 flowering cherry trees are in bloom.

The elegant Secretariat building is showing its age and plans for renovation are underway, which means the UN will have to temporarily relocate. Where? Possibly Brooklyn, with the rest of many former Manhattanites.

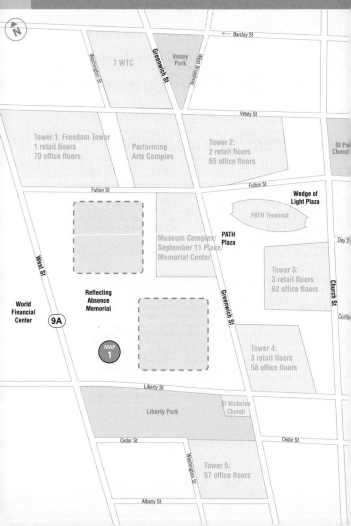

As we edge closer to half a decade passing since 9-11, it's tough to not want to call your buddies over, borrow some hammers, and start filling the void still apparent in the Financial District.

In early spring 2006, construction crews were scheduled to break ground on the first large-scale projects: the Freedom Tower and September 11th Memorial. To clear the area for a $2.2 billion transit hub designed by Santiago Calatrava to connect Manhattan and New Jersey a dozen subway lines, relocating power lines is on the agenda as well. In 2007, these construction feats should be visually apparent, and even more so in 2008, since projected completion hovers around 2009. You can call your buddies mid-2009 if construction stalls.

Why has it taken this long? Numerous groups vied to make their vision of the rebuilding of the World Trade Center site become reality. The Port Authority originally built the buildings, and just before September 11th, they were leased to Larry Silverstein. As leaseholder, he had the right to collect insurance and redevelop the site. Created by Governor Pataki, the Lower Manhattan Development Corporation was assigned the task of overseeing the development of the site. The families of victims and the rest of the public have been vocal in expressing their desires for the rebuilding project as well.

In the fall of 2002, a single design was selected from over 400 submissions to the LMDC. Studio Daniel Libeskind's proposal, "Memory Foundations," achieved the nearly impossible task of getting the approval of the LMDC, Port Authority, city, and state of New York. Despite the Libeskind design being accepted as the official master plan, Silverstein hired architect Larry Childs. Feuds over designs dissolved late in the year, and Libeskind and Childs emerged with an amicable compromise, changing the arrangement of the buildings and parks on the ground and altering the look of the Freedom Tower. What will it look like? The spire-like Freedom Tower will climb roughly 1,800 feet in the sky. Its footprint will match the footprints of the Twin Towers at 200 feet by 200 feet. Boasting 2.6 million square feet of office space, restaurants, an observation deck, and broadcasting facilities for the MTVA, it will be environmentally-sound and ultra-safe. If it ever gets built, that is.

And the memorial? Michael Arad designed "Reflecting Absence" as waterfalls flowing into the sunken "footprints" of the twin towers, cascading onto the names etched in stone of those who died there. The plans also include a performing arts and museum space designed by Norwegian firm Snohetta.

Debate still rages regarding many aspects of the project, from the height and look of the other towers to how many streets will be allowed to run through the site (many were demapped when the WTC was originally built). Also raging are class action lawsuits alleging inadequate protection against toxins for workers.

Transit has been restored to pre-September 11th order, with all subway lines resuming service to the area, along with PATH service to the newly constructed PATH station.

Useful Websites

• The World Trade Center Health Registry will track the health survey of thousands of people directly exposed to the events of 9/11: www.nyc.gov/html/doh/html/wtc/index.html

• The findings of the the National Commission on Terrorist Attacks Upon the United States (the 9/11 Commission): www.9-11commission.gov

• Website of the largest Sept. 11 advocacy group, representing the WTC memorial position of over 4,000 Sept. 11 family members, survivors, rescue workers, and others: www.coalitionof911families.org

• "New York New Visions," is a coalition of several groups looking at different options for rebuilding the area: http://nynv.aiga.org

• The New York Skyscraper Museum continues to add information about the WTC and downtown NYC in general; they also contributed to the historical panels placed on the viewing wall around the site: www.skyscraper.org

• A second 9/11 families group: www.911wvfa.org

Hudson River

Taxi/Bus Dropoff

Chelsea Waterside Park

Southbound Parking Entrance

Pier 62

13 Roller Rinks

12

Northbound Parking Entrance

4

11

Field House

Pier 61

9 Sky Rink

MAP 8

7

5

Pier 60

10

8 Sports Center **6**

3

AMF Chelsea Piers Bowling

Pier 59

2 Golf Club

West Side Hwy

25th St
24th St
23rd St
Eleventh Ave
22nd St
21st St
20th St
19th St
18th St
17th St
16th St
Tenth Ave

Overview

Website: www.chelseapiers.com

Opened in 1910 as a popular port for trans-Atlantic ships, Chelsea Piers found itself neglected and deteriorating by the 1960s. In 1992, Roland W. Betts began the plan to renovate and refurbish the piers as a gargantuan 30-acre sports and entertainment center. In 1995, Chelsea Piers re-opened its doors to the public at a final cost of $120 million—all private money. The only hitch from the state was a very generous 49-year lease. By 1998, Chelsea Piers was the third-most popular attraction in New York City, after Times Square and the Map Room at the NY Public Library.

How to Get There

Unless you live in Chelsea, it's a real pain to get to the Piers. The closest subway is the **C E** to 23rd Street and Eighth Avenue, and then it's still a three-avenue block hike there. If you're lucky, you can hop a **23** bus on 23rd Street and expedite the last leg of your journey. **L** train commuters should get off at the Eighth Avenue stop and take the **16** bus across to the West Side Highway where you'll be dropped off at 18th Street.

If you drive, entering from the south can be a little tricky. It's pretty well signed, so keep your eyes peeled. Basically you exit right at Eleventh Avenue and 22nd Street, turn left onto 24th Street, and then make a left onto the West Side Highway. Enter Chelsea Piers the same way you would if you were approaching from the north. Parking costs $10 for the first hour, $13 for two, $17 for three. Street parking in the West 20s is an excellent alternative in the evenings after 6 pm.

Facilities

Chelsea Piers is amazing. There are swimming pools, ice skating rinks, a bowling alley, spa, restaurants, shops, batting cages—you name it. So, what's the catch? Well, it's gonna cost ya. Like Manhattan rents, only investment bankers can afford this place.

1 **Chelsea Brewing Company** · 212-336-6440. Micro-brewery and restaurant. Try the amber ale, wings, na-chos, spinach dip, and cheesy fries—all excellent.

2 **Golf Club** · 212-336-6400. Aside from potentially long wait times, the 200-yard driving range with 52 heated stalls and automated ball-feed (no buckets or bending over!) is pretty awesome. $25 buys you 100 balls (peak) or 148 balls (off-peak). If you don't bring your own, club hire is $4/one club, $5/two, $6/three, or $12/ten. Before 5 pm on weekdays, you can whack all the balls you want for an hour for $20 plus free club rental.

3 **AMF Chelsea Piers** · 212-835-BOWL. A very schmancy 40-lane bowling alley equipped with video games and bar. $7.50/game plus $4.50 shoe rental.

4 **Ruthy's Bakery & Café** · 212-336-6333. Pastries and sandwiches.

5 **New York Presbyterian Sports Medicine Center** · 212-366-5100.

6 **The Spa at Chelsea Piers** · 212-336-6780. It's not Canyon Ranch. A basic 50-minute massage is $100, a basic 50-minute facial is $80. They also have a range of scrubs, wraps, polishes, manicures, pedicures, and waxes.

7 **College Sports Television** · Street-level broadcast center accessible to the public with interactive events and activities for college sports fans.

8 **The Sports Center** · 212-336-6000. A very expensive, monster health club with a 10,000-square-foot climb-ing wall, a quarter-mile track, a swimming pool, and enough fitness equipment for a small army in training. If you have to ask how much the membership is, you can't afford it.

9 **Sky Rink** · 212-336-6100. Two 24/7 ice rinks mainly used for classes, training, and bar mitzvahs.

10 **The Lighthouse** · 212-336-6144. 10,000-square-foot event space for private gatherings catered by Abigail Kirsch.

11 **The Field House** · 212-336-6500. The Field House is an 80,000-square-foot building with a 30-foot climbing wall, a gymnastics training center, four batting cages, two basketball courts, and two indoor soccer fields. A season (ten games plus playoffs) of league soccer costs $225/person, league basketball costs $160/person, rock-climbing costs $18/class, and gymnastics costs $25/class.

12 **Spirit Cruise** · 212-727-7735; www.spiritofnewyork.com. Ships run out of Chelsea Piers and Weehawken, NJ. Dinner cruises are approximately $67/person, and if you're having a big function, you can rent the entire boat!

13 **Roller Rinks** · 212-336-6200. Two regulation-size out-door skating rinks and an "extreme" skate park. The Skate Park costs $10/day for members, otherwise each session costs $14 (on weekends, sessions are only three hours long). Closed from October 31 until spring.

Unfortunately, but not surprisingly, there are no golf courses on the island of Manhattan. Thankfully, there are two driving ranges where you can at least smack the ball around until you can get to a real course, as well as a golf simulator at Chelsea Piers that lets you play a full round "at" various popular courses (Pebble Beach, St. Andrews, etc.). NYC has a number of private and public courses throughout the outer boroughs and Westchester; however, they don't even come close to satisfying the area's huge demand for courses.

Golf Courses

	Borough	Address	Phone	Par	Fee
Mosholu Golf Course	Bronx	3700 Jerome & Bainbridge Ave	718-655-9164	9 holes, par 30	9 holes-$10, 18 holes-$14, twilight-$7.50
Pelham/Split Rock Golf Course	Bronx	870 Shore Rd	718-885-1258	18 holes, par71	For NYC residents: $30 M-F, after 12pm $26 M-F, twilight $15.50, weekends & holidays $36.50, twilight $15.50, Non-residents: add $8, add $6 for twilight
Van Cortlandt Golf Course	Bronx	Van Cortlandt Pk S & Bailey Ave	718-543-4595	18 holes, par 70	Green fees are $38 weekdays $44.50 weekend, $15 cart
Dyker Beach Golf Course	Brooklyn	86th St & Seventh Ave	718-836-9722	18 holes, par 71,	Weekend fees: $43 resident, $36.50 non-resident, weekdays: fluctuates between $35 - $38
Marine Park Golf Club	Brooklyn	2880 Flatbush Ave	718-338-7149	18 holes, par 72	Weekend fees: $36 resident, $44.50 non-resident, weekdays: $30 resident, $38 non-resident
Golf Simulator	Manhattan (see previous Chelsea Piers page)	Chelsea Piers Golf Club			$45 for one hour, $340 for 10 hour package
LaTourette Golf Course	Staten Island	1001 Richmond Hill Rd	718-351-1889	18 holes, par 72	$22 per hour walk, $40 per hour cart
Silver Lake Golf Course	Staten Island	15 Victory Blvd	718-447-5686	18 holes, par 69	Around 35 dollars during the week, call for exact rates.
South Shore Golf Course	Staten Island	200 Huguenot Ave	718-984-0101	18 holes, par 72	Weekday $30, twilight $15.50, Weekend $36.50,twilight $16.50
Kissena Park Golf Course	Queens	164-15 Booth Memorial Ave	718-939-4594	18 holes, par 64	Weekdays before 12 pm $30; after 12 pm: $26; Weekends: $36.50 all day; carts $30, carts after 4 pm $18.75, reservation fee $3
Clearview Golf Course	Queens	202-12 Willets Point Blvd	718-229-2570	18 holes, par 70,	Weekdays: before 12 pm $30; after 12 pm $26; weekends & holidays: $26.50 all day; twilight rate: $15.50 weekdays; $16.50 weekends. carts $30, reservation fee $3
Douglaston Golf Course	Queens	63-20 Marathon Pkwy	718-428-1617	18 holes, par 67,	Weekdays before 12 pm: $30; after 12 pm: $26; weekends: 36.50 all day; carts $30, reservation fee $3
Forest Park Golf Course	Queens	101 Forest Park Dr	718-296-0999	18 holes, par 70	Weekdays before 12 pm: $30; after 12 pm: $26; after 4 pm: $15.50; weekends: $36.50; after 4 pm $16.50; carts $30 for 2 people, reservation fee $3

Driving Ranges

	Borough	Address	Phone	Fee
Randall's Island Golf Center	New York	1 Randalls Rd	212-427-5689	$8/bucket of 68, $12/l bucket of 150
Chelsea Piers: Pier 59	New York	Pier 59	212-336-6400	$20/118 balls, $25/148, after 5pm-$20/80 balls, $25/100balls, clubs: 1 for $4, 2 for $5, 3 for $6, 10 for $12
Brooklyn Sports Center	Brooklyn	3200 Flatbush Ave	718-253-6816	$10 for 180 balls, $12 for 285 balls

For swimming pools in Manhattan, you pretty much have two options: Pay exorbitant gym fees or health club fees in order to use the private swimming facilities, or wait until the summer to share the city's free outdoor pools with freely, urinating summer camp attendees. OK, so it's not that bad! Some YMCAs and YWCAs have nice indoor pools, and their fees are reasonable. And several of the same New York public recreation centers that have outdoor pools (and some that do not) have indoor pools for year-round swimming. Though plenty of kids use the pools, there are dedicated adult swim hours in the mornings, at lunch time, and in the evenings (pee-free if you get there early).

Then there's the Hudson. Yes, we're serious. There are about eight races in the Hudson each year, and the water quality is tested before each race. New York City also has some great beaches for swimming, including Coney Island, Manhattan Beach, and the Rockaways. If you prefer your swimming area enclosed, check out the pool options in Manhattan:

Pools

	Address	Phone	Type	Fees	Map
14th Street Y	344 E 14th St	212-780-0800	Indoor	$20/day	13
All Star Fitness Club	75 West End Ave	212-265-8200	Indoor	$25/day	14
Asphalt Green	555 E 90th St	212-369-8890	Indoor	Adults $25/day, children $8/day, seniors $15/day; $1000/year	17
Asser Levy Recreation Center	E 23rd St & Asser Levy Pl	212-447-2020	Indoor/Outdoor	Indoor - $75/year (not open during summer) / Outdoor - Free*	10
Athletic and Swim Club at the Equitable Center	787 Seventh Ave	212-265-3490	Indoor	Call for membership fees	12
Bally's Sports Club	139 W 32nd St	212-465-1750	Indoor	$25/day	9
Bally's Sports Club	335 Madison Ave	212-983-5320	Indoor	$25/day	12
Bally's Sports Club	350 W 50th St	212-265-9400	Indoor	$25/day	11
Battery Park Swim & Fitness Center	375 South End Ave	212-321-1117	Indoor	Call for membership fees	p202
Chelsea Piers Sports Center	Pier 60	212-336-6000	Indoor	$50/day	8
Dry Dock Swimming Pool	408 E 10th St	212-677-4481	Outdoor	Free	7
Excelsior Athletic Club	301 E 57th St	212-688-5280	Indoor	$25/day	7
Gravity Fitness and Spa	119 W 56th St	212-708-7340	Indoor	$50/day	12
Hamilton Fish Recreation Center	128 Pitt St	212-387-7687	Outdoor, summer only	Free	23
Hansborough Recreation Center	35 W 134th St	212-234-9603	Indoor	$75/year	11
Highbridge	2301 Amsterdam Ave	212-927-2400	Outdoor	Free	21
Holiday Inn	440 W 57th St	212-581-8100	Indoor	Call for rate information	11
Jackie Robinson Pool	89 Bradhurst Ave	212-234-9607	Outdoor, summer only	Free	21
John Jay	E 77th St & Cherokee Pl	212-794-6566	Outdoor, summer only	Free	15
Lasker Pool	110th St & Lenox Ave	212-534-7639	Outdoor, summer only	Free	19
Lenox Hill Neighborhood House	331 E 70th St	212-744-5022	Indoor	$595/year	15
Manhattan Plaza Health Club	482 W 43rd St, 2nd Fl	212-563-7001	Indoor, summer only	$35/day	11
Marcus Garvey Swimming Pool	13 E 124th St	212-410-2818	Outdoor, summer only	Free	20
Monterey Sports Club	175 E 96th St	212-996-8200	Indoor	Call for membership fees	17
New York Health & Racquet Club	110 W 56th St	212-541-7200	Indoor	$50/day or $99/month	12
New York Health & Racquet Club	115 E 57th St	212-826-9650	Indoor	$50/day or $99/month	13
New York Health & Racquet Club	132 E 45th St	212-986-3100	Indoor	$50/day or $99/month	13
New York Health & Racquet Club	1433 York Ave	212-737-6666	Indoor	$50/day or $99/month	15
New York Health & Racquet Club	20 E 50th St	212-593-1500	Indoor	$50/day or $99/month	13
New York Health & Racquet Club	24 E 13th St	212-924-4600	Indoor	$50/day or $99/month	6
New York Health & Racquet Club	39 Whitehall St	212-269-9800	Indoor	$50/day or $99/month	1
New York Sports Club Crowne Plaza Hotel	1605 Broadway	212-977-4000	Indoor	$25/day	12
New York Sports Club	1605 Broadway	212-977-8880	Indoor	$25/day	12
New York Sports Club	1637 Third Ave	212-987-7200	Indoor	$25/day	17
New York Sports Club	614 Second Ave	212-213-5999	Indoor	Call for membership fees	10
Paris Health Club	752 West End Ave	212-749-3500	Indoor	call for membership fees	16
Recreation Center 54	348 E 54th St	212-754-5411	Indoor	$75/year	13
Recreation Center 59	533 W 59th St	212-397-3159	Indoor	$75/year	11
Reebok Sports Club	160 Columbus Ave	212-362-6800	Indoor	$188/month	14
Riverbank State Park	679 Riverside Dr	212-694-3600	Indoor, summer only	$2/day	21
Sheltering Arms	W 129th St & Amsterdam Ave	212-662-6191	Outdoor	$40/day, free for hotel guests	18
Sheraton New York Health Club	811 Seventh Ave	212-621-8591	Indoor	$40/day	12
Thomas Jefferson Swimming Pool	2180 First Ave	212-860-1372	Outdoor, summer only	Free	20
Tompkins Square Mini Pool	500 E 9th St	212-387-7685	Outdoor, summer only	Free	7
Tony Dapolito Recreation Center	1 Clarkson St	212-242-5228	Indoor/Outdoor	$75/year for indoor use, Outdoor free - summer months only	5
UN Plaza Health Club	1 UN Plz 41st Floor	212-702-5016	Indoor	$35/day	13
YMCA	1395 Lexington Ave	212-415-5700	Indoor	$30/day or $86/month	17
YMCA	180 W 135th St	212-281-4100	Indoor	$30/day or $86/month	19
YMCA	224 E 47th St	212-756-9600	Indoor	$30/day	13

General Information

Manhattan Parks Dept: 212-360-8131 • website: www.nycgovparks.org
Permit Locations: The Arsenal, 830 5th Ave @ 64th St; Paragon Sporting Goods Store, 867 Broadway & 18th St

Overview

There are more tennis courts on the island of Manhattan than you might think, although getting to them may be a bit more than you bargain for. Most of the public courts in Manhattan are either smack in the middle of Central Park or are on the edges of the city—East River Park, for instance, and Riverside Park. These courts in particular can make for some pretty windy playing conditions.

Tennis

	Address	Phone	Type/# of Cts./Surface	Map
Coles Center, NYU	181 Mercer St	212-998-2020	Schools, 9 courts, Rubber	3
East River Park Tennis Courts	FDR Dr & Broome St	212-387-7678	Public, Outdoor, 12 courts, Hard	7
Midtown Tennis Club	341 Eighth Ave	212-989-8572	Private, 8 courts, Har-Tru	8
Manhattan Plz Racquet Club	450 W 43rd St	212-594-0554	Private, 5 courts, Cushioned Hard	11
Millennium UN Plaza Hotel Gym	44th & First Ave	212-758-1234	Private, 1 court, Supreme	13
River Club	447 E 52nd St	212-751-0100	Private, 2 courts, Clay	13
The Tennis Club	15 Vanderbilt Ave, 3rd Fl	212-687-3841	Private, 2 courts, Hard	13
Town Tennis Club	430 E 56th St	212-752-4059	Private, 2 courts, Clay, Hard	13
Rockefeller University	1230 York Ave	212-327-8000	Schools, 1 court, Hard	15
Sutton East Tennis Club	York Ave & 60th St	212-751-3452	Private, 8 courts, Clay, Available Oct-April.	15
Central Park Tennis Center	96th St & Central Park W	212-280-0205	Public, Outdoor, 30 Courts Fast-Dry, Hard	16
Riverside Park	Riverside Dr & W 119th St	212-978-0277	Public, Outdoor, 10 courts, Hard	16
PS 146	421 E 106th St	n/a	Schools, 3 courts, Hard	17
Tower Tennis Courts	1725 York Ave	212-860-2464	Private, 2 courts, Hard	17
PS 125	425 W 123rd St	n/a	Schools, 3 courts, Hard	18
Riverside Park	Riverside Dr & W 96th St	212-469-2006	Public, Outdoor, 10 courts, Clay	18
PS 144	134 W 122nd St	n/a	Schools, 4 courts, Hard	19
Riverbank State Park	W 145th St & Riverside Dr	212-694-3600	Public, Outdoor, 1 court, Hard	21
F Johnson Playground	W 151st St & Seventh Ave	212-234-9609	Public, Outdoor, 8 courts, Hard	22
Fort Washington Park	Hudson River & 170th St	212-304-2322	Public, Outdoor, 10 courts, Hard	23
PS 187	349 Cabrini Blvd	n/a	Schools, 4 courts, Hard	24
Columbia Tennis Center	575 W 218th St	212-942-7100	Private, 6 courts, Hard	25
Inwood Park	207th St & Seaman Ave	212-304-2381	Public, Outdoor, 9 courts, Hard	25
Roosevelt Island Racquet Club	281 Main St	212-935-0250	Private, 12 courts, Clay	p226
Randall's Island	East & Harlem Rivers	212-860-1827	Public, Outdoor, 11 courts, Hard	p218
Randall's Island Indoor Tennis	Randall's Island Park	212-427-6150	Private, 4 courts, Hard, Available Oct-April.	P218

Getting a Permit

The tennis season, according to the NYC Parks Department, lasts from April 7 to November 18. Permits are good for use until the end of the season at all public courts in all boroughs, and are good for one hour of singles or two hours of doubles play. Fees are:

Juniors (17 yrs and under) $10		Adults (18-61 yrs) $100
Senior Citizen (62 yrs and over) $20		Single-play tickets $7

Yoga

Finding a Class

When it comes to yoga, New York City has it better than other places in the country, where yoga is often confined to sweaty, ping-pong-table-inhabited back rooms in makeshift recreation centers. Luckily, New Yorkers have an array of charming, airy, sometimes even glossy studios in which to practice—as well as what seems to be an infinite variety of yoga styles to choose from. You can mellow out in meditation, relax in Restorative, practice Pranayama, kick-it Kundalini style, vie for the Vinyasa vibe, jive with Jivamukti, awaken your spirit with Ashtanga, investigate

Iyengar, or bend it like Bikram—just to name a few. To get you started, here's a short list of places to try. Remember, it's always a good idea to contact studios in advance for information about their different approaches to classes, what branches of yoga they teach, class sizes, appropriate attire, cost, and schedules.

Word to the wise: You may want to begin with an introductory class wherever you land. Even seasoned yogis will want to familiarize themselves with the methods of each studio before jumping into headstand first.

	Address	Phone	Website	Map
Kula Yoga Project	28 Warren St, 4th Fl	212-945-4460	www.kulayoga.com	2
Dance New Amsterdam	451 Broadway	212-625-8369	www.dancespace.com	3
Virayoga	580 Broadway, Ste 1109	212-334-9960	www.virayoga.com	3
Flow Yoga Center	240 W 14th St	212-255-7588	www.flowyoganyc.com	5
Integral Yoga Institute	227 W 13th St	212-929-0586	www.integralyogany.org	5
Jivamukti Yoga Studio	707 Washington St	212-675-9642	www.jivamuktiyoga.com	5
Mahayogi Yoga Mission	228 Bleeker St	212-807-8903	www.mahayogiyogamission.com	5
Yamuna	132 Perry St	212-633-2143	www.yamunastudio.com	5
Himalayan Institute– Yoga Science	78 Fifth Ave	212-243-5995	www.hinyc.org	6
Jivamukti Yoga Center	404 Lafayette St	212-353-0214	www.jivamuktiyoga.com	6
Lila Yoga and Wellness	302 Bowery	212-254-2130	www.lilawellness.com	6
New York Open Center	83 Spring St	212-219-2527	www.opencenter.org	6
OM Yoga Center	826 Broadway, 6th Fl	212-254-9642	www.omyoga.com	6
Three Jewels Yoga	61 Fourth Ave	212-475-6650	www.threejewels.org	6
Yoga Mandali	560 Broadway	212-473-9001	www.yogamandali.com	6
Ashtanga Yoga Shala	295 E 8th St	212-614-9537	www.ashtangayogashala.net	7
Ramakrishnananda Classic Yoga Society	96 Ave B	646-436-7010	www.ramakrishnananda.com	7
Abundant Bodies Yoga	18 W 18th St	212-304-1230	www.healingplay.com	9
Bikram Yoga NYC	182 Fifth Ave	212-206-9400	www.bikramyoganyc.com	9
Dahn Center	830 Sixth Ave	212-725-3262	www.dahnyoga.com	9
Iyengar Yoga Institute	150 W 22nd St	212-691-9642	www.iyengarnyc.org	9
Kundalini Yoga East	873 Broadway	212-982-5959	www.kundaliniyogaeast.com	9
Laughing Lotus	59 W 19th St, 3rd Fl	212-414-2903	www.laughinglotus.com	9
Movements Afoot	151 W 30th St	212-904-1399	www.movementsafoot.com	9
Panetta Movement Center	214 W 29th St	212-239-0831	www.panettamovementcenter.com	9
Raja Yoga Center	306 Fifth Ave	212-564-9533		9
Shambhala Meditation Center of New York	118 W 22nd St	212-675-6544		9
Sivananda Yoga Vedanta Center	243 W 24th St	212-255-4560	www.sivananda.org	9
The Breathing Project	15 W 26th St	212-979-9642	www.breathingproject.org	9
Universal Force Yoga	7 W 24th St	917-606-1730	www.universalforceyoga.com	9
Yoga Moves	1026 Sixth Ave	212-278-8330		9
Yoga Works	138 Fifth Ave	212-647-9642	www.yogaworks.com	9
Dharma Yoga Center: Shri Dharma Mittra	297 Third Ave	212-889-8160	www.dharmayogacenter.com	10
NY Underground Fitness	440 W 57th St	212-957-4781	www.nyundergroundfitness.com	11
Sonic Yoga	754 Ninth Ave	212-397-6344	www.sonicyoga.com	11
Bikram Yoga NYC	797 Eighth Ave	212-245-2525	www.bikramyoganyc.com	12
BR Yoga	532 Madison Ave	212-935-5777		12
exhale	150 Central Park S	212-561-7400	www.exhalespa.com	12
Healthy Tao	250 W 49th St	212-586-2100		12
Levitate Yoga	780 Eighth Ave	212-974-2288	www.levitateyoga.com	12
Prana Mandir	316 E 59th St	212-803-5446	www.pranamandir.com	13
Yoga Works	160 E 56th St	212-935-9642	www.yogaworks.com	13
BeYoga	37 W 65th St	212-769-9642	www.yogaworks.com	14
Bikram Yoga NYC	208 W 72nd St	212-724-7303	www.bikramyoganyc.com	14
Life In Motion	371 Amsterdam Ave	212-666-0877	www.lifeinmotion.com	14
Little Yoga Space	102 W 85th St	212-501-8010		14
Practice Yoga	140 W 83rd St	212-724-4884	www.practiceyoga.com	14

	Address	Phone	Website	Map
Steps	2121 Broadway	212-874-2410	www.stepsnyc.com	14
World Yoga Center	265 W 72nd St	212-787-4908	www.worldyogacenter.com	14
exhale	980 Madison Ave	212-561-6400	www.exhalespa.com	15
MonQi Fitness	201 E 67th St	212-327-2170	www.monqifitness.com	15
New York Yoga HOT	132 E 85th St	212-717-9642	www.newyorkyoga.com	15
Yoga Works	1319 Third Ave	212-650-9642	www.yogaworks.com	15
Baby Om	250 Riverside Dr #25	212-615-6935	www.babyom.com	16
New York Yoga	1629 York Ave	212-717-9642	www.newyorkyoga.com	17
Riverside Church Wellness Center	490 Riverside Dr	212-870-6758	www.theriversidechurchny.org	18
Ta Yoga House	71 W 128th St	212-289-6363	www.ta-life.com	19

Billiards

Whether you're looking for a new hobby or need a new atmosphere in which to booze (that isn't your 300 sq. ft. apartment), a good pool-hall is a great way to get the job done. Or perhaps you simply enjoy a hearty game of 8-ball, and it's as simple as that; in any case, an eclectic mix of options dot the island of Manhattan.

If you're in search of a laid-back, nonsense-free setting, **SoHo Billiards (Map 6)** and **Corner Billiards (Map 6)** are best. Each occupies a large space with a ton of tables, cheap rates and plenty, small crowds, and a low-key, local scene. Extra points should be awarded to Corner for its great music—on most nights a D.J. spins your latest indie favorites, and it's not unheard of for the actual band-members to be playing at a table nearby. **Fat Cat Billiards (Map 5)** is another great option if you're looking for a chill setting—located underground in a dim basement, it holds 20 tables and offers an hourly rate of $4.50 (not to mention the $2.00 Pabst). For those of you who tire of shiny balls and green felt, there are multiple Scrabble, checkers, and chess stations scattered about—and if that's not enough, there are nightly jazz and comedy performances in the performance room.

In what appears to be a new breed of pool hall, **Slate Bar** and **Billiards (Map 9)** actually has a velvet rope outside, as if to suggest there's something legitimately exclusive about it. Alas, the SoHo House it's not, although there are two levels with plenty of tables, a clean and comfy lounge setting around the bar, plenty of top-shelf liquor—and extremely loud Top-40 hits blasting on the speakers. Accordingly, the staff can have a bit of an attitude, which is more bewildering than anything else. If you're uptown, check out the recently renovated **East Side Billiards and Bar (Map 16)**, where in addition to the 13 tables, you can also play ping-pong. Or ditch your friends and wander into the attached video game arcade, the largest of its kind outside of Times Square. On the other hand, if you don't have any friends to begin with, think about signing up for one of the East Side seasonal pool leagues—where you not only get to compete and socialize, but receive additional discounts. Last but not least is **Amsterdam Billiards Club (Map 14)**—Manhattan's swankiest pool parlor. With its mahogany bar, multiple fireplaces, and extensive wine list, the club is best suited for corporate events and private parties (for 20 to 200 people). It also boasts the largest coed league in the country and offers lessons for all skill levels.

So what are you waiting for? Turn off the latest Real World/Road Rules challenge (or whatever crap you're watching), get off the couch, and give yourself a real challenge—play some pool!

	Address	Phone	Fee	Hours
Fat Cat Billiards	75 Christopher St	212-675-6056	$5 per person/hour	5
Corner Billiards	110 E 11th St	212-995-1314	$7-9 per person/hour	6
Pressure	110 University Pl	212-352-1161	$26 per table/hour	6
Soho Billiards	298 Mulberry St	212-925-3753	$7-12 per person/hour	6
Mammoth Billiards	558 Eighth Ave	212-535-0331	$3-$4 per person/hour	8
Broadway Billiard Café	10 E 21st St	212-388-1582	$4 per person/hour	9
Q Lounge	220 W 19th St	212-206-7665	$15-18 per person/hour	9
Slate Restaurant Bar Billiards	54 W 21st St	212-989-0096	$15/hour M-F, $17/hour weekends	9
Amsterdam Billiards & Bar	344 Amsterdam Ave	212-496-8180	$5-7.50 /hour	14
East Side Billiard Club	163 E 86th St	212-831-7665	$5- $6.50 per person/hour	16
Chung Haeum	566 W 181st St	212-928-8235	$10 per person/hour	23
Guys & Gals Billiard Parlor	500 W 207th St	212-567-9279	$5/hour	25
Post Billiards Café	154 Post Ave	212-569-1840	$7 per person/hour	25

If you want to go bowling in Manhattan, you have three solid options. Keep in mind that there's just about no way to bowl cheaply, so if you're struggling to keep a positive balance in your bank account, you may want to find another activity or head out to New Jersey.

The most affordable bowling experience can be found at **Leisure Time Bowl (Map 12)**. Connected to the Port Authority (remember this in case you have a long wait for a bus), Leisure Time has 30 lanes, a full bar and pub menu, and two game-rooms. At Chelsea Piers, you'll find the **AMF Bowling Center (Map 8)**. Part of a massive national chain of bowling alleys, AMF offers 40 lanes. On weekend nights, the center plays host to "Xtreme Bowling," a glow-in-the-dark "bowling party" featuring music, fog machines, and an "enhanced" rate of $8.25 per person per game.

Honestly, if you're looking for "extreme" glow-in-the-dark bowling, skip Chelsea Piers and go downtown to **Bowlmor Lanes (Map 6)**. On Monday nights, "Night Strike" is the place to be. Twenty dollars per person provides shoes and all the games you can bowl—assuming you can handle the sometimes long wait (not such a big deal since they offer free pool upstairs!). Nevertheless, this really is a great deal—normal rates are $7.95 per person, per game. The scene (made up of college kids, after-work partiers, and standard bar-hoppers) is a bit surreal—although this is a bowling alley, it's going for the feel of a high-class lounge. Just don't take the setting as seriously as the people who run the place might, order a few drinks (but know that they are way over-priced), and bowl to your heart's content (or your wallet's limit— that is unless it's "Night Strike"). Unless you're internally wired to not have fun, Bowlmor Lanes is the sure thing.

	Address	Phone	Fee	Map
AMF Chelsea Piers Bowl	Pier 60	212-835-2695	$7.50-$8.25 per person/game $4.50 for shoes	8
Bowlmor Lanes	110 University Pl b/w 12th & 13th Sts	212-255-8188	$8.45 per game, $5 for shoes	6
Leisure Time	Port Authority 625 Eighth Ave, 2nd Fl	212-268-6909	$8 per person/game, $5 for shoes	12

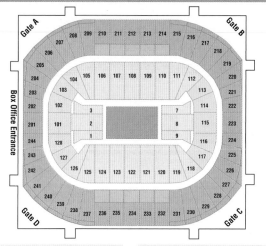

General Information

Address: East Rutherford, NJ 07073
Website: www.meadowlands.com/coarenafaq.asp
Devils: www.newjerseydevils.com
Nets: www.nba.com/nets
Ticketmaster: 212-307-7171, www.ticketmaster.com

Overview

Once upon a time, this place was called Brendan Byrne Arena and was the home of two very bad pro teams: the New Jersey Nets and the New Jersey Devils. Today, it's called the Continental Airlines Arena and is the home of two suddenly very good teams. Though things seem to be going well game-wise for the Nets, they've been engulfed in financial troubles for quite sometime. NJ Nets management is currently in talks to sell and move the team to Brooklyn. Developer Bruce Ratner hopes to move the team to a proposed $435-million arena as a part of a residential, shopping, and office complex development to be built in the Prospect Heights area within the next five years. Residents who don't want their brownstone neighborhoods infringed upon by this mammoth complex are protesting the plan. The NJ Storm lacrosse team up and relocated to Anaheim, CA as well. And then there were two.

How to Get There—Driving

Continental Airlines Arena is only five miles from the Lincoln Tunnel. Luckily, since the fan base for the teams that play hails primarily from New Jersey, you won't have to deal with the same New York City and Long Island traffic that plagues Giants Stadium games. Additionally, attendance rates are much smaller than for football, even on the rare occasions when the Nets or Devils sell out. You can take the Lincoln Tunnel to Route 3 W to Route 120 N, or you can try either the Holland Tunnel to the New Jersey Turnpike (North) to Exit 16W, or the George Washington Bridge to the New Jersey Turnpike (South) to Exit 16W. Accessing the stadium from Exit 16W feeds you directly into the parking areas.

How to Get There–Mass Transit

The direct bus from the Port Authority Bus Terminal to the arena costs $7 round trip for advance-purchase tickets, and $4 each way on the bus, which accepts exact change only. Buses usually start running two hours before game time.

How to Get Tickets

The box office is open Monday–Saturday from 11 am to 6 pm and is closed Sunday, unless there is an event. For ticket information, call 201-935-3900. To purchase tickets without going to the box office, call Ticketmaster at 212-307-7171, or visit their website.

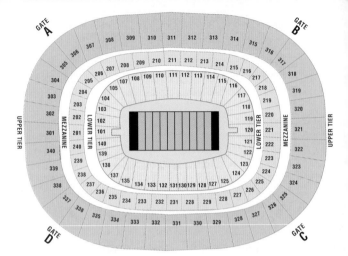

General Information

Address:	East Rutherford, NJ 07073
Phone:	201-935-3900
Website:	www.giantsstadium.com
Giants:	www.giants.com
Jets:	www.newyorkjets.com
Red Bulls:	www.newyorkredbulls.com
Ticketmaster:	212-307-7171, www.ticketmaster.com

Overview

Giants Stadium, located in New Jersey's scenic and smelly Meadowlands Sports Complex, is the home of both the New York Giants and New York Jets football teams. It's the only stadium in the country that hosts two professional football teams, and it looks to stay that way unless Bloomberg resurrects the west side stadium nonsense again. For now, the two NFL teams play on alternating Sundays throughout the fall, and the only way to get regular-priced tickets is to inherit them, since both teams are sold out through the next ice age (even though at least one of the teams—ok, usually the Jets—stinks in any given year). Giants Stadium also houses Major League Soccer's Red Bulls (for which many, many tickets are available) and is the site of several concerts and other sporting and religious events throughout the year. The stadium's field is made of synthetic FieldTurf.

How to Get There—Driving

Giants Stadium is only five miles from the Lincoln Tunnel (closer to Midtown than Shea Stadium, even), but leave early if you want to get to the game on time—remember that the Giants and the Jets are a) sold out for every game and b) have tons of fans from both Long Island and the five boroughs. You can take the Lincoln Tunnel to Route 3 W to Route 120 N, or you can try either the Holland Tunnel to the New Jersey Turnpike N to Exit 16W, or the George Washington Bridge to the New Jersey Turnpike S to Exit 16W. Accessing the stadium from Exit 16W allows direct access to parking areas. Parking costs $15 for most events.

How to Get There–Mass Transit

Less stressful than driving to Giants Stadium is taking a bus from the Port Authority Bus Terminal directly to the stadium. Pre-paid bus trips cost $7 round trip (and $4 each way when purchased on the bus), and buses usually start running two hours before kickoff.

How to Get Tickets

For the Jets and the Giants, scalpers and friends are the only options. For the Red Bulls and for concerts, you can call Ticketmaster or visit the website.

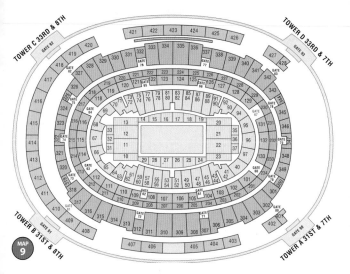

General Information

NFT Map: 9
Address: 4 Pennsylvania Plz
New York, NY 10001
Phone: 212-465-6741
Website: www.thegarden.com
Knicks: www.nyknicks.com
Liberty: www.nyliberty.com
Rangers: www.newyorkrangers.com
Ticketmaster: 212-307-7171, www.ticketmaster.com

Overview

Once resembling the Doge's Palace in Venice (c.1900), the since-relocated Altoid 'tween Seventh and Eighth Avenues atop Penn Station remains one of the legendary venues in sport, becoming so almost solely by way of the sport of boxing. It now, for good and ill, houses the NBA's Knicks, NHL's Rangers, The Liberty of the WNBA, St. John's University's Red Storm, as well as concerts, tennis tournaments, dog shows, political conventions, and, for those of you with 2+ years of graduate school, monster truck rallies and "professional" wrestling. Check out MSG's website for a full calendar of events.

How to Get There–Mass Transit

MSG is right above Penn Station, which makes getting there very easy. You can take the **A C E** and **1 2 3** lines to 34th Street and Penn Station, or the **N R Q W**, **B D F V**, and PATH lines to 34th Street and 6th Avenue. The Long Island Rail Road also runs right into Penn Station.

How to Get Tickets

For single seats for the Knicks and the Rangers, you can try Ticketmaster, but a better bet would be to try the "stand-by" line (show up a half-hour before game time and wait). The ubiquitous ticket scalpers surrounding the Garden are a good last resort for when your rich out-of-town friends breeze in to see a game. Liberty tickets (and tickets for other events) are usually available through Ticketmaster.

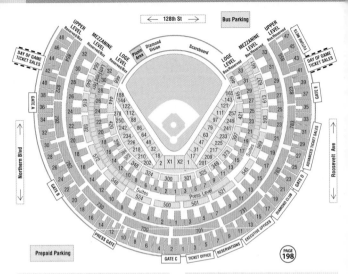

General Information

Address: 126th St & Roosevelt Ave,
Flushing, Queens

Shea Stadium Box Office: 718-507-TIXX

Website: www.mets.com

Mets Clubhouse Shops: 143 E 54th St & 11 W 42nd St

Ferry: 800-BOATRIDE
or 732-872-2628

Overview

Some would consider this House of New York's Mets a second class abode to the gray bowl in the Bronx. However, disregarding the incessant air traffic overhead of LaGuardia, the train journey is more "picturesque" (quotes required) and the surroundings better suited to tailgate. Unless near season's end and the Mets atop the table, tickets come easy and cheaply. Decide at 4 pm on a Wednesday you feel like a game, hop the 7 train to Willets Point—a mere 7 stops express from Grand Central—bring $50 and have a night.

How To Get Tickets

You can order Mets tickets by phone through the Mets' box office, on the internet through the Mets' website, or at the Mets Clubhouse Shops.

How To Get There—Driving

Driving to Shea Stadium is easy, although commuter traffic during the week can cause tie-ups. You can take the Triborough Bridge to the Grand Central Parkway; the Mid-Town Tunnel to the Long Island Expressway to the Grand Central; or the Brooklyn-Queens Expressway to the LIE to the Grand Central. If you want to try and avoid the highways, get yourself over to Astoria Boulevard in Queens, make a right on 108th Street, then a left onto Roosevelt Avenue.

How To Get There—Mass Transit

The good news is that the 7 train runs straight to Shea Stadium. The bad news is: it's the only train that goes there. However, it will get you there and back (eventually), and the 7 is accessible from almost all the other train lines in Manhattan. Alternately, you can take the E, F, G, or R to Roosevelt Avenue and pick up the 7 there, saving about 30 minutes. Also, New York Waterway runs a ferry service (the "Mets Express") to Shea from the South Street Seaport, E 34th Street, and E 94th Street. The other option is the Port Washington LIRR from Penn Station, which stops at Shea on game days.

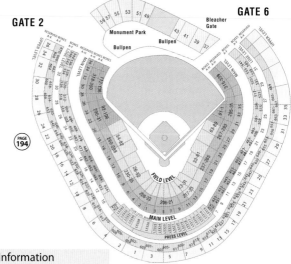

GATE 2

GATE 6

Bleacher Gate

Monument Park

Bullpen

Bullpen

Bullpen

Reserved Boxes

Upper Level

Main Level

Field Level

Main Level

Press Level

PAGE 194

General Information

Address: 161st St & River Ave, Bronx
Box Office: 718-293-6000
Website: www.yankees.com
Yankees Store: 393 Fifth Ave
Ferry: 800-53-FERRY
Ticketmaster: 212-307-7171; www.ticketmaster.com

Overview

Arguably the globe's most famous ballpark, Yankee Stadium—not built by Ruth but broken in by him—sits brazen in the Bronx, usually boiling come October. Opened in 1923, the field, once a veritable prairie, has diminished to better suit the affinities of today's fan. Interestingly, New York's Football Giants began renting in 1956 only to eventually succumb to the lure of floral Jersey and its Meadowlands. Obviously, promises made by the city and the team to rehabilitate the neighborhood surrounding have proved illusions...we await the new ballpark with the standard mixture of doubt and hope.

How to Get There—Driving

Driving to Yankee Stadium from Manhattan isn't as bad as you might think. Your best bet is to take the Willis Avenue Bridge from either First Avenue or FDR Drive and get on

GATE 4

the Major Deegan for about one mile until you spot the stadium exit. From the Upper West Side, follow Broadway up to 155th Street and use the Macombs Dam Bridge to cross over the river to the stadium (thus avoiding cross-town traffic). Parking (in contrast to ticket prices) is cheap, especially at lots a few blocks away from the stadium.

How to Get There—Mass Transit

Getting to the stadium by subway is easy. The ④, ⑧, and the ⑩ (on weekdays) all run express to the stadium, and you can easily hook up with those lines at several junctions in Manhattan. It should take no more than 45 minutes to get to the stadium from any point in Manhattan—even less from Midtown. New York Waterway also runs a wonderful ferry (the "Yankee Clipper") from South Street Seaport, E 34th Street, and E 94th Street.

How to Get Tickets

You can purchase tickets by phone through Ticketmaster, at the box office or the Yankee store, or online through either Ticketmaster or the Yankees web site.

Airline	Phone	JFK	EWR	LGA
Aer Lingus	888-474-7424	■		
Aeroflot	800-340-6400	■		
Aerolineas Argentinas	800-333-0276	■		
Aeromexico	800-237-6639	■		
Aerosvit Ukranian	212-661-1620	■		
Air Canada	888-247-2262	■	■	■
Air China	800-982-8802	■		
Air France	800-237-2747	■	■	
Air India	212-751-6200	■	■	
Air Jamaica	800-523-5585	■	■	
Air Plus Comet	877-999-7587	■	■	
Air Tahiti Nui	866-835-9286	■		
Air Tran	800-247-8726		■	■
Alaska Airlines	800-426-0333	■		
Alitalia	800-223-5730	■	■	
All Nippon	800-235-9262	■		
Allegro	800-903-2779	■		
America West (domestic)	800-235-9292	■	■	
America West (international)	800-363-2597	■		
American (domestic)	800-433-7300	■	■	■
American (international)	800-433-7300	■	■	
American Eagle	800-433-7300	■	■	■
Asiana	800-227-4262	■		
ATA	800-435-9282			■
Austrian Airlines	800-843-0002	■		
Avianca	800-284-2622	■		
Azteca	212-289-6400	■		
Biman Bangladesh	212-808-4477	■		
British Airways	800-247-9297	■	■	
BWIA	800-538-2942	■		
CanJet	800-809-7777			■
Casino Express	775-738-6040		■	
Cathay Pacific	800-233-2742	■		
Chautauqua	317-484-6000		■	
China Airlines	800-227-5118	■		
Colgan	800-428-4322			■
Comair	800-354-9822	■	■	■
Continental (domestic)	800-525-0280	■	■	■
Continental (international)	800-231-0856		■	
Copa Airlines	800-892-2672	■		
Corsair (seasonal)	800-677-0720	■		
Czech Airlines	212-765-6545	■	■	
Delta (domestic)	800-221-1212	■	■	■
Delta (international)	800-241-4141	■	■	
Delta Express	800-235-9359	■	■	■
Egyptair	212-315-0900	■		
El Al	800-223-6700	■	■	
Emirates	800-777-3999	■		
EOS	888-357-3677	■		
Eurofly	800-459-0581	■		
Eva Airways	800-695-1188		■	
Flybe British European	800-525-0280	■		
Finnair	800-950-5000	■		
Frontier Airlines	800-432-1359			■
Ghana Airways	800-404-4262	■		

Airline	Phone	JFK	EWR	LGA
Hooters Air	888-359-4668	■		
Iberia	800-772-4642	■		
Icelandair	800-223-5500		■	
Israir	877-477-2471	■		
Japan Airlines	800-525-3663	■		
Jet Blue	800-538-2583	■	■	■
KLM	800-374-7747	■	■	
Korean Air	800-438-5000	■		
Kuwait Airways	800-458-9248	■		
Lacsa	800-225-2272	■		
Lan Chile	800-735-5526	■		
Lan Ecuador	866-526-3279	■		
Lan Peru	800-735-5590	■		
LOT Polish	800-223-0593	■	■	
LTU	866-266-5588	■		
Lufthansa	800-645-3880	■	■	
Malaysia	800-582-9264		■	
Malev Hungarian	800-223-6884	■		
MaxJet	888-435-9626	■		
Mexicana	800-531-7921	■	■	
Miami Air (charter)	305-871-3300	■	■	
Midwest Express	800-452-2022		■	■
National Airlines	888-757-5387	■		
North American	718-656-2650	■		
Northwest (domestic)	800-225-2525	■	■	■
Northwest (international)	800-447-4747	■		
Olympic	800-223-1226	■		
Pakistan Int'l Airlines	212-370-9157	■		
Qantas	800-227-4500	■	■	
Royal Air Maroc	800-344-6726	■		
Royal Jordanian	212-949-0050	■		
SAS	800-221-2350		■	
Saudi Arabian Airlines	800-472-8342	■		
Singapore Airlines	800-742-3333	■		
SN Brussels	516-622-2248	■		
Song	800-359-7664	■		■
South African Airways	800-722-9675	■		
Spirit	800-772-7117			■
Sun Country	800-359-6786	■		
Swiss Airlines	800-221-4750	■	■	
TACA	800-535-8780	■		
TAM	888-235-9826	■		
Tap Air Portugal	800-221-7370		■	
Thai Airways	800-560-0840	■		
Travel Spain	800-817-6177	■		
Turkish	800-874-8875	■		
United Airlines (domestic)	800-241-6522	■	■	■
United Airlines (international)	800-241-6522	■		
Universal	718-441-4900	■		
US Airways	800-428-4322		■	■
USA3000	800-577-3000	■	■	
Uzbekistan	212-245-1005	■		
Varig	800-468-2744	■		
Virgin Atlantic	800-862-8621	■	■	

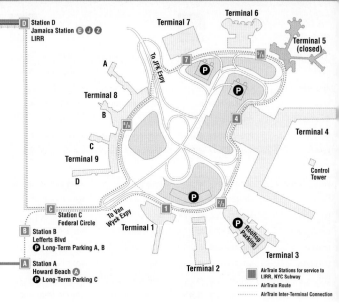

Station D
Jamaica Station E J Z
LIRR

Terminal 7
Terminal 6
Terminal 5 (closed)

To JFK Expy

A

Terminal 8

B

C

Terminal 9

D

Station C
Federal Circle

To Van Wyck Expy

Terminal 4

Control Tower

Station B
Lefferts Blvd
P Long-Term Parking A, B

Terminal 1

Station A
Howard Beach A
P Long-Term Parking C

Terminal 2

Rooftop Parking

Terminal 3

■ AirTrain Stations for service to LIRR, NYC Subway
······ AirTrain Route
----- AirTrain Inter-Terminal Connection

Airline	Terminal
Aer Lingus	4
Aero Mexico	1
Aeroflot	1
Aerolineas Argentinas	4
Aerosvit Ukrainian	4
Air Canada	7
Air China	1
Air France	1
Air India	4
Air Jamaica	4
Air Plus Comet	1
Air Tahiti Nui	4
Alitalia	1
All Nippon Airways	7
Allegro (Seasonal)	1
America West	7
America West (int'l, Canada, Mexico)	7
American (dom/ San Juan)	9
American (intl/Carib)	8
American Eagle	9
Asiana	4

Airline	Terminal
Austrian Airlines	1
Avianca	4
Azteca	4
Biman Bangladesh	4
British Airways	7
BWIA	4
Cathay Pacific	7
China Airlines	1
Comair	3
Continental Airlines	2
Continental Express	2
Copa Airlines	4
Corsair (Seasonal)	4
Czech Airlines	3
Delta	3
Delta Connection	3
Egypt Air	4
El Al	4
Emirates	4
EOS	4
Eurofly	4
Finnair	8
Ghana Airways	4
Iberia	7

Airline	Terminal
Icelandair	7
Israir	4
Japan	1
JetBlue (dom)	6
JetBlue (int'l)	4
KLM	4
Korean	1
Kuwait	4
Lacsa	4
Lan Chile	4
Lan Ecuador	4
Lan Peru	4
LOT Polish	4
LTU	4
Lufthansa	1
Malev	3
MaxJet	1
Mexicana	4
Miami Air	3
National	4
North American	4
Northwest	4
Olympic	1
Pakistan	4

Airline	Terminal
Qantas	7
Royal Air Maroc	1
Royal Jordanian	3
Saudi Arabian Airlines	3
Singapore	4
SN Brussels Airlines	8
Song	2
South African	4
Sun Country	3
Swiss International	4
TACA International	4
TAM	4
Thai Airways Int'l	4
Travel Span	4
Turkish	1
United	7
Universal	4
USA 3000	4
Uzbekistan Airlines	4
Varig	4
Virgin Atlantic	4

General Information

Address: JFK Expy
                      Jamaica, NY 11430
Phone: 718-244-4444
Lost & Found: 718-244-4225
Website: www.kennedyairport.com
AirTrain: www.airtrainjfk.com
AirTrain Phone: 718-570-1048
Long Island Rail Road: www.mta.info/lirr

Overview

Ah, JFK. It's long been a nemesis to Manhattanites due to the fact that it's the farthest of the three airports from the city. Nonetheless, more than 32 million people use JFK every year. A $9.5-billion expansion and modernization program will transform the airport, with JetBlue taking about $900 million of that for its gigantic, 26-gate, new HQ to address the ten million of you who, in spite of JFK's distance, wake up an hour earlier to save a buck.

JetBlue's new terminal will rise just behind the landmark TWA building, which if you have time to kill after getting up an hour earlier, you should check out. Its bubblicious curves makes this 1950s gem a glam spaceship aptly prepared to handle any swanky NY soiree. Top that, Newark.

Rental Cars (On-Airport)

The rental car offices are all located along the Van Wyck Expressway near the entrance to the airport. Just follow the signs.
1 · **Avis** · 718-244-5406 or 800-230-4898
2 · **Budget** · 718-656-6010 or 800-527-0700
3 · **Dollar** · 718-656-2400 or 800-800-4000
4 · **Hertz** · 718-656-7600 or 800-654-3131
5 · **Enterprise** · 718-659-1200 or 800-RENT-A-CAR
6 · **National** · 718-632-8300 or 800-CAR-RENT

Hotels

Crown Plaza JFK · 151-20 Baisley Blvd · 718-489-1000
Comfort Inn JFK · 144-36 153rd Ln · 718-977-0001
Holiday Inn JFK Airport · 144-02 135th Ave · 718-659-0200
Radisson Hotel at JFK · 135-40 140th St · 718-322-2300
Ramada Plaza Hotel · Van Wyck Expy · 718-995-9000

Car Services & Taxis

All County Express · 914-381-4223 or 800-914-4223
Classic Limousine · 631-567-5100 or 800-666-4949
Dial 7 Car & Limo Service · 212-777-7777 or 800-222-9888
Super Saver by Carmel · 800-924-9954 or 212-666-6666
Tel Aviv Limo Service · 800-222-9888 or 212-777-7777

Taxis from the airport to Manhattan cost a flat $45 + tolls, while fares to the airport are metered + tolls. The SuperShuttle (800-258-3826) will drop you anywhere between Battery Park and 227th, including all hotels, for $17-$19 but it could end up taking a while, depending on where your fellow passengers are going—nevertheless, a good option if you want door-to-door service, have a lot of time to kill, but not a lot of cash.

How to Get There–Driving

You can take the lovely and scenic Belt Parkway straight to JFK, as long as it's not rush hour. The Belt Parkway route is about 30 miles long, even though JFK is only 15 or so miles from Manhattan. You can access the Belt by taking the Brooklyn-Battery Tunnel to the Gowanus (the best route) or by taking the Brooklyn, Manhattan, or Williamsburg Bridges to the Brooklyn-Queens Expressway to the Gowanus. If you're sick of stop-and-go highway traffic, and you prefer an alternate route using local roads, take Atlantic Avenue in Brooklyn and drive east until you hit Conduit Avenue. Follow this straight to JFK—it's direct and fairly simple. You can get to Atlantic Avenue from any of the three downtown bridges (look at one of our maps first!). From Midtown, you can take the Queens Midtown Tunnel to the Long Island Expressway to the Van Wyck Expressway S (there's never much traffic on the LIE, of course…). From uptown, you can take the Triboro Bridge to the Grand Central Parkway to the Van Wyck Expressway S. JFK also has two new AM frequencies solely devoted to keeping you abreast of all of the airport's endeavors that may affect traffic. Tune into 1630AM for general airport information and 1700AM for construction updates en route to your next flight. It might save you a sizeable headache.

How to Get There—Mass Transit

This is your chance to finish *War and Peace*. The new AirTrain will make your journey marginally smoother, but it will also make your wallet a little lighter. Where there was once a free shuttle bus service from the Howard Beach/JFK Airport stop on the Ⓐ subway line, the AirTrain will now whisk you across for a mere five bucks extra. Depending on where you're traveling from in Manhattan, Queens or Brooklyn, the Ⓔ, Ⓙ, and Ⓜ subway lines to Sutphin Blvd/Archer Ave also connect with the AirTrain.

All subway-AirTrain combos will set you back a total of $7. If you're anywhere near Penn Station and your time is valuable, the LIRR to Jamaica will cost you $5 off-peak, $7 during peak times, and the journey takes roughly 20 minutes. The AirTrain portion of the trip will still cost you an additional $5 and round out your travel time to less than an hour.

If you want to give your MetroCard a workout, you can take the Ⓔ or the Ⓕ to the Turnpike/Kew Gardens stop, and transfer to the Ⓠ. Another possibility is the Ⓐ to New Lots Avenue, where you transfer to the Ⓑ to JFK. The easiest and most direct option is to take a New York Airport Service Express bus (718-875-8200) from either Grand Central Station, Penn Station, or the Port Authority for $15 or you can hop on the Trans-Bridge Bus Line (800-962-9135) at Port Authority for $12. Since the buses travel on service roads, Friday afternoon is not an advisable time to try them out.

Parking

Daily rates for the Central Terminal Area lots cost $3 for the first half-hour, $6 for up to one hour, $3 for every hour after that, up to $30 per day. Long-term parking costs $15 for the first 24 hours, and $5 for each 8-hour period thereafter. Be warned, though—many of the ongoing construction projects at JFK affect both their short-term and long-term lots, so be sure to allow extra time for any unpleasant surprises. For updated parking availability, call (718) 244-4080.

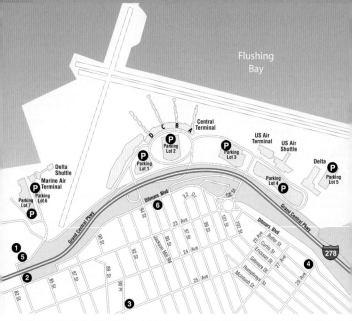

Airline	Terminal
Air Canada	A
Air Tran	B
American	D
American Eagle	C
ATA	B
Canjet	A
Colgan	US Airways
Comair	Delta
Continental	A
Continental Express	A
Delta	Delta
Delta Shuttle	Marine

Airline	Terminal
Delta Connection	Delta
Frontier Airlines	A
JetBlue Airways	A,B
Midwest Express	B
Northwest	Delta
Song	Delta
Spirit	B
United	C
United Express	C
US Airways	US Airways
US Airways Express	US Airways
US Airways Shuttle	US Air Shuttle

General Information

Address:	LaGuardia Airport
	Flushing, NY 11371
Recorded Information:	718-533-3400
Lost & Found:	718-533-3988
Police:	718-533-3900
Website:	www.laguardiaairport.com

Overview

Remember when you got stuck in Kansas in a barn of an airport with one row of lounge chairs? Well, like that Kansas experience, LaGuardia is the JFK sister who never got asked to the prom.

If you're one for a less-harrowing travel day, its smaller terminals actually make it simpler for your car service to find you. You won't be on the phone repeating, "I'm wearing a black jacket and have blue luggage," like you do at JFK. Plus, you can always hang out in the Crown Room, while they find your luggage.

All said, LaGuardia, though miles away from any subway, has that homely appeal to it that has made it rather attractive when Newark is booked solid.

How to Get There—Driving

LaGuardia is mere inches away from Grand Central Parkway, which can be reached from both the Brooklyn-Queens Expressway (BQE) or from the Triboro Bridge. From Lower Manhattan, take the Brooklyn, Manhattan, or Williamsburg Bridges to the BQE to Grand Central Parkway E. From Midtown Manhattan, take FDR Drive to the Triboro to Grand Central. A potential alternate route (and money-saver) would be to take the 59th Street Bridge to 21st Street in Queens. Once you're heading north on 21st Street, you can make a right on Astoria Boulevard and follow it all the way to 94th Street, where you can make a left and drive straight into LaGuardia. This alternate route is good if the FDR and/or the BQE is jammed, although that probably means that the 59th Street Bridge won't be much better.

How to Get There—Mass Transit

Alas, no subway line goes to LaGuardia (although there SHOULD be one running across 96th Street in Manhattan, through Astoria, and ending at LaGuardia—but that's another story). The closest the subway comes is the 🟡 🟠 🟣 🟢 Ⓡ Jackson Heights/Roosevelt Avenue/ 74th Street stop in Queens, where you can transfer to the 🟥 or 🟪 bus to LaGuardia. Sound exciting? Well, it's not. A better bus to take is the M60, which runs across 125th Street to the airport. An even better bet would be to pay the extra few bucks and take the New York Airport Service Express Bus ($12 one-way, 718-875-8200) from Grand Central Station. It departs every 20-30 minutes and takes approximately 45 minutes; also catch it on Park Avenue between 41st and 42nd Streets, Penn Station, and the Port Authority Bus Terminal. The improbably named SuperShuttle Manhattan is a shared mini-bus that picks you up anywhere within the city limits ($13-$22 one-way, 212-258-3826). Or you could just pay a cab driver with your firstborn.

How to Get There—Really

Two words: car service. Call them, they'll pick you up at your door and drop you at the terminal. Simple. Allstate Car and Limousine: 212-333-3333 ($30 in the am & $38 in the pm + tolls from Union Square); Tri-State: 212-777-7171 ($30 + tolls from Union Square; best to call in the morning); Tel Aviv: 212-777-7777 ($30 in the am & $40 in the pm + tolls from Union Square).

Parking

Daily parking rates at LaGuardia cost $3 for the first half-hour, $6 for up to one hour, $3 for every hour thereafter, and up to $30 per day. Long-term parking is $30 for each of the first two days, then $5 for each 8-hour period thereafter (though only in Lot 3). Another option is independent parking lots, such as Clarion Airport Parking (Ditmars Blvd & 94th St, 718-335-6713) and AviStar (23rd Ave & 90th St, 718-507-8162). They run their own shuttle buses from their lots, and they usually charge $14-$17 per day. If all the parking garages onsite are full, follow the "P" signs to the airport exit and park in one of the off-airport locations.

Rental Cars

1 Avis · LGA		800-230-4898
2 Budget · 83-34 23rd Ave		800-527-0700
3 Dollar · 90-05 25th Ave		800-800-4000
4 Enterprise · 104-04 Ditmars Blvd		718-457-2900
5 Hertz · LGA		800-654-3131
6 National · Ditmars Blvd & 95th St		800-227-7368

Hotels

Clarion · 94-00 Ditmars Blvd · 718-335-1200
Courtyard · 90-10 Grand Central Pkwy ·
   718-446-4800
Crowne Plaza · 104-04 Ditmars Blvd · 718-457-6300
Best Western · 113-10 Corona Ave · 718-699-4500
LaGuardia Marriott · 102-05 Ditmars Blvd ·
   718-565-8900
Paris Suites · 109-17 Horace Harding Expy ·
   718-760-2820
Sheraton · 135-20 39th Ave · 718-460-6666
Wyndham Garden · 100-15 Ditmars Blvd ·
   718-426-1500

Transit • **Newark Liberty Airport**

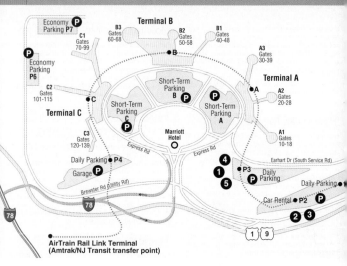

Airline	Terminal
Air Canada	A
Air France	B
Air India	B
Air Jamaica	B
Air Plus Comet (seasonal)	B
Air Tran	A
Alaska Airlines	A
Alitalia	B
America West	A
American (domestic)	A
American (international)	A/B*
American Eagle	A
British Airways	B
Casino Express (charter)	A
Chautauqua	A
Comair	B
Continental	C
Continental (Atlanta/Chicago/ Dallas/Washington DC)	A
Continental (Baton Rouge)	A
Continental (Boston)	A
Czech Airlines	B
Delta	B
Delta Express	B
El Al	B

Airline	Terminal
Eva Airways	B
Express Jet – Continental	C
Flybe British European	C
Hooters Air	B
Jet Blue	A
KLM Royal Dutch Airlines	B
LoT Polish	B
Lufthansa	B
Malaysia	B
Mexicana	B
Miami Air (Charter)**	B
Midwest Express	B
Northwest	B
Qantas	A
SAS	B
Singapore Airlines	B
Swiss International Air Lines	B
TAP Portugal	B
United (domestic)	A
United (international)	A/B*
United Express	A
USA3000	B
US Airways	A
US Airways Express	A
Virgin Atlantic	B

* Departs Terminal A, arrives Terminal B.
** Charter Airlines: For departure/arrival information, contact the airline or travel agent.

General Information

Address:	10 Toler Pl, Newark, NJ 07114
Phone:	888-EWR-INFO
Police/Lost & Found:	973-961-6230
Airport Information:	973-961-6000
Transportation Info:	800-AIR-RIDE (247-7533)
Radio Station:	530 AM
Website:	www.newarkairport.com

Overview

Newark Airport is easily the nicest of the three major metropolitan airports. The monorail and the AirTrain link from Penn Station, as well as a diverse food court, make it the city's preferred point of departure and arrival. Newark's burgeoning international connections are increasing its popularity, which means you might be languishing in Holland Tunnel traffic long after your plane has left the ground.

If your flight gets delayed or you find yourself with time on your hands, check out the new d-parture spa in Terminal C, Gate 92 (with another new location at Gate 48 in Terminal B). They offer everything from massage and facials to haircuts and make-up, and their friendly staff watches the clock so you don't have to. www.departurespa.com, 973-242-3444.

How to Get There–Driving

The route to Newark Airport is easy—just take the Holland Tunnel or the Lincoln Tunnel to the New Jersey Turnpike South. You can use either Exit 14 or Exit 13A. If you want a cheaper and slightly more scenic (from an industrial standpoint) drive, follow signs for the Pulaski Skyway once you exit the Holland Tunnel. It's free, it's one of the coolest bridges in America, and it leads you to the airport just fine. If possible, check a traffic report before leaving Manhattan—sometimes there are viciously long tie-ups, especially at the Holland Tunnel. It's always worth it to see which outbound tunnel has the shortest wait.

How to Get There–Mass Transit

If you're allergic to traffic, try taking the AirTrain service from Penn Station. It's run by Amtrak ($27–$35 one-way) and NJ Transit ($11.55 one-way). If you use NJ Transit, choose a train that runs on the Northeast Corridor or North Jersey Coast Line with a scheduled stop for Newark Airport. If you use Amtrak, choose a train that runs on the Northeast Corridor Line with a scheduled stop for Newark Airport. You can also catch direct buses departing from Port Authority Bus Terminal (with the advantage of a bus-only lane running right out of the station and into the Lincoln Tunnel), Grand Central Terminal, and Penn Station (the New York version) on Olympia for $13. The SuperShuttle will set you back $19, and a taxi from Manhattan will cost you around $50.

How to Get There–Car Services

Car services are always the simplest option, although they're a bit more expensive for Newark Airport than they are for LaGuardia. Allstate Car and Limousine: 212-333-3333 ($44 in the am & $52 in the pm + tolls from Union Square); Tri-State: 212-777-7171 ($43 + tolls from Union Square; best to call in the morning); Tel Aviv: 212-777-7777 ($44 in the am & $49 in the pm + tolls from Union Square).

Parking

Regular parking rates are $3 for the first half-hour, $6 for up to one hour, $3 for every hour after that, and now an excessive $24 per day for the P1, P3, and P4 monorail-serviced lots. The P6 parking lot is much farther away, only serviced by a shuttle bus, and costs $12 per day. There are some off-airport lots, but they are not easy to get to and they're really not any cheaper for the most part. Valet parking costs $36 per day.

Rental Cars

1 · **Avis**	800-230-4898
2 · **Budget**	800-527-0700
3 · **Dollar**	800-800-3665
4 · **Hertz**	800-654-3131
5 · **National**	800-227-7368
6 · **Alamo** (Off-Airport)	800-522-9696
7 · **Enterprise** (Off-Airport)	800-261-7331

Hotels

Marriott (On-Airport) · 973-623-0006
Courtyard Marriott · 600 Rte 1 9 S · 973-643-8500
Hilton · 1170 Spring St · 908-351-3900
Howard Johnson · 50 Port St · 973-344-1500
Sheraton · 128 Frontage Rd · 973-690-5500
Hampton Inn · 1128-38 Spring St · 908-355-0500
Best Western · 101 International Wy · 973-621-6200
Holiday Inn North · 160 Frontage Rd · 973-589-1000
Days Inn · 450 Rte 1 South · 973-242-0900
Ramada Inn · US Hwy 1/9 & Haynes Ave · 973-824-4000
Four Points Sheraton · 901 Spring St · 908-527-1600

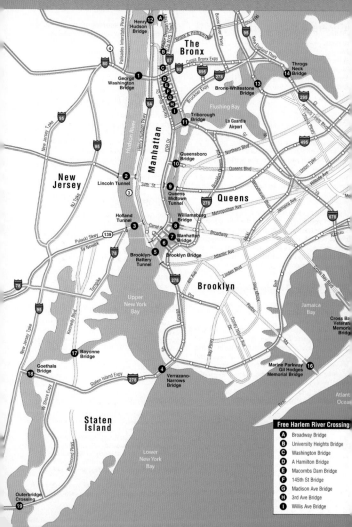

Henry
Hudson
Bridge

The Bronx

George
Washington
Bridge

New
Jersey

Manhattan

Lincoln Tunnel

Holland
Tunnel

Throgs
Neck
Bridge

Bronx-Whitestone
Bridge

Flushing Bay

La Guardia
Airport

Triborough
Bridge

Queensboro
Bridge

Queens
Midtown
Tunnel

Queens

Williamsburg
Bridge

Brooklyn-
Battery Tunnel

Manhattan
Bridge

Brooklyn Bridge

Brooklyn

Upper
New York
Bay

Jamaica
Bay

Bayonne
Bridge

Goethals
Bridge

Verrazano-
Narrows
Bridge

Marine Parkway
Gil Hodges
Memorial Bridge

Cross Ba
Veteran
Memori
Bridge

Staten
Island

Lower
New York
Bay

Atlant
Ocea

Outerbridge
Crossing

Free Harlem River Crossing

- **A** Broadway Bridge
- **B** University Heights Bridge
- **C** Washington Bridge
- **D** A Hamilton Bridge
- **E** Macombs Dam Bridge
- **F** 145th St Bridge
- **G** Madison Ave Bridge
- **H** 3rd Ave Bridge
- **I** Willis Ave Bridge

General Information

Port Authority of NY and NJ: www.panynj.gov
DOT: www.ci.nyc.ny.us/html/dot/home.html · 212 or 718-CALLDOT
MTA: www.mta.info
EZPass: www.e-zpassny.com · 800-333-TOLL
Transportation Alternatives: www.transalt.org
Best overall site: www.nycroads.com

Overview

Since NYC is an archipelago, it's no wonder there are so many bridges and four major tunnels. Most of the bridges listed in the chart below are considered landmarks, either for their sheer beauty or because they were the first of their kind at one time. The traffic-jammed Holland Tunnel, finished in 1927, was the first vehicular tunnel connecting New Jersey and New York. King's Bridge, built between Manhattan and the Bronx in 1693, was sadly demolished in 1917. Highbridge, the oldest existing bridge in NYC (built in 1843), is no longer open to vehicles or pedestrians. Brooklyn Bridge, built in 1883, is the city's oldest functioning bridge, still open to vehicles and pedestrians alike, and is considered one of the most beautiful bridges ever built.

The '70s was a decade of neglect for city bridges. Inspections in the '80s and maintenance and refurbishment plans in the '90s/'00s have made the bridges stronger and safer than ever before. On certain holidays when the weather permits, the world's largest free-flying American flag flies from the upper arch of the New Jersey tower on the George Washington Bridge.

		Toll/EZPass peak/EZPass off-peak	# of lanes	Pedestrians/bicyclists?	# of vehicles/day (in thousands)	Original cost (in millions)	Engineer	Main span	Operated by	Opened to traffic
1	Geo. Washington Bridge	6.00/5.00/4.00 (inbound only)	14	yes	300	59	Othmar H. Ammann	4,760'	PANYNJ	10/25/31
2	Lincoln Tunnel	6.00/5.00/4.00 (inbound only)	6	no	120	75	Othmar H. Ammann Ole Singstad	8,216'	PANYNJ	12/22/37
3	Holland Tunnel	6.00/5.00/4.00 (inbound only)	4	no	100	54	Clifford Holland/ Ole Singstad	8,558'	PANYNJ	11/13/27
4	Verrazano-Narrows Bridge	* 4.50/4.00	12	no	190	320	Othmar H. Ammann	4,260'	MTA	11/21/64
5	Brooklyn-Battery Tunnel	4.50/4.00	4	no	60	90	Ole Singstad	9,117'	MTA	5/25/50
6	Brooklyn Bridge	free	6	yes	140	15	John Roebling/ Washington Roebling	1,595.5'	DOT	5/24/1883
7	Manhattan Bridge	free	7	yes	150	31	Leon Moisseiff	1,470'	DOT	12/31/09
8	Williamsburg Bridge	free	8	yes	140	24.2	Leffert L. Buck	1,600'	DOT	12/19/03
9	Queens-Midtown Tunnel	4.50/4.00	4	no	80	52	Ole Singstad	6,414'	MTA	11/15/40
10	Queensboro Bridge	free	10	yes	200	20	Gustav Lindenthal	1,182'	DOT	3/30/09
11	Triboro Bridge	4.50/4.00	8/ 6/8	yes	200	60.3	Othmar H. Ammann	1,380'	MTA	7/11/36
12	Henry Hudson Bridge	2.25/1.75	7	no	75	5	David Steinman	840'	MTA	12/12/36
13	Whitestone Bridge	4.50/4.00	6	no	110	20	Othmar H. Ammann	2300'	MTA	4/29/39
14	Throgs Neck Bridge	4.50/4.00	6	no	100	92	Othmar H. Ammann	1800'	MTA	1/11/61
15	Cross Bay Veterans Memorial Bridge	2.25/1.50	6	yes	20	29	n/a	n/a	MTA	5/28/70
16	Marine Parkway Gil Hodges Memorial Bridge	2.25/1.50	4	no	25	12	Madigan and Hyland	540'	MTA	7/3/37
17	Bayonne Bridge	6.00/5.00/4.00	4	yes	20	13	Othmar H. Ammann	5,780'	PANY/NJ	11/13/31
18	Goethals Bridge	6.00/5.00/4.00	4	no	75	7.2	Othmar H. Ammann	8,600'	PANY/NJ	6/29/28
19	Outerbridge Crossing	6.00/5.00/4.00	4	no	80	9.6	Othmar H. Ammann	750'	PANY/NJ	6/29/28

* $9.00/$8.00 with EZPass to Staten Island ($6.40/4.80 for registered Staten Island residents with EZPass), $2.25 with three or more occupants—cash only). Free to Brooklyn.

Transit · **Ferries**

Commuter Ferry Services
- NY NY Waterway
- SI Staten Island
- SS Sea Streak
- TX Water Taxi

Central Park

Hudson River

East River

MANHATTAN

QUEENS

WEEHAWKEN

HOBOKEN

JERSEY CITY

BROOKLYN

NY Port Imperial

TX Pier 84 44th St

NY Lincoln Harbor

Pier 78 38th St NY

NY Hoboken North

Pier 63 W 23rd St
TX

SS 34th St

TX Hunters Point

NY Hoboken South

TX Pier 45 W 10th St

NY Newport

NY Harborside

World Financial Center NY TX

South Street Seaport NY

SS TX Pier 11 Wall St

Fulton Ferry Landing

TX

NY Colgate

NY Paulus Hook

NY Liberty Harbor

TX A SI B

Red Hook TX

(Weekday Rush Hours Only)

NY Port Liberte

Brooklyn Army Terminal TX

Staten Island Belford

Atl Highlands Highlands

A Battery Park/Slip 6
B Whitehall Terminal

Ferries/Boat Tours, Rentals, & Charters

Name	Contact Info
Staten Island Ferry	311 • www.nyc.gov/html/dot/html/masstran/ferries/statferry.html
	This free ferry travels between Battery Park and Staten Island. On weekdays it leaves every 15-30 minutes from 12 am-11:30 pm. On weekends, it leaves every hour between 1:30 am-11:30 am and every half-hour at all other times.
NY Waterway	800-53-FERRY • www.nywaterway.com
	The largest ferry service in NY, NYWaterway offers many commuter routes (mostly from New Jersey), sightseeing tours, and shuttles to Yankees and Mets games. However, recent financial troubles have them closing many commuter lines.
NY Water Taxi	212-742-1969 • www.nywatertaxi.com
	Available for commuting, sightseeing, and charter. Commuter tickets range between $4.50 and $6 and tours cost $20 to $25. For chartered trips or tours, call for a quote.
Sea Streak	800-BOAT-RIDE • www.seastreakusa.com
	Catamarans that go pretty fast from the Highlands in NJ to Wall Street and E 34th Street.
Circle Line	212-269-5755 • www.circleline.com
	Circle Line offers many sightseeing tours, including a visit to Ellis Island (departs from Pier 16 at South Street Seaport - $11 for adults, $4.50 for kids)
Spirit of New York	212-727-7735 • www.spiritcruises.com
	Offers lunch and dinner cruises. Prices start at $43. Leaves from Pier 62 at Chelsea Piers. Make a reservation at least one week in advance, but the earlier the better.
Loeb Boathouse	212-517-2233 • www.centralparknyc.org/virtualpark/thegreatlawn/loebboathouse/
	You can rent rowboats from March through October at the Lake in Central Park, open seven days a week, weather permitting. Boat rentals cost $10 for the first hour and $2.50 for every additional 15 minutes (rentals also require a $30 cash deposit). The boathouse is open 10 am-5 pm, but the last boat goes out at 4:30 pm. Up to five people per boat. No reservations needed.
World Yacht Cruises	212-630-8100 or 800-498-4271 • www.worldyacht.com
	These fancy, three-hour dinner cruises start at $69.95 per person. The cruises depart from Pier 81 (41st Street) and require reservations. The cruise boards at 6 pm, sails at 7 pm, and returns at 10 pm. There's also a Sunday brunch cruise April–December that costs $41.90 per person.

Marinas/Passenger Ship Terminal

Name	Contact Info	Map
Surfside III	212-336-7873 • www.surfside3.com	8
	Dockage at Chelsea Piers. They offer daily, weekly, and seasonal per foot rates (there's always a waiting list).	
NY Skyports Inc	212-686-4546	10
	Located on the East River at E 23rd Street. Transient dockage costs $3 per foot.	
79th St Marina	212-496-2105	14
	This city-operated dock is filled with long-term houseboat residents. It's located at W 79th Street and the Hudson River. Open from May to October.	
Dyckman Marina	212-942-4179	25
	Transient dockage on the Hudson River at 348 Dyckman Street	
Passenger Ship Terminal	212-246-5450 • www.nypst.com	11
	If *Love Boat* re-runs aren't enough and you decide to go on a cruise yourself, you'll leave from the Passenger Ship Terminal. W 55th Street at 12th Avenue. Take the West Side Highway to Piers 88-92.	
North Cove Yacht Harbor	212-786-1200 • www.thenorthcove.com	p202
	A very, very fancy place to park your yacht in Battery Park City.	

Helicopter Services

Name	Contact Info	Map
Helicopter Flight Services	212-355-0801 • www.heliny.com	3, 8
	For a minimum of $129, you can hop on a helicopter at the Downtown Manhattan Heliport at Pier 6 on the East River on weekdays, or at the W 30th Street Heliport on weekends and spend 15 minutes gazing down on Manhattan. Reservations are recommended, and there's a minimum of two passengers per flight.	
Liberty Helicopter Tours	212-967-6464 • www.libertyhelicopters.com	3, 8
	Leaves from the heliport at W 30th Street and 12th Avenue (9 am-9 pm) or the Downtown Manhattan Heliport at Pier 6 on the East River (9 am-6:30 pm). Prices start at $69, and reservations are needed only when boarding at the Seaport. Flights depart every 5-10 minutes. Minimum of four passengers per flight.	
Wall Street Helicopter	212-943-5959 • www.wallstreetheli.qpg.com	3
	Leaves from any heliport in Manhattan. Executive/corporate helicopter and twin engine aircraft charters. No sightseeing.	

General Information

E-ZPass Information:	800-333-TOLL
Radio Station Traffic Updates:	1010 WINS on the 1s for a 5 boroughs focus and 880 on the 8s for a suburbs focus
DOT Website:	www.ci.nyc.ny.us/html/dot/html/motorist/motorist.html
Real-Time Web Traffic Info:	www.metrocommute.com

Driving in Manhattan

Avoid it. Why drive when you can see the city so well on foot or by bus. (We don't count the subway as seeing the city, but rather as a cultural experience in and of itself.) We know that sometimes you just *have* to drive in the city, so we've made you a list of essentials.

- Great auto insurance that doesn't care if the guy who hit you doesn't have insurance and doesn't speak any English.
- Thick skin on driver, passengers, and car. Needed for the fender benders and screamed profanity from the cabbies that are ticked anyone but cabbies are on the road.
- Meditation CD to counteract cardiac arrest-inducing "almost" accidents.
- NFT. But we know you would never leave home without it.
- E-ZPass. Saves time and lives. Maybe not lives, but definitely time and some money.
- New York State license plates. Even pedestrians will curse you out if you represent anywhere other than the Empire State, especially NJ or CT.
- A tiny car that can fit into a spot slightly larger than a postage stamp or tons of cash for parking garages.
- Patience with pedestrians—they own the streets of New York. Well, co-own them with the cabbies.

The following are some tips that we've picked up over the years:

Hudson River Crossings

In the Bridge or Tunnel battle, the Bridge almost always wins. The George Washington Bridge is by far the best Hudson River crossing. It's got more lanes and better access than either tunnel with a fantastic view to boot. If you're going anywhere in the country that's north of central New Jersey, take it. The Lincoln Tunnel is decent inbound, but check 1010 AM (WINS) if you have the chance—even though they can be horribly inaccurate and frustrating. Avoid the Lincoln like the plague during evening rush hour (starts at about 3:30 pm). If you have to take the Holland Tunnel outbound, try the Broome Street approach, but don't even bother between 5 and 7 pm on weekdays.

East River Crossings

Brooklyn
Pearl Street to the Brooklyn Bridge is the least-known approach. Only the Williamsburg Bridge has direct access (i.e. no traffic lights) to the northbound BQE in Brooklyn, and only the Brooklyn Bridge has direct access to the FDR Drive in Manhattan. Again, listen to the radio if you can, but all three bridges can be disastrous as they seem to be constantly under construction (or, in a fabulous new twist, having one lane closed by the NYPD to for some unknown (terrorism?) reason). The Williamsburg is by far the best free route into Brooklyn, but make sure to take the outer roadway to keep your options open in case the BQE is jammed. Your best option to go anywhere in Brooklyn is usually the Brooklyn-Battery Tunnel, which can be reached from the FDR as well as the West Side Highway. Fun fact: The water you pass was so dirty in the '50s that it used to set on fire. The tunnel is not free ($4.50), but if you followed our instructions you've got E-ZPass anyway ($4).

The bridges from north to south are B-M-W, but they are not as cool as the cars that share the intials.

Queens
There are three options for crossing into Queens by car. The Queens Midtown Tunnel is usually miserable, since it feeds directly onto the parking lot known as the Long Island Expressway. The 59th Street Bridge (known as the Queensboro to mapmakers) is the only free crossing to Queens. The best approach to it is First Avenue to 57th Street (after that, follow the signs). If you're in Queens and want to go downtown in Manhattan, you can take the lower level of the 59th Street Bridge since it will feed directly onto Second Avenue, which of course goes downtown. The Triborough Bridge is usually the best option (especially if you're going to LaGuardia, Shea, Astoria for Greek food, or Flushing for dim sum). The FDR to the Triborough is good except for rush hour—then try Third Avenue to 124th Street.

Harlem River Crossings

The Triborough ($4.50) will get you to the Bronx in pretty good shape, especially if you are heading east on the Bruckner towards 95 or the Hutchinson (which will take you to eastern Westchester and Connecticut). To get to Yankee Stadium, take the Willis or the Macomb's Dam (which are both free). When you feel comfortable maneuvering the tight turns approaching the Willis, use it for all travel to Westchester and Connecticut in order to save toll money. The Henry Hudson Bridge ($2.25) will take you up to western Westchester along the Hudson, and, except for the antiquated and completely unnecessary toll plaza, is pretty good. It wins the fast and pretty prize for its beautiful surroundings. The Cross-Bronx Expressway will take years off your life. Avoid it at all costs.

Manhattan's "Highways"

There are two so-called highways in Manhattan—the Harlem River Drive/FDR Drive (which prohibits commercial vehicles) and the Henry Hudson Parkway/West Side Highway. The main advantage of the FDR is that it has no traffic lights, while the West Side Highway has lights from Battery Park up through 57th Street. The main disadvantages of the FDR are (1) the potholes and (2) the narrow lanes. If there's been a lot of rain, both highways will flood, so you're out of luck. Although the West Side Highway can fly, we would rather look at Brooklyn and Queens than Jersey, so the FDR wins.

Driving Uptown

The 96th Street transverse across Central Park is usually the best one, although if there's been a lot of rain, it will flood. If you're driving on the west side, Riverside Drive is the best route, followed next by West End Avenue. People drive like morons on Broadway, and Columbus jams up in the mid 60s before Lincoln Center. Amsterdam is a good uptown route if you can get to it. For the east side, you can take Fifth Avenue downtown to about 65th Street, whereupon you should bail out and cut over to Park Avenue for the rest of the trip. Do NOT drive on Fifth Avenue below 65th Street within a month of Christmas, and check the parade schedules before attempting it on weekends throughout the year. The 96th Street entrance to the FDR screws up First and Third Avenues going north and the 59th Street Bridge screws up Lexington and Second Avenues going downtown. Getting stuck in 59th Street Bridge traffic is one of the most frustrating things in the universe because there is absolutely no way out of it.

Driving in Midtown

Good luck! Sometimes Broadway is best because everyone's trying to get out of Manhattan, jamming up the west side (via the Lincoln Tunnel) and the east side (via the 59th Street Bridge and the Queens Midtown Tunnel). Friday nights at 9:30 pm can be a breeze, but from 10 pm-midnight, you're screwed as shows let out. The "interior" city is the last place to get jammed up—it's surprisingly quiet at 8 am. At 10 am, however, it's a parking lot. Those who plan to drive in Midtown on weekends from about March–October should check parade schedules for Fifth AND Sixth Avenues.

The demarcation of several "THRU Streets" running east-west in Midtown has been with the city for a couple of years and folks are finally getting the hang of it. Still, it may screw you up. See the next page for more information.

Driving in the Village

People still get confused walking in the village, so you can imagine how challenging driving can be in the maze of one ways and short streets. Beware. If you're coming into the Village from the northwest, 14th Street is the safest crosstown route heading west. However, going west, take 13th Street. Houston Street is usually okay in both directions and has the great benefit of direct access to

FDR Drive, both getting onto it and coming off of it. If you want to get to Houston Street from the Holland Tunnel, take Hudson Street to King Street to the Avenue of the Americas to Houston Street (this is the **only** efficient way to get to the Village from the Holland Tunnel). First Avenue is good going north and Fifth Avenue is good going south. Washington Street is the only way to make any headway in the West Village.

Driving Downtown

Don't do it unless you have to. Western TriBeCa is okay and so is the Lower East Side—try not to "turn in" to SoHo, Chinatown, or the Civic Center. Canal Street is a complete mess during the day (avoid it), since on its western end, everyone is trying to get on to the Holland Tunnel, and on its eastern end, everyone is mistakenly driving over the Manhattan Bridge (your only other option when heading east on Canal is to turn **right** on Bowery!). Watch the potholes!

DMV Locations in Manhattan

If you're going to the DMV to get your first NY license (including drivers with other states' licenses), you'll need extensive documentation of your identity. The offices have a long list of accepted documents, but your best bet is a US passport and a Social Security card. If you don't have these things, birth certificates from the US, foreign passports, and various INS documents will be okay under certain conditions. Do not be surprised if you are turned away the first time. This trip requires great amounts of patience. Plan on spending three to six hours here. We're not kidding. This is not a lunch-hour errand.

Greenwich Street Office
11 Greenwich St
New York, NY 10004
(Cross Streets Battery Park Pl & Morris St)
M-F 8:30 am-4 pm
212-645-5550 or 718-966-6155

Harlem Office
159 E 125th St, 3rd Fl
New York, NY 10035
(Lexington and Third)
M, T, W & F 8:30 am-4 pm, Thursday 10 am-6 pm
212-645-5550 or 718-966-6155

Herald Square Office
1293-1311 Broadway, 8th Fl
New York, NY 10001
(Between W 33 & W 34 Sts)
* To exchange an out-of-state license for a New York license, you must go to License X-Press.
M-F 8:30 am-4 pm
212-645-5550 or 718-966-6155

Manhattan
License X-Press Office*
300 W 34th St
New York, NY 10001
(Between Eighth & Ninth Ave)
*Service Limited: Only NY State renewals. You also can't renew your boat or snowmobile license here, only stuff for cars and trucks.
M-F 8:30 am-4 pm
212-645-5550 or 718-966-6155

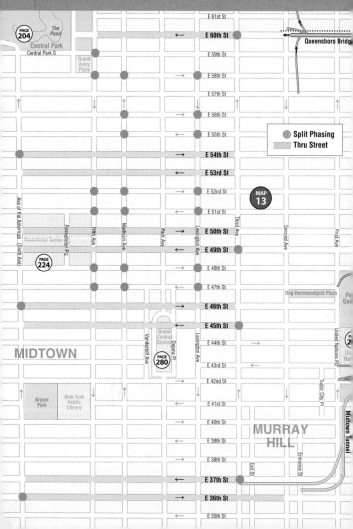

Central Park

PAGE 204

The Pond

Central Park S

Grand Army Plaza

E 61st St

E 60th St

Queensboro Bridge

E 59th St

E 58th St

E 57th St

E 56th St

E 55th St

E 54th St

E 53rd St

E 52nd St

MAP 13

E 51st St

E 50th St

E 49th St

E 48th St

E 47th St

E 46th St

E 45th St

E 44th St

E 43rd St

E 42nd St

E 41st St

E 40th St

E 39th St

E 38th St

E 37th St

E 36th St

E 35th St

Ave of the Americas (Sixth Ave)

Rockefeller Center

Rockefeller Plz

Fifth Ave

Madison Ave

Park Ave

Lexington Ave

Third Ave

Second Ave

First Ave

PAGE 224

MIDTOWN

Vanderbilt Ave

Depew Pl

Grand Central Station

PAGE 280

Lexington Ave

Dag Hammarskjold Plaza

United Nations Plz

MURRAY HILL

Tudor City Pl

Exit St

Entrance St

Midtown Tunnel

Bryant Park

New York Public Library

● Split Phasing

▨ Thru Street

General Information

DOT Website: www.nyc.gov/html/dot/html/motorist/streetprog.html
DOT Phone: 311

Overview

In the tradition of "don't block the box" and other traffic solutions (such as randomly arresting political protesters), the city introduced "THRU Streets", a program initially tested in 2002, as a permanent fixture in Midtown in 2004. The plan was implemented on some crosstown streets in Midtown in order to reduce travel times, relieve congestion, and provide a safer environment for pedestrians and cyclists. They are still working on cleaning up the exhaust fume issue for those concerned about said environment.

On certain streets, cars are not allowed to make turns between Sixth and Third Avenues (with the exception of Park Avenue). The regulations are in effect between 10 am and 6 pm on weekdays. The affected streets are:

    36th & 37th Streets
    45th & 46th Streets
    49th & 50th Streets
    53rd & 54th Streets
    60th Street (between Third and Fifth Avenues)

The good news is that turns from 59th Street are permitted. Oh joy.

The above streets are easily identifiable by big, purple "THRU Streets" signs. With everything that's going on in midtown Manhattan though, you'd be forgiven for missing a sign (by us, not by the NYPD). If you happen to unwittingly find yourself on a THRU Street and can't escape on Park Avenue, you're going to have to suck it up until you get to Sixth Avenue or Third Avenue, depending on the direction you're heading. If you attempt to turn before the designated avenue, you'll find yourself with an insanely expensive ticket. Of course, if you're trying to drive crosstown, it's in your best interests to take one of these streets.

Both sides of almost every non-THRU street in this grid have been stuck with "No Standing Except Trucks Loading and Unloading" regulations, supposedly creating up to 150 spaces for truck loading (if you were ever stuck behind a truck in morning rush hour on a THRU street in 2004, you would rejoice at this news). Additionally, one side of each non-THRU street has been "daylighted" for 80-100 feet in advance of the intersection. We are not exactly sure how they came up with the term "daylighted", but the DOT tells us it allows space for turning vehicles.

According to the DOT, THRU Streets are working—since the program began, travel times have fallen by 25% (as people have decided to emigrate to New Zealand) and vehicle speeds have increased by an average of 33% (from 4 mph to 5.3 mph). The THRU Streets combined now carry 4,854 vehicles per hour (up from 4,187), which means that each of the THRU Streets accommodates an average of 74 additional vehicles per hour.

Split Signal Phasing

Another traffic innovation in Midtown is "split signal phasing," which allows pedestrians to cross the street without having to worry about vehicles turning in their path at about 40 non-THRU street intersections in this same grid. Of course, this system assumes that both pedestrians and drivers follow the rules of the road. In spite of the disregard that most New Yorkers display for crossing signals, the number of pedestrian accidents in the eight-month trial period (compared to the eight months prior to implementation) fell from 81 to 74. The number of cycling accidents fell from 30 to 17. Accidents not related to pedestrians or bikes fell from 168 to 102. We don't know if this accounts for accidents caused by drivers who became confused by the pretty purple signs. We have to admit that something must be working—though there would be no accidents if no one ever left their house.

Now if the DOT and NYPD could get traffic to flow smoothly onto bridges and into tunnels, they might actually be onto something. They can save you 1.5 minutes getting crosstown, just don't try leaving the city. Ever.

Information

Department of Transportation (DOT): 3-1-1 (24 hours) or
212-NEW-YORK (Out-of-state)
TTY Hearing-Impaired: 212-504-4115
Website: www.ci.nyc.ny.us/html/dot/
Parking Violations Help Line: 3-1-1
TTY Automated Information
for the Hearing Impaired: 718-802-8555
Website: www.ci.nyc.ny.us/finance (parking ticket info)

Standing, Stopping and Parking Rules

In "No Stopping" areas, you **can't** wait in your car, drop off passengers, or load/unload.

In "No Standing" areas, you **can't** wait in your car, but you **can** drop off passengers or load/unload.

In "No Parking" areas, you **can't** wait in your car or drop off passengers, but you **can** load/unload.

Parking Meter Zones

On holidays when street cleaning rules are suspended (see calendar), the "no parking" cleaning regulations for metered parking are also suspended. You can park in these spots but have to pay the meters. Also, metered spots are still subject to rules not suspended on holidays (see below). On MLH (major legal holidays), meter rules are suspended (so no need to feed the meter).

Meters

At a broken meter, parking is allowed only up to one hour. Where a meter is missing, parking is still allowed for the maximum time on the posted sign (an hour for a one-hour meter, two hours for a two-hour meter, etc.).

Instead of old-fashioned individual meters, Midtown has "muni-meters." The machines let you purchase time-stamped slips which you stick in your windshield to show you paid. These machines accept coins, parking cards and some (we wish it was all!) accept credit cards (for example, the machines in the theater district). In the case of a non-functional muni-meter, the one-hour time limit applies.

The DOT sells parking cards that come in $20 and $50 denominations and can be used in muni-meters, municipal parking lots and some single-space meters (look for a yellow decal). The cards can be purchased through the DOT website (http://www.nyc.gov/html/dot/home.html), by calling 718-786-7042/6334, or by going to the Staten Island Ferry Terminal or one of the two City Stores.

As of spring 2006, you don't have to pay meters on Sunday, even if the signs say you do (unless the law changes again with the political winds).

Signs

New York City Traffic Rules state that one parking sign per block is sufficient notification. Check the entire block and read all signs carefully before you park. Then read them again.

If there is more than one sign posted for the same area, the more restrictive sign takes effect (of course). If a sign is missing on a block, the remaining posted regulations are the ones in effect.

The Blue Zone

The Blue Zone is a "No Parking" (Mon–Fri 7 am–7 pm) area in Lower Manhattan. Its perimeter has been designated with blue paint; however, there are no individual "Blue Zone" signs posted. Any other signs posted in that area supersede Blue Zone regulations. Confused yet?

General

- All of NYC was designated a Tow Away Zone under the State's Vehicle & Traffic Law and the NYC Traffic Rules. This means that any vehicle parked or operated illegally, or with missing or expired registration or inspection stickers, may, and probably will, be towed.

- On major legal holidays, stopping, standing, and parking are permitted except in areas where stopping, standing, and parking rules are in effect seven days a week (for example, "No Standing Anytime").

- Double-parking of passenger vehicles is illegal at all times, including street-cleaning days, regardless of location, purpose, or duration. Everyone, of course, does this anyway.

- It is illegal to park within 15 feet of either side of a fire hydrant. The painted curbs at hydrant locations do not indicate where you can park. Isn't New York great?

- If you think you're parked legally in Manhattan, you're probably not, so go and read the signs again.

- Cops will now just write you parking tickets and mail them to you if you are parked in a bus stop; so you won't even know it's happening unless you're very alert.

- There is now clearly an all-out effort to harass everyone who is insane enough to drive and/or park during the day in downtown Manhattan. Beware.

Alternate Side Parking Suspension Calendar 2006-2007 (estimated*)

2006 Holiday	Date	Day	Rules
Labor Day	Sept 4	Mon	MHL
Rosh Hashanah, 1st/2nd Day	Sept 23-24	Sat-Sun	ASP
Yom Kippur	Oct 2	Mon	ASP
Succoth, 1st/2nd Day	Oct 7-8	Sat-Sun	ASP
Columbus Day	Oct 9	Mon	ASP
Shemini Atzereth	Oct 14	Sat	ASP
Simchat Torah	Oct 15	Sun	ASP
Diwali	Oct 21	Sat	ASP
Idul-Fitr	Oct 22-24	Sun-Tues	ASP
All Saints Day	Nov 1	Wed	ASP
Election Day	Nov 7	Tues	ASP
Veterans Day (Observed)	Nov 10	Fri	ASP
Veterans Day	Nov 11	Sat	ASP
Thanksgiving Day	Nov 23	Thurs	MHL
Immaculate Conception	Dec 8	Fri	ASP
Christmas Day	Dec 25	Mon	MHL
Idul-Adha	Dec 30-Jan 1	Sat-Mon	ASP

2007 Holiday	Date	Day	Rules
New Year's Day 2007	Jan 1	Mon	MHL
New Year's Day (Observed)	Jan 2	Tues	MHL
Idul-Adha	Jan 10-12	Wed-Fri	ASP
Martin Luther King Jr's Birthday	Jan 15	Mon	ASP
Lincoln's Birthday	Feb 12	Mon	ASP
Asian Lunar New Year	Feb 18	Sun	ASP
President's Day	Feb 19	Mon	ASP
Ash Wednesday	Feb 21	Wed	ASP
Purim	Mar 4	Sun	ASP
Passover, 1st/2nd Day	April 3-4	Tues-Wed	ASP
Holy Thursday	Apr 5	Thurs	ASP
Good Friday	Apr 6	Fri	ASP
Passover, 7th/8th Day	April 9-10	Mon-Tues	ASP
Solemnity of Ascension	May 17	Thurs	ASP
Shavuot, 1st/2nd Day	May 23-24	Wed-Thurs	ASP
Memorial Day	May 28	Mon	MHL
Independence Day	July 4	Wed	MHL
Assumption of the Blessed Virgin	Aug 15	Wed	ASP
Labor Day	Sept 3	Mon	MHL
Rosh Hashanah, 1st/2nd Day	Sept 13-14	Thurs-Fri	ASP
Yom Kippur	Sept 22	Sat	ASP
Succoth, 1st/2nd Day	Sept 27-28	Thurs-Fri	ASP
Shemini Atzereth	Oct 4	Thurs	ASP
Simchas Torah	Oct 5	Fri	ASP
Columbus Day	Oct 8	Mon	ASP
Idul-Fitr	Oct 11-13	Thurs-Sat	ASP
All Saints Day	Nov 1	Thurs	ASP
Election Day	Nov 6	Tues	ASP
Diwali	Nov 9	Fri	ASP
Veterans Day	Nov 11	Sun	ASP
Veterans Day (Observed)	Nov 12	Mon	ASP
Thanksgiving Day	Nov 22	Thurs	MHL
Immaculate Conception	Dec 8	Sat	ASP
Christmas Day	Dec 25	Tues	MHL
Idul-Adha	Dec 19-21	Wed-Fri	ASP

* *Note:* We go to press before the DOT issues its official calendar. However, using various techniques, among them a Ouija Board, a chainsaw, and repeated phone calls to said DOT, we think it's pretty accurate. Nonetheless, caveat parkor.

- **Street Cleaning Rules** (SCR)
  Most SCR signs are clearly marked by the "P" symbol with the broom through it. Some SCR signs are the traditional 3-hour ones ("8 am-11 am" etc.) but many others vary considerably. Check the times before you park. Then check them again.
- **Alternate Side Parking Suspended** (ASP)
  "No Parking" signs in effect one day a week or on alternate days are suspended on days designated ASP; however, all "No Stopping" and "No Standing" signs remain in effect.
- **Major Legal Holiday Rules** (MHL)
  "No Parking" and "No Standing" signs that are in effect fewer than seven days a week are suspended on days designated MLH in the above calendar.
- If the city finds that a neighborhood keeps its streets clean enough, it may lessen the number of street cleaning days, or even eliminate them all together. So listen to your mother and don't litter.

Tow Pounds

Manhattan
Pier 76 at W 38th St & Twelfth Ave
Monday: 7 am-11 pm,
open 24 hours: Tuesday 7 am-Sunday 6 am
212-971-0771 or 212-971-0772
Bronx
745 E 141st St b/w Bruckner Expy & East River
Monday-Friday: 8 am-9 pm, Saturday: 8 am-3 pm,
Sunday: Closed; 718-585-1385 or 718-585-1391
Brooklyn
Brooklyn Navy Yard; corner of Sands St & Navy St
Monday-Friday: 8 am-9 pm, Saturday: 8 am-4 pm,
Sunday: 12 pm-8 pm; 718-694-0696
Queens
Under the Kosciusko Bridge at 56th Rd & Laurel Hill Blvd
Monday-Friday: 8 am-6 pm, Sunday: 7 am-3 pm,
Sunday: 12 pm-8 pm; 718-786-7122, 718-786-7123, or
718-786-7136

Find out if your car was towed (and not stolen or disintegrated): 718-422-7800 or 718-802-3555

http://nycserv.nyc.gov/NYCServInquiry/NYCSERVMain

Once you've discovered that your car has indeed been towed, your next challenge is to find out which borough it's been towed to. This depends on who exactly towed your car—the DOT, the Marshal, etc. Don't assume that since your car was parked in Manhattan that they will tow it to Manhattan—always call first.

So you've located your car, now come the particulars: If you own said towed car, you're required to present your license, registration, insurance, and payment of your fine before you can collect the impounded vehicle. If you are not the owner of the car, you can usually get it back with all of the above, if your last name matches the registration (i.e. the car belongs to a relative or spouse); otherwise, you'll need a notarized letter with the owner's signature authorizing you to take the car. The tow fee is $185, plus $20 for each day it's in the pound. If they've put a boot on it instead, it's still $185. You can pay with cash or debit card; if you own the car, you can also pay by credit card or certified check. We recommend bringing a wad of cash and a long Russian novel for this experience.

269

General Information

New York City: 718-217-LIRR
Nassau County: 516-822-LIRR
Suffolk County: 631-231-LIRR
TTY Information (Hearing Impaired): 718-558-3022
Group Travel and Tours: 718-558-7498
(M-F 8 am-4 pm)
Mail & Ride: 800-649-NYNY
MTA Police Eastern Region: 718-558-3300
or 516-733-3900
Lost & Found (M-F 7:20 am-7:20 pm): 212-643-5228
Ticket Refunds (M-F 8 am-4 pm): 718-558-3488
Ticket Machine Assistance: 877-LIRR-TSM
Hamptons Reserve Service: 718-558-8070
Website: www.mta.info/lirr

Overview

The Long Island Railroad is the busiest railroad in North America. It has eleven lines with 124 stations stretching from Penn Station in midtown Manhattan, to the eastern tip of Long Island, Montauk Point. An estimated 81 million people ride the LIRR every year. If you enjoy traveling on overcrowded, smelly trains with intermittent air-conditioning, then the LIRR is for you. If you are going anywhere on Long Island and you don't have a car, the LIRR is your best bet. Don't be surprised if the feeling of being in a vaguely uncomfortable bar creeps over you during evening rush—the commuters like their beers on the train.

If you're not a regular LIRR user, you might find yourself taking the train to Shea Stadium for a Mets game (Port

Washington Branch), Long Beach for some summer surfing (Long Beach Branch), or to Jamaica to transfer to the AirTrain to JFK (tip—the subway is cheaper). For the truly adventurous, take the LIRR all the way out to the Hamptons beachhouse you are visiting for the weekend (Hamptons Reserve seating is available during the summer for passengers taking 6 or more trips). Bring a book as it is a long ride.

Fares and Schedules

Fares and schedules can be obtained by calling one of the general information lines, depending on your area. They can also be found on the LIRR website. Make sure to buy your ticket before you get on the train at a ticket window or at one of the ticket vending machines in the station. Otherwise it'll cost you an extra $4.75 to $5.50 depending on your destination. As it is a commuter railroad, the LIRR offers weekly and monthly passes, as well as ten-trip packages for on- or off-peak hours.

Pets on the LIRR

Trained service animals accompanying passengers with disabilities are permitted on LIRR trains. Other small pets are allowed on trains, but they must be confined to closed, ventilated containers.

Bikes on the LIRR

You need a permit ($5) to take your bicycle onto the Long Island Railroad. Pick one up at a ticket window, or online at the LIRR website.

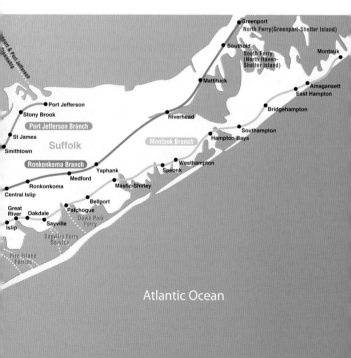

General Information

NYC Phone:	212-532-4900
All other areas:	800-METRO-INFO
Website:	www.mta.info/mnr
Lost and Found (Grand Central):	212-712-2555
MTA Inspector General:	800-MTA-IG4U

Overview

Metro-North is an extremely accessible and efficient railroad with three of its main lines (Hudson, Harlem, and New Haven) originating in Grand Central Station in Manhattan (42nd St & Park Ave). Those three lines east of the Hudson River, along with two lines west of the Hudson River that operate out of Hoboken, NJ (not shown on map), form the second-largest commuter railroad system in the US. Approximately 250,000 commuters use the tri-state Metro-North service each day for travel between New Jersey, New York, and Connecticut. Metro-North rail lines cover roughly 2,700 square miles of territory.

Fares and Schedules

Fare information is available on Metro-North's extraordinarily detailed website (along with in-depth information on each station, full timetables, and excellent maps) or at Grand Central Station. The cost of a ticket to ride varies depending on your destination so you should probably check the website before setting out. If you wait until you're on the train to pay, it'll cost you an extra $4.75-$5.50. Monthly and weekly rail passes are also available for commuters. Daily commuters save 50% on fares when they purchase a monthly travel pass.

Hours

Train frequency depends on your destination and the time of day that you're traveling. On weekdays, peak-period trains east of the Hudson River run every 20-30 minutes; off-peak trains run every 30-60 minutes; and weekend trains run hourly. Hours of operation are approximately 5 am to 3 am.

Bikes on Board

If you're planning on taking your two-wheeler on-board, you'll need to apply for a bicycle permit first. An application form can be found on the Metro-North website at http://mta.info/mnr/html/mnrbikepermit. htm. The $5 permit fee and application can either be mailed into the MTA, or processed right away at window 27 at Grand Central Terminal.

Common sense rules for taking bikes on board include: no bikes on escalators, no riding on the platform, and board the train after other passengers have boarded. Unfortunately there are restrictions on bicycles during peak travel times. Bicycles are not allowed on trains departing from Grand Central Terminal 7 am-9 am and 3:01 pm-8:15 pm. Bikes are not permitted on trains arriving at Grand Central 5 am-10 am and 4 pm-8 pm. Don't even think about taking your bike with you on New Year's Eve, New Year's Day, St. Patrick's Day, Mother's Day, eve of Rosh Hashanah, eve of Yom Kippur, eve of Thanksgiving, Thanksgiving Day, Christmas Eve, or Christmas Day—they're not allowed. The Friday before any long weekend is also a no-no. There's a limit of two bikes per carriage, and four bikes per train at all times. What happens if there are five riders waiting on the platform? Rock, paper, scissors?

Riders of folding bikes do not require a permit and do not have to comply with the above rules, provided that the bike is folded at all times at stations and on trains.

Pets

Only seeing-eye dogs and small pets, if restrained or confined, are allowed aboard the trains.

One-Day Getaways

Metro-North offers "One-Day Getaway" packages on its website. Packages include reduced rail fare and discounted entry to destinations along MNR lines including Dia:Beacon ($27), Foxwoods Casino ($41.25), Hudson River Museum/Andrus Planetarium ($14.50), Maritime Aquarium at Norwalk ($28.25), Mohegan Sun Casino ($38.25), New York Botanical Garden ($18.25), and Nyack ($14.50). The website also suggests one-day hiking and biking excursions.

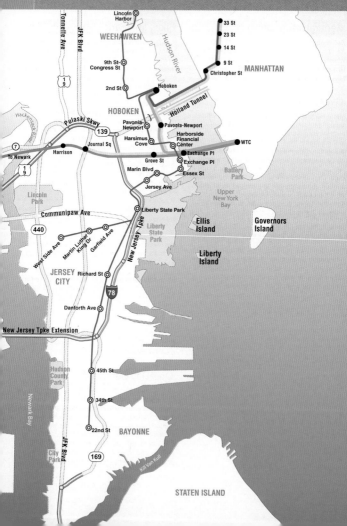

PATH Train

General Information

Website: www.panynj.gov/path
Phone: 800-234-7284
Police/Lost & Found: 201-216-6078

Overview

The PATH (Port Authority Trans-Hudson Corp.) is an excellent small rail system that services Newark, Jersey City, Hoboken, and Manhattan. There are a few basic lines that run directly between 33rd Street (Herald Square) in Manhattan & Hoboken, 33rd Street & Jersey City, and Newark & the WTC. Transfers between the lines are available at most stations. The PATH can be quite useful for commuters on the west side of Manhattan when the subway isn't running, say, due to a transit strike or mysterious police investigation. Additionally, you can catch the PATH to Newark and then either jump in a cheap cab or take New Jersey Transit one stop to Newark Airport. It's a more economical option than taking a car all the way in from Manhattan; and you can take it back to the Village late at night when you've finished seeing a show at Maxwell's in Hoboken.

Check the front or the sides of incoming trains to determine their destination. Don't be fooled by the TV screens installed at stations, they occasionally announce the time of the next arrival, but as their main purpose is low-quality advertising, they are often incorrect. Also, don't assume that if a Journal Square train just passed through, the next train is going to Hoboken. Often there will be two Journal Square trains in a row, followed by two Hoboken trains.

The Port Authority is in the process of installing seven new escalators at the Journal Square Station. Each one will take approximately 6 months to install, so expect some disruption over the next few years.

Fares

The PATH costs a buck fifty one-way. Regular riders can purchase 11-trip, 20-trip, and 40-trip QuickCards, which reduce the fare per journey to $1.20–$1.36. The fare for seniors (65+) is $1 per ride. You can also use pay-per-ride MTA MetroCards (finally!) for easy transition between the PATH and subway.

Hours

The PATH runs 24/7 (although a modified service operates between 11pm and 6am, M-F, and 7:30pm and 9am, S,S,H). Daytime service is pretty consistent, but the night schedule for the PATH is a bit confusing, so make sure to look at the map. You may be waiting

underground for up to a half an hour. because during off hours the train runs on the same track through the tunnel. This allows for maintenance to be completed on the unused track.

Hudson-Bergen Light Rail

General Information

Website: www.njtransit.com
Phone: 800-772-2222

Overview

The Hudson-Bergen Light Rail system (HBLR, operated by NJ Transit) is the newest rail line in the New York area, and has brought about some exciting changes (a.k.a. "gentrification") in Jersey City, though Bayonne remains (for the moment) totally, well…Bayonne. Currently there are 20 1/2 stops (Port Imperial is only operational on the weekends) in the system, including service to Jersey City, Hoboken, and Weehawken. Transfer at the Hoboken stop for the PATH into Manhattan. Expansion plans include a Bergenline Avenue stop in Union City, and a Tonnelle Avenue station in North Bergen. We're psyched.

Fares

The Light Rail is $1.50 per trip; reduced fare is 85 cents. Ten-trip tickets are $15, monthly passes cost $53, and monthly passes with parking are $93. Unless you have a monthly pass, you need to validate your ticket before boarding at a Ticket Validating Machine (TVM). Once validated, tickets are only valid for 90 minutes, so don't buy too far in advance. The trains and stations have random fare inspection and the fine for fare evasion is $100.

Hours

Light rail service operates between 5 am and 1:30 am. Check the website for exact schedules on each line.

Bikes on Board

Bikes are allowed (no permit or fee required) on board during off-peak times—weekdays from 9:30 am to 4 pm and 7 pm to 6 am, and all day Saturday, Sunday, and NJ state holidays. Bicycles have to be accompanied on the low-floor vestibule section of each rail car.

Pets

Small pets are allowed, as long as they're confined to a carry container. Service animals are permitted at all times.

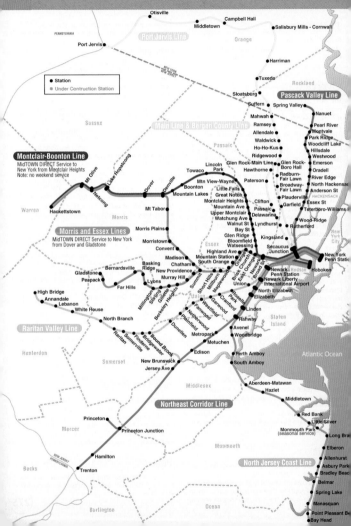

General Information

Address:	1 Penn Plz E
	Newark, NJ 07105
Phone:	973-491-7000 or
	800-772-2222
Website:	www.njtransit.com
Quik-Tik (monthly passes):	800-648-0215
Emergency Hotline:	973-378-6565
Newark Lost and Found:	973-961-6230
Hoboken Lost and Found:	201-714-2739
New York Lost and Found:	212-630-7389
AirTrain:	973-491-7600
Atlantic City Terminal:	609-343-7174

Overview

NJ Transit carries hundreds of thousands of New Jersey commuters to New York every morning—well, almost. The trains are usually clean (and immune to the weirdness that plagues the LIRR), but some lines (like the Pascack Valley Line) seem to just creep along, and many lines involve transfers before reaching the Big Apple. But with many new stations, including the renovated transfer station at Secaucus, and an expanded Light Rail system (see PATH page), NJ Transit is staying competitive with all other modes of transportation into and out of the city. NJ Transit also runs an AirTrain to Newark Airport. While NJ Transit won't be competing with Japanese rail systems any time soon, riding their rails still beats waiting in traffic at the three measly Hudson River automobile crossings. NJ Transit also offers bus lines to Hoboken and Newark for areas not served by train lines.

Secaucus Transfer Station

The new, three-level train hub at Secaucus cost around $450 million and took 14 years to complete. The new building is dedicated to Democratic New Jersey senator, Frank R. Lautenberg, who was responsible for securing the federal funds necessary for construction. The former Secaucus Transfer Station is now officially known as the Frank R. Lautenberg Station at Secaucus Junction. We're certain that most commuters will adopt this new name whenever referring to the station.

For riders, the biggest advantage of the new station is that they no longer have to travel out to Hoboken to get to Penn Station. (Secaucus is just an 8-minute ride from Penn Station.) The Secaucus hub connects ten of NJ Transit's 11 rail lines, and also offers service to Newark Airport, downtown Newark, Trenton, and the Jersey Shore.

Fares and Schedules

Fares and schedules can be obtained at Hoboken, Newark, Penn Station, on NJ Transit's website, or by calling NJ Transit. If you wait to pay until you're on the train, you'll pay extra for the privilege. NJ Transit also offers discounted monthly, weekly, weekend, and ten-trip tickets for regular commuters.

Pets

Only seeing-eye dogs and small pets in carry-on containers are allowed aboard the trains and buses.

Bikes

You can take your bicycle onboard a NJ Transit train only during off-peak hours (weekdays from 9:30 am to 4 pm, and from 7 pm to 5 am) and during all hours on the weekends. Bikes are not allowed on board on most holidays; however, a folding frame bicycle can be taken onboard at any time. Most NJ Transit buses participate in the "Rack 'n Roll" program, which allows you to load your bike right on to the front of the bus.

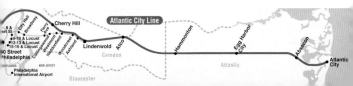

Overview

Phone: 800-USA-RAIL
Website: www.amtrak.com

General Information

Amtrak is our national train system, and while it's not particularly punctual or affordable, it *will* take you to many major northeastern cities in half a day or less. Cheap airlines like Southwest and JetBlue have made flying to many cities faster and cheaper than Amtrak. But if you plan a trip at the last minute and miss the requisite advance on buying airline tickets or just can't handle another trip through the LaGuardia security line, you might want to shop Amtrak's fares. Bonus: Amtrak allows you to talk on cell phones in most cars and has plugs for laptop computers at your seat.

Amtrak was created by the federal government in 1971. Today, Amtrak services 500+ stations in 46 states (Alaska, Hawaii, South Dakota, and Wyoming sadly do not have the pleasure of being serviced by Amtrak). Amtrak serves over 24 million passengers a year, employs 22,000 people, and provides "contract-commuter services" for several state and regional rail lines.

Amtrak in New York

In New York City, Amtrak runs out of Pennsylvania Station, which is currently located in a rat's maze underneath Madison Square Garden. We treat the station like our annoying little brother, calling it Penn for short and avoiding it when we can. But don't despair—chances are, the city you'll wind up in will have a very nice station, and, if all goes well, so will we, once the front half of the Farley Post Office is converted to a "new" Penn Station. Warning: If you hop in a cab to get to Amtrak, specify that you want to be dropped off at Eighth Avenue and 33rd Street in order to avoid LIRR and Madison Square Garden foot traffic.

Popular Destinations

Many New Yorkers use Amtrak to get to Boston, Philadelphia, or Washington, DC. Amtrak also runs a line up to Montreal and through western New York state (making stops in Buffalo, Rochester, Albany, etc.) Check Amtrak's website for a complete listing of all Amtrak stations.

Going to Boston

Amtrak usually runs 18 trains daily to Boston, MA. One-way fares cost $54–$73, and the trip, which ends at South Station in downtown Boston, takes about four-and-a-half hours door-to-door. For $95 one-way, you can ride the high speed Acela ("acceleration" and "excellence" combined into one word, though perhaps "expensive" would have been more appropriate) and complete the journey in three to three-and-a-half hours.

Going to Philadelphia

About 40 Amtrak trains pass through Philadelphia every day. One-way tickets cost about $42–$56 on a regular Amtrak train; if you're really in a hurry, you can take the special "Metroliner" service for $87, which will get you there in an hour and fifteen minutes, or the Acela for $109, which takes about one hour from station to station. The cheapest rail option to Philly is actually to take NJ Transit to Trenton and then hook up with Eastern Pennsylvania's excellent SEPTA service—this will take longer, but will cost you under $25. Some commuters take this EVERY day. Thank your lucky stars you're probably not one of them.

Going to Washington, DC

(Subtitle: *How Much is Your Time Worth?*)
Amtrak runs over 40 trains daily to DC and the prices vary dramatically. The cheapest trains cost $63 one-way and take just under four hours. The Acela service costs more than double at $152 one-way, and delivers you to our nation's capital in less than three hours (sometimes). Worth it? Only you can say. Depending on what time of day you travel, you may be better off taking the cheaper train when the Acela will only save you 30 minutes.

A Note About Fares

While the prices quoted above for Boston, Philly, and DC destinations tend to remain fairly consistent, fare rates to other destinations, such as Cleveland, Chicago, etc., can vary depending on how far in advance you book your seat. For "rail sales" and other discounts, check www.amtrak.com. Military IDs will save you a bundle, so use them if you have them.

Baggage Check
(Amtrak Passengers)

A maximum of three items may be checked up to thirty minutes before departure. Up to three additional bags may be checked for a fee of $10 (two carry-on items allowed). No electronic equipment, plastic bags, or paper bags may be checked. See the "Amtrak Policies" section of their website for details.

General Information

NFT Map:	9
Address:	7th Ave & 33rd St
General Information (Amtrak):	800-872-7245
MTA Subway Stops:	① ② ③ Ⓐ Ⓒ Ⓔ
MTA Bus Lines:	④ ⑩ ⑯ ⑭
Train Lines:	LIRR, Amtrak, NJ Transit
Newark Airport Bus Service:	Olympia, 212-964-6233, $13
LaGuardia Airport Bus Service:	NY Airport Service, 718-706-9658, $10
JFK Airport Bus Service:	NY Airport Service, 718-706-9658, $13
Passengers per day:	600,000

Overview

Penn Station, designed by McKim, Mead & White (New York's greatest architects), is a Beaux Arts treasure, filled with light and…oh wait, that's the one that was torn down. Penn Station is essentially a basement, complete with well-weathered leather chairs, unidentifiable dust particles, and high-cholesterol snack food. If the government gods are with us, the plan to convert the eastern half of the Farley Post Office (also designed by McKim, Mead, & White) next door to an above-ground, light-filled station will come to fruition. With bureaucracy at hand, we aren't holding our collective breath. Until then, Penn Station will go on being the country's busiest railway station, servicing 600,000 people per day in the crappy terminal under Madison Square Garden.

Penn Station services Amtrak, the LIRR, and NJ Transit trains. Amtrak, which is surely the worst national train system of any first-world country, administers the station. How is it that the Europeans all have bullet trains and it still takes 3 or more hours to get from NYC to DC? While we're hoping the new station proposal will come through, will it help the crazed LIRR commuters struggling to squish down stairwells to catch the 6:05 to Ronkonkoma? We can only hope.

Dieters traveling through Penn Station should pre-pack snacks. The fast food joints are just too tempting. Donuts and ice cream and KFC, oh my! Leave yourself time to pick up some magazines and a bottle of water for your train trip. It may turn out to be longer than you think.

Terminal Shops

On the LIRR Level

Food & Drink
Auntie Anne's Soft
  Pretzels
Blimpie
Caruso's Pizza
Carvel
Cinnabon
Colombo Frozen Yogurt
Dunkin' Donuts
Europan Café
Haagen Dazs
Hot & Crusty
Hot Dog Stand
KFC
Knot Just Pretzels
Le Bon Café
McDonald's
Nedick's
Pizza Hut
Primo! Cappuccino
Rose Pizza and Pasta
Salad Chef/Burger Chef
Seattle Coffee Roasters
Soup King
Soup Man/Smoothie
  King (2)
Starbucks
Subway
TGI Friday's
Tracks Raw Bar & Grill

Other
Carlton Cards
Dreyfus Financial Center
Duane Reade
GNC
Hudson News (4)
K-Mart
Petal Pusher
Penn Books
Perfumania
Soleman—Shoe repair,
  locksmith
Verizon Wireless

On the Amtrak Level
Food & Drink

Auntie Anne's Soft Pret-
  zels (2) Baskin Robbins
Deli
Dunkin' Donuts
Don Pepi Pizza
Houlihan's Restaurant
  & Bar
Nathan's/Carvel
Kabooz's Bar and Grille
Krispy Kreme Doughnuts
Penn Sushi
Pizza Hut
Primo! Cappuccino (3)
Roy Rogers
Soup Man/Smoothie
  King/Sodutto Ice Cream
Zaro's Bread Basket (2)

Other
Book Corner
Duane Reade
Elegance
Gifts & Electronics
GNC

Hudson News (3)
Joseph Lawrence
  Jewelers
New York New York
Shoetrician—Shoe repair
  and shine
Tiecoon
The Petal Pusher
Staples
Tourist Information
  Center
Verizon Wireless

There is a Wachovia 24-hour ATM and a PNC Bank ATM located on the Amtrak level. There is a Bank of America 24-hour ATM and a 24-hour HSBC ATM located on the LIRR level, in addition to the generic (money-thieving) ATMs located in several stores throughout the station.

Temporary Parcel/Baggage Check

The only facility for storing parcels and baggage in Penn Station is at the Baggage Check on the Amtrak level (to the left of the ticket counter). There are no locker facilities at Penn Station. The Baggage Check is open from 5:15 am until 10 pm and costs $4.50 per item for each 24-hour period.

Transit · Grand Central Terminal

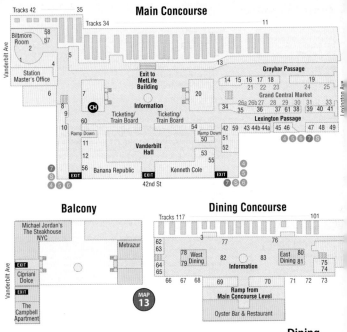

Main Concourse

Balcony

Dining Concourse

MAP 13

Stores

1. Eddie's Shoe Repair
2. Eastern News
3. Dahlia
4. Junior's
5. Starbucks
6. New York Transit Museum
7. Zaro's Bread Basket
8. Discovery Channel Store
9. Posman Books
10. Rite Aid
11. Central Market
12. Hot & Crusty
13. Zaro's Bread Basket
14. Olivers & Co
15. Grande Harvest Wines
16. Cobbler & Shine
17. Stop'N Go Wireless
18. O' Henry's Film Works
19. GNC
20. Hudson News
21. Greenwich Produce
22. Koglin German Hams
23. Murray's Cheese
24. Ceriello Fine Foods
25. Greenwich Produce
26. Pescatore Seafood Company
26b. Dishes at Home
27. Li-Lac Chocolates
28. Oren's Daily Roast
29. Adriana's Caravan
30. Zaro's Bread Basket
31. Wild Edibles
32. Corrado Bread & Pastry
33. Forever Silver
34. Grand Central Optical
35. Tumi
37. L'Occitane
38. Bose
39. Our Name is Mud
40. Aveda
41. Starbucks
42. Swatch
43. Origins
44a. Children's General Store
44b. Leeper Kids
45. Altitunes
46. Pink Slip
47. TOTO
48. LaCrasia Gloves & Creative Accessories
49. Godiva Chocolatier
50. Super Runners Shop
51. Papyrus
52. Oren's Daily Roast
53. Douglas Cosmetics
54. Joon Stationary
55. Super Runners Shop
56. Neuhaus Boutique
57. Grand Central Raquet
58. Central Watch Band Stand
59. Flowers on Lexington
60. Hudson News
61. Access Artisans

Dining Concourse

62. Paninoteca Italiana
63. Chirping Chicken
64. Eata Pita
65. Feng Shui
66. Mendy's Kosher Deli
67. Mendy's Kosher Dairy
68. Masa Sushi
69. Juniors
70. Zócalo
71. Central Market Grill
72. Jacques-imo's To Geaux
73. Brother Jimmy's BBQ
74. Two Boots Pizza
75. Café Spice
76. Golden Krust Patties
77. New York Pretzel
78. Ciao Bella Gelateria
79. Hale and Hearty Soups
80. Zaro's Bread Basket
81. Little Pie Company
82. Dishes
83. Caffé Peppe Rosso

General Information

NFT Map:	13
Address:	42nd St & Park Ave
General Information:	212-340-2210
Lost and Found:	212-712-2555
Website:	www.grandcentralterminal.com
MTA Subway Stops:	④⑤⑥⑦⑤
MTA Bus Lines:	①②③④ 42 ⑨⑩ ⑩② ⑩④ ⑩
Other Rail Lines:	Metro North
Newark Airport Bus Service:	Olympia, 212-964-6233, $13
LaGuardia Airport Bus Service:	NY Airport Express, 718-875-8200, $10
JFK Airport Bus Service:	NY Airport Express, 718-875-8200, $13

Overview

Grand Central Terminal, designed in the Beaux Arts style by Warren & Wetmore, is by far the most beautiful of Manhattan's major terminals, and is considered one of the most stunning terminals in the world. Its convenient location (right in the heart of Midtown) and its refurbishments only add to its intrinsic appeal. The only downside is that the station only services Metro North—you'll have to venture over to ugly Penn Station for LIRR and NJ Transit trains.

If you ever find yourself underestimating the importance of the Grand Central renovations, just take a peek at the ceiling towards the Vanderbilt Avenue side—the small patch of black shows how dirty the ceiling was previously. And it was really dirty…

If you've got time for a drink, check out the exceptionally cool and snotty (no sneakers!) bar, The Campbell Apartment, near the Vanderbilt Avenue entrance. You can also snag some seafood at the Oyster Bar & Restaurant, then go right outside its entrance to hear a strange audio anomaly: If you and a friend stand in opposite corners and whisper, you'll be able to hear each other clearly.

Grand Central Station offers three tours: the hour-long LaSalle Tour (212-340-2347), the Municipal Arts Society Tour (212-935-3960), and the Grand Central Partnership Tour (212-833-2420). The last two tours are free.

ATMs

Chase
Numerous generic (money-thieving) ATMs at stores throughout the station.

East Dining

Brother Jimmy's BBQ
Café SpiceCentral Market Grill
Golden Krust Patties
Jaques-Imo's to Geaux
Little Pie Company
Pepe Rosso
Two Boots
Zaro's Bread Basket
Zócalo Bar and Restaurant

West Dining

Dishes
Ciao Bella Gelateria
Chirping Chicken
Eata Pita
Feng Shui
Hale and Hearty Soups
Junior's
Masa Sushi
Mendy's Kosher Dairy
Mendy's Kosher Delicatessen
New York Pretzel
Paninoteca Italiana

General Information

NFT Map:	11
Address:	41st St & 8th Ave
General Information:	212-564-8484
Kinney Garage:	212-502-2341
Website:	www.panynj.gov/tbt/pabframe.HTM
Subway:	A C E Port Authority
	1 2 3 7 N R Q W S Times Square
MTA Bus Lines:	10 11 16 20 27 42 104
Newark Airport Bus Service:	Olympia, 212-964-6233, $13
LaGuardia Airport Bus Service:	NY Airport Express, 718-875-8200, $12
JFK Airport Bus Service:	NY Airport Express, 718-875-8200, $15

Overview

Devised as a solution to New York City's horrendous bus congestion, the Port Authority Bus Terminal was completed in 1950. The colossal structure consolidated midtown Manhattan's eight, separate interstate bus stations into one convenient drop-off and pick-up point. It was then, and remains, the world's busiest bus terminal, as well as the largest bus terminal in the United States. The Port Authority is located on the north and south sides of W 41st Street between Eighth Avenue and Ninth Avenue in a neighborhood that real-estate agents haven't yet graced with an official name.

There are plenty of things to do should you find that you've got some time to kill at the Port Authority. Send a post card from the post office, donate blood at the blood bank on the main floor, use the refurbished bathrooms, or bowl a few frames (and experience the 70s) at Leisure Time Bowl. There are also many other souvenir carts, newsstands, and on-the-go restaurants, as well as a statue of beloved bus driver, Ralph Kramden, located outside of the south wing. The grungiest area of the terminal is the lower bus level, which is a dirty, exhaust-filled space, best visited just a few minutes before you need to board your bus. The chart on the right shows which bus companies run out of the Port Authority and provides a basic description of their destinations.

If you can, avoid interstate bus rides from the Port Authority on the busiest travel days of the year. The lines are long, the people are cranky and some of the larger bus companies hire anyone who shows up with a valid bus operator's license and their very own bus (apparently, easier to obtain than you might think) to drive their popular routes. The odds of having a disastrous trip skyrocket when the driver is unfamiliar with the usual itinerary.

On Easter Sunday, Christmas Eve, or Thanksgiving, one can see all the angst-ridden sons and daughters of suburban New Jersey parents joyfully waiting in cramped, disgusting corridors for that nauseating bus ride back to Leonia or Morristown or Plainfield or wherever. A fascinating sight.

Terminal Shops

South Wing—Lower Bus Level
Green Trees
Hudson News

South Wing—Subway Mezzanine
Au Bon Pain
Hudson News
Music Explosion

South Wing—Main Concourse
Au Bon Pain
Auntie Anne's
Casa Java
Deli Plus
Duane Reade
GNC
Hudson News

Hudson News Book Corner
Marrella Men's Hair Stylist
NY Blood Center
Radio Shack
Ruthie's Hallmark
Stop 'n Go Wireless
Strawberry
US Postal Service
Villa Pizza
World's Fare Restaurant Bar
Zaro's Bakery

South Wing—Second Floor
Café Metro
Drago Shoe Repair
Bank of America
Hudson News Book Corner
Kelly Film Express

Leisure Time Bowling Center
McAnn's Pub
Mrs Fields Bakery Café
Munchy's Gourmet
Sak's Florist
Sweet Factory

South Wing—Fourth Floor
First Stop-Last Stop Café
Hudson News

North Wing-Lower Bus Level
Snacks-N-Wheels
North Wing—Subway Mezzanine
Bank of America (ATM)
Green Trees
Hudson News

North Wing—Main Concourse
Continental Airlines
Hudson News
Mrs Fields Cookies

North Wing—on 42nd Street
Big Apple Café

North Wing—Second Floor
Bank of America (ATM)
Hudson News
Jay's Hallmark Bookstore
Tropica Juice Bar
USO
US Postal Service

North Wing—Third Floor
Hudson News
Tropica Juice Bar

Bus Company	Phone	Area Served
Academy Bus Transportation	800-242-1339	Serves New York City, including Staten Island, Wall Street and Port Authority, and New Jersey, including Hoboken. www.academybus.com
Adirondack New York & Pine Hill Trailways	800-858-8555	Serves all of New York State with coach connections throughout the U.S. www.trailwaysny.com
Bonanza Bus	800-556-3815	Serves many points between New York and New England, including Cape Cod and the Berkshires. www.bonanzabus.com
Capitol Trailways	800-333-8444	Service between Pennsylvania, Virginia, New York State, and New York City. www.capitoltrailways.com
Carl Bieber Bus	800-243-2374	Service to and from Port Authority and Wall Street in New York and Reading, Kutztown, Wescosville, Hellertown, and Easton, Pennsylvania. www.biebertourways.com
Coach USA	800-522-4514	Service between New York City and W Orange, Livingston, Morristown, E Hanover, Whippany, and Floram Park, New Jersey. www.coachusa.com
DeCamp Bus	800-631-1281	Service between New York City and New Jersey, including the Meadowlands. www.decamp.com
Greyhound Bus	800-229-9424	Serves most of the US and Canada. www.greyhound.com
Gray Line Bus	212-397-2620	Service offered throughout the US and Canada. www.grayline.com
Lakeland Bus	973-366-0600	Service between New York and New Jersey. www.lakelandbus.com
Martz Group	800-233-8604	Service between New York and Pennsylvania. www.martzgroup.com
New Jersey Transit	800-772-2222 (NJ) 973-762-5100 (all other)	Serves New York, New Jersey, and Philadelphia. www.njtransit.com
NY Airport Service	212-875-8200	Service between Port Authority and Kennedy and LaGuardia Airports. www.nyairportservice.com
Olympia Trails	212-964-6233	Provides express bus service between Manhattan and Newark Airport. Makes stops all over New York City, including Penn Station, Grand Central, and many connections with hotel shuttles. www.olympiabus.com
Peter Pan Lines	800-343-9999	Serves the East, including New Hampshire, Maine, Philly, DC. Also goes to Canada. www.peterpanbus.com
Rockland Coaches (NY)	845-356-0877	Services New York's Port Authority, GW bridge, 44th Street, and 8th Street to and from most of Bergen County and upstate New York. www.coachusa.com/rockland
ShortLine Bus	800-631-8405	Serves the New York City airports, Atlantic City, and the Hudson Valley. www.shortlinebus.com
Suburban	732-249-1100	Offers commuter service from Central New Jersey to and from Port Authority and Wall Street. Also services between the Route 9 Corridor and New York City. www.coachusa.com/suburban
Susquehanna Trailways	800-692-6314	Service to and from New York City and Newark (Gr Terminal) and Summerville, New Jersey and many stops in Central Pennsylvania, ending in Williamsport and Lock Haven. www.susquehannabus.com
Trans-Bridge Lines	610-868-6001 800-962-9135	Offers service between New York, Pennsylvania, and New Jersey, including Newark and Kennedy airports.
Red & Tan Hudson County (NJ)	201-876-9000	Serves New York City and Hudson County, New Jersey. www.coachusa.com/redandtan

General Information

NFT Map:	23
Address:	4211 Broadway & 178th St
Phone:	800-221-9903 or 212-564-8484
Website:	www.panynj.gov/tbt/gwbframe.htm
Subway:	Ⓐ (175th St), Ⓐ ① (181st St)
Buses:	ⓦ ⑩ ⑤ ④ ③ Ⓨ

Overview

Completed in 1963, the George Washington Bridge Bus Terminal, located between 178th and 179th Streets on Fort Washington Avenue, is a bit like the bastard sibling of the 42nd Street terminal. It's fairly reminiscent of its downtown brother, but for the wrong reasons: the omni-present smell of gasoline, assorted strange people hanging around, and a slightly seedy aura. To be fair, it's better than it once was thanks to some timely renovations, but any place where one of the centerpiece establishments is OTB has a long way to go.

Stores

Concourse:
ATM
Bridge Stop Newsstand
Dentists—Howard Bloom, DDS; Steve Kaufman DDS
E-Z Visions Travel
Food Plus Café
GW Books and Electronics
HealthPlus Healthcare
Neighborhood Trust Federal Credit Union
New York National Bank
Off-Track Betting
Pizza Palace
Terminal Barber Shop
Washington Heights Optical

Street Level:
Blockbuster Video
Rite-Aid Pharmacy
Urban Pathways—Homeless Outreach Office
Port Authority Business Outreach Center
  (179th St underpass)

Bus Companies

Air Brook · 800-800-1990 ·
www.airbrook.com
To Atlantic City

Astro-Eastern Bus Company · 201-865-2230 ·
www.easternbuses.com
Trips to Florida (purchase tickets on the upper level).

Express Bus Service · 973-881-9122 ·
www.expressbusservice.com
To Clifton, Passaic, Paterson, and Willowbrook Mall.

New Jersey Transit · 800-772-2222 ·
www.njtransit.com/sf_bus.shtm
To 60th St, Bergenfield, Bogota, Cliffside Park, Coytesville, Dumont, Edgewater (including Edgewater Commons Mall), Englewood, Englewood Cliffs, West Englewood, Fair Lawn (including the Radburn section), Fairview, Fort Lee, Glen Rock, Guttenberg, Hackensack (including NJ Bus Transfer), Hoboken, North Hackensack (Riverside Square), Irvington, Jersey City, Kearney, Leonia, Maywood, Newark, North Bergen, Paramus (including the Bergen Mall and Garden State Plaza), Paterson (including Broadway Terminal), Ridgewood, Rochelle Park, Teaneck (including Glenpointe and Holy Name Hospital), Union City, Weehawken, and West New York.

Rockland Coaches/Coach USA · 845-356-0877 ·
www.coachusa.com/rockland
To Alpine, Bergenfield, Blauvelt, Bradlees Shopping Center, Closter, Congers, Creskill, Demarest, Dumont, Emerson, Englewood, Englewood Cliffs, Grandview, Harrington Park, Haverstraw, Haworth, Hillsdale, Linwood Park, Montvale, Nanuet, (including Nanuet Shopping Mall), Nauraushaun, New City, New Milford, Northvale (including Northvale Industrial Park), Norwood, Nyack, Oradell, Orangeburg, Palisades, Park Ridge, Pearl River, Piermont, Rivervale, Rockland Lake, Rockland Psych Center, Rockleigh (including Rockleigh Industrial Park), South Nyack, Sparkill, Spring Valley, Stony Point, Tappan, Tenafly, Upper Nyack, Valley Cottage, West Haverstraw, Westwood, and Woodcliff Lake.

Shortline/Coach USA · 800-631-8405 ·
www.shortlinebus.com
To, Harriman, Paramus, Park Ridge, and Ridgewood.

Vanessa Express · 201-583-0999.
To Cliffside Park, Jersey City, North Bergen, Union City, and West New York.

General Information

NFT Map: 3
Websites: www.chinatown-bus.com
            www.chinatown-bus.org

Overview

There are several inexpensive bus lines running from China-town in New York City to the respective Chinatowns in Boston, Philadelphia, Washington DC, Richmond, and Atlanta. They'll even take you to the outlet malls in Jersey. If you're lucky, you'll catch a kung-fu movie on board. Tickets usually cost $15-20 each way, and can be purchased online or in person at pick-up locations.

Cheaper than planes and trains, the Chinatown buses have become extraordinarily popular. They are in such demand that Greyhound and Trailways have lowered their online fares to compete. That said, the Chinatown buses are still less expensive than mainstream buses, and they're an infinitely more adventurous mode of transportation. The odds are high that you'll experience at least one problem during the course of your trip including, but not limited to, poor customer service, unmarked bus stops, late departures, less than ideal bus conditions, and hucking or spitting from other passengers. More pertinent problems include cancelled or delayed trips without warning, breakdowns, fires, broken bathrooms (or none at all), stolen luggage, and drop-offs on the side of the road near the highway because bus companies don't have permission to deliver passengers to central transportation hubs, though this particular problem is slowly improving. On the other hand, many people have enjoyed dirt-cheap, hassle-free experiences on the Chinatown buses. So if you thrive on the unpredictable and you need to save some cash, give it a try.

Passengers should arrive at least 30 minutes prior to scheduled departure and buy tickets before boarding the bus. Schedules and prices are subject to change at a moment's notice, so it's helpful to call or consult the company's website right before you leave. If you walk down East Broadway under the Manhattan Bridge, chances are you'll be solicited by people on the street without even having to ask. Buses vary in quality from company to company and even from day to day. Fung Wah has been around the longest and is generally considered the best line. To read user reviews, visit www.chinatown-bus.com.

Bus Companies

Fung Wah Transportation Inc. · 212-925-8889 · www.fungwahbus.com
- To Boston every hour on the hour between 7 am-10 pm. From **139 Canal Street** to South Station: one-way $15, round trip $30.

Lucky Star Bus Transportation · 617-426-8801 · www.luckystarbus.com.
- To Boston every hour 7 am-10 pm. From **69 Chrystie St** to South Station: one-way $15, round trip $30.

Boston Deluxe · 917-662-7552 or 646-773-3816· www.bostondeluxe.com

- To Boston at 9 am, 12:30 pm, and 6 pm. From **1250 Broadway & 32nd St** or **88 E Broadway** to 175 Huntington Ave: one-way $15, round trip $30.
- To Hartford at 8:30 am and 5:30 pm. From the same pick-up points to 365 Capital Ave: one-way $15, round trip $30.

Washington Deluxe · 866-BUS-NY-DC · www.washny.com
- To Washington several times a day; From **34th St & 8th Ave**. Additional departures from **Delancey & Allen Sts**, and several locations in **Williamsburg** to various locations in DC. Schedule varies by day of the week, so it's recommended that you check the website for info. One-way $20, round-trip $35.

Dragon Deluxe · 212-608-6406 · www.dragondeluxe.com
- To Washington seven times a day between 7:30 am and 11:30 pm. From **153 Lafayette St** or **Broadway & W 34th St-Herald Square** to 14th & L Sts: one-way $20, round trip $35.
- To Baltimore seven times a day between 7:30 am and 11:30 pm. From the same pick-up points to 5600 O'Donnell St: one-way $20, round trip $35.
- To Albany five times a day between 8 am and 9 pm. From the same pick-up points to Madison Ave (between the New York State Museum and Empire State Plaza): one-way $20, round trip $35
- To Woodbury Commons five times a day between 8 am and 9 pm. From the same pick-ups points to Woodbury Commons: one-way $10, round trip $20.

Eastern Travel · 212-244-6132 · www.easternshuttle.com
- To Washington DC 6-12 times a day between 7:30 am and 7:30 pm; From **88 E Broadway, 430 7th Ave at W 34th St**, or **5 Times Square (in front of the Ernst &Young Building)** to 715 H Street in Washington DC: one-way $20, round trip $35.
- To Baltimore 6-12 times a day between 7:30 am and 7:30 pm. From same pickup-point to 5501 O'Donnell Ave Cut Off: one-way $20, round trip $35.

New Century Travel · 215-627-2666 · www.2000coach.com
- To Philadelphia every hour between 7 am and 11 pm. From **88 E Broadway** or **5994 8th Ave, Williamsburg** (7 am only) to 55 N 11th St: one-way $12, round trip $20.
- To DC eight times between 7 am and 11 pm; From **88 E Broadway** to 513 H St NW: one-way $20, round trip $35.
- To Richmond at 5 pm and 1 am. From **88 E Broadway** to 2808 W Broad St: one-way $40, round-trip $60.

Today's Bus · 212-964-2666 · www.todaysbus.com
- To Philadelphia everyhour between 7:15 am and 11 pm. From **88 E Broadway** to 1041 Race St: one-way $12, round trip $20.
- To DC 11 times a day between 7:15 am and 11 pm. From **88 E Broadway** to 610 I St NW: one-way $20, round trip $30.
- To Atlantic City at 10 am, 1 pm, and 11 pm. From **37 Division St** to Resorts Casino: round trip $20 (but they give you $25 cash back and $20 in chips if you're over 21).
- To Norfolk, VA at 6 pm. From **13 Allen St** to 649 Newton Rd: one-way $35, round trip $60.
- To Richmond, VA at 5 pm. From **88 E Broadway** to 5215 W Broad St: one-way $40, round trip $60.
- To Atlanta, GA at 8 pm. From **109 E Broadway** to 5150 Buford Hwy NE: one-way $90, round trip $170.

···· Bike Lane
(on-street)

···· Recommended Route
(sufficient width and/or light traffic)

···· Greenway
(off-street or designated path in parks)

THE BRONX

Broadway Bridge

W 217 St

Sedgwick Ave

Broadway

10th Ave

Univ Heights Bridge

St Nicholas Ave

Dyckman St

Nagle Ave

Hudson River Greenway

Broadway

Fort Washington

W 185 St

W 184 St

Amsterdam Ave

Washington Bridge

W 178 St

George Washington Bridge

Haven Ave

W 177 St

High Bridge

W 172 St

W 171 St

W 165 St

W 155 St

St Nicholas Ave

Macombs Dam Bridge

W 145 St

W 142 St

Convent Ave

145th St Bridge

W 141 St W 139 St

W 138 St

Madison Ave Bridge

3rd Ave Bridge

Willis Ave Bridge

W 125 St

Adam C Powell Ave

E 127 St

Triboro Bridge

E 124 St

RANDALL'S ISLAND

W 120 St

Hudson River Greenway

E 121 St

E 120 St

3rd Ave

E 119 St

1st Ave

WARDS ISLAND

W 110 St

E 111 St

2nd Ave

E 110 St

NEW JERSEY

Riverside Dr

West End Ave

W 100 St

Central Park W

Fifth Ave

E 105 St

Pedestrian Bridge

E 102 St

Hudson River

W 91 St

W 90 St

Central Park

E 91 St

East River

E 90 St

QUEEN

General Information

Bicycle Defense Fund: www.bicycledefensefund.org
Bike New York, Five Borough Bike Tour: www.bikenewyork.org
Century Road Club Association (CRCA): www.crca.net
Department of City Planning: www.ci.nyc.ny.us/html/dcp/html/bike
Department of Parks & Recreation: www.nycgovparks.org
Department of Transportation: www.nyc.gov/html/dot/html/bikeped/bikemain.html
Empire Skate Club: www.empireskate.org
Fast & Fabulous Lesbian & Gay Bike Club: www.fastnfab.org
Five Boro Bicycle Club: www.5bbc.org
League of American Bicyclists: www.bikeleague.org
New York Bicycle Coalition: www.nybc.net
New York Cycle Club: www.nycc.org
Time's Up! Bicycle Advocacy Group: www.times-up.org
Transportation Alternatives: www.transalt.org

Overview

While not for the faint of heart, biking and skating around Manhattan can be one of the most efficient and exhilarating forms of transportation. Transportation Alternatives estimates that over 120,000 New Yorkers hop on a bike each day—an all-time high for the city. Manhattan is relatively flat, and the fitness and environmental advantages of using people power are incontrovertible. However, there are also some downsides, including, but not limited to: psychotic cab drivers, buses, traffic, pedestrians, pavement with potholes, glass, and debris, and poor air quality. In 1994, the Bicycle Network Development Program was created to increase bicycle usage in the NYC area. Since then, many bike lanes have been created on streets and in parks (see map on previous page). These tend to be the safest places to ride, though they sometimes get blocked by parked or standing cars. Central Park is a great place to ride, as are the newly developed paths from Battery Park that run along the Hudson River. East River Park is another nice destination for recreational riding and skating—just not after dark! In addition to bicycle rentals, Pedal Pusher Bike Shop (1306 Second Ave, 212-288-5592) offers recorded tours of Central Park, so you can learn about the park and exercise at the same time.

Recreational skating venues in Manhattan include Wollman and Lasker Rinks in Central Park, Chelsea Piers, The Roxy (515 W 18th St), Riverbank State Park (Riverside Drive at 145th St), and Rivergate Ice Rink (401 E 34th St). If you're looking for a place to get your skates sharpened to your own personal specifications before hitting the ice, contact Westside Skate & Stick (174 Fifth Avenue, 212-228-8400), a custom pro shop for hockey and figure skaters that's by appointment only. For more information on skating venues throughout the boroughs, check out www.skatecity.com. For organized events, visit the Empire Skate Club at www.empireskate.org.

Bikes are sometimes less convenient than skates. Where skates can be tucked in a bag and carried onto subways, indoors, or on buses, bikes have to be locked up on the street and are always at risk of being stolen. Unfortunately, bike racks are hard to come by in NYC, so you may need to get creative on where to park. Always lock them to immovable objects and don't skimp on a cheap bike lock. With

over 40,000 bikes a year stolen in NYC, the extra cost for a top of the line bike lock is worth it. On the upside, bikes provide a much faster, less demanding form of transportation around the city.

Crossing the Bridges by Bike

Crossing the Brooklyn, Manhattan, or Williamsburg Bridges by bike is a great way for Brooklynites to commute to work (unless, of course, it's really windy and cold out). Riding across these bridges also makes for a great weekend outing for Manhattanites and Brooklynites alike. All bridges afford amazing views of the Manhattan and Brooklyn skylines and waterfronts. In the fall of 2003, the DOT estimated that nearly 4,000 cyclists crossed the East River bridges each day. It just isn't healthy to stay underground so much, so gear up and give it a go.

Brooklyn Bridge

Separate bicycle and pedestrian lanes run down the center of the bridge, with the bicycle lane on the north side and the pedestrian lane on the south. Cyclists should beware of wayfaring tourists taking photographs. We do not recommend rollerblading across the bridge—the wooden planks make for quite a bumpy ride. The bridge is quite level and, aside from the tourists and planks, fairly easy to traverse.

Brooklyn Access: Stairs to Cadman Plaza East and Prospect Street, ramp to Johnson and Adams Streets.
Manhattan Access: Park Row and Centre Street, across from City Hall Park

Manhattan Bridge

The last of the Brooklyn crossings to be outfitted with decent pedestrian and bike paths, the Manhattan Bridge bike and pedestrian paths are on separate sides of the bridge. The walking path is on the south side, and the bike path is on the north side of the bridge. The major drawback to walking across the Manhattan Bridge is that you have to climb a steep set of stairs on the Brooklyn side (not the best conditions for lugging around a stroller or suitcase). Fortunately, the bike path on the north side of the bridge is ramped on both approaches. However, be careful on Jay Street when accessing the bridge in Brooklyn due to the dangerous, fast moving traffic.

Brooklyn Access: Jay St & Sands St
Manhattan Access: Bike Lane–Canal St & Forsyth St
Pedestrian Lane–Bowery, just south of Canal St

Williamsburg Bridge

Rejoice! The dangerous steel bumps have finally been removed from the Williamsburg Bridge. Riders can now smoothly zip into Williamsburg from the Lower East Side without fearing for their lives. The Williamsburg has the widest pedestrian/bike path of the three bridges to Brooklyn. The path on the north side, shared by cyclists and pedestrians, is 12 feet wide. The southern path, at eight feet wide, is also shared by bikers and walkers Unfortunately, only one of the paths seems to be open at any given time for some illogical reason. However, during the 2005 transit strike both sides were open, and hopefully this will become the norm. As a bonus fitness feature, the steep gradient on both the Manhattan and Brooklyn sides of the bridge gives bikers and pedestrians a good workout.
Brooklyn Access: North Entrance–Driggs Ave, right by the Washington Plz
South Entrance–Bedford Ave b/w S 5th & S 6th Sts
Manhattan Access: Delancey St & Clinton St/Suffolk St

George Washington Bridge

Bikers get marginalized by the pedestrians on this crossway to New Jersey. The north walkway is for pedestrians only, and the south side is shared by pedestrians and bikers. Cyclists had to fight to keep their right to even bike on this one walkway, as city officials wanted to institute a "walk your bike across" rule to avoid bicycle/pedestrian accidents during construction. The bikers won the battle but are warned to "exercise extra caution" when passing pedestrians.
Manhattan Access: W 178th St & Fort Washington Ave
New Jersey Access: Hudson Terrace in Fort Lee

Triborough Bridge

Biking is officially prohibited on this two-mile span that connects the Bronx, Queens, and Manhattan. Unofficially, people ride between the boroughs and over to Wards Island all the time. The bike path is quite narrow, compared to the paths on other bridges, and the lighting at night is mediocre at best. The tight path sees less pedestrian/cycling traffic than other bridges, which, paired with the insufficient lighting, gives the span a rather ominous feeling after dark. If you're worried about safety, or keen on obeying the laws, the 103rd Street footbridge provides an alternative way to reach Wards Island sans car. This pedestrian pass is open only during the warmer months, and then only during daylight hours. See page 208 for more information about the footbridge schedule.
Bronx Access: 134th St & Cypress Ave
Manhattan Access: Ramps–124/126th Sts & First Ave Stairs–Second Avenue and 124/126 Streets
Queens Access: 26th St & Hoyt Ave (beware of extremely steep stairs).

Queensboro Bridge

The north outer roadway of the Queensboro Bridge is open exclusively to bikers, 24 hours a day, seven days a week, except for the day of the New York Marathon. More than 2,500 cyclists and pedestrians per day traverse the bridge. Bikers complain about safety issues on the Manhattan side of the bridge: With no direct connection from Manhattan onto the bridge's West Side, bikers are forced into an awkward five-block detour to get to Second Avenue, where they can finally access the bridge.
Manhattan Entrance: 60th St, b/w First Ave & Second Ave
Queens Entrance: Queens Plz & Crescent St

Bike Rentals (and Sales)

Metro Bicycle Stores:
• 88th St & Lexington Ave • 212-427-4450 • Map 17
• 360 W 47th St & Ninth Ave • 212-581-4500 • Map 11
• 213 W 96th St & Broadway • 212-663-7531 • Map 16
• 14th St, b/w First & Second Aves • 228-4344 • Map 6
• Sixth Ave & W 15th St • 255-5100 • Map 9
• Sixth Ave b/w Canal & Grand • 212-334-8000 • Map 2
Anewgen Bicycles • 832 Ninth Ave • 757-2418 • Map 11
Toga Bike Shop • 110 West End Ave & 64th St • 212-799-9625 • Map 14
Gotham Bikes • 112 W Broadway • 212-732-2453 • Map 2
Bicycle Habitat • 244 Lafayette St b/w Spring & Prince Sts • 212-625-1347 • Map 6
Bicycle Heaven • 348 E 62 St b/w First & Second Aves • 212-230-1919 • Map 15
Bike Works • 106 Ridge St b/w Stanton & Rivington Sts • 212-388-1077 • Map 7
City Bicycles • 315 W 38th St b/w Eighth & Ninth Aves • 212-563-3373 • Map 11
Eddie's Bicycles Shop • 490 Amsterdam Ave b/w 83rd & 84th Sts • 212-580-2011 • Map 14
Larry and Jeff's Bicycles Plus • 1690 Second Ave b/w 87th & 88th Sts • 212-722-2201 • Map 17
Pedal Pusher Bike Shop • 1306 Second Ave b/w 68th & 69th Sts • 212-288-5592 • Map 15
Manhattan Bicycles • 791 Ninth Ave b/w 52nd & 53rd Sts • 212-262-0111 • Map 11
New York Cyclist • 301 Cathedral Pkwy • 212-864-4449 • Map 16

Bikes and Mass Transit

Surprisingly, you can take your bike on trains and some buses—just make sure it's not during rush hour and you are courteous to other passengers. The subway requires you to carry your bike down staircases, use the service gate instead of the turnstile, and board at the very front or back end of the train. To ride the commuter railroads with your bike, you may need to purchase a bike permit. For appropriate contact information, see transportation pages.

Amtrak: Train with baggage car required.
LIRR: $5 permit required.
Metro-North: $5 permit required.
New Jersey Transit: No permit required.
PATH: No permit required.
New York Water Taxi: No fee or permit required
NY Waterway: $1 fee.
Staten Island Ferry: Enter at lower level.
Bus companies: Call individual companies.

Television

2	WCBS (CBS)	www.cbsnewyork.com
4	WNBC (NBC)	www.wnbc.com
5	WNYW (FOX)	www.fox5ny.com
7	WABC (ABC)	abclocal.go.com/wabc
9	WWOR (UPN)	www.upn9.com
11	WPIX (WB)	www.wb11.com
13	WNET (PBS)	www.thirteen.org
21	WLIW (Long Island Public)	www.wliw.org
25	WNY (Public)	
31	PXN (Pax)	www.pax.tv
41	WXTV (Univision)	www.univision.com
47	WNJU (Telemundo)	www.telemundo.com
49	CPTV (Conn. Public)	www.cptv.org
50	WNJN (NJ Public)	www.njn.net
55	WLNY (Public)	www.wlnytv.com
63	WMBC (Religious)	www.wmbctv.com

AM Stations

570	WFME	Religious
620	WSNR	Sports
660	WFAN	Sports
710	WOR	Talk
770	WABC	Talk
820	WNYC	Talk
880	WCBS	Talk
930	WPAT	Talk
1010	WINS	News
1050	WEVD	Sports
1130	WBBR	Talk
1190	WLIB	Talk
1280	WADO	Sports
1600	WWRL	Talk
1660	WWRU	Talk

FM Stations

88.1	WCWP Jazz	
88.3	WBGO	Jazz
88.7	WRHU College	
88.9	WSIA	College
89.1	WFDU	College
89.1	WNYU	College
89.5	WSOU	Alternative/Hard Rock
89.9	WKCR	Jazz/College/ Experimental
90.3	WHCR	College
90.3	WHPC	College
90.7	WFUV	Adult Alternative
90.9	WKPB	College
91.1	WFMU	Independent free-form!
91.5	WNYE	Talk
92.3	WXRK	Alternative/Hard Rock
92.7	WLIR	Latin
93.1	WPAT	Latin
93.9	WNYC	Talk
94.7	WFME	Religious
95.5	WPLJ	Top 40
96.3	WQXR	Classical
97.1	WQHT	Hip-Hop/R&B
97.9	WSKQ	Latin
98.7	WRKS	Hip-Hop/R&B
99.5	WBAI	Talk
100.3	WHTZ	Top 40
101.1	JACK FM	
101.9	WQCD	Jazz
102.3	WBAB	Classic Rock
102.7	WNEW	Top 40
103.5	WKTU	Top 40/Dance
104.3	WAXQ	Classic Rock
105.1	WWPR	Hip-Hop/R&B
105.9	WWPR	Latin
106.7	WLTW	Adult Comtemporary
107.1	WCAA	Latin
107.5	WBLS	R&B

Print Media

amNY	145 W 30th St, 9th Fl	212-239-5398	Free daily; general news.
Daily News	450 W 33rd St	212-210-2100	Daily tabloid; rival of the Post. Good sports.
El Diario	345 Hudson St	212-807-4600	Daily; America's oldest Spanish-language newspaper.
Metro NYC	44 Wall St	212-952-1500	Free daily; pick it up at the subway.
New York Observer	54 E 64th St	212-755-2400	Weekly.
New York Post	1211 Avenue of the Americas	212-997-9272	Daily tabloid; known for its sensationalist headlines.
New York Sun	105 Chambers St	212-406-2000	Daily; only a couple of years old.
New York Times	229 W 43rd St	212-556-1234	Daily; one of the world's best-known papers.
Newsday	235 Pinelawn Rd,	516-843-2700	Daily; based in Long Island.
NY Press	333 Seventh Ave	212-244-2282	Free weekly; mostly opinion/editorial.
The Onion	515 W 20th St	212-627-1972	Weekly; news satire & listings.
The Village Voice	36 Cooper Sq	212-475-3300	Free, alternative weekly.
Wall Street Journal	200 Liberty St	212-416-2500	Daily; famous financial paper.
New York Magazine	444 Madison Ave	212-508-0700	Broad-based upscale weekly.
New York Review of Books	1755 Broadway	212-757-8070	Bi-weekly; intellectual lit review. Recommended.
The New Yorker	4 Times Square	212-286-5400	Weekly; intellectual news, lit, and arts.
Time Out New York	627 Broadway, 7th Fl	212-539-4444	Weekly; the best guide to goings-on in the city.

January

• Winter Antiques Show	Park Ave at 67th St	Selections from all over the country.
• Three Kings Day Parade	El Museo del Barrio	Features a cast of hundreds from all over the city dressed as kings or animals–camels, sheep, and donkeys (early Jan).
• Outsider Art Fair	Corner of Lafayette & Houston	Art in many forms of media from an international set. $15 admits one for one day.
• National Boat Show	Jacob Javits Convention Center	Don't go expecting a test drive (early Jan).
• Chinese New Year	Chinatown	Features dragons, performers, and parades.

February

• Empire State Building Run-Up	Empire State Building	Run until the 86th floor (0.2 miles) or heart seizure.
• The Art Show	Park Ave at 67th St	A very large art fair.
• Westminster Dog Show	Madison Square Garden	Fancy canines.
• Seventh on Sixth Fall Fashion Show	Bryant Park	Weeklong celeb-studded event.

March

• International Cat Show	Madison Square Garden	Fine felines.
• St Patrick's Day Parade	Fifth Avenue	Irish pride (March 17). We recommend fleeing.
• Orchid Show	Bronx River Parkway	Brought to you by the New York Botanical Garden.
• Ringling Brothers Circus	Madison Square Garden	Greatest Show on Earth (March–April).
• Whitney Biennial	Whitney Museum	Whitney's most important American art, every other year (March–June).
• Greek Independence Day Parade	Fifth Avenue	Floats and bands representing area Greek Orthodox churches and Greek federations and organizations (Late March).
• Small Press Book Fair	Small Press Center	Sometimes-interesting fair of small publishers and self-published authors.
• Macy's Flower Show	Broadway and 34th St	Flowers and leather-clad vixens. Okay, just flowers really.
• The Armory Show	West Side Piers	Brilliant best-of-galleries show—recommended.
• New Directors/New Films	MoMA	Film festival featuring new films by emerging directors.

April

• Easter Parade	Fifth Avenue	Starts at 11 am, get there early (Easter Sunday).
• New York Antiquarian Book Fair	Park Ave at 67th St	170 international booksellers exhibition.
• New York International Auto Show	Jacob Javits Convention Center	Traffic jam.
• Spring Spectacular	Radio City Music Hall	The Rockettes in bunny costumes? (Easter week).
• New York City Ballet Spring Season	Lincoln Center	Features new and classical ballet (April–June).

May

• Tribeca Film Festival	Various locations including Regal 16 at BPC, BMCC Chambers St, Battery Park	Festival includes film screenings, panels, lectures, discussion groups, and concerts (Early May).
• The Great Five Boro Bike Tour	Battery Park to Staten Island	Tour de NYC (first Sunday in May).
• Ninth Avenue International Food Festival	Ninth Ave from 37th to 57th Sts	Decent but overrated.
• Fleet Week	USS Intrepid	Boats and sailors from many navies (last week in May).
• New York AIDS Walk	Central Park	10K walk whose proceeds go toward finding a cure.
• Lower East Side Festival of the Arts	Theater for the New City, 155 First Ave	Celebrating Beatniks and Pop Art (last weekend in May).
• Spring Flower Exhibition	NY Botanical Garden, Bronx	More flowers.
• Cherry Blossom Festival	Brooklyn Botanic Garden	Flowering trees and Japanese cultural events.
• Martin Luther King, Jr Parade	Fifth Avenue	Celebration of equal rights (third Sunday in May).
• Thursday Night Concert Series	South Street Seaport	Free varied concerts (May–September).

June

- Toyota Comedy Festival — Various locations — Japan's dullest cars, America's funniest comics.
- Puerto Rican Day Parade — Fifth Avenue — Puerto Rican pride (First Sunday in June).
- Metropolitan Opera Parks Concerts — Various locations — Free performances through June and July.
- Museum Mile Festival — Fifth Avenue — Museum open-house (second Sunday in June).
- Gay and Lesbian Pride Parade — Columbus Circle, Fifth Ave & Christopher St — Commemorates the 1969 Stonewall riots (last Sunday in June).
- New York Jazz Festival — Various locations — All kinds of jazz.
- JVC Jazz Festival — Various locations — Descends from the Newport Jazz Festival.
- Mermaid Parade — Coney Island — Showcase of sea-creatures and freaks—basically, Brooklynites.
- Feast of St Anthony of Padua — Little Italy — Patron saint of expectant mothers, mail, Portugal, seekers of lost articles, shipwrecks, Tigua Indians, and travel hostesses, among other things (Saturday before summer solstice).
- Central Park SummerStage — Central Park — Free concerts (June–August).
- Bryant Park Free Summer Season — Sixth Ave at 42nd St — Free music, dance, and film (June–August).
- Midsummer Night Swing — Lincoln Center — Performances with free dance lessons (June–July).

July

- Macy's Fireworks Display — East River — Independence Day's literal highlight (July 4).
- American Crafts Festival — Lincoln Center — Celebrating quilts and such (first two weekends in July).
- Washington Square Music Festival — W 4th St at LaGuardia Pl — Open-air concert (July–August).
- New York Philharmonic Concerts — Various locations — Varied programs (July–August).
- Summergarden — MoMA — Free classical concerts (July–August).
- Celebrate Brooklyn! Performing Arts Festival — Prospect Park Bandshell — Nine weeks of free outdoor events (July–August).
- Mostly Mozart — Lincoln Center — The name says it all (July–August).
- New York Shakespeare Festival — Delacorte Theater in Central Park — Two free plays every summer (July–August)—Zounds!
- Music on the Boardwalk — Coney Island — "Under the Boardwalk" not on the set list, presumably… (July–August).
- PS 1 Warm Up — PS 1 Contemporary Art Center — An assortment of musical performances every Saturday afternoon (July–August).
- Village Voice Siren Music Festival — Coney Island — Free outdoor show featuring renowned and emerging artists. For the alternative minded (July).

August

- Harlem Week — Harlem — Black and Latino culture. The celebration lasts all month.
- Hong Kong Dragon Boat Festival — Flushing-Meadows Park Lake, Queens — 39-foot boats race.
- Greenwich Village Jazz Festival — Greenwich Village — Ten-day festival ending with a free concert in Washington Square Park.
- The Fringe Festival — Various locations, Lower East Side — Avant-garde theater.
- US Open Tennis Championships — USTA National Tennis Center, Flushing — Final Grand Slam event of the year (August–September).
- Howl Festival — Tompkins Square Park — Jazz, East Village merchants, art, etc. Recommended.
- Lincoln Center Out of Doors — Lincoln Center — Free outdoor performances throughout the month.

September

- West Indian Day Carnival — Eastern Parkway from Utica—Grand Army Plaza, Brooklyn — Children's parade on Saturday, adult's parade on Labor Day (Labor Day Weekend).
- Richmond County Fair — 441 Clarke Ave, Staten Island — Best agricultural competitions (Labor Day).
- Wigstock — Pier 54 b/w 12th–13th Sts, west side — Celebration of drag, glamour, and artificial hair (Labor Day Weekend).
- Feast of San Gennaro — Little Italy — Plenty of greasy street food (third week in September).
- Downtown Arts Festival — Various locations, SoHo — Mammoth art exhibitions.
- Broadway on Broadway — Times Square — Sneak peek at old and new plays.

September—*continued*

• Brooklyn BeerFest	N 11th St between Berry and Wythe, Brooklyn	Taste test of over 100 beers. Yum!
• Atlantic Antic	Brooklyn Heights	Multicultural street fair (last Sunday in September).
• New York Is Book Country	Fifth Avenue	Publishers and bookstores from around NYC (third Sunday in September).
• Race for the Mayor's Cup	NY Harbor	And the winner gets to find out what he's been drinking! (September–November)
• New York City Opera Season	Lincoln Center	Popular and classical operas.

October

• New York Film Festival	Lincoln Center	Features film premieres (early October).
• Fall Crafts Park Avenue	Seventh Regiment Armory on Park Avenue, b/w 66th and 67th Sts	Display and sale of contemporary American crafts by 175 of the nation's finest craft artists.
• Columbus Day Parade	Fifth Avenue	Celebrating the second person to discover America (Columbus Day).
• Halloween Parade	West Village	Brings a new meaning to costumed event (October 31).
• Fall Antique Show	Pier 92	Look at old things you can't afford.
• Chrysanthemum and Bonsai Festival	NY Botanical Garden, Bronx	Even more flowers.
• Blessing of the Animals	St John the Divine, Morningside Heights	Where to take your gecko.
• Big Apple Circus	Lincoln Center	Step right up! (October–January)
• Hispanic Day Parade	Fifth Ave b/w 44th and 86th Sts	A celebration of Latin America's rich heritage (mid-October).

November

• New York City Marathon	Verrazano to Central Park	26 miles of NYC air (first Sunday of November).
• Veteran's Day Parade	Fifth Ave from 42nd St to 79th St	Service at Eternal Light Memorial in Madison Square Park following the parade.
• Macy's Thanksgiving Day Parade	Central Park West at 79th St to Macy's	Santa starts the holiday season.
• Chase Championships, Corel WTA Tour	Madison Square Garden	Women's tennis.
• The Nutcracker Suite	Lincoln Center	Christmas tradition (November–December).
• Singing Christmas Tree	South Street Seaport	Warning: might scare small children, family pets, and stoners (November–December).
• Christmas Spectacular	Radio City Music Hall	Rockettes star (November–January).
• A Christmas Carol	Madison Square Garden	Dickens a la New York City (Nov–Jan).
• Origami Christmas Tree	Museum of Natural History	Hopefully not decorated with candles (Nov–Jan).

December

• Christmas Tree Lighting Ceremony	Rockefeller Center	Most enchanting spot in the city during the holidays.
• Messiah Sing-In	Call 212-333-5333	Handel would be proud.
• New Year's Eve Fireworks	Central Park	Hot cider and food available (December 31).
• New Year's Eve Ball Drop	Times Square	Welcome the new year with a freezing mob (Dec 31).
• Blessing of the Animals	Central Presbyterian Church	Where to take your other gecko (December 24).
• Menorah Lighting	Fifth Avenue	Yarmulke required.
• Kwanzaa Holiday Expo	Jacob Javits Convention Center	Black pride retail.
• New Year's Eve Midnight Run	Central Park	5k for the brave.
• John Lennon Vigil	Strawberry Fields, Central Park	Anniversary of the singer/songwriter's death. Yoko showed up last year (December 9).
• Alvin Ailey American Dance Theater	New York City Center	Dance at its best.

"New York is the concentrate of art and commerce and sport and religion and entertainment and finance, bringing to a single compact arena the gladiator, the evangelist, the promoter, the actor, the trader and the merchant." —E.B. White

Useful Phone Numbers

Emergencies: 911
General City Information: 311
City Board of Elections: 212-VOTE-NYC
Con Edison: 800-752-6633
Time Warner Cable: 212-358-0900 (Manhattan);
                             718-358-0900   (Queens);

Brooklyn);

                             718-816-8686 (Staten Island)
Cablevision: 718-617-3500
Verizon: xxx-890-1550 (add 1 and your
local area code plus the seven digit number)
Police Headquarters: 646-610-5905
Public Advocate: 212-669-7200

Bathrooms

When nature calls, New York can make your life excruciatingly difficult. The city-sponsored public bathroom offerings, including dodgy subway restrooms and the sporadic experimentation with self-cleaning super porta-potties, leave a lot to be desired. Your best bet, especially in an emergency, remains bathrooms in stores and other buildings that are open to the public.

The three most popular bathroom choices for needy New Yorkers (and visitors) are Barnes & Noble, Starbucks, and any kind of fast food chain. Barnes & Noble bathrooms are essentially open to everyone (as long as you're willing to walk past countless shelves of books during your navigation to the restrooms). They're usually clean enough, but sometimes you'll find yourself waiting in line during the evening and weekends. Although Starbucks bathrooms are more prevalent, they tend to be more closely guarded (in most places you have to ask for a key) and not as clean as you'd like. Fast food restrooms are similarly unhygienic, but easy to use inconspicuously without needing to purchase anything.

For a comprehensive listing of bathrooms in NYC (including hours and even ratings), try www.allny.com (look under "NYC Bathroom Guide") and the Bathroom Diaries at www.thebathroomdiaries.com/usa/new+york.

If you're busting to go and there's no Barnes & Noble, Starbucks, or fast food joint in sight, consider the following options:

- **Public buildings**—including train stations (Grand Central, Penn Station) and malls (South Street Seaport, World Financial Center, Manhattan Mall, The Shops at Columbus Circle).
- **Government buildings**—government offices, courthouses, police stations.
- **Department stores**—Macy's, Bloomingdale's, Saks, Kmart, etc.
- **Other stores**—Old Navy, Bed Bath & Beyond, FAO Schwartz, NBA store, The Strand, etc.
- **Supermarkets**—Pathmark, Food Emporium, D'Agostino, Gristedes, Key Food, etc. You'll probably have to ask, because the restrooms in supermarkets are usually way in the back amongst the employee lockers.

- **Bars**—a good choice at night when most other places are closed. Try to choose a busy one so as not to arouse suspicion. Most bars have those intimidating signs warning you that the restrooms are for customers only!
- **Museums**—most are closed at night, and most require an entry fee during the day. How desperate are you?
- **Colleges**—better if you're young enough to look like a student.
- **Parks**—great during the day, closed at night.
- **Hotels**—you might have to sneak past the desk though.
- **Times Square visitors centers**—1560 Broadway and 810 Seventh Avenue.
- **Places of worship**—unpredictable hours, and not all have public restrooms.
- **Subways**—how bad do you have to go? Your best bets are express stops on the IND lines, for example, 34th Street and 6th Avenue. Some stations have locked bathrooms, with keys available at the booths.
- **Gyms**—i.e. places where you have a membership.
- **Outdoor public bathrooms**—try these once in a while (if you can find one)—apparently the city signed on for 20 of them in 2004.

Websites

www.allny.com · The most detailed and varied site about anything you can imagine that relates to NY.
www.curbed.com · Keeps track of the daily developments in New York real estate.
www.downtowninfocenter.org · Current listing of Downtown events.
www.downtownny.com/gettingaround/?sid=19 · Information and map of the free Downtown Connection bus service between Battery Park City and the South Street Seaport with many stops in between.
www.fieldtrip.com/ny/index_ny.htm · Hundreds of suggestions for places to visit in the city.
www.forgotten-ny.com · Fascinating look at the relics of New York's past.
www.gothamist.com · Blog detailing various daily news and goings-on in the city.
www.lowermanhattan.info · An excellent resource for information about what's happening in Lower Manhattan.
www.menupages.com · Menus for almost every restaurant in Manhattan below 96th Street.
www.newyork.citysearch.com · Fairly comprehensive overview of businesses, landmarks, and attractions in the city, though too many paid listings and other ads get in the way.
www.newyork.craigslist.org · Classifieds for every area, including personals, apartments, musicians, jobs and more.
www.notfortourists.com/ny-home.aspx · The ultimate NYC website.
www.ny1.com · Local news about the city; weather.
www.nyc.gov · New York City government resources.
www.nycsubway.org · Complete history and overview of the subways.
www.nycvisit.com · The official NYC tourism site.

New York Timeline — a timeline of significant events in New York history (by no means complete)

1524: Giovanni de Verrazano enters the New York harbor.
1609: Henry Hudson explores what is now called the Hudson River.
1625: The Dutch purchase Manhattan and New Amsterdam is founded.
1647: Peter Stuyvesant becomes Director General of New Amsterdam.
1664: The British capture the colony and rename it New York.
1754: King's College/Columbia founded.
1776: British drive colonial army from New York and hold it for the duration of the war.
1776: Fire destroys a third of the city.
1788: Washington takes the Oath of Office as the first President of the United States.
1801: Alexander Hamilton founds the *New-York Evening Post*, still published today as the *New York Post*.
1811: The Commissioners Plan dictates a grid plan for the streets of New York.
1812: City Hall completed.
1825: Completion of the Erie Canal connects New York City commerce to the Great Lakes.
1835: New York Herald publishes its first edition.
1835: Great Fire destroys 300 buildings and kills 30 New Yorkers.
1854: First Tammany Hall-supported mayor Fernando Woods elected
1859: Central Park opens.
1863: The Draft Riots terrorize New York for three days.
1868: Prospect Park opens.
1871: Thomas Nast cartoons and *New York Times* exposes lead to the end of the Tweed Ring.
1880: The population of Manhattan reaches over 1 million.
1883: Brooklyn Bridge opens.
1886: The Statue of Liberty is dedicated, inspires first ticker tape parade.
1888: The Blizzard of '88 incapacitates the city for two weeks.
1892: Ellis Island opens; 16 million immigrants will pass through in the next 32 years.
1897: Steeplechase Park opens, first large amusement park in Coney Island.
1898: The City of Greater New York is founded when the five boroughs are merged.
1904: The subway opens.
1906: First New Year's celebration in Times Square.
1911: Triangle Shirtwaist Fire kills 146, impels work safety movement.
1920: A TNT-packed horse cart explodes on Wall Street, killing 30; the crime goes unsolved.
1923: The Yankees win their first World Championship.
1929: Stock market crashes, signaling the beginning of the Great Depression.
1929: The Chrysler Building is completed.
1930: The Empire State Building is built, the tallest in the world.
1927: The Holland Tunnel opens, making it the world's longest underwater tunnel.
1931: The George Washington Bridge is completed.
1933: Fiorello LaGuardia elected mayor.
1934: Robert Moses becomes Parks Commissioner.
1939: The city's first airport, LaGuardia, opens.
1950: United Nations opens.
1955: Dodgers win the World Series; they move to LA two years later.
1964: The Verrazano-Narrows Bridge is built, at the time the world's longest suspension bridge.
1965: Malcolm X assassinated in the Audubon Ballroom.
1965: Pennsylvania Station is demolished to the dismay of many; preservation efforts gain steam.
1965: Blackout strands hundreds of thousands during rush hour.
1969: The Stonewall Rebellion marks beginning of the gay rights movement.
1969: The Miracle Mets win the World Series.
1970: Knicks win their first championship.
1970: First New York City Marathon takes place.
1971: World Trade Center opens.
1975: Ford to City: Drop Dead.
1977: Thousands arrested for various mischief during a city-wide blackout.
1977: Ed Koch elected mayor to the first of three terms.
1987: Black Monday—stock market plunges.
1993: Giuliani elected mayor.
1993: A bomb explodes in the parking garage of the World Trade Center, killing 5.
1994: Rangers win the Stanley Cup after a 40-year drought.
2000: NFT publishes its first edition.
2000: Yankees win their 26th World Championship.
2001: The World Trade Center is destroyed in a terrorist attack; New Yorkers vow to rebuild.
2003: Tokens are no longer accepted in subway turnstiles.
2004: Yankees lose the LCS to the Boston Red Sox. We don't want to talk about it.
2005: Bloomberg sees his West Side Stadium proposal quashed.
2006: Ground is broken on the WTC memorial.

Essential New York Songs

"Sidewalks of New York" — Various, written by James Blake and Charles Lawlor, 1894

"Give My Regards to Broadway" — Various, written by George Cohan, 1904

"I'll Take Manhattan" — Various, written by Rodgers and Hart, 1925

"Puttin' on the Ritz" — Various, written by Irving Berlin, 1929

"42nd Street" — Various, written by Al Dubin and Harry Warren, 1932

"Take the A Train" — Duke Ellington, 1940

"Autumn in New York" — Frank Sinatra, 1947

"Spanish Harlem" — Ben E. King, 1961

"Car 54 Where Are You?" — Nat Hiken and John Strauss, 1961

"On Broadway" — Various, written by Weil/Mann/Leiber/Stoller, 1962

"Talkin' New York" — Bob Dylan, 1962

"Up on the Roof" — The Drifters, 1963

"59th Street Bridge Song" — Simon and Garfunkel, 1966

"I'm Waiting for My Man" — Velvet Underground, 1967

"Brooklyn Roads" — Neil Diamond, 1968

"Crosstown Traffic" — Jimi Hendrix, 1969

"Personality Crisis" — The New York Dolls, 1973

"New York State of Mind" — Billy Joel, 1976

"53rd and 3rd" — The Ramones, 1977

"Shattered" — Rolling Stones, 1978

"New York, New York" — Frank Sinatra, 1979

"Life During Wartime" — Talking Heads, 1979

"New York New York" — Grandmaster Flash and the Furious 5, 1984

"No Sleep Til Brooklyn" — Beastie Boys, 1987

"Christmas in Hollis" — Run-D.M.C., 1987

"New York" — U2, 2000

"I've Got New York" — The 6th's, 2000

"New York, New York" — Ryan Adams, 2001

"New York" — Ja Rule f. Fat Joe, Jadakiss, 2004

Essential New York Movies

The Crowd (1928)
42nd Street (1933)
King Kong (1933)
Miracle on 34th Street (1947)
On the Town (1949)
On the Waterfront (1954)
The Blackboard Jungle (1955)
An Affair to Remember (1957)
The Apartment (1960)
Breakfast at Tiffany's (1961)
West Side Story (1961)
Barefoot in the Park (1967)
Midnight Cowboy (1969)

French Connection (1970)
Shaft (1971)
Mean Streets (1973)
Godfather II (1974)
The Taking of Pelham One Two Three (1974)
Dog Day Afternoon (1975)
Taxi Driver (1976)
Saturday Night Fever (1977)
Superman (1978)
Manhattan (1979)
The Warriors (1979)
Fame (1980)

Escape From New York (1981)
Nighthawks (1981)
Ghostbusters (1984)
The Muppets Take Manhattan (1984)
Wall Street (1987)
Moonstruck (1987)
Working Girl (1988)
Do the Right Thing (1989)
When Harry Met Sally (1989)
A Bronx Tale (1993)
Men in Black (1997)
Gangs of New York (2002)
Spider-Man (2002)

Essential New York Books

A Tree Grows in Brooklyn, by Betty Smith	Coming of age story set in the slums of Brooklyn.
The Bonfire of the Vanities, by Tom Wolfe	The story of a Wall Street tycoon, set in New York in the 1980's.
Bright Lights, Big City, by Jay McInerney	1980s yuppie and the temptations of the city.
Catcher in the Rye, by J.D. Salinger	Classic portrayal of teenage angst.
The Cricket in Times Square, by George Selden	Classic children's book.
The Death and Life of Great American Cities, by Jane Jacobs	Influential exposition on what matters in making cities work.
The Encyclopedia of New York City, . by Kenneth T. Jackson, ed	Huge and definitive reference work.
Gotham: A history of New York City to 1898, by Edwin G. Burrows and Mike Wallace	Authorative history of New York.
Here is New York, by E.B. White	Reflections on the city.
House of Mirth, by Edith Wharton	Climbing the social ladder in upper crust, late 19th-century NY.
Knickerbocker's History of New York, by Washington Irving	Very early (1809) whimsical "history" of NY.
Manchild in the Promised Land by Claude Brown	*Autobiographical tale of growing up in Harlem.*
The Power Broker, by Robert Caro	Biography of Robert Moses, you'll never look at the city the same way after reading it.
Washington Square, by Henry James	Love and marriage in upper-middle-class 1880s NY.

The Best of the Best

With all the culture the city has to offer, finding activities to amuse children is easy enough. From fencing classes to the funnest parks, our guide will provide you with great ideas for entertaining your little ones.

★ **Neatest Time-Honored Tradition:** The Central Park Carousel (830 Fifth Ave, 212-879-0244) features the largest hand-carved figures ever constructed and has been in residence in the park since 1950. $1 will buy you a memory to last forever. Open 10 am to 6 pm on weekdays and 10 am to 7 pm weekends, weather permitting.

★ **Coolest Rainy Day Activity:** Our Name is Mud (59 Greenwich Ave, 212-647-7899) is a paint-your-own pottery studio, with four locations throughout the city. Pick out what you want to paint, and the studio will provide paint, stencils, and all the other equipment to produce a masterpiece. A great activity for creative kids and a fantastic destination for birthday parties.

★ **Sweetest Place to Get a Cavity:** Dylan's Candy Bar (1011 Third Ave, 646-735-0078) is a two-story candy land, chock full of every confectionary delight you can think of, plus a tasty ice cream bar. A great place for birthday parties, they'll provide enough candy-related activities to keep kids on a permanent sugar high. Watch out, Willy Wonka. Open Sun-Thurs: 10 am–9 pm, Fri-Sat: 10 am–6 pm.

★ **Best Spots for Sledding:** Central Park's Pilgrim Hill and Cedar Hill. Snow pray for a snow day for the chance to try out this slick slope. BYO sled or toboggan.

★ **Funnest Park:** Hudson River Park Playground (Pier 51, Gansevoort St) With a beautiful view of the Hudson River, the park features several sprinklers, a winding "canal" and a boat-themed area complete with prow, mast, and captain's wheel.

★ **No Tears Hair Cuts:** Whipper Snippers (106 Reade St, 212-227-2600) is a children's salon that calms the most fearful of scissor-phobes. An on-site toy store helps to distract timid tots and promises a prize for the well-behaved. The salon also offers birthday parties.

★ **Best Halloween Costume Shopping:** Halloween Adventure (104 Fourth Ave, 212-673-4546) is the city's costume emporium that has every disguise you can possibly imagine, along with wigs, make-up supplies, and magic tricks to complete any child's dress-up fantasy. Open year round.

★ **Best Place for Sunday Brunch:** Church Lounge (2 Avenue of the Americas, 212-519-6600) in the Tribeca Grand Hotel is spacious enough to accommodate a Bugaboo onslaught, and the colossal buffet will tempt even the pickiest eaters. The best part: They screen kid flicks in theaters downstairs.

Rainy Day Activities

When splashing in puddles has lost its novelty and ruined far too many of their designer duds:

• **American Museum of Natural History** (Central Park West and 79th St, 212- 769-5100) Fantastic for kids of all ages, with something to suit every child's interest. From the larger-than-life dinosaur fossils and the realistic animal dioramas to the out-of-this-world Hayden Planetarium, all attention will be rapt. The hands-on exhibits of the Discovery Room and the IMAX theatre are also worth a visit. Open 10 am–5:45 pm daily.

• **Bowlmor Lanes** (110 University Pl, 212-255-8188) Great bowling alley with a retro décor that kids will love. Bumpers are available to cut down on those pesky gutter balls. Children are welcome any day before 5 pm and all day Sunday—a popular birthday spot.

• **Brooklyn Children's Museum** (145 Brooklyn Ave, 718-735-4400) The world's first museum for children (opened in 1899) engages kids in educational hands-on activities and exhibits. Kids can learn about life in New York in the *Together in the City* exhibit and find out why snakes are so slimy in the *Animal Outpost*.

• **Children's Museum of the Arts** (182 Lafayette St, 212-941-9198) Through special exhibitions, workshops, and activities, as well as after school art classes in music, ceramics, painting, and mixed media, the museum provides a creative outlet for children, aged 1–12. The museum is open Wed-Sun, 12 pm–5 pm, Thurs, 12 pm–6 pm.

• **Children's Museum of Manhattan** (212 W 83rd St, 212-721-1234) As soon as you arrive at the museum, sign up for some of the day's activities. While you're waiting, check out the other exhibits in the museum. There's the Word Play area designed for the younger children in your group and the Time/Warner Media Center for the older set, where kids can produce their own television shows. The museum is open Wed–Fri, 10 pm–5 pm and Sat-Sun 9 am–5 pm.

• **Intrepid Sea Air Space Museum** (Pier 86, 46th St and 12th Ave, 212-245-0072) Tour the *Growler*, a real submarine that was once a top-secret missile command center, or take a virtual trip on one of the simulator rides. After you've taken a look at the authentic aircrafts on deck, visit the museum of the *Intrepid* for an extensive model airplane collection and a Cockpit Challenge flight video game for those aspiring pilots. The museum is open Mon–Fri, 10 am–5pm, and Sat-Sun, 10 am–6 pm.

• **Lower East Side Tenement Museum** (108 Orchard St, 212-431-0233) The museum offers insight into immigrant life in the late 19th and early 20th centuries by taking groups on tours of an historic tenement building on the Lower East Side. One tour called *Visit the Confino Family* is led by "Victoria Confino" a young girl dressed in authentic costume who teaches children about the lives of immigrants in the early 1900s. A great place to take your kids if they haven't already been there on a school field trip.

• **The Metropolitan Museum of Art** (1000 Fifth Ave, 212-535-7710) A great museum to explore with audio guides designed specifically for children. From the armor exhibits to the Egyptian Wing, the museum offers art exhibits from all historical periods.

• **Noguchi Museum** (9-01 33rd Road (at Vernon Boulevard), Long Island City, 718-204-7088) This newly renovated museum that features the works of Japanese American artist Isamu Noguchi offers interesting tours and hands-on workshops for toddlers to teens. The fees are nominal, but you must register beforehand.

• **The Museum of Modern Art** (11 W 53rd St, 212-708-9400) Besides the kid-friendly audio guides that make this renowned museum enjoyable for tykes, the MoMA has a lot of exciting weekend family programs that get kids talking about art and film. Lots of fun hands-on programs too. Registration is a must—these programs book up fast.

• **Sydney's Playground** (66 White St, 212-431-9125) A 6,000 square foot indoor playground featuring a bouncy house, climbing play town, and a book nook. There's also a Womb Room, a quiet, dimly lit space with a view of the play area for moms who need to quiet baby while big brother plays.

Shopping Essentials

Kid's designer couture sounds like a recipe for disaster, with threats of grass stains, paint stains, and dirt lurking around every corner. But it exists and thrives in New York City, nonetheless (eg. Julian & Sara). buybuyBaby has nursing rooms which are very helpful. Here's a list of shops for the best party clothes and party gifts and everything in between:

- **American Girl Place** · 609 Fifth Ave · 877-AGPLACE · dolls
- **Bambini** · 1088 Madison Ave · 212-717-6742 · European clothing
- **A Bear's Place** · 789 Lexington Ave · 212-826-6465 · furniture & toys
- **Bellini** · 1305 Second Ave · 212-517-9233 · furniture
- **Bombalulus** · 101 W 10th St · 212-463-0897 · unique clothing & toys
- **Bonpoint** · pricey clothing
  - 1269 Madison Ave · 212-722-7720
  - 811 68th St · 212-879-0900
- **Books of Wonder** · 18 W 18th St · 212-989-3270 · books
- **Boomerang Toys** · 173 West Broadway · 212-226-7650 · infant toys
- **Bu and the Duck** · 106 Franklin St · 212-431-9226 · vintage-inspired clothing/toys
- **buybuyBABY** · 270 Seventh Ave · 917-344-1555 · furniture/clothing/toys
- **Calypso Enfant & Bebe** · 426 Broome St · 212-966-3234 · hand-made clothing
- **Catimini** · 1284 Madison Ave · 212-987-0688 · French clothing
- **The Children's General Store** · Central Passage Grand Central Terminal · 212-682-0004 · toys
- **The Children's Place** · chain clothing store
  - 1460 Broadway · 212-398-4416
  - 901 Sixth Ave · 212-268-7696
  - 173 E 86th St · 212-831-5100
  - 22 W 34th St · 212-904-1190
  - 2187 Broadway · 917-441-9807
  - 36 Union Sq E · 212-529-2201
  - 600 W 181 St · 212-923-7244
  - 1164 Third Ave · 212-717-7187
  - 248 W 125th St · 212-866-9616
  - 650 Sixth Ave · 917-305-1348
  - 163 E 125th St · 212-348-3607
  - 142 Delancey St · 212-979-5071
- **Dinosaur Hill** · 306 E 9th St · 212-473-5850 · toys & clothes
- **Disney Store** · 711 Fifth Ave · 212-702-0702 · Disney merchandise
- **Discovery Channel Store** · Grand Central Station · 212-808-9144 · educational toys
- **East Side Kids** · 1298 Madison Ave · 212-360-5000 · shoes
- **EAT Gifts** · 1062 Madison Ave · 212-861-2544 · toys & trinkets
- **Estella** · 493 Sixth Ave · 212-255-3553 · boutique clothing
- **FAO Schwarz** · 767 Fifth Ave · 212-644-9400 · toy land
- **Funky Fresh Children's Boutique** · 9 Clinton St · 212-254-5584 · unique clothing

- **GapKids/baby Gap** · chain clothing store
  - 1 Astor Pl · 212-253-0145
  - 11 Fulton St · 212-374-1051
  - 1535 Third Ave · 212-423-0033
  - 750 Broadway · 212-674-1877
  - 2300 Broadway · 212-873-2044
  - 335 Columbus Ave · 212-875-9196
  - 734 Lexington Ave · 212-327-2614
  - 225 Liberty St · 212-945-4090
  - 1988 Broadway · 212-721-5304
  - 122 Fifth Ave · 917-408-5580
  - 250 W 57th St · 212-315-2250
  - 545 Madison Ave · 212-980-2570
  - 657 Third Ave · 212-697-3590
  - 680 Fifth Ave · 212-977-7023
  - 60 W 34th St · 212-760-1268
  - 1212 Sixth Ave · 212-730-1087
  - 1466 Broadway · 212-382-4500
- **Geppetto's Toy Box** · 10 Christopher St · 212 620-7511 · toys
- **Granny-Made** · 381 Amsterdam Ave · 212-496-1222 · hand-made sweaters
- **Greenstone's** · hats & clothing
  - 442 Columbus Ave · 212-580-4322
  - 1184 Madison Ave · 212-427-1665
- **Gymboree** · chain clothing store
  - 1049 Third Ave · 212- 688-4044
  - 2015 Broadway · 212- 595-7662
  - 1332 Third Ave · 212-517-5548
  - 2271 Broadway · 212- 595-9071
  - 1120 Madison Ave · 212-717-6702
- **Halloween Adventure** · 104 Fourth Ave · 212-673-4546 · costumes & magic tricks
- **Jacadi** · expensive French clothing
  - 1296 Madison Ave · 212-369-1616
  - 787 Madison Ave · 212-535-3200
  - 1260 Third Ave · 212-717-9292
- **Jay Kos** · boys' clothing
  - 986 Lexington Ave · 212-327-2382
  - 475 Park Ave · 212-319-2770
- **Julian & Sara** · 103 Mercer St · 212-226-1989 · European clothing
- **Just for Tykes** · 83 Mercer St · 212-274-9121 · clothing & furniture
- **KB Toys** · chain toy store
  - 901 Sixth Ave · 212-629-5386·
- **Karin Alexis** · 490 Amsterdam Ave · 212-769-9550 · clothing & toys
- **Kidding Around** · 60 W 15th St · 212-645-6337 · toy store
- **Kidrobot** · 126 Prince St · 212-966-6688 · toy store
- **Leeper Kids** · Grand Central Station, Lexington Terminal · 212-499-9111 · pricey clothing & toys
- **Lester's** · clothing · 1522 Second Ave · 212-734-9292
- **Lilliput** · pricey clothing
  - 240 Lafayette St · 212-965-9201
  - 265 Lafayette St · 212-965-9567

- **Little Eric** · 1118 Madison Ave · 212-717-1513 · shoes
- **Lucky Wang** · clothing
  - 82 7th Ave · 212-229-2900
  - 799 Broadway · 212-353-2850
- **Magic Windows** · 1186 Madison Ave · 212-289-0181 · clothing
- **Manhattan Dollhouse Shop** · 428 Second Ave · 212-725-4520 · dolls
- **Mary Arnold Toys** · 1010 Lexington Ave · 212-744-8510 · toys
- **Oilily** · 820 Madison Ave · 212-772-8686 · unique clothing
- **Oshkosh B'Gosh** · 586 Fifth Ave · 212-827-0098 · play clothes
- **Peanut Butter and Jane** · 617 Hudson St · 212-620-7952 · clothing & toys
- **Penny Whistle Toys** · toys & trinkets
  - 448 Columbus Ave · 212-873-9090
  - 1283 Madison Ave · 212-369-3868
- **Pipsqueak** · 248 Mott St · 212-226-8824 · clothing
- **Planet Kids** · infant gear
  - 247 E 86th St · 212-426-2040
  - 2688 Broadway · 212-864-8705
- **Pokemon Center** · 10 Rockefeller Plz · 212-307-0900 · Pokemon
- **Promises Fulfilled** · 1592 Second Ave · 212-472-1600 · toys & accessories
- **ShooFly** · 42 Hudson St · 212-406-3270 · shoes & accessories
- **Space Kiddets** · 46 E 21st St · 212-420-9878 · girls' clothing
- **Spring Flowers** · shoes & clothes
  - 538 Madison Ave · 212-207-4606
  - 905 Madison Ave · 212-717-8182
  - 1050 Third Ave · 212-758-2669
- **Talbot's Kids and Babies** · clothing
  - 527 Madison Ave · 212-758-4152
  - 1523 Second Ave · 212-570-1630
- **Tannen's Magical Development Co** · 45 W 34st,Ste 608 · 212-929-4500 · magic shop
- **The Scholastic Store** · 557 Broadway · 212-343-6166 · books & toys
- **Tigers, Tutu's and Toes** · fun clothing & shoes
  - 128 Second Ave · 212-228-7990
  - 56 University Pl · 212-375-9985
- **Tiny Doll House** · 1179 Lexington Ave · 212-744-3719 · dolls
- **Toys R Us** · toy superstore
  - 1514 Broadway · 800-869-7787
- **West Side Kids** · 498 Amsterdam Ave · 212-496-7282 · toys
- **Yoya** · 636 Hudson St · 646-336-6844 · clothing
- **Z'baby** · clothing
  - 100 W 72nd St · 212-579-BABY
  - 996 Lexington Ave · 212-472-BABY
- **Zitomar** · 969 Madison Ave, 3rd Fl · 212-737-2040 · toys & books

Outdoor *and* Educational

They can't learn *everything* from the Discovery Channel.

• **Central Park Zoo** • 830 Fifth Ave, 212-439-6500 • Houses more than 1,400 animals, including some endangered species. Take a walk through the arctic habitat of the polar bears and penguins to the steamy tropical Rain Forest Pavilion. The Tisch Children's Zoo nearby is more suited for the younger crowd with its smaller, cuddlier animals.

• **Fort Washington Park** • W 155 St to Dyckman, at the Hudson River • 301-763-4600 • Call the Urban Park Rangers to arrange a tour of the little red lighthouse located at the base of the George Washington Bridge. The lighthouse affords some spectacular views—better than anything they'd see from atop Dad's shoulders. The park offers a "Junior Ranger Program" for kids, as well as a playground in Picnic Area "B."

• **Historic Richmond Town** • 441 Clarke Ave, Staten Island • 718-351-1611 • A 100-acre complex with over 40 points of interest and a museum that covers over three centuries of the history of Staten Island. People dressed in authentic period garb lead demonstrations and tours.

• **New York Botanical Garden** • 200th St and Kazimiroff Blvd, Bronx • 718-817-8777 • 250 acres and 50 different indoor and outdoor gardens and plant exhibits to explore. The Children's Adventure Garden changes each season, and kids can get down and dirty in the Family Garden. Keen young botanists can join the Children's Gardening Program and get their own plot to care for.

Classes

With all of their after school classes and camps, the children of New York City are some of the most well-rounded (and programmed) in the country. Help them beef up their college applications with some fancy extracurriculars. It's never too early…

• **92nd Street Y After-School Programs** • 1395 Lexington Ave, 212-415-5500 • The center provides children of all ages with tons of activities, ranging from music lessons and chess to flamenco and yoga. 92nd St is known as "the Y to beat all Ys."

• **Abrons Arts Center/Henry Street Settlement** • 466 Grand St, 212-598-0400 • The Arts Center offers classes and workshops for children of all ages in music, dance, theater, and visual arts.

• **Archikids** • 44 E 32 St, 718-768-6123 • After-school classes and summer camp for children five and up that teach kids about architecture through hands-on building projects.

• **The Art Farm** • 419 E 91st St, 631-537-1634 • "Mommy & Me" art and music classes, baking courses, and small animal care for the very young.

• **Asphalt Green** • 1750 York Ave, 212-369-8890 • Swimming and diving lessons, gymnastics, teams sports and art classes. They've got it all for kids one and up.

• **Baby Moves** • 139 Perry St, 212-255-1685 • A developmental play space that offers classes for infants to six year-olds in movement, music, and play.

• **Children and Art** • 747 Amsterdam Ave, 917-841-9651 • After-school art lessons for children five and up that focus on art history and developing the skills to create masterpieces.

• **The Children's Studio** • 307 E 84th St, 212-737-3344 • The Studio offers hands-on courses in art, science, and yoga, with an emphasis on process and discovery.

• **Church Street School for Music and Art** • 74 Warren St, 212-571-7290 • This community arts center offers a variety of classes in music and art involving several different media, along with private lessons and courses for parents and children.

• **Claremont Riding Academy** • 175 W 89th St, 212-724-5100 • Horseback riding lessons offered by the oldest continuously operating stable in the United States.

• **Dieu Donné Papermill** • 433 Broome St, 212-226-0573 • Workshops in hand papermaking offered for children ages seven and up.

• **Greenwich House Music School** • 27 Barrow St, 212-242-4140 • Group classes and private lessons in music and ballet for children of all ages.

• **Greenwich Village Center** • 219 Sullivan St, 212-254-3074 • Run by the Children's Aid Society, the center provides arts and after-school classes ranging from gymnastics to origami, as well as an early childhood program and nursery school.

• **Hamilton Fish Recreation Center** • 128 Pitt St, 212-387-7687 • The center offers free swimming lessons in two outdoor pools along with free after-school programs with classes like astronomy and photography.

• **Hi Art!** • 601 W 26th St, Studio 1425I, 212-362-8190 • For children ages 2-12, the classes focus on the exploration of art in museums and galleries in the city and giving kids the freedom to develop what they've seen into new concepts in a spacious studio setting.

• **Institute of Culinary Education** • 50 W 23rd St, 212-847-0700 • Hands-on cooking classes.

• **Irish Arts Center** • 553 W 51st St, 212-757-3318 • Introductory Irish step dancing classes for children five and up.

• **Jewish Community Center** • 334 Amsterdam Ave, 646-505-4444 • The center offers swimming lessons, team sports, and courses in arts and cooking. There's even a rooftop playground.

• **Kids at Art** • 1349 Lexington Ave, 212-410-9780 • Art program that focuses on the basics in a non-competitive environment for kids ages 2-11.

• **Marshall Chess Club** • 23 W 10th St, 212-477-3716 • Membership to the club offers access to weekend chess classes, summer camp, and tournaments for children ages five and up.

• **Metropolis Fencing** • 45 W 19st St, 212-463-8044 • Fencing classes offered for children ages seven and up.

• **Tannen's Magical Development Co** • 24 W 25th St, 2nd Fl, 212-929-4500 • Private magic lessons for children eight and up on weekday evenings or group lessons of three to four teens on Monday nights. Their week-long summer sleep-away camp is also very popular.

• **The Mixing Bowl** • 243 E 82nd St, 212-585-2433 • Cooking classes for the aspiring young chef, ages two and up.

• **The Techno Team** • 160 Columbus Ave, 212-501-1425 • Computer technology classes for children ages 3-12.

• **Trapeze School** • West St, south of Canal, 917-797-1872 • Kids ages six and up can learn how to fly through the air with the greatest of ease.

Babysitting/Nanny Services

Baby Sitter's Guild • 60 E 42nd St, 212-682-0227
Barnard College of Babysitting Services • 11 Milbank Hall, 212-854-2035
My Child's Best Friend • 239 E 73rd St, 212-396-4090
New York City Explorers • 212-591-2619

Where to go for more info

www.gocitykids.com

Whether you are devout, trying to do the right thing, or simply seeking, there may be a time when you need to find a place of worship in the city. Perhaps it's a need to feel connected on Christmas or the fact that you never set foot in synagogue after your bar mitzvah, but let's face it-even the most jaded New Yorker sometimes needs a little sympathy in the city.

The faiths practiced in New York are as diverse as the people who live here. Jews, Buddhists, Muslims, even (gasp!) Evangelical Christians all seek the answer to the timeless question "Is this all there is?" For people on a spiritual quest, there are plenty of options. Even if the notion of organized religion makes you cringe, there are numerous opportunities to find a community that suits you, and many places of worship are worth visiting for their significant historical, cultural, or architectural appeal. Some notable places of worship:

Abyssinian Baptist Church—famous politically active Harlem church. Previous pastors include Adam Clayton Powell Sr. and Jr. [Map 22]

African Methodist Episcopal—first African-American church in the city, played a crucial role in the Underground Railroad. [Map 21]

Brooklyn Tabernacle—home of the famous Brooklyn Tabernacle Choir. [Map 30]

Cathedral of St. John the Divine—largest Gothic cathedral in the world. [Map 18]

Mosque no. 7/Masjid Malcolm Shabazz—Malcolm X served as imam here from 1954-1965. [Map 19]

Riverside Church—boasts the world's largest carillon bell tower. [Map 18]

St. Patrick's Cathedral—largest Roman Catholic cathedral in the US. [Map 12]

St. Paul's Chapel—NY's only church built before the Revolution; relief center during 9/11 aftermath. [Map 1]

Temple Emanu-El—largest Jewish house of worship in the world. [Map 15]

Trinity Church—downtown landmark since 1698; current building dates to 1846. [Map 1]

The Watchtower—international headquarters of the Jehovah's Witnesses. [Map 30]

Denomination Key:

B=Baptist	Mo=Morman
Bu=Buddhist	Mu=Muslim
C=Catholic	ND=Non-denominational
E=Episcopal	O=Orthodox
J=Jewish	OP=Other Protestant
L=Lutheran	P=Presbyterian
M=Methodist	Pe=Pentacostal

Map 1 · Financial District

C	Our Lady of Victory Church	60 William St
C	St Elizabeth Ann Seton Shrine	7 State St
M	St John's United Methodist Church	44 John St
C	St Joseph's Chapel	385 South End Ave
E	St Paul's Church	209 Broadway
E	Trinity Church	Broadway & Wall St
Bu	True Buddha Diamond Temple	105 Washington St

Map 3 · City Hall / Chinatown

B	Chinese Conservative Baptist	103 Madison St
M	Chinese United Methodist Church	69 Madison St
	Church of Jesus Christ of Latter Day Saints	401 Broadway
E	Church Our Saviour	48 Henry St
J	Civic Center Synagogue (Orthodox)	49 White St
Bu	Eastern States Buddhist Temple	64 Mott St
Bu	Faith Vow Ded Buddhist Association	130 Lafayette St # 2
P	First Chinese Presbyterian Church	61 Henry St
Bu	Mahayana Temple Buddhist Association	133 Canal St
C	Mariners' Temple Baptist Church	3 Henry St
C	Most Precious Blood Church	113 Baxter St
C	Seamens Church	241 Water St
Bu	Society of Buddhist Studies	214 Centre St
C	St Andrew's Roman Catholic Church	20 Cardinal Hayes Pl
O	St Barbara Greek Orthodox Church	27 Forsyth St
C	St Joseph's Church	5 Monroe St
C	Transfiguration Catholic Church	29 Mott St
Bu	Transworld Buddhist Association	7 East Broadway
L	True Light Lutheran Church	195 Worth St

Map 4 · Lower East Side

J	Mesivtha Tiferath Jerusalem (Orthodox)	145 East Broadway
Pe	Primitive Christian Church	207 East Broadway
E	St Augustine's Episcopal Church	333 Madison St
C	St Mary's Church	440 Grand St
C	St Teresa's Church	141 Henry St
J	Young Israel Synagogue	225 East Broadway

Map 5 · West Village

J	A Greenwich Village Synagogue	53 Charles St
B	Legree Baptist Church	362 W 125th St
OP	Manhattan Seventh Day Adventist Church	232 W 11th St
M	Metropolitan-Duane United Church	201 W 13th St
C	Our Lady of Guadalupe Catholic Church	328 W 14th St
C	Our Lady of Pompeii Church	25 Carmine St
E	St John's in the Village	224 Waverly Pl
L	St John's Lutheran Church	81 Christopher St
E	St Luke in the Fields Church	487 Hudson St
N	Village Church	232 W 11th St

Map 6 · Washington Square / NYU / NoHo / SoHo

N Abounding Grace	9 E 7th St
Baha'i Faith	53 E 11th St
OP Christian Science Church 10th	171 MacDougal St
M Church of All Nations	48 St Marks Pl
E Church of the Ascension	Fifth Ave & 10th St
J Conservative Synagogue-5th Ave	11 E 11th St
Dianetics Hubbard	4 W 43rd St
E First Presbyterian Church	12 W 12th St
E Grace Church	802 Broadway
Judson Memorial Church	55 Washington Sq
OP Middle Church (Dutch Reformed)	50 E 7th St
C Nativity Church	44 Second Ave
OP NY Chinese Alliance Church	162 Eldridge St
C Old St Patrick's Cathedral	263 Mulberry St
C Our Lady-Loreto	18 Bleecker St
O Russian Orthodox Cathedral of the Holy Virgin Protection	59 E 2nd St
St Cyril's Church	62 St Marks Pl
C St George's Ukrainian Catholic	30 E 7th St
M Washington Square United Methodist	135 W 4th St

Map 7 · East Village / Lower East Side

OP Church of Christ	257 E 10th St
C Church of Mary Help-Christians	440 E 12th St
Pe Citylight Church	121 E 7th St
J Congregation Meseritz Synagogue (Orthodox)	451 E 6th St
OP De Witt Reformed Church	280 Rivington St
N East Side Tabernacle	6163 Rivington St
N Father's Heart Church	545 E 11th St
B Greater New Hope Missionary Baptist Church of Christ	507 E 11th St
C Immaculate Conception Church	414 E 14th St
Islamic Council of America	401 E 11th St
C Most Holy Redeemer Church	173 E 3rd St
C St Emeric's Church	740 E 13th St
C St Stanislaus B & M Church	101 E 7th St
J Trinity Lower East Side Lutheran	602 E 9th St

Map 8 · Chelsea

N Chelsea Community Church	346 W 20th St
J Congregation Beth Israel (Modern Orthodox)	347 W 34th St
E Holy Apostles Episcopal Church	296 Ninth Ave
N Metropolitan Community Church	446 W 36th St
C St Columba Church	343 W 25th St
C St Michael's Catholic Church	424 W 34th St
E St Peter's Episcopal Church	346 W 20th St

Map 9 · Flatiron / Lower Midtown

N Aquarian Foundation	139 W 35th St
C Church of Holy Innocents	128 W 37th St
C Church of St Francis	135 W 31st St
E Church of the Incarnation	209 Madison Ave
OP Community Church of New York (Unitarian)	40 E 35th St
J Congregation Emunath Israel (Orthodox)	236 W 23rd St
OP French Evangelical Church	126 W 16th St
J Japanese American United Church	255 Seventh Ave
B Madison Avenue Baptist Church	129 Madison Ave
J Metropolitan Synagogue of NY (Reformed)	40 E 35th St
Bu Shambhala Meditation Center of NY (Tibetan)	118 W 22nd St #6
C St Francis Xavier Church	30 W 16th St
C St Vincent de Paul Church	116 W 24th St
J United Synagogue of America	155 Fifth Ave

(Conservative)	
OP Unity Church of New York	230 W 29th St
J Young Israel of 5th Avenue (Orthodox)	3 W 16th St

Map 10 · Murray Hill / Gramercy

OP Armenian Evangelical Church	152 E 34th St
L Christ Lutheran Church (Evangelical)	355 E 19th St
C Church of Our Saviour	59 Park Ave
O Diocese of the Armenian Church	630 Second Ave
E East End Temple (Reformed)	245 E 17th St
OP First Moravian Church	154 Lexington Ave
O Greek Orthodox Church of St John the Baptist	143 E 17th St
L Lutheran Church of Gustavus	155 E 22nd St
OP Manhattan Mennonite Fellowship	15th St & Second Ave
C Our Lady of the Scapular & St Stephen's Church	149 E 29th St
P Remnant Presbyterian Church	206 E 29th St
C Sacred Hearts Church	307 E 33rd St
J Society of Jewish Science	109 E 39th St
E St Ann's Church for the Deaf	209 E 16th St
O St Illuminators Cathedral (Armenian)	221 E 27th St

Map 11 · Hell's Kitchen

C Church of the Sacred Heart of Jesus	457 W 51st St
J Congregation Ezrath Israel (Conservative)	339 W 47th St
OP Crossroads Seventh Day Church	410 W 45th St
P First Prebyterian Church	424 W 51st St
B Metro Baptist Church	410 W 40th St
N Rauschenbusch Memorial United Church in Christ	422 W 57th St
E St Clement's Episcopal Church	423 W 46th St
C St Paul the Apostle Church	415 W 59th St
P Trinity Presbyterian Church	422 W 57th St

Map 12 · Midtown

J Chabad Lubavitch of Midtown (Orthodox)	509 Fifth Ave
OP Christian Science Church	9 E 43rd St
P Fifth Avenue Presbyterian Church	7 W 55th St
OP Fifth Church of Christ Scientist	5 E 43rd St
OP First Church of Religious Science (Metaphysical)	14 E 48th St
B First Corinthian Baptist Church	1912 Seventh Ave
J Garment Congregation (Modern Orthodox)	205 W 40th St
N Harvest Christian Fellowship	130 W 56th St
OP Lamb's Church of the Nazarene	130 W 44th St
M Salem United Methodist Church	2190 Seventh Ave
B Shiloh Baptist Church	2226 Seventh Ave
O St George Greek Orthodox Church	307 W 54th St
L St Luke's Lutheran Church	308 W 46th St
E St Mary the Virgin Church	145 W 46th St
C St Patrick's Cathedral	460 Fifth Ave
E St Thomas Church Fifth Ave	1 W 53rd St
L Swedish Seamens Church	5 E 48th St

Map 13 · East Midtown

J Central Synagogue	123 E 55th St
C Church of St Agnes	143 E 43rd St
J Conservative Synagogue (Conservative)	308 E 55th St
J Holy Family Church	315 E 47th St
OP Sacred Center for Spiritual Living (New Thought Church)	111 E 59th St
C St John Evangelist Church	348 E 55th St
L St Peter's Lutheran Church	619 Lexington Ave

Map 14 • Upper West Side (Lower)

E	All Angels Church	251 W 80th St
C	Blessed Sacrament Church	152 W 71st St
OP	Christian Science Church	10 W 68th St
N	Church of Humanism & Humanist	250 W 85th St
E	Church-St Matthew & St Timothy	26 W 84th St
OP	Collegiate Reformed Church	368 West End Ave
J	Congregation Habonim (Conservative)	44 W 66th St
J	Congregation Rodeph Sholom (Reformed)	7 W 83rd St
J	Congregation Shearith Israel (Sephardic Orthodox)	8 W 70th St
B	First Baptist Church	265 W 79th St
P	Good Shepherd-Faith Church	152 W 66th St
L	Holy Trinity Lutheran Church	3 W 65th St
C	Holy Trinity Roman Catholic	213 W 82nd St
Bu	Karma Thegwum Choling	412 West End Ave
J	Lincoln Square Synagogue (Modern Orthodox)	200 Amsterdam Ave
L	Lutheran Church of the Holy Trinity	65 Central Park W
P	Rutgers Church	236 W 73rd St
E	St Matthew & St Timothy Church	26 W 84th St
N	Vision Church	2 W 64th St
J	West End Synagogue (Reconstructionist)	190 Amsterdam Ave
J	West Side Synagogue (Modern Orthodox)	120 W 76th St
OP	World Wide Church of God (Evangelical)	2 W 64th St

Map 15 • Upper East Side (Lower)

M	Christ Church United Methodist	520 Park Ave
OP	Christian Science Church	103 E 77th St
OP	Christian Science Church	583 Park Ave
E	Church of the Epiphany	1393 York Ave
E	Church of the Resurrection	115 E 74th St
J	Congregation of Zarua (Conservative Traditional)	127 E 82nd St
J	Congregation Zichron Ephraim (Orthodox)	164 E 68th St
	Dianetics Foundation Hubbard	65 E 82nd St
J	Fifth Avenue Synagogue (Modern Orthodox)	5 E 62nd St
O	Greek Orthodox Cathedral	319 E 74th St
O	Hellenic Eastern Orthodox Church (Greek)	319 E 74th St
O	Holy Trinity Cathedral (Greek)	319 E 74th St
M	Koryo United Methodist Church	150 E 62nd St
M	Lexington United Methodist Church	150 E 62nd St
J	Lisker Congregation	163 E 69th St
P	Madison Avenue Presbyterian Church	921 Madison Ave
J	Manhattan Sephardic Congregation (Orthodox)	325 E 75th St
C	Our Lady of Peace	237 E 62nd St
C	St Catherine of Siena Church	411 E 68th St
C	St Ignatius Church (Jesuit)	53 E 83rd St
C	St James' Episcopal Church	865 Madison Ave
C	St Jean Baptiste Church	184 E 76th St
C	St John Nepomucene Church	411 E 66th St
C	St Monica's Church	413 E 79th St
C	St Stephens of Hungary Church	414 E 82nd St
J	Temple Emanu-El (Reformed)	1 E 65th St
J	Temple Israel-City-NY (Reformed)	112 E 75th St
J	Temple Shaaray Tefila (Reformed)	250 E 79th St
J	Temple-Universal Judaism (Reformed)	1010 Park Ave
B	Trinity Baptist Church	250 E 61st St

OP	Unitarian Church of All Souls	1157 Lexington Ave
Bu	Zen Studies Society	223 E 67th St
L	Zion St Marks Church	424 E 84th St

Map 16 • Upper West Side (Upper)

L	Advent Lutheran Church	2504 Broadway
J	Ansche Chesed Temple (Conservative)	251 W 100th St
C	Ascension Catholic Church	221 W 107th St
C	Central Baptist Church of NY	166 W 92nd St
C	Church of St Gregory	144 W 90th St
J	Congregation Ohab Zedek (Orthodox)	118 W 95th St
J	Congregation Shaare Zedek (Conservative)	212 W 93rd St
O	Evangelismos Greek Orthodox	302 W 91st St
O	Greek Orthodox Community	149 W 105th St
Bu	New York Buddhist Church	332 Riverside Dr
P	Second Presbyterian Church	6 W 96th St
B	Southern Baptist Church	12 W 108th St
E	St Ignatius Episcopal Church	552 West End Ave
M	St Paul & St Andrew Methodist	West End Ave & W 86th St
L	Trinity Lutheran Church	168 W 100th St
P	West End Presbyterian Church	165 W 105th St
P	West Park Presbyterian Church	165 W 86th St

Map 17 • Upper East Side / East Harlem

OP	Bethany Christian Church (Spanish-speaking Assembly of God)	131 E 103rd St
P	Brick Presbyterian Church	62 E 92nd St
OP	Church of Advent Hope (Seventh Day Adventist)	111 E 87th St
C	Church of St Thomas More	65 E 89th St
E	Church of the Heavenly Rest	2 E 90th St
C	Church of the Holy Agony	1834 Third Ave
E	Church of the Holy Trinity	316 E 88th St
E	Church of the Holy Trinity	316 E 88th St
OP	Church of the Living Hope (United Church of Christ)	161 E 104th St
N	Church of the Resurrection	325 E 101st St
N	City Church New York	111 E 87th St
B	East Ward Missionary Baptist	2011 First Ave
Pe	Healing Stream Deliverance Church	121 E 106th St
E	Immanuel Lutheran Church	122 E 88th St
C	Our Lady of Good Counsel Church	230 E 90th St
M	Park Avenue Church	106 E 86th St
J	Park Avenue Synagogue (Conservative)	50 E 87th St
	Ramakrishna-Vivekananda Center	17 E 94th St
C	St Cecilia's Parish Service	125 E 105th St
E	St Edward the Martyr	14 E 109th St
C	St Francis De Sales Church	135 E 96th St
C	St Joseph's Church	404 W 87th St
C	St Lucy Catholic Church	344 E 104th St
O	Synod of Bishops Russian Church	75 E 93rd St

Map 18 • Columbia / Morningside Heights

C	Annunciation Rectory	88 Convent Ave
B	Antioch Baptist Church	515 W 125th St
P	Broadway Presbyterian Church	601 W 114th St
E	Cathedral of St John the Divine	1047 Amsterdam Ave
C	Church of Notre Dame	405 W 114th St
J	Congregation Ramath Orah (Orthodox)	550 W 110th St
C	Corpus Christi Catholic Church	529 W 121st St
M	Emanuel African Methodist Episcopal Church	3741 W 119th St
Pe	Gethsemane Revival Holiness	463 W 125th St

M	Korean Methodist Church	633 W 115th St
N	Manhattan Grace Tabernacle	2929 Broadway
Pe	Manhattan Pentecostal Church	541 W 125th St
N	Riverside Church	91 Claremont Ave
B	St Luke Baptist Church	103 Morningside Ave
E	St Mary's Episcopal Church	521 W 126th St
C	Timplo Biblico Church	503 W 126th St

Map 19 · Harlem (Lower)

E	All Souls Church	88 St Nicholas Ave
M	Bethel African Methodist Episcopal Church	60 W 132nd St
N	Bethelite Community Church	38 W 123rd St
B	Beulah Baptist Church	125 W 130th St
B	Canaan Baptist Church	132 W 116th St
B	Christ Temple Baptist Church	161 W 131st St
OP	Ephesus 7th Day Adventist Church of Harlem	101 W 123rd St
N	Faith Mission Christian Church	160 W 129th St
B	Friendship Baptist Church	144 W 131st St
B	Greater Central Baptist Church	2152 Fifth Ave
B	Greater Metropolitan Baptist Church	147 W 123rd St
N	Harlem Grace Tabernacle	180 W 135th St
B	Kelly Temple Church-God in Christ	8 E 130th St
OP	Lively Stone Church-Apostolic	161 W 122nd St
L	Lutheran Church of Transfiguration	74 W 126th St
	Masjid Malcolm Shabazz Mosque	102 W 116th St
B	Memorial Baptist Church	141 W 115th St
B	Metropolitan Baptist Church	151 W 128th St
B	Mt Nebo Baptist Church	1883 Seventh Ave
B	Mt Pisgah Baptist Church	30 W 126th St
N	New Covenent Life Christian	2433 Eighth Ave
OP	NY United Sabbath Day Church (Seventh Day Adventist)	145 W 110th St
Pe	Pilgrim Cathedral of Harlem	15 W 126th St
Pe	Refuge Temple Church	2081 Seventh Ave
N	Salvation & Deliverance Church	37 W 116th St
B	Second Canaan Baptist Church	10 Lenox Ave
B	Second Providence Baptist Church	11 W 116th St
OP	Shiloh Church of Christ	5 W 128th St #7
	St Ambrose Episcopal Church	9 W 130th St
E	St Andrew's Episcopal Church	2067 Fifth Ave
M	St James African Methodist Episcopal Church	2010 Fifth Ave
E	St Martin's Episcopal Church	230 Lenox Ave
E	St Philips Church	204 W 134th St
C	St Thomas the Apostle	262 W 118th St
OP	Tabernacle of Prayer	139 W 126th St
Pe	United House of Prayer For All	2320 Eighth Ave

Map 20 · El Barrio

C	All Saints Church	47 E 129th St
Pe	Christ Apostolic Church	160 E 112th St
	Church of Scientology	2250 Third Ave
B	Church of the Crucified Church	350 E 120th St
C	Church-Our Lady of Mt Carmel	448 E 116th St
Pe	Community Pentecostal Church	214 E 111th St
OP	Elmendorf Reformed Church	171 E 121st St
Pe	Greater Highway Church of Christ	132 E 111th St
N	Holy Tabernacle Church	407 E 114th St
N	Hosanna City Church	240 E 123rd St
OP	Kingdom Hall-Jehovah's Witness	1763 Madison Ave
M	Madison Avenue United Methodist Church	1723 Madison Ave
M	Metropolitan Community Church	1975 Madison Ave
C	St Ann's Roman Catholic Church	312 E 110th St
C	United Moravian Church	200 E 127th St

Map 21 · Manhattanville / Hamilton Heights

Pe	Bethel Holy Church-Mt Sinai	922 St Nicholas Ave
OP	Christian Science Church	555 W 141st St
C	Church of Our Lady-Esperanza (Spanish speaking)	624 W 156th St
E	Church of the Intercession	550 W 155th St
B	Convent Avenue Baptist Church	420 W 145th St
B	Jehovah-Jireh Baptist Church	536 W 148th St
B	Macedonia Baptist Church	452 W 147th St
M	Mt Calvary Methodist Church	116 Edgecombe Ave
N	North Presbyterian Church	525 W 155th St
C	Our Lady of Lourdes Church	463 W 142nd St
O	Russian Holy Fathers Church	524 W 153rd St
P	St James Presbyterian Church	409 W 141st St
B	St John Baptist Church	448 W 152nd St
E	St Luke's Episcopal Church	435 W 141st St
M	United Methodist Church	53 Edgecombe Ave

Map 22 · Harlem (Upper)

B	Abyssinian Baptist Church	132 W 138th St
E	African Methodist	140 W 137th St
B	Bethany Baptist Church	303 W 153rd St
N	Calvery Christian Fellowship	2350 Fifth Ave
C	Church of St Mark	65 W 138th St
Pe	First Emmanuel Church-Jesus	270 W 153rd St
N	Harlem Tabernacle	2350 Fifth Ave
M	Mt Calvary Baptist Church	231 W 142nd St
P	Rendall Memorial Presbyterian	59 W 137th St
C	Resurrection Roman Catholic Church	276 W 151st St
C	St Charles Church	211 W 141st St
C	St Thomas Liberal Catholic Church	147 W 144th St

Map 23 · Washington Heights

M	Christ United Church	4140 Broadway
C	Christ United Church & the United Palace	4140 Broadway
C	Church of the Incarnation	1290 St Nicholas Ave
OP	Collegiate Reformed Church	729 W 181st St
J	Congregation Shaare (Orthodox)	711 W 179th St
OP	Correa Miguel (Evangelical)	507 W 159th St
B	Primera Iglesia Baptista	96 Wadsworth Ave
C	St Rose of Lima Church	510 W 165th St
O	St Spyridon Church (Greek)	124 Wadsworth Ave
O	Washington Heights Hellenic Orthodox (Greek)	124 Wadsworth Ave

Map 24 · Fort George / Fort Tryon

J	Congregation K'Hal Adath Jeshurun (Orthodox)	85 Bennett Ave
J	Fort Tryon Jewish Center (Reformed)	524 Ft Washington Ave
C	Our Lady Queen of Martyrs	71 Arden St
L	Our Saviors Atonement	178 Bennett Ave
C	St Elizabeth's Church	268 Wadsworth Ave
B	Wadsworth Avenue Baptist Church	210 Wadsworth Ave

Map 25 · Inwood

C	Church of the Good Shepherd	4967 Broadway
E	Holy Trinity Episcopal Church	20 Cumming St
M	Manhattan Bible Church	3816 Ninth Ave
Pe	Narrow Door Church	161 Sherman Ave
C	St Jude's Roman Catholic Church	431 W 204th St
	The Church of Jesus Christ of Latter Day Saints (Inwood 1st Ward) Roosevelt Ave	1815 Riverside Dr
C	Sacred Heart of Jesus Church	206 Main St
C	St Mary's Roman Catholic Church	201 Main St

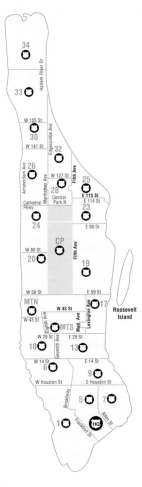

Important Phone Numbers

All Emergencies:	911
Non-Emergencies:	311
Terrorism Hot Line:	888-NYC-SAFE
Crime Stoppers:	800-577-TIPS
Crime Stoppers (Spanish):	888-57-PISTA
Sex Crimes Report Line:	212-267-RAPE
Crime Victims Hotline:	212-577-7777
Cop Shot:	800-COP-SHOT
Missing Persons Case Status:	646-610-6914
Missing Persons Squad:	212-473-2042
Operation Gun Stop:	866-GUNSTOP
Organized Crime Control Bureau Drug Line:	888-374-DRUG
Complaints (Internal Affairs):	212-741-8401
Website:	www.ci.nyc.ny.us/html/nypd/home.html

Statistics	2005	2003	2002	2001	2000
Uniformed Personnel	39,110	37,200			39,778
Murders	540	596	584	643	671
Rapes	1,640	1,877	2,013	1,917	2,067
Robberies	24,417	25,890	27,124	27,863	32,231
Felony Assaults	17,336	18,717	20,700	22,994	25,854
Burglaries	23,997	29,120	31,250	32,663	38,241
Grand Larcenies	47,619	46,518	45,461	46,115	49,381
Grand Larcenies (cars)	17,865	23,144	26,339	29,619	35,602

Precinct		Phone	Map
1st Precinct	16 Ericsson Pl	212-334-0611	2
5th Precinct	19 Elizabeth St	212-334-0711	3
7th Precinct	19 1/2 Pitt St	212-477-7311	4
6th Precinct	233 W 10th St	212-741-4811	5
9th Precinct	130 Ave C	212-477-7811	7
Mid-Town South	357 W 35th St	212-239-9811	8
10th Precinct	230 W 20th St	212-741-8211	9
13th Precinct	230 E 21st St	212-477-7411	10
Mid-Town North	306 W 54th St	212-760-8300	11
17th Precinct	167 E 51st St	212-826-3211	13
20th Precinct	120 W 82nd St	212-580-6411	14
19th Precinct	153 E 67th St	212-452-0600	15
24th Precinct	151 W 100th St	212-678-1811	16
23rd Precinct	162 E 102nd St	212-860-6411	17
26th Precinct	520 W 126th St	212-678-1311	18
28th Precinct	2271 Frederick Douglass Blvd	212-678-1611	19
32nd Precinct	250 W 135th St	212-690-6311	19
25th Precinct	120 E 119th St	212-860-6511	20
30th Precinct	451 W 151st St	212-690-8811	21
33rd Precinct	2207 Amsterdam Ave	212-927-3200	p23-24
34th Precinct	4295 Broadway	212-927-9711	24
Central Park Precinct	86th St & Transverse Rd	212-570-4820	p204

Self-Storage

	Address	Phone	Map
Manhattan Mini Storage	161 Varick St	800-786-7243	5
Manhattan Mini Storage	260 Spring St	800-786-7243	5
Whitehall Storage	303 W 10th St	212-929-3537	5
Whitehall Storage	330 Hudson St	212-645-4080	5
Manhattan Mini Storage	28 Second Ave	800-786-7243	6
Keepers Self Storage	444 E 10th St	212-674-2166	7
American Self Storage	500 Tenth Ave	212-714-9300	8
Bulwark Mini Storage	239 Eleventh Ave	212-255-5832	8
Chelsea Mini Storage	224 12th Ave	212-564-7735	8
Manhattan Mini Storage	510 W 21st St	800-786-7243	8
Manhattan Mini Storage	520 Eighth Ave	800-786-7243	8
Manhattan Mini Storage	520 W 17th St	800-786-7243	8
Manhattan Mini Storage	524 W 23rd St	800-786-7243	8
Manhattan Mini Storage	541 W 29th St	800-786-7243	8
Tuck It Away	517 W 29th St	212-368-1717	8
U-haul Center Of Chelsea	562 W 23rd St	212-620-4177	8
Whitehall Storage	511 W 25th St	212-989-9668	8
Manhattan Mini Storage	451 Ninth Ave	800-786-7243	11
Manhattan Mini Storage	543 W 43rd St	800-786-7243	11
Manhattan Mini Storage	645 W 44th St	800-786-7243	11
Whitehall Storage	610 W 52nd St	212-489-1733	11
Sofia Brothers	475 Amsterdam Ave	212-873-3600	14
Manhattan Mini Storage	420 E 62nd St	800-786-7243	15
Manhattan Mini Storage	108 W 107th St	800-786-7243	16
Manhattan Mini Storage	570 Riverside Dr	800-786-7243	18
Tuck It Away	3261 Broadway	212-368-1717	18
Tuck It Away	3330 Broadway	212-694-7390	18
Tuck It Away	655 W 125th St	212-663-4784	18
Big Apple Mini Storage West	157 W 124th St	212-865-4899	19
Manhattan Mini Storage	401 E 110th St	800-786-7243	20
Tuck It Away	1901 Park Ave	212-831-5545	20
American Self Storage	9 W 141st St	212-283-5500	22
Storage USA	58 W 143rd St	212-694-0849	22
Sofia Brothers	4396 Broadway	212-923-4300	24

Van & Truck Rental

	Address	Phone	Map
Budget Truck Rental	510 W 35th St	212-465-1911	8
Budget Truck Rental	415 W 45th St	212-397-2893	11
Budget Truck Rental	220 E 117th St	212-987-3642	20
Penske Manhattan	451 Tenth Ave	212-741-9800	8
U-Haul • Straight Hardware	613 Ninth Ave	212-581-9395	11
U-Haul • All State Leasing	535 W 44th St	212-643-8076	11
U-Haul	3270 Broadway	212-491-7723	18
U-Haul Center Chelsea	562 W 23rd St	212-620-4177	8

If you have to get to a hospital, it's best to go to the closest one. However, as a quick reference, the following is a list of the largest hospitals by neighborhood, complete with the name of its corresponding map. But no matter which hospital you drag yourself into, for heaven's sake make sure you have your insurance card.

Lower Manhattan: NYU Downtown Hospital • William & Beekman Sts, just south of the Brooklyn Bridge • [Map 3]

West Village/Chelsea: St Vincent's • Seventh Ave & 12th St [Map 5]

East Village: Beth Israel Medical Center • 14th St & Broadway/Union Square • [Map 10]

Murray Hill: Bellevue Hospital Center • First Ave & 27th St [Map 10] ; NYU College of Dentistry • First Ave & 24th St [Map 10]

Hell's Kitchen/Upper West Side: St Luke's Roosevelt Hospital • 10th Ave & 58th St [Map 10]

East Side: New York Presbyterian • York Ave & 68th St [Map 15]; Lenox Hill Hospital • Lexington Ave & 77th St [Map 15]; Mt Sinai Medical Center • Madison Ave & 101st St [Map 17]

Columbia/Morningside Heights: St Luke's Hospital Center • Amsterdam Ave & 114th St [Map 18]

El Barrio: North General Hospital • Madison Ave & 125th St [Map 20]

Farther Uptown: Columbia Presbyterian Medical Center • 168th St & Broadway [Map 23]

If you have a condition that isn't immediately threatening, certain hospitals in New York specialize and excel in specific areas of medicine:

Cancer: Memorial Sloan-Kettering

Birthing Center/Labor & Delivery: St Luke's Roosevelt

Digestive Disorders: Mt Sinai

Dentistry: NYU College of Dentistry

Ear, Nose and Throat: Mt Sinai

Eyes: New York Eye and Ear Infirmary

Geriatrics: Mt Sinai, New York Presbyterian

Heart: New York Presbyterian

Hormonal Disorders: New York Presbyterian

Kidney Disease: New York Presbyterian

Mental Health: Bellevue

Neurology: New York Presbyterian, NYU Medical Center

Orthopedics: Hospital for Special Surgery, New York Presbyterian

Pediatrics: Children's Hospital of New York Presbyterian

Psychiatry: New York Presbyterian, NYU Medical Center

Rheumatology: Hospital for Special Surgery, Hospital for Joint Diseases Orthopedic Institute, NYU Medical Center

Emergency Rooms	Address	Phone	Map
Bellevue Hospital Center	462 First Ave	212-562-4141	10
Beth Israel Medical Center	281 First Ave	212-420-2000	10
Cabrini Medical Center	227 E 19th St	212-995-6000	10
Columbia-Presbyterian Allen Pavilion	5141 Broadway	212-932-4000	25
Columbia-Presbyterian Medical Center	622 W 168th St	212-305-2500	23
Harlem Hospital Center	506 Lenox Ave	212-939-1000	22
Hospital for Joint Diseases	301 E 17th St	212-598-6000	10
Lenox Hill	110 E 77th St	212-434-2000	15
Manhattan Eye, Ear & Throat	210 E 64th St	212-838-9200	15
Metropolitan	1901 First Ave	212-423-6262	17
Mt Sinai Medical Center	1468 Madison Ave	212-241-6500	17
New York Eye & Ear Infirmary	310 E 14th St	212-979-4000	6
New York PresbyterianNWeill Cornell Medical Center	525 E 68th St	212-746-5454	15
North General	1879 Madison Ave	212-423-4000	20
NYU Downtown	170 William St	212-312-5000	3
NYU Medical Center: Tisch	560 First Ave	212-263-7300	10
St Luke's	1111 Amsterdam Ave	212-523-4000	18
St Luke's Roosevelt Hospital Center	1000 Tenth Ave	212-523-4000	11
St Vincent's	153 W 11th St	212-604-7000	5
St Vincent's Midtown	426 W 52nd St	212-586-1500	11
VA Hospital	423 E 23rd St	212-686-7500	10

Other Hospitals	Address	Phone	Map
Beth Israel – Phillips Ambulatory Care Center	10 Union Sq E	212-844-8000	10
Coler Goldwater–Coler Campus	900 Main St	212-848-6000	p226
Coler Goldwater–Goldwater Campus	1 Main St	212-848-6000	p226
Gouverneur	227 Madison St	212-238-7000	4
Gracie Square	420 E 76th St	212-988-4400	15
Hospital for Special Surgery	535 E 70 St	212-606-1000	15
Memorial Sloan-Kettering Cancer Center	1275 York Ave	212-639-2000	15
Renaissance Diagnostic and Treatment Center	215 W 125th St	212-932-6500	18
The Floating Hospital	232 East Broadway	212-514-7447	4

Beginner's mistake: Walk into the main branch of the New York Public Library at Bryant Park and ask how to check out books. Trust us; it's happened. Recognizable for its reclining stone lions Patience and Fortitude, the famous building is a research library with non-circulating materials that you can peruse only in the iconic reading room. If you want to read *War and Peace* or *The DaVinci Code*, it's best to go to your local branch (there are 80 branch and five central libraries). But, if it's reference material you're after, there are several specialized research libraries to help. **The Schomburg Center for Research in Black Culture (Map 22)** is a wealth of material on the history of African-Americans. **The Science, Industry, and Business Library (Map 9)** is perhaps the newest and swankiest of all of Manhattan's libraries. **The Library for the Performing Arts (Map 14)** contains a wonderful archive of New York City theater on film and tape. **The Early Childhood Resource and Information Center (Map 5)** runs workshops for parenting and reading programs for children. The aforementioned main branch of the **New York Public Library (Map 12)** (one of Manhattan's architectural treasures, designed by Carrere and Hastings in 1897) has several special collections and services, such as the Humanities and Social Sciences Library, the Map Division, Exhibition galleries, and divisions dedicated to various ethnic groups. The main branch contains 88 miles of shelves and has more than 10,000 current periodicals from almost 100 countries. Research libraries require an ACCESS card, which you can apply for at the library and which allows you to request materials in any of the reading rooms. In addition to the above, there is also the **Andrew Heiskell Braille and Talking Book Library (Map 9)**, designed to be barrier-free. The library contains large collections of special format materials and audio equipment for listening to recorded books and magazines. You can check out the full system online at www.nypl.org.

Library	Address	Phone	Map
115th St (temporarily location)	2011 Adam Clayton Powell Jr Blvd	212-666-9393	19
115th Street (temporarily closed)	203 W 115th St	212-666-9393	19
125th St	224 E 125th St	212-534-5050	20
58th St	127 E 58th St	212-759-7358	13
67th St	328 E 67th St	212-734-1717	15
96th Street	112 E 96th St	212-289-0908	17
Aguilar	174 E 110th St	212-534-2930	20
Andrew Heiskell Library for the Blind	40 W 20th St	212-206-5400	9
Bloomingdale	150 W 100th St	212-222-8030	16
Chatham Square	33 East Broadway	212-964-6598	3
Columbus	742 Tenth Ave	212-586-5098	11
Countee Cullen	104 W 136th St	212-491-2070	22
Donnell Library Center	20 W 53rd St	212-621-0618	12
Early Childhood Resource & Information Center	66 Leroy St	212-929-0815	5
Epiphany	228 E 23rd St	212-679-2645	10
Fort Washington	535 W 179th St	212-927-3533	23
George Bruce	518 W 125th St	212-662-9727	18
Hamilton Fish Park	415 E Houston St	212-673-2290	7
Hamilton Grange	503 W 145th St	212-926-2147	21
Harlem	9 W 124th St	212-348-5620	19
Hudson Park	66 Leroy St	212-243-6876	5
Humanities & Social Sciences Library	42nd St & Fifth Ave	212-930-0830	12
Inwood	4790 Broadway	212-942-2445	25
Jefferson Market	425 Sixth Ave	212-243-4334	5
Kips Bay	446 Third Ave	212-683-2520	10
Macomb's Bridge	2650 Adam Clayton Powell Jr Blvd	212-281-4900	22
Mid-Manhattan Library	455 Fifth Ave	212-340-0833	12
Morningside Heights Library	2900 Broadway	212-864-2530	18
Muhlenberg	209 W 23rd St	212-924-1585	9
New Amsterdam	9 Murray St	212-732-8186	3
New York Academy of Medicine Library	1216 Fifth Ave	212-822-7200	17
New York Public Library for the Performing Arts	40 Lincoln Center Plz	212-870-1630	14
New York Society Library	53 E 79th St	212-288-6900	15
NYC Municipal Archives	31 Chambers St	212-788-8580	3
Ottendorfer	135 Second Ave	212-674-0947	6
Riverside	127 Amsterdam Ave	212-870-1810	14
Roosevelt Island	524 Main St	212-308-6243	p226
Schomburg Center for Research in Black Culture	515 Lenox Ave	212-491-2200	22
Science, Industry, and Business Library	188 Madison Ave	212-592-7000	9
Seward Park	192 East Broadway	212-477-6770	4
St Agnes	444 Amsterdam Ave	212-877-4380	14
Terence Cardinal Cooke-Cathedral	560 Lexington Ave	212-752-3824	13
Tompkins Square	331 E 10th St	212-228-4747	7
Washington Heights	1000 St Nicholas Ave	212-923-6054	23
Webster	1465 York Ave	212-288-5049	15
Yorkville	222 E 79th St	212-744-5824	15

General Information · LGBT

From the "Muscle Marys" of Chelsea to the grungy rock-and-rollers of the East Village, New York boasts a diverse range of gay men and places for them to play. Strangely, the gay scene in NYC is barely visible in daylight, as most bars and clubs don't get busy before midnight. One of the more popular mostly-gay boy mod parties, Misshapes, can be found Saturday nights at **Don Hill's**. The new-and-improved Cock can always be counted on for a good time (which moved, so appropriately, into the bar formerly known as "The Hole" on 2nd and 2nd). Otherwise, enjoy the museums and SoHo shopping before taking your disco-nap to explore the city that never sleeps—perhaps as a result of all the "Tina" in this town.

If you're a lesbian venturing into New York City with high hopes of finding a hot soccer mom, turn around, girlfriend, because they live on the other side of the tunnel. And if you think your dream girl might be found sipping a Miller Light at old **Henrietta Hudson**, stay away, because the bar is notorious for its intolerable bathroom line. There are few venues in Manhattan that cater to the lesbian crowd full-time—instead you'll need to hit the weeknight girl parties dotted around the island. Check out Snapshot at Bar 13 on Tuesday nights for steamy Sapphic scenesters, **Starlight** on Sunday nights for the L-Word-esque hotties. And **Libation** on Thursday nights for all sorts of Lower East Side lovelies. For an up-to-the-minute list, visit www.gonycmagazine.com. In Brooklyn, check out the patio at **Ginger's** (363 Fifth Ave, Brooklyn), the roofdeck at **Cattyshack**, or Wednesday ladies' night at the low-key neighborhood boys spot, **Metropolitan**.

Websites

The Lesbian, Gay, Bisexual & Transgender Community Center: www.gaycenter.org — Information about center programs, meetings, publications, and events.

Out & About: www.outandabout.com — Travel website for gays and lesbians including destination information, a gay travel calendar, health information, and listings of gay tour operators.

Gayellow Pages: www.gayellowpages.com — Yellow pages of gay/lesbian-owned and gay/lesbian-friendly businesses in the US and Canada.

Dyke TV: www.dyketv.org — Whether you're interested in viewing or contributing, this website has all the info you'll need.

Edwina: www.edwina.com — A NY online meeting place for gays and lesbians looking for love, lust, or just friendship.

Publications

Free at gay and lesbian venues and shops, and some street corners.

HX — Weekly magazine featuring information about bars, clubs, restaurants, events, meetings, and loads of personals. www.hx.com

Gay City News (formerly LGNY) — Newspaper for lesbian and gay New Yorkers including current local and national news items. www.gaycitynews.com

The New York Blade — NYC's only gay-owned and operated weekly newspaper featuring local and national news coverage, as well as guides to theater, nightlife, food, and local arts and entertainment. www.nyblade.com

GO NYC — Monthly magazine for the urban lesbian on the go with free arts and entertainment listings, weekly event picks, plus information on community organizations and LGBT-owned and LGBT friendly-businesses. www.gonycmagazine.com

Bookshops

Creative Visions, 548 Hudson St (212-645-7573) — Gay and lesbian magazines and videos. http://www.creativevisionsbooks.com

Bluestockings, 172 Allen St (212-777-6028) — Lesbian/radical bookstore and activist center with regular readings and a fair-trade café. www.bluestockings.com

Health Centers and Support Organizations

Callen-Lorde Community Health Center, 356 W 18th St (212-271-7200) — Primary Care Center for GLBT New Yorkers. www.callen-lorde.org

Gay Men's Health Crisis, 119 W 24th St (212-367-1000; Hotline: 212-807-6655) — Non-profit organization dedicated to AIDS awareness and support for those with the disease. www.gmhc.org

The Lesbian, Gay, Bisexual & Transgender Community Center, 208 W 13th (212-620-7310) — The largest LGBT multi-service organization on the East Coast. www.gaycenter.org

Gay and Lesbian National Hotline, (212-989-0999) — Switchboard for referrals, advice, and counseling. www.glnh.org

PFLAG, 109 E 50th St (212-463-0629) — Parents, Families, and Friends of Lesbians and Gays meet on the second Sunday of every month 3 pm-5 pm for mutual support. www.pflagnyc.org

Lesbian and Gay Immigration Rights Task Force (LGIRTF), 350 W 31st St, Ste 505 (212-714-2904) — Advocates for changing US policy on immigration of permanent partners. www.lgirtf.org

GLAAD (Gay and Lesbian Alliance Against Defamation), 248 W 35th St, 8th fl (212-629-3322) — These are the folks who go to bat for you in the media. www.glaad.org

OUTdancing @ Stepping Out Studios, 37 W 26th St (646-742-9400) — The first GLBT partner dance program in the US. www.steppingoutstudios.com

Annual Events

Pride Week — Usually the last full week in June; www.hopinc.org (212-807-7433)

New York Gay and Lesbian Film Festival — Showcase of international gay and lesbian films, May/June; www.newfestival.org (212-571-2170)

Mass Blue Ribbon Ride — Replacing the old NYC to Boston AIDS ride, this version is a two-day ride across Massachusetts. The 2006 ride begins in Pittsfield and finishes in Weston, mid-August; www.acc.org (617-450-1100 or 888-MASSRIDE)

Venues — Lesbian

- **Bar 13** • (Tues) 35 E. 13th St. • 212-979-6677 • www.bar13.com
- **Cattyshack** • 249 Fourth Ave, Brooklyn • 718-230-5740 • www.cattyshackbklyn.com
- **Club Fahrenheit** • (second, fourth Fri) • 95 Leonard St • 917-299-1975
- **Cubbyhole** • 281 W 12th St • 212-243-9041
- **Escuelita** (Fri) • 301 W 39th St • 212-631-0588 • www.enyclub.com
- **49 Grove** (first Mon) • 49 Grove St • 212-727-1100
- **Heaven** (Wed, Fri, Sat) • 579 Sixth Ave • 212-243-6100
- **Henrietta Hudson** • 438 Hudson St • 212-924-3347 • www.henriettahudson.com
- **Nowhere** (Mon) • 322 E 14th St • 212-477-4744
- **Opaline** (Fri) • 85 Avenue A • 212-995-8684
- **Rubyfruit** • 531 Hudson St • 212-929-3343
- **Slipper Room** (Tues) • 167 Orchard St • 212-253-7246 • www.slipperroom.com
- **Starlight** (Sun) • 167 Avenue A • 212-475-2172 • www.starlightbarlounge.com

Venues — Gay

- **Avalon** • (Sun. Nights) 47 W 20th St • 212-807-7780 • www.avalonnewyorkcity.com
- **Barracuda** • 275 W 22nd St • 212-645-8613
- **Barrage** • 401 W 47th St • 212-586-9390
- **Boots & Saddle** • 76 Christopher St • 212-929-9684
- **Chi Chiz** • 135 Christopher St • 212-462-0027
- **Cleo's Ninth Avenue Salon** • 656 Ninth Ave • 212-307-1503
- **Crobar** • 530 W 28th St • 212-629-9000 • www.crobar.com
- **Dick's Bar** • 192 Second Ave • 212-475-2071
- **The Dugout** • 185 Christopher St • 212-242-9113
- **The Duplex** • 61 Christopher St • 212-255-5438 • www.theduplex.com
- **Eagle** • 554 W 28th St • 646-473-1866 • www.eaglenyc.com
- **Escuelita** • 301 W 39th St • 212-631-0588 • www.enyclub.com
- **G Lounge** • 225 W 19th St • 212-929-1085 • www.glounge.com
- **GYM Sports Bar** • 167 8th Ave. bet. 18th and 19th St • 212.337-2439
- **Hangar Bar** • 115 Christopher St • 212-627-2044
- **Heaven** • 579 Sixth Ave • 212-243-6100
- **Marie's Crisis** • 59 Grove St • 212-243-9323
- **Metropolitan** • 559 Lorimer St. 718.599-4444
- **The Monster** • 80 Grove St • 212-924-3558 • www.manhattan-monster.com
- **Nowhere** • 322 E 14th St • 212-477-4744
- **OW Bar** • 221 E 58th St • 212-355-3395 • www.owbar.com
- **Pegasus** • 119 E 60th St • 212-888-4702
- **The Phoenix** • 447 E 13th St • 212-477-9979
- **Pieces Bar** • 8 Christopher St • 212-929-9291 • www.piecesbar.com
- **Posh** • 405 W 51st St • 212-957-2222
- **Pyramid Club** • 101 Avenue A • 212-228-4888 • www.thepyramidclub.com
- **Rawhide** • 212 Eighth Ave • 212-242-9332
- **Roxy** • 515 W 18th St • 212-645-5156 • www.roxynyc.com
- **The Slide** • 356 Bowery • 212-420-8885 • www.theslidebar.com
- **Splash** (SBNY) • 50 W 17th St • 212-691-0073 • www.splashbar.com
- **Starlight** • 167 Avenue A • 212-475-2172 • www.starlightbarlounge.com
- **Stonewall** • 53 Christopher St • 212-463-0950 • www.stonewall-place.com
- **Tenth Avenue Lounge** • 642 Tenth Ave • 212-245-9088
- **Therapy** • 348 W 52nd St • 212-397-1700 • www.therapy-nyc.com
- **Tool Box** • 1742 Second Ave • 212-348-1288
- **Townhouse** • 236 E 58th St • 212-754-4649 • www.townhouseny.com
- **Ty's** • 114 Christopher St • 212-741-9641
- **Urge** • 33 Second Ave • 212-533-5757
- **View Bar** • 232 Eighth Ave • 212-929-2243 • www.viewbarnyc.com
- **The Web** • 40 E 58th St • 212-308-1546
- **XL** • 357 W 16th St • 646-336-5574 • www.XLnewyork.com

Beyond the obvious crowd-pleasers, New York City landmarks are super-subjective. One person's favorite cobblestoned alley is some developer's idea of prime real estate for a luxury condo. Bits of old New York disappear to differing amounts of fanfare and make room for whatever it is we'll be romanticizing in the future. Ain't that just the circle of life? The landmarks discussed here are highly idiosyncratic choices, and this list is by no means complete or even typical, but we've included an array of places, from world famous to little known, all worth visiting.

Coolest Skyscrapers

Most visitors to New York go to the top of the **Empire State Building (Map 9)**, but it's far more familiar to New Yorkers from afar—as a directional guide, or as a tip-off to obscure holidays (blue & red lights mean Happy Equal Parents Day!). If you want an actual view of the Empire State Building, ascend to the **Top of the Rock (Map 12)**, aka Rockefeller Center's swanky observation deck, recently reopened. If it's class you're looking for, the **Chrysler Building (Map 13)** has it in spades. Unfortunately, this means that only the "classiest" are admitted to the top floors. Other midtown highlights include the **Citicorp Center (Map 13)**, a building that breaks out of the boxy tower form, and the **RCA Building (Map 12)**, one of the steepest-looking skyscrapers in the city. More neck-craning excitement can be found in the financial district, including the **Woolworth Building (Map 3)**, the **American International Building (Map 1)** at 70 Pine Street (with private spire rooms accessible only to the connected), **40 Wall Street (Map 1)**, the **Bankers Trust Company Building (Map 1)**, and **20 Exchange Place (Map 1)**.

Best Bridges

The **Brooklyn Bridge** is undoubtedly the best bridge in New York—aesthetically, historically, and practically; you can walk or bike across on a wooden sidewalk high above the traffic. It's also worth walking across the **George Washington Bridge (Map 23)**, though it takes more time than you'd expect (trust us). The **Henry Hudson Bridge (Map 25)** expresses the tranquility of that part of the island—view it from Inwood Hill Park to see its graceful span over to Spuyten Duyvil. The **Verrazano-Narrows Bridge** between Brooklyn and Staten Island is the most awe-inspiring in the city.

Great Architecture

The Beaux Arts interior of Grand Central Terminal **(Map 13)** is full of soaring arches and skylights. Head to SoHo to see the **Singer Building (Map 6)** and other gorgeous cast-iron structures. You can find intricately carved faces and creatures on the tenement facades of the Lower East Side. The **Flatiron (Map 9)**, once among the tallest buildings in the city, remains one of the most distinctive, so long as they keep the H&M ads off of it. The **Lever House (Map 13)** and the **Seagram's Building (Map 13)** redefined corporate architecture and are great examples of Modernism. The **Ellis Island Main Building (take the**

ferry from Battery Park, Map 1), devoted solely to the immigrant experience, features domed ceilings and Gustavino tiled arches. The **Guggenheim (Map 17)** is one of New York's most unique and distinctive buildings (apparently there's some art inside, too). The **Cathedral of St. John the Divine (Map 18)** has a very medieval vibe and is the world's largest unfinished cathedral. It's home to a new-agey giant quartz crystal, amongst other secular stuff, and it's a much cooler destination than the eternally crowded **St. Patrick's Cathedral (Map 12)**.

Great Public Buildings

Once upon a time, the city felt that public buildings should inspire civic pride through great architecture. Head downtown to view **City Hall (Map 3)** (1812), **Tweed Courthouse (Map 3)** (1880), **Jefferson Market Courthouse (Map 5)** (1877—now a library), the **Municipal Building (Map 3)** (1914), and a host of other courthouses built in the early 20th century. The **Old Police Headquarters (Map 3)** now a posh condo, would be a more celebrated building if it wasn't located on a little-trafficked block of Centre Street in Little Italy/Chinatown. And what are the chances a firehouse built today would have the same charm as the **Great Jones Firehouse (Map 6)**? If the guys are around outside, they're more than happy to let you in to look around.

Outdoor Spaces

Central Park obviously. **Madison Square Park (Map 9)** is not as well known as many other central city parks, but is home to the Shake Shack, where you can grab a burger, a shake, and a bit of peace and quiet on the grass. For better or worse, **Washington Square (Map 6)** is a landmark (the arch is nice to look at, and the fountain is nice to play in), although it pretty much functions as the NYU campus. There's all kinds of interesting folk around **Tompkins Square (Map 7)**, which makes it ideal for people watching. In addition to **Union Square (Map 9)** housing a bunch of great statues (Gandhi, Washington, Lincoln), it also hosts an amazing Farmer's Market (Mon, Wed, Fri, and Sat) and is close to great shopping. **Bryant Park (Map 12)** attracts a chi-chi lunch crowd (it's a wi-fi hotspot), and hosts movies in the summer. Next door, people lounge on the **New York Public Library (Map 12)** steps and reminisce about their favorite scene from *Ghostbusters*, no doubt. **Rockefeller Center (Map 12)** tends to get overrun by tourists, but it's still deserving of a visit, especially to view the Art Deco styling. The **Cloisters (Map 25)** and **Inwood Hill Park (Map 25)** are great uptown escapes. Thanks to Stuyvesant Street's diagonal path, **St. Marks-in-the-Bowery (Map 6)** gets a nice little corner of land in front for a park, which gives a hint of its rural past. **Wave Hill** is 28 acres of garden oasis in the Bronx.

Lowbrow Landmarks

The **Chinatown Ice Cream Factory (Map 3)** is worth a slog through Chinatown crowds on a hot day. Just around the corner is **Doyers Street (Map 3)**, which retains the slight air of danger from its gang war past. Among other positive attributes, **CBGB's (Map 6)** is dingy, dark, loud, and most likely evicted, but the nearby nook known as **Joey Ramone Place (Map 6)** still stands. Some classic and historic New York bars, known mainly for their famous patrons of drinks past, include **McSorley's (Map 6)**, Pete's **Tavern (Map 10)**, the **White Horse Tavern (Map 5)**, **Chumleys (Map 5)**, and the **Ear Inn (Map 5)**.

Lame, Bad & Overrated Landmarks

Even the most cynical New Yorker would have to admit that **Times Square (Map 12)** is a unique place, but the truth is that it's no fun to compete for sidewalk space with tourists in search of dinner at the Bubba Gump Shrimp Company. **South Street Seaport (Map 1)** is essentially a lame mall with some old ships parked nearby. **Madison Square Garden (Map 9)** doesn't really deserve its status as a great sports arena. Aside from a few shining moments, the teams mostly stink, and the architecture is mostly banal. The worst part is that the gorgeous old Penn Station was torn down to make room for it. You can see

pictures of the old station when you walk through the new **Penn Station (Map 9)**, which is famous not for its totally drab and depressing environs, but because of the sheer volume of traffic it handles. The **Cross Bronx Expressway (Map 23)** gets a mention as the worst highway ever.

Underrated Landmarks

Many of these get overlooked because they are uptown. **Grant's Tomb (Map 18)** was once one of New York's most famous attractions, but these days it's mostly a destination for history buffs. The **City College (Map 18)** campus is quite beautiful, even though a few newer buildings muck things up. Farther north, **Sylvan Terrace (Map 23)** and the **Morris Jumel Mansion (Map 23)**, a unique block of small row houses and a revolutionary war era house, offer a truer glimpse of old New York than the Seaport or Fraunces Tavern. Memorialized in a beloved children's book, a visit to **The Little Red Lighthouse (Map 23)** will make you feel like you're on the coast of Maine and not actually standing under the George Washington Bridge.

Map 1 · Financial District

20 Exchange Place	20 Exchange Pl	Check out the cool facade with its bronze depictions of various modes of both ancient and modern transportation.
40 Wall St	40 Wall St	The tallest building in the world upon its completion in 1930... for a day, until the Chrysler went up. Oh and Trump owns it.
American International Building	70 Pine St	Great Art Deco skyscraper.
American Stock Exchange	86 Trinity Pl · 212-306-1000	New York's other stock exchange.
Bankers Trust Company Building	16 Wall St	More neck-craning excitement from NYC skyline!
Battery Maritime Building	10 South St	Ready-to-be-converted riverfront building.
Bowling Green	Broadway & State St	Watch the tourists take pics of the bull. New York's first park.
Canyon of Heroes	Broadway b/w Bowling Green & City Hall Park	Markers in the sidewalk remember those honored with a ticker tape parade.
Charging Bull	Bowling Green Park	Rub his cojones for luck.
Cunard Building	25 Broadway · 212-363-9490	Former Cunard headquarters, former post office, currently a locked building with great ceiling mosaics.
Customs House/Museum of the American Indian	1 Bowling Green · 212-514-3700	Stately Cass Gilbert building; check out the oval staircases.
Delmonico's Building	56 Beaver St · 212-509-3130	Once the site of THE restaurant in New York.
Ellis Island		Besides the museum, the main building features beautiful domed ceilings and Gustavino tiled arches.
Equitable Building	120 Broadway · 212-490-0666	Its massiveness gave momentum to zoning laws for skyscrapers.
Federal Hall	26 Wall St · 212-825-6888	Where George the First was inaugurated.
The Federal Reserve Bank	33 Liberty St · 212-720-6130	Where Die Hard 3 took place.
The First JP Morgan Bank	23 Wall St	Still visibly scarred from an anarchist bombing in 1920.
New York Stock Exchange	20 Broad St · 212-656-5168	Where Wall Street took place.
South Street Seaport	South St · 212-732-7678	Mall with historic ships as backdrop.
St Paul's Chapel & Cemetery	Broadway & Fulton St · 212-602-0874	Old-time NYC church and cemetery.
Standard Oil Building	26 Broadway	Sweeping wall of a building overlooking Bowling Green.
Trinity Church & Cemetery	Broadway & Wall St	Formerly the tallest building in New York.
Vietnam Veterans Plaza	Coenties Slip & Water St	A nice quiet spot to contemplate our faded dreams of empire.
World Trade Center Site	Church St & Vesey St	We still can't believe what happened.

Map 2 • TriBeCa

The Dream House	275 Church St • 212-925-8270	Cool sound + light installation by LaMonte Young. Closed during summer.
Duane Park	Duane St & Hudson St	One of the nicest spots in all of New York.
Ghostbusters Firehouse	14 N Moore St	Are you the gatekeeper?
Harrison Street Row Houses	Harrison St & Greenwich St	Some old houses.
Washington Market Park	Greenwich St • 212-274-8447	One of the city's oldest marketplaces.

Map 3 • City Hall / Chinatown

African Burial Ground	Duane St & Broadway	Colonial burial ground for 20,000+ African-American slaves.
Bridge Café	279 Water St • 212-227-3344	The oldest bar in NYC. Great vibe, good food too.
Brooklyn Bridge	Chambers St & Centre St	The granddaddy of them all. Walking towards Manhattan at sunset is as good as it gets.
Chinatown Visitors Kiosk	Canal, Baxter, & Walker St	Good meeting point. Just lookout for the dragon.
Chinatown Ice Cream Factory	65 Bayard St • 212-608-4170	The best mango ice cream, ever.
City Hall	Park Row & Broadway • 212-788-6879	Beautiful and now heavily barricaded.
Criminal Courthouse	100 Centre St • 212-374-4423	Imposing.
Doyers Street (Bloody Angle)	Doyers St	One of the few angled streets in New York. Has a decidedly otherworldly feel.
Eastern States Buddhist Temple	64 Mott St • 212-966-6229	The oldest Chinese Buddhist temple on the east coast.
Hall of Records/Surrogate's Court	Chambers St & Park Row	Great lobby and zodiac-themed mosaics.
Municipal Building	Chambers St & Park Row	Wonderful McKim, Mead and White masterpiece.
Not For Tourists	2 East Broadway • 212-965-8650	Where the sh** goes down!
Old Police Headquarters	240 Centre St	A beautiful building in the center of the not so beautiful Little Italy/Chinatown area.
Shearith Israel Cemetery	55 St James Pl	Oldest Jewish cemetery in New York.
Tweed Courthouse	Chambers St & Broadway	Great interior dome, but will we ever see it?
Woolworth Building	233 Broadway	A Cass Gilbert classic. The top half's being converted to condos.

Map 4 • Lower East Side

Bialystoker Synagogue	7 Bialystoker Pl • 212-475-0165	The oldest building in NY to currently house a synagogue. Once a stop on the Underground Railroad.
Eldridge Street Synagogue	12 Eldridge St	The first large-scale building constructed by Eastern European immigrants in NY.
Essex Street Market	120 Essex St	Lots of shops and stalls offering great food and other items.
Gouverneur Hospital	Gouverneur Slip & Water St	One of the oldest hospital buildings in the world.
Lower East Side Tenement Museum	90 Orchard St • 212-431-0233	Great illustration of turn-of-the-century (20th, that is) life.

Map 5 • West Village

Chumley's	86 Bedford St • 212-675-4449	Former speakeasy; still one of the coolest bars around.
The Cage (basketball court)	320 Sixth Ave at W 4th St	Where everybody's got game…
The Ear Inn	Washington & Spring Sts • 212-226-9060	Second-oldest bar in New York; great space.
Jefferson Market Courthouse	425 Sixth Ave • 212-243-4334	Now a library.
Old Homestead	56 Ninth Ave • 212-242-9040	Said to be NY's oldest steakhouse, circa 1868.
Patchin Place	W 10th St b/w Sixth Ave & Greenwich Ave	Tiny gated enclave, once home to e.e. cummings.
Stonewall Inn	53 Christopher St • 212-463-0950	Site of a very important uprising in the late '60s.
Westbeth Building	Washington St & Bethune St • 212-989-4650	Cool multifunctional arts center.
White Horse Tavern	567 Hudson St • 212-243-9260	Another old, cool bar. Dylan Thomas drank here (too much).

Map 6 · Washington Square / NYU / NoHo / SoHo

11 Spring St	Spring St & Elizabeth St	Mysterioius building with no discernable doors, famously covered in street art.
The Alamo (The Cube)	Astor Pl & Fourth Ave	Give it a spin sometime…
Asch Building (Brown Building)	23-29 Washington Pl	Site of the Triangle Shirtwaist Fire.
Bayard-Condict Building	65 Bleecker St	Louis Sullivan's only New York building.
CBGB & OMFUG	315 Bowery · 212-982-4052	Punk mecca, most likely evicted by the time you read this.
Colonnade Row	428 Lafayette St	Remains of a very different era.
Con Edison Building	145 E 14th St	Cool top.
Cooper Union	30 Cooper Sq · 212-353-4195	Great brownstone-covered building.
Gem Spa	131 Second Ave · 212-995-1866	Magazine stand that serves fantastic egg creams.
Grace Church	802 Broadway · 212-254-2000	Another old, small, comfortable church.
Great Jones Fire House	Great Jones St & Bowery	The coolest firehouse in NYC.
Joey Ramone Place	Bowery & E 2nd St	It's Joey Ramone's place. Period.
Lombardi's	32 Spring St · 212-941-7994	Said to be the first pizzeria in the U.S., circa 1905.
Mark Twain House	14 W 10th St	Mark Twain lived here. It's also NYC's most haunted portal.
McSorley's	15 E 7th St	One of the oldest bars in Manhattan, and some would say one of the best. Others…
Milano's	51 E Houston St · 212-226-8844	One of our faves. An utter dump.
New York Marble Cemetery	41 Second Ave	Oldest public non-sectarian cemetery in New York City.
Old Merchant's House	29 E 4th St	The merchant is now dead.
The Public Theater	425 Lafayette St · 212-260-2400	Great building, great shows.
Salmagundi Club	47 Fifth Ave · 212-255-7740	Cool building.
Singer Building	561 Broadway	Now houses Kate's Paperie; a fine building by Ernest Flagg.
St Mark's-in-the-Bowery Church	131 E 10th St · 212-674-6377	Old church with lots of community ties.
The Strand Bookstore	828 Broadway · 212-473-1452	One of a kind. All others are imitations.
Wanamaker's	Broadway & E 8th St	Once the classiest department store in the city, now houses a Kmart.
Washington Mews	University Pl (entrance)	Where horses and servants used to live. Now coveted NYU space.
Washington Square Park	Washington Sq	Dime bag, anyone?

Map 7 · East Village / Lower East Side

Charlie Parker House	151 Ave B & Tompkins Sq Pk	The Bird lived here. Great festival every summer in Tompkins Square.
General Slocum Monument	Tompkins Sq Park	Memorial to one of the worst disasters in NYC history.
Katz's Deli	205 E Houston St · 212-254-2246	Classic NY deli, interior hasn't changed in decades.
Nuyorican Poets Café	236 E 3rd St · 212-505-8183	Home of the poetry slam, among other things.
Pyramid Club	Ave A b/w 6th & 7th Sts · 212-473-7184	Classic 80s and 90s club.
Tompkins Square Park	Ave A & E 9th St · 212-387-7685	Home to many.

Map 8 · Chelsea

General Theological Seminary	175 Ninth Ave · 212-243-5150	Oldest seminary of the Episcopal Church; nice campus.
High Line Elevated Railroad	Gansevoort to 34th St, west of Tenth Ave	Abandoned elevated railroad trestle, soon to be a park.
JA Farley Post Office	441 Eighth Ave · 212-967-2781	Another McKim, Mead and White masterpiece.
Jacob K Javits Convention Center	36th St & Eleventh Ave · 212-216-2000	IM Pei's attempt to make sense out of New York. Love the location.
Starrett-Lehigh Building	27th St & Eleventh Ave	One of the coolest factories/warehouses ever built.

Map 9 · Flatiron / Lower Midtown

Chelsea Hotel	23rd St b/w Seventh & Eighth Aves · 212-243-3700	The scene of many, many crimes.
Empire State Building	34th St & Fifth Ave · 212-736-3100	The roof deck at night is unmatched by any other view of New York.

Flatiron Building	175 Fifth Ave • 212-633-0200	A lesson for all architects: design for the actual space.
Flower District	28th St b/w Sixth & Seventh Aves	Lots of flowers by day, lots of nothing by night.
Garment District	West 30s south of Herald Sq	Clothing racks by day, nothing by night. Gritty, grimy.
Macy's Herald Square	151 W 34th St • 212-494-4662	13 floors of wall-to-wall tourists! Sound like fun?
Madison Square Garden	4 Penn Plz • 212-465-6000	Crappy, uninspired venue for Knicks, Rangers, Liberty, and over-the-hill rock bands.
Madison Square Park	23rd St & Broadway • 212-360-8111	One of the most underrated parks in the city. Lots of great weird sculpture.
Metropolitan Life Insurance Co	1 Madison Ave • 212-578-3700	Cool top, recently refurbished.
Penn Station	31st St & Eighth Ave	Well, the old one was a landmark, anyway…
Theodore Roosevelt Birthplace	28 E 20th St • 212-645-1242	Teddy was born here, apparently.
Tin Pan Alley	W 28th St b/w Sixth Ave & Broadway	Where all that old-timey music came from.
Union Square	14th St-Union Sq	Famous park for protests and rallys. Now bordered on all sides by chain stores.

Map 10 • Murray Hill / Gramercy

Gramercy Park	Irving Pl & 20th St	New York's only keyed park. This is where the revolution will doubtlessly start.
National Arts Club	15 Gramercy Park S • 212-477-2389	One of two beautiful buildings on Gramercy Park South.
Pete's Tavern	129 E 18th St • 212-473-7676	Where O Henry hung out. And so should you, at least once.
The Players	16 Gramercy Park S	The other cool building on Gramercy Park South.
Sniffen Court	36th St & Third Ave	Great little space.
Tammany Hall/Union Sq Theater	100 E 17th St • 212-307-4100	Once housed NYC's Democratic political machine, now it's a theater.

Map 11 • Hell's Kitchen

Intrepid Sea, Air & Space Museum	Twelfth Ave & 45th St • 212-957-3700	Lots of tourists.
Theatre Row	42nd St b/w Ninth & Tenth Aves	This is that "Broadway" place that everyone keeps talking about, isn't it?

Map 12 • Midtown

Bryant Park	42nd St & 6th Ave	Summer movies, winter ice-skating, hook-ups year round.
Carnegie Deli	854 Seventh Ave • 212-757-2245	Serving pastrami since 1937.
Carnegie Hall	154 W 57th St • 212-247-7800	Great classic performance space. The Velvet Underground's first gig was here.
Dahesh Museum of Art	580 Madison Ave • 212-759-0606	Europe.
The Debt Clock	Sixth Ave & 44th St	How much Bush has borrowed—thanks again, Dubya.
Museum of Modern Art (MoMA)	11 W 53rd St • 212-708-9400	The renovation worked! Admire the beauty of architecture and art.
New York Public Library	Fifth Ave & 42nd St • 212-930-0787	A wonderful Beaux Arts building. Great park behind it. The Map Room rules.
Plaza Hotel	768 Fifth Ave • 212-759-3000	Now anyone can be Eloise with her own Plaza condo.
RCA Building	30 Rockefeller Plz	The tallest building at Rock Center, home of the famous (and pricy) Rainbow Room restaurant.
Rockefeller Center	600 Fifth Ave • 212-632-3975	Sculpture, ice skating, and a mall!
Royalton Hotel	44th St b/w Fifth Ave & Sixth Ave • 212-869-4400	Starck + Schrager = cool.
St Patrick's Cathedral	Fifth Ave & 50th St • 212-753-2261	NYC's classic cathedral. Always empty.
Times Square	42nd St-Times Sq	It looks even cooler than it does on TV!
Top of the Rock	600 Fifth Ave • 212-698-2000	Reopened after 19 years, gorgeous view of the Empire State.

Map 13 • East Midtown

Central Synagogue	123 E 55th St • 212-838-5123	NYC's oldest continuous use Jewish house of worship. Architectural gem.
Chrysler Building	405 Lexington Ave • 212-682-3070	The stuff of Art Deco dreams. Wish the Cloud Club was still there.

General Information • Landmarks

Citicorp Center	153 E 53rd St	How does it stand up?
Grand Central Terminal	42nd St • 212-340-2583	Another Beaux Arts masterpiece by Warren and Wetmore. Ceiling, staircases, tiles, clock, Oyster Bar, all great.
The Lever House	390 Park Ave	A great example of architectural modernism, but even better, it's so fresh and so clean!
Roosevelt Island Tram	E 59th St & Second Ave	The only tramway of its kind in North America used for mass transit.
Seagram Building	375 Park Ave	Or, "how to be a modernist in 3 easy steps!"
United Nations	First Ave b/w 42nd & 48th Sts • 212-963-8687	The diplomatic version of the World Cup.
Waldorf Astoria	301 Park Ave • 212-355-3000	Great hotel, although the public spaces aren't up to the Plaza's.

Map 14 • Upper West Side (Lower)

Ansonia Hotel	2109 Broadway • 212-724-2600	Truly unique residence on Broadway.
The Dorilton	Broadway & 71st St	Cool, weird arch. Flashy facade.
Lincoln Center	Broadway & 64th St • 212-875-5000	A rich and wonderful complex. Highly recommended movies, theater, music, opera.
The Majestic	115 Central Park W	Great brick by Chanin.
Museum of Natural History	Central Park W & 79th St • 212-769-5100	Includes the new planetarium and lots and lots of stuffed animals.
New-York Historical Society	2 W 77th St • 212-873-3400	Oldest museum in New York City.
Rotunda at 79th St Boat Basin	W 79th St • 212-496-2105	Rotunda arcade arches great location.
The Dakota	Central Park W & W 72nd St	Classic Central Park West apartment building, designed by Henry J Hardenbergh.
The San Remo	Central Park W & 74th St • 212-877-0300	Emery Roth's contribution to the Upper West Side skyline.

Map 15 • Upper East Side (Lower)

Asia Society	725 Park Ave • 212-288-6400	Small-scale modernism.
Bemelman's Bar	Carlyle Hotel 35 E 76th St • 212-744-1600	Features lovely mural by creator of Madeline books, Ludwig Bemelmans.
Breakfast at Tiffany's Apartment Building	169 E 71st St	Where Holly Golightly and "Fred" lived in *Breakfast at Tiffany's*.
Butterfield Market	1114 Lexington Ave • 212-288-7800	UES gourmet grocer circa 1915.
Café Carlyle	Carlyle Hotel, 35 E 76th St • 212-744-1600	Cabaret café and home of the late, great, Bobby Short.
Frank E Campbell Funeral Chapel	1076 Madison Ave • 212-288-3500	Undertaker to the famously deceased, including John Lennon and Joan Crawford.
Frick Collection	1 E 70th St • 212-288-0700	Lots of furniture.
The Jeffersons High-rise	185 E 85th St	"We're movin' on up…to a dee-luxe apartment in the sky-hi."
Lascoff Apothecary	1209 Lexington Ave • 212-288-9500	Delightfully well-preserved apothecary circa 1899.
The Manhattan House	200 E 66th St	Seminal UES "white-brick" building.
Metropolitan Museum of Art	1000 Fifth Ave • 212-879-5500	The mother of all art musuems. Check out: temple, roof garden, Clyfford Still room, baseball cards.
Mount Vernon Hotel Museum	421 E 61st St • 212-838-6878	Nice old building.
New York Society Library	53 E 79th St • 212-288-6900	A 250-year-old library. Wow!
Temple Emanu-El	1 E 65th St • 212-744-1400	Way cool building.
Whitney Museum of American Art	945 Madison Ave • 212-570-3676	It almost always has something to talk about—not the least of which is their typically controversial Biennial.
Zion-St Mark's Evangelical Lutheran Church	339 E 84th St • 212-479-7808	Last "Germantown" church (see the General Slocum memorials inside).

Map 16 • Upper West Side (Upper)

Fireman's Memorial	W 100th St & Riverside Dr	Memorial to fallen fire fighters.
Pomander Walk	261 W 94th St	Great little hideaway.
Soldiers and Sailors Monument	Riverside Dr & 89th St	It's been seen in *Law & Order*, along with everything else in New York.

General Information · Landmarks

Map 17 · Upper East Side / East Harlem

Cooper-Hewitt Museum	2 E 91st St · 212-860-8400	Great design shows; run by the Smithsonian.
Glaser's Bake Shop	1670 First Ave · 212-289-2562	Best black-and-white cookies for more than a century.
Gracie Mansion	Carl Schulz Park & 88th St · 212-570-4751	Our own Buckingham Palace, and right above the FDR Drive.
Henderson Place	East End Ave & E 86th St	Charming Queen Anne-style apartment houses circa 1881-82.
Jewish Museum	1109 Fifth Ave · 212-423-3200	Over 28,000 artifacts of Jewish culture and history.
Museo del Barrio	Fifth Ave & 104th St · 212-831-7272	NYC's only Latino museum.
Museum of the City of New York	Fifth Ave & 103rd St · 212-534-1672	Nice space, but we were excited when they were going to move to the Tweed Courthouse.
Old Municipal Asphalt Plant (Asphalt Green)	90th St & FDR Dr · 212-369-8890	Industrial architecture turned sports facility.
Papaya King	179 E 86th St · 212-369-0648	Dishing out damn good dogs since 1932.
Schaller & Weber	1654 Second Ave	A relic of old Yorkville with great German meats.
Solomon R Guggenheim Museum	1071 Fifth Ave · 212-423-3500	Wright's only building in NYC, but it's one of the best.
St Nicholas Russian Orthodox Cathedral	15 E 97th St	This UES cathedral, built in 1902, remains the center of Russian Orthodoxy in the US.

Map 18 · Columbia / Morningside Heights

Cathedral of St John the Divine	112th St & Amsterdam Ave · 212-316-7540	Our favorite cathedral. Completely unfinished and usually in disarray, just the way we like it.
City College	138th St & Convent Ave · 212-650-7000	Once known for academic excellence and free tuition, now has open admissions and hefty fees.
Columbia University	116th St & Broadway · 212-854-1754	Peaceful verdant campus. A nice little sanctuary amid the roiling masses.
Grant's Tomb	122nd St & Riverside Dr · 212-666-1640	Interesting, great grounds—a totally underrated experience.
Riverside Church	490 Riverside Dr	Gothic, great views from 392-foot tower.

Map 19 · Harlem (Lower)

Alhambra Theatre and Ballroom	2116 Adam Clayton Powell Jr Blvd · 212-222-6940	Last Harlem dance hall.
Apollo Theater	253 W 125th St · 212-531-5300	Live, the Hardest Working Man in Show Business, Mr James Brown!
Duke Ellington Circle	110th St & Fifth Ave	Nice monument to a jazz great.
Harlem YMCA	180 W 135th St · 212-281-4100	Sidney Poitier, James Earl Jones, and Eartha Kitt have performed at this Y's "Little Theatre."
Langston Hughes Place	20 E 127th St · 212-534-5992	Where the prolific poet lived and worked 1947-1967.
Marcus Garvey Park	E 120-124th Sts & Madison Ave · 212-201-PARK	Appealingly mountainous park.
Sylvia's	328 Lenox Ave · 212-996-0660	This restaurant is worth the trip.

Map 20 · El Barrio

Church of Our Lady of Mt Carmel	448 E 115th St · 212-534-0681	The first Italian parish in NYC.
Harlem Courthouse	170 E 121st St	Cool.
Harlem Fire Watchtower	Marcus Garvey Park	It's tall.
Keith Haring "Crack is Wack" Mural	Second Ave & 127th St	Keith was right.
Thomas Jefferson Swimming Pool	2180 First Ave · 212-860-1372	Major pool.

Map 21 · Manhattanville / Hamilton Heights

Audubon Terrace	Broadway & W 155th St	American Academy and Institute of Arts and Letters, American Numismatic Museum, Hispanic Society of America. Pleasant, if lonely, Beaux Arts complex. What's it doing here?

Hamilton Grange National Memorial	287 Convent Ave • 212-368-9133	Elegant buildings on a serene street.
Hamilton Heights Historic District	W 141st- W 145th Sts & Convent Ave	Hamilton's old dig moved here from its original location and now facing the wrong way. Damn those Jeffersonians.
Hispanic Society Museum	613 W 155th St & Broadway • 212-690-0743	Free museum (Tues-Sat) with Spanish masterpieces.
Trinity Church Cemetery's Graveyard of Heroes	3699 Broadway	Hilly, almost countryish cemetery.

Map 22 · Harlem (Upper)

Abyssinian Baptist Church	132 Odell Clark Pl • 212-862-7474	NY's oldest black congregation.
The Dunbar Houses	Frederick Douglass Blvd & W 149th St	Historic multi-family houses.
St Nicholas Historic District	202 W 138th St	Beautiful neo-Georgian townhouses.
The 369th Regiment Armory	2366 Fifth Ave	Home of the Harlem Hellfighters.

Map 23 · Washington Heights

Cross Bronx Expressway		Worst. Highway. Ever.
George Washington Bridge	W 178th St	Try to see it when it's lit up. Drive down from Riverdale on the Henry Hudson at night and you'll understand.
Little Red Lighthouse	under the George Washington Bridge • 212-304-2365	It's there, really!
Morris-Jumel Mansion	Edgecombe Ave & 161st St • 212-923-8008	The oldest building in New York, at least until someone changes it again.
Sylvan Terrace	b/w Jumel Ter & St Nicholas Ave	The most un-Manhattanlike place in the borough.

Map 24 · Fort George / Fort Tryon

Fort Tryon Park	Ft Washington Ave	A totally beautiful and scenic park on New York's north edge.
Yeshiva University Main Building (Zysman Hall)	Amsterdam Ave & W 187th St • 212-960-5224	Interesting Byzantine-style building.

Map 25 · Inwood

The Cloisters	Ft Tryon Park • 212-923-3700	The Met's storehouse of medieval art. Great herb garden, nice views.
Dyckman House	4881 Broadway • 212-643-1527	Needs some work.
Henry Hudson Bridge		Affords a nice view from the Inwood Hill Park side.
Inwood Hill Park		The last natural forest and salt marsh in Manhattan!
West 215th St Step Street	W 215th St	Elevation of sidewalk requires steps.

Battery Park City

Manhattan Sailing Club	North Cove (Liberty St & North End Ave) • 212-786-3323	Membership required.
Mercantile Exchange	1 North End Ave	A great, big financial building in Battery Park.
Museum of Jewish Heritage	36 Battery Pl • 646-437-4200	A living memorial to the Holocaust.
Police Memorial	Liberty St & South End Ave	A fountain commemorating the career of a policeman and those killed in the line of duty.
Skyscraper Museum	39 Battery Pl • 212-968-1961	The place to go to learn what's up in New York.
The Irish Hunger Memorial	Vesey St & North End Ave	A memorial to the "The Great Irish Famine and Migration" to the US in the mid-1800s.
The Real World Sculptures		Tom Otterness sculptures of a tiny, whimsical society. Cooler than Smurfs.
Winter Garden	37 Vesey St	A cavernous marble and glass atrium.

Roosevelt Island

Blackwell House	591 Main St	Fifth-oldest wooden house in New York City.
Blackwell's Lighthouse		Built by institutionalized 19th-century convicts, just like the rest of NYC.
Chapel of the Good Shepherd		1888 Chapel given as a gift to island inmates and patients.

Smallpox Hospital		New York City's only landmarked ruin.
Tramway	Tramway Plz	Short but great thrill ride; see *Nighthawks* for more thrills.

Map 26 · Astoria

American Museum of the Moving Image	36-01 35th Ave · 718-784-4520	Learn about film and television, or catch screenings of classic films.
Astoria Park and Pool	19th St & 23rd Dr · 718-626-8621	City's oldest and largest public pool surrounded by 65 acres of waterfront parkland.
Buzzer Thirty	38-01 23rd Ave · 646-523-8582	Community arts organization with an exhibition space.
Kaufman-Astoria Studios	34-12 36th St · 718-706-5300	The US's largest studio outside of Los Angeles sits on a 13-acre plot with 8 sound stages.
Socrates Sculpture Park	Broadway & Vernon Blvd · 718-956-1819	Cool, gritty sculpture park with events and films.

Map 27 · Long Island City

5 Pointz/Crane Street Studios	Jackson Ave & Crane St	7 train riders will see this graffiti-covered studio building from afar; PS 1 visitors should take a closer look.
Center for the Holographic Arts	45-10 Court Sq · 718-784-5065	Promotes the art of holography.
The Chocolate Factory	5-49 49th Ave · 718-482-7069	Performance space for experimental theater.
Citicorp Building	1 Court Sq	This 48-story structure is the tallest New York building outside of Manhattan.
Fisher Landau Center for Art	38-27 30th St · 718-937-0727	Temporary exhibits plus a world-class permanent collection of contemporary art.
Gantry State Park	50-50 Second St · 718-786-6385	Waterfront park and piers with breathtaking skyline views.
Hunter's Point Historic District	45th Ave b/w 21st St & 23rd St	Well-preserved homes from LIC's first heyday in the late 1800s.
Local Project	21-36 44th Rd · 718-433-2779	Nonprofit performance venue and gallery space.
Long Island City Courthouse	25-10 Court Sq · 718-298-1000	Built in 1876 and rebuilt in 1904, an architectural gem.
The Noguchi Museum	9-01 33rd Rd · 718-204-7088	Showcases Noguchi's work in a converted factory with a beautiful garden.
NY Center for Media Arts	45-12 Davis St	Exhibition space for emerging artists.
PS 1 Contemporary Art Center	22-25 Jackson Ave · 718-784-2084	MoMA's contemporary art space with dance parties every summer Saturday.
SculptureCenter	44-19 Purves St · 718-361-1750	An artist-run nonprofit and gallery supporting experimental sculpture since 1928.
Silvercup Studios	42-22 22nd St · 718-906-2000	Former bakery is now a busy film and television studio.
The Space	42-16 West St	Organization to encourage public arts in Long Island City.

Map 29 · Williamsburg

Brooklyn Brewery	79 N 11th St · 718-486-7422	Connect with your beer by witnessing its birth; free samples also encourage closeness.

Map 30 · Brooklyn Heights / DUMBO / Downtown

Brooklyn Borough Hall	209 Joralemon St · 718-802-3700	Built in the 1840s, this Greek Revival landmark was employed as the official City Hall when Brooklyn was an independent city.
Brooklyn Bridge	Adams St & East River	If you haven't walked over it yet, you're not cool.
Brooklyn Heights Promenade	n/a	The best place to really see Manhattan. It's the view that's in all the movies.
Brooklyn Historical Society	128 Pierrepont St · 718-222-4111	This newly renovated historical landmark building houses a new exhibition, *Brooklyn Works: 300 Years of Making a Living in Brooklyn*.
Brooklyn Ice Cream Factory	Fulton Ferry Pier · 718-246-3963	Expensive, old-fashioned ice cream beneath the bridge.
Brooklyn Navy Yard	Waterfront	Nation's first navy yard employed 70,000 people during WWII. Today, it houses a diverse range of businesses.
Brooklyn Tabernacle	290 Flatbush Ave · 718-783-0942	Home of the Grammy Award-winning Brooklyn Tabernacle Choir.
Fulton Street Mall	Fulton St b/w Flatbush Ave & Boerum Hall	The shopping experience, Brooklyn-style. Hot sneakers can be had for a song.

Jetsons Building	110 York St	View this sculptural roof from the Manhattan Bridge at night when it's lit with colored lights (As though you could ignore it.)
Junior's Restaurant	386 Flatbush Ave · 800-458-6467	For the only cheesecake worth its curds and whey. (Free pickles, great if you're preggers.)
New York Transit Museum	Boerum Pl & Schermerhorn St · 718-243-8601	Everything one can say about the MTA.

Map 31 · Fort Greene / Clinton Hill

Brooklyn Academy of Music	30 Lafayette Ave · 718-636-4100	America's oldest continuously-operating performing arts center. Never dull.
Brooklyn Masonic Temple	317 Clermont Ave · 718-638-1256	You can't actually enter, but it only adds to the mystery of what goes on behind those giant doors.
Fort Greene Park	DeKalb Ave & Washington Park	Liquor store proximity is a plus on a warm afternoon when you visit this welcome chunk of green.
Lafayette Avenue Presbyterian Church	85 S Oxford St · 718-625-7515	Nationally-known church with performing arts; former Underground Railroad stop.
Long Island Rail Road Station	Hanson Pl & Flatbush Ave · 718-217-5477	A low red-brick building that is used by more than 20 million passengers annually. A total craphole.
Pratt Institute Power Plant	200 Willoughby Ave · 718-636-3600	This authentic steam generator gets fired up a few times a year to impress the parents. Cool.
Steiner Studios	15 Washington Ave	Spanking new film studios in the Brooklyn Navy Yard.
Williamsburg Savings Bank Building	1 Hanson Pl	Still the tallest building in the borough and when you're lost, a sight for sore eyes.

Map 32 · BoCoCa / Red Hook

Gowanus Canal	n/a	Brooklyn's answer to the Seine.
Phone Booth	Huntington Street & Hamilton Ave	Where hookers, pimps, and dealers call mom for money.
Red Hook Grain Terminal	n/a	Visit just to wonder what it's doing there.
Warren Place	Warren Pl	Public housing from the 1870s.

Map 33 · Park Slope / Prospect Heights / Windsor Terrace

Brooklyn Botanic Garden	900 Washington Ave · 718-623-7200	A beautiful and peaceful spot inside and out. Cherry blossoms in spring are awe inspiring.
Brooklyn Conservatory of Music	58 Seventh Ave · 718-622-3300	This five-story Victorian Gothic brownstone hosts regular performances by its students and guest artists.
Brooklyn Public Library (Central Branch)	Grand Army Plz · 718-230-2100	The building looks like a book!
Grand Army Plaza	Flatbush Ave & Plaza St	Site of John H. Duncan's Soldiers' and Sailors' Memorial Arch.
Park Slope Food Co-op	782 Union St · 718-622-0560	Any of these farm fresh veggies will do for those in search of their peck of dirt. Rinse.

Map 34 · Hoboken

First recorded baseball game	Elysian Fields	On 19 June 1846, the first officially recorded, organized baseball match was played on Hoboken's Elysian Fields.
Frank Sinatra's Childhood House Location	415 Monroe St	A brick arch built by fans marks the spot where Sinatra spent his childhood.
Hoboken Historical Museum	1301 Hudson St · 201-656-2240	The zipper was invented in Hoboken.
Hoboken Terminal	1 Hudson Pl · 800-772-2222	Gorgeous Beaux-Arts combination railroad and ferry terminal.
Willow Terrace	6th & 7th St b/w Willow Ave & Clinton St	Ye Olde Hoboken Towne.

Map 35 · Jersey City

| Colgate Clock | 105 Hudson St | The world's largest clock's dial--looks cool from Manhattan! |
| Powerhouse | 344 Washington St | This coal-powered railway powerhouse connected New York to New Jersey by train via Hudson River tunnels. Today the Powerhouse is being considered for residential development. |

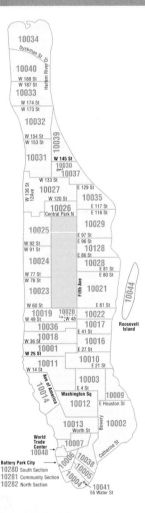

Branch	Address	Phone	Map
Wall Street	73 Pine St	212-425-5875	1
Canal Street	350 Canal St	212-925-3378	2
Church Street	90 Church St	212-330-5001	2
Chinatown	6 Doyers St	212-267-3510	3
Peck Slip	1 Peck Slip	212-964-1054	3
Knickerbocker	128 East Broadway	212-608-3598	4
Pitt Station	185 Clinton St	212-254-9270	4
Village	201 Varick St	212-645-0327	5
West Village	527 Hudson St	212-989-5084	5
Cooper	93 Fourth Ave	212-254-1390	6
Patchin	70 W 10th St	212-475-2534	6
Prince	124 Greene St	212-226-7868	6
Peter Stuyvesant	432 E 14th St	212-677-2112	7
Tompkins Square	244 E 3rd St	212-673-6415	7
James A Farley	421 Eighth Ave	212-330-2902	8
London Terrace	234 Tenth Ave	800-275-8777	8
Port Authority	76 Ninth Ave	800-275-8777	8
Empire State	19 W 33rd St	212-736-8282	9
Greeley Square	39 W 31st St	212-244-7055	9
Midtown	223 W 38th St	212-819-9604	9
Old Chelsea	217 W 18th St	212-675-0548	9
Station 138 (Macy's)	151 W 34th St	212-494-2688	9
Madison Square	149 E 23rd St	212-673-3771	10
Murray Hill	205 E 36th St	212-545-0836	10
Murray Hill Finance	115 E 34th St	212-689-1124	10
Radio City	322 W 52nd St	212-265-3672	11
Times Square	340 W 42nd St	212-502-0421	11
Bryant	23 W 43rd St	212-279-5960	12
Rockefeller Center	610 Fifth Ave	212-265-3854	12
Dag Hammarskjold	884 Second Ave	800-275-8777	13
Franklin D Roosevelt	909 Third Ave	800-275-8777	13
Grand Central Station	450 Lexington Ave	212-330-5722	13
Tudor City	5 Tudor City Pl	800-275-8777	13
Ansonia	178 Columbus Ave	212-362-1697	14
Columbus Circle	27 W 60th St	212-265-7858	14
Planetarium	127 W 83rd St	212-873-5698	14
Cherokee	1483 York Ave	212-517-8361	15
Gracie	229 E 85th St	212-988-6680	15
Lenox Hill	217 E 70th St	212-330-5561	15
Cathedral	215 W 104th St	212-662-0355	16
Park West	693 Columbus Ave	800-275-8777	16
Yorkville	1617 Third Ave	212-369-2747	17
Columbia University	534 W 112th St	800-275-8777	18
Manhattanville	365 W 125th St	212-662-1540	18
Morningside	232 W 116th St	800-275-8777	19
Oscar Garcia Rivera	153 E 110th St	212-860-1896	20
Triborough	167 E 124th St	212-534-0381	20
Hamilton Grange	521 W 146th St	212-281-1538	21
College Station	217 W 140th St	212-283-7096	22
Colonial Park	99 Macombs Pl	212-368-9849	22
Lincolnton	2266 Fifth Ave	212-281-9781	22
Audubon	511 W 165th St	212-568-2387	23
Sergeant Riayan A Tejeda	555 W 180th St	212-568-2690	23
Fort George	4558 Broadway	212-942-5266	24
Inwood Post Office	90 Vermilyea Ave	212-567-7821	25
Roosevelt Island	694 Main St	800-275-8777	p226

The latest FedEx dropoffs are at 9:30 pm Monday-Friday at 880 Third Ave (Map 13), 606 W 49th St and 621 W 48th St (Map 11), 130 Leroy (Map 5), and 537 W 33rd St (Map 8). However, many Manhattan FedEx delivery trucks have a drop-off slot on the side of the truck itself, in case you're on your way to a service center at 9:15 pm and see one. Please note that locations, hours of operation, and pickup times may change. If in doubt, call 1-800-Go-FedEx or visit www.FedEx.com.

Map 1 · Financial District

Drop Box	1 Chase Manhattan Plz	
Drop Box	1 New York Plz	8:30 PM
Drop Box	1 State St Plz	8 PM
Drop Box	11 Broadway	8 PM
Drop Box	120 Broadway	7 PM
Drop Box	150 Broadway	8 PM
Drop Box	17 Battery Pl	8 PM
Drop Box	180 Maiden Ln	8:30 PM
Drop Box	26 Broadway	8 PM
Drop Box	32 Old Slip	8:30 PM
Drop Box	4 New York Plz	8 PM
Drop Box	40 Exchange Pl	8 PM
Drop Box	40 Rector St	7:30 PM
Drop Box	85 Broad St	8:30 PM
Drop Box	90 Broad St	8 PM
Drop Box	95 Wall St	8 PM
FedEx Staffed	100 Wall St	8 PM
FedEx Staffed	100 William St	9 PM
FedEx Staffed	110 Wall St	9 PM
FedEx Staffed	110 William St	9 PM
FedEx Staffed	55 Broadway	9 PM
PostNet	29 John St	7:30 PM
Self-Service	125 Maiden Ln	8 PM
Self-Service	14 Wall St	8 PM
Self-Service	33 Liberty St	7:30 PM
Self-Service	44 Wall St	8 PM
Self-Service	60 Wall St	8 PM
Self-Service	7 Hanover Sq	8 PM
Self-Service	73 Pine St	5 PM
Self-Service	88 Pine St	8:30 PM

Map 2 · TriBeCa

Bestype Imaging	285 W Broadway	6 PM
Drop Box	145 Hudson St	7:30 PM
Drop Box	32 Ave of The Americas	8 PM
Mail Boxes Etc	295 Greenwich St	5:30 PM
PostNet	130 Church St	5:30 PM

Map 3 · City Hall / Chinatown

Drop Box	109 Lafayette St	8 PM
Drop Box	401 Broadway	8:30 PM
EC Shipping Center	230 Grand St	7 PM
Far East Shipping Service	28 Bowery	6:30 PM
FedEx Staffed	105 Duane St	9 PM
FedEx Staffed	4 Barclay St	9 PM

Howard Shipping	33 Howard St	8:30 PM
IBS Group	88 E Broadway, Ste 114-115	6 PM
Quick Global Shipping		
Self-Service	11 Park Pl	8:30 PM
Self-Service	488 Broadway # 92	6 PM
Self-Service	6 Doyers St	4:30 PM
Thriftway Beekman Pharmacy	19 Beekman St	5 PM
WJRD	125 Canal St Frnt 1	6 PM

Map 4 · Lower East Side

Drop Box	357 Grand St	8 PM

Map 5 · West Village

Authorized Ship Center	332 Bleecker St	5:45 PM
Drop Box	315 Hudson St	7:30 PM
Drop Box	350 Hudson St	8:30 PM
Drop Box	375 Hudson St	8:30 PM
Drop Box	80 Eighth Ave	8 PM
Drop Box	95 Morton St	8 PM
FedEx Staffed	130 Leroy St	9:30 PM
FedEx Staffed	229 W 4th St	9 PM
Mail Boxes Etc	315 Bleecker St	5:15 PM
Mail Boxes Etc	511 Ave of the Americas	8 PM
Mailbox Etc	302 W 12th St	5:30 PM
Self-Service	139 Charles St	7:30 PM
Self-Service	201 Varick St	8 PM
Village Copy	520 Hudson St	7 PM

Map 6 · Washington Square / NYU / NoHo / SoHo

Drop Box	270 Lafayette St	8 PM
Drop Box	580 Broadway	8 PM
Drop Box	799 Broadway	8:30 PM
FedEx Staffed	70 Spring St	9 PM
First Prince Copy Center	2 Prince St	6 PM
Mail Call	341 Lafayette St	4:30 PM
Self-Service	124 Greene St	4:30 PM
Self-Service	21 Astor Pl	8 PM
Self-Service	375 Lafayette St	8:30 PM
Self-Service	5 Union Sq W	5 PM
United Shipping and Packaging	200 E 10th St	6:30 PM
Village Postal Center	532 LaGuardia Pl	5 PM

Map 7 · East Village / Lower East Side

FedEx Staffed	250 E Houston St	9 PM
Keepers Packaging & Shipping	444 E 10th St	6 PM
Little Village Postal	151 First Ave	5 PM

Map 8 · Chelsea

Direct Rush	356 W 37th St	8 PM
Drop Box	111 Eighth Ave	5:30 PM
Drop Box	322 Eighth Ave	8 PM
Drop Box	450 W 15th St	8 PM
Drop Box	450 W 33rd St	6 PM
Drop Box	505 Eighth Ave	8 PM
Drop Box	519 Eighth Ave	8 PM
Drop Box	520 Eighth Ave	8 PM
Drop Box	545 Eighth Ave	8 PM
Drop Box	547 W 27th St	7:30 PM
Drop Box	75 Ninth Ave	8 PM
FedEx Staffed	537 W 33rd St	9:30 PM
FedEx Staffed	538 W 34th St	9 PM
Mail Boxes	245 Eighth Ave	8 PM
Self-Service	234 Tenth Ave	4:30 PM
Self-Service	508 W 26th St	8 PM

Map 9 · Flatiron / Lower Midtown

Drop Box	1133 Broadway	8 PM
Drop Box	121 W 27th St	8 PM
Drop Box	1250 Broadway	7 PM
Drop Box	132 W 31st St	7:30 PM
Drop Box	1370 Broadway	7:30 PM
Drop Box	1407 Broadway	7 PM
Drop Box	21 Penn Plz	8 PM
Drop Box	220 Fifth Ave	8 PM
Drop Box	220 W 19th St	5 PM
Drop Box	230 Fifth Ave	8 PM
Drop Box	28 E 28th St	7 PM
Drop Box	330 Fifth Ave	6 PM
Drop Box	37 E 28th St	8 PM
Drop Box	390 Fifth Ave	8 PM
Drop Box	41 Madison Ave	8 PM
Drop Box	45 W 18th St	8 PM
Drop Box	450 Seventh Ave	8 PM
Drop Box	463 Seventh Ave	8 PM
Drop Box	5 W 37th St	7:30 PM
Drop Box	875 Ave of the Americas	8 PM
FedEx Staffed	1 Penn Plz	9 PM

FedEx Staffed	112 W 39th St	9 PM
FedEx Staffed	125 Fifth Ave	9 PM
FedEx Staffed	125 W 33rd St	9 PM
FedEx Staffed	1350 Broadway	9 PM
FedEx Staffed	157 W 35th St	9 PM
FedEx Staffed	191 Madison Ave	6 PM
FedEx Staffed	20 E 20th St	9 PM
FedEx Staffed	245 Seventh Ave	2 PM
FedEx Staffed	261 Madison Ave	9 PM
FedEx Staffed	326 Seventh Ave	9 PM
FedEx Staffed	350 Fifth Ave	9 PM
FedEx Staffed	525 Seventh Ave	9 PM
FedEx Staffed	650 Sixth Ave	7:30 PM
FedEx Staffed	8 E 23rd St	9 PM
PostNet	200 W 39th St	6 PM
PostNet	800 Ave of the Americas	6 PM
Self-Service	100 W 33rd St	7 PM
Self-Service	1385 Broadway	7:30 PM
Self-Service	149 Madison Ave	9 PM
Self-Service	16 E 34th St	6 PM
Self-Service	19 W 33rd St	4:30 PM
Self-Service	207 W 25th St	8 PM
Self-Service	217 W 18th St	5 PM
Self-Service	223 W 38th St	5 PM
Self-Service	225 W 34th St	8 PM
Self-Service	233 W 18th St	5 PM
Self-Service	239 Seventh Ave	5 PM
Self-Service	366 Fifth Ave	6 PM
Self-Service	39 W 31st St	4:30 PM
Self-Service	485 Seventh Ave	8 PM
Self-Service	5 Penn Plz	8 PM
Self-Service	50 W 34th St	7 PM
Self-Service	500 Seventh Ave	8 PM
Self-Service	650 Ave of the Americas	8 PM
Self-Service	699 Ave of the Americas	7 PM

Map 10 • Murray Hill / Gramercy

Backofficenyc	345 E 18th St	7 PM
Drop Box	192 Lexington Ave	7 PM
Drop Box	200 Park Ave S	8:15 PM
Drop Box	220 E 23rd St	8 PM
Drop Box	240 E 38th St	7:30 PM
Drop Box	3 Park Ave	8 PM
Drop Box	3G Waterside Plz	8 PM
Drop Box	345 Park Ave S	8 PM
Drop Box	475 Park Ave S	8 PM
Drop Box	545 First Ave	8 PM
FedEx Staffed	108 E 28th St	9 PM
FedEx Staffed	2 Park Ave	9 PM
FedEx Staffed	257 Park Ave S	8 PM
FedEx Staffed	4 Union Sq E	9 PM
FedEx Staffed	600 Third Ave	9 PM
FedEx Staffed	90 Park Ave	9 PM
Mail Boxes	350 Third Ave	6 PM
Mail Boxes Etc	303 Park Ave S	6:30 PM
Self-Service	200 Lexington Ave	8 PM
Self-Service	225 Park Ave S Fl 13	8 PM

Self-Service	345 Park Ave S	5 PM
Self-Service	425 E 25th St	7 PM
Self-Service	550 First Ave	8 PM
Self-Service	600 Third Ave	8 PM
Self-Service	660 First Ave	6 PM
SX/Moonlite Courier	125 E 23rd St	8 PM
The Villager	338 First Ave	7 PM

Map 11 • Hell's Kitchen

Drop Box	630 Ninth Ave	8 PM
FedEx Staffed	560 W 42nd St	9:30 PM
FedEx Staffed	621 W 48th St	9:30 PM
Mail Boxes	331 W 57th St	5 PM
Mail Boxes Etc	676 Ninth Ave	5 PM
Self-Service	322 W 52nd St	7 PM
Self-Service	340 W 42nd St	4:30 PM
Self-Service	405 W 55th St	8 PM
Self-Service	429 W 53rd St	8 PM
Self-Service	432 W 58th St	6 PM

Map 12 • Midtown

Drop Box	10 E 40th St	8 PM
Drop Box	1095 Sixth Ave	7:30 PM
Drop Box	120 W 45th St	8 PM
Drop Box	1325 Sixth Ave	8:30 PM
Drop Box	1350 Ave of the Americas	8 PM
Drop Box	1370 Ave of the Americas	8 PM
Drop Box	1466 Broadway	8 PM
Drop Box	1500 Broadway	8 PM
Drop Box	1501 Broadway	8 PM
Drop Box	152 W 57th St	8 PM
Drop Box	1700 Broadway	8:30 PM
Drop Box	1775 Broadway	8 PM
Drop Box	3 E 54th St	8 PM
Drop Box	41 W 48th St	8 PM
Drop Box	477 Madison Ave	8 PM
Drop Box	488 Madison Ave	8 PM
Drop Box	500 Fifth Ave	8 PM
Drop Box	51 W 52nd St Fl 21	8:30 PM
Drop Box	530 Fifth Ave	8 PM
Drop Box	555 Madison Ave	8 PM
Drop Box	575 Madison Ave	8 PM
Drop Box	600 Madison Ave	8 PM
Drop Box	712 Fifth Ave	8 PM
Drop Box	745 Fifth Ave	8 PM
Drop Box	787 Seventh Ave	8 PM
Drop Box	825 Eighth Ave	8 PM
FedEx Staffed	10 E 53rd St	8 PM
FedEx Staffed	1120 Ave of the Americas	9 PM
FedEx Staffed	1211 Ave of the Americas	9 PM
FedEx Staffed	1290 Ave of the Americas	9 PM
FedEx Staffed	135 W 50th St	9 PM
FedEx Staffed	1440 Broadway	9 PM

FedEx Staffed	16 E 52nd St	8 PM
FedEx Staffed	200 W 57th St	9 PM
FedEx Staffed	233 W 54th St	9 PM
FedEx Staffed	240 Central Park S	8 PM
FedEx Staffed	43 W 42nd St	9 PM
FedEx Staffed	437 Madison Ave	8 PM
FedEx Staffed	51 E 44th St	6:30 PM
FedEx Staffed	6 W 48th St	9 PM
FedEx Staffed	767 Fifth Ave	6 PM
Fifth Avenue Pack & Ship	666 Fifth Ave	5:30 PM
La Boutique	2 E 55th St	7 PM
Self-Service	1065 Sixth Ave	7 PM
Self-Service	1185 Ave of the Americas	8 PM
Self-Service	1285 Ave of the Americas	8 PM
Self-Service	1515 Broadway	8:30 PM
Self-Service	156 W 56th St	7:30 PM
Self-Service	224 W 57th St	8 PM
Self-Service	23 W 43rd St	4:30 PM
Self-Service	335 Madison Ave	7:30 PM
Self-Service	444 Madison Ave	8 PM
Self-Service	57 W 57th St	7 PM
Self-Service	590 Madison Ave	8 PM
Self-Service	60 W 40th St	8 PM
Self-Service	610 Fifth Ave	4:30 PM

Map 13 • East Midtown

Drop Box	150 E 42nd St	7 PM
Drop Box	150 E 58th St	8:30 PM
Drop Box	211 E 43rd St	7 PM
Drop Box	220 E 42nd St	7:30 PM
Drop Box	270 Park Ave	9:15 PM
Drop Box	350 Park Ave	7 PM
Drop Box	353 Lexington Ave	7:30 PM
Drop Box	500 Park Ave	7 PM
Drop Box	575 Lexington Ave	7 PM
Drop Box	630 Third Ave	8 PM
Drop Box	633 Third Ave	8 PM
Drop Box	805 Third Ave	7 PM
Drop Box	866 United Nations Plz	8 PM
Drop Box	979 Third Ave	8 PM
FedEx Staffed	153 E 53rd St	7 PM
FedEx Staffed	230 Park Ave	8 PM
FedEx Staffed	405 Park Ave	8 PM
FedEx Staffed	450 Lexington Ave	8 PM
FedEx Staffed	641 Lexington Ave	8:30 PM
FedEx Staffed	747 Third Ave	8 PM
FedEx Staffed	750 Third Ave	8 PM
FedEx Staffed	880 Third Ave	9:30 PM
Mail Boxes Etc	1040 First Ave	5 PM
Mail Boxes Etc	847 Second Ave	5 PM
Self-Service	100 Park Ave	8 PM
Self-Service	135 E 57th St	7 PM
Self-Service	205 E 42nd St	6 PM
Self-Service	280 Park Ave	8:45 PM
Self-Service	299 Park Ave	8:30 PM

Self-Service	355 Lexington Ave	8 PM
Self-Service	420 Lexington Ave	8 PM
Self-Service	425 Lexington Ave	6 PM
Self-Service	45 E 49th St	5 PM
Self-Service	450 Lexington Ave	8 PM
Self-Service	55 E 59th St	8 PM
Self-Service	60 E 42nd St	8:15 PM
Self-Service	885 Third Ave	8 PM
Self-Service	909 Third Ave	6:30 PM

Map 14 · Upper West Side (Lower)

Drop Box	101 West End Ave	6:30 PM
FedEx Staffed	156 W 72nd St	5 PM
FedEx Staffed	221 W 72nd St	8 PM
FedEx Staffed	2211 Broadway	9 PM
Mail Boxes Etc	163 Amsterdam Ave	6 PM
Mail Boxes Etc	459 Columbus Ave	6 PM
Self-Service	127 W 83rd St	6 PM
Self-Service	168 Columbus Ave	6:30 PM
Self-Service	211 W 61st St	6 PM
Self-Service	2248 Broadway	5 PM
Self-Service	27 W 60th St	3:30 PM
Self-Service	517 Amsterdam Ave	7 PM
The Padded Wagon	215 W 85th St	5 PM

Map 15 · Upper East Side (Lower)

Big Apple Art Gallery	1456 Second Ave	5 PM
Drop Box	667 Madison Ave	8:30 PM
Drop Box	968 Lexington Ave	6 PM
FedEx Staffed	1122 Lexington Ave	8:30 PM
Mail Boxes Etc	1461 First Ave	6 PM
Mail Boxes Etc	954 Lexington Ave	5:45 PM
Postal Express	1382 Third Ave	6 PM
Self-Service	1300 York Ave	8:30 PM
Self-Service	217 E 70th St	6 PM
Self-Service	425 E 61st St	5:30 PM
Self-Service	428 E 72nd St	6 PM
Self-Service	445 E 69th St	5:30 PM
Self-Service	525 E 68th St	8 PM
Self-Service	650 Madison Ave	7:30 PM
Self-Service	695 Park Ave	7:30 PM
Senderos	1471 Third Ave	6 PM
The Padded Wagon Budget	1569 Second Ave	6 PM

Map 16 · Upper West Side (Upper)

Columbia Copy Center	2790 Broadway	8 PM
Copy Experts	2440 Broadway	7:30 PM
Foxy Graphic Services	211 W 92nd St	5 PM
Mail Boxes Etc	2444 Broadway	6 PM
Mail Boxes Etc	2565 Broadway	6 PM
Self-Service	70 W 86th St	8 PM

Map 17 · Upper East Side / East Harlem

Compu Signs Plus	1598 Third Ave	6 PM
Cross County Pharmacy	1514 Madison Ave	3 PM
Mail Boxes Etc	1369 Madison Ave	6 PM
Mail Boxes Etc	1710 First Ave	6 PM
SDS Duplicating	2069 Second Ave	6 PM
Self-Service	1 E 104th St	6:30 PM
Self-Service	1280 Lexington Ave	8 PM
Self-Service	1619 Third Ave	5 PM
Self-Service	225 E 95th St	8:30 PM

Map 18 · Columbia / Morningside Heights

Drop Box	475 Riverside Dr	7 PM
FedEx Staffed	600 W 116th St	9 PM
Self-Service	3022 Broadway	8 PM
Self-Service	435 W 116th St	8 PM
Self-Service	525 W 120th St	8 PM

Map 19 · Harlem (Lower)

Self-Service	163 W 125th St	7 PM
Self-Service	55 W 125th St	7 PM

Map 20 · El Barrio

Self-Service	1879 Madison	6:45 PM

Map 21 · Manhattanville / Hamilton Heights

La National	3351 Broadway	6 PM
La National	3480 Broadway	6 PM
La National	3609 Broadway	6 PM

Map 23 · Washington Heights

Doc Q Pack	2201 Amsterdam Ave	7 PM
Drop Box	161 Ft Washington Ave	7 PM
Drop Box	722 W 168th St	7:30 PM
La National	1342 St Nicholas Ave	6 PM
La National	113 Audubon Ave	6 PM
La National	2174 Amsterdam Ave	6 PM
La National	3914 Broadway	6 PM
Rel Express Pack	2140 Amsterdam Ave	6 PM
Self-Service	100 Haven Ave	7 PM
Self-Service	1051 Riverside Dr	7:30 PM
Self-Service	1150 St Nicholas Ave	6:30 PM
Self-Service	177 Ft Washington Ave	7 PM
Self-Service	3960 Broadway	7 PM
Self-Service	60 Haven Ave	7 PM
Self-Service	622 W 168th St	7 PM
Self-Service	630 W 168th St	7 PM
Self-Service	701 W 168th St	7 PM
Self-Service	710 W 168th St	7 PM

Map 24 · Fort George / Fort Tryon

La National	1443 St Nicholas Ave	6 PM
La National	1533 St Nicholas Ave	6 PM
Mibandera Cargo Express	570 W 189th St	5 PM
Quisqueyana Express	4468 Broadway	6:30 PM

Map 25 · Inwood

Adam Enterprises	165 Sherman Ave	4:30 PM
Atlas Travel Group	4742 Broadway	5 PM
La Nacional	566 W 207th St	3 PM

Battery Park City

Drop Box	3 World Financial Ctr	8 PM

Pharmacies <small>Closing Time (Prescription Counter) Address</small>

Pharmacy	Closing Time	Address	Phone	Map
Rite Aid		408 Grand St	212-529-7115	4
Duane Reade	9 PM	378 Sixth Ave	212-674-5357	5
Duane Reade	9 PM	123 Third Ave	212-529-7140	6
Duane Reade	10 PM	24 E 14th St	212-989-3632	6
Duane Reade	8:30 PM	598 Broadway	212-343-2567	6
Duane Reade	8:30 PM	769 Broadway	646-602-8274	6
Walgreen's		145 Fourth Ave	212-677-0054	6
Duane Reade	10 PM	460 Eighth Ave	212-244-4026	8
Duane Reade	9 PM	180 W 20th St	212-243-0129	9
Duane Reade	8 PM	358 Fifth Ave	212-279-0208	9
Walgreen's		33 E 23rd St	212-685-2047	9
Walgreen's		350 Fifth Ave	212-868-5790	9
CVS Pharmacy		342 E 23rd St	212-505-1555	10
Duane Reade	8:30 PM	155 E 34th St	212-683-3042	10
Duane Reade	8 PM	300 Park Ave S	212-533-7580	10
Rite Aid		542 Second Ave	212-213-9887	10
CVS Pharmacy		400 W 58th St	212-245-0617	11
Duane Reade	8 PM	100 W 57th St	212-956-0464	12
Duane Reade	10 PM	1627 Broadway	212-586-0374	12
Duane Reade		224 W 57th St	212-541-9708	12
Duane Reade	7 PM	4 Times Sq	646-366-8047	12
Duane Reade	7:30 PM	625 Eighth Ave	212-273-0889	12
Duane Reade	8 PM	661 Eighth Ave	212-977-1562	12
Duane Reade	9 PM	900 Eighth Ave	212-582-3463	12
Rite Aid		301 W 50th St	212-247-8384	12
CVS Pharmacy		630 Lexington Ave	917-369-8688	13
Duane Reade	8 PM	1076 Second Ave	212-223-1130	13
Duane Reade	8 PM	401 Park Ave	212-213-9730	13
Duane Reade	8 PM	405 Lexington Ave	212-808-4743	13
Duane Reade	8:30 PM	485 Lexington Ave	212-682-5338	13
Duane Reade	9 PM	852 Second Ave	212-983-1810	13
Duane Reade	9 PM	866 Third Ave	212-759-9412	13
Duane Reade	9 PM	2025 Broadway	212-579-9955	14
Duane Reade	8:30 PM	253 W 72nd St	212-580-0497	14
Duane Reade	10 PM	380 Amsterdam Ave	212-579-7246	14
Duane Reade	9 PM	4 Amsterdam Ave	212-581-5527	14
Duane Reade	9 PM	4 Columbus Cir	212-265-2302	14
Rite Aid		210 Amsterdam Ave	212-787-2903	14
CVS Pharmacy		1396 Second Ave	212-249-5699	15
Duane Reade	9 PM	1191 Second Ave	212-355-5944	15
Duane Reade		1279 Third Ave	212-744-2668	15
Duane Reade	9 PM	1345 First Ave	212-535-9816	15
Duane Reade	9 PM	1498 York Ave	212-879-8990	15
Duane Reade	9 PM	773 Lexington Ave	212-829-0651	15
Walgreen's		1328 Second Ave	212-734-6076	15
CVS Pharmacy		540 Amsterdam Ave	212-712-2821	16
CVS Pharmacy		743 Amsterdam Ave	212-280-0582	16
Duane Reade		2522 Broadway	212-663-1580	16
Duane Reade	9 PM	2589 Broadway	212-864-5246	16
Duane Reade		609 Columbus Ave	212-724-4270	16
Rite Aid		2833 Broadway	212-663-3135	16
CVS Pharmacy		1622 Third Ave	212-876-7016	17
Duane Reade	9 PM	1231 Madison Ave	212-360-6586	17
Duane Reade	9 PM	125 E 86th St	212-996-5261	17
Duane Reade	9 PM	1675 Third Ave	212-348-7400	17
Duane Reade	9:30 PM	401 E 86th St	917-492-8801	17
Rite Aid		146 E 86th St		17
Duane Reade	9 PM	2864 Broadway	212-316-5113	18

Copying

	Address	Phone	Map
Acro Photo Printing	90 Maiden Ln	212-809-8999	1
Administrative Resources	60 Broad St, 25th Fl	212-480-3892	1
Printech Business Systems	519 Eighth Ave	212-290-2542	8
Exact	1 W 34th St	212-643-6699	9
FedEx Kinko's	191 Madison Ave	212-685-3449	9
Kinko's	245 Seventh Ave	212-929-0623	9
Metropolitan Duplicating & Imaging	216 W 18th St	212-620-0087	9
Village Copier	10 E 39th St	212-599-3344	9
On-Site Sourcing	443 Park Ave S Fl 3	212-252-9700	10
Xact	333 W 52nd St	212-581-9595	11
Discovery Copy Services	45 W 45th St	212-827-0039	12
FedEx Kinko's	233 W 54th St	212-977-2679	12
Kinko's	1211 Sixth Ave	212-391-2679	12
Kinko's	16 E 52nd St	212-308-2679	12
Kinko's	240 Central Park S	212-258-3750	12
Kinko's	60 W 40th St	212-921-1060	12
Kopy Kween	25 W 45th St	212-944-7350	12
Skyline Duplication	151 W 46th St	212-302-5153	12
Kinko's	641 Lexington Ave	212-572-9995	13
Kinko's	747 Third Ave	212-753-7778	13
Kinko's	221 W 72nd St	212-362-5288	14
FedEx Kinko's	1122 Lexington Ave	212-628-5500	15
The Village Copier	2872 Broadway	212-666-0600	18

Post Office

	Address	Phone	Map
JA Farley GPO	421 Eighth Ave	212-330-2902	8

Hardware Store

	Address	Phone	Map
HomeFront	202 E 29th St	212-545-1447	10

Plumbers

	Address	Phone	Map
Sanitary Plumbing and Heating	211 E 117th St	212-734-5000	20
Effective Plumbing	Multiple Locations	212-545-0100	n/a
New York Plumbing & Heating Service	Multiple Locations	212-496-9191	n/a
Roto-Rooter Plumbing	Multiple Locations	212-687-1661	n/a

Gyms

	Address	Phone	Map
24/7 Fitness Club	107 Chambers St	212-267-7949	2
New York Sports Clubs	125 Seventh Ave S	212-206-1500	5
24/7 Fitness Club	47 W 14th St	212-206-1504	6
New York Sports Clubs	113 E 23rd St	212-982-4400	10
New York Sports Clubs	2527 Broadway	212-665-0009	16

Veterinary

	Address	Phone	Map
Animal Emergency Clinic	1 W 15th St	212-924-3311	9
Animal Medical Center	510 E 62nd St	212-838-8100	15
Center for Veterinary Care	236 E 75th St	212-734-7480	15
Park East Animal Hospital	52 E 64th St	212-832-8417	15

Gas Stations

		Map			Map
Mobil	2 Pike St	4	Independent	619 W 125th St	18
Lukoil	63 Eighth Ave	5	Mobil	3260 Broadway	18
Mobil	140 Sixth Ave	5	Exxon	2040 Frederick Douglass Blvd	19
Mobil	290 West St	5	Shell	235 St Nicholas Ave	19
Exxon	24 Second Ave	6	Amoco	2276 First Ave	20
Mobil	253 E 2nd St	7	Getty	155 St Nicholas Ave	21
Exxon	110 Eighth Ave	8	Mobil	3740 Broadway	21
Getty	239 Tenth Ave	8	Mobil	800 St Nicholas Ave	21
Mobil	309 Eleventh Ave	8	Amoco	232 W 145th St	22
Mobil	70 Tenth Ave	8	Hess	128 W 145th St	22
Mobil	718 Eleventh Ave	11	Mobil	150 W 145th St	22
Mobil	1132 York Ave	15	Shell	2420 Amsterdam Ave	23
Exxon	303 W 96th St	16	BP	3936 Tenth Ave	25
Amoco	1599 Lexington Ave	17	Getty	242 Dyckman St	25
BP	1855 First Ave	17	Getty	4880 Broadway	25
Getty	348 E 106th St	17	Shell	3761 Tenth Ave	25

Newsstands

	Map		Map
Sixth Ave & 3rd St	5	59th St & Third Ave	13
Sixth Ave (South of W 8th St)	5	First Ave & 57th St	13
Second Ave & St Marks Pl	6	72nd St & Broadway	14
St Marks Pl & Bowery	6	76th St & Broadway	14
Delancey & Essex Sts	7	Columbus Ave & 81st St	14
23rd St & Third Ave	10	79th St & York (First Ave)	15
Third Ave (34th/35th Sts)	10	First Ave & 63rd St	15
42nd St & Seventh Ave	12	Second Ave (60th/61st Sts)	15
49th St & Eighth Ave	12	86th St & Lexington Ave	17
Broadway & 50th St	12	Broadway & 116th St	18

Delivery and Messengers *Phone*

Alliance Courier & Freight	212-302-3422
Moonlite Courier	212-473-2246
Need It Now	212-989-1919
Parkes Messenger Service	212-997-9023
Same Day Express	800-982-5910
Urban Express	212-855-5555

Private Investigators *Phone*

Matthew T Cloth, PI	718-449-4100
North American Investigations	800-724-8080
Sherlock Investigations	212-579-4302/ 888-354-2174

Locksmiths *Phone*

A&V Locksmith	212-226-0011	East Manhattan Locksmiths	212-369-9063
Aaron-Hotz Locksmith	212-243-7166	Emergency Locksmith 24 Hours	212-231-7627
Abbey Locksmiths	212-535-2289	LockDoctors	212-935-6600
Advantage Locksmith	212-398-5500	Lockmasters Locksmith	212-690-4018
Always Ready Locksmiths	888-490-4900	Night and Day Locksmith	212-722-1017
American Locksmiths	212-888-8888	Paragon Security & Locksmith	212-620-9000
CBS Locksmith	212-410-0090	Speedway Locksmith	877-917-6500
Champion Locksmiths	212-362-7000		

Restaurants

	Address	Phone	Map
Jin Market	111 Hudson St		2
Wo Hop	17 Mott St	212-267-2536	3
Florent	69 Gansevoort St	212-989-5779	5
French Roast	78 W 11th St	212-533-2233	5
Around the Clock	8 Stuyvesant Pl	212-598-0402	6
Cozy Soup & Burger	739 Broadway	212-477-5566	6
Knicks Lunch East	1732 Second Ave	212-426-8400	6
Veselka	144 Second Ave	212-228-9682	6
7A	109 Ave A	212-673-6583	7
Bereket Turkish Kebab House	187 E Houston St	212-475-7700	7
Odessa	119 Ave A	212-253-1470	7
Yaffa Café	97 St Marks Pl	212-674-9302	7
Cheyenne Diner	411 Ninth Ave	212-465-8750	8
Empire Diner	210 Tenth Ave	212-243-2736	8
Skylight Diner	402 W 34th St	212-244-0395	8
Tick Tock Diner	481 Eighth Ave	212-268-8444	8
Cafeteria	119 Seventh Ave	212-414-1717	9
Kang Suh	1250 Broadway	212-564-6845	9
Kum Gang San	49 W 32nd St	212-967-0909	9
Kunjip	9 W 32nd St	212-216-9487	9
Woo Chon	8 W 36th St	212-695-0676	9
Gemini Diner	641 Second Ave	212-532-2143	10
Gramercy Restaurant	184 Third Ave	212-982-2121	10
L'Express	249 Park Ave S	212-254-5858	10
Sarge's Deli	548 Third Ave	212-679-0442	10
H&H Bagels	639 W 46th St	212-765-7200	11
Morningstar	401 W 57th St	212-246-1593	11
Big Nick's	2175 Broadway	212-362-9238	14
French Roast	2340 Broadway	212-799-1533	14
Gray's Papaya	2090 Broadway	212-799-0243	14
H&H Bagels	2239 Broadway	212-595-8003	14
Manhattan Diner	2180 Broadway	212-877-7252	14
City Diner	2441 Broadway	212-877-2720	16
IHOP	2294 Adam Clayton Powell Jr Blvd	212-234-4747	19
New Caporal	3772 Broadway	212-862-8986	21
El Malecon	4141 Broadway	212-927-3812	23
Tipico Dominicano	4177 Broadway	212-781-3900	23
Bobby's Fish and Seafood Market and Restaurant	3842 Ninth Ave	212-304-9440	25

Supermarkets

	Address	Phone	Map
Jubilee Marketplace	99 John St	212-233-0808	1
Gristede's	460 Third Ave	212-251-9670	10
Gristede's	907 Eighth Ave	212-582-5873	12
Westside Market	2171 Broadway	212-595-2536	14
Gristede's	1446 Second Ave	212-535-4925	15
Gristede's	2704 Broadway	646-352-4676	16
Gristede's Mega Store	262 W 96th St	212-663-5126	16
Gristede's Mega Store	350 E 86th St	212-535-1688	17
Gristede's	315 South End Ave	212-233-7797	p202

Laundromats

	Address	Phone	Map
69 Avenue C Laundromat	69 Ave C	212-388-9933	7
Classic Laundry	262 W 145th St	917-507-4865	22
106 Audubon Avenue Laundromat	106 Audubon Ave	212-795-8717	23

General Information • **Dog Runs**

Useful websites: www.doglaw.com, www.nycparks.org, www.urbanhound.com

It's good to be a dog in New York. NYC's pooches are among the world's most pampered: They celebrate birthdays, don expensive sweaters, and prance down Fifth Avenue in weather-appropriate gear. But for the rest of us, who would rather step in dog doo than dress our pups in Burberry raincoats, there's still reason to smile. NYC is full of dog runs—both formal and informal—scattered throughout the city's parks and neighborhood community spaces. Good thing too, as the fine for having a dog off-leash can run upwards of $100, and park officials are vigilant. While the city takes no active role in the management of the dog runs, it provides space to the community groups who do. These community groups are always eager for help (volunteer time or financial contributions) and many post volunteer information on park bulletin boards. Each run is different, but pet lovers can check out www.urbanhounds.com for descriptions. It's good to know, for example, that Riverside Park at 87th Street has a fountain and hose to keep dogs cool in the summer. Formal runs are probably the safest bet for pets, as most are enclosed and maintained. For safety reasons, choke or pronged collars are forbidden, and identification and rabies tags should remain on the flat collar. Most runs prohibit dogs in heat, aggressive dogs, and dogs without up-to-date shots.

There are no dog runs in Central Park, but before 9am the park is full of people walking their dogs off-leash. While this is a strict no-no for the rest of the day (and punishable by hefty fines), park officials unofficially tolerate the practice as long as dogs maintain a low profile, and are leashed immediately at 9am.

Map	Name • Address • Comments
2	**P.S. 234** • 300 Greenwich St at Chambers St • Private run. $50/year membership. www.doglaw.com
3	**Fish Bridge Park** • Pearl and Dover Sts • Concrete-surfaced runs. Features water hose, wading pool, and lock box with newspapers. www.nycgovparks.org
5	**West Village D.O.G. Run** • Little W 12th St • Features benches, water hose, and drink bowl. Membership costs $40 annually, but there's a waiting list. www.manhattan.about.com
6	**Washington Square Park** • MacDougal St at W 4th St • Located in the southwest corner of the park, this is a large, gravel-surfaced run with many spectators. This popular run gets very crowded, but is well-maintained nonetheless. www.nycgovparks.org
6	**LaGuardia Place** • Mercer St at Houston St • This is a private run with a membership (and a waiting list). The benefits to this run include running water and a plastic wading pool for your dog to splash in. www.mhdra.org
6	**Union Square** • Broadway at 16th St • Crushed stone surface. www.nycgovparks.org
7	**Tompkins Square Park** • Avenue B at 10th St • New York City's first dog run is quite large and has a wood chip surface. Toys, balls, frisbees, and dogs in heat are all prohibited. This community-centered run offers lots of shade, benches, and running water. www.nycgovparks.org
7	**Thomas Smith Triangle** • Eleventh Ave at 23rd St • Concrete-surfaced run. www.nycgovparks.org
8	**Chelsea** • 18th St at the West Side Hwy
10	**Madison Square Park** • Madison Ave at 25th St • Medium-sized run with gravel surface and plenty of trees. www.nycgovparks.org
11	**DeWitt Clinton Park** • Eleventh Ave at 52nd & 54th Sts • Two small concrete-surfaced runs. www.nycgovparks.org
11	**Hell's Kitchen/Clinton Dog Run** • W 39th St at Tenth Ave • A private dog run (membership costs $15 a year) featuring chairs, umbrellas, fenced garden, and woodchip surface. www.urbanhound.com
13	**E 60th Street Pavilion** • 60th St at the East River • Concrete-surfaced run. www.doglaw.com
13	**Peter Detmold Park** • Beekman Pl at 51st St • Large well-maintained run with cement and dirt surfaces and many trees. www.nycgovparks.org
13	**Robert Moses Park** • First Ave and 42nd St • Concrete surface. www.nycgovparks.org
14	**Theodore Roosevelt Park** • Central Park W at W 81st St • Gravel surface. www.nycgovparks.org
14	**Riverside Park** • Riverside Dr at 72nd St www.nycgovparks.org
14	**Margaret Mead Park** • Columbus Ave at 81st St www.leashline.com
15	**Balto Dog Monument** • Fifth Ave at E 67th St (Central Park)
15,17	**Carl Schurz Park** • East End Ave at 85/86th Sts • Medium-sized enclosed run with pebbled surface and separate space for small dogs. This run has benches and shady trees, and running water is available in the bathrooms. www.nycgovparks.org
16	**Riverside Park** • Riverside Dr at 87th St • Medium-sized run with gravel surface. www.nycgovparks.org
16	**Riverside Park** • Riverside Dr at 105/106th Sts • Medium-sized run with gravel surface. www.nycgovparks.org
18	**Morningside Park** • Morningside Ave b/w 114th & 119th Sts www.nycgovparks.org
20	**Thomas Jefferson Park** • E 112nd St at First Ave • Wood chips surface.
21	**Harlem** • Riverside Dr at 140th St www.doglaw.com
23	**J. Hood Wright Park** • Haven Ave at W 173rd St • An enclosed dirt-surfaced run. www.nycgovparks.org
24	**Fort Tryon Park** • Margaret Corbin Dr, Washington Heights www.nycgovparks.org
25	**Inwood Hill Dog Run** • Dyckman St and Payson Av • Gravel surface. www.nycgovparks.org
p202	**Battery Park City (south end)** • Third Pl at Battery Pl • This long, narrow, concrete-surfaced enclosed run is located along the West Side Highway and offers a pleasant view of the river and some shade.
p202	**Battery Park City** • Along River Ter between Park Pl W and Murray St • Concrete-surfaced run with a view of the river. www.manhattan.about.com

If you're reading this you're probably not a tourist, and if you're not a tourist you probably don't need a hotel. However, chances are good that at some point your obnoxious friend or relative from out of state will suddenly come a-knockin', bearing news of their long-awaited arrival to the big city. "So I thought I'd stay at your place," they will suggest casually, displaying their complete ignorance of the number of square feet in an average New York apartment—and simultaneously realizing their greatest fear of playing host to someone you greatly dislike. Or there's the possibility that your place is infested with mice, bed-bugs, or pigeons and you need to escape, pronto. Or maybe you're just looking for a romantic (or slightly less than romantic) getaway without leaving the city. Whatever the case, be assured that there is a seemingly endless array of possibilities to suit all your overnight desires and needs.

Obviously, your options run from dirt cheap (that's "dirt cheap" by NYC standards) to disgustingly offensive. For those of you with money to spare and/or a respect for high status, there are the elite luxury chains—**The Ritz Carlton** (cheaper to stay at the one in Battery Park (**Map 100**) than Central Park (**Map 12**)), **The Four Seasons** (**Map 12**)(E 57th St), **The W** (Union Square (**Map 10**), Times Square (**Map 12**), E 39th St (**Map 10**), and Lexington Ave at 49th St (**Map 13**)), **Le Parker Meridien** (**Map 12**)(W 57th St), **The Peninsula** (**Map 12**)(5th Ave at 55th St), **The St. Regis** (**Map 12**)(E 55th St), **Swissotel** (**Map 13**)(Park Ave at 56th St), and **The Mandarin-Oriental (14**)(Columbus Circle).

Those hotels that are more unique to Manhattan include: **The Lowell (Map 15)**, a fortress of pretentiousness nestled beside Central Park, which successfully captures the feel of a snobby, high-class gentleman's club. For a similar feeling, only with a heavy dose of Renaissance Italy and a design dating back to 1882, check into **The New York Palace (Map 12)**(E 51st St). If you prefer more modern surroundings, the swank-tastic **Bryant Park Hotel (Map 12)** on W 40th St (once the landmark Radiator building before it was transformed) is a favorite amongst entertainment and fashion industry folks. Similarly, **The Regency (Map 15)**(Park Ave at 61st), nicknamed "Hollywood East" in the 1960's, is a must for all celeb-stalkers hangers-on alike. Meanwhile, **The Algonquin (Map 12)**(W 44th St) offers complimentary delivery of the New Yorker, as if to suggest that they cater to a more literary crowd (maybe in the 1920s, but whether or not that's the case today is up for debate). If you're feeling fabulous, there's **The Muse Hotel (Map 12)**(W 46th St), located in the heart of Times Square, mere steps away from the bright lights of Broadway (*Movin' Out*, anyone?). If you're more comfortable with the old-money folks (or if you're a nostalgic member of the nouveau-riche), check out the apartment-size rooms at **The Carlyle (Map 15)** on E 76th St. Be a bit easier on your wallet and get a room at **The Excelsior Hotel (Map 14)**(W 81st St)—it may be a tad less indulgent, but get over it, you're still right on Central Park. Yet more affordable and not an ounce less attractive is **The Hudson (Map 11)**(W 58th St), a chic boutique hotel from Ian Schrager. Then there's **The Shoreham (Map 12)**(5th Ave at 55th St), which offers complimentary champagne at the front desk (so it's definitely worth a shot to pose as a guest) in addition to a fantastically retro bar, that looks like it's straight out of *A Clockwork Orange*. Last but not least, dance on over to the famous **Waldorf Astoria (Map 13)**(Park Ave at 49th), where the unrivaled service and $200 million in renovations more than justify the cost of staying.

There are also plenty of places to stay downtown, perfect for those of you who plan on stumbling home after a long night of bar-hopping. The sexier of these hotels include: **The Hotel Gansevoort (Map 5)**, a sleek tower of luxury, located steps away from the Meatpacking District—New York's very own version of Miami Beach! Nearby, you'll find **The Maritime Hotel (Map 10)**, which does a great impression of a cruise ship, replete with porthole-shaped windows and La Bottega, an Italian restaurant with a massive outdoor patio that feels like the deck of a Carnival liner. In trendy Soho, you'll find **The Mercer Hotel**, **60 Thompson (Map 6)**, and **The Soho Grand (Map 2)**(there's also its sister, **The Tribeca Grand (Map 2)**, further south)—which vary ever-so-slightly in degrees of coolness, depending on your demands. A little ways north, next to Gramercy Park, you'll find **The Inn at Irving Place (Map 10)**—things are a tad less modern at this upscale bed and breakfast (it consists of two restored 19th-century townhouses), but the Cibar lounge, the company (It's a favorite of rock and fashion royalty), and the lack of any visible sign outside, are all sure to validate your sense of hip.

Let's just be honest, shall we? The truth of the matter is that you're poor. All you want is a bargain—and believe it or not, we get it. Thus, behold the most affordable splendors of the New York hotel experience: **The Gershwin Hotel (Map 9)**(5th Ave at 27th St, Lowest possible rate: $44.00), **Herald Square Hotel (Map 9)**(W 31st St, LPR: $69.00), **Super 8 Times Square (Map 12)**(LPR: $85.49), **Red Roof Inn (Map 9)**(E 32nd St, LPR: $89.99), **Second Home on Second Avenue (Map 6)**(btw 13th and 14th, LPR: $80.00), **The Chelsea Savoy (Map 9)**(W 23rd St, LPR: $99.00) and **The Howard Johnson Express (Map 6)**(E Houston St, LPR: $119).

More mid-range options include: **Hotel Thirty Thirty (Map 9)**(E 30th St), **The Abington Guest House (Map 5)**(8th Ave at 12th St), **The Hotel Roger Williams (Map 9)**(Madison Ave at 31st St), **Portland Square Hotel (Map 12)**(W 47th St), **Comfort Inn (Map 9)**(W 46th St), **Clarion Hotel (Map 10)**(E 40th St), and **The New Yorker Hotel (Map 8)**(8th Ave at 34th St).

Be aware that prices are generally highest during the holiday season and the summer, and lowest during the in-between times. Not all hotels have a star rating, and those that are sometimes inaccurate. The quoted rates will give you a pretty good idea of the quality of each hotel. Rates are ballpark and subject to change—go to one of the many travel websites (Hotels.com, Priceline, Hotwire, Travelocity, Expedia, etc.) or individual company websites (hilton.com, spg.com, holiday-inn.com) to get the best rates. Or call the hotel and ask if they have any specials. The bottom line is that, as is the case with everything in New York, you have plenty of options, few of them cheap.

Map 1 · Financial District

	Address	Phone	Rate $	Rating
Holiday Inn Wall Street	15 Gold St	212-232-7700	187	
Manhattan Seaport Suites	129 Front St	212-742-0003	149	
Millenium Hilton	55 Church St	212-693-2001	332	★★★★
New York Marriott Financial Center	85 West St	212-385-4900	155	★★★
Providence Hotel	125 Broadway	212-226-5818	40	
Wall Street Inn	9 S William St	212-747-1500	219	★★★

Map 2 · TriBeCa

	Address	Phone	Rate $	Rating
Cosmopolitan Hotel	95 West Broadway	212-566-1900	145	★★★
Soho Grand Hotel	310 West Broadway	212-965-3000	396	
Tribeca Grand Hotel	2 Sixth Ave	212-519-6600	309	★★★★

Map 3 · City Hall / Chinatown

	Address	Phone	Rate $	Rating
Best Western Seaport Inn	33 Peck Slip	212-766-6600	159	★★★
Grand Hotel	143 Bowery	212-226-6655	25	
Hampton Inn Seaport	320 Pearl St	212-571-4400	195	
Holiday Inn Downtown	138 Lafayette St	212-966-8898	165	★★★
New World Hotel	101 Bowery	212-226-5522	85	
Sohotel	341 Broome St	212-226-1482	89	
Sun Hotel	140 Hester St	212-226-7070	15	
Windsor Hotel	108 Forsyth St	212-226-3009	155	★★

Map 5 · West Village

	Address	Phone	Rate $	Rating
Abingdon Guest House	21 Eighth Ave	212-243-5384	154	
Chelsea Pines Inn	317 W 14th St	212-929-1023	109	
Hotel Gansevoort	18 Ninth Ave	212-206-6700	395	★★★★
Hotel Riverview	113 Jane St	212-929-0060	40	
Incentra Village House	32 Eighth Ave	212-206-0007	119	
Jane-West Hotel	507 West St	212-929-8632	45	
Liberty Inn	51 Tenth Ave	212-741-2333	2 hr-$52, 3 hr-$59, $129	
Mini Suites of Minetta	9 Minetta St	212-475-6952	150	
Rooms to Let	83 Horatio St	212-675-5481	175	
West Eleventh	278 W 11th St	212-675-7897	175	

Map 6 • Washington Square / NYU / NoHo / SoHo

60 Thompson	60 Thompson St	212-431-0400	279	★★★★
Howard Johnson Express Inn	135 E Houston St	212-358-8844	119	★★
Larchmont Hotel	27 W 11th St	212-989-9333	75	
Off Soho Suites Hotel	11 Rivington St	800-633-7646	99	
Second Home on Second Avenue	221 Second Ave	212-677-3161	105	
St Marks Hotel	2 St Marks Pl	212-674-0100	110	
Union Square Inn	209 E 14th St	212-614-0500	99	
Village House	45 W 9th St	212-473-5500	145	
Washington Square Hotel	103 Waverly Pl	212-777-9515	155	★★★
White House Hotel	340 Bowery	212-477-5623	32	

Map 7 • East Village / Lower East Side

East Village Bed & Coffee	110 Ave C	212-533-4175	85	
Hotel on Rivington	107 Rivington St	212-475-2600	350	★★★

Map 8 • Chelsea

Allerton Hotel	302 W 22nd St	212-243-6017	98	
Best Western Convention Center Hotel	522 W 38th St	212-405-1700	208	★★
Chelsea Inn	184 Eleventh Ave	212-929-4096	55	
Chelsea International Hostel	251 W 20th St	212-647-0010	70 private, 28 dorm	
Chelsea Lodge Suites	318 W 20th St	212-243-4499	195	
Chelsea Star Hotel	300 W 30th St	212-244-7827	35 dorm, 89 private	
Colonial House Inn	318 W 22nd St	212-243-9669	95	
Manhattan Inn Hostel	303 W 30th St	212-629-4064	36	
New Yorker Ramada Hotel	481 Eighth Ave	212-971-0101	129	★★★
Vigilant Hotel	370 Eighth Ave	212-594-5246	130 weekly	

Map 9 • Flatiron / Lower Midtown

Affinia Manhattan	371 Seventh Ave	212-563-1800	119	★★★
Americana Inn	69 W 38th St	212-840-6700	70	
The Avalon	16 E 32nd St	212-299-7000	225	★★★
Broadway Plaza Hotel	1155 Broadway	212-679-7665	119	★★★
Carlton Hotel	88 Madison Ave	212-532-4100	289	★★★★
Chelsea Hotel	222 W 23rd St	212-243-3700	195	
Chelsea Inn	46 E 17th St	212-645-8989	89	
Chelsea Savoy Hotel	204 W 23rd St	212-929-9353	99	
Churchill Residence Suites	50 W 34th St	212-697-8970	119	
Comfort Inn	18 W 25th St	212-645-3990	85-100	★★★
Comfort Inn Manhattan	42 W 35th St	212-947-0200	159	★★
Comfort Inn New York	442 W 36th St	212-714-6699	109	★★
Four Points by Sheraton Chelsea	160 W 25th St	212-627-1888	279	★★★
Gershwin Hotel	21 E 26th St	212-545-8000	40	
Hampton Inn Manhattan/Chelsea	108 W 24th St	212-414-1000	175	★★★
Hampton Inn-Madison Square Garden	116 W 31st St	212-947-9700	187	★★★
Herald Square Hotel	19 W 31st St	212-279-4017	89	
Holiday Inn Martinique on Broadway	49 W 32nd St	212-736-3800	169	
Hotel Chandler	12 E 31st St	212-889-6363	210	★★★
Hotel Grand Union	34 E 32nd St	212-683-5890	140	★★
Hotel Metro	45 W 35th St	212-947-2500	175	
Hotel Stanford	43 W 32nd St	212-563-1500	99	
Hotel Thirty Thirty	30 E 30th St	212-689-1900	159	★★★
Inn on 23rd	131 W 23rd St	212-463-0330	219	
Jolly Hotel Madison Towers	22 E 38th St	212-802-0600	245	★★★
La Quinta Inn–Manhattan	17 W 32nd St	212-736-1600	170	★★★
La Semana	25 W 24th St	212-255-5944	159	
Latham Hotel	4 E 28th St	212-685-8300	79	
Madison Hotel on the Park	21 E 27th St	212-532-7373	99	
Manhattan Broadway Hotel	273 W 38th St	212-921-9791	89	
Morgan's Hotel	237 Madison Ave	212-686-0300	259	★★★★
New York Hotel Pennsylvania	401 Seventh Ave	212-736-5000	109	★★
Red Roof Inn	6 W 32nd St	212-643-7100	109	

Map 9 · Flatiron / Lower Midtown—*continued*

Regency Inn & Suites	215 W 34th St	212-594-4732	119	★★
Roger Williams Hotel	131 Madison Ave	212-448-7000	260	★★★★
Senton Hotel	39 W 27th St	212-684-5800	79	
Wolcott Hotel	4 W 31st St	212-268-2900	120	★★★

Map 10 · Murray Hill / Gramercy

70 Park Avenue Hotel	70 Park Ave	212-687-7050	295	★★★
Affinia Dumont	150 E 34th St	212-481-7600	299	
Carlton Arms Hotel	160 E 25th St	212-679-0680	77	
Clarion Park Avenue	429 Park Ave S	212-532-4860	139	★★
Deauville Hotel	103 E 29th St	212-683-0990	125	
Eastgate Tower	222 E 39th St	212-687-8000	159	
Envoy Club	377 E 33rd St	212-481-4600	229	
Gramercy Park Hotel	2 Lexington Ave	212-201-2161		
Hotel 17	225 E 17th St	212-475-2845	79	
Hotel 31	120 E 31st St	212-685-3060	95	
Hotel Giraffe	365 Park Ave S	212-685-7700	295	
Inn at Irving Place	56 Irving Pl	212-533-4600	325	★★★
Kitano Hotel New York	66 Park Ave	212-885-7000	210	
Marcel Hotel	201 E 24th St	212-696-3800	125	
Maritime Hotel	363 W 16th St	212-242-4300	295	
Murray Hill East Suites	149 E 39th St	212-661-2100	249	
Murray Hill Inn	143 E 30th St	212-683-6900	89	
Park South Hotel	122 E 28th St	212-448-0888	129	★★★
Ramada Inn Eastside	161 Lexington Ave	212-545-1800	99	
Shelburne Murray Hill	303 Lexington Ave	212-689-5200	179	★★★
W New York–The Court	130 E 39th St	212-685-1100	329	★★★★
W New York–The Tuscany	120 E 39th St	212-686-1600	429	★★★★★
W Union Square	201 Park Ave S	212-253-9119	419	★★★★★

Map 11 · Hell's Kitchen

414 Inn New York	414 W 46th St	212-399-0006	130	★★★
Belvedere Hotel	319 W 48th St	212-245-7000	174	★★★
Elk Hotel	360 W 42nd St	212-563-2864	45	★★
Holiday Inn Midtown	440 W 57th St	212-581-8100	159	★★★
Hudson Hotel	356 W 58th St	212-554-6000	300	★★★
Skyline Hotel	725 Tenth Ave	212-586-3400	159	★★★
Travel Inn	515 W 42nd St	212-695-7171	165	★★
Washington Jefferson Hotel	318 W 51st St	212-246-7550	139	★★★
Westpark Hotel	308 W 58th St	212-445-0200	119-149	★★

Map 12 · Midtown

Algonquin Hotel	59 W 44th St	212-840-6800	249	★★★
Ameritania Hotel	230 W 54th St	212-247-5000	125	★★★
Amsterdam Court Hotel	226 W 50th St	212-459-1000	115	
Best Western President Hotel	234 W 48th St	212-246-8800	120	★★
Big Apple Hostel	119 W 45th St	212-302-2603	98 private/ 38 dorm	
Blakely Hotel	136 W 55th St	212-245-1800	245	★★★
Broadway Inn	264 W 46th St	212-997-9200	125	★★★
Bryant Park Hotel	40 W 40th St	212-869-0100	410	★★★★
Buckingham Hotel	101 W 57th St	212-246-1500	239	★★★
The Carnegie Hotel	229 W 58th St	212-245-4000	169	★★★
Carter Hotel	250 W 43rd St	212-944-6000	89	
Casablanca Hotel	147 W 43rd St	212-869-1212	239	
Chambers Hotel	15 W 56th St	212-974-5656	450	★★★★

Hotel	Address	Phone	Price	Rating
City Club Hotel	55 W 44th St	212-921-5500	275	★★★★
Comfort Inn Midtown	129 W 46th St	212-221-2600	149	
Courtyard Times Square South by Marriott	114 W 40th St	212-391-0088	259	★★★
Crowne Plaza Times Square	1605 Broadway	212-977-4000	239	★★★
Da Vinci Hotel	244 W 56th St	212-489-4100	120	
Days Inn Hotel Manhattan Midtown	790 Eighth Ave	212-581-7000	129-149	★★
Doubletree Guest Suites	1568 Broadway	212-719-1600	290	★★★
Dream	210 W 55th St	212-247-2000	269	★★★★
Dylan Hotel	52 E 41st St	212-338-0500	269	★★★
Flatotel International	135 W 52nd St	212-887-9400	335	★★★★
Four Seasons Hotel	57 E 57th St	212-758-5700	595	★★★★★
Hampton Inn-Times Square North	851 Eighth Ave	212-581-4100	219	★★★
Helmsley Park Lane Hotel	36 Central Park S	212-371-4000	235	★★★★
Hilton New York	1335 Sixth Ave	212-586-7000	243	★★★
Hilton Times Square	234 W 42nd St	212-840-8222	293	★★★
Holiday Inn Express	15 W 45th St	212-302-9088	169	
Hotel 41	206 W 41st St	212-703-8600	189	
Hotel Edison	228 W 47th St	212-840-5000	165	★★
Hotel Shoreham	33 W 55th St	212-247-6700	249	★★★★
Hotel St James	109 W 45th St	212-221-3600	145	
Iroquois Hotel	49 W 44th St	212-840-3080	385	★★★★
Jumeirah Essex House	160 Central Park S	212-247-0300	279	★★★★
Le Parker Meridien	119 W 57th St	212-245-5000	425	★★★★
Library Hotel	299 Madison Ave	212-983-4500	279	★★★★
Mansfield Hotel	12 W 44th St	212-277-8700	209	★★★
Marriott Courtyard Fifth Avenue	3 E 40th St	212-447-1500	199	★★★
Mayfair Hotel	242 W 49th St	212-586-0300	125	
Michelangelo	152 W 51st St	212-765-0505	240	★★★★
Milford Plaza Hotel	270 W 45th St	212-869-3600	149	★★★
Millennium Broadway	145 W 44th St	212-768-4400	260	★★★★
Moderne Hotel	243 W 55th St	212-397-6767	107	
The Muse	130 W 46th St	877-692-6873	289	★★★★
New York Inn	765 Eighth Ave	212-247-5400	99	★★
New York Marriott Marquis	1535 Broadway	212-398-1900	241	★★★
New York Palace Hotel	455 Madison Ave	212-888-7000	269	★★★★
Novotel New York	226 W 52nd St	212-315-0100	219	★★★
Omni Berkshire Place	21 E 52nd St	212-753-5800	318	★★★★
Oxbridge Apts Theater District	30 W 46th St	212-348-8100	200	
Paramount Hotel	235 W 46th St	212-764-5500	266	★★★
Park Central Hotel	870 Seventh Ave	212-247-8000	199	★★★
Park Savoy Hotel	158 W 58th St	212-245-5755	115	
Peninsula New York	700 Fifth Ave	212-956-2888	685	★★★★
Portland Square Hotel	132 W 47th St	212-382-0600	89	
The Premier	133 W 44th St	212-789-7670	399	★★★★
Quality Hotel Times Square	157 W 47th St	212-768-3700	129	★★
Radio City Suites Hotel	142 W 49th St	212-730-0728	150	
Renaissance New York Times Square	714 Seventh Ave	212-765-7676	239	★★★★
Rihga Royal New York	151 W 54th St	212-387-5000	299	★★★★
The Ritz Carlton, Central Park	50 Central Park S	212-308-9100	495	★★★★
Royalton Hotel	44 W 44th St	212-869-4400	279	★★★
Salisbury Hotel	123 W 57th St	212-358-6206	165	★★
Sheraton Manhattan	790 Seventh Ave	212-581-3300	279	★★★
Sheraton New York Hotel and Towers	811 Seventh Ave	212-581-1000	250	★★★
Sherry Netherland Hotel	781 Fifth Ave	212-355-2800	300	★★★★★
Sofitel	45 W 44th St	212-354-8844	249	★★★★
St Regis	2 E 55th St	212-753-4500	575	★★★★★
Super 8 Times Square	59 W 46th St	212-719-2300	89	★★★
The Time	224 W 49th St	212-246-5252	219	★★★★
W New York Times Square	1567 Broadway	212-930-7400	385	★★★
Warwick New York	65 W 54th St	212-247-2700	185	★★★
Wellington Hotel	871 Seventh Ave	212-247-3900	129	★★★
Westin New York at Times Square	270 W 43rd St	212-201-2700	299	★★★★

Map 13 · East Midtown

Hotel	Address	Phone	Price	Rating
Affinia 50	155 E 50th St	212-751-5710	165	★★
Alex Hotel	205 E 45th St	212-867-5100	429	
Bedford Hotel	118 E 40th St	212-697-4800	160	★★★
Beekman Tower Hotel	3 Mitchell Pl	212-355-7300	179	★★★
The Benjamin	125 E 50th St	212-715-2500	329	★★★★
Best Western Hospitality House	145 E 49th St	212-753-8781	183	
Courtyard by Marriott Midtown East	866 Third Ave	212-644-1300	199	★★★
Crowne Plaza at the United Nations	304 E 42nd St	212-986-8800	189	★★★
Doubletree Metropolitan Hotel	569 Lexington Ave	212-752-7000	177	★★★
Fitzpatrick Grand Central Hotel	141 E 44th St	212-351-6800	239	★★★
Fitzpatrick Manhattan Hotel	687 Lexington Ave	212-355-0100	239	★★★
Grand Hyatt Hotel	109 E 42nd St	212-883-1234	245	★★★
Helmsley Middletowne Hotel	148 E 48th St	212-755-3000	160	
Hotel 57	130 E 57th St	212-753-8841	325	
Hotel Elysee	60 E 54th St	212-753-1066	295	★★★
Hotel Inter-Continental–The Barclay	111 E 48th St	212-755-5900	329	★★★
Hotel Lombary	111 E 56th St	212-753-8600	245	★★★
Kimberly Hotel	145 E 50th St	212-702-1600	249	
Korman Communities-Manhattan	234 E 46th St	212-867-2357		
Marriott New York City East Side	525 Lexington Ave	212-755-4000	199	★★★
Millenium UN Plaza	1 United Nations Plz	212-758-1234	239	★★★★
The New York Helmsley	212 E 42nd St	212-490-8900	199	★★★
Pickwick Arms Hotel	230 E 51st St	212-355-0300	89	
Radisson Lexington	511 Lexington Ave	212-755-4400	139	★★★
Roger Smith Hotel	501 Lexington Ave	212-755-1400	189	★★★
Roosevelt Hotel	45 E 45th St	212-661-9600	325	★★★
San Carlos Hotel	150 E 50th St	212-755-1800	300	
Seton Hotel	144 E 40th St	212-889-5301	65	
Swissotel The Drake	440 Park Ave	212-421-0900	228	★★★
W New York	541 Lexington Ave	212-755-1200	185	★★★
Waldorf Towers	100 E 50th St	212-355-3100	449	★★★★
Waldorf-Astoria	301 Park Ave	212-872-4534	299	★★★★★
YMCA Vanderbilt Hotel	224 E 47th St	212-756-9600	80	

Map 14 · Upper West Side (Lower)

Hotel	Address	Phone	Price	Rating
Amsterdam Inn	340 Amsterdam Ave	212-579-7500	79	
Amsterdam Residence	207 W 85th St	212-873-9402	275 weekly	
Comfort Inn Central Park West	31 W 71st St	212-721-4770	179	★★★
Country in the City	270 W 77th St	212-580-4183	190	
Excelsior Hotel	45 W 81st St	212-362-9200	169	★★★★
Hayden Hall Hotel	117 W 79th St	212-787-4900	89	
Hotel Beacon	2130 Broadway	212-787-1100	169	★★
Hotel Lucerne	201 W 79th St	212-875-1000	210	★★★★
Hotel Riverside Studios	342 W 71st St	212-873-5999	50	
Imperial Court Hotel	307 W 79th St	212-787-6600	99	
Inn New York City	266 W 71st St	212-580-1900	475	
Mandarin Oriental New York	80 Columbus Cir	212-805-8800	499	★★★★★
Milburn Hotel	242 W 76th St	212-362-1006	139	
On the Ave Hotel	2178 Broadway	212-362-1100	300	★★★
Phillips Club	155 W 66th St	212-835-8800	6600 Monthly	
Riverside Tower Hotel	80 Riverside Dr	212-877-5200	94	★★
Trump International	1 Central Park W	212-299-1000	475	★★★★
YMCA West Side Branch	5 W 63rd St	212-875-4100	80	
Your Stay Central Park	240 W 73rd St	212-874-1600	150	

Map 15 · Upper East Side (Lower)

Hotel	Address	Phone	Price	Rating
1871 House	130 E 62nd St	212-756-8823	250	
Affinia Gardens	215 E 64th St	212-355-1230	259	★★★★
Anco Studios	1202 Lexington Ave	212-717-7500	150	

Bentley Hotel	500 E 62nd St	212-644-6000	135	★★★
Carlyle Hotel	35 E 76th St	212-744-1600	600	★★★★
Gracie Inn	502 E 81st St	212-628-1700	129	
Helmsley Carlton	680 Madison Ave	212-838-3000	450	★★★★
Hotel Plaza Athenee	37 E 64th St	212-734-9100	525	★★★★
Lowell Hotel	28 E 63rd St	212-838-1400	495	★★★★
The Mark New York	25 E 77th St	212-744-4300	410	
The Pierre	2 E 61st St	212-838-8000	695	★★★★
Regency Hotel	540 Park Ave	212-759-4100	271	★★★★
Surrey Hotel	20 E 76th St	212-288-3700	540	★★★★

Map 16 · Upper West Side (Upper)

Central Park Hostel	19 W 103rd St	212-678-0491	29	
Days Hotel Broadway	215 W 94th St	212-866-6400	99	★★★
Hostelling International New York	891 Amsterdam Ave	212-932-2300	35 dorm, 135 private	
Hotel Belleclaire	250 W 77th St	212-362-7700	139	★★
Hotel Dexter House	345 W 86th St	212-873-9600	70	
Hotel Newton	2528 Broadway	212-678-6500	95	★★
Jazz on the Park	36 W 106th St	212-932-1600	75	
Malibu Hotel	2688 Broadway	212-222-2954	99	★★
Morningside Inn	235 W 107th St	212-316-0055	90	
The Riverside	312 W 109th St	212-678-4820		
Riverside Inn	319 W 94th St	212-316-0656	70	
West End Studios	850 West End Ave	212-749-7104	20 dorm / 109 private	
West Side Inn	237 W 107th St	212-866-0061	90 private, 20 dorm	

Map 17 · Upper East Side / East Harlem

92nd Street Y de Hirsch Residence	1395 Lexington Ave	212-415-5660	60	
Courtyard by Marriott	410 E 92nd St	212-410-6777		
Franklin Hotel	164 E 87th St	212-369-1000	210	
The Marmara-Manhattan	301 E 94th St	212-427-3042	4500 monthly	
Wales Hotel	1295 Madison Ave	212-876-6000	249	★★★★

Map 18 · Columbia / Morningside Heights

International House of NY	500 Riverside Dr	212-316-6300	120	

Map 19 · Harlem (Lower)

102 Brownstone	102 W 118th St	212-662-4223	250	
Efuru Bed & Breakfast	106 W 120th St	212-961-9855	100	
YMCA of Greater NY	180 W 135th St	212-281-4100	50	

Map 21 · Manhattanville / Hamilton Heights

Alga Hotel	828 St Nicholas Ave	212-368-0700	40	
Hamilton Heights Casablanca Hotel	511 W 145th St	212-491-0488	65 shared bath, 85 private bath	
Hotel Caribe	515 W 145th St	212-368-9915	85	
Sugar Hill Harlem Inn	460 W 141st St	917-464-3528	150	

Map 22 · Harlem (Upper)

Harlem Vista Hotel	75 Macombs Pl	917-507-4140	77	

Battery Park City

Embassy Suites New York City	102 North End Ave	212-945-0100	279	★★★
Ritz-Carlton New York Battery Park	2 West St	212-344-0800	345	★★★★★

Internet

Some New Yorkers harbor the theory that Kinko's raison d'etre is to make our lives more miserable. Your disk never works in the drive, or maybe the printer ran out of toner again. To add insult to injury, the overwhelmed employees are often too busy to offer immediate help. Nevertheless, it is a great comfort that—should you need to check your e-mail at 2 in the morning—those same employees are there and waiting. Several locations, including the Bryant Park address on W 40th Street (Map 12), never close. That convenience comes at a hefty price, though. All Kinko's offer Internet access for 30-45 cents per minute, depending on which location you visit and which machine you use (it works out to $18-$27 per hour). For service with a personal touch (and a cup of coffee), try an alternative such as News Bar on University Place (Map 6). At 18 cents a minute, it's a much cheaper option. In Brooklyn, Williamsburg's Internet Garage (Map 29) is a good bet.

Wi-Fi

For those with a laptop or PDA that has wireless access, there are a ton of free public "Wi-Fi" connections available throughout the city. The majority of the listed hotspots are maintained by private citizens, though a few are run by organizations such as the Downtown Alliance, including great spots at Bowling Green, City Hall, South Street Seaport, and the Winter Garden (www.downtownny.com/discover/wifi). More than 50 branches of the NY Public Library in Manhattan and the Bronx (and six on Staten Island) offer Wi-Fi access (www.nypl. org/branch/services/wifi.html), and the rest are sure to follow. Both www.wififreespot.com/ny.html and www. auscillate.com/wireless/manhattan are good starting points for locating a free hotspot. Of course, it's always an option to simply plug in or turn on your wireless card and see what networks are available. If it doesn't offend your sense of ethics, you can often tap into other people's Wi-Fi networks for free.

With so many options that don't cost a dime, it's beyond us why you'd want to pay for a connection. There are, however, plenty of fee-based services out there. T-Mobile Hotspot subscribers ($6 per hour, $10 a day, or $40 per month/$30 per month paid annually gives you unlimited access) can find access at most Kinko's, Borders, and Starbucks. McDonald's offers Wi-Fi access at dozens of locations in Manhattan: check out www.mcdwireless. com. Free Wi-Fi is offered at Penn Station for AT&T Wireless customers. Everyone else can surf for as little as $6 per day. If you're just visiting NYC, visit www.jwire.com for a list of hotels (as well as cafes and libraries) that provide both paid and free Wi-Fi. The site offers a Hotspot Search function where you can search for locations throughout the city.

It seems plausible that recent talk of a citywide Wi-Fi network in New York could come to fruition. Philadelphia and New Orleans are already implementing plans, and New Yorkers never like to be second-best.

Internet Café	Address	Phone	Map	Wi-Fi	Computers
Cosi	54 Pine St	212-809-2674	1	■	
Cosi	55 Broad St	212-344-5000	1		
Internet Café NYC	17 John St	212-217-6043	1	■	■
Leonidas	74 Trinity Pl	212-233-1111	1		
Pecan	130 Franklin St	646-613-8293	2	■	
Blue Spoon Coffee	76 Chambers St	212-619-7230	3		
Caffe Del Arte	143 Mulberry St	212-219-9799	3	■	
Universal News	484 Broadway	212-965-0730	3	■	
Full City Coffee	409 Grand St	212-260-2363	4	■	
Cosi	504 Sixth Ave	212-462-4188	5	■	
Grounded	28 Jane St	212-647-0943	5	■	
Sant Ambroeus	259 W 4th	212-604-9254	5		
Snice	45 Eighth Ave	212-645-0310	5	■	
Anyway Café	34 E 2nd St	212-533-3412	6	■	
Cosi	841 Broadway	212-614-8544	6	■	
Cyberfelds	20 E 13th St	212-647-8830	6		■
Gametime Nation	111 E 12th St	212-228-4260	6	■	
Mission Café	82 Second Ave	212-505-6616	6	■	
Mr Fresh Bread, Inc	116 Second Ave	212-253-1046	6	■	
Tasti D-Lite	137 Fourth Ave	212-228-5619	6	■	
Tea Spot St	127 MacDougal	212-832-7768	6	■	
Village Juice Bar	200 E 14th St	212-673-0005	6	■	
web2zone	54 Cooper Sq	212-614-7300	6	■	■
altcoffee	139 Ave A	212-529-2233	7	■	
Café Pick Me Up	145 Avenue A	212-673-7231	7	■	
Coffee Pot	41 Ave A	212-614-0815	7	■	
Kudo Beans	49 1/2 First Ave	212-353-1477	7	■	
Sympathy for the Kettle	109 St Marks Pl	212-979-1650	7	■	
Antique Café	55 W 26th St	212-213-5723	9	■	
Brooklyn Bagel Café	319 Fifth Ave	212-532-0007	9	■	
Café Bonjour	20 E 39th St	212-481-1224	9	■	
Café Express	138 W 32nd St	212-714-9401	9	■	
Café Muse	43 W 32nd St	212-290-1414	9	■	
Cosi	498 Seventh Ave	212-947-1005	9	■	
Guy & Gallard	1001 Sixth Ave	212-730-0010	9	■	
Guy & Gallard	180 Madison Ave	212-725-2392	9	■	
Guy & Gallard	245 W 38th St	212-302-7588	9	■	
Guy & Gallard	469 Seventh Ave	212-695-0006	9	■	

Internet Café	Address	Phone	Map	Wi-Fi	Computers
Hotel Grand Union	34 E 32nd St	212-683-5890	9	■	
News Bar	2 W 19th St	212-255-3996	9	■	
Universal News	50 W 23rd St	212-647-1761	9	■	■
Cosi	257 Park Ave S	212-598-4070	10	■	
Cosi	461 Park Ave S	212-634-3467	10	■	
Guy & Gallard	120 E 34th St	212-684-3898	10	■	
Sunburst	157 E 18th St	212-674-1702	10	■	
Sunburst	206 Third Ave	212-674-1702	10	■	
Coffee Pot	350 W 49th St	212-265-3566	11	■	
Rocket Wrapps	609 Ninth Ave	212-333-2600	11	■	
The Bread Factory Café	600 Ninth Ave	212-974-8100	11	■	
Café Metro	625 Eighth Ave	212-714-9342	12	■	
City Chow	1633 Broadway	212-445-0600	12	■	
Cosi	11 W 42nd St	212-399-6662	12	■	
Cosi	1633 Broadway	212-397-9838	12	■	
Cosi	61 W 48th St	212-265-7579	12	■	
Cyber Café	250 W 49th St	212-333-4109	12	■	■
Fluffy's Café & Bakery	855 Seventh Ave	212-247-0234	12	■	
Universal News	977 Eighth Ave	212-459-0932	12	■	
Ambrosia Café	158 E 45th St	212-661-1717	13	■	
Cosi	38 E 45th St	212-370-0705	13	■	
Cosi	60 E 56th St	212-588-1225	13	■	
Cosi	685 Third Ave	212-697-8329	13	■	
Mambi Lounge	933 Second Ave	212-832-3500	13	■	
Beard Papa	2167 Broadway	212-799-3770	14	■	
Cosi	2160 Broadway	212-595-5616	14	■	
Lenny's Café Ave	302 Columbus	212-580-8300	14	■	
Sensuous Bean	66 W 70th St	212-724-7725	14	■	
DT * UT	1626 Second Ave	212-327-1327	15	■	
Gotham Coffee House	1298 Second Ave	212-717-0457	15	■	
M Rohrs	303 E 85th St	212-396-4456	15	■	■
Telegraphe Café	260 E 72nd St	212-288-1544	15	■	
Broadway Bagel	2658 Broadway	212-662-0231	16	■	
Saurin Parke Café	301 w 110th St	212-222-0683	19	■	
Society Coffee Juice	2104 Frederick Douglass Blvd	212-222-3323	19	■	
Astron Coffee Shop	3795 Broadway	212-368-1837	21	■	
Jou Jou	603 W 168th St	212-781-2222	23	■	
Cosi	200 Vesey St	212-571-2001	100		

Overview

If you want to see cutting edge art, go to New York City's galleries. There are more than 500 galleries in the city, with artwork created in every conceivable medium (and of varying quality) on display. SoHo, Chelsea, DUMBO, and Williamsburg are the hot spots for gallery goers, but there are also many famous (and often, more traditional) galleries and auction houses, like **Christie's (Map 12)** and **Sotheby's (Map 15)**, uptown. With so much to choose from, there's almost always something that's at least *provocative*, if not actually *good*.

The scene at the upscale galleries is sometimes intimidating, especially if you look like you are on a budget. If you aren't interested in buying, they aren't interested in you being there. Some bigger galleries require appointments. Cut your teeth at smaller galleries; they aren't as scary. Also, put your name on the mailing lists. You'll get invites to openings so crowded that no one will try to pressure you into buying (and there's free wine). The Armory Show, an annual show of new art, is also a great way to see what the galleries have to offer without intimidation.

SoHo Area

Five years ago, there were still hundreds of art galleries in SoHo. Now, it's swiftly becoming an outdoor mall. However, there are still some permanent artworks in gallery spaces, such as Walter DeMaria's excellent *The Broken Kilometer* (a Dia-sponsored space at 393 West Broadway), and his sublime *New York Earth Room* at 141 Wooster Street. And a short jaunt down to TriBeCa will land you in LaMonte Young's awesome aural experience *Dream House* at the **MELA Foundation (Map 2)**. Artist's Space **(Map 2)**, one of the first alternative art galleries in New York, is also in TriBeCa. The **HERE Arts Center (Map 5)** showcases works of all types, and usually has some interesting things going on.

Chelsea

In case you weren't sure where all the galleries went after SoHo prices exploded, this is it. Over 200 galleries now reside in Chelsea, and there is always something new to see. Our recommendation is to hit at least two streets—W 24th Street between Tenth and Eleventh Avenues, and W 22nd Street between Tenth and Eleventh Avenues. W 24th Street is anchored by the almost-always-brilliant **Gagosian Gallery (Map 8)** and also includes the **Luhring Augustine (Map 8)**, **Charles Cowles (Map 8)**, **Mary Boone (Map 8)**, **Barbara Gladstone (Map 8)**, and **Matthew Marks (Map 8)** galleries. W 22nd has the brilliant **Dia: Chelsea (Map 8)**, as well as the architecture-friendly **Max Protech (Map 8)** gallery and the **Julie Saul (Map 8)**, **Leslie Tonkonow (Map 8)**, **Marianne Boesky (Map 8)**, **Pace Wildenstein (Map 8)**, and **Yancey Richardson (Map 8)** galleries. Also, check out the famous "artists" bookstore **Printed Matter (535 W 22nd St) (Map 8)**.

Perhaps the final nail in the coffin for SoHo's art scene was **Exit Art's (Map 8)** move to 475 Tenth Avenue a couple years back. This gallery is well-known for brilliant group shows, exhibiting everything from album covers to multimedia installations, and killer openings. It's highly recommended.

Other recommendations are the Starrett-Lehigh Building (601 W 26th St), not only for the art but also for the great pillars, windows, and converted freight elevators, **Esso Gallery (Map 8)** (531 W 25th St) for Pop Art, and the **Daniel Reich Gallery (Map 8)**

Map 1 • Financial District

AngelliniArte Italiana	80 Wall St	212-422-2474
Water Street Gallery	241 Water St	212-349-9090

Map 2 • TriBeCa

A Taste of Art	147 Duane St	212-964-5493
Adelphi University	75 Varick St, 2nd Fl	212-965-8340
Anthem Gallery	41 Wooster St	347-249-4525
Apex Art	291 Church St	212-431-5270
Arcadia Fine Arts	51 Greene St	212-965-1387
Art at Format	50 Wooster St	212-941-7995
Artists Space	38 Greene St, 3rd Fl	212-226-3970
The Atlantic Gallery	40 Wooster St, 4th Fl	212-219-3183
Brooke Alexander Editions	59 Wooster St	212-925-4338
Cheryl Hazan Gallery	35 N Moore St	212-343-8964
Cheryl Pelavin Fine Art	13 Jay St	212-925-9424
Coda Gallery	472 Broome St	212-334-0407
Dactyl Foundation for the Arts & Humanities	64 Grand St	212-219-2344
Deitch Projects	76 Grand St	212-343-7300
DFN Gallery	176 Franklin St	212-334-3400
The Drawing Center	35 Wooster St	212-219-2166
Ethan Cohen Fine Arts	18 Jay St	212-625-1250
Gallery 402	19 Hudson St	212-219-9213
Gallery Gen	158 Franklin St	212-226-7717
Location One	26 Greene St	212-334-3347
Mela Foundation	275 Church St, 3rd Fl	212-925-8270
The Painting Center	52 Greene St	212-343-1060
SE Feinman Fine Arts	448 Broome St	212-431-6820
Spencer Brownstone Gallery	39 Wooster St	212-334-3455
Woodward Gallery	476 Broome St, 5th Fl	212-966-3411

Map 3 • City Hall / Chinatown

55 Mercer Gallery	55 Mercer St	212-226-8513
Agora Gallery Soho	415 West Broadway	212-226-4151
Animazing Art	461 Broome St	212-226-7374
Art in General	79 Walker St	212-219-0473
Broome Street Gallery	498 Broome St	212-226-6085
Canada	55 Chrystie St	212-925-4631
CVZ Contemporary	446 Broadway	212-625-0408
The Gallery at Dieu Donne Papermill	433 Broome St	212-226-0573
Gallery 456	456 Broadway, 3rd Fl	212-431-9740
Gigantic Art Space	59 Franklin St	212-226-6762
Globe Institute Gallery	291 Broadway	212-349-4330
Grant Gallery	7 Mercer St	212-343-2919
KS Art	73 Leonard St	212-219-9918
Museum Salvador Rosillo	18 Reade St	212-349-7068
Rhonda Schaller Studio	59 Franklin St	212-226-0166
Ronald Feldman Fine Arts	31 Mercer St	212-226-3232
Studio 18 Gallery	18 Warren St	212-385-6734
Swiss Institute Contemporary Art	495 Broadway, 3rd Fl	212-925-2035
Synagogue for the Arts	49 White St	212-966-7141

Map 4 · Lower East Side

Abrons Art Center	466 Grand St	212-498-0400
maccarone	45 Canal St	212-431-4977
Michelle Birnbaum Fine Art	220 South St	212-427-8250

Map 5 · West Village

14th Street Painters	110 W 14th St	212-627-9893
Akira Ikeda	17 Cornelia St, #1C	212-366-5449
Baron/Boisante	421 Hudson St	212-924-9940
Casey Kaplan	416 W 14th St	212-645-7335
Charles Street Gallery	160 Charles St	212-645-9700
Cooper Classics Collection	137 Perry St	212-929-3909
CVB Space	407 W 13th St	646-336-8387
Doma	17 Perry St	212-929-4339
Elliot Smith Contemporary Art	327 W 11th St	212-675-7164
Gavin Brown's Enterprise	620 Greenwich St	212-627-5258
Hal Katzen Gallery	459 Washington St	212-925-9777
Heller Gallery	420 W 14th St	212-414-4014
HEREArt	145 Sixth Ave	212-647-0202
hpgrp	32 Little W 12th St	212-727-2491
Jane Hartsook Gallery at Greenwich House Pottery	16 Jones St	212-242-4106
Parkett Editions	155 Sixth Ave, 2nd Fl	212-673-2660
Plane Space	102 Charles St	917-606-1268
Pratt Manhattan Gallery	144 W 14th St, 2nd Fl	212-647-7778
Sperone Westwater	415 W 13th St	212-999-7337
Synchronicity Fine Arts	106 W 13th St	212-238-8199
Tracy Williams Ltd	313 W 4th St	212-229-2757
Westbeth Gallery	57 Bethune St	212-989-4650
White Columns	320 W 13th St	212-924-4212
Wooster Projects	418 W 15th St	646-336-1999

Map 6 · Washington Square / NYU / NoHo / SoHo

80 Washington Square East Galleries	80 Washington Sq E	212-998-5747
A/D	560 Broadway	212-966-5154
Agora Gallery Chelsea	530 W 25th St	212-226-4151
American Indian Community House Gallery	708 Broadway	212-598-0100
American Primitive	594 Broadway #205	212-966-1530
Andrei Kushnir/ Michele Taylor	208 E 6th St	212-254-2628
Axelle Fine Arts Ltd	148 Spring St	212-226-2262
Bond Gallery	5 Rivington St	212-253-7600
Bottom Feeders Studio Gallery	195 Chrystie St, 2nd Fl	917-974-9664
Broadway Windows	Broadway & E 10th St	212-998-5751
Bronfman Center Gallery at NYU	7 E 10th St	212-998-4114
Caldwell Snyder Gallery	451 West Broadway	212-387-0208
Cavin-Morris	560 Broadway Ste #405B	212-226-3768
CFM	112 Greene St	212-966-3864
Chaim Gross Studio	526 LaGuardia Pl	212-529-4906
Deitch Projects	18 Wooster St	212-343-7300
Dia Center for the Arts– The Broken Kilometer	393 West Broadway	212-989-5566
Dia Center for the Arts– New York Earth Room	141 Wooster St	212-473-8072
Eleanor Ettinger	119 Spring St	212-925-7474
Exhibit A	160 Mercer St	212-343-0230
Franklin Bowles Galleries	431 West Broadway	212-226-1616
Gallery Juno	568 Broadway #604B	212-431-1515
Gracie Mansion Fine Art	407 E 6th St #2	212-505-9577
Grey Art Gallery	100 Washington Sq E	212-998-6780
ISE Foundation	555 Broadway	212-925-1649
Jacques Carcanagues	21 Greene St	212-925-8110
Janet Borden	560 Broadway	212-431-0166
John Szoke Editions	591 Broadway, 3rd Fl	212-219-8300
June Kelly	591 Broadway	212-226-1660
Kerrigan Cambell Art +	317 E 9th St	212-505-7196

Projects		
Leslie-Lohman Gay Art Foundation	127B Prince St	212-673-7007
Louis K Meisel	141 Prince St	212-677-1340
Margarete Roeder Gallery	545 Broadway, 4th Fl	212-925-6098
Martin Lawrence	457 West Broadway	212-995-8865
Michael Ingbar Gallery of Architectural Art	568 Broadway	212-334-1100
Mimi Ferzt	114 Prince St	212-343-9377
Molloy-Blitz Tribal	594 Broadway	212-219-9822
Moss Gallery	152 Greene St	212-204-7104
Multiple Impressions	128 Spring St	212-925-1313
Nancy Hoffman	429 West Broadway	212-966-6676
National Association of Women Artists Fifth Avenue Gallery	80 Fifth Ave #1405	212-675-1616
New York Studio School	8 W 8th St	212-673-6466
Nolan/Eckman	560 Broadway Ste 604	212-925-6190
OK Harris Works of Art	383 West Broadway	212-431-3600
Opera Gallery	115 Spring St	212-966-6675
The Pen & Brush	16 E 10th St	212-475-3669
Peter Blum Gallery	526 W 29th St	212-343-0441
Peter Freeman	560 Broadway Ste 602	212-966-5154
Phyllis Kind Gallery	136 Greene St	212-925-1200
pop international galleries	473 West Broadway	212-533-4262
Rosenberg + Kaufman Fine Art	115 Wooster St	212-431-4838
Salmagundi Club	47 Fifth Ave	212-255-7740
Sculptors Guild	110 Greene St Ste 603	212-431-5669
Silo	1 Freeman Aly	212-505-9156
Sragow	73 Spring St	212-219-1793
Staley-Wise Gallery	560 Broadway Ste 305	212-966-6223
Storefront for Art and Architecture	97 Kenmare St	212-431-5795
Sumi NY	458 W Broadway	212-274-0064
Sundaram Tagore Gallery	137 Greene St	212-677-4520
Susan Teller Gallery	568 Broadway, Ste 103A	212-941-7335
Tenri Cultural Institute	43A W 13th St	212-645-2800
Terrain Gallery	141 Greene St	212-777-4490
Tobey Fine Arts	580 Broadway, Ste 902	212-431-7878
Ward-Nasse Gallery	178 Prince St	212-925-6951
Washington Square Windows	80 Washington Sq E	212-998-5751
Watson & Spierman Fine Art	636 Broadway	212-253-9991
Westwood Gallery	568 Broadway	212-925-5700
Wooster Arts Space	147 Wooster St	212-777-6338
Xanadu	217 Thompson St	646-319-8597

Map 7 · East Village / Lower East Side

BlueSky/Eickholt Gallery	93 St Marks Pl	646-613-9610
Gallery Onetwentyeight	128 Rivington St	212-674-0244
MF Gallery	157 Rivington St	917-446-8681
The Phatory	618 E 9th St	212-777-7922
Rivington Arms	102 Rivington St	646-654-3213

Map 8 · Chelsea

303 Gallery	525 W 22nd St	212-255-1121
511 Gallery	529 W 20th St	212-255-2885
ACA Galleries	529 W 20th St, 5th Fl	212-206-8080
AIR Gallery	511 W 25th St	212-255-6651
Alexander and Bonin	132 Tenth Ave	212-367-7474
Allen Sheppard Gallery	530 W 25th St	212-989-9919
Alona Kagan Gallery	540 W 29th St	212-560-0670
Amos Eno Gallery	530 W 25th St, 6th Fl	212-226-5342
Amsterdam Whitney	511 W 25th St	212-255-9050
Andrea Meislin Gallery	526 W 26th St	212-627-2552
Andrea Rosen Gallery	525 W 24th St	212-627-6000
Andrew Edlin Gallery	529 W 20th St, 6th Fl	212-206-9723

(339)

Map 8 · Chelsea—*continued*

Andrew Kreps	558 W 21st St	212-741-8849
Anton Kern	532 W 20th St	212-367-9663
Ariel Meyerowitz Gallery	120 Eleventh Ave, 2nd Fl	212-414-2770
Art of this Century	530 W 25th St, 6th Fl	212-352-8131
Atelier A/E	323 W 22nd St	212-620-8103
Bon a Tirer	651 W 20th St	212-868-8484
Bose Pacia Modern	508 W 26th St, 11th Fl	212-989-7074
Bound & Unbound	601 W 26th St #1201	212-463-7348
Bowery Gallery	530 W 25th St, 4th Fl	646-230-6655
Briggs Robinson Gallery	527 W 29th St	212-560-9075
Bruce Silverstein Gallery	535 W 24th St	212-627-3930
Bryce Wolkowitz Gallery	601 W 26th St #1240	212-243-8830
BUIA Gallery	541 W 23rd St	212-366-9915
Caelum Gallery	526 W 26th St, Ste 315	212-924-4161
Camhy Studio Gallery	526 W 26th St	212-741-9183
Caren Golden Fine Art	539 W 23rd St	212-727-8304
Ceres	547 W 27th St, 2nd Fl	212-947-6100
Chambers Fine Art	210 Eleventh Ave, 2nd Fl	212-414-1169
Chapel of Sacred Mirrors/ COSM NYC	540 W 27th St	212-564-4253
Chappell Gallery	526 W 26th St, #317	212-414-2673
Charles Cowles Gallery	537 W 24th St	212-925-3500
Cheim & Read	547 W 25th St	212-242-7727
Christopher Henry Gallery	550 W 29th St	212-244-6004
Claire Oliver Gallery	513 W 26th St	212-929-5949
Clementine Gallery	526 W 26th St, 2nd Fl	212-243-5937
Cohan and Leslie	138 Tenth Ave	212-206-8710
CRG Gallery	535 W 22nd St, 3rd Fl	212-229-2766
Cue Art Foundation	511 W 25th St	212-206-3583
Cynthia Broan Gallery	546 W 29th St	212-760-0809
D'Amelio Terras	525 W 22nd St	212-352-9460
Danese	535 W 24th St	212-223-2227
Daniel Cooney Fine Art	511 W 25th St	212-255-8158
Daniel Reich Gallery	537 W 23rd St	212-924-4949
David Krut Fine Art	526 W 26th St	212-255-3094
David Zwirner	525 W 19th St	212-727-2070
DCA Gallery	525 W 22nd St	212-255-5511
DCKT Contemporary	552 W 24th St	212-741-9955
Denise Bibro Fine Art	529 W 20th St, 4th Fl	212-647-7030
Derek Eller Gallery	615 W 27th St	212-206-6411
Dia: Chelsea (closed for renovations)	548 W 22nd St	212-989-5566
Dinter Fine Art	547 W 25th St	212-947-2818
DJT Fine Art/Dom Tagliatalatela	511 W 25th St, 2nd Fl	212-367-0881
Dorfman Projects	529 W 20th St, 7th Fl	212-352-2272
Edition Schellmann	210 Eleventh Ave, 8th Fl	212-219-1821
Edward Thorp	210 Eleventh Ave, 6th Fl	212-691-6565
Elizabeth Dee Gallery	545 W 20th St	212-924-7545
Elizabeth Harris	529 W 20th St	212-463-9666
Esso Gallery	531 W 26th St	212-560-9728
Exit Art	475 Tenth Ave	212-966-7745
Eyebeam	540 W 21st St	718-222-3982
Feature	530 W 25th St	212-675-7772
Feigen Contemporary	535 W 20th St	212-929-0500
First Street Gallery	526 W 26th St #915	646-336-8053
Fischbach Gallery	210 Eleventh Ave #801	212-759-2345
Flomenhaft Gallery	547 W 27th St	212-268-4952
Florence Lynch Gallery	539 W 25th St	212-924-3290
Fredericks Freiser Gallery	536 W 24th St	212-633-6555
Frederieke Taylor Gallery	535 W 22nd St, 6th Fl	646-230-0992
Freight + Volume	542 W 24th St	212-989-8700

Friedrich Petzel	535 W 22nd St	212-680-9467
Gagosian Gallery	555 W 24th St	212-741-1111
Galeria Ramis Barquet	532 W 24th St	212-675-3421
Galerie Lelong	528 W 26th St	212-315-0470
Gallery Henoch	555 W 25th St	917-305-0003
George Adams	525 W 26th St	212-644-5665
George Billis Gallery	511 W 25th St	212-645-2621
Goff and Rosenthal	537B W 23rd St	212-675-0461
GR N'Namdi Gallery	526 W 26th St	212-929-6645
Greene Naftali	526 W 26th St, 8th Fl	212-463-7770
Haim Chanin Fine Arts	210 Eleventh Ave, Ste 201	646-230-7200
Heidi Cho Gallery	522 W 23rd St	212-255-6783
Henry Urbach Architecture	526 W 26th St	212-627-0974
Howard Scott	529 W 20th St, 7th Fl	646-486-7004
I-20 Gallery	529 W 20th St	212-645-1100
In Camera	511 W 25th St #401	212-647-7667
InterArt Gallery	225 Tenth Ave	212-647-1811
International Poster Center	601 W 26th St	212-787-4000
International Print Center	526 W 26th St, Rm 824	212-989-5090
New York J Cacciola Galleries	531 W 25th St	212-462-4646
Jack Shainman Gallery	513 W 20th St	212-645-1701
James Cohan	533 W 26th St	212-714-9500
Jeff Bailey Gallery	511 W 25th St #808	212-989-0156
Jim Kempner Fine Art	501 W 23rd St	212-206-6872
John Connelly Presents	625 W 27th St	212-337-9563
John Stevenson Gallery	338 W 23rd St	212-352-0070
Jonathan LeVine Gallery	529 W 20th St	212-243-3822
Josee Bievenu Gallery	529 W 20th St	212-206-8494
Josee Bievenu Gallery	529 W 20th St, 2nd Fl	212-206-7990
Joseph Helman	601 W 26th St	212-929-1545
Julie Saul Gallery	535 W 22nd St, 6th Fl	212-627-2410
Kashya Hildebrand Gallery	531 W 25th St	212-366-5757
Katherine Markel Fine Arts	529 W 20th St	212-366-5368
Kent Gallery	541 W 25th St	212-627-3680
Kim Foster	529 W 20th St	212-229-0044
Kimcherova	532 W 25th St	212-929-9720
The Kitchen Gallery	512 W 19th St	212-255-5793
Klemens Gasser & Tanja Grunert	524 W 19th St, 2nd Fl	212-807-9494
Klotz Sirmon Gallery	511 W 25th St	212-741-4764
Kravets/Wehby Gallery	521 W 21st St	212-352-2238
Kustera Tilton Gallery	520 W 21st St	212-989-0082
Larissa Goldston Gallery	530 W 25th St	212-206-7887
Lehmann Maupin	540 W 26th St	212-937-6581
Lemmons Contemporary	210 Eleventh Ave	212-337-0025
Lennon, Weinberg	514 W 25th St	212-941-0012
Leo Koenig	545 W 23rd St	212-334-9255
Leslie Tonkonow Artworks and Projects	535 W 22nd St, 6th Fl	212-255-8450
Lohin Geduld Gallery	531 W 25th St	212-675-2656
Lombard-Freid Projects	531 W 26th St	212-967-8040
Lost Art	515 W 29th St PH	212-594-5450
Lucas Schoormans	508 W 26th St #11B	212-243-3159
Luhring Augustine	531 W 24th St	212-206-9100
Luise Ross	511 W 25th St	212-343-2161
Lyons Wier Gallery	511 W 25th St #205	212-242-6220
Magnan Projects	317 Tenth Ave	212-244-2344
Margaret Thatcher Projects	511 W 25th St #404	212-675-0222
Marianne Boesky Gallery	535 W 22nd St	212-680-9889
Marvelli Gallery	526 W 26th St	212-627-3363
Mary Boone Gallery	541 W 24th St	212-752-2929
Massimo Audiello	526 W 26th St #519	212-675-9082
Matthew Marks Gallery	523 W 24th St	212-243-0200
Max Protech	511 W 22nd St	212-633-6999
Maya Stendhal Gallery	545 W 20th St	212-366-1549
McKenzie Fine Art	511 W 25th St, 2nd Fl	212-989-5467
Medialia: Rack & Hamper Gallery	335 W 38th St, 4th Fl	212-971-0953
Messineo Wyman Projects	525 W 22nd St	212-414-0827
Metro Pictures	519 W 24th St	212-206-7100
Michael Steinberg Fine Art	526 W 26th St	212-924-5770
Mike Weiss Gallery	520 W 24th St	212-691-6899
Mixed Greens	531 W 26th St	212-331-8888
Montserrat	547 W 27th St	212-268-0088

Morgan Lehman	317 Tenth Ave	212-268-6699
Moti Hasson Gallery	330 W 38th St	212-268-4444
Murray Guy	453 W 17th St	212-463-7372
Museum Works Gallery	511 W 25th St	800-386-2785
MY Art Prospects	547 W 27th St 2nd Fl	212-268-7132
Nancy Margolis Gallery	523 W 25th St	212-242-3013
New Art Center	580 Eighth Ave	212-354-2999
New Century Artists	530 W 25th St Ste 406	212-367-7072
Newman/Popiashvili Gallery	504 W 22nd St	212-274-9166
Nicole Klagsbrun Gallery	526 W 26th St #213	212-243-3335
NoHo Galleries in Chelsea	530 W 25th St, 4th Fl	212-367-7063
Pace Wildenstein	534 W 25th St	212-929-7000
Paul Kasmin Gallery	293 Tenth Ave	212-563-4474
Paul Kasmin Gallery	511 W 27th St	212-563-4474
Paul Morris Gallery	525 W 26th St	212-727-2752
Paul Rodgers/9W	529 W 20th St, 9th Fl	212-414-9810
Paul Sharpe Contemporary Art	525 W 26th St	646-613-1252
Paula Cooper Gallery	534 W 21st St	212-255-1105
Pavel Zoubok Gallery	533 W 23rd St	212-675-7490
Perry Rubenstein Gallery	527 W 23rd St	212-627-8000
Phoenix	210 Eleventh Ave, 9th Fl	212-226-8711
Pleiades Gallery	530 W 25th St	646-230-0056
Plum Blossoms Gallery	555 W 25th St	212-719-7008
Postmasters Gallery	459 W 19th St	212-727-3323
PPOW	555 W 25th St	212-941-8642
PPOW	555 W 25th St, 2nd Fl	212-647-1044
Prince Street Gallery	530 W 25th St, 4th Fl	646-230-0246
Printed Matter	195 Tenth Ave	212-925-0325
The Proposition	559 W 22nd St	212-242-0035
Qui New York/Zwicker Collective USA	601 W 26th St	212-691-2240
R Duane Reed Gallery	529 W 20th St #7W	212-462-2600
Randel Gallery	287 Tenth Ave, 2nd Fl	212-239-3330
Rare	521 W 26th St	212-268-1520
Reeves Contemporary	535 W 24th St, 2nd Fl	212-714-0044
Remy Toledo Gallery	529 W 20th St	212-242-7552
Ricco/Maresca Gallery	529 W 20th St, 3rd Fl	212-627-4819
Robert Mann Gallery	210 Eleventh Ave	212-989-7600
Robert Miller	524 W 26th St	212-366-4774
Robert Steele Gallery	511 W 25th St	212-243-0165
Rush Arts Gallery & Resource Center	526 W 26th St #311	212-691-9552
Sandra Gering Gallery	534 W 22nd St	646-336-7183
Sara Meltzer Gallery	516 W 20th St	212-727-9330
Sara Tecchia Roma New York	529 W 20th St	212-741-2900
Sean Kelly Gallery	528 W 29th St	212-239-1181
Sears-Peyton Gallery	210 Eleventh Ave #802	212-966-7469
Sherry French	601 W 26th St	212-647-8867
Sikkema, Jenkins & Co	530 W 22nd St	212-929-2262
Silas Seandel Studio	551 W 22nd St	212-645-5286
Skoto Gallery	529 W 20th St	212-352-8058
SoHo 20 Chelsea	511 W 25th St Ste 605	212-367-8994
Sonnabend	536 W 22nd St	212-627-1018
Spike Gallery	547 W 20th St	212-627-4100
Stefan Stux Gallery	530 W 25th St	212-352-1600
Stellan Holm Gallery	524 W 24th St	212-627-7444
Stephen Haller	542 W 26th St	212-741-7777
Steven Kasher	521 W 23rd St	212-966-3978
Stricoff Fine Art	564 W 25th St	212-219-3977
Studio 601	511 W 25th St	212-367-7300
Susan Conde Gallery	511 W 25th St	212-367-9090
Susan Inglett Gallery	511 W 25th St	212-647-9111
SVA Main Gallery	601 W 26th St	212-592-2145
Tanya Bonakdar Gallery	521 W 21st St	212-414-4144
Team	527 W 26th St	212-279-9219
Thomas Erben Gallery	516 W 20th St	212-645-8701
Thomas Werner Gallery	526 W 26th St #712	646-638-2883
Tony Shafrazi Gallery	544 W 26th St	212-274-9300
Van De Weghe Fine Art	521 W 23rd St	212-929-6633
Virgil De Voldere Gallery	530 W 25th St, #407	917-535-9694
Viridian Artists	530 W 25th St, #407	212-414-4040
Von Lintel Gallery	555 W 25th St, 2nd Fl	212-242-0599
Walter Wickiser Gallery	210 Eleventh Ave	212-941-1817

Weisspollack Galleries	521 W 25th St	212-989-3708
White Box	525 W 26th St	212-714-2347
Yancey Richardson Gallery	535 W 22nd St	646-230-9610
Yossi Milo Gallery	525 W 25th St	212-414-0370
Yvon Lambert	564 W 25th St	212-242-3611
Zach Fuer Gallery (LFL)	530 W 24th St	212-989-7700
Zieher Smith	531 W 25th St	212-229-1088
ZONEchelsea, Center for the Arts	601 W 26th St	212-205-2177

Map 9 · Flatiron / Lower Midtown

A-forest Gallery	134 W 29th St	212-673-1168
Alp Galleries	291 Seventh Ave, 5th Fl	212-206-9108
Art Center of the Graduate Center CUNY	365 Fifth Ave	212-817-7386
Christine Burgin Gallery	243 W 18th St	212-462-2668
Diapason	1026 Sixth Ave	212-719-4393
Gallery ArtsIndia	206 Fifth Ave	212-725-6092
H Heather Edelman Gallery	141 W 20th St	646-230-1104
Illustration House	110 W 25th St	212-966-9444
Jack Tilton	520 W 21st St	212-989-0082
Marlborough Chelsea	211 W 19th St	212-463-8634
Merton D Simpson Gallery	38 W 28th St, 5th Fl	212-686-6735
Nabi Gallery	137 W 25th St	212-929-6063
Senior & Shopmaker	21 E 26th St	212-213-6767
Sepia International	148 W 24th St	212-645-9444
Space B	257B W 19th St	917-518-2385

Map 10 · Murray Hill / Gramercy

Artefact Gallery Pardo	119 E 31st St	212-686-3643
Baruch College/Sidney Mishkin Gallery	135 E 22nd St	212-802-2690
East-West Gallery	573 Third Ave	212-687-0180
Hayato New York	125 E 23rd St	212-673-7373
The National Arts Club	15 Gramercy Park S	212-475-3424
Nyehaus	15 E 20th St	212-995-1783
School of Visual Arts	209 E 23rd St	212-592-2144
So Hyun Gallery	350 Fifth Ave	212-355-6669
Swann Galleries	104 E 25th St	212-254-4710
Talwar Gallery	108 E 16th St	212-673-3096
Tepper Galleries	110 E 25th St	212-677-5300

Map 11 · Hell's Kitchen

Art for Healing NYC / Art for Healing Gallery	405 W 50th St	212-977-1165
Fountain Gallery	702 Ninth Ave	212-262-2756
Gallery MC	549 W 52nd St	212-581-1966
Hunter College/Times Square Gallery	450 W 41st St	212-772-4991
Jadite	413 W 50th St	212-315-2740
NYCoo Gallery	408 W 46th St	212-489-0461

Map 12 · Midtown

AFP Galleries	41 E 57th St	212-230-1003
Alexandre Gallery	41 E 57th St, 13th Fl	212-755-2828
Ameringer & Yohe Fine Art	20 W 57th St, 2nd Fl	212-445-0051
Anthony Grant	37 W 57th St, 2nd Fl	212-755-0434
Art Students League of NY	215 W 57th St, 2nd Fl	212-247-4510
Austrian Cultural Forum	11 E 52nd St	212-319-5300
AXA Gallery	787 Seventh Ave	212-554-4818
Babcock	724 Fifth Ave, 11th Fl	212-767-1852
Barbara Mathes	22 E 80th St	212-570-4190
Bernarducci-Meisel	37 W 57th St, 6th Fl	212-593-3757
Berwald Oriental Art	5 E 57th St	212-751-1612
Bill Hodges Gallery	24 W 57th St	212-333-2640

(341)

Arts & Entertainment · **Art Galleries**

Map 12 · Midtown—*continued*

Bonni Benrubi	41 E 57th St, 13th Fl	212-517-3766
China 2000 Fine Art	5 E 57th St	212-588-1198
Christie's	20 Rockefeller Plz	
Cohen Amador	41 E 57th St	212-759-6740
David Findlay Jr Fine Art	41 E 57th St Ste 1120	212-486-7660
DC Moore	724 Fifth Ave, 8th Fl	212-247-2111
Edwynn Houk	745 Fifth Ave, 4th Fl	212-750-7070
Forum	745 Fifth Ave, 5th Fl	212-355-4545
Franklin Parrasch	20 W 57th St	212-246-5360
Galeria Ramis Barquet	41 E 57th St, 5th Fl	212-644-9090
Galerie St Etienne	24 W 57th St Ste 802	212-245-6734
Gallery: Gertrude Stein	56 W 57th St, 3rd Fl	212-535-0600
Garth Clark	24 W 57th St #305	212-246-2205
Gemini GEL at Joni Moisant Weyl	58 W 58th St #21B	212-308-0924
Greenberg Van Doren Gallery	730 Fifth Ave	212-445-0444
Hammer Galleries	33 W 57th St	212-644-4400
Herbert Arnot	250 W 57th St	212-245-8287
Howard Greenberg	41 E 57th St, 14th Fl	212-334-0010
Jain Marunouchi	24 W 57th St, 6th Fl	212-969-9660
James Goodman	41 E 57th St, 8th Fl	212-593-3737
Jason McCoy	41 E 57th St	212-319-1996
Joan T Washburn	20 W 57th St, 8th Fl	212-397-6780
Julian Jacono Francis	37 W 57th St #601	212-757-6660
Katharina Rich Perlow	41 E 57th St, 13th Fl	212-644-7171
Kennedy Galleries	730 Fifth Ave	212-541-9600
Kraushaar	724 Fifth Ave	212-307-5730
Lang Fine Art	41 E 57th St	212-980-2400
Latincollector	37 W 57th St	718-334-7813
Laurence Miller	20 W 57th St	212-397-3930
Leo Kaplan Modern	41 E 57th St, 7th Fl	212-872-1616
Leonard Hutton	41 E 57th St, 3rd Fl	212-751-7373
Littleton & Hennessey Asian Art	724 Fifth Ave	212-586-4075
Lori Bookstein Fine Art	37 W 57th St	212-750-0949
Marian Goodman	24 W 57th St, 4th Fl	212-977-7160
Marlborough	40 W 57th St, 2nd Fl	212-541-4900
Mary Boone	745 Fifth Ave, 4th Fl	212-752-2929
Mary Ryan	24 W 57th St, 2nd Fl	212-397-0669
Maxwell Davidson	724 Fifth Ave	212-759-7555
McKee	745 Fifth Ave, 4th Fl	212-688-5951
Michael Rosenfeld	24 W 57th St, 7th Fl	212-247-0082
Neuhoff	41 E 57th St, 4th Fl	212-838-1122
Nippon Gallery	145 W 57th St	212-581-2223
Nohra Haime	41 E 57th St, 6th Fl	212-888-3550
O'Hara	41 E 57th St, 13th Fl	212-355-3330
Pace MacGill	32 E 57th St, 9th Fl	212-759-7999
Pace Primitive	32 E 57th St, 7th Fl	212-421-3688
Pace Prints	32 E 57th St, 3rd Fl	212-421-3237
PaceWildenstein	32 E 57th St	212-421-3292
Patricia Laligant Gallery	24 W 57th St	
Peter Findlay	41 E 57th St, 3rd Fl	212-644-4433
The Project	37 W 57th St, 3rd Fl	212-688-4673
Projectile	37 W 57th St	212-688-1585
Reece	24 W 57th St Ste 304	212-333-5830
Rehs Galleries	5 E 57th St	212-355-5710
Rita Krauss/Meridian Gallery	41 E 57th St	212-980-2400
Scholten Japanese Art	145 W 58th St #2H	212-585-0474
Susan Sheehan	20 W 57th St, 7th Fl	212-489-3331
Tibor de Nagy	724 Fifth Ave, 12th Fl	212-262-5050
Tina Kim Fine Art	41 E 57th St	212-716-1100
UBS Art Gallery	1285 Sixth Ave	212-713-2885
UMA Gallery	30 W 57th St, 6th Fl	212-757-7240
Zabriskie	41 E 57th St, 4th Fl	212-752-1223

Map 13 · East Midtown

Dai Ichi Arts	249 E 48th St	212-230-1680
Gallery Korea	460 Park Ave, 6th Fl	212-759-9550
Japan Society	333 E 47th St	212-832-1155
National Sculpture Society	237 Park Ave	212-764-5645
Spanierman Gallery	45 E 58th St	212-832-0208
St Peter's Lutheran Church	619 Lexington Ave	212-935-2200
Throckmorton Fine Art	145 E 57th St, 3rd Fl	212-223-1059
Trygve Lie Gallery	317 E 52nd St	212-319-0370
Ubu Gallery	416 E 59th St	212-753-4444
Wally Findlay Galleries	124 E 57th St	212-421-5390

Map 14 · Upper West Side (Lower)

Cork Gallery	W 65th St & Broadway	212-564-2656
Frederick Schultz Ancient Art	325 W 82nd St	212-721-6007
Littlejohn Contemporary	245 W 72nd St	212-980-2323

Map 15 · Upper East Side (Lower)

Achim Moeller Fine Art	167 E 73rd St	212-988-4500
Acquavella	18 E 79th St	212-734-6300
Adam Baumgold	74 E 79th St	212-861-7338
Adelson Galleries	25 E 77th St, 3rd Fl	212-439-6800
American Illustrators Gallery	18 E 77th St Ste 1A	212-744-5190
Andrew Roth	160A E 70th St	212-717-9067
Anita Friedman Fine Arts	980 Madison Ave	212-472-1527
Anita Shapolsky	152 E 65th St	212-452-1094
Barry Friedman	32 E 67th St	212-794-8950
Bernard Goldberg Fine Arts	667 Madison Ave	212-813-9797
Berry-Hill	11 E 70th St	212-744-2300
Bruton	40 E 61st St	212-980-1640
Cavalier Gallery	1100 Madison Ave	212-570-4696
CDS	76 E 79th St	212-772-9555
China Institute Gallery	125 E 65th St	212-744-8181
Conner & Rosenkranz	19 E 74rd St	212-517-3710
Cook Fine Art	1063 Madison Ave	212-737-3550
Craig F Starr Associates	5 E 73rd St	212-570-1739
D Wigmore Fine Art	22 E 76th St	212-794-2128
David Finlay	984 Madison Ave	212-249-2909
Davis & Langdale	231 E 60th St	212-838-0333
De Vos and Giraud	21 E 67th St	212-396-1501
Debra Force Fine Art	14 E 73rd St Ste 4B	212-734-3636
Dickinson Roundell	19 E 66th St	212-772-8083
Ekstrom & Ekstrom	417 E 75th St	212-988-8857
Elkon Gallery	18 E 81st St	212-535-3940
Ezair	905 Madison Ave	212-628-2224
Faggionato Fine Art	42 E 76th St	212-737-9761
Flowers	1000 Madison Ave, 2nd Fl	212-439-1700
Francis M Naumann Fine Art	22 E 80th St	212-472-6800
Friedman & Vallois	27 E 67th St	212-517-3820
Frost & Reed	21 E 67th St	212-717-2201
Gagosian	980 Madison Ave	212-744-2313
Galerie Rienzo	20 E 69th St #4C	212-288-2226
Gallery 71	974 Lexington Ave	212-744-7779
Gallery Pahk	988 Madison Ave	212-861-3303
Gallery Schlesinger	24 E 73rd St, 2nd Fl	212-734-3600
Gerald Peters	24 E 78th St	212-628-9760
Gitterman Gallery	170 E 75th St	212-734-0868
Godel & Co	39A E 72nd St	212-288-7272
Goedhuis Contemporary	42 E 76th St	212-535-6954

Hall & Knight	21 E 67th St	212-772-2266
Hilde Gerst	987 Madison Ave	212-288-3400
Hirschl & Adler Galleries	21 E 70th St	212-535-8810
Hollis Taggart Galleries	958 Madison Ave	212-628-4000
Hoorn-Ashby	766 Madison Ave, 2nd Fl	212-628-3199
Hubert Gallery	1046 Madison Ave	212-628-2922
Hunter College/Bertha & Karl Leubsdorf Gallery	E 68th St & Lexington	212-772-4991
Irena Hochman Fine Art	1100 Madison Ave	212-772-2227
Island Weiss Gallery	201 E 69th St	212-861-4608
Jacobson Howard	22 E 72nd St	212-570-2362
James Francis Trezza	39 E 78th St Ste 603	212-327-2218
James Graham & Sons	1014 Madison Ave	212-535-5767
Jan Krugier	958 Madison Ave	212-755-7288
Jane Kahan	922 Madison Ave, 2nd Fl	212-744-1490
Janos Gat Gallery	1100 Madison Ave	212-327-0441
Kate Ganz USA	25 E 73rd St	212-535-1977
Keith De Lellis	47 E 68th St	212-327-1482
Knoedler & Co	19 E 70th St	212-794-0550
Kouros	23 E 73rd St	212-288-5888
L&M Arts	45 E 78th St	212-861-0020
L'Arc En Seine	15 E 82nd St	212-585-2587
Leila Taghinia-Milani Heller Gallery	22 E 72nd St	212-249-7695
Leo Castelli	18 E 77th St	212-249-4470
Leon Tovar Gallery	9 E 71st St	212-585-2400
Linda Hyman Fine Arts	44 E 67th St	212-399-0112
M Sutherland Fine Arts	55 E 80th St, 2nd Fl	212-249-0428
M&R Sayer Fine Arts	129 E 71st St	212-517-8811
Marc Jancou Fine Art	801 Madison Ave	212-717-1700
Mark Murray Fine Paintings	39 E 72nd St	212-585-2380
Martha Parrish & James Reinish	25 E 73rd St, 2nd Fl	212-734-7332
Mary-Anne Martin Fine Art	23 E 73rd St	212-288-2213
McGrath Galleries	9 E 77th St	212-737-7396
Megan Moynihan & Franklin Riehlman	24 E 73rd St	212-879-2545
Menconi & Schoelkopf Fine Art	13 E 69th St	212-879-8815
Meredith Ward Fine Art	60 E 66th St	212-744-7306
Michael Werner	4 E 77th St	212-988-1623
Michail-Lombardo Gallery	19 E 69th St Ste 302	212-472-2400
Michelle Rosenfeld	16 E 79th St	212-734-0900
Mitchell-Innes & Nash	1018 Madison Ave, 5th Fl	212-744-7400
MMC Gallery	221 E 71st St	212-517-0692
MME Fine Art	74 E 79th St	212-439-6600
Nancy Schwartz Fine Art	710 Park Ave	212-988-6709
Neptune Fine Art & Brand X Projects	50 E 72nd St	212-628-0501
Paul Thiebaud Gallery	42 E 76th St	212-737-9759
Praxis International Art	25 E 73rd St, 4th Fl	212-772-9478
Questroyal Fine Art	903 Park Ave Ste 3A & B	212-744-3586
Rachel Adler Fine Art	24 E 71st St	212-308-0511
Richard Gray	1018 Madison Ave, 4th Fl	212-472-8787
Richard L Feigen & Co	34 E 69th St	212-628-0700
Salander-O'Reilly	20 E 79th St	212-879-6606
Schiller & Bodo	19 E 77th St	212-772-8627
Shepherd & Derom Galleries	58 E 79th St	212-861-4050
Skarstedt Fine Art	1018 Madison Ave, 3rd Fl	212-737-2060
Solomon & Co Fine Art	959 Madison Ave	212-737-8200
SothebyÒs	1334 York Ave	212-606-7000
Soufer	1015 Madison Ave	212-628-3225
Tilton Gallery	8 E 76th St	212-737-2221
Ukrainian Institute of	2 E 79th St	212-288-8660

America		
Ursus Prints	981 Madison Ave	212-772-8787
Uta Scharf	42 E 76th St	212-744-3840
Vivian Horan Fine Art	35 E 65th St, 2nd Fl	212-517-9410
Wildenstein	19 E 64th St	212-879-0500
William Secord	52 E 76th St	212-249-0075
Winston Wachter Mayer Fine Art	39 E 78th St, Ste 301	212-327-2526
Yoshii	17 E 76th St, Ste 1R	212-744-5550
Zwirner & Wirth	32 E 69th St	212-517-8677

Map 16 · Upper West Side (Upper)

Catherine Dail Fine Art	40 W 86th St	212-595-3550

Map 17 · Upper East Side / East Harlem

Allan Stone Gallery	113 E 90th St	212-987-4997
Casa Linda Galleries	300 E 95th St	212-860-8016
Doyle New York	175 E 87th St	212-427-2730
Gallery at the Marmara-Manhattan	301 E 94th St	212-427-3100
Jeffrey Myers Primitive & Fine Art	12 E 86th St	212-472-0115
Neue Galerie New York	1048 Fifth Ave	212-628-6200
Salon 94	12 E 94th St	646-672-9212
Samson Fine Arts	1150 Fifth Ave	212-369-6677
Taller Boricua Galleries	1680 Lexington Ave	212-831-4333
Uptown Gallery	1194 Madison Ave	212-722-3677

Map 18 · Columbia / Morningside Heights

Galleries at the Interchurch Center	475 Riverside Dr	212-870-2200
Miriam & Ira D Wallach Art Gallery	116th & Broadway, 8th Fl	212-854-7288

Map 19 · Harlem (Lower)

PCOG Gallery	1902 Adam Clayton Powell Jr Blvd	212-932-9669

Battery Park City

World Financial Center Courtyard Gallery	220 Vesey St	212-945-2600

Jersey City

Kearon-Hempenstall Gallery`	536 Bergen Ave [Harrison]	201-333-8855
New Jersey City University	2039 Kennedy Blvd [Culver]	201-200-3246

Overview

In case you haven't noticed, New York caters to a wide array of tastes, and music is no exception. From the indie rock clubs of the Lower East Side to the history-steeped jazz clubs in the Village, the world-class orchestral stages of Lincoln Center to the hot dance floors of the Copa, your musical thirst can be quenched in seemingly every possible way. One of the disadvantages of living in a city where there's so much going on is that the choices can be overwhelming. New York's top weeklies—*The Village Voice* and *Time Out New York*—constantly offer suggestions, but it's hard to say whether you should trust them or the e-mail newsletters such as *Flavorpill* (www.flavorpill. net), *DailyCandy* (www.dailycandy.com), and *Nonsense NYC* (www.nonsensenyc.com) who each week urge your attendance at various concerts, multimedia events, and recently opened bars. While more and more places are opening up throughout the isle of Manhattan and the outer boroughs, the majority of these watering holes are still tucked comfortably between 14th and Canal streets, with new bars sprouting like weeds east of Avenue A and south of Houston in the East Village/Lower East Side. But nightlife consists of more than just guzzling beer (although we love to do that, too): LVHRD hosts monthly themed parties at secret locations (www.lvhrd.com); Rubulad throws a Brooklyn loft party in a space that looks like Timothy Leary was the interior decorator; and hipsters dance to notable guest DJs every Saturday night in the West Village (www. misshapes.com). In the following paragraphs, we've taken the liberty of selecting a few choice destinations for your basic nightlife variables: the dive, best beer selection, outdoor space, jukebox, smoker-friendly, music venue, dance club, and a few favorites where you won't mind dishing out some extra dollars. Here are a few of the highlights.

Dive Bars

There are a LOT of dumps in this city, so we've done our best to single out the darkest and the dirtiest. A popular choice among our staff is the oh-so derelict **Mars Bar (Map 6)**—clean-freaks beware of the bathroom! Other favorites include **Milano's (Map 6)**, **The Subway Inn (Map 15)**, **Grassroots Tavern (Map 6)**, and **Cherry Tavern (Map 7)**. If you need to get down and dirty in Brooklyn, check out the **Turkey's Nest (Map 29)** in Williamsburg.

Best Beer Selection

When it comes to sheer beer selection, there are a number of worthy contenders. The heavily-trodden **Peculier Pub (Map 6)** offers an expensive, yet extensive, beer list. Visit this one on a weekday if you want some genuine one-on-one time with the bartender. **The Ginger Man (Map 9)** in lower Midtown stocks over 100 kinds of bottled brew, and has over 60 options on tap. **Vol de Nuit (Map 5)** has a large number of Belgian beers and a warm but reclusive atmosphere. Flatiron's **Silver Swan (Map 9)** offers a slew of beer choices to wash down its German fare. Hipster-fave **Otherroom (Map 5)** has a surprising selection, too. Other places to try are **Blind Tiger Ale House (Map 5)** and **The Waterfront Ale House (Map 10)** (located in both Manhattan and Brooklyn). **Spuyten Duyvil (Map 29)**, which offers many rare finds among its 100-plus beers, is worth the trip to Brooklyn.

Outdoor Spaces

What could be better than sipping a cocktail under the stars? How about sipping a cocktail *with a smoke* under the stars? That's right—bars with outdoor patios have circumvented the no-smoking legislation. Not only do these outdoor spaces offer solace to those cranky puffing pariahs, they provide us all with a short intermission from the commotion and clamor of city life…that is until the next fire truck screams by. We love the aptly named **Gowanus Yacht Club (Map 32)** in Carroll Gardens. This intimate beer garden serves up cold ones with dogs and burgers in a cook-out setting. Other patios to check out are **B Bar (Map 6)**, **Sweet & Vicious (Map 6)**, **The Porch (Map 7)**, **The Park (Map 8)**, and the **Heights Bar & Grill (Map 18)**. **Croxley Ales (Map 7)** on Avenue B has a great outdoor garden that serves large groups well. Some other goodies in Brooklyn are **The Gate (Map 33)** in Park Slope and Williamsburg's **Pete's Candy Store (Map 29)** and **Union Pool (Map 29)**.

Best Jukebox

Again, this is truly a matter of personal taste, but here is a condensed list of NFT picks. For Manhattan: **Ace Bar (Map 7)** (indie rock/rock), **Cherry Tavern (Map 7)** (punk/rock), **HiFi (Map 7)** (a huge and diverse selection), **Lakeside Lounge (Map 7)** (a little something for everybody), **7B (Map 7)** (rock all the way), **Rudy's Bar & Grill (Map 11)** (blues), **Welcome to the Johnsons (Map 7)** (indie rock/punk). For Brooklyn: **The Charleston (Map 29)** (Williamsburg old school), **Great Lakes (Map 33)** (Park Slope—indie rock), **The Boat (Map 32)** (Carroll Gardens—indie rock), **The Levee (Map 29)** (Williamsburg—good all around), and the **Brooklyn Social Club (Map 32)** (Carroll Gardens—country/soul goodness).

Smoker-Friendly

Despite Bloomberg's efforts to create a smoker-free New York, there are a few loopholes in the current legislation. You can still light up in cigar bars and hookah bars, bars with outdoor spaces, and privately-owned establishments. **Hudson Bar & Books (Map 5)** is our favorite place to puff. Smoking is also permitted at its sister uptown location, **Lexington Bar & Books (Map 15)** (jacket required). On the Upper East Side, **Club Macanudo (Map 15)** suggests a country-club atmosphere. Also try **Circa Tabac (Map 2)** (cigar bar). A good number of the city's non-smoking bars will permit the act late at night, but that's entirely up to the establishment. Some have developed clever solutions: in Brooklyn **Larry Lawrence (Map 29)**, a lofted patio allows smokers to keep an eye on the action in the bar below.

Dance Clubs

For those of you who don't believe in paying to dance, there are a number of great places to boogie for free. We like **Lit (Map 6)**, **Good World (Map 4)**, **Luke & Leroys (Map 5)**, **Rififi (Map 6)** (free-$5), the **APT (Map 5)** (sometimes free, sometimes $5-10), and **Cielo (Map 5)**. If you don't mind shelling out the dough, definitely look into the cozy dance space at **Sapphire Lounge (Map 6)** ($5 after 10:30 pm) and the new gargantuan-sized **Crobar (Map**

8) ($30-40). Some other new-ish clubs worth mentioning: **Avalon (Map 9)** (formerly Limelight) and **Capitale (Map 3)** (located in the old Bowery Savings Bank). On the weekends, entry into these clubs doesn't come without paying your dues in long lines and pricey cover charges ($20-$30), but many of them have reduced rates on weeknights. If you need to shake your tail feather in Williamsburg, we suggest checking out the lively dance scene at **Boogaloo (Map 29)** ($5). **Supreme Trading, Black Betty (Map 29)**, and **Royal Oak** are also good options in Brooklyn.

Costly Cocktails

If you don't mind spending a few extra bucks on your drinking habit, try these favorites: Phillippe Starck's brilliant **Royalton (Map 12)** and **Paramount (Map 12)** bars, **Bar Veloce (Map 6)** (a great selection of wine and grappa), **Little Branch (Map 5)** (a unique underground space from the guy who brought us **Milk & Honey**); and **Employees Only (Map 5)**, which has some of the best cocktails we've tasted (think vodka and honey and figs together in one glass)!

Classical Music

Lincoln Center (Map 14) is the focus of most of the classical music performance in the city—see the "Lincoln Center" page in the "Parks and Places" section for info. **Carnegie Hall (Map 12)** also hosts a classical concert, along with more contemporary popular music. Farther uptown, Columbia University's **Miller Theatre (Map 18)** puts on many classical performances in its space and nearby locales (such as Riverside Church). On a nice day, a trip up to bucolic **Wave Hill** in the Bronx for a concert can be a delight. For a more "downtown" classical experience, try the **Amato Opera (Map 6)**. The **Monkey (Map 24)** is the place to go if you like classical guitar, along with some more avant-garde approaches to the instrument. **BAM (Map 31)** in Fort Greene is the home of the Brooklyn Philharmonic. And don't miss **Bargemusic** in Brooklyn, classical concerts on a former coffee-hauling harbor vessel overlooking downtown Manhattan.

Jazz, Blues, Folk and Country

There are plenty of places to see jazz in the city, starting off with classic joints like the **Village Vanguard (Map 5)**, **Birdland (Map 11)**, the **Blue Note (Map 6)** and the **Iridium (Map 12)**, which all draw top notch talent. For a smaller (and cheaper) jazz experience, try and the **Lenox Lounge (Map 19)** and **St. Nick's Pub (Map 21)** in Harlem, or the **Bar Next Door (Map 6)**, **Arthur's Tavern (Map 4)** and **Smalls (Map 5)** in the Village. The **Nuyorican Poets Café (Map 7)** has frequent jazz performances. **Tonic (Map 7)** also plays host to many jazz artists. In Brooklyn, your best bets are the **BAM Café (Map 31)** and the **Up Over Jazz Café (Map 33)**.

The big change for jazz in NYC has been the new **Jazz at Lincoln Center (Map 14)** complex in the Time Warner Center on Columbus Circle. It has three rooms: the 1,000+ seat, designed-for-jazz **Rose Theater**, the **Allen Room**, an amphitheater with a great view of the park, and the nightclub-esque **Dizzy's Club Coca Cola**.

The blues can make an appearance in all sorts of clubs, but **Terra Blues (Map 6)** focuses on the art form and features reliably excellent music on an otherwise tired Bleecker Street scene. The **Baggot Inn (Map 6)** is good for folk, folk-rock, blues and blues-rock, with some country leanings thrown in. The **Sidewalk Café (Map 7)** hosts a steady stream of folky acts and has a weekly open mic on Sundays. The **Living Room (Map 6)** gets some top singer-songwriter talent. For country, try **Rodeo Bar (Map 10)** or **Hank's Saloon (Map 33)**.

Rock and Pop

It's been a tough couple of years for Manhattan rock clubs. LES favorite Luna Lounge got priced out of the scene it helped to create and moved to Brooklyn. CBGB's future is uncertain. The Continental took the Brownie's approach and stopped featuring live music. Still, there's plenty going on, even if it's more and more concentrated in one area.

Bowery Ballroom (Map 6) remains the top live venue, featuring big acts but with excellent sound and a good layout. **Irving Plaza (Map 10)** is a good place to see a show as well. The **Beacon Theater (Map 14)** is the best place to see a show uptown, though it doesn't usually get the newest acts (OK, almost never). **Roseland (Map 12)** is a decent venue in midtown.

The best small club is **Mercury Lounge (Map 7)**, which gets great acts right before they're ready to move up to Bowery, and features a big stage and audience area (the bar can be really cramped though). **Pianos (Map 7)** gets some of the best acts, but the scene can be a bit soul crushing and the small music room literally crushing when packed. The upstairs lounge is great for some quieter fare. As far as the rest of the Lower East Side/East Village area goes, it comes down to how you like your rock clubs. (Faux) punky basement? Try **Lit (Map 6)**, **Cake Shop (Map 7)** or the **Delancey (Map 7)**. Big, loud, clangy space off the main drag? **Sin-é (Map 7)** or **Rothkos**. Or you can head to Brooklyn—try the **Hook (Map 32)**, **Magnetic Field (Map 32)**,**Northsix (Map 29)** (Williamsburg), **Southpaw (Map 33)** or **Trash (Map 29)**. And **Maxwell's (Map 34)** is still your best bet in Hoboken.

Obviously, **MSG (Map 9)** is the place for the big shows, and it's pretty standard issue for an arena venue (boomy sound, a wide range in the quality of seating, pricey refreshments). But U2's not going to play Ludlow Street anytime soon, so whatcha gonna do?

Experimental

A number of venues in New York provide a place for experimental music to get exposure. **Diapason (Map 9)** and **Experimental Intermedia (Map 3)** and **Roulette (Map 2)** are fully dedicated to showcasing the avant-garde, while places like **Tonic (Map 7)** and the **Monkey (Map 24)** mix experimental fare in with more conventional performers. Jon Zorn's relatively-new place, **The Stone (Map 7)**, takes an experimental approach towards the performance space as well as the music, with a different artist acting as curator for an entire month, no drinks or food, and the artists taking in 100% of door proceeds.

Other Music

A few places run the gamut of musical genres. The **Knitting Factory (Map 3)** can have everything from jazz to metal (and three stages to boot). **Town Hall (Map 12)** gets folksy artists one night, hot Latin tango the next, and a slew of comedy, spoken word, and other acts. **Joe's Pub (Map 6)** has a good variety of popular music styles. **The Cutting Room's (Map 9)** offerings include jazz, soul, rock, vocal, and other types of music. And as you might guess, **BAM (Map 31)** has all kinds of musical offerings.

For cabaret or piano-bar, try **Don't Tell Mama's (Map 11)** or **Duplex (Map 5)**. For a more plush experience, try the **Café Carlyle (Map 15)** or **Oak Room (Map 12)** at the Algonquin Hotel. If you're seeking some R&B or soul, check out the **Apollo Theater (Map 19)** and **B.B. Kings (Map 12)**,

though they mostly get "oldies" acts. The Apollo's Amateur Night on Wednesday is your chance to see some up-and-comers. The **Bowery Poetry Club (Map 6)** does a freestyle and DJing competition night on the fourth Friday of every month. Many dance clubs feature hip-hop DJs.

Barbes (Map 33) in Park Slope hosts a wide palette of "world music" (for lack of a better term), including Latin America, Europe, and traditional US styles, plus more experimental fare. For more sounds of the south, **SOB's (Map 5)** has live South American music and dancing; **Café Creole (Map 20)** has Cajun and Caribbean music; **Remy Lounge (Map 1)** has DJs spinning Latin pop, house, salsa, merengue, and more. And don't forget about the **Copacabana (Map 8)**!

Map 1 · Financial District

John Street Bar & Grill	17 John St	212-349-3278	Nightmarish underground nonsense.
Kilarney Rose	80 Beaver St	212-422-1486	Irish pub where you can pregame for the Staten Island Ferry.
Liquid Assets	Millennium Hilton Hotel, 55 Church St	212-693-2001	Plush seating and soft lighting.
Papoos	55 Broadway	212-809-3150	Popular Wall Street bar.
Remy Lounge	104 Greenwich St	212-267-4646	Latin lounge with late-night dancing.
Ryan Maguire's Ale House	28 Cliff St	212-566-6906	Decent Irish pub.
Ryan's Sports Bar & Restaurant	46 Gold St	212-385-6044	Downtown sports bar.
Ulysses	95 Pearl St	212-482-0400	Slightly hipper downtown bar.
White Horse Tavern	25 Bridge St	212-668-9046	Downtown dive.

Map 2 · TriBeCa

46 Grand	46 Grand St	212-219-9311	Cramped and lacking in libations.
Anotheroom	249 West Broadway	212-226-1418	Sister to Room on Sullivan. Missed ConEd bill, too.
Brandy Library	25 North Moore St	212-226-5545	Refined but cozy.
Bubble Lounge	228 West Broadway	212-431-3433	Champagne bar.
Buster's Garage	180 West Broadway	212-226-6811	Sports bar for shitheads.
Church Lounge	Tribeca Grand Hotel, 25 Walker St	212-519-6600	Luxurious space with pricey drinks and occasional live music.
Circa Tabac	32 Watts St	212-941-1781	Smoker-friendly lounge.
Lucky Strike	59 Grand St	212-941-0772	Hipsters, locals, ex-smoky.
Naked Lunch	17 Thompson St	212-343-0828	Average lounge.
Nancy Whisky Pub	1 Lispenard St	212-226-9943	Good dive.
Puffy's Tavern	81 Hudson St	212-766-9159	Locals, hipsters.
Roulette	228 W Broadway	212-219-8242	For the experimental at heart.
Soho Grand Hotel	310 West Broadway	212-965-3000	Swank sophistication.
Tribeca Tavern	247 West Broadway	212-941-7671	Good enough for us.
Walker's	16 N Moore St	212-941-0142	Where old and new Tribeca neighbors mix.

Map 3 · City Hall / Chinatown

Capitale	130 Bowery	212-334-5500	Formerly the Bowery Savings Bank. Cool space.
Double Happiness	173 Mott St	212-941-1282	Downstairs hipster bar.
Experimental Intermedia	224 Centre St	212-431-5127	Experimental art/performance art shows, usually involving a variety of artistic media.
Happy Ending	302 Broome St	212-334-9676	Still taking the edge off.
Knitting Factory	74 Leonard St	212-219-3132	Great downstairs bar.
Metropolitan Improvement Company	3 Madison St	212-962-8219	Where the cops drink.
Milk & Honey	134 Eldridge St		Good luck finding the phone number.
The Beekman Pub	15 Beekman St	212-732-7333	Guinness on tap and karaoke nights.
The Paris Café	119 South St	212-240-9797	By far the best bar in a 10-block radius.
Winnie's	104 Bayard St	212-732-2384	Chinese gangster karaoke!

Map 4 · Lower East Side

Bar 169	169 East Broadway	212-473-8866	Sometimes good, sometimes not.
Clandestino	35 Canal St	212-475-5505	Pate and wine, anyone?
Good World	3 Orchard St	212-925-9975	Great dance parties on the weekends, nice patio.
King Size	21 Essex St	212-995-5464	Laid-back hipsters groove to funky beats.
Lolita	266 Broome St	212-966-7223	Hipster-haven.

Map 5 · West Village

2i's	248 W 14th St	212-807-1775	Hip-hop dance club.
APT	419 W 13th St	212-414-4245	If it makes you feel cool.
Art Bar	52 Eighth Ave	212-727-0244	Great spaces, cool crowd.
Automatic Slims	733 Washington St	212-645-8660	LOUD. Yes, that loud.
Barrow's Pub	463 Hudson St	212-741-9349	Low-key, old man bar.
Chumley's	86 Bedford St	212-675-4449	Former speakeasy. Top 10 bar.
Cielo	18 Little W 12th St	212-645-5700	Too much 'tude.
Cornelia Street Café	29 Cornelia St	212-989-9319	Cozy live music.
Culture Club	179 Varick St	212-243-1999	Bachelorette party heaven.
Daddy-O	44 Bedford St	212-414-8884	Good for a first date or after-work drinks.
Don Hill's	511 Greenwich St	212-219-9850	Live rock music and dancing.
Duplex	61 Christopher St	212-255-5438	Everything's still fun.
The Ear Inn	326 Spring St	212-226-9060	2nd oldest bar in NYC. A great place.
Employees Only	510 Hudson St	212-242-3021	Classy cocktails for big bucks.
Gaslight Lounge	400 W 14th St	212-807-8444	Laidback attitude.
Henrietta Hudson	438 Hudson St	212-924-3347	Good lesbian vibe.
Hudson Bar and Books	636 Hudson St	212-229-2642	Like *Cheers* for a hipper, more sophisticated crowd.
Jazz Gallery	290 Hudson St	212-242-1063	Jazz venue.
Johnny's Bar	90 Greenwich Ave	212-741-5279	Occassional celeb sightings at this popular dive.
Kettle of Fish	59 Christopher St	212-414-2278	Cozy couches and darts.
Little Branch	20 Seventh Ave	212-929-4360	Clever cocktails in an intimate, cavernous setting.
Lotus	409 W 14th St	212-243-4420	Don't forget your Seven pass.
Luke and Leroy	21 Seventh Ave S	212-645-0004	DJs, dancing, debauchery.
Smalls	183 W 10th St		Classic New York jazz; under $10 downstairs.
SOB's	204 Varick St	212-243-4940	World music venue with salsa lessons on Mondays.
The Otherroom	143 Perry St	212-645-9758	Surprisingly decent beer selection.
Village Vanguard	178 Seventh Ave S	212-255-4037	Classic NYC jazz venue. Not to be missed.
Vol de Nuit	148 W 4th St	212-982-3388	Belgian beers, cool vibe.
West	425 West St	212-242-4175	Lounge with a view.
White Horse Tavern	567 Hudson St	212-989-3956	Another NYC classic.
Wogie's	39 Greenwich Ave	212-229-2171	Supposedly an amazing cheesesteak.

Map 6 · Washington Square / NYU / NoHo / SoHo

Ace of Clubs	9 Great Jones St	212-420-1934	Decent space, can be fun with a good band.
Baggot Inn	82 W 3rd St	212-477-0622	Live bluegrass on Wednesdays.
Bar Next Door	129 Macdougal St	212-529-5945	For serious jazz enthusiasts with a penchant for wine and crispy pizza.
Bar Veloce	175 Second Ave	212-260-3200	Sip grappa on a first date. Also in Chelsea.
Beauty Bar	231 E 14th St	212-539-1389	Just a little off the top, dahling?
Blue & Gold	79 E 7th St	212-473-8918	Another fine East Village establishment.
Blue Note	131 W 3rd St	212-475-2462	Classic jazz venue. Pricey.
Bowery Ballroom	6 Delancey St	212-533-2111	Great space that attracts great bands.
Bowery Poetry Club	308 Bowery	212-614-0505	Slam poetry.
CBGB & OMFUG	315 Bowery	212-982-4052	Punk classic. Most likely closed by now.
Cedar Tavern	82 University Pl	212-741-9754	Classic NYU/actor hangout.
Central Bar	109 E 9th St	212-529-5333	Student-filled yet spicy dance party.
Comedy Cellar	117 MacDougal St	212-254-3480	Big names make surprise appearances.
Continental	25 Third Ave	212-529-6924	Good for up-and-comers. Sometimes.
Crash Mansion	199 Bowery		Good live music in posh basement.
Detour	349 E 13th St	212-533-6212	No-cover jazz.
Fanelli's	94 Prince St	212-226-9412	Old-time SoHo haunt. Nice tiles.
Gibraltar Lounge	20 Prince St	212-996-8886	Libation-serving lounge attached to Jacque's.
Grassroots Tavern	20 St Marks Pl	212-475-9443	That mass of fur in the corner is a cat.
Holiday Lounge	75 St Marks Pl	212-777-9637	Where to go to lose your soul.
Joe's Pub	425 Lafayette St	212-539-8776	Good accts in problematic space.
KGB	85 E 4th St	212-505-3360	Former CP HQ. Meet your comrades.
Lit	93 Second Ave	212-777-7987	Live rock and cavernous dancing.
Loreley	7 Rivington St	212-253-7077	Tons of beer, individual pitchers optional.
Mannahatta	316 Bowery	212-253-8644	Newish lounge with huggable poles for dancing.
Marion's Continental	354 Bowery	212-475-7621	Classic cocktails with occasional live tunes.
Mars Bar	25 E 1st St	212-473-9842	The king of grungy bars. Recommended.
McSorley's Old Ale House	15 E 7th St	212-473-9148	Lights or darks?
Milady's	160 Prince St	212-226-9340	The only bar of its kind in this 'hood.
Milano's	51 E Houston St	212-226-8844	Grungy, narrow, awesome.
Nevada Smith's	74 Third Ave	212-982-2591	GooooaaaaaalllllllLLLL!
Peculier Pub	145 Bleecker St	212-353-1327	Large beer selection. NYU hangout.

Map 6 · Washington Square / NYU / NoHo / SoHo—*continued*

The Dove	228 Thompson St	212-254-1435	Diverse crowd but not a scene, chill but not a dive.
The Fish Bar	237 E 5th St	212-475-4949	Friendly dive, lots of neighborhood characters.
Pravda	281 Lafayette St	212-226-4944	Sophisticated lounge serving up inventive martinis.
Red Bench	107 Sullivan St	212-274-9120	Tiny, classy, quiet (sometimes).
Rififi	332 E 11th St	212-677-1027	Decent dancing.
Sapphire Lounge	249 Eldridge St	212-777-5153	Intimate dance floor.
Spring Street Lounge	48 Spring St	212-965-1774	All-ESPN-watchin' post-college moochers.
Sweet & Vicious	5 Spring St	212-334-7915	Great outdoor space.
Terra Blues	149 Bleecker St	212-777-7776	Live blues.
Urge Lounge	33 Second Ave	212-533-5757	Monday night means Drag Queen Money Wheel featuring Miss Cashetta.
Village Underground	130 W 3rd St	212-777-7745	Average rock venue.
Webster Hall	125 E 11th St	212-353-1600	Dance club/ music venue. Amateur strip night.

Map 7 · East Village / Lower East Side

11th Street Bar	510 E 11th St	212-982-3929	Darts, Irish, excellent.
151	151 Rivington St	212-228-4139	2 for 1 until 10pm.
2A	25 Ave A	212-505-2466	Great upstairs space.
7B	108 Ave B	212-473-8840	*Godfather II* shot here. What can be bad?
Ace Bar	531 E 5th St	212-979-8476	Loud, headbanger-y, good.
Arlene Grocery	95 Stanton St	212-995-1652	Cheap live tunes.
Back Room	102 Norfolk St	212-228-5098	Drink vodka from teacups in this hidden speakeasy.
Barramundi	67 Clinton St	212-529-6900	Great garden in summer.
Boss Tweed's Saloon	115 Essex St	212-475-9997	Oaken bartop. Jukebox divine. Surprisingly obnoxious, then.
Bouche Bar	540 E 5th St	212-420-9265	Small, intimate.
Bua	122 St Marks Pl	212-979-6276	Weekend crowds of pretty people on St. Marks.
Cake Shop	152 Ludlow St	212-253-0036	Coffee, records, beer, rock shows, and a "Most Radical Jukebox".
Cheap Shots	140 First Ave	212-254-6631	Ridiculously cheap drinks without the sleaze. How do they do it?
Cherry Tavern	441 E 6th St	212-777-1448	Get the Tijuana Special.
The Delancey	168 Delancey St	212-254-9920	Overrated, but the roof is cool if you can get up there.
The Edge	95 E 3rd St	212-477-2940	Biker hangout. Don't bring your camera.
The Hanger	217 E 3rd St	212-228-1030	Cute DJ on Monday nights.
Hi-Fi	169 Ave A	212-420-8392	THE best jukebox in town.
Joe's Bar	520 E 6th St	212-473-9093	Classic neighborhood hangout. A favorite.
Korova Milk Bar	200 Ave A	212-254-8838	Everyone goes here.
Lakeside Lounge	162 Ave B	212-529-8463	Great jukebox, live music, décor, everything.
Laugh Lounge NYC	151 Essex St	212-614-2500	Where to get your HaHas on the LES.
Living Room	154 Ludlow St	212-533-7235	Live music in your living room.
The Magician	118 Rivington St	212-673-7851	Hipster haven.
Manitoba's	99 Ave B	212-982-2511	Punk scene.
Max Fish	178 Ludlow St	212-529-3959	Where the musicians go.
Mercury Lounge	217 E Houston St	212-260-4700	Rock venue with occasional top-notch acts.
Mona's	224 Ave B	212-353-3780	Depressing. Recommended.
Motor City	127 Ludlow St	212-358-1595	Faux biker bar. Still good, though.
NuBlu	62 Ave C	212-979-9925	Sexy lounge with world music, nice ambience and outdoor porch.
Nuyorican Poet's Café	236 E 3rd St	212-505-8183	Slam poetry.
Parkside Lounge	317 E Houston St	212-673-6270	Good basic bar, live acts in the back.
Pianos	158 Ludlow St	212-505-3733	Painful scene with decent live tunes.
The Phoenix	447 E 13th St	212-477-9979	$1 Wednesdays!
The Porch	115 Ave C	212-982-4034	Just like back at home.
Rothko	116 Suffolk St	no phone	Bleh.
Scenic	25 Ave B	212-253-2595	Trannies and cute girls.
Sidewalk	94 Ave A	212-473-7373	Classic open mic.
Sin-e	150 Attorney St	212-388-0077	Cozy live music.
Sophie's	507 E 5th St	212-228-5680	More crowded counterpart to Joe's.
The Stone	Ave C & E 2nd St		All the front door proceeds go to the avant-garde and experimental artists, so go. Right now.
Three of Cups Lounge	83 First Ave	212-388-0059	Live music and tasty pizza.
Tonic	107 Norfolk St	212-358-7501	Great avant-garde space just saved from eviction!
Welcome to the Johnsons	123 Rivington St	212-420-9911	Great décor, but too crowded mostly.
Zum Schneider	107 Ave C	212-598-1098	Get weisse, man.

Map 8 · Chelsea

Billymark's West	332 Ninth Ave	212-629-0118	Down and dirty dive.
Blarney Stone	340 Ninth Ave	212-502-4656	The only bar in purgatory.
Cajun	129 Eighth Ave	212-691-6174	A little taste of the French Quarter.
Chelsea Brewing Company	Pier 59	212-336-6440	When you're done playing basketball.
Copacabana	560 W 34th St	212-239-2672	Salsa Tuesdays with free buffet.
Crobar	530 W 28th St	212-629-9000	Hangar-like space for dancing.
Half King	505 W 23rd St	212-462-4300	Always the perfect drinking choice in Chelsea. Amazing brunch.
Hammerstein Ballroom	311 W 34th St	212-279-7740	Lofty rock venue.
Molly Wee Pub	402 Eighth Ave	212-967-2627	You may just need a pint after a trip to Penn Station.
The Park	118 Tenth Ave	212-352-3313	Good patio.
Red Rock West	457 W 17th St	212-366-5359	F'ing loud!
Roxy	515 W 18th St	212-645-5156	Roller disco Wednesdays.
West Side Tavern	360 W 23rd St	212-366-3738	Local mixture.

Map 9 · Flatiron / Lower Midtown

Avalon	660 Sixth Ave	212-807-7780	You gotta go at least once.
Blarney Stone	106 W 32nd St	212-502-5139	The only bar in purgatory.
Club Shelter	20 W 39th St	212-719-4479	Dance until dawn.
Cutting Room	19 W 24th St	212-691-1900	Large, usually mellow vibe.
Ginger Man	11 E 36th St	212-532-3740	Where button-down midtown types loosen up over bitter beers
Gotham Comedy Club	208 W 23rd St	212-367-9000	In a new, shiny location.
Kavehaz	37 W 26th St	212-343-0612	Jazz venue.
Live Bait	14 E 23rd St	212-353-2400	Still a great feel. A mainstay.
Merchants	112 Seventh Ave	212-366-7267	Good mixed space.
Old Town Bar & Restaurant	45 E 18th St	212-529-6732	Excellent old-NY pub. Skip the food.
Peter McManus	152 Seventh Ave	212-929-9691	Refreshingly basic.
Satalla	37 W 26th St	212-576-1155	World music venue.
Skybar at La Quinta Hotel	17 W 32nd St	212-736-1600	Rooftop bar with affordable drinks and a kickass view of the ESB.
Splash Bar	50 W 17th St	212-691-0073	Men dancing in waterfalls.
Suede	161 W 23rd St	212-633-6113	Be seen.
Tir Na Nog	5 Penn Plz	212-630-0249	Penn Station hangout.
Under The Volcano	12 E 36th St	212-213-0093	Relaxed, subdued; large selection of tequilas.

Map 10 · Murray Hill / Gramercy

Bar 515	515 Third Ave	212-532-3300	Local pseudo-frat hangout.
Belmont Lounge	117 E 15th St	212-533-0009	Be seen.
Irving Plaza	17 Irving Pl	212-777-6800	Staple rock venue.
The Jazz Standard	116 E 27th St	212-576-2232	Jazz venue.
Joshua Tree	513 Third Ave	212-689-0058	Murray Hill meat market.
Mercury Bar	493 Third Ave	212-683-2645	Lots of TVs for sports. You make the call.
Molly's	287 Third Ave	212-889-3361	Great Irish pub with a fireplace.
New York Comedy Club	241 E 24th St	212-696-5233	...and the bartender asks, "where did you get that?"
Paddy Reilly's Music Bar	519 Second Ave	212-686-1210	Sunday night means pints of Guinness and live Irish fiddlin'.
Revival	129 E 15th St	212-253-8061	Low maintenance beer drinking.
Rocky Sullivan's	129 Lexington Ave	212-725-3871	Lackadaisical trivia on Thursday nights. Free.
Rodeo Bar & Grill	375 Third Ave	212-683-6500	As close to a honky-tonk as you'll get, partner.
Waterfront Ale House	540 Second Ave	212-696-4104	Decent local vibe.

Map 11 · Hell's Kitchen

Bellevue Bar	538 Ninth Ave		A dirty dive, winos and all.
Birdland	315 W 44th St	212-581-3080	Top-notch jazz.
Bull Moose Saloon	357 W 44th St	212-956-5625	Good local hangout.
Don't Tell Mama	343 W 46th St	212-757-0788	Good cabaret space.
Hudson Hotel Library	356 W 58th St	212-554-6000	Super-super-super pretentious.
Rudy's Bar & Grill	627 Ninth Ave	212-974-9169	Classic Hell's Kitchen. Recommended.
Siberia Bar	356 W 40th St	212-333-4141	Brrrr, it's cold out there.
Vintage	Chelsea Market, 753 Ninth Ave	212-581-4655	Ginormous martini menu. Good beers.
Xth	642 Tenth Ave	212-245-9088	Good local vibe.

Map 12 · Midtown

BB King Blues Club	237 W 42nd St	212-997-4144	Check out the live gospel brunch on Sundays.
Blue Bar	59 W 44th St	212-842-6800	If you're in the mood for a Harvey Wallbanger.
Carolines on Broadway	1626 Broadway	212-757-4100	Laughs in Times Square.
Chicago City Limits	318 W 53rd St	212-888-5233	Improv.

Map 12 · Midtown—*continued*

China Club	268 W 47th St	212-398-3800	Think *Night at the Roxbury*.
Flute	205 W 54th St	212-265-5169	Munch on strawberries and cream with your bubbly.
Heartland Brewery	127 W 43rd St	646-366-0235	Heartland HeartLAND HEARTLAND!
Heartland Brewery	1285 Sixth Ave	212-582-8244	Heartland HeartLAND HEARTLAND!
Iridium	1650 Broadway	212-582-2121	Good mainstream jazz venue. Pricey.
Jimmy's Corner	140 W 44th St	212-221-9510	This cozy dive is the only place you should be tipping in Times Square, trust us.
Paramount Bar	235 W 46th St	212-764-5500	Tiny, pretentious, unavoidable.
Roseland	239 W 52nd St	212-247-0200	Big-time rock venue.
The Royalton	44 W 44th St	212-869-4400	Phillippe Starck is the SHIT!
Russian Vodka Room	265 W 52nd St	212-307-5835	Russian molls and cranberry vodka. Awesome.
Show	135 W 41st St	212-278-0988	Show off your goods.
St Andrews	120 W 44th St	212-840-8413	Great bar in the front of this restaurant.
Town Hall	123 W 43rd St	212-840-2824	Attracts great musical acts.

Map 13 · East Midtown

Blarney Stone	710 Third Ave	212-490-0457	The only bar in purgatory.
The Campbell Apartment	Grand Central Terminal	212-953-0409	Awesome space, awesomely snooty!
Fubar	305 E 50th St	212-872-1325	The best option in the area by far.
Kate Kearney's	251 E 50th St	212-935-2045	Irish shenanigans.
Metro 53	307 E 53rd St	212-838-0007	Celebrities and suits.
Sutton Place	1015 Second Ave	212-207-3777	Fabulous roofdeck makes it worth the climb.

Map 14 · Upper West Side (Lower)

All-State Café	250 W 72nd St	212-874-1883	Great underground space.
Beacon Theater	2124 Broadway	212-496-7070	Official venue of the Allman Bros.
Bourbon Street	407 Amsterdam Ave	212-721-1332	Not like N'Awlins, except for the drunken fratboys.
Café Des Artistes	1 W 67th St	212-877-3500	Endless wine menu. Snack on hard-boiled eggs at the bar.
Dead Poet	450 Amsterdam Ave	212-595-5670	Good Irish feel.
Dublin House	225 W 79th St	212-874-9528	Great dingy Irish pub. Recommended.
Emerald Inn	205 Columbus Ave	212-874-8840	Another good Irish pub!
The Evelyn Lounge	380 Columbus Ave	212-724-2363	Candlelight upstairs, dancing downstairs.
Jake's Dilemma	430 Amsterdam Ave	212-580-0556	Sort of okay sometimes.
Makor	35 W 67th St	212-601-1000	Lots of different stuff.
P&G	279 Amsterdam Ave	212-874-8568	Depressing dive. Recommended.
Prohibition	503 Columbus Ave	212-579-3100	Cool space, music, people, etc.
Stand-up NY	236 W 78th St	212-595-0850	The frog replies, "Brooklyn—they're a dime a dozen out there!"
Yogi's	2156 Broadway	212-873-9852	Cheap drinks and a country-western jukebox.

Map 15 · Upper East Side (Lower)

Banshee Pub	1373 First Ave	212-717-8177	Good, fun Upper East Sider.
The Bar at Etats-Unis	247 E 81st Ave	212-396-9928	Hands down the best bar eats you'll find anywhere.
Bemelman's Bar	Carlyle Hotel, 35 E 76th St	212-744-1600	Features lovely mural by creator of Madeline books, Ludwig Bemelman.
Brandy's Piano Bar	235 E 84th St	212-650-1944	Good ol' New York vibe.
Brother Jimmy's	1485 Second Ave	212-288-0999	Crowded meat market.
Café Carlyle	Carlyle Hotel, 35 E 76th St	212-744-1600	Classic cabaret venue. Hellishly expensive.
Club Macanudo	26 E 63rd St	212-752-8200	A perfect environment for smokers (and non-smokers)
Comic Strip Live	1568 Second Ave	212-861-9386	A rabbi walks into a bar with a frog on his shoulder...
Dangerfield's	1118 First Ave	212-593-1650	No amateurs here.
David Copperfield's	1394 York Ave	212-734-6152	Go for the beer.
Feinstein's at the Regency	540 Park Ave	212-339-4095	Cabaret.
Finnegan's Wake	1361 First Ave	212-737-3664	Standard Irish pub. Therefore, good.
Fondue Lounge	303 E 80th St	212-772-2390	Tiny, low-seated lounge for dunking sticks into cheese.
Lexington Bar & Books	1020 Lexington Ave	212-717-3902	Sexy spot to sip cognac and smoke a stogie.
Session 73	1359 First Ave	212-517-4445	Live music and yuppies.
Ship of Fools	1590 Second Ave	212-570-2651	Loud sports with every vittles.
Subway Inn	143 E 60th St	212-223-8929	Sad, bad, glare, worn-out, ugh. Totally great.
Tin Lizzy	1647 Second Ave	212-288-7983	Love those inebriated kids from Jersey dancing on the bar!
Vudu	1487 First Ave	212-249-9540	They dance on the Upper East Side?

Map 16 · Upper West Side (Upper)

Abbey Pub	237 W 105th St	212-222-8713	Cozy Columbia hangout.
Broadway Dive	2662 Broadway	212-865-2662	Where everyone who reads this book goes.
The Ding Dong Lounge	929 Columbus Ave	212-663-2600	Downtown punk brought Uptown. Happy hour all day Tuesdays.

Dive Bar	732 Amsterdam Ave	212-749-4358	Columbia hangout.
La Negrita	999 Columbus Ave		Latin-themed cocktails.
Night Café	938 Amsterdam Ave	212-864-8889	This is what a real dive looks like.
The Parlour	250 W 86th St	212-580-8923	Irish pub, two spaces, good hangout.
Roadhouse	988 Amsterdam Ave	212-666-2337	Happy hour until 9pm & all-you-can-drink specials.
Sip	998 Amsterdam Ave	212-316-2747	Organic coffee by day, cool mojitos by night.
Smoke	2751 Broadway	212-864-6662	Local jazz hangout.

Map 17 · Upper East Side / East Harlem

Auction House	300 E 89th St	212-427-4458	Stylin' uptown lounge.
Big Easy	1768 Second Ave	212-348-0879	Cheap college dive. Beer Pong anyone?
Cavatappo Wine Bar	1728 Second Ave	212-426-0919	Jewel-box-sized spot to sip wine and nibble appetizers.
Kinsale Tavern	1672 Third Ave	212-348-4370	Right-off-the-boat Irish staff. Good beers.
Marty O'Brien's	1696 Second Ave	212-722-3889	Where kilted firefighters go to enjoy pints on St. Paddy's.
Rathbones Pub	1702 Second Ave	212-369-7361	Basic pub.
Tool Box	1742 Second Ave	212-348-1288	Perhaps the official gay bar on the UES.

Map 18 · Columbia / Morningside Heights

Cotton Club	656 W 125th St	212-663-7980	Good, fun swingin' uptown joint.
Heights Bar & Grill	2867 Broadway	212-866-7035	Fun rooftop bar in summer.
Nacho Mama's Kitchen Bar	2893 Broadway	212-665-2800	Get your nacho on.
West End	2911 Broadway	212-662-8830	Long-time Columbia hangout.

Map 19 · Harlem (Lower)

Apollo Theater	253 W 125th St	212-531-5300	The one and the only.
Lenox Lounge	288 Lenox Ave	212-427-0253	Old-time Harlem hangout, recently redone.

Map 20 · El Barrio

Café Creole	2167 Third Ave	212-876-8838	Creole cuisine and live entertainment, satisfaction guaranteed!

Map 21 · Manhattanville / Hamilton Heights

St Nick's Pub	773 St Nicholas Ave	212-283-9728	Great vibe, go for African Saturday nights.
The Hide-A-Way	3578 Broadway	212-283-8384	Possibly the least pretentious bar you've ever been to.

Map 24 · Fort George / Fort Tryon

The Monkey Room	589 Ft Washington Ave	212-543-9888	Quirky, doubles as a coffee shop by day.

Map 25 · Inwood

Keenan's Bar	4878 Broadway	212-567-9016	A friendly neighborhood bar.
Piper's Kilt	4944 Broadway	212-569-7071	Irish pub and sports bar.

Battery Park City

Rise Bar	Ritz Carlton, 2 West St	212-344-0800	Great harbor and park views.

Map 26 · Astoria

Bohemian Hall & Beer Garden	29-19 24th Ave	718-274-4925	Nearly a century old, there's room for 500 drinkers at the last of the city's beer gardens.
Brick Café	30-95 33rd St	718-267-2735	Faux French café with lovely outdoor seating.
Café Bar	32-90 36th St	718-204-5273	Funky place for coffee or cocktails serving Mediterranean food.
Cronin & Phelan	38-14 Broadway	718-545-8999	Typical Irish bar popular with locals.
Fatty's Café	25-01 Ditmars Blvd	718-267-7071	Hip bar and restaurant with nice backyard garden.
Irish Rover	37-18 28th Ave	718-278-9372	A well-loved hangout with live music, quiz nights, and Irish sports.
Mary McGuire's	38-04 Broadway	718-728-3434	Irish pub, OTB, and great burgers.
McCaffrey & Burke	28-54 31st St	718-278-7651	Dive bar complete with colorful regulars, billiards, and darts.
McCann's Pub & Grill	36-15 Ditmars Blvd	718-278-2621	Bustling sports bar that attracts the young and the loud.
Rapture	34-27 28th Ave	718-626-8044	Swank lounge with a Manhattan vibe and prices.
The Albatross	36-19 24th Ave	718-204-9045	Fun lesbian bar that welcomes all.
The Sparrow	24-01 29th St	718-606-2260	A hipster outpost from the folks who brought us Tupelo.

Map 27 · Long Island City

Dominie's Hoek	48-17 Vernon Blvd	718-706-6531	No-frills bar with backyard patio and live music.
LIC Bar	45-58 Vernon Blvd	718-786-5400	Vintage New York saloon with serene backyard patio.
McReilly's	46-42 Vernon Blvd	718-786-7727	Local pub with the best burgers in LIC.
PJ Leahy's	50-02 Vernon Blvd	718-472-5131	Sports bar with a flat-screen TV at every table.
Sunswick Limited	35-02 35th St	718-752-0620	Lively beer bar close to AMMI.
The Cave	10-93 Jackson Ave	718-706-8783	Subterranean lounge with music and performance nights.
Water Taxi Beach	Waterfront, 2nd St & Borden Ave	No phone	Tropical drinks and grilled snacks on an artifical sand beach in summer.

Map 28 · Greenpoint

Enid's	560 Manhattan Ave	718-349-3859	Greenpoint's finest.
Europa	98 Meserole Ave	718-383-5723	Strobe light extravaganza.
Kingsland Tavern	244 Nassau Ave	718-383-9883	Live music occasionally.
The Mark Bar	1025 Manhattan Ave	718-349-2340	Wide selection of beer.
Matchless	557 Manhattan Ave	718-383-5333	Rock 'n roll trivia nights are a must.
Pencil Factory	142 Franklin St	718-609-5858	Great beer, great vibe.
Tommy's Tavern	1041 Manhattan Ave	718-609-5044	Super-dive with live music on weekends.
Warsaw	261 Driggs Ave	718-387-0505	Brooklyn's best concert venue.

Map 29 · Williamsburg

The Abbey	536 Driggs Ave	718-599-4400	Great jukebox and staff.
Alligator Lounge	600 Metropolitan Ave	718-599-4440	Corny, but free pizza is free pizza.
Art Land	609 Grand St	718-599-9706	Low-key bar.
Barcade	388 Union Ave	718-302-6464	Gamer's paradise.
Bembe	81 S 6th St	718-387-5389	Hookahville.
Black Betty	366 Metropolitan Ave	718-599-0243	Dark, exotic, and inviting.
Boogaloo	168 Marcy Ave	718-599-8900	Intimate dancing to live music and DJs.
Brooklyn Ale House	103 Berry St	718-302-9811	When you just want to drink some beer.
Brooklyn Brewery	79 N 11th St	718-486-7422	Open Friday nights only. Tours on Saturdays.
Capone's	221 N 9th St	718-599-4044	Free pizza!
Charleston	174 Bedford Ave	718-782-8717	Old-school bar with pizza, or vice-versa. The first live music venue in Williamsburg.
Daddy's	437 Graham Ave	718-609-6388	Friendly hipster hideaway.
East River Bar	97 S 6th St	718-302-0511	Fun interior, patio, live music.
Galapagos	70 N 6th St	718-782-5188	Reflecting pools, candles, and attractive people.
Greenpoint Tavern	188 Bedford Ave	718-384-9539	Cheap beer in Styrofoam cups.
Iona	180 Grand St	718-384-5008	Plenty of choices on tap.
Laila Lounge	113 N 7th St	718-486-6791	Roomy space with pool and live music.
Larry Lawrence	295 Grand St	718-218-7866	Laid back bar with a lovely loft space.
Mugs Ale House	125 Bedford Ave	718-486-8232	Surprisingly good food, great beer selection, cheap.
Northsix	66 N 6th St	718-599-5103	Great bands almost every night.
Pete's Candy Store	709 Lorimer St	718-302-3770	Live music, trivia nights, awesome back room, and Scrabble.
R Bar	451 Meeker Ave	718-486-6116	Locals call it "our bar."
Red and Black	135 N 5th St	718-302-4535	Fashionistas galore.
Royal Oak	594 Union Ave	718-388-3884	It seems like everybody ends up here.
Southside Lounge	41 Broadway	718-387-3182	Dive bar supreme.
Spike Hill	184 Bedford Ave	718-218-9737	Grab a scotch before jumping on the L.
Spuyten Duyvil	359 Metropolitan Ave	718-963-4140	Join the Belgian beer cult.
Supreme Trading	213 N 8th St	718-218-6538	Oh so hip.
Surf Bar	139 N 6th St	718-302-4441	Sandy-floored seafood joint.
Tainted Lady Lounge	318 Grand St	718-302-5514	Burlesque-inspired bar.
Trash	256 Grand St	718-599-1000	Punk rock and PBRs.
Turkey's Nest	94 Bedford Ave	718-384-9774	Best dive in Williamsburg.
Union Pool	484 Union Ave	718-609-0484	Good starting point or finishing point.

Map 30 · Brooklyn Heights / DUMBO / Downtown

68 Jay Street Bar	68 Jay St	718-260-8207	Arty local bar.
Dumba	57 Jay St	718-858-4886	Punk rock, performance art and DJs.
Henry St Ale House	62 Henry St	718-522-4801	Cozy, dark space with good selections on tap.
Low Bar	81 Washington St	718-222-1569	Asian-themed basement bar.
St Ann's Warehouse	38 Water St	718-254-8779	Live music, theater—cool all around.
Water Street Bar	66 Water St	718-625-9352	Roomy Irish pub.

Map 31 · Fort Greene / Clinton Hill

BAMcafé	30 Lafayette Ave	718-636-4100	Fine food, cocktails, and live music in a classy cavernous space.
Frank's Lounge	660 Fulton St	718-625-9339	When you need to get funky.
Moe's	80 Lafayette Ave	718-797-9536	Laid-back friendly fun.
Reign Bar & Lounge	46 Washington Ave	718-643-7344	Posh, pricey club.
Rope	415 Myrtle Ave	718-522-2899	Scenester spot with jukebox.
Sputnik	262 Taaffe Pl	718-398-6666	Fabulously furnished Pratt hangout.
Stonehome Wine Bar	87 Lafayette Ave	718-624-9443	Dark cave for serious oenophiles

Map 32 · BoCoCa / Red Hook

Boat	175 Smith St	718-254-0607	Nice and dark with great tunes.
Brazen Head	228 Atlantic Ave	718-488-0430	Decent beer, mixed crowd.
Brooklyn Inn	148 Hoyt St	718-625-9741	When you're feeling nostalgic.
Brooklyn Social	335 Smith St	718-858-7758	Classy and cool. NFT pick.
Camp	179 Smith St	718-852-8086	Relive summer camp with games and s'mores.
Floyd	131 Atlantic Ave	718-858-5810	Indoor bocce ball court!
Gowanus Yacht Club	323 Smith St	718-246-1321	Dogs, burgers, and beer. Love it.
The Hook	18 Commerce St	718-797-3007	Red Hook's best live music space.
Kili	81 Hoyt St	718-855-5574	Nice space and cool vibe.
Last Exit	136 Atlantic Ave	718-222-9198	Still trying to win trivia night. Pails of PBR for $10.
Liberty Heights Tap Room	34 Van Dyke St	718-246-1793	A Red Hook must.
Lillie's	46 Beard St	718-858-9822	Retro hideaway. Nice outdoor space.
Magnetic Field	97 Atlantic Ave	718-834-0069	Great décor, live music on the weekends.
Mini Bar	482 Court St	718-852-8086	Wine, bourbon and friendly conversation. Nice.
Montero's	73 Atlantic Ave	718-624-9799	A taste of what things used to be like.
Moonshine	317 Columbia St	718-422-0563	Great atmosphere and garden.
Pioneer Bar-B-Q	318 Van Brunt St	718-624-0700	Great garden, excellent grub.
Red Hook Bait & Tackle	320 Van Brunt St	718-797-4892	Kitschy, comfy pub with cheap drinks and good beers on tap.
Sugar Lounge	147A Columbia St	718-643-2880	Hammocks, hummus, and happy people.
Sunny's	253 Conover St	718-625-8211	No longer pay-what-you-wish, but still cheap and good.
Waterfront Ale House	155 Atlantic Ave	718-522-3794	Standard but solid food and beer.

Map 33 · Park Slope / Prospect Heights / Windsor Terrace

Bar Sepia	234 Underhill Ave	718-399-6680	Neighborhood fave.
Bar Toto	411 11th St	718-768-4698	Great bar food.
Barbes	376 9th St	718-965-9177	Smart-looking space with eclectic entertainment.
Buttermilk	577 Fifth Ave	718-788-6297	Hippest on the block.
Cattyshack	249 Fourth Ave	718-230-5740	Lesbian bar with pool table, smoking deck, and lots of party nights.
Excelsior	390 Fifth Ave	718-832-1599	Decent bar with mixed gay crowd.
Farrell's	215 Prospect Park W	718-788-8779	No-frills bar filled with firefighters.
Freddy's	485 Dean St	718-622-7035	Music and readings and way-coolness.
The Gate	321 Fifth Ave	718-768-4329	Large outdoor section, twenty beers on tap.
Ginger's	363 Fifth Ave	718-788-0924	Nice and casual for comfort.
Great Lakes	284 Fifth Ave	718-499-3710	Laid-back hipster dive. Great jukebox, cheap beer.
Half	626 Vanderbilt Ave	718-783-4100	Intimate wine bar.
Hank's Saloon	46 Third Ave	718-625-8003	Sweaty, hillbillyesque.
Lighthouse Tavern	243 Fifth Ave	718-788-8070	Don't miss Local Yokel night on Monday.
Loki Lounge	304 Fifth Ave	718-965-9600	Darts and billiards tone down the classic wood bar. Good music.
Lucky 13 Saloon	273 13th St	718-499-7553	Park Slope's only punk/metal dive bar.
Mooney's Pub	353 Flatbush Ave	718-783-6406	The real old Brooklyn deal smells of many spilt beers.
O'Connor's	39 Fifth Ave	718-783-9721	Friendly dive in need of a designer..
Park Slope Ale House	356 Sixth Ave	718-788-1756	Good pub grub and beer selection.
Patio Lounge	179 Fifth Ave	718-857-3477	Verdant boozing.
Puppet's Jazz Bar	294 Fifth Ave	718-499-2627	Jazz and wine preside in this web club.
Royale	506 Fifth Ave	718-840-0089	Moroccan boudoir with Brits.
Soda	629 Vanderbilt Ave	718-230-8393	Old-timey ice cream parlor turned bar.
Southpaw	125 Fifth Ave	718-230-0236	Best live music in the Slope.
Up Over Jazz Café	351 Flatbush Ave	718-398-5413	Serious jazz at late hours.

Map 34 · Hoboken

Black Bear	205 Washington St	201-656-5511	Ordinary food but the bands and atmosphere compensate.
City Bistro	56 14th St	201-963-8200	Great summer scene, rooftop views to the city.
Leo's Grandezvous	200 Grand St	201-659-9467	Hoboken's Rat Pack bar. Bring a dame and have some booze.
Maxwell's	1039 Washington St	201-653-1703	A storied live music venue—if the band is good, it's worth the trek.
Mile Square	221 Washington St	201-420-0222	Preppy bar where the food is good and the scene is lively.
Oddfellows	80 River St	201-656-9009	Happening happy hour. Close to the PATH so it catches the commuter crowd.
Texas Arizona	76 River St	201-420-0304	You can eat, you can drink, you can catch a band.

Map 35 · Jersey City

Dennis and Maria's Bar	322 1/2 7th St	201-217-6607	Popular with the locals.
Hamilton Park Ale House	708 Jersey Ave	201-659-9111	Relaxed *Cheers*-esque atmosphere with yummy food.
Lamp Post Bar and Grille	382 2nd St	201-222-1331	Look for the lamp post on the street to find this friendly neighborhood bar.
LITM	140 Newark Ave	201-536-5557	Artsy, laid-back lounge.
Markers	Harborside Financial Ctr, Plz II	201-433-6275	Happy hour heaven. The upscale after-work crowd selects from excellent beers on tap.
The Merchant	279 Grove St	201-200-0202	Classy bar where businessmen go to cut loose.
PJ Ryan's	172 1st St	201-239-7373	A real Irish pub—see your favorite sporting event w/ a pint.
White Star	230 Brunswick St	201-653-9234	Great bar and good eats.

The New York City book scene has taken a sharp decline in terms of diversity in recent years, with many excellent bookshops—including A Different Light, Academy, A Photographer's Place, Rizzoli SoHo, Tower Books, Brentano's, Pageant, Spring Street Books, and Shortwave—all going the way of the dodo. The remaining independent stores are now the last outposts before everything interesting or alternative disappears altogether. And some of NYC's richest cultural neighborhoods—such as the East Village and the Lower East Side—don't have enough bookstores to even come close to properly serving their populations of literate hipsters. So we thought we'd take this opportunity to list some of our favorite remaining shops…

General New/Used

The **Strand (Map 6)** on Broadway, arguably the city's most popular independent bookstore, has recently undergone serious renovations. Glossy white walls, new floors, and an expanded art section on the second floor are among the improvements. The changes have made the store easier to navigate, but the Strand is still a great place to get lost in the stacks on a Sunday afternoon. For rare books (like signed first editions), don't miss the third floor. **Gotham Book Mart (Map 12)** remains Midtown's major literary watering hole, and **St. Mark's Bookshop (Map 6)** anchors the border between the NYU crowd and the East Village hipster contingent. Both Gotham and St. Mark's have excellent literary journal selections. **Argosy Book Store (Map 13)** on 59th Street is still a top destination for books and prints. **Coliseum Books (Map 12)** is a worthwhile stop in Midtown. Uptown, **Morningside Bookshop (Map 18)** and **Labyrinth (Map 18)** serve the Columbia area well. With four locations around the city, the punchy **Shakespeare & Company (Map 1, Map 6, Map 10, Map 15)** is a local chain that somehow manages to maintain an aura of independence. In the West Village, **Three Lives and Co. (Map 5)** should be your destination. The **Barnes & Noble (Map 9)** on Union Square has a signature store and has a great feel. The **Housing Works Used Book Café (Map 6)** has a vintage coffeehouse feel and is one of our favorite bookstores—all of the profits go to help homeless New Yorkers living with HIV/AIDS.

Small Used

Fortunately there are still a lot of used bookstores tucked away all over the city. **Mercer Street Books (Map 6)** serves NYU, **Last Word (Map 18)** covers Columbia, **East Village Books (Map 7)** takes care of hipster heaven, and **Skyline (Map 9)** remains a good Chelsea destination. In Brooklyn, **Park Slope Books**, aka 7th Avenue Books, is a fun browse.

Travel

The city's travel book selection is possibly its greatest strength—from the **Hagstrom Map & Travel (Map 12)** near Bryant Park to several independents, such as the elegant **Complete Traveler Bookstore (Map 9)** and SoHo's **Traveler's Choice Bookstore (Map 2)**.

Art

Printed Matter (Map 8) houses one of the best collections of artists' books in the world and is highly recommended. The **New Museum of Contemporary Art Bookstore (Map 8)** also offers a brilliant selection of both artists' and art books. If you aren't on a budget and have a new coffee table to fill, try **Ursus (Map 15)** in Chelsea.

NYC/Government

The City Store in the Municipal Building is small, but carries a solid selection (and is still the only store we've seen that sells old taxicab medallions). The **Civil Service Bookstore (Map 3)** on Worth Street has all the study guides you'll need when you want to change careers and start driving a bus. The **United Nations Bookshop (Map 13)** has a great range of international and governmental titles. The **New York Transit Museum (Map 12)** shop at Grand Central also has an excellent range of books on NYC.

Specialty

Books of Wonder (Map 9) in Chelsea has long been a downtown haven for children's books. Mystery shops **Murder Ink (Map 16)**, **The Mysterious Book Shop (Map 2)**, and **Partners & Crime (Map 5)** slake the need for whodunits. The **Drama Book Shop (Map 12)** is a great source for books on acting and the theater. **Biography Book Shop (Map 5)** speaks for itself. **Urban Center Books (Map 12)** is well-known for its architecture collection.

Readings

Anyone can read great authors, but lucky for New Yorkers, we have beaucoup chances to meet the literati, too. The four-story Barnes & Noble in Union Square regularly hosts major writers (Tom Wolfe, Jonathan Safran Foer, and Bret Easton Ellis are examples of recent guests). Housing Works Used Book Café features the author2author series in which, you guessed it, two accomplished authors read and discuss their tomes. Nearly all bookstores present readings, even if irregularly; check a store's Web page for listings. Literary blogs like www.maudnewton.com list weekly events for bookworms. Even bars have taken a literary turn for the better: KGB Bar features fiction and nonfiction readings each week (www.kgbbar.com) and One Story magazine hosts an excellent monthly reading series at Pianos (www.pianosnyc.com). In Brooklyn, Pete's Candy Store is a good bet for your weekly dose of literature.

Arts & Entertainment · **Bookstores**

Map 1 · Financial District

Borders	100 Broadway	212-964-1988	Chain
Metropolitan Museum of Art Bookshop	12 Fulton St	212-248-0954	Specialty -Art books.
Shakespeare & Co	1 Whitehall St	212-742-7025	Chain
Strand	95 Fulton St	212-732-6070	Used; Remainders

Map 2 · TriBeCa

Manhattan Books	150 Chambers St	212-385-7395	New and used textbooks.
The Mysterious Book Shop	58 Warren St	212-587-1011	Specialty - Mystery
NY Law School Bookstore	47 Worth St	212-334-2412	Specialty - Law textbooks
Sufi Books	227 West Broadway	212-334-5212	Specialty - Spiritual
Traveler's Choice	2 Wooster St	212-941-1535	Specialty - Travel

Map 3 · City Hall / Chinatown

Civil Service Book Shop	89 Worth St	212-226-9506	Specialty - Civil Services
Computer Book Works	78 Reade St	212-385-1616	Specialty - Computer
Ming Fay Book Store	42 Mott St	212-406-1957	Specialty - Chinese
New York City Store	1 Centre St	212-669-8246	Specialty - NYC books and municipal publications
Oriental Books Stationery & Arts	29 East Broadway	212-962-3634	Specialty - Chinese
Oriental Culture Enterprises	13 Elizabeth St	212-226-8461	Specialty - Chinese
Pace University Bookstore	41 Park Row	212-349-8580	Academic - General
Zakka	147 Grand St	212-431-3961	Specialty - Graphic design books

Map 4 · Lower East Side

Eastern Books	15 Pike St	212-964-6869	Specialty - Chinese

Map 5 · West Village

Barnes & Noble	396 Sixth Ave	212-674-8780	Chain
Biography Book Shop	400 Bleecker St	212-807-8655	Specialty - Biography
Bonnie Slotnick Cookbooks	163 W 10th St	212-989-8962	Specialty - Out of print cookbooks
Drougas Books	34 Carmine St	212-229-0079	Used, political, Eastern religious, etc.
Joanne Hendricks Cookbooks	488 Greenwich St	212-226-5731	Specialty - Wine & Cooking
Left Bank Books	304 W 4th St	212-924-5638	Used; Antiquarian
Libreria Lectorum	137 W 14th St	212-741-0220	Specialty - Spanish
Macondo Books	221 W 14th St	212-741-3108	Specialty - Spanish
Oscar Wilde Memorial Bookshop	15 Christopher St	212-255-8097	Specialty - Gay/Lesbian
Partners & Crime Mystery Booksellers	44 Greenwich Ave	212-243-0440	Specialty - Mystery
Three Lives and Co	154 W 10th St	212-741-2069	General Interest

Map 6 · Washington Square / NYU / NoHo / SoHo

12th Street Books & Records	11 E 12th St	212-645-4340	Used
Alabaster Bookshop	122 Fourth Ave	212-982-3550	Used
Barnes & Noble	4 Astor Pl	212-420-1322	Chain
Benjamin Cardozo School of Law Bookstore	55 Fifth Ave	212-790-0339/0200	Academic - Law
East West Books	78 Fifth Ave	212-243-5994	Specialty - Spirituality; Self-Help
Forbidden Planet	840 Broadway	212-473-1576/ 212-475-6161	Specialty - Fantasy/Sci-fi
Housing Works Used Book Café	126 Crosby St	212-334-3324	Used
McNally Robinson	50 Prince St	212-274-1160	General Interest
Mercer Street Books and Records	206 Mercer St	212-505-8615	Used
New Museum of Contemporary Art Bookstore (Re-opens Fall 2007)	235 Bowery	212-219-1222	
New York Open Center Bookstore	83 Spring St	212-219-2527x109	Specialty - New Age; Spiritual
New York University Book Center-Main Branch	18 Washington Pl	212-998-4667	Academic - General
New York University Book Center- Professional Bookstore	530 LaGuardia Pl	212-998-4680	Academic - Management
Pageant Book & Print Shop	69 E 4th St	212-674-5296	Used and rare.
Scholastic Store	557 Broadway	212-343-6166	Specialty - Educational.
SF Vanni	30 W 12th St	212-675-6336	Specialty - Italian

(355)

Shakespeare & Co	716 Broadway	212-529-1330	Chain
St Mark's Bookshop	31 Third Ave	212-260-7853	General Interest
Strand	828 Broadway	212-473-1452	Used; Remainders
Surma Book & Music	11 E 7th St	212-477-0729	Specialty - Ukrainian
Village Comics	214 Sullivan St	212-777-2770	Specialty - Comics
Virgin Megastore	52 E 14th St	212-598-4666	Chain

Map 7 • East Village / Lower East Side

Bluestockings Bookstore Café and Activist Center	172 Allen St	212-777-6028	Specialty - Political
East Village Books and Records	99 St Marks St	212-477-8647	Messy pile of used stuff
May Day Books	155 First Ave		Anarchist bookstore and collective
St Mark's Comics	11 St Mark's Pl	212-598-9439	Specialty - Comics

Map 8 • Chelsea

Aperture Book Center	547 W 27th St	212-505-5555	Specialty - Photography
Polish American	333 W 38th St	212-594-2386	Specialty - Polish
Printed Matter	195 Tenth Ave	212-925-0325	Specialty - Artist Books

Map 9 • Flatiron / Lower Midtown

Barnes & Noble	33 E 17th St	212-253-0810	Chain
Barnes & Noble	675 Sixth Ave	212-727-1227	Chain
Barnes & Noble College Bookstore	6 E 18th St	212-675-5500	Textbook mayhem.
Books of Wonder	16 W 18th St	212-989-3270	Specialty - Children's
Center for Book Arts	28 W 27th St, 3rd Fl	212-481-0295	Specialty - Artist/Handmade
Compleat Strategist	11 E 33rd St	212-685-3880	Specialty - Fantasy/ SciFi
Complete Traveller	199 Madison Ave	212-685-9007	Specialty - Vintage travel books
Cosmic Comics	10 E 23rd St	212-460-5322	Comics
Fashion Design Books	250 W 27th St	212-633-9646	Specialty - Fashion design
Hudson News	Penn Station	212-971-6800	Chain
Jim Hanley's Universe	4 W 33rd St	212-268-7088	Specialty - Comics; SciFi
Koryo Books	35 W 32nd St	212-564-1844	Specialty - Korean
Metropolis Comics and Collectibles	873 Broadway	212-260-4147	Specialty - Comics
Penn Books	1 Penn Plz	212-239-0311	General interest
Revolution Books	9 W 19th St	212-691-3345	Specialty - Political
Rudolf Steiner Bookstore	138 W 15th St	212-242-8945	Specialty - Metaphysics
Russian Bookstore 21	174 Fifth Ave	212-924-5477	Specialty - Russian/Russia
Samuel French	45 W 25th St, 2nd Fl	212-206-8990	Specialty - Plays and theater books
Skyline Books	13 W 18th St	212-759-5463	Used

Map 10 • Murray Hill / Gramercy

Baruch College Bookstore	55 Lexington Ave	646-312-4850	Academic - General
Borders	576 Second Ave	212-685-3938	Chain
Metropolitan Museum of Art Bookshop	151 E 34th St	212-268-7266	Specialty -Art books.
New York University Book Store– Health Sciences	333 E 29th St	212-998-9990	Academic - Health Sciences
Shakespeare & Co	137 E 23rd St	212-505-2021	Chain

Map 11 • Hell's Kitchen

Hudson News	Port Authority Bldg, North Wing	212-563-1030	Chain

Map 12 • Midtown

AMA Management Bookstore	1601 Broadway	212-903-8286	Specialty - Management
Barnes & Noble	555 Fifth Ave	212-697-3048	Chain
Barnes & Noble	600 Fifth Ave	212-765-0590	Chain
Bauman Rare Books	535 Madison Ave	212-751-0011	Antiquarian
Bookoff	14 E 41st St	212-685-1410	Used Japanese and English
Chartwell Booksellers Churchill	55 E 52nd St	212-308-0643	Specialty - books about Winston
Coliseum Books	11 W 42nd St	212-803-5890	
Collector's Universe	31 W 46th St	212-398-2100	Specialty - Comics
Dahesh Heritage Fine Books	1775 Broadway, Ste 501	212-265-0600	General interest
Drama Book Shop	250 W 40th St	212-944-0595	Specialty - Theater & Drama
FAO Schwarz Book Department	767 Fifth Ave	212-644-9400	Specialty - Children's
Gotham Bookmart and Gallery	16 E 46th St	212-719-4448	Used; New
Hagstrom Map and Travel Center	51 W 43rd St	212-398-1222	Specialty - Travel/Maps
J N Bartfield-Fine Books	30 W 57th St	212-245-8890	Rare and antiquarian.
Kinokuniya	10 W 49th St	212-765-7766	Specialty - Japanese
Libraire de France	610 Fifth Ave	212-581-8810	French and Spanish books, maps, foreign language dictionaries.
Metropolitan Museum of Art Bookshop at Rockefeller Center	15 W 49th St	212-332-1360	Specialty - Art books
Midtown Comics–Times Square	200 W 40th St	212-302-8192	Specialty - Comics
New York City Store	810 Seventh Ave	212-669-8246	Specialty - NYC books and municipal publications
New York Transit Museum	Grand Central Station	212-878-0106	Specialty - NYC/Transit
Rakuza	16 E 41st St	212-686-5560	Specialty - Japanese
Rizzoli	31 W 57th St	212-759-2424/800-52-BOOKS	Specialty - Art/Design
Urban Center Books	457 Madison Ave	212-935-3595	Specialty - Architecture; Urban Planning
Virgin Megastore	1540 Broadway, Level B2	212-921-1020x296	Chain
Waldenbooks	30 Rockefeller Plz	212-245-6921	Chain

Map 13 • East Midtown

Argosy Book Store	116 E 59th St	212-753-4455	Rare and Antiquarian.
Asahiya	360 Madison Ave	212-883-0011	Specialty - Japanese
Barnes & Noble	160 E 54th St	212-750-8033	Chain
Borders	461 Park Ave	212-980-6785	Chain
Come Again	353 E 53rd St	212-308-9394	Specialty - Erotica; Gay/Lesbian
Hudson News	89 E 42nd St	212-687-0833	Chain
Midtown Comics–Grand Central	459 Lexington Ave	212-302-8192	Specialty - Comics
Posman Books	9 Grand Central Terminal	212-983-1111	General Interest
Potterton Books	979 Third Ave	212-644-2292	Specialty - Decorative Arts/Architecture/Design
Quest Book Shop	240 E 53rd St	212-758-5521	Specialty - New Age
Richard B Arkway Books	59 E 54th St, Ste 62	212-751-8135	Specialty - Rare maps and books
United Nations Bookshop	First Ave & 42nd St	212-963-7680/800-553-3210	Good range of everything

Map 14 • Upper West Side (Lower)

Barnes & Noble	1972 Broadway	212-595-6859	Chain
Barnes & Noble	2289 Broadway	212-362-8835	Chain
Borders	10 Columbus Cir	212-823-9775	Chain
Fordham University Bookstore	113 W 60th St	212-636-6080	Academic - General
Juilliard School Bookstore	60 Lincoln Center Plz	212-799-5000	Academic - Music
New York Institute of Technology	1855 Broadway	212-261-1551	Specialty - Technical
Westsider	2246 Broadway	212-362-0706	Used; Antiquarian

Map 15 · Upper East Side (Lower)

Asia Society Bookstore	725 Park Ave	212-327-9217	Specialty - Asian
The Black Orchid Bookshop	303 E 81st St	212-734-5980	Specialty - Mystery/Crime
Blue Danube	217 E 83rd St	212-794-7099	Specialty - Hungarian
Bookberries	983 Lexington Ave	212-794-9400	General Interest
Bookstore Of The NY Psychoanalytic Institution	247 E 82nd St	212-772-8282	Specialty - Psychoanalysis
Choices Bookshop- Recovery	220 E 78th St	212-794-3858	Specialty - Self-help and recovery
Cornell University Medical College Bookstore	424 E 70th St	212-988-0400	Academic - Medical
Crawford Doyle Booksellers	1082 Madison Ave	212-288-6300	General Interest
Hunter College Bookstore	695 Park Ave	212-650-3970	Academic - General
Imperial Fine Books	790 Madison Ave, Ste 200	212-861-6620	Antiquarian
James Cummins Book Seller	699 Madison Ave, 7th Fl	212-688-6441	Antiquarian
Metropolitan Museum of Art Bookshop	Fifth Ave & 82nd St	212-650-2911	Specialty - Art books
Shakespeare & Co	939 Lexington Ave	212-570-0201	Chain
Ursus Books	981 Madison Ave	212-772-8787	Specialty - Art
Whitney Museum of American Art Bookstore	945 Madison Ave	212-570-3614	Specialty - Art/ Artists Books

Map 16 · Upper West Side (Upper)

Funny Business Comics	660B Amsterdam Ave	212-799-9477	Specialty - Comics
Murder Ink	2486 Broadway	212-362-8905	Mystery and general.

Map 17 · Upper East Side / East Harlem

Barnes & Noble	1280 Lexington Ave	212-423-9900	Chain
Barnes & Noble	240 E 86th St	212-794-1962	Chain
Corner Bookstore	1313 Madison Ave	212-831-3554	General Interest
Kitchen Arts & Letters	1435 Lexington Ave	212-876-5550	Specialty - Books on food and wine

Map 18 · Columbia / Morningside Heights

Bank Street College Bookstore	610 W 112th St	212-678-1654	Academic - Education/Children
City College Book Store	138th St & Convent Ave	212-368-4000	General - Academic
Columbia University Bookstore	2922 Broadway	212-854-4132	Academic - General
Labyrinth Books	536 W 112th St	212-865-1588	General Interest
Last Word Used Books	1181 Amsterdam Ave	212-864-0013	Used
Morningside Bookshop	2915 Broadway	212-222-3350	General Interest; New and used
Teachers College Bookstore (Columbia University Graduate School of Education)	1224 Amsterdam Ave	212-678-3920	Academic - Education

Map 19 · Harlem (Lower)

Hue-Man	2319 Frederick Douglass Blvd	212-665-7400	African-American

Map 20 · El Barrio

J P Medical Books	53 E 124th St	212-410-0593	Academic - Medical

Map 21 · Manhattanville / Hamilton Heights

Sisters Uptown	1942 Amsterdam Ave	212-862-3680	African-American books

Map 23 · Washington Heights

Columbia Medical Books	3954 Broadway	212-923-2149	Academic - Medical

Map 24 • Fort George / Fort Tryon

Libreria Caliope	170 Dyckman St	212-567-3511	Spanish and English
Metropolitan Museum of Art Bookshop- Cloisters Branch	799 Ft Washington Ave	212-650-2277	Specialty - Art books

Map 25 • Inwood

Libreria Continental	628 W 207th St	212-544-9004	Specialty - Spanish

Map 26 • Astoria

Book Value	33-18 Broadway	718-267-7929	Bestsellers, discount.
Silver Age Comics	22-55 31st St	718-721-9691	Comics.

Map 28 • Greenpoint

Ex Libris Polish Book Gallery	140 Nassau Ave	718-349-0468	Polish.
Polish American Bookstore	648 Manhattan Ave	718-349-3756	Polish.
Polish Bookstore	739 Manhattan Ave	718-383-0739	Polish.
Polish Bookstore & Publishing	161 Java St	718-349-2738	Polish.
Polonia Book Store	882 Manhattan Ave	718-389-1684	Polish.

Map 29 • Williamsburg

Clovis Press	229 Bedford Ave	718-302-3751	General.
The Read Café	158 Bedford Ave	718-599-3032	Used.
Spoonbill & Sugartown	Mini Mall, 218 Bedford Ave	718-387-7322	Art, architecture, design, philosophy, and literature. New and used.

Map 30 • Brooklyn Heights / DUMBO / Downtown

A&B Books	146 Lawrence St	718-596-0872	African-American books.
Barnes & Noble	106 Court St	718-246-4996	Chain.
Heights Books	109 Montague St	718-624-4876	Rare, out of print, used.
St Mark's Comics	148 Montague St	718-935-0911	Comics.
Trazar's Variety Book Store	40 Hoyt St	718-797-2478	African-American books.

Map 31 • Fort Greene / Clinton Hill

Big Deal Books	973 Fulton St	718-622-4420	General.
Dare Books	33 Lafayette Ave	718-625-4651	General.
Pratt Bookstore	550 Myrtle Ave	718-709-1105	Art books.
Shakespeare & Co	BAM, 30 Lafayette Ave	718-636-4136	Art books.

Map 32 • BoCoCa / Red Hook

Anwaar Bookstore	428 Atlantic Ave	718-875-3791	Arabic books.
Book Court	163 Court St	718-875-3677	General.
Community Book Store	212 Court St	718-834-9494	Used.
Freebird Books	123 Columbia St	718-643-8484	Used.
Rocketship	208 Smith St	718-797-1348	Comic books and graphic novels.

Map 33 • Park Slope / Prospect Heights / Windsor Terrace

Barnes & Noble	267 Seventh Ave	718-832-9066	Chain.
Community Book Store	143 Seventh Ave	718-783-3075	General.
Park Slope Books	200 Seventh Ave	718-499-3064	Mostly used.
Seventh Avenue Books	202 Seventh Ave	718-840-0020	Used.

Multiplexes abound in NYC, but unlike everywhere else, you'll need to cash in a savings bond to cover the steep $10.75 ticket price, the ridiculously expensive popcorn drenched in artificial grease, and costly carbonated syrup water. Needless to say, a trip to the movies here is a rather exorbitant affair, but hey, we don't live in the Big Apple 'cause it's cheap! No matter what kind of flick you're in the mood for, the city's bound to have a theater that'll suit your needs.

If you're after a first-run Hollywood blockbuster, we highly recommend the **Regal 16** in Battery Park City. It has spacious theaters with large screens, big sound, comfortable seats, plenty of aisle room, and most importantly, fewer people! The **Regal Union Square 14 (Map 6)** is gargantuan, too, but frequently so packed that the lines spill out onto the sidewalk. Stadium seating and an IMAX theater make **Loews Lincoln Square (Map 14)** a great place to catch a huge film, and its ideal location offers loads of after-movie options—we recommend grabbing a bite at the Whole Foods Market in the fancy new Time-Warner Center. If you'd like to save a little money and don't mind seeing a movie a few months after it's released, check out what's playing at the **Loews State (Map 12)** in the basement of the Times Square Virgin Megastore. The theater is a little threadbare, but they have popcorn, and you can see a movie for half the regular price.

For the independent or foreign film, the **Landmark Sunshine (Map 6)** on Houston and Forsyth has surpassed the **Angelika (Map 6)** as the superior downtown movie house. Don't get us wrong—the Angelika still presents some great movies, but the theater itself is a far cry from Sunshine. Any list of hip venues wouldn't be complete without mentioning the **Two Boots Pioneer (Map 7)**, operated by the folks at Two Boots. The Pioneer specializes in the independent scene, featuring documentaries, short films, cool film series, and festivals (www.twoboots.com/pioneer). The best revival house is the **Film Forum (Map 5)**—especially now that both the Screening Room and Cinema Classics are gone.

The most decadent and enjoyable movie experiences can be had at the theaters that feel the most "New York." Unfortunately, the Upper East Side's Beekman—where Annie meets Alvy in *Annie Hall*, was just sickeningly demolished thanks to leaseholder Sloan-Kettering. (Does no one in this city give a damn about anything?) **Clearview's Ziegfeld (Map 12)** on 54th Street is a vestige from a time long past when movie theaters were real works of art. This space is so posh with its gilding and red velvet, you'll feel like you're crossing the Atlantic on an expensive ocean liner. The **Paris Theatre (Map 12)** on 58th Street is one of our favorite theaters in the city—it has the best balcony, hands down!

Oh, and don't forget to use Moviefone (777-FILM; www.moviefone.com) or Fandango (www.fandango.com) to reserve your tickets ahead of time on an opening weekend!

Manhattan

	Address	Phone	Map	
92nd Street Y	Lexington Ave & 92nd St	212-415-5500	17	Upper East Side / East Harlem
AMC Empire 25	234 W 42nd St	212-398-3939	12	Midtown
American Museum of Natural History IMAX	Central Park W & 79th St	212-769-5100	14	Upper West Side (Lower)
Angelika Film Center	18 W Houston St	777-FILM #531	6	Washington Square / NYU / NoHo / SoHo
Anthology Film Archives	32 Second Ave	212-505-5181	6	Washington Square / NYU / NoHo / SoHo
Asia Society	725 Park Ave	212-327-9276	15	Upper East Side (Lower)
Bryant Park Summer Film Festival (outdoors)	Bryant Park, b/w 40th & 42nd Sts	212-512-5700	12	Midtown
Cinema Village	22 E 12th St	212-924-3363	6	Washington Square / NYU / NoHo / SoHo
City Cinemas 1, 2, 3	1001 Third Ave	777-FILM #635	13	East Midtown
City Cinemas: East 86th Street	210 E 86th St	212-744-1999	17	Upper East Side / East Harlem
City Cinemas: Village East Cinemas	189 Second Ave	777-FILM #922	6	Washington Square / NYU / NoHo / SoHo
Clearview's 62nd & Broadway	1871 Broadway	777-FILM #864	14	Upper West Side (Lower)
Clearview's Beekman One & Two	1271 Second Ave	212-249-4200	15	Upper East Side (Lower)
Clearview's Chelsea	260 W 23rd St	212-691-5519	9	Flatiron / Lower Midtown
Clearview's Chelsea West	333 W 23rd St	212-989-0060	8	Chelsea
Clearview's First & 62nd Street	400 E 62nd St	777-FILM #957	15	Upper East Side (Lower)
Clearview's Ziegfeld	141 W 54th St	777-FILM #602	12	Midtown
Czech Center	1109 Madison Ave	212-288-0830	15	Upper East Side (Lower)
Film Forum	209 W Houston St	212-966-8163	5	West Village
French Institute	55 E 59th St	212-355-6160	13	East Midtown
IFC Center	323 Sixth Ave	212-924-7771	5	West Village
Instituto Cervantes	122 E 42nd St	212-308-7720	13	East Midtown
Italian Academy	1161 Amsterdam Ave	212-854-3570	18	Columbia / Morningside Heights
Japan Society	333 E 47th St	212-752-3015	13	East Midtown
Landmark Sunshine Cinema	141 E Houston St	212-330-8182	6	Washington Square / NYU / NoHo / SoHo
Leonard Nimoy Thalia	2537 Broadway	212-864-5400	16	Upper West Side (Upper)
Lincoln Plaza Cinemas	30 Lincoln Plz	212-757-2280	14	Upper West Side (Lower)
Loews 19th Street East	890 Broadway	212-260-8000	9	Flatiron / Lower Midtown

Loews 34th Street	312 W 34th St	212-244-8686	8	Chelsea
Loews 42nd Street E Walk	247 W 42nd St	212-50-LOEWS #572	12	Midtown
Loews 72nd Street East	1230 Third Ave	212-50-LOEWS #704	15	Upper East Side (Lower)
Loews 84th St	2310 Broadway	212-50-LOEWS #701	14	Upper West Side (Lower)
Loews Cineplex Orpheum	1538 Third Ave	212-50-LOEWS #964	17	Upper East Side / East Harlem
Loews Cineplex Village VII	66 Third Ave	212-50-LOEWS #952	6	Washington Square / NYU / NoHo / SoHo
Loews Kips Bay	550 Second Ave	212-50-LOEWS #558	10	Murray Hill / Gramercy
Loews Lincoln Square & IMAX Theatre	1992 Broadway	212-336-5000	14	Upper West Side (Lower)
Loews State	1540 Broadway	212-50-LOEWS	12	Midtown
Magic Johnson Harlem USA	300 W 125th St	212-665-8742	19	Harlem (Lower)
Makor	35 W 67th St	212-601-1000	14	Upper West Side (Lower)
Metropol@Rififi	332 E 11th St	212-677-1027	6	Washington Square / NYU / NoHo / SoHo
Metropolitan Museum of Art	1000 Fifth Ave	212-535-7710	15	Upper East Side (Lower)
MOMA	11 W 53rd St	212-708-9480	12	Midtown
Museum of TV and Radio	25 W 52nd St	212-621-6800	12	Midtown
New Coliseum Theatre	701 W 181st St	212-740-1545	23	Washington Heights
New York Public Library Jefferson Market Branch	425 Sixth Ave	212-243-4334	5	West Village
New York Public Library-Donnell Library Center	20 W 53rd St	212-621-0618	12	Midtown
NYU Cantor Film Center	36 E 8th St	212-998-4100	6	Washington Square / NYU / NoHo / SoHo
Paris Theatre	4 W 58th St	212-688-3800	12	Midtown
Quad Cinema	34 W 13th St	212-255-8800	6	Washington Square / NYU / NoHo / SoHo
Regal Battery Park City 16	102 North End Ave Embassy Suites	800-326-3264 #629	p202	Battery Park City
Regal Union Square Stadium 14	850 Broadway	212-253-6266	6	Washington Square / NYU / NoHo / SoHo
Scandinavia House	58 Park Ave	212-779-3587	10	Murray Hill / Gramercy
Solomon R Guggenheim Museum	1071 Fifth Ave	212-423-3500	17	Upper East Side / East Harlem
The ImaginAsian	239 E 59th St	212-371-6682	13	East Midtown
Tribeca Cinemas	54 Varick St	212-966-8163	2	TriBeCa
Two Boots Pioneer Theater	155 E 3rd St	212-591-0434	7	East Village / Lower East Side
UA East 85th Street	1629 First Ave	212-249-5100	15	Upper East Side (Lower)
UA Gemini	1210 Second Ave	212-832-1670	15	Upper East Side (Lower)
Walter Reade Theater	70 Lincoln Plz	212-875-5600	14	Upper West Side (Lower)
Whitney Museum	945 Madison Ave	1-800-WHITNEY	15	Upper East Side (Lower)

Queens

	Address	Phone	Map	
The American Museum of the Moving Image	36-01 35th Ave	718-784-4520	26	Astoria
Kaufman Studios Cinema 14	35-30 37th St	718-786-2020	27	Long Island City
Regal Entertainment Group	35-30 38th St	718-786-2020	26	Astoria

Brooklyn

	Address	Phone	Map	
BAM Rose Cinemas	30 Lafayette Ave BAM	718-636-4100	31	Fort Greene / Clinton Hill
Cobble Hill Cinemas	265 Court St	718-596-9113	32	BoCoCa / Red Hook
Ocularis	Galapagos Art Space, 70 N 6th St	718-388-8713	29	Williamsburg
Pavilion Brooklyn Heights	70 Henry St	718-596-7070	30	Brooklyn Heights / DUMBO / Downtown
Pavilion Movie Theatres	188 Prospect Park W	718-369-0838	33	Park Slope / Prospect Heights / Windsor Terrace
Regal/UA Court Street	108 Court St	718-246-7995	30	Brooklyn Heights / DUMBO / Downtown
Rooftop Films	various locations	718-417-7362	n/a	

New Jersey

	Address	Phone	Map	
Loews Cineplex Newport Center II	30 Mall Dr W	201-626-3200	35	

Arts & Entertainment · **Museums**

Make a resolution: Go to at least one museum in New York City every month. There are over 100 museums in the five boroughs, from the **Metropolitan Museum of Art (Map 15)** to the **Dyckman Farmhouse Museum (Map 25)**, an 18th-century relic in upper Manhattan. Many of these museums have special programs and lectures that are open to the public, as well as children's events and summer festivals. When you've found your favorite museums, look into membership. Benefits include free admission, guest passes, party invites, and a discount at the gift shop.

The famous Museum Mile includes eight world-class museums along Fifth Avenue between 82nd Street and 105th Street, including the **Met (Map 15)**, the **Museum of Modern Art (Map 12)**, and Frank Lloyd Wright's architectural masterpiece, the **Guggenheim (Map 17)**. **The Whitney Museum of American Art (Map 15)**, which showcases contemporary American artists, **El Museo del Barrio (Map 17)**, devoted to early Latin American art, **The Museum of the City of New York (Map 17)**, the **Cooper-Hewitt National Design Museum (Map 17)** (housed in the Andrew Carnegie's Mansion), and the **Jewish Museum (Map 17)** are also along the mile.

See gothic art at the **Cloisters (Map 24)** (also a famous picnic spot), exhibitions of up and coming African-American artists at the **Studio Museum in Harlem (Map 19)**, and **P.S. 1 (Map 27)** (MoMA's satellite) for contemporary art. Take the kids to the **Brooklyn Children's Museum** or the **Children's Museum of Manhattan (Map 14)**. The **Lower East Side Tenement Museum (Map 4)** and the **Ellis Island Immigration Museum (Map 1)** stand as reminders of the past, while the **Hayden Planetarium (Map 14)** offers visions of the future. The treasures of the Orient are on display at the **Asia Society (Map 15)**, and coach potatoes can watch the tube all day at the **Museum of Television and Radio (Map 12)**. **The Brooklyn Museum of Art** has edgy exhibitions and has recently been restored.

Just about every museum in the city is worth a visit. Other favorites include the **New York Transit Museum (Map 30)**, the **Morgan Library (Map 9)** (with copies of Guttenberg's Bible on display), the **American Museum of the Moving Image (Map 27)**, **The Museum of Sex (Map 9)**, **The New Museum of Contemporary Art (Map 6)** and the **Queens Museum of Art** (specifically the panorama of New York City).

Manhattan

	Address	Phone	Map	
American Academy of Arts & Letters	633 W 155th St	212-368-5900	21	Manhattanville / Hamilton Heights
American Folk Art Museum	45 W 53rd St	212-265-1040	12	Midtown
American Friends of Tel Aviv	545 Madison Ave	212-319-0555	12	Midtown
American Geographical Society	120 Wall St	212-422-5456	1	Financial District
American Institute of Graphic Arts	164 Fifth Ave	212-807-1990	9	Flatiron / Lower Midtown
American Museum of Natural History	Central Park W at 79th St	212-769-5100	15	Upper East Side (Lower)
American Numismatic Society	96 Fulton St	212-571-4470	1	Financial District
Americas Society	680 Park Ave	212-249-8950	15	Upper East Side (Lower)
Anthology Film Archives	32 Second Ave	212-505-5181	6	Washington Square / NYU / NoHo / SoHo
Arsenal Gallery	830 Fifth Ave	212-360-8163	15	Upper East Side (Lower)
Art in General	79 Walker St	212-219-0473	3	City Hall / Chinatown
Asia Society & Museum	725 Park Ave	212-288-6400	15	Upper East Side (Lower)
Asian American Arts Centre	26 Bowery	212-233-2154	3	City Hall / Chinatown
Bard Graduate Center for Studies in the Decorative Arts	18 W 86th St	212-501-3000	16	Upper West Side (Upper)
Chaim Gross Studio Museum	526 LaGuardia Pl	212-529-4906	6	Washington Square / NYU / NoHo / SoHo
Chelsea Art Museum	556 W 22nd St	212-255-0719	8	Chelsea
Children's Galleries for Jewish Culture	515 W 20th St	212-924-4500	8	Chelsea
Children's Museum of Manhattan	The Tisch Building, 212 W 83rd St	212-721-1234	14	Upper West Side (Lower)
Children's Museum of the Arts	182 Lafayette St	212-941-9198	3	City Hall / Chinatown
Children's Museum of the Native Americans	550 W 155th St	212-283-1122	21	Manhattanville / Hamilton Heights
China Institute	125 E 65th St	212-744-8181	15	Upper East Side (Lower)
The Cloisters	Ft Tryon Park	212-923-3700	24	Fort George / Fort Tryon
Constitution Works	Federal Hall National Memorial, 26 Wall St	212-785-1989	1	Financial District
Cooper Union for the Advancement of Science and Art	Foundation Bldg, 7 E 7th St	212-353-4195	6	Washington Square / NYU / NoHo / SoHo
Cooper-Hewitt National Design Museum	2 E 91st St	212-849-8400	17	Upper East Side / East Harlem
Czech Center	1109 Madison Ave	212-288-0830	15	Upper East Side (Lower)
Dahesh Museum	580 Madison Ave	212-759-0606	12	Midtown
Dia: Chelsea (closed for renovations)	548 W 22nd St	212-989-5566	8	Chelsea

Name	Address	Phone	Map	Neighborhood
Drawing Center	35 Wooster St	212-219-2166	2	TriBeCa
Dyckman Farmhouse Museum	4881 Broadway	212-304-9422	25	Inwood
El Museo del Barrio	1230 Fifth Ave	212-831-7272	17	Upper East Side / East Harlem
Ellis Island Immigration Museum	Ellis Island, via ferry at Battery Park	212-269-5755	1	Financial District
Exit Art	475 Tenth Ave	212-966-7745	8	Chelsea
Fraunces Tavern Museum	54 Pearl St	212-425-1778	1	Financial District
Frick Collection	1 E 70th St	212-288-0700	15	Upper East Side (Lower)
Goethe-Institut	1014 Fifth Ave	212-439-8700	15	Upper East Side (Lower)
Gracie Mansion	East End Ave at 88th St	212-570-4751	17	Upper East Side / East Harlem
Grant's Tomb	W 122nd St & Riverside Dr		18	Columbia / Morningside Heights
Grey Art Gallery	NYU Silver Ctr, 100 Washington Sq E	212-998-6780	6	Washington Square / NYU / NoHo / SoHo
Guggenheim Museum	1071 Fifth Ave	212-423-3500	17	Upper East Side / East Harlem
Hayden Planetarium	Central Park & W 79th St	212-769-5100	14	Upper West Side (Lower)
Hispanic Society of America	613 W 155th St	212-926-2234	21	Manhattanville / Hamilton Heights
International Center of Photography (ICP)	1133 Sixth Ave	212-857-0000	12	Midtown
Intrepid Sea, Air and Space Museum	Pier 86, W 46th St & 12th Ave	212-245-0072	11	Midtown
Japan Society	333 E 47th St	212-832-1155	13	East Midtown
Jewish Museum	1109 Fifth Ave	212-423-3200	17	Upper East Side / East Harlem
Lower East Side Tenement Museum	108 Orchard St	212-982-8420	4	Lower East Side
Madame Tussauds NY	234 W 42nd St	800-246-8872	12	Midtown
Merchant's House Museum	29 E 4th St	212-777-1089	6	Washington Square / NYU / NoHo / SoHo
Metropolitan Museum of Art	1000 Fifth Ave	212-535-7710	15	Upper East Side (Lower)
Morgan Library	29 E 36th St	212-590-0300	9	Flatiron / Lower Midtown
Morris-Jumel Mansion	65 Jumel Ter	212-923-8008	23	Washington Heights
Mount Vernon Hotel Museum and Garden	421 E 61st St	212-838-6878	15	Upper East Side (Lower)
Municipal Art Society	457 Madison Ave	212-935-3960	12	Midtown
Museum at the Fashion Institute of Technology	Seventh Ave & 27th St	212-217-5800	9	Flatiron / Lower Midtown
Museum of American Financial History	28 Broadway	212-908-4110	1	Financial District
Museum of American Illustration	128 E 63rd St	212-838-2560	15	Upper East Side (Lower)
Museum of Arts & Design	40 W 53rd St	212-956-3535	12	Midtown
The Museum of Biblical Art	1865 Broadway	212-408-1500	14	Upper West Side (Lower)
Museum of Chinese in the Americas	70 Mulberry St	212-619-4785	3	City Hall / Chinatown
Museum of Jewish Heritage	36 Battery Pl	646-437-4200	p202	Battery Park City
Museum of Modern Art (MoMA)	11 W 53rd St	212-708-9400	12	Midtown
Museum of Sex	233 Fifth Ave	212-689-6337	9	Flatiron / Lower Midtown
Museum of Television and Radio	25 W 52nd St	212-621-6800	12	Midtown
Museum of the City of New York	1220 Fifth Ave	212-534-1672	17	Upper East Side / East Harlem
National Academy of Design	1083 Fifth Ave	212-369-4880	17	Upper East Side / East Harlem
National Museum of Catholic Art & History	443 E 115th St	212-828-5209	20	El Barrio
National Museum of the American Indian	Alexander Hamilton US Custom House, 1 Bowling Green	212-514-3700	1	Financial District
Neue Galerie: Museum for German and Austrian Art	1048 Fifth Ave	212-628-6200	17	Upper East Side / East Harlem
New Museum of Contemporary Art	235 Bowery	212-219-1222	6	Washington Square / NYU / NoHo / SoHo
New York City Fire Museum	278 Spring St	212-691-1303	5	West Village
New York Historical Society	170 Central Park W	212-873-3400	14	Upper West Side (Lower)
New York Police Museum	100 Old Slip	212-480-3100	1	Financial District
The New York Public Library	Fifth Ave & 42nd St	212-930-0830	12	Midtown
New York Public Library for the Performing Arts	40 Lincoln Center Plz	212-870-1630	14	Upper West Side (Lower)
New York Unearthed	17 State St	212-748-8772	1	Financial District
Nicholas Roerich Museum	319 W 107th St	212-864-7752	16	Upper West Side (Upper)
Rose Museum	154 W 57th St	212-247-7800	12	Midtown
Rubin Museum of Art	150 W 17th St	212-620-5000	9	Flatiron / Lower Midtown
Scandinavia House	58 Park Ave	212-879-9779	10	Murray Hill / Gramercy
School of Visual Arts Museum	209 E 23rd St	212-592-2145	10	Murray Hill / Gramercy
Skyscraper Museum	39 Battery Pl	212-968-1961	1	Financial District
Sony Wonder Technology Lab	550 Madison Ave	212-833-8100	12	Midtown
South Street Seaport Museum	12 Fulton St	212-748-8600	1	Financial District
Statue of Liberty Museum	Liberty Island, via ferry at Battery Park	212-363-3200	1	Financial District
Studio Museum in Harlem	144 W 125th St	212-864-4500	19	Harlem (Lower)
Humanities & Social Sciences Library				
Tibet House	22 W 15th St	212-807-0563	9	Flatiron / Lower Midtown

Manhattan-continued

	Address	Phone	Map	
Ukrainian Museum	222 E 6th St	212-228-0110	6	Washington Square / NYU / NoHo / SoHo
US Archives of American Art	1285 Sixth Ave	212-399-5015	12	Midtown
Whitney Museum of American Art	945 Madison Ave	212-570-3676	15	Upper East Side (Lower)
Whitney Museum of American Art at Altria	120 Park Ave	917-663-2453	13	East Midtown
Yeshiva University Museum	15 W 16th St	212-294-8330	24	Fort George / Fort Tryon

Brooklyn

	Address	Phone	Map	
Brooklyn Children's Museum	145 Brooklyn Ave	718-735-4400	n/a	Prospect-Lefferts Gardens / Crown Heights
Brooklyn Historical Society	128 Pierrepont St	718-222-4111	30	Brooklyn Heights / DUMBO / Downtown
Brooklyn Museum of Art	200 Eastern Pkwy	718-638-5000	n/a	Prospect-Lefferts Gardens / Crown Heights
City Reliquary	370 Metropolitan Ave	n/a	2	Williamsburg
Doll & Toy Museum of NYC	280 Cadman Plz W	718-243-0820	30	Brooklyn Heights / DUMBO / Downtown
Harbor Defense Museum	Ft Hamilton , 230 Sheridan Loop	718-630-4349	n/a	Bay Ridge
Jewish Childrens' Museum	792 Eastern Pkwy	718-467-0600	n/a	Prospect-Lefferts Gardens / Crown Heights
Kurdish Library and Museum	144 Underhill Ave	718-783-7930	33	Park Slope / Prospect Heights / Windsor Terrace
New York Aquarium	502 Surf Ave	718-265-3474	n/a	Coney Island
New York Transit Museum	Boerum Pl & Schermerhorn St	718-694-1600	30	Brooklyn Heights / DUMBO / Downtown
The Old Stone House	First Ave b/w 3rd St & 4th St	718-768-3195	33	Park Slope / Prospect Heights / Windsor Terrace
Simmons Collection African Arts Museum	1063 Fulton St	718-230-0933	31	Fort Greene / Clinton Hill
Waterfront Museum	290 Conover St	718-624-4719	32	BoCoCa / Red Hook
Wyckoff Farmhouse Museum	5816 Clarendon Rd	718-629-5400	n/a	East Flatbush

Queens

	Address	Phone	Map	
American Museum of the Moving Image	36-01 35th Ave	718-784-4520	26	Astoria
Bowne House	37-01 Bowne St	718-359 0528	n/a	Flushing
Fisher Landau Center for Art	38-27 30th St	718-937-0727	27	Long Island City
King Manor Museum	King Park, 150th St & Jamaica Ave	718-206-0545	n/a	Jamaica
Kingsland Homestead	Weeping Beech Park, 143-35 37th Ave	718-939-0647	n/a	Flushing
Louis Armstrong Museum	34-56 107th St	718-478-8297	n/a	Elmhurst
The Museum for African Art	36-01 43rd Ave (temporary location)	718-784-7700	27	Long Island City
New York Hall of Science	47-01 111th St	718-699-0005	n/a	Elmhurst
The Noguchi Museum	9-01 33rd Rd	718-204-7088	27	Long Island City
PS 1 Contemporary Art Center	22-25 Jackson Ave	718-784-2084	27	Long Island City
Queens Museum of Art	New York City Building, Flushing Meadows Corona Park	718-592-9700	n/a	

New Jersey

	Address	Phone	Map	
Jersey City Museum	350 Montgomery St [Monmouth]	201-413-0303	35	Jersey City

General Information

NFT Map: 12
Address: 11 W 53rd St
Phone: 212-708-9400
Website: www.moma.org
Hours: Sun, Mon, Wed, Thurs, Sat: 10:30 am-5:30 pm; Fri 10:30 am-8 pm; closed Tues, Thanksgiving, and Christmas
Admission: $20 for adults, $16 for seniors, $12 for students; free to members and children under 16 accompanied by an adult

Overview

The Museum of Modern Art opened in 1929, back when impressionism and surrealism were truly modern art. Starting out in the Heckscher Building at 730 Fifth Avenue, MoMA moved to its current address on W 53rd Street in 1932. What started out as a townhouse eventually expanded into an enormous space, with new buildings and additions in 1939 by Phillip L. Goodwin and Edward Durell Stone), 1953 (including a sculpture garden by Phillip Johnson), 1964 (another Johnson garden), and 1984 (by Cesar Pelli). During the summer of 2002, the museum closed its Manhattan location and moved temporarily to Long Island City. After a major expansion and renovation by Yoshio Taniguchi, MoMA reopened in September 2004. Taniguchi's new design is understated to the degree of actual boredom, but the art is the point, right?

Wrong. Museums are one of the last great bastions of inventive, exciting, fun, not-necessarily-practical architecture. Taniguchi's design uses all available space, which, considering the price of midtown real estate, must have been a selling point for his design. Other than that, you'll have to trek up to the Guggenheim, fly off to Bilbao, and/or wait for the New Museum of Contemporary Art to move in to its new Bowery digs to see better marriages of art and design.

The re-Manhattanized museum charges $20. If crowds on a typical Saturday afternoon are any indication, the hefty entry fee is not keeping patrons away. Art lovers take note: The yearly $75 membership ($120 for a dual and $150 for a family) is the way to go. Members get a 10% discount at MoMA stores, and you're free to pop in whenever you want to see your favorite Picasso (or use the restroom).

What to See

The fourth and fifth floors are where the big names reside—Johns, Pollack, Warhol (fourth floor), Braque, Cezanne, Dali, Duchamp, Ernst, Hopper, Kandinsky, Klee, Matisse, Miro, Monet, Picasso, Rosseau, Seurat, Van Gogh, and Wyeth (fifth floor). More recent works can be found in the contemporary gallery on the second floor. Special exhibitions are featured on the third and sixth floors. The surrealism collection is definitely the bomb; however, we suspect that MoMA is only showing about 5% of its pop art collection. Well, you can't have everything…

Moving downstairs to the third floor, it's clear that the photography collection is, as always, one of the centerpieces of the museum and is highly recommended (although the Gursky pieces are actually dotted throughout the building). The architecture and design gallery has all kinds of cool consumer product designs, from chairs to cars to airport arrival boards—there is a LOT more to see here than at the old museum, and it's by far, the most fun thing to see at the new MoMA.

Breakdown of the Space

Floor One: Lobby, Sculpture Garden, Museum Store, Restaurant
Floor Two: Contemporary Galleries, Media Gallery, Prints and Illustrated Books, Café
Floor Three: Architecture and Design, Drawing, Photography, Special Exhibitions
Floor Four: Painting and Sculpture II
Floor Five: Painting and Sculpture I, Café
Floor Six: Special Exhibitions
There are two theater levels below the first floor.

Amenities

Bags are not allowed in gallery spaces, and the free coat check can become messy when the check-in and check-out lines become intertwined. Leave large items at home.

Bathrooms and water fountains are on floors one through five, and on the lower theater level. We don't think that there are enough of them, and the bathrooms themselves are way too small to handle the crowds.

There are three places to get food in the museum—you'll pay heavily for the convenience and Danny Meyer experience. Café 2, located on the second floor, offers "seasonal Roman fare," also known as "snooty Italian." They also have an espresso bar. Terrace 5, which overlooks the beautiful sculpture garden, has desserts, chocolates, and sandwiches, along with wine, cocktails, coffee, and tea. Both cafes open half an hour after the museum opens its doors and close half an hour before the museum closes.

For the ultimate museum dining experience, The Modern features the cuisine of Gabriel Kreuther. It has two main rooms—the Dining Room overlooks the sculpture garden, and the Bar Room is more casual and overlooks the bar. An outdoor terrace is also made available when the weather permits. The Modern serves French and New American food and features wild game menu items—sounds great if you've got a platinum card.

The Modern is open beyond museum hours, with the Dining Room closing at 11 pm Monday-Thursday, and 11:30 pm on Friday and Saturday. The Bar Room closes at 11:30 pm Monday-Saturday and 10:30 on Sunday. There's a separate street entrance to allow diners access to The Modern after the museum closes.

Metropolitan Museum of Art

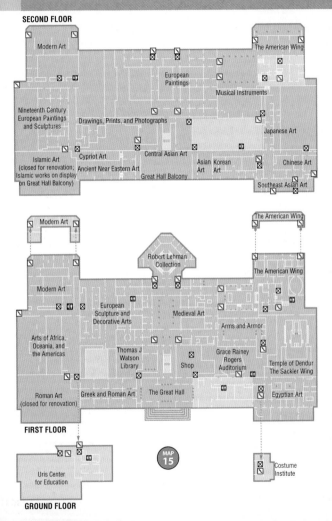

SECOND FLOOR

Modern Art

The American Wing

European Paintings

Musical Instruments

Nineteenth Century
European Paintings
and Sculptures

Drawings, Prints, and Photographs

Japanese Art

Islamic Art
(closed for renovation;
Islamic works on display
on Great Hall Balcony)

Cypriot Art

Central Asian Art

Ancient Near Eastern Art

Asian   Korean
Art   Art

Chinese Art

Great Hall Balcony

Southeast Asian Art

Modern Art

The American Wing

Robert Lehman
Collection

The American Wing

Modern Art

European Sculpture and
Decorative Arts

Medieval Art

Arms and Armor

Arts of Africa,
Oceania, and
the Americas

Thomas J
Watson
Library

Shop

Grace Rainey
Rogers
Auditorium

Temple of Dendur
The Sackler Wing

Roman Art
(closed for renovation)

Greek and Roman Art

The Great Hall

Egyptian Art

FIRST FLOOR

MAP
15

Uris Center
for Education

Costume
Institute

GROUND FLOOR

General Information

NFT Map: 15
Address: 1000 Fifth Ave at 82nd St
Phone: 212-535-7710
Website: www.metmuseum.org
Hours: Sun, Tues-Thurs: 9:30 am-5:30 pm;
                Fri & Sat: 9:30 am-9 pm; Mon,
                New Year's Day, Christmas &
                Thanksgiving: closed. The museum
                is open on select "Holiday Mondays"
                throughout the year.
Admission: A suggested $15 donation for adults,
                $10 for students, and $10 for senior
                citizens. Admission includes the
                Main Building and The Cloisters on
                the same day. Free to members and
                children under twelve with an adult.

Overview

The Metropolitan Museum of Art is touted as the largest and most comprehensive museum in the Western hemisphere. Established by a group of American businessmen, artists, and thinkers back in 1870, the museum was created to preserve and stimulate appreciation for some of the greatest works of art in history.

In the first few years of its inception, the museum moved from its original location at 681 Fifth Avenue to the Douglas Mansion at 128 W 14th Street, and then finally to its current Central Park location in 1880.

Calvert Vaux and Jacob Wrey Mold designed the museum's Gothic Revival red-brick facade, which was later remodeled in 1926 into the grand, white-columned front entrance that you see today. Part of the original facade was left intact and can still be seen from the Robert Lehman Wing looking toward the European Sculpture and Decorative Arts galleries.

The Met's annual attendance reaches over 5 million visitors who flock to see the more than 2 million works of art housed in the museum's permanent collection. You could visit the museums many times and not see more than a small portion of the permanent collection. The vast paintings anthology had a modest beginning in 1870 with a small donation of 174 European paintings and has now swelled to include works spanning 5,000 years of world culture, from the prehistoric to the present and from every corner of the globe.

The Met is broken down into a series of smaller museums within each building. For instance, the American Wing contains the most complete accumulation of American paintings, sculpture, and decorative arts, including period rooms offering a look at domestic life throughout the nation's history. The Egyptian collection is the finest in the world outside of Cairo, and the Islamic art exhibition remains unparalleled, as does the mass of 2,500 European paintings and Impressionist and Post-Impressionist works. Sadly, only a tiny portion of Islamic art is on display throughout the museum, as the permanent gallery is undergoing renovations until 2008. On a positive note, the final phase of renovation of the Greek & Roman collection is scheduled to be complete sometime in 2007. The redesigned galleries will display works that have been in storage for decades, including the museum's newly-restored, world-famous, non-gas-guzzling **Etruscan chariot**.

Other major collections include the arms and armor, Asian art, costumes, European sculpture and decorative arts, medieval and Renaissance art, musical instruments, drawings, prints, ancient antiquities from around the world, photography, and modern art. Add to this the many special exhibits the museums offers throughout the year, and you have a world-class museum with Central Park as its backyard.

The Greatest Hits

You can, of course, spend countless hours at the Met. Pick any style of art and chances are you will find a piece here. But if you're rushed for time, check out the sublime space that houses the **Temple of Dendur** in the Sackler Wing, the elegant **Frank Lloyd Wright Room** in the American Wing, the fabulous **Tiffany Glass** and **Tiffany Mosaics**, also in the American Wing, the **choir** screen in the Medieval Sculpture Hall, the **Caravaggios** and **Goyas** in the Renaissance Rooms, the **Picassos** and **Pollocks** in Modern Art, and that huge **canoe** in Arts of Africa and Oceania. When it's open, we highly recommend the **Roof Garden**, which has killer views of Central Park as a side dish to cocktails and conversation.

How to Get There–Mass Transit

Subway
Take the ④ ⑤ ⑥ to the 86th Street stop and walk three blocks west to Fifth Avenue.

Bus
Take the ④ bus along Fifth Avenue (from uptown locations) to 82nd Street or along Madison Avenue (from downtown locations) to 83rd Street.

Museum of Natural History

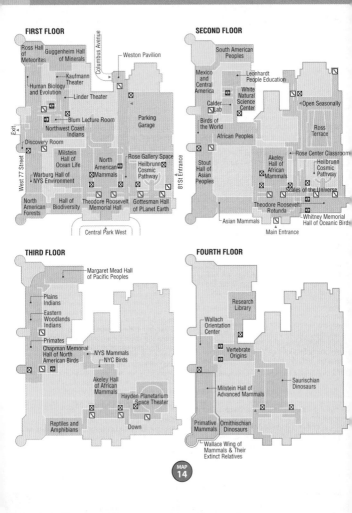

FIRST FLOOR

Columbus Avenue

Ross Hall of Meteorites
Guggenheim Hall of Minerals
Weston Pavilion
Kaufmann Theater
Human Biology and Evolution
Linder Theater
Blum Lecture Room
Northwest Coast Indians
Parking Garage
Discovery Room
Milstein Hall of Ocean Life
North American Mammals
Rose Gallery Space
Heilbrunn Cosmic Pathway
Warburg Hall of NYS Environment
North American Forests
Hall of Biodiversity
Theodore Roosevelt Memorial Hall
Gottesman Hall of Planet Earth
Exit
West 77 Street
81St Entrance
Central Park West

SECOND FLOOR

South American Peoples
Mexico and Central America
Leonhardt People Education
White Natural Science Center
Calder Lab
Birds of the World
African Peoples
Stout Hall of Asian Peoples
Akeley Hall of African Mammals
Scales of the Universe
Theodore Roosevelt Rotunda
Asian Mammals
Open Seasonally
Ross Terrace
Rose Center Classroom
Heilbrunn Cosmic Pathway
Whitney Memorial Hall of Oceanic Birds
Main Entrance

THIRD FLOOR

Margaret Mead Hall of Pacific Peoples
Plains Indians
Eastern Woodlands Indians
Primates
Chapman Memorial Hall of North American Birds
NYS Mammals
NYC Birds
Akeley Hall of African Mammals
Hayden Planetarium Space Theater
Reptiles and Amphibians
Down

FOURTH FLOOR

Research Library
Wallach Orientation Center
Vertebrate Origins
Milstein Hall of Advanced Mammals
Saurischian Dinosaurs
Primitive Mammals
Ornithischian Dinosaurs
Wallace Wing of Mammals & Their Extinct Relatives

MAP 14

General Information

NFT Map: 14
Address: Central Park West at 79th Street
Phone: 212-769-5100
Website: www.amnh.org
Hours: Daily, 10:00 am–5:45 pm The Rose Center stays open until 8:45pm the first Friday of every month. Christmas & Thanksgiving: closed.
Admission: Suggested general admission is $14 for adults, $8 for children (2-12), and $10.50 for senior citizens and students. Special exhibitions, IMAX movies, and the space show are extra; packages are available. Free to members.

Overview

Admit it. You secretly TiVo the Discovery Channel and the History Channel, and (gulp, yes even) have left on *Star Trek* through more than one commercial. Something about African beetles, famous dead guys, and the universe unknown strokes your inner Einstein. Put your microscope on this one, smarty pants: the American Museum of Natural History. Oh, but what are we saying…You're already a chief benefactor! Don't worry. This, and your living-room secrets are safe with us.

Decades before anyone knew what an atom was, when relativity was just a twinkle in Einstein's eye, Albert Smith Bickmore established the AMNH. Completed in 1869, the museum held grand exhibition numero uno in the Central Park Arsenal a few years later, garnering enough respect to acquire space on your favorite and ours, Central Park West. Then, architects, Calvert Vaux and J. Wrey Mould, (somewhat of scientists in their own right) designed a new, posh building on limited Benjamins and opened it to the public in 1877. Key additions followed: The Hayden Planetarium, 1935; Theodore Roosevelt Memorial Hall and Rotunda, 1936; Rose Center for Earth and Space, 2000.

Today, as your favorite Saturday morning museum-going ritual tells you, it's crowded as sh**. On those days, you dodge out-of-towners, eyes wide, mouths gaping. And see much of the same on weekdays, in rowdy school kids on field trips. How to avoid the Excedrine-inducing atmosphere? Two words: permanent collection. Hey, don't knock the live-ins. Even the Met can back up the value of an Alaskan Brown Bear Diorama.

The Greatest Hits

Five floors of star-lovin', mammal-gazin', bird-watchin', fossil-fuelin' science await. Rain forest fever? Check out the Hall of Biodiversity. Jonesing to brush off the suit and trade it for the aquatic life? A 94-foot long great blue whale welcomes you to the Milstein Hall of Ocean Life. Moby teamed up with MTV2 and the Hayden Planetarium in The Rose Center for Earth and Space to produce SonicVision, an animated alternative music show that poses the question: How do you see your music? If you see it enough on your own, thank you very much, consider the next mind boggler headed by Harrison Ford at the Rose Center: The search for life; are we alone? Or, if you'd rather just can the intellect for a while, check out the gigantic meteorites at the Arthur Ross Hall of Meteorites or the Theodore Roosevelt Rotunda with a phenomenal, five-story tall dinosaur display, the largest free-standing beast in the world, as part of two dinosaur halls with the largest collection of vertebrate fossils, also, in the world. Not down with T-rex? The AMNH also churns out Angelika-worthy features in Imax. Pretend you're in your own self-titled film, wearing the bling from the Hall of Gems, home to the Star of India, the largest star sapphire, again, in the world. And, for a recreation of *The Birds* with a lesser evil, visit The Butterfly Conservatory. Tropical butterflies flit all around you from, you guessed, all over the world. It's enough to put TiVo on pause.

How To Get There

Subway
Take the B/C to the 81st Street stop. Or take the 1 to 79th Street and walk two blocks east.

Bus
The 7 10 and 11 all stop within a block of the museum. Take the M79 across Central Park if you are coming from the East Side.

Eating out in New York. Why do we do it? Because cooking is probably only 15% cheaper. Or at least that's what we tell ourselves when we're spending $41 on a hamburger (**Old Homestead Steakhouse (Map 5)**), or $45 on pizza (**Otto (Map 6)**), or god knows what else. But hey—if you're into cooking, that's great. Just move where groceries are cheaper—say, Kansas.

As for the rest of us, eating out is a way of life, an art form, a topic of endless discussion. *Zagat Survey* restaurant ratings, which started as a photocopied sheet handed out to friends in the 1970s, is now an institution in NYC. Half the time we think it's cool to actually even *find* a restaurant that's not "Zagat Rated." The other half of the time, it makes us very, very nervous.

But we *like* that nervous feeling; we can't wait to try a new cuisine; we don't mind eating in places that would clearly fail a Board of Health test—it's all part of eating out in New York. It never gets old—in fact, it's been said that, in New York City, you could eat out at a different restaurant every night for the rest of your life without ever having to go to the same place twice. Whether it's true or not, we may never know, but we'll all certainly have a great time finding out!

Eating Old

When it comes to NYC dining, it's easy to get swept away by the ever-changing hype of the "next big thing." But when you need a break from the Parmesan cheese ice cream with pesto foam in a braised kale emulsion, you can check out these anything-but-boring, time-tested stalwarts. Rub elbows with the who's-who at the posh **'21' Club (Map 12)** (circa 1929); sink your teeth into the original $41 hamburger at **Old Homestead Steakhouse (Map 5)** (circa 1868); dine on New American cuisine at the near-ancient, 213 year-old **Bridge Café (Map 3)**; slurp fresh-shucked oysters under the vaulted, tiled ceiling at Grand Central Station's **Oyster Bar (Map 12)** (circa 1913); pull up a stool at the venerable Midtown watering hole **P.J. Clarke's (Map 13)** (since 1884); or expand your culinary horizons with calf's spleen and cheese on a roll at **Ferdinando's Focaccetta (Map 32)** (circa 1904).

Eating Cheap

Eating cheap is becoming more stylish thanks to the recent trend of highbrow chefs and restaurateurs going lowbrow. At Danny Meyer's **Shake Shack (Map 9)**, you can grab a cheeseburger for $3.69 or one of their legendary Chicago Dogs (a meal in itself) for only $2.77. Waldy Malouf (Beacon) fires up inexpensive pizzas and pastas with snip-your-own-herbs at **Waldy's Wood-Fired Pizza & Penne (Map 9)**. In addition to its brick-and-mortar location, **Daisy May's BBQ USA (Map 11)**, co-owned by Adam Perry Lang (Le Cirque, Daniel, Chanterelle), has mobile push carts throughout the city where you can fetch a hearty bowl of award-winning "Bowl'O Red" Texas-style chili for $7. Naturally, you can never go wrong with ethnic fare when eating on the cheap. Vietnamese (**Nicky's Vietnamese Sandwiches (Map 7)**, **Saigon Grill (Map 16)**), Chinese (**Mandarin Court (Map 3)**, **Wo Hop (Map 3)**, **Joe's Shanghai (Map 3 , Map 12)**), Middle Eastern (**Mamoun's Falafel (Map 6)**, **Sam's Falafel (Map 1) – a street cart**), and burrito joints (**Blockheads (Map 10)**, **Burritoville (Map 1, Map 8, Map 9, Map 11)**) are always sure-fire options when your wallet's running on the thin side. And now, thanks to a new influx of hip hot dog joints, your prospects for avoiding dirty water dogs have improved. With the recent openings of **Broomedogs (Map 4)**, **Dash Dogs (Map 7)**, and the Manhattan branch of **Sparky's (Map 6)**, hot dog lovers of all stripes can savor the affordable, inside-the-bun affair. Last, but not least, there's always the old, but never forgotten staples of NYC eats—bagels and knishes. For bagels, go with perennial winners **Ess-a-Bagel (Map 10, 13)** and **H&H Bagels (Map 11, 14)**, or take our two favorites: **David's Bagels (Map 7,10)** and **Kossar's Bialys (Map 4)**. For knishes, nothing beats the **Yonah Schimmel Knish Bakery (Map 7)**.

Eating Hip

Eating hip usually involves the food of the moment (tacos, lobster rolls, Asian street food), beautiful people (those who often look like they never met), and some kind of exclusivity (ridiculously long waits, unpublished phone numbers, impossible-to-come-by reservations, or no reservations at all). That being said, the ultimate in cool dining is, of course, **Rao's (Map 20)**—or so we hear. But unless you're the Mayor, the Governor, or Woody Allen, you probably won't be getting a reservation anytime soon, so don't hold your breath. Special patrons of P.J. Clarke's upstairs dining room **Sidecar (Map 13)** can enter the restaurant using the exclusive "Sidecar card" (us common folk have to make a reservation and ring the doorbell). Judging from the many stoops stacked with bleary-eyed, wait-listed people who will do practically anything for a lobster roll, **Pearl Oyster Bar (Map 5)** and **Mary's Fish Camp (Map 5)** definitely fit the "hip dining" bill. **Employees Only (Map 5)** easily makes the cut because drinking and dining to the tunes of the Clash and Lou Reed (while garter-clad waitresses wearing vintage headwear sexily saunter around) is very cool. Speaking of "Employees Only," that's what the unassuming door leading to the "secret" subterranean restaurant says at **La Esquina (Map 6)**. While anyone can belly-up to the taco stand (or eat at the cantina around the corner), scoring a coveted underground reservation is a rarity. **Momofuku Noodle Bar (Map 7)**, a stool-lined, plywood-walled sliver of a space, has emerged as a wildly popular spot to buck the waning low-carb craze and dive head first into a steaming bowl of noodles. The decadent Judeo-Latino cuisine at **Mo Pitkin's House of Satisfaction (Map 7)** probably has a few cardiologists on alert, but you gotta try the deep-fried macaroni and cheese, a Mo Burger (a beef burger smeared with chopped chicken liver topped with a fried egg and onions), and a gin-spiked Orange Julius at least once. And when you factor in that Debbie Harry as well as *Saturday Night Live's* Rachel Dratch and Amy Poehler are among those who've performed in the space upstairs—it's quite the hip spot.

Eating Late

Kang Suh's (Map 9) Korean barbeque runs all night, as well as **Bereket** (Map 7), **Odessa** (Map 7), **Florent** (Map 5) (weekends only), **7A** (Map 7), **Yaffa Café** (Map 7), and a host of generic diners. For the suburban-style, late-night dining experience you can always go to the IHOP (Map 19) in Harlem. **Employees Only** (Map 5) serves a special "$11 Staff Meal" only available after midnight and served until 4 am. Likewise, **La Esquina** (Map 6) turns out tacos until the wee small hours of the morning. And, of course, **Blue Ribbon** (Map 6) is still one of the best places to eat after midnight.

Eating Pizza

We New Yorkers are very opinionated about our pizza—that's why it deserves its very own category. Most New Yorkers consider the coal oven joints the best: **Grimaldi's** (Map 30), **Lombardi's** (Map 6), and the original **Patsy's** (Map 20) in East Harlem. What makes having a coal oven extra special is that they are no longer permitted except for the few (at the above mentioned places) that were already in operation when the law was passed. The brick oven places, such as **John's Pizzeria (Map 5, Map 15)**, **Nick's** (Map 17), **Franny's** (Map 33), **Slice of Harlem** (Map 19) and **Totonno's Pizzeria Napolitano** (Map 10, **Map 15)**, certainly have no shortage of fans either. For a classic Village scene, check out **Arturo's** (Map 6) on Houston St. And there is always, of course, the ordinary, greasy, saucy, cheesy, mouth-watering by-the-slice pies that cause New Yorkers to miss home anytime they go away, like the slices at **Mimi's (Map 15)**, **DeMarco's (Map 6)**, **Joe's (Map 5)**, **Ben's (Map 6)** and **Lil' Frankie's (Map 7)**.

Eating Ethnic

New York has not only an example of every type of cuisine on the planet, but also a *good* version of every type of cuisine on the planet. To wit: **Sammy's Roumanian (Map 6)**, **Katz's Delicatessen (Map 7)**, and **Carnegie Deli (Map 12)** (Jewish); **Shun Lee (Map 13)**, **Grand Sichuan International (Map 6, Map 8, Map 11)**, and **Chef Ho's Peking Duck Grill (Map 17)** (Chinese); **Banjara (Map 7)**, **Tabla (Map 9)**, and **Indian Tandoor Oven (Map 15)** (Indian); **Alma (Map 32)**, **Maya (Map 15)**, and **Rosa Mexicano (Map 13, Map 14)** (Mexican); **Kang Suh (Map 9)** and **Dok Suni's (Map 7)** (Korean); **Holy Basil (Map 6)** (Thai); **Nobu (Map 2)**, **Blue Ribbon Sushi (Map 6)**, and about 40 others (Japanese); **Il Giglio (Map 2)**, **Il Palazzo (Map 2)**, **Babbo (Map 6)**, **John's of 12th Street (Map 6)**, **Il Bagatto (Map 7)**, **Il Mulino (Map 6)**, **Carino (Map 17)**, and about 20 others (Italian); **Ghenet (Map 6)** and **The Ethiopian Restaurant (Map 15)** (Ethiopian); **Eight Mile Creek (Map 6)** (Australian); **Balthazar (Map 6)**, **Chanterelle (Map 2)**, **La Luncheonette (Map 8)**, **Le Gamin (Map 5, Map 7, Map 8)**, **Jules (Map 6)**, **French Roast (Map 5, Map 14)**, and 50 others (French); **Good World (Map 4)** and **Aquavit (Map 12)** (Scandinavian); **Heidelberg (Map 15)** and **Hallo Berlin (Map 11)** (German); **Charles' Southern Style (Map 22)**, **Sylvia's (Map 19)**, and **Old Devil Moon (Map 7)** (Southern); **Stamatis (Map 26)** (Greek); **Mingala Burmese (Map 6)** (Burmese); etc. etc. etc.

Eating Meat

New York is, of course, home to perhaps the world's best steakhouse, **Peter Luger's** (Map 29). But getting closer to that quality every day is the new **Mark Joseph Steakhouse** (Map 3), as well as favorites like **Frank's Restaurant** (Map 8), **Sparks** (Map 13), **Palm** (Map 13), **Smith & Wollensky** (Map 13), **Angelo & Maxie's** (Map 10), and, a top NFT pick, the **Strip House** (Map 6). For the Brazilian-style "all you can eat meatfest," **Churrascaria Plataforma** (Map 11) is the place. For poor man's steak (read: hamburger), nothing really comes close to **Corner Bistro** (Map 5), although **Burger Joint at Le Parker Meridien** (Map 12), **J.G. Melon** (Map 15), **Island Burgers 'N Shakes** (Map 11), **7A** (Map 7), **Cozy Soup & Burger** (Map 6), **Big Nick's** (Map 14), and even **Jackson Hole** (Map 10, Map 14, Map 15, Map 17) have many admirers. And for those who like their meats smoky and sopping with sauce, several barbecue joints have popped up on the culinary landscape fairly recently including **Blue Smoke** (Map 10), **Dinosaur Bar-B-Que** (Map 18), and **RUB BBQ** (Map 9).

Eating Meatless

We're not sure, but we think the first McDonald's "veggie burger" ever sold was in the one on St. Mark's Place and Third Avenue. However, for less disgusting fare, try the veggie burgers at **Dojo East** (Map 6) and **West** (Map 6), the great faux-sausages at **Kate's Joint** (Map 7), a whole range of vegan/macrobiotic at **Angelica Kitchen** (Map 6), the quality Indian fare at **Pongal** (Map 10), and, for high-end eats, **Candle 79** (Map 15) and **Hangawi** (Map 9). A fun alternative to the usual vegetarian fare is **Peanut Butter & Co.** (Map 6), where they have every kind of peanut butter sandwich imaginable. While some do include meat, most don't—and peanut butter is a great source of protein.

Eating Your Wallet

Here's the rant: You can easily spend over $100 (per person) at any one of these places without even blinking an eye. Is it worth it? Sometimes, little grasshopper, sometimes. But it's almost always at least close at: **Craft** (Map 9), **Gotham** (Map 6), **Per Se** (Map 12), **Gramercy Tavern** (Map 9), **Chanterelle** (Map 2), **Le Bernardin** (Map 12), **Bouley** (Map 2), **Oceana** (Map 13), **Union Square Café** (Map 9), **March** (Map 13), **Jean-Georges** (Map 14), **Babbo** (Map 6), **Danube** (Map 2), and a handful of other places. But you can eat at Joe's Shanghai for a full week for the same amount of money. So here we say: Choose wisely.

Our Favorite Restaurant

It's **Blue Ribbon (Map 6)** on Sullivan Street. Why? A million reasons: It's open 'till 4 am, it's where the chefs of other restaurants go, it's got fondue, it's got beef marrow, it's got fried chicken, it's got pigeon, it's got a great vibe, great liquor, great service, and not-so-hellish prices. It's everything that's good, and it's why we're in New York. Period.

Key: $: Under $10 / $$: $10–$20 / $$$: $20–$30 / $$$$: $30–$40 / $$$$$: $40+; *: Cash only / †: Accepts only American Express. / †† Accepts only Visa/Mastercard. Time refers to hour kitchen closes on weekends.

Map 1 • Financial District

The 14 Wall St Restaurant	14 Wall St	212-233-2780	$$$$$	8 pm	Top-end French from high-up.
Battery Gardens	Battery Park, across from 17 State St	212-809-5508	$$$$$	10 pm	Panoramic views of NY harbor with a wood-burning fireplace.
Bayards	1 Hanover Sq	212-514-9454	$$$	10 pm	Elegant Continental cuisine in the historic India House
Burritoville	36 Water St	212-747-1100	$	10 pm	Takeout Mexican.
Carmela's	30 Water St	212-809-0999	$	8 pm	Superior quick slices.
Cassis on Stone	52 Stone St	212-425-3663	$$	11 pm	A mini European vacation.
Cosi Sandwich Bar	54 Pine St	212-809-2674	$	4:30 pm	Sandwiches for the masses.
Cosi Sandwich Bar	55 Broad St	212-344-5000	$	5 pm	Sandwiches for the masses.
Daily Soup	41 John St	212-791-7687	$	3 pm	Soup!
Financier Patisserie	62 Stone St	212-344-5600	$$	8 pm	Have your cake and a light meal too.
Giovanni's Atrium	100 Washington St	212-513-4133	$$$$$	11 pm	Owner grows fresh herbs for meals!
The Grotto	69 New St	212-809-6990	$$	7:30 pm	More quick, tasty Italian. Less nudity than that other grotto.
Heartland Brewery	93 South St	646-572-2337	$$	10 pm	Decent pub grub.
Lemongrass Grill	84 William St	212-809-8038	$$	10:15 pm	Serviceable Thai.
Les Halles	15 John St	212-285-8585	$$$	12 am	Excellent French steakhouse.
MJ Grill	110 John St	212-346-9848	$$$	11 pm	Steaks, burgers, loud.
Papoos	55 Broadway	212-809-3150	$$$$	9 pm	Good, if pricey, Italian cuisine.
Red	19 Fulton St	212-571-5900	$$	10 pm	Acceptable Mexican.
Romi	19 Rector St	212-809-1500	$$	3 am	Tapas and sandwiches.
Rosario's	38 Pearl St	212-514-5763	$$	3 pm	Italian. Go for the small portions.
Roy's New York	130 Washington St	212-266-6262	$$$	10 pm	Hawaiian fusion seafood.
Sam's Falafel (street cart)	Liberty Plz	NA	$*		Super cheap (and good) falafel.
Sophie's	73 New St	212-809-7755	$*	4 pm	Great cheap Cuban/Carribean.
St Maggie's Café	120 Wall St	212-943-9050	$$$	9 pm	Downtown lunch option.
Zaitzeff	72 Nassau St	212-571-7272	$$	10 pm	Quick and organic lunch.
Zeytuna	59 Maiden Ln	212-742-2436	$$	10 pm	Gourmet take-out. NFT fave.

Map 2 • TriBeCa

66	241 Church St	212-925-0202	$$$$$		Trendy Asian fusion: beware the scene.
A&M Roadhouse	57 Murray St	212-385-9005	$$$	2 am	Down-south barbecue ribs meet Maine lobsters.
Azafran	77 Warren St	212-284-0578	$$$$	11:30 pm	Upscale tapas and Spanish dishes.
Bouley	120 W Broadway	212-964-2525	$$$$$	11:30 pm	Absolute top NYC dining. Love the apples in the foyer.
Bread Tribeca	301 Church St	212-334-8282	$$	12 am	Country-style Italian.
Bubby's	120 Hudson St	212-219-0666	$$	11 pm	Great atmosphere—good home-style eats and homemade pies.
Café Noir	32 Grand St	212-431-7910	$$	4 am	Tapas. Open 'til 4am.
Capsouto Frères	451 Washington St	212-966-4900	$$$		Excellent brunch, great space, oldish (in a good way) vibe.
Centrico	211 West Broadway	212-431-0700	$$$	11 pm	Cha cha upscale Mexican makes you forget the ka-ching.
Chanterelle	2 Harrison St	212-966-6960	$$$$$	11 pm	Sublime French with prices to match.
Church Lounge, Tribeca Grand Hotel	2 Ave of the Americas	212-519-6600	$$$	4 am	Sunday buffet brunch is great.
City Hall	131 Duane St	212-227-7777	$$$$	12 am	Bright, expensive, lots of suits, but still cool.
Columbine	229 West Broadway	212-965-0909	$	6 pm	Sandwiches made fresh to order; worth the wait.
Cupping Room Café	359 West Broadway	212-925-2898	$$$	1 am	Keeps the mimosas flowing at brunch.
Danube	30 Hudson St	212-791-3771	$$$$$	11:30 pm	Excellent food with an Austrian twist. Go for the tasting menu.
Dekk	134 Reade St	212-941-9401	$$$	12 am	New American/Italian. This close to having potential.
Della Rovere	250 West Broadway	212-334-3470	$$$$$	1 am	Booked until hell freezes over, apparently.
Duane Park Café	157 Duane St	212-732-5555	$$$$	10:30 pm	Underrated New American.
Dylan Prime	62 Laight St	212-334-4783	$$$$$	12 am	Excellent steakhouse, great location, TriBeCa prices.
Edward's	136 West Broadway	212-233-6436	$$		Middle-of-the-road, kid's menu, mostly locals, sometimes great.
Elixir Juice Bar	95 West Broadway	212-233-6171	$	7 pm	Fresh squeezed juices!
Félix	340 West Broadway	212-431-0021	$$$†		Buzzing Brazilian with French overtones, see and be seen.
Flor de Sol	361 Greenwich St	212-366-1640	$$$$	1 am	Tapas with—of course—a scene.
fresh	105 Reade St	212-406-1900	$$$$$	11:30 pm	Excellent seafood.
The Harrison	355 Greenwich St	212-274-9310	$$$$$	11:30 pm	Great New American—understandably popular.

Il Giglio	81 Warren St	212-571-5555	$$$$$	10:30 pm	Stellar Italian. Trust us.
Ivy's Bistro	385 Greenwich St	212-343-1139	$$	11 pm	Down-to-earth neighborhood Italian.
Karahi	508 Broome St	212-965-1515	$$	10 pm	Authentic, delicious Indian.
Kitchenette	80 West Broadway	212-267-6740	$$	10 pm	Great breakfast. Try the bacon.
Kori	253 Church St	212-334-4598	$$$	10:30 pm	Korean.
Landmarc	179 West Broadway	212-343-3883	$$$	2 am	Modern American with extensive wine list.
Lucky Strike	59 Grand St	212-941-0772	$$	2:30 am	Good bar in front, reliable food in back.
Lupe's East LA Kitchen	110 Sixth Ave	212-966-1326	$*	12 am	Tex-Mex. Quaint.
Montrachet	239 West Broadway	212-219-2777	$$$$$	11 pm	Wonderful French.
Nobu	105 Hudson St	212-219-0500	$$$$$	10:15 pm	Designer Japanese. When we have 100 titles, we'll go there.
Nobu, Next Door	105 Hudson St	212-334-4445	$$$$$	1 am	Nobu's cheaper neighbor.
Odeon	145 West Broadway	212-233-0507	$$$	2 am	We can't agree about this one, so go and make your own decision.
Pakistan Tea House	176 Church St	212-240-9800	$	4 am	The real deal. Where cabbies eat.
Palacinka	28 Grand St	212-625-0362	$$*	12 am	A tasty load of crepe. NFT face.
Petite Abeille	134 West Broadway	212-791-1360	$	11 pm	Belgian waffle chain, great beer selection. Try the stoemp.
Roc	190 Duane St	212-625-3333	$$$	1 am	Lovely Italian, good for weekend brunch.
Salaam Bombay	317 Greenwich St	212-226-9400	$$	11 pm	Indian; excellent lunch buffet.
Sosa Borella	460 Greenwich St	212-431-5093	$$	11 pm	Louche Argentines and brilliant french toast.
Spaghetti Western	59 Reade St	212-513-1333	$$		Cheap Italian food and bar.
Square Diner	33 Leonard St	212-925-7188	$*	9 pm	Classic neighborhood diner.
Thalassa	179 Franklin St	212-941-7661	$$$	12 am	Greek. Beautiful and better in Astoria.
Tribeca Grill	375 Greenwich St	212-941-3900	$$$$$	11 pm	Are you looking at me?
Viet Café	345 Greenwich St	212-431-5888	$$$	11 pm	Glossy out of a magazine.
Walker's	16 N Moore St	212-941-0142	$$	1 am	Surprisingly good food for a pub!
wichcraft	397 Greenwich St	212-780-0577	$*	6 pm	Sandwiches, soups, and sweets from Tom Colicchio of Craft.
Yaffa's	353 Greenwich St	212-274-9403	$$	1 am	Cooly eclectic. Food 'til 1am.
Zutto	77 Hudson St	212-233-3287	$$	10:30 pm	Neighborhood Japanese.

Map 3 • City Hall / Chinatown

Bridge Café	279 Water St	212-227-3344	$$$$$	12 am	Now extremely expensive.
Canton	45 Division St	212-226-4441	$$$$*	10 pm	Top-shelf Chinese.
Cendrillon	45 Mercer St	212-343-9012	$$$	11 pm	Flippin' Filipino. Try the young coconut pie.
Cup & Saucer	89 Canal St	212-925-3298	$*	5 pm	Good greasy countertop burgers.
Dim Sum Go Go	5 East Broadway	212-732-0797	$$	10:45 pm	New, hip, inventive dim sum; essentially, post-modern Chinese.
Excellent Dumpling House	111 Lafayette St	212-219-0212	$*	9 pm	Excellent dumplings, really.
Ferrara	195 Grand St	212-226-6150	$	1 am	Classic Little Italy patisserie.
Fuleen Seafood	11 Division St	212-941-6888	$$	4 am	Chinese seafood shack.
Golden Unicorn	18 E Broadway	212-941-0911	$$	11 pm	Dim sum—great for medium-sized groups.
Goodies	1 East Broadway	212-577-2922	$$	11 pm	Almost as good as Joe's and one-eighth as crowded. 18 different soup varieties.
Il Palazzo	151 Mulberry St	212-343-7000	$$$	12 am	Excellent mid-range Italian.
Joe's Shanghai	9 Pell St	212-233-8888	$$*	11:15 pm	Great crab soup dumplings, crowded.
L'Ecole	462 Broadway	212-219-3300	$$$$	9:30 pm	The restaurant of the French Culinary Institute; new student menu every 6 weeks.
L'Orange Bleue	430 Broome St	212-226-4999	$$$†	12 am	Belly dancing with a side of frites.
Le Pain Quotidien	100 Grand St	212-625-9009	$$	7 pm	Excellent breads.
Lily's	31 Oliver St	212-766-3336	$$	10:30 pm	Official Japanese/Chinese takeout of NFT management.
Mandarin Court	61 Mott St	212-608-3838	$$	11 pm	Consistently good dim sum.
Mark Joseph Steakhouse	261 Water St	212-277-0020	$$$$		Luger's wannabe: damn close, actually, and they take plastic.
New York Noodle Town	28 Bowery	212-349-0923	$*	5 am	Cheap Chinese.
Nha Trang	148 Center St	212-914-9292	$	10 pm	Ever wonder where district attorneys go for cheap, tasty Vietnamese?
Nha Trang	87 Baxter St	212-233-5948	$$	9:30 pm	The best cheap Vietnamese.
Pho Viet Huong	73 Mulberry St	212-233-8988	$$	10:30 pm	Very good Vietnamese—get the salt & pepper squid.
Ping's	22 Mott St	212-602-9988	$$	12 am	Eclectic Asian seafood.
Pongsri Thai	106 Bayard St	212-349-3132	$$	11 pm	Great, spicy Thai. Go for the jungle curry.
Positano	122 Mulberry St	212-334-9808	$$	12 am	Good northern Italian fare.
Quartino	21 Peck Slip	212-349-4433	$$	11:30 pm	Good, clean pizza and pasta.
The Paris Café	119 South St	212-240-9797	$$$	12 am	Good burgers and seafood, a bit pricey though.
Triple Eight Palace	88 East Broadway	212-941-8886	$$	10 pm	Dim sum madness under the Manhattan Bridge.
Umberto's Clam House	178 Mulberry St	212-343-2053	$$	4 am	Spicy red sauce joint. Standout calamari.
Wo Hop	17 Mott St	212-267-2536	$*	24 Hrs	Chinatown mainstay.

Arts & Entertainment • **Restaurants**

Key: $: Under $10 / $$: $10–$20 / $$$: $20–$30 / $$$$: $30–$40 / $$$$$: $40+; *: Cash only / † : Accepts only American Express. / † † Accepts only Visa/Mastercard. Time refers to hour kitchen closes on weekends.

Map 4 • Lower East Side

88 Orchard	88 Orchard St	212-228-8880	$$	8 pm	Bridges the gap so you don't have to walk to the East Village.
Barrio Chino	253 Broome St	212-228-6710	$$†	1 am	Started life as a tequila bar, but now more of a restaurant.
Broomedoggs	250 Broome St	917-453-6013	$*	4 am	Hot dogs of all breeds—turkey, tofu, Black
Congee Village	100 Allen St	212-941-1818	$$	12 am	Good neighborhood Asian.
El Bocadito	79 Orchard St	212-343-3331	$$	10:30 pm	Hip, new LES joint for guac, taquitos, and cactus salad.
El Castillo de Jagua 2	521 Grand St	212-254-6150	$*	11:30 pm	Dirt cheap, tasty, Dominican food.
Good World Bar & Grill	3 Orchard St	212-925-9975	$$	12 am	Excellent Scandinavian finger food.
Il Laboratorio del Gelato	95 Orchard St	212-343-9922	$*	6 pm	Mind-bogglingly incredible artisanal gelato.
Kossar's Bagels and Bialys	367 Grand St	212-473-4810	$*	9 pm	Where the NFT office gets their morning bialys & bagels.
Les Enfants Terribles	37 Canal St	212-777-7518	$$$	12 am	Cozy French-African. Recommended.
Little Giant	85 Orchard St	212-226-5047	$$$$$	12 am	Quirky expensive LES newcomer.
Noah's Arc	399 Grand St	212-674-2200	$$	4 pm	Great Jewish deli.
Pho Bang	3 Pike St	212-233-3947	$	9 pm	Vietnamese.

Map 5 • West Village

A Salt & Battery	112 Greenwich Ave	212-691-2713	$	10:30 pm	Great take-out fish 'n chips.
Agave	140 Seventh Ave S	212-989-2100	$$$	1 am	Surprisingly good Southwest-Mex.
AOC	314 Bleecker St	212-675-9463	$$$	1:30 am	A fine French replacement for Grove.
Aquagrill	210 Spring St	212-274-0505	$$$$$	12 am	Excellent seafood.
August	359 Bleecker St	212-929-4774	$$$$	1 am	Bistro more like October. Crisp and rustic.
Benny's Burritos	113 Greenwich Ave	212-727-3560	$$	12 am	A NYC Mexican institution.
Blue Ribbon Bakery	33 Downing St	212-337-0404	$$$	2 am	Another Blue Ribbon success.
Bonsignour	35 Jane St	212-229-9700	$$	10 pm	Over-priced but tasty café, celeb-sighting likely.
Café Asean	117 W 10th St	212-633-0348	$$*	11 pm	Pan-Asian, via Mr. Wong.
Caffe Torino	139 W 10th St	212-675-5554	$$	12 am	Comfy, relaxed Italian.
Chez Brigitte	77 Greenwich Ave	212-929-6736	$*	10:30 pm	You never thought a chicken sandwich could be this good.
Chumley's	86 Bedford St	212-675-4449	$$	3 am	Former speakeasy, great atmosphere and food.
Corner Bistro	331 W 4th St	212-242-9502	$*	3:30 am	Top NYC burgers. Open 'til 4am.
Cowgirl	519 Hudson St	212-633-1133	$$	12 am	Good chicken fried steak.
Day-O	103 Greenwich Ave	212-924-3160	$$	12:30 am	Island fave, great cocktails.
Diablo Royale	189 W 10th St	212-620-0223	$$$*	2 am	West Village taqueria and cantina—interesting crema salsas to choose from.
Do Hwa	55 Carmine St	212-414-1224	$$$$	11:30 pm	Hot-off-the-barbie Korean with friends.
Dragonfly	47 Seventh Ave	212-255-2848	$$	2 am	Try the Filipino specialties.
Employees Only	510 Hudson St	212-242-3021	$$$$	3:30 am	Deco-decorated eatery with a damn good bar.
Fatty Crab	643 Hudson St	212-352-3590	$$$	12 am	A new West Village favorite for Malaysian street food.
Florent	69 Gansevoort St	212-989-5779	$$$$*	24 hrs	One of the best places on the planet.
French Roast	78 W 11th St	212-533-2233	$$	24 hrs	Open 24 hours. French comfort food.
Gonzo Restaurant	140 W 13th St	212-645-4606	$$$	12 am	Cool Italian bistro with hearty food.
Gradisca	126 W 13th St	212-691-4886	$$$	12 am	Romantic Italian.
Grey Dog's Coffee	33 Carmine St	212-462-0041	$$	11:30 pm	Happy coffee, huge sandwiches.
Gusto	60 Greenwich Ave	212-924-8000	$$$$	11 pm	Great Italian.
Havana Alma de Cuba	94 Christopher St	212-242-3800	$$$	1 am	Cheap, authentic Cuban fare, with live entertainment and sweet sweet mojitos to boot.
Home	20 Cornelia St	212-243-9579	$$$	11 pm	There's no place like it.
Hong Kong Noodle Bar	26 Carmine St	212-524-6800	$$$*	11 pm	Yumcha closed, but the owners opened this place around the corner.
Ivo & Lulu	558 Broome St	212-226-4399	$$	12 am	Tiny inventive French-Caribbean (BYOB).
Jefferson Grill	121 W 10th St	212-255-3333	$$$$	11:30 pm	Wong's American take.
Joe's Pizza	233 Bleecker St	212-366-1182	$*	5 am	Excellent slices.
John's Pizzeria	278 Bleecker St	212-243-1680	$$*	12:30 am	Quintessential NY pizza.
Jonez	41 Greenwich Ave	212-255-3606	$$$$	12 am	Unbelievably delicious mac 'n cheese.
La Palapa Rockola	359 Sixth Ave	212-243-6870	$$	11 pm	Former Dorothy Parker hangout with strong margaritas.
Le Gamin	27 Bedford St	212-243-2846	$$	11 pm	New digs, same great food.
MaMa Buddha	578 Hudson St	212-924-2762	$$	11 pm	Magically greaseless Chinese food.
Mary's Fish Camp	64 Charles St	646-486-2185	$$$	11 pm	At least as good as Pearl Oyster Bar.

Mercadito	100 Seventh Ave S	212-647-0410	$$$$	3 am	Inventive Mexican with great fish taco choices.
Mirchi	29 Seventh Ave S	212-414-0931	$$	12 am	Spicy Indian.
Moustache	90 Bedford St	212-229-2220	$$*	12 am	Excellent sit-down falafel.
Old Homestead	56 Ninth Ave	212-242-9040	$$$$$	12:45 am	Said to be NY's oldest steakhouse, circa 1868.
One If By Land, TIBS	17 Barrow St	212-228-0822	$$$$$	11:15 pm	Exudes romance.
Ony	357 Sixth Ave	212-414-9885	$$	12:30 am	Noodles, sushi, NYU hangout.
Pastis	9 Ninth Ave	212-929-4844	$$$$	3 am	Great French vibe; LOUD.
Pearl Oyster Bar	18 Cornelia St	212-691-8211	$$$	11 pm	For all your lobster roll cravings. NFT fave.
Perry Street	176 Perry St	212-352-1900	$$$$$	11 pm	Satisfyingly simplified New French from Jean-Georges Vongerichten.
Petite Abeille	466 Hudson St	212-741-6479	$$	11 pm	Tintin-infused waffle chain. Try the stoemp.
Philip Marie	569 Hudson St	212-242-6200	$$$	1 am	Romantic—and with great steak!
Pink Teacup	42 Grove St	212-807-6755	$$*	12:45 am	Authentic Southern cuisine.
Po	31 Cornelia St	212-645-2189	$$$	11 pm	Creative Italian.
Risottoria	270 Bleecker St	212-924-6664			Delicious risotto and other gluten-free goodies.
Sapore	55 Greenwich Ave	212-229-0551	$$*	11 pm	Decent Italian, good lunch deal.
Shopsin's	54 Carmine St	212-924-5160	$$*		Huge menu, delicious food, no cell phones allowed.
Snack Taverna	63 Bedford St	212-929-3499	$$$	11 pm	Greek for hipsters. More upscale than its sister restaurant on Thompson.
sNice	45 Eighth Ave	212-645-0310	$*	10 pm	Coffee, wraps, and such.
Souen	210 Sixth Ave	212-807-7421	$$$	10:30 pm	High-end vegetarian.
Spice Market	403 W 13th St	212-675-2322	$$$$$	12 am	Another Jean-George joint. Thai-Malaysian street food and beautiful people.
Spotted Pig	314 W 11th St	212-620-0393	$$$	2 am	We're still waiting on line.
Tea & Sympathy	108 Greenwich Ave	212-989-9735	$$$	10:30 pm	Eccentric English. Cult favorite.
Tortilla Flats	767 Washington St	212-243-1053	$$	1 am	Fun Mexican place. Free shot of tequila on your birthday!
Two Boots	201 W 11th St	212-633-9096	$	1 am	Cajun pizza.
Voyage Restaurant	117 Perry St	212-255-9191	$$	12 am	Low key and intimate, just like the West Village.
Yama	38 Carmine St	212-989-9330	$$$	11:30 pm	Sushi deluxe.

Map 6 • Washington Square / NYU / NoHo / SoHo

12 Chairs	56 MacDougal St	212-254-8640	$$	11 pm	Rough around the edges. Fantabulous blintzes and pirogis.
A Salt & Battery	80 Second Ave	212-254-6610	$	11 pm	Fish. Chips. More chips.
Acme Bar & Grill	9 Great Jones St	212-420-1934	$$	11 pm	Workmanlike Southern.
Angelica Kitchen	300 E 12th St	212-228-2909	$$$*	10:30 pm	Vegan/macrobiotic heaven.
Aroma	36 E 4th St	212-375-0100	$$$$	1 am	Quaint, lovely Italian place with excellent service.
Around the Clock	8 Stuyvesant St	212-598-0402	$$	24 Hrs	NYU hangout.
Arturo's Pizzeria	106 W Houston St	212-677-3820	$$	1 am	Classic NYC pizza joint.
Babbo	110 Waverly Pl	212-777-0303	$$$$	11:30 pm	Super Mario—eclectic Italian, fabulous wine list.
Balthazar	80 Spring St	212-965-1414	$$$$$	2 am	Simultaneously pretentious and amazing.
Bellavitae	21 Minetta Ln	212-473-5121	$$$	12 am	Food is delicious and the wine list is even better.
Ben's Pizza	177 Spring St	212-966-4494	$*	12 am	Decent pizza.
Blue 9 Burger	92 Third Ave	212-979-0053	$*	4 am	Fresh burgers and shakes made from actual milk.
Blue Green Organic Juice Café	248 Mott St	212-334-0805	$$	11 pm	Super healthy juices and mostly raw eats in hip surroundings.
Blue Hill	75 Washington Pl	212-539-1776	$$$$$	11 pm	Wonderful food in an unexpected location.
Blue Ribbon	97 Sullivan St	212-274-0404	$$$$	4 am	Open 'til 4am. Everything's great.
Blue Ribbon Sushi	119 Sullivan St	212-343-0404	$$$$$	2 am	Great sushi.
Café Colonial	73 E Houston St	212-274-0044	$$	11 pm	Excellent American/Brazilian.
Café Gitane	242 Mott St	212-334-9552	$$*	12 am	Brunch with beautiful people.
Café Habana	17 Prince St	212-625-2001	$$$	12 am	Excellent Cuban takeout joint.
Café Spice	72 University Pl	212-253-6999	$$$	11:30 pm	Designer Indian.
Cha An Tea House	230 E 9th St	212-228-8030	$$*	12 am	Japanese tea ceremonies Fridays and Sundays. Must reserve.
Chick-fil-A Express	Weinstein Hall, 5 University Pl		$*		Boneless chicken delights tucked away in NYU's Weinstein Hall.
ChikaLicious	203 E 10th St	212-995-9511	$$	11:30 pm	Dessert bar.
Colors	417 Lafayette St	212-777-8443	$$$$$	10:30 pm	Owned by former staff of Windows on the World (WTC).
Cozy Soup & Burger	739 Broadway	212-477-5566	$	24 Hrs	Great burgers!
Cubana Café	110 Thompson St	212-966-5366	$$*	11:30 pm	Café Habana on Prince full? Plan B.

Key: $: Under $10 / $$: $10–$20 / $$$: $20–$30 / $$$$: $30–$40 / $$$$$: $40+; *: Cash only / † : Accepts only American Express. / †† Accepts only Visa/Mastercard. Time refers to hour kitchen closes on weekends.

Map 6 · Washington Square / NYU / NoHo / SoHo–*continued*

DeMarco's	146 West Houston St	212-253-2290	$	12 am	Top Brooklyn pizza comes to Houston. NFT Pick.
Dojo East	24 St Marks Pl	212-674-9821	$*	1 am	Cheap and cheerful in Studentville.
Dojo West	14 W 4th St	212-505-8934	$*	12:30 am	Cheap and cheerful in Studentville.
Eight Mile Creek	240 Mulberry St	212-431-4635	$$$$	1 am	Awesome Australian.
Five Points	31 Great Jones St	212-253-5700	$$$$	12 am	Excellent NoHo destination.
Frank	88 Second Ave	212-420-0202	$$*	2 am	Good food, great breakfast.
Ghenet	284 Mulberry St	212-343-1888	$$	11 pm	Excellent, unpretentious Ethiopian.
Gotham Bar & Grill	12 E 12th St	212-620-4020	$$$$$	11:30 pm	Excellent New American—one of the best.
Great Jones Café	54 Great Jones St	212-674-9304	$$	1 am	Classic soul food. Sort of.
Hampton Chutney Co	68 Prince St	212-226-9996	$	9 pm	Good take-out dosas.
Holy Basil	149 Second Ave	212-460-5557	$$$	12 am	Holy sh*t this is good Thai!
Hummus Place	99 MacDougal St	212-533-3089	$††	12 am	Authentic! Best hummus this side of Tel Aviv.
Il Buco	47 Bond St	212-533-1932	$$$$$	1 am	Lovely Italian food. Great wines by the glass.
Il Mulino	86 W 3rd St	212-673-3783	$$$$	11 pm	Fine Italian dining at fine Italian dining prices.
Indian Bread Co	194 Bleecker St	212-228-1909	$	1 am	Tandoori and curry-stuffed flatbreads on the cheap.
Jane	100 W Houston St	212-254-7000	$$$$	12 am	Good all-around!
Jean Claude	137 Sullivan St	212-475-9232	$$$*	11:30 pm	Mmmm mussels. Good date place.
Jeollado	116 E 4th St	212-260-7696	$$*	1 am	Cheap sushi with REAL crabmeat.
John's of 12th Street	302 E 12th St	212-475-9531	$$*	11:30 pm	Classic Italian. Get the rollatini.
Jules	65 St Marks Pl	212-477-5560	$$$	1 am	Small French bistro with live unimposing jazz.
Kelley & Ping	127 Greene St	212-228-1212	$$	11 pm	Noodles and killer tea selection.
Khyber Pass	34 St Marks Pl	212-473-0989	$$	11:30 pm	Good Afghani.
Kittichai	60 Thompson St	212-219-2000	$$$$	12 am	Thai me up, Thai me down at this hotel spot.
L'Ulivo Focaccaria	184 Spring St	212-343-1445	$$$	12 am	Good personal pizzas, quaint.
La Esquina	106 Kenmare St	646-613-7100		12 am	Taqueria trifecta: taco stand, corner cantina, and secret subterranean abode.
Lombardi's	32 Spring St	212-941-7994	$$$*	12 am	Said to be the first pizzeria in the U.S., circa 1905. Incredible!
Mamoun's Falafel	119 MacDougal St	212-674-8685	$*	5 pm	You've never been? You haven't lived. $2 falafel.
Mara's Homemade	342 E 6th St	212-598-1110	$$	12 am	Ragin' Cajun. Recommended.
Melampo Imported Foods	105 Sullivan St	212-334-5179	$*	6 pm	Excellent sandwiches.
Mercer Kitchen	99 Prince St	212-966-5454	$$$$	1 am	Psuedo-famous New American with a French accent.
Mingala Burmese	21 E 7th St	212-529-3656	$$	12 am	Burmese.
Olive's	120 Prince St	212-941-0111	$	7 pm	Killer soups/sandwiches. A must, great for take-out, too.
Otto	1 Fifth Ave	212-995-9559	$$$	11:30 pm	$45 pizza? Absolutely!
Paul's Palace	131 Second Ave	212-529-3097	$*	12 am	Burger heaven.
Peanut Butter & Co	240 Sullivan St	212-677-3995	$	10 pm	Peanut butter every way you can imagine (and beyond)!!
Peep	177 Prince St	212-254-7337	$$$	12 am	Stylin' Thai. See-through bathroom mirrors.
Penang	109 Spring St	212-274-8883	$$$	12 am	Snooty but good Malaysian.
Pepe Rosso	149 Sullivan St	212-677-4555	$	11 pm	Italy on a budget. Fast.
Pizza Box	176 Bleecker St	212-979-0823	$*	1 am	Plain old delicious pizza that doesn't involve anyone named Ray.
Pommes Frites	123 Second Ave	212-674-1234	$*	1 am	Fries—medium, large, or double—with tons of tasty sauces to choose from.
Room 4 Dessert	17 Cleveland Pl	212-941-5405	$$	12 am	Downtown dessert destination tasting delights by pastry chef Will Goldfarb.
Sala	344 Bowery	212-979-6606	$$		Wonderful décor, good tapas.
Sammy's Roumanian	157 Chrystie St	212-673-0330	$$$$	11 pm	An experience not to be missed.
Souen	28 E 13th St	212-627-7150	$$	11 pm	Macrobiotic and delicious.
Spice	60 University Ave	212-982-3758	$$	11:30 pm	Trendy Thai.
Strip House	13 E 12th St	212-328-0000	$$$$$	12 am	Super downtown steakhouse. NFT favorite.
Temple	81 St Marks Pl	212-979-9300	$$	1 am	Cheap Korean excellence, beware of crowds.
Tomoe Sushi	172 Thompson St	212-777-9346	$$$	11 pm	Good sushi, long line.
Vegetarian's Paradise 2	144 W 4th St	212-260-7130	$$	12 am	Tastes like chicken.
Veselka	144 Second Ave	212-228-9682	$	24 hrs	Pierogies absorb beer. At 4 am that's all you need to know.
Yakitori Taisho	5 St Mark's Pl	212-228-5086	$	5:30 am	Skewered chicken and pan-fried noodles washed down with Asahi.

Map 7 · East Village / Lower East Side

1492	60 Clinton St	646-654-1114	$$$	12:30 am	Tapas. It's cool.
7A	109 Ave A	212-673-6583	$$	24 hrs	Great burgers.
Azul Bistro	152 Stanton St	646-602-2004	$$	1 am	Argentinean fare.
B3	33 Ave B	212-614-9755	$$$	2 am	Great default date restaurant.
Banjara	97 First Ave	212-477-5956	$$$	12 am	Best Indian on 6th Street, hands-down.
Benny's Burritos	93 Ave A	212-254-2054	$	1 am	A NYC Mexican institution.
Bereket Turkish Kebab House	187 E Houston St	212-475-7700	$*	24 hrs	Middle Eastern delights. Open late.
Boca Chica	13 First Ave	212-473-0108	$$	12 am	Excellent, fun South American.
Café Mogador	101 St Marks Pl	212-677-2226	$$	1:30 am	Perfect place for hummus and a latte.
Caracas Arepa Bar	91 E 7th St	212-228-5062	$$	11 pm	Authentic Venezuelan.
Clinton St Baking Company	4 Clinton St	646-602-6263	$$	11 pm	Homemade buttermilk everything. LES laid back.
Dash Dogs	127 Rivington St	212-254-8885	$*	4 am	Cool spot for hot dogs.
David's Bagels	228 First Ave	212-533-8766	$*	8 pm	Bagels. Some say the best. Cheaper than H&H.
Dawgs on Park	178 E 7th St	212-598-0667	$*	10 pm	Just try asking for a tofu dog from a street vendor.
Dok Suni's	119 First Ave	212-477-9506	$$$*	12 am	Excellent Korean fusion.
El Castillo de Jaqua	113 Rivington St	212-982-6412	$*	1 am	Great cheap Dominican.
El Sombrero	108 Stanton St	212-254-4188	$$*	3 am	Cheap margaritas. Dates back to earlier days of the LES.
Esashi	32 Ave A	212-505-8726	$$	11:30 pm	Simple but always good neighborhood sushi.
Essex Restaurant	120 Essex St	212-533-9616	$$$	12 am	Great space, OK food.
Flea Market Café	131 Ave A	212-358-9282	$$	1 am	French, good brunch.
Flor's Kitchen	149 First Ave	212-387-8949	$$	11 pm	Authentic South American.
Hummus Place	109 St Marks Pl	212-529-9198	$$	12 am	Authentic! Best hummus this side of Tel Aviv.
Il Bagatto	192 E 2nd St	212-228-0977	$$$	12:45 am	Packed Italian.
Il Posto Accanto	190 E 2nd St	212-228-3562	$$$††	1 am	Tiny, rustic Italian enoteca.
inoteca	98 Rivington St	212-614-0473	$$	3 am	Late-night tapas mafia-style.
Kate's Joint	58 Ave B	212-777-7059	$$	1 am	Inventive vegetarian and vegan.
Katz's Delicatessen	205 E Houston St	212-254-2246	$$	3 am	Great corned beef, fries, and Dr. Brown's.
Kuma Inn	113 Ludlow St	212-353-8866	$$*	12 am	Spicy southeast Asian tapas.
Kura Sushi	67 First Ave	212-979-6646	$$	12:30 am	Good sushi, good atmosphere, good music.
La Caverna	122 Rivington St	212-475-2126	$$$††	12 am	It's got stalactites and stalagmites!
Lavagna	545 E 5th St	212-979-1005	$$$	12 am	We hear it's great!
Le Frenchy Diner	188 Orchard St	212-677-5200	$†	12 am	Cozy, inexpensive French brasserie where the owner serves your quiche.
Le Gamin	536 E 5th St	212-254-8409	$$	1 am	Great French Toast, overall brunch, etc.
Le Pere Pinard	175 Ludlow St	212-777-4917	$$$$	2 am	Cool, hip, swank French bistro with lovely back patio.
Lil' Frankie's Pizza	19 First Ave	212-420-4900	$$*	2 am	Cheap, good pizzas and Italian.
The Lite Touch Restaurant	151 Ave A	212-420-8574	$	4am	Authentic Moroccan and Middle Eastern.
Mama's Food Shop	200 E 3rd St	212-777-4425	$*	10 pm	Great home-cooking and take-out. NFT Pick.
Mo Pitkin's House of Satisfaction	34 Ave A	212-777-5660	$$	2 am	Quirky Judeo-Latino cantina and performance space.
Momofuku	163 First Ave	212-475-7899	$$$	12 am	Fresh noodles!
Moustache	265 E 10th St	212-228-2022	$*	12 am	Excellent Middle Eastern.
Nicky's Vietnamese Sandwiches	150 E 2nd St	212-388-1088	$*	9 pm	Dirt-cheap Vietnamese treats.
Odessa	119 Ave A	212-253-1470	$	24 hrs.	Diner. Awesome pirogies.
Old Devil Moon	511 E 12th St	212-475-4357	$$	12 am	Good southern food. Great biscuits.
Panna II Indian Restaurant	93 First Ave	212-598-4610	$	11:30 pm	Indian food so good they don't allow it on 6th.
Pylos	128 E 7th St	212-473-0220	$$	1 am	Delicious Greek, cool hanging-pot ceiling.
Raga	433 E 6th St	212-388-0957	$$$	11:30 pm	Good Indian fusion.
Sapporo East	245 E 10th St	212-260-1330	$$	12:45 am	Cheap and cheerful sushi.
Schiller's	131 Rivington St	212-260-4555	$$$	3 am	Loud, good, loud, good.
Share	406 E 9th St	212-777-2425	$$$$	10:30 pm	Seasonal American.
Sidewalk	94 Ave A	212-473-7373	$$	24 Hrs	When 7A's wait is too long...
St Dymphna's	118 St Marks Pl	212-254-6636	$$	4 am	A great Irish pub doesn't need shamrocks.
The Sunburnt Cow	137 Ave C	212-529-0005	$$	12 am	Aussie cooking featuring backyard garden.
Supper	156 E 2nd St	212-477-7600	$$$*	12 am	Spaghetti con limone is yummy. Great brunch. Otherworldly atmosphere.
Takahachi	85 Ave A	212-505-6524	$$$	12:30 am	Super-good Japanese and sushi.
Tasting Room	72 E 1st St	212-358-7831	$$$$$	11 pm	Relatively pretentious.
Teany	90 Rivington St	212-475-9190	$$	12 am	Tea room and Moby hang-out.
Thor	107 Rivington St	212-796-8040	$$$$$	11 pm	Kurt Gutenbrunner's sleek eatery inside The Hotel on Rivington.
Two Boots	37 Ave A	212-505-2276	$	1 am	Cajun Pizza.
Yaffa Café	97 St Marks St	212-674-9302	$$	24 Hrs	Eclectic food/decor. Open 24 hours.
Yonah Schimmel's Knishery	137 E Houston St	212-477-2858	$	9 pm	Dishing delish knish since 1910.
Yuca Bar	111 Ave A	212-982-9533	$$$	2 am	Amazing Latin-style brunch, less amazing Latin-style dinner.
Zum Schneider	107 Ave C	212-598-1098	$$*	11 pm	Finally some downtown wurst.

Key: $: Under $10 / $$: $10–$20 / $$$: $20–$30 / $$$$: $30-$40 / $$$$$: $40+; *: Cash only / †: Accepts only American Express. / †† Accepts only Visa/Mastercard. Time refers to hour kitchen closes on weekends.

Map 8 · Chelsea

202 Café	Chelsea Market, 75 Ninth Ave	646-638-1173	$$	10 pm	Simple European eats (and fancy dishware boutique).
Better Burger Chelsea	178 Eighth Ave	212-989-6688	$	1 am	Ostrich burger? Check. Soy burger? Check. Antibiotic meat? Check.
Blue Moon Mexican Café	150 Eighth Ave	212-463-0560	$$$	11:15 pm	Great Mexican.
Bottino	246 Tenth Ave	212-206-6766	$$$	11 pm	Good, clean Italian.
Bright Food Shop	216 Eighth Ave	212-243-4433	$$$	11 pm	Small, Asian-Mexican experience.
Buddakan	Chelsea Market, 75 Ninth Ave	212-989-6699	$$$$$		New NYC branch of Stephen Starr's insanely popular Philadelphia behemoth.
Burritoville	352 W 39th St	212-563-9088	$	10 pm	Takeout Mexican.
Chelsea Bistro & Bar	358 W 23rd St	212-727-2026	$$$$	11:30 pm	Charming French.
Cheyenne Diner	411 Ninth Ave	212-465-8750	$	24 Hrs	NYC diner. You know the score.
Cola's Italian	148 Eighth Ave	212-633-8020	$††	11:30 pm	Intimate and inexpensive.
Cookshop	156 Tenth Ave	212-924-4440		12 am	New, loft-like, local ingredient-focused eatery.
Cupcake Café	522 Ninth Ave	212-465-1530	$*	7:30 pm	Three words: sweet potato doughnuts.
El Cid	322 W 15th St	212-929-9332	$$$	11:30 pm	Spanish/tapas.
Empire Diner	210 Tenth Ave	212-243-2736	$$	24 Hrs	A Chelsea institution. 24 hours.
Frank's Restaurant	410 W 16th St	212-243-1349	$$$$	11 pm	Noisy beef-fest.
Grand Sichuan Int'l	229 Ninth Ave	212-620-5200	$$	11:30 pm	Some of the best Chinese in NYC. Recommended.
Havana Chelsea	190 Eighth Ave	212-243-9421	$$*	10:30 pm	Great Cuban sandwiches.
La Luncheonette	130 Tenth Ave	212-675-0342	$$$	11 pm	A truly great French restaurant. Recommended.
La Taza de Oro	96 Eighth Ave	212-243-9946	$$*	10:30 pm	Great local Puerto Rican.
Le Gamin	183 Ninth Ave	212-243-8864	$$	12 am	Great French toast.
Manganaro Foods	488 Ninth Ave	212-563-5331	$$	7 pm	Locals-only Italian sandwich joint. Recommended.
Matsuri, Maritime Hotel	369 W 16th St	212-243-6400	$$$$$	1 am	Gigantic, luxurious Japanese restaurant tucked beneath The Maritime Hotel.
Moonstruck Diner	400 W 23rd St	212-924-3709	$$	24 Hrs	Not diner-cheap, but the portions are generous.
Morimoto	88 Tenth Ave	212-989-8883	$$$$$	12 am	Stephen Starr's couture Japanese temple. Iron Chef-prepared cuisine.
Pepe Giallo	253 Tenth Ave	212-242-6055	$$	11 pm	Takeout Italian.
The Red Cat	227 Tenth Ave	212-242-1122	$$$$	12 am	Hip and expensive.
Sandwich Planet	534 Ninth Ave	212-273-9768	$	8:30 pm	Unlimited sandwich selection.
Skylight Diner	402 W 34th St	212-244-0395	$	24 Hrs	24-hour diner.
Soul Fixin's	371 W 34th St	212-736-1345	$$	10 pm	It would be an injustice not to include this soul food eatery.
Spice	199 Eighth Ave	212-989-1116	$$	11:30 pm	Good, straightforward Thai.
Tick Tock Diner	481 Eighth Ave	212-268-8444	$	24 Hrs	24-hour diner.
Viceroy	160 Eighth Ave	212-633-8484	$$$		Stargazin' American.

Map 9 · Flatiron / Lower Midtown

Basta Pasta	37 W 17th St	212-366-0888	$$$$	11 pm	Pac-rim Italian.
Blaggard's Pub	8 W 38th St	212-382-0089	$	4 am	Smells like last night's vomit. Overpriced, awful service.
BLT Fish	21 W 17th St	212-691-8888	$$$$$	11:30 pm	Downstairs: New England clam shack fare. Upstairs: High-brow seafood.
Blue Water Grill	31 Union Sq W	212-675-9500	$$$$$	1 am	Seafood. Overrated.
Bolo	23 E 22nd St	212-228-2200	$$$$$	11 pm	Chef Bobby Flay's flavorful Flatiron Spanish.
Burritoville	264 W 23rd St	212-367-9844	$	1 am	Mexcellent and cheap.
Butterfield 8	5 E 38th St	212-679-0646	$$$	11 pm	Walnut-paneled Murray Hill American with cool, Hitchcockian cityscape mural.
Cafeteria	119 Seventh Ave	212-414-1717	$$$	24 Hrs	Comfort food, open all night.
Chat 'n Chew	10 E 16th St	212-243-1616	$$	12 am	Home cookin'.
City Bakery	3 W 18th St	212-366-1414	$$	7 pm	Stellar baked goods.
Coffee Shop	29 Union Sq W	212-243-7969	$$$	5:30 am	Diner.
Craft	43 E 19th St	212-780-0880	$$$$$	11 pm	Outstanding. A top-end place worth the $.
Eisenberg's Sandwich Shop	174 Fifth Ave	212-675-5096	$$	7 pm	Old-school corned beef and pastrami.
Eleven Madison Park	11 Madison Ave	212-889-0905	$$$$$	11 pm	Where the elite meet to greet.
Elmo	156 Seventh Ave	212-337-8000	$$	12 am	Good for cocktails and oysters, in whatever order.
Evergreen Shang HAI Restaurant	10 E 38th St	212-448-1199	$	10:30 pm	Their scallion pancakes are worth the wait, and they know it.
Francisco's Centro Vasco	159 W 23rd St	212-645-6224	$$$	12 am	Fun Spanish.
Giorgio's of Gramercy	27 E 21st St	212-477-0007	$$$	11:30 pm	Cozy Italian.
Gramercy Tavern	42 E 20th St	212-477-0777	$$$$$	11 pm	Expensive, but good, New American.
Hangawi	12 E 32nd St	212-213-0077	$$$$	10:30 pm	Serene Korean.
Kang Suh	1250 Broadway	212-564-6845	$$$	24 Hrs	Late-night Korean. Go for the private rooms.

Koryodang	31 W 32nd St	212-967-9661	$	2:00 am	Bakery with mocha-filled eclairs and green tea popsicles. Yum.
Kum Gang San	49 W 32nd St	212-967-0909	$$$	24 Hrs	Another late-night Korean paradise.
Kunjip	9 W 32nd St	212-216-9487	$$	24 Hrs	The best Korean food in Manhattan; try the Bo Bim.
La Fenice	120 W 23rd St	212-989-3071	$$$	9:30 pm	Good Italian.
Le Pain Quotidien	38 E 19th St	212-673-7900	$$	7 pm	Excellent breads and such.
Le Zie 2000	172 Seventh Ave	212-206-8686	$$$	11:30 pm	Venetian. That means it's Italian.
Luna Park	50 E 17th St	212-475-8464	$$$		Have meals May-October in Union Square Park.
Mayrose	920 Broadway	212-533-3663	$$	11 pm	Upscale diner.
Mesa Grill	102 Fifth Ave	212-807-7400	$$$$$	11 pm	Southwest heaven.
Minado	6 E 32nd St	212-725-1333	$$		All-you-can-eat sushi a la Las Vegas.
Periyali	35 W 20th St	212-463-7890	$$$$	11:30 pm	Upscale Greek.
Petite Abeille	107 W 18th St	212-604-9350	$$	6 pm	Tintin-infused waffle chain. Try the stoemp.
Republic	37 Union Sq W	212-627-7172	$$	11:30 pm	Noisy noodles.
RUB BBQ	208 W 23rd St	212-524-4300	$$$	11 pm	Smokin' 'cue from Kansas City pit master Paul Kirk.
Salute	270 Madison Ave	212-213-3440	$$	11 am	Generous portions of old-world Italian cuisine.
Shake Shack	Madison Sq Park	212-889-6600	$	4 pm	Shakes 'n burgers March-October (and, lately, through September).
Silver Swan	41 E 20th St	212-254-3611	$$$$	11 pm	Beer, brats, 'n schnitzel.
Tabla	11 Madison Ave	212-889-0667	$$$$$	10:30 pm	Inventive Indian-inspired American. Recommended.
Tamarind	41 E 22nd St	212-674-7400	$$$	12 am	Lovely, intimate upscale Indian.
Toledo	6 E 36th St	212-696-5036	$$$$	10:30 pm	Classy Spanish.
Tocqueville	1 E 15th St	212-647-1515	$$$$	10:30 pm	Lovely everything—and you can actually hear each other speak!
Uncle Moe's	14 W 19th St	212-727-9400	$	9 pm	Solid lunchtime burrito joint.
Union Square Café	21 E 16th St	212-243-4020	$$$$$	10:45 pm	Someday we'll get in and like it.
Waldy's Wood Fired Pizza	800 Sixth Ave	212-213-5042	$$	11 pm	Where former Beacon chef fires up gourmet penne and pie.
Woo Chon	8 W 36th St	212-695-0676	$$$	24 Hrs	All-night Korean.

Map 10 · Murray Hill / Gramercy

71 Irving	71 Irving Pl	212-995-5252	$	12 am	Good coffee, great treats, superior service.
Angelo & Maxie's	233 Park Ave S	212-220-9200	$$$	12 am	Excellent steaks, burgers, etc.
AQ Café	Scandinavia House, 58 Park Ave	212-847-9745	$	5 pm	Nordic museum café. Menu by Aquavit's Marcus Samuelsson—brilliant!
Artisanal	2 Park Ave	212-725-8585	$$$$	12 am	Eat the fondue and leave.
Bar Jamon	52 Irving Pl	212-253-2773	$	12 am	Tiny tapas bar.
Blockheads Burritos	499 Third Ave	212-213-3332	$	12 am	Damn good burritos, a little pricey.
BLT Prime	111 E 22nd St	212-995-8500	$$$$$	11:30 pm	Steakhouse with Craft-like, a-la-carte sides.
Blue Smoke	116 E 27th St	212-447-7733	$$$	1 am	Finger lickin' BBQ, Danny Meyer style (with downstairs jazz club).
Butai	115 E 18th St	212-387-8885	$$$	1 am	Impressive Japanese cuisine.
Candela	116 E 16th St	212-254-1600	$$$	12 am	Sushi scene in *Frankenstein* novel.
Coppola's	378 Third Ave	212-679-0070	$$	12 am	Neighborhood Italian.
Curry Leaf	99 Lexington Ave	212-725-5558	$$$	11 pm	Best basic Indian.
David's Bagels	331 First Ave	212-780-2308	$*	8 pm	Bagels. Some say the best. Cheaper than H&H.
El Parador Café	325 E 34th St	212-679-6812	$$$	11 pm	NY's oldest and friendliest Mexican.
Ess-a-bagel	359 First Ave	212-260-2252	$	9 pm	Bagels with attitude.
Friend of a Farmer	77 Irving Pl	212-477-2188	$$	11 pm	Chic country cooking.
Gemini Diner	641 Second Ave	212-532-2143	$$	24 Hrs	Open 24 hours. Diner.
Gramercy Restaurant	184 Third Ave	212-982-2121	$$	24 Hrs	Open 24 hours. Diner.
Haandi	113 Lexington Ave	212-685-5200	$	4 pm	Stellar Pakistani grilled meats.
I Trulli	122 E 27th St	212-481-7372	$$$$$	10:30 pm	Italian. Great garden.
Jackson Hole	521 Third Ave	212-679-3264	$$	1:30 am	Extremely large burgers.
Jaiya Thai	396 Third Ave	212-889-1330	$$$	12 am	Inventive, spicy Thai.
L'aanam	393 Third Ave	212-686-5168	$$	12:30 am	Cheap and quick Vietnamese, good—but not for serious enthusiasts.
L'Express	249 Park Ave S	212-254-5858	$$	24 Hrs	Always open French bistro.
Les Halles	411 Park Ave S	212-679-4111	$$$	12 am	Steak frites and French vibe.
Mexico Lindo	459 Second Ave	212-679-3665	$$$	12 am	Famous Mexican food.
Paquitos	160 E 28th St	212-685-9815	$	11 pm	Cheap burritos, better than most.
Park Avenue Country Club	381 Park Ave S	212-685-3636	$$	11 pm	Somewhat sharkish sports bar.
Patsy's Pizzeria	509 Third Ave	212-689-7500	$$*	11:45 pm	Classic NY pizza.
Penelope	159 Lexington Ave	212-481-3800	$$*	11 pm	Gingham décor but oh, what a menu!
Pete's Tavern	129 E 18th St	212-473-7676	$$$$	1 am	Good pub food, especially after drinking!
Pongal	110 Lexington Ave	212-696-9458	$$	10 pm	Possibly NY's best Indian. Vegetarian.
Pongsri Thai	311 Second Ave	212-477-2727	$$	11 pm	Great, spicy Thai.
Posto	310 Second Ave	212-716-1200	$$	12 am	Savory thin crust pizza, salads.
Pure Food and Wine	54 Irving Pl	212-477-1010	$$$	9:30 pm	The raw vegan food craze hits New York.
Rare Bar & Grill, Shelbourne Murray Hill Hotel	303 Lexington Ave	212-481-1999	$$	12 am	Top-rated NYC burger.
Rice	115 Lexington Ave	212-686-5400	$$*	12 am	Trendy and creative Indian goodies.

Arts & Entertainment • **Restaurants**

Key: $: Under $10 / $$: $10–$20 / $$$: $20–$30 / $$$$: $30-$40 / $$$$$: $40+; *: Cash only / †: Accepts only American Express. / †† Accepts only Visa/Mastercard. Time refers to hour kitchen closes on weekends.

Map 10 • Murray Hill / Gramercy—*continued*

Rodeo	375 Third Ave	212-683-6500	$$	4 am	Rockabilly, beer, and chicken fried steak for homesick Texans.
Sarge's Deli	548 Third Ave	212-679-0442	$$	24 Hrs	Open 24 hours. Jewish deli.
Totonno's Pizzeria Napolitano	462 Second Ave	212-213-8800	$$	1 am	Manhattan wing of classic Coney Island Pizza.
Tracy J's Watering Hole	106 E 19th St	212-674-5783	$	2 am	Perfect place to watch the game.
Turkish Kitchen	386 Third Ave	212-679-6633	$$$	11:30 pm	Excellent Turkish, great décor. NFT pick!
Via Emilia	240 Park Ave S	212-505-3072	$$$*	11:30 pm	Emilia-Romagnan specialties.
Water Club	500 E 30th St	212-683-3333	$$$$	11 pm	Romantic, good brunch.
Yama	122 E 17th St	212-475-0969	$$$	11 pm	Sushi deluxe.
Zen Palate	34 Union Sq E	212-614-9291	$$$	11:20 pm	Dependable vegetarian.
				11:30 pm	

Map 11 • Hell's Kitchen

Afghan Kebab House	764 Ninth Ave	212-307-1612	$$	11 pm	Great kebabs.
Ariana Afghan Kebab	787 Ninth Ave	212-262-2323	$		Afghan.
Burrito Box	885 Ninth Ave	212-489-6889	$	11:30 pm	Cheap and tasty Mexican with killer guac.
Burritoville	625 Ninth Ave	212-333-5352	$	1 am	Takeout Mexican.
Chipotle	620 Ninth Ave	212-247-3275	$	10 pm	Cheap, fat, Mex-American goodness.
Churruscaria Plataforma	316 W 49th St	212-245-0505	$$$$	12 am	Popular but uneven Brazilian.
Daisy May's BBQ USA	623 Eleventh Ave	212-977-1500	$$	8 pm	Takeout BBQ and sides Mon-Fri. Plus, various Manhattan street carts!
Don Giovanni	358 W 44th St	212-581-4939	$$	2 am	One of the better cheap pies in the city.
Eatery	798 Ninth Ave	212-765-7080	$$	1 am	A Hell's Kitchen comfort food favorite. All de-lish.
Grand Sichuan Int'l	745 Ninth Ave	212-582-2288	$$	11 pm	Excellent weird Szechuan. Recommended.
H&H Bagels	639 W 46th St	212-765-7200	$*	24 hrs	A cultural landmark. They make bagels too.
Hallo Berlin	626 Tenth Ave	212-977-1944	$$	11 pm	The best wurst in the city! Check out their street cart at 54th and Fifth.
Hell's Kitchen	679 Ninth Ave	212-977-1588	$$$	12 am	Haute cuisine, Mexican style. Packed.
Hudson Cafeteria, Hudson Hotel	356 W 58th St	212-554-6000	$$$	12 am	Lovely and pricey and goody.
Island Burgers 'N Shakes	766 Ninth Ave	212-307-7934	$$*	11 pm	Aptly named.
Jezebel	630 Ninth Ave	212-582-1045	$$$$	12 am	Southern charm.
Joe Allen	326 W 46th St	212-581-6464	$$$	12 am	De rigueur stargazing, open late.
Les Sans Culottes	347 W 46th St	212-247-4284	$$$	11:30 pm	Friendly French.
Marseille	630 Ninth Ave	212-333-2323	$$$$	12 am	True to the name, an expatriate's delight.
Meskerem	468 W 47th St	212-664-0520	$$	11:30 pm	Standard Ethiopian.
Morningstar	401 W 57th St	212-246-1593	$	24 Hrs	French toast with ice-cream at midnight, terrible diner.
The Nook	746 Ninth Ave	212-247-5500	$$$*	12 am	Delicious New American (with after-hours parties).
Old San Juan	765 Ninth Ave	212-262-6761	$$	11 pm	Good, Puerto Rican-Argentinean fare.
Orso	322 W 46th St	212-489-7212	$$$$	11:45 pm	Popular busy Italian.
Puttanesca	859 Ninth Ave	212-581-4177	$$$	1 am	Serious Italian with light-hearted prices.
Ralph's	862 Ninth Ave	212-581-2283	$$	6 pm	Classic Italian cuisine.
Taboon	773 Tenth Ave	212-713-0271	$$$	11:30 pm	Great bang for your buck. Middle Eastern/ Mediterranean.
Tony Luke's	576 Ninth Ave	212-967-3005	$	10 pm	Philly cheese steak without the snobbery. Extra Cheez Whiz, please.
Tout Va Bien	311 W 51st St	212-265-0190	$$$	11:30 pm	Warm, homey, pre-theater, French. NFT Pick.
Turkish Cuisine	631 Ninth Ave	212-397-9650	$$	12 am	Turkish food, in case you were wondering.
Uncle Nick's	747 Ninth Ave	212-245-7992	$$$	11 pm	Greek, noisy.
Zen Palate	663 Ninth Ave	212-582-1669	$$$	10:30 pm	Dependable vegetarian.

Map 12 • Midtown

'21' Club	21 W 52nd St	212-582-7200	$$$$$	10 pm	Old, clubby New York.
Alain Ducasse	155 W 58th St	212-265-7300	$$$$$	9:30 pm	Crème de la crème, dude.
Aquavit	13 W 54th St	212-307-7311	$$$$$	11:30 pm	Stellar dining experience: top-drawer Scandinavian.
Baluchi's	240 W 56th St	212-397-0707	$$	11 pm	Slightly above-average Indian.
BG	754 Fifth Ave	212-872-8977	$$$$$	8 pm	Another reason to spend the whole day at Bergdorf's.
Brasserie 8 1/2	9 W 57th St	212-829-0812	$$$$$	12 am	A must for brunch. Lovely for cocktails and dinner too.
Burger Joint, Parker Meridien	119 W 56th St	212-708-7414	$*	12 am	Fancy hotel lobby leads to unexpected burger dive.

Carnegie Deli	854 Seventh Ave	212-757-2245	$$$*	3:30 am	Still good.
Coldstone Creamery	253 W 42nd St	212-398-1882	$	12 am	Because ice cream without trendiness ain't worth a lick.
Cosi	11 W 42nd St	212-398-6662	$	8:30 pm	Sandwiches for the masses.
Cosi	1633 Broadway	212-397-9838	$	12 am	Sandwiches for the masses.
Gallagher's Steak House	228 W 52nd St	212-245-5336	$$$$	12 am	Dine on fancy steak with grizzled old New Yorkers.
Haru	205 W 43rd St	212-398-9810	$$$$	12 am	Excellent mid-range Japanese. Loud, good.
Joe's Shanghai	24 W 56th St	212-333-3868	$$	10:30 pm	Uptown version of killer dumpling factory.
La Bonne Soupe	48 W 55th St	212-586-7650	$$	12 am	Ooh la la, the best salad dressing accompanies my soupe a l'oignon.
Le Bernardin	155 W 51st St	212-554-1515	$$$$$	11 pm	Top NYC seafood.
Molyvos	871 Seventh Ave	212-582-7500	$$$$	12 am	Top Greek.
Mont Blanc	306 W 48th St	212-582-9648	$$$	10 pm	Classic fondue spot. Remember—drink wine, not water!
Nation Restaurant & Bar	12 W 45th St	212-391-8053	$$$	12 am	Loud, pretentious, good.
Nobu 57	40 W 57th St	212-757-3000	$$$$	11:15 pm	Uptown branch of wildly popular and renowned downtown sushi joints.
Norma's	Parker Meridien Hotel, 118 W 57th St	212-708-7460	$$$$	3 pm	Inventive and upscale brunch.
Per Se	10 Columbus Cir	212-823-9335	$$$$$	10 pm	Divine but you practically have to sell a kidney to afford it!
Petrossian	182 W 58th St	212-245-2214	$$$$$	11:15 pm	The décor's not updated, but the fare is FINE.
Pongsri Thai	244 W 48th St	212-582-3392	$$	11:30 pm	Great, spicy Thai.
Pret a Manger	135 W 50th St		$	6 pm	British sandwich chain.
Pret a Manger	1350 Sixth Ave	212-307-6100	$*	6 pm	British sandwich chain.
Primeburger	5 E 51st St	212-759-4729	$*	7 pm	Truly retro diner with kitschy swiveling-tray seating.
Pump Energy Food	40 W 55th St	212-246-6844	$	10 pm	Just what you think it is.
Redeye Grill	890 Seventh Ave	212-541-9000	$$$	12:30 am	Sprawling and diverse.
Seppi's	123 W 56th St	212-708-7444	$$$	2 am	Chocolate brunch every weekend.
Shelly's New York	104 W 57th St	212-245-2422	$$$	12:45 am	Come starve, leave stuffed.
Spanky's BBQ	127 W 43rd St	212-575-5848	$$	12 am	The real BBQ deal, just don't try and compare it to actual Texas BBQ.
Virgil's Real BBQ	152 W 44th St	212-921-9494	$$$	12 am	It's real.
wichcraft, Bryant Park	Sixth Ave b/w 40th & 42nd St	212-780-0577	$$	6 pm	4 Kiosks: Sandwiches, soups, and sweets from Craft's Tom Colicchio.

Map 13 · East Midtown

BLT Steak	106 E 57th St	212-752-7470	$$$$$	11:30 pm	Pricey and good, not great.
Caffé Buon Gusto	1009 Second Ave	212-755-1476	$$	11 pm	The bread is addictive. Sop it in sauce.
Chola	232 E 58th St	212-688-4619	$$$	11 pm	Pricey south Indian cuisine.
Cosi Sandwich Bar	60 E 56th St	212-588-1225	$	6 pm	Sandwiches for the masses.
Dawat	210 E 58th St	212-355-7555	$$$$	11:15 pm	Top-end Indian.
Docks Oyster Bar	633 Third Ave	212-986-8080	$$$	12 am	Great seafood, good atmosphere.
Ess-a-bagel	831 Third Ave	212-980-1010	$	5 pm	Bagels with attitude.
F&B	150 E 52nd St	212-421-8600	$	10 pm	Belgian street food that makes our carts look nasty.
Felidia	243 E 58th St	212-758-1479	$$$$	11:30 pm	Top Northern Italian.
Four Seasons	99 E 52nd St	212-754-9494	$$$$$	9:30 pm	Designer everything.
March	405 E 58th St	212-754-6272	$$$$$	10:45 pm	Lovely. It's actually 8 dollar signs.
Menchanko-tei	131 E 45th St	212-986-6805	$$	12:30 am	Japanese noodle shop.
Metropolitan	959 First Ave	212-759-5600	$$$	10:30 pm	American fare on the far east side never disappoints.
Nikki	151 E 50th St	212-753-1144	$$$	3 am	Eclectic Miami vice with pillows.
Oceana	55 E 54th St	212-759-5941	$$$$$	10:30 pm	Le Bernardin Jr.
Organic Harvest Café	235 E 53rd St	212-421-6444	$$	9:30 pm	Vegetarian.
Oyster Bar	Grand Central, Lower Level	212-490-6650	$$$	9:30 pm	Classic New York seafood joint.
Palm	837 Second Ave	212-687-2953	$$$$$	11 pm	Steak.
Pershing Square	90 E 42nd St	212-286-9600	$$$	10:30 pm	Excellent food and awesome space.
PJ Clarke's	915 Third Ave	212-317-1616	$$$	3 am	Pub grub.
Rosa Mexicano	1063 First Ave	212-753-7407	$$$	11 pm	Inventive Mexican. Great guac.
Shun Lee Palace	155 E 55th St	212-371-8844	$$$$	11:30 pm	Top-end Chinese.
Sidecar	205 E 55th St	212-317-2044	$$$$$	11:30 pm	PJ. Clarke's quieter, more refined restaurant sibling.
Smith & Wollensky	797 Third Ave	212-753-1530	$$$$$	11 pm	Don't order the fish.
Sparks Steak House	210 E 46th St	212-687-4855	$$$$$	11:30 pm	If you can't go to Luger's.
Vong	200 E 54th St	212-486-9592	$$$$	11 pm	$38 pre-theater menu. Top Pan-Asian.
Zarela	953 Second Ave	212-644-6740	$$$	11:30 pm	Go for the guac at the bar.

Key: $: Under $10 / $$: $10–$20 / $$$: $20–$30 / $$$$: $30–$40 / $$$$$: $40+; *: Cash only / †: Accepts only American Express. / †† Accepts only Visa/Mastercard. Time refers to hour kitchen closes on weekends.

Map 14 · Upper West Side (Lower)

The 79th St Boat Basin Café (seasonal)	W 79th St	212-496-5542	*	11:30 pm	Dog and family friendly.
All-State Café	250 W 72nd St	212-874-1883	$$	3 am	Very comfy and friendly downstairs joint.
Asiate	80 Columbus Cir, 35th fl	212-805-8881	$$$$$	10 pm	Highest-end Japanese/French.
Baluchi's	283 Columbus Ave	212-579-3900	$$	11:30 pm	Slightly above-average Indian.
Big Nick's	2175 Broadway	212-362-9238	$$	24 Hrs	Death by burger. Recommended.
Blondies	212 W 79th St	212-362-4360	$$	3 am	Pair wings with a salad to save your arteries.
Café Des Artistes	1 W 67th St	212-877-3500	$$$$$	12 am	A fine romance.
Café Lalo	201 W 83rd St	212-496-6031	$$	4am	Packed dessert and coffee destination.
Café Luxembourg	200 W 70th St	212-873-7411	$$$$$	12 am	Top-end bistro.
China Fun	246 Columbus Ave	212-580-1516	$$	12 am	Uptown dim sum option.
Crumbs	321 Amsterdam Ave	212-712-9800	$	12 am	MMM, cupcakes.
Edgar's Café	255 W 84th St	212-496-6126	$$*	2 am	Salads, desserts, and atmosphere.
EJ's Luncheonette	447 Amsterdam Ave	212-873-3444	$$	11 pm	Homey diner.
Epices du Traiteur	103 W 70th St	212-579-5904	$$$	12 am	Charming atmosphere, eclectic and flavorful food.
Fairway Café	2127 Broadway	212-595-1888	$$$	10 pm	When it's all too much.
The Firehouse	522 Columbus Ave	212-595-3139	$$	2 am	Where to go for after-softball wings.
French Roast	2340 Broadway	212-799-1533	$$	24 Hrs	Good croque monsieur.
Gabriel's	11 W 60th St	212-956-4600	$$$	12 am	Local-draw; good all-around.
Gari	370 Columbus Ave	212-362-4816	$$$$	11:30 pm	Why UWS sushi snobs no longer have to take the cross-town bus.
Gray's Papaya	2090 Broadway	212-799-0243	$*	24 Hrs	An institution.
H&H Bagels	2239 Broadway	212-595-8003	$*	24 hrs	A cultural landmark. They make bagels too.
Harry's Burrito Junction	241 Columbus Ave	212-580-9494	$$	1 am	What could they possibly serve here?
Hunan Park	235 Columbus Ave	212-724-4411	$$	11:30 pm	Dependable Chinese.
Jackson Hole	517 Columbus Ave	212-362-5177	$$	2 am	Extremely large burgers.
Jean Georges	1 Central Park W	212-299-3900	$$$$$	11 pm	$20 prix fixe summer lunch!
Jean-Luc	507 Columbus Ave	212-712-1700	$$$$	12 am	Classy, expensive bistro.
Josie's	300 Amsterdam Ave	212-769-1212	$$$		Good vegetarian option.
Kinoko	165 W 72nd St	212-580-5900	$$$	11:30 pm	All-you-can-eat sushi for $19.95.
La Caridad 78	2197 Broadway	212-874-2780	$$*	1 am	Cheap Cuban paradise.
Land Thai Kitchen	450 Amsterdam Ave	212-501-8121	$$	10:45 pm	Standard Thai.
Le Pain Quotidien	50 W 72nd St	212-712-9700	$$	7 pm	Good breads and such.
Lenge	200 Columbus Ave	212-799-9188	$$	11:30 am	Serviceable Japanese.
Manhattan Diner	2180 Broadway	212-877-7252	$	24 Hrs	Diner.
Penang	240 Columbus Ave	212-769-3988	$$$	12:45 am	Snooty but good Malaysian.
Picholine	35 W 64th St	212-724-8585	$$$$	12 am	Go for the cheese.
Planet Sushi	380 Amsterdam Ave	212-712-2162	$$$	3 am	Decent sushi in a cheap raw fish no-man's land.
Rain	100 W 82nd St	212-501-0776	$$$	12 am	Asian fusion with a magnificent bar.
Rosa Mexicano	61 Columbus Ave	212-977-7700	$$$$	11:30 pm	Inventive Mexican. Great guac.
Ruby Foo's Dim Sum & Sushi Palace	2182 Broadway	212-724-6700	$$$	12:30 am	Your parents will love it.
Santa Fe	73 W 71st St	212-724-0822	$$$	12 am	Calm Southwest.
Sarabeth's	423 Amsterdam Ave	212-496-6280	$$$	11 pm	Go for brunch.
Taco Grill	146 W 72nd St	212-501-8888	$*	11 pm	Mexican.
Vince and Eddie's	70 W 68th St	212-721-0068	$$$$	11 pm	Cozy comfort food.
Vinnie's Pizza	285 Amsterdam Ave	212-874-4382	$*	12 am	Good slice of pizza.
Whole Foods Café	10 Columbus Cir, downstairs	212-823-9600	$	10 pm	Very good and by far the cheapest eats in Time Warner Center.

Map 15 · Upper East Side (Lower)

Afghan Kebab House II	1345 Second Ave	212-517-2776	$$	10:30 pm	Great kebabs.
Atlantic Grill	1341 Third Ave	212-988-9200	$$$$$	12:30 am	Seafood galore.
Aureole	34 E 61st St	212-319-1660	$$$$$	11 pm	Well-done but unimaginative.
Baluchi's	1149 First Ave	212-371-3535	$$	11 pm	Slightly above-average Indian.
Baluchi's	1565 Second Ave	212-288-4810	$$	11 pm	Slightly above-average Indian.
The Bar at Etats-Unis	247 E 81st St	212-396-9928	$$$	11 pm	Hands down—the best bar eats you'll find anywhere.
Barking Dog Luncheonette	1453 York Ave	212-861-3600	$$*	11 pm	Good diner/café food.
Beyoglu	1431 Third Ave	212-650-0850	$$$	12 am	Make a meal out of meze.
Blue Green Organic Juice Café	203 E 74th St	212-744-0940	$$	11 pm	Super healthy juices and mostly raw eats in hip surroundings.
Brunelli	1409 York Ave	212-744-8899	$$$	10:30 pm	Old-world Italian.
Burger Heaven	804 Lexington Ave	212-838-3580	$	9:30 pm	Nuff said.
Burke Bar Café	1000 Third Ave	212-705-3800	$$$$	11 pm	Chef David Burke's elegant, inside-Bloomingdale's café with cheeky menu.

Name	Address	Phone	Price	Hours	Notes
Burke in the Box at Bloomingdale's	1000 Third Ave	212-705-3800	$$	10 pm	Chef David Burke's offbeat take-out eatery inside Bloomies.
Café Boulud, Surrey Hotel	20 E 76th St	212-772-2600	$$$$$	11 pm	Elegant, slightly more relaxed sibling of Daniel.
Café Mingala	1393 Second Ave	212-744-8008	$	11 pm	Burmese. $5.50 lunch special!
Café Sabarsky	1048 Fifth Ave	212-288-0665	$$$	9 pm	Beautiful wood-paneled surroundings for sipping Viennese coffee.
Candle 79	154 E 79th St	212-537-7179	$$$$	10:30 pm	Upscale vegetarian cuisine in luxurious surroundings.
Candle Café	1307 Third Ave	212-472-0970	$$$	10:30 pm	Delicious vegetarian café next door to Le Steak.
Canyon Road	1470 First Ave	212-734-1600	$$$	11:30 pm	Southwest haven.
Cilantro	1321 First Ave	212-537-4040	$$	12 am	Where transplanted Texans satiate cravings for Southwestern fare.
Daniel	60 E 65th St	212-288-0033	$$$$$	11 pm	Overrated $150+ meal.
Davidburke & Donatella	133 E 61st St	212-813-2121	$$$$$	11:30 pm	Multi-level New American with consistently great reviews.
Donguri	309 E 83rd St	212-737-5656	$$$$	9:45 pm	"Transcendent," UES Japanese standout.
EAT	1064 Madison Ave	212-772-0022	$$$	10 pm	Great brunch spot—part of the Eli Zabar empire.
Eat Here Now	839 Lexington Ave	212-751-0724	$$	9 pm	Clean, classic diner. Fast, friendly service.
EJ's Luncheonette	1271 Third Ave	212-472-0600	$$*	11 pm	Homey diner.
Elio's	1621 Second Ave	212-772-2242	$$$$$	12 am	UES Italian where schmoozing with the "who's-who" goes down.
Etats-Unis	242 E 81st St	212-517-8826	$$$$	11 pm	A jewel on the UES food map—exceptional New American.
Ethiopian Restaurant	1582 York Ave	212-717-7311	$$$	11 pm	Ethiopian in a sea of mediocre Italian.
Haru	1329 Third Ave	212-452-2230	$$		Sushi. Takeout recommended.
Heidelberg	1648 Second Ave	212-628-2332	$$$	11:30 pm	Dirndls and lederhosen serving colossal beers and sausage platters.
Indian Tandoor Oven Restaurant	175 E 83rd St	212-628-3000	$$	12 am	Delectable Indian specialties in cozy, color-draped surroundings.
Jackson Hole	1611 Second Ave	212-737-8788	$$	3 am	Extremely large burgers.
Jackson Hole	232 E 64th St	212-371-7187	$$	1:30 am	Extremely large burgers. Cozy.
Jacque's Brasserie	204 E 85th St	212-327-2272	$$$	12 am	UES spot for tasty moules frites and Stella on tap.
JG Melon	1291 Third Ave	212-744-0585	$$*	2:30 am	Excellent burgers. Always crowded.
John's Pizzeria	408 E 64th St	212-935-2895	$$	11:30 pm	Quintessential NY pizza.
JoJo	160 E 64th St	212-223-5656	$$$$	11 pm	Charming French bistro.
King's Carriage House	251 E 82nd St	212-734-5490	$$$$$	11 pm	Romantic fine dining in a charming, old carriage house.
Le Pain Quotidien	1131 Madison Ave	212-327-4900	$$	7 pm	Great breads and such.
Le Pain Quotidien	1336 First Ave	212-717-4800	$$	7 pm	Great breads and such.
Le Pain Quotidien	833 Lexington Ave	212-755-5810	$$	7:30 pm	Great breads and such.
Lexington Candy Shop / Luncheonette	1226 Lexington Ave	212-288-0057	$	7 pm	Charming old-timey soda shop with twirly stools.
Malaga	406 E 73rd St	212-737-7659	$$$	11 pm	Sleeper Spanish joint dishing up terrific tapas and swell sangria.
Mary Ann's	1503 Second Ave	212-249-6165	$$	11:45 pm	Good Mex, good margaritas.
Maya	1191 First Ave	212-585-1818	$$$$	11:30 pm	Top-drawer Mexican.
Mimi's Pizza & Restaurant	1248 Lexington Ave	212-861-3363	$$	11 pm	Said to be Paul McCartney's favorite NYC pizza.
Orsay	1057 Lexington Ave	212-517-6400	$$$$$	11:30 pm	Upscale brasserie popular with "about-town" uptowners.
Our Place	1444 Third Ave	212-288-4888	$$$$	11 pm	Next level Chinese.
Park Avenue Café	100 E 63rd Ave	212-644-1900	$$$$	11 pm	Wonderful expensive American.
Payard Patisserie & Bistro	1032 Lexington Ave	212-717-5252	$$$$$	11 pm	For tea and tarts (or tarts in Ts).
Penang	1596 Second Ave	212-585-3838	$$$	1 am	Snooty but good Malaysian.
Pintaile's Pizza	1443 York Ave	212-717-4990	$	10:30 pm	Tasty thin-crust stuff.
Pintaile's Pizza	1577 York Ave	212-396-3479	$	9:30 pm	Tasty thin-crust stuff.
Post House	28 E 63rd St	212-935-2888	$$$$$		Good bet: steak.
River	345 Amsterdam Ave	212-579-1888	$$	11:30 pm	Divine rice dishes from Thailand and Vietnam.
Sarabeth's at the Whitney	945 Madison Ave	212-570-3670	$$$	4 pm	Shorter lines for those with Sarabeth's cravings.
Serafina	29 E 61st St	212-702-9898	$$	3 am	Good pizza and pasta.
Serendipity 3	225 E 60th St	212-838-3531	$$	1 am	Home of the legendary "Frrrozen Hot Chocolate."
Sette Mezzo	969 Lexington Ave	212-472-0400	$$$$$*	11:30 pm	Oprah's fave.
Slice, The Perfect Food	1413 Second Ave	212-249-4353	$$	11 pm	Gluten-free pizza, except it tastes much better than that.
Sushi of Gari	402 E 78th St	212-517-5340	$$$$$	10:45 pm	Sure to please even the snootiest sushi snobs.
Totonno Pizzeria Napolitano	1544 Second Ave	212-327-2800	$$	1 am	Quality pizza.
Viand	1011 Madison Ave	212-249-8250	$$	10 pm	Basic diner.
Viand	673 Madison Ave	212-751-6622	$$*	10 pm	Basic diner.

Key: $: Under $10 / $$: $10–$20 / $$$: $20–$30 / $$$$: $30–$40 / $$$$$: $40+; *: Cash only / †: Accepts only American Express. / † † Accepts only Visa/Mastercard. Time refers to hour kitchen closes on weekends.

Map 16 · Upper West Side (Upper)

A	947 Columbus Ave	212-531-1643	$$*	11 pm	French-Caribbean café. BYOB on your first date!
AIX	2398 Broadway	212-874-7400	$$$$$	11 pm	Upscale uptown French.
Awash	947 Amsterdam Ave	212-961-1416	$$	1:00 am	Tasty Ethiopian.
Barney Greengrass	541 Amsterdam Ave	212-724-4707	$$$*	5 pm	Classic deli.
Bella Luna	584 Columbus Ave	212-877-2267	$$	11 pm	Italian.
Café Con Leche	726 Amsterdam Ave	212-678-7000	$$	12 am	Cuban-Dominican haven.
Carmine's	2450 Broadway	212-362-2200	$$$	12 am	Large-portion Italian.
City Diner	2441 Broadway	212-877-2720	$$	24 Hrs	Neighborhood joint.
Docks Oyster Bar	2427 Broadway	212-724-5588	$$$$	12 am	Consistently good seafood.
Flor de Mayo	2651 Broadway	212-663-5520	$$	12 am	Cuban-Chinese-Chicken-Chow.
Gabriela's	688 Columbus Ave	212-961-0574	$$		Cheery Mexican.
Gennaro	665 Amsterdam Ave	212-665-5348	$$$*	11 pm	Crowded Italian.
Henry's	2745 Broadway	212-866-0600	$$$	11 pm	Friendly uptown joint.
Jerusalem Restaurant	2715 Broadway	212-865-2295	$*	4 am	Good Middle Eastern, friendly service, open late.
Lemongrass Grill	2534 Broadway	212-666-0888	$$	11:30 am	Serviceable Thai.
Mary Ann's	2452 Broadway	212-877-0132	$$	11:30 pm	Good Mex, order margaritas.
Miss Mamie's Spoonbread Too	366 W 110th St	212-865-6744	$$	10:30 pm	Soul food spectacular.
Pampa	768 Amsterdam Ave	212-865-2929	$$*	12 am	Argentinean.
Popover Café	551 Amsterdam Ave	212-595-8555	$$	10 pm	Kind of fun. Whatever.
Restaurant Broadway	2664 Broadway	212-865-7074	$*	10 pm	Great breakfast and sandwiches, good place to start the day.
Saigon Grill	620 Amsterdam Ave	212-875-9072	$$	12 am	Busy Vietnamese. Great food, dirt cheap.
Talia's Steakhouse	668 Amsterdam Ave	212-580-3770	$$$	2:30 am on Saturdays. Closed on Fridays.	Your basic kosher steakhouse.
Trattoria Pesce & Pasta	625 Columbus Ave	212-579-7970	$$$	11 pm	Italian.

Map 17 · Upper East Side / East Harlem

Barking Dog Luncheonette	1678 Third Ave	212-831-1800	$$*	11 pm	Good diner/café food.
Bella Cucina	1293 Lexington Ave	212-289-9004	$$$	10:30 pm	Non-Zagat rated Italian with great fish specials.
Carino	1710 Second Ave	212-860-0566	$$	11 pm	Mama Carino's divine, home-style Sicilian kitchen.
Chef Ho's Peking Duck Grill	1720 Second Ave	212-348-9444	$$$	11 pm	Creative gourmet-ish Chinese cuisine. Try the Banana Chicken - delicious!
Choux Factory	1685 First Ave	212-289-2023		10 pm	Kona coffee and filled-to-order Japanese cream puffs.
Cilantro	1712 Second Ave	212-722-4242	$$$	1 am	Where transplanted Texans satiate cravings for Southwestern fare.
El Paso Taqueria	1642 Lexington Ave	212-831-9831	$	1 am	Mexican.
Elaine's	1703 Second Ave	212-534-8103	$$$$	2 am	Ignore the naysayers! Great food and fun center-of-it-all vibe.
Jackson Hole	1270 Madison Ave	212-427-2820	$$	11 pm	Extremely large burgers.
Kebap G	1830 Second Ave	212-860-5960	$	10 pm	Bright, hip joint for Turkish-style gyros, falafel, and hummus.
Knick's Lunch East	1732 Second Ave	212-426-8400	$	24 Hrs	Delightfully lowbrow fare dished out in modest digs 24/7.
La Fonda Boricua	169 E 106th St	212-410-7292	$$	9 pm	Puerto Rican home-cookin'.
Luca Restaurant	1712 First Ave	212-987-9260	$$$$$	11 pm	Northern Italian standout with loyal neighborhood following.
Nick's Restaurant & Pizzeria	1814 Second Ave	212-987-5700	$$$	11:30 pm	Piping hot, thin-crust, brick oven pizza (and pasta).
Nina's Argentinean Pizzeria	1750 Second Ave	212-426-4627	$$	11 pm	Italian with an Argentinean accent.
Papaya King	179 E 86th St	212-369-0648	$*	1 am	Dishing out damn good dogs since 1932.
Pinocchio	1748 First Ave	212-828-5810	$$$$$	11 pm	Itty bitty sleeper Italian with rave reviews and loyal fans.
Pintaile's Pizza	26 E 91st St	212-722-1967	$$	9:30 pm	Tasty thin-crust stuff.
Sabora Mexico	1744 First Ave	212-289-2641	$$††	11 pm	Small, home-cooked, cheap & delicious.
Saigon Grill	1700 Second Ave	212-996-4600	$$	11:30 pm	Busy Vietnamese. Great food, dirt cheap.
Sarabeth's	1295 Madison Ave	212-410-7335	$$$	10 pm	Good breakfast, if you can get in.
Viand	300 E 86th St	212-879-9425	$$	24 Hrs	
York Grill	1690 York Ave	212-772-0261	$$$$$	11:30 pm	Way-out-yonder Yorkville New American.
Yura & Company	1292 Madison Ave	212-860-8060	$$	5 pm	Take-out and bakery branch with hot breakfast station.
Yura & Company	1645 Third Ave	212-860-8060		9:30 pm	Brisk brunch spot with dine-in and take-out options.
Yura & Company	1659 Third Ave	212-860-8060	$	8 pm	Take-out baked goods and sandwiches with airy, open kitchen.
Zebu Grill	305 E 92nd St	212-426-7500	$$$$$	11:30 pm	Candlelit Brazilian bistro with exposed brick and earthy wooden tables.

Map 18 · Columbia / Morningside Heights

Bistro Ten 18	1018 Amsterdam Ave	212-662-7600	$$$	11:30 pm	Excellent uptown American bistro.
Dinosaur Bar-B-Que	646 W 131st St	212-694-1777	$$$	12 am	Not just for 'cue fans. Head WAY uptown.
Hungarian Pastry Shop	1030 Amsterdam Ave	212-866-4230	$*	11:30 pm	Exactly what it is—and excellent.
Kitchenette	1272 Amsterdam Ave	212-531-7600	$$	11 pm	Good for everything.
Koronet Pizza	2848 Broadway	212-222-1566	$*	4 am	Just one slice. Really. That's all you'll need.
Le Monde	2885 Broadway	212-531-3939	$$	1:30 am	Brasserie.
M&G Soul Food Diner	383 W 125th St	212-864-7326	$$*	12 am	A soulful diner.
Massawa	1239 Amsterdam Ave	212-663-0505	$$	11 pm	Neighborhood joint.
Max	1274 Amsterdam Ave	212-531-2221	$$	12 am	The Italian genius of Max, uptown.
Mill Korean	2895 Broadway	212-666-7653	$$	10:30 pm	Great neighborhood Korean.
Ollie's	2957 Broadway	212-932-3300	$$	2 am	Only if you must.
P + W Sandwich Shop	1030 Amsterdam Ave	212-222-2245	$*	8 pm	Fresh deli meats.
Pisticci	125 La Salle St	212-932-3500	$$	11 pm	Wonderful cozy Italian.
Sezz Medi	1260 Amsterdam Ave	212-932-2901	$$	12 am	Popular pizza/pasta place.
Symposium	544 W 113th St	212-865-1011	$$	11 pm	Good traditional Greek.
Terrace in the Sky	400 W 119th St	212-666-9490	$$$$$	10:30 pm	Rooftop French.
Toast	3157 Broadway	212-662-1144	$$	12 am	Great diverse café menu. Recommended.
V&T Pizzeria	1024 Amsterdam Ave	212-666-8051	$		Columbia pizza heaven.

Map 19 · Harlem (Lower)

African Kine Restaurant	256 W 116th St	212-666-9400		2 am	Senegalese.
Amy Ruth's	113 W 116th St	212-280-8779	$$	11 pm	Soul food, incredible fried chicken.
Bayou	308 Lenox Ave	212-426-3800	$$$	11 pm	Cajun, with a good bar, too.
Ginger Restaurant	1400 Fifth Ave	212-423-1111	$$$	10:30 pm	New Harlem spot dishing creative, healthy Chinese cuisine.
Home Sweet Harlem Café	270 W 135th St	212-926-9616	$	7 pm	Breakfast/lunch spot.
IHOP	2294 Adam Clayton Powell Jr Blvd	212-234-4747	$$	24 hrs	Pancakes, etc.
Keur Sokhna	225 W 116th St	212-864-0081	$††	2 am	Good cheap Senegalese.
Manna's Too	486 Lenox Ave	212-234-4488	$*	10 pm	Soul food buffet!
Native	101 W 118th St	212-665-2525	$	12 am	Excellent soul food.
Papaya King	121 W 125th St	212-665-5732	$*	9 pm	Dawgs for all you dawgs.
Slice of Harlem	308 Lenox Ave	212-426-7400	$	10 pm	Harlem brick-oven pizza. Cool.
Sylvia's	328 Lenox Ave	212-996-0660	$$$	10:30 pm	An institution. Not overrated.
Yvonne Yvonne	301 W 135th St	212-862-1223	$*	8 pm	Excellent Jamaican chicken, ribs, etc.

Map 20 · El Barrio

Camaradas	2241 First Ave	212-348-2703	$$*	3 am	Spanish/Puero Rican/tapas/music.
Creole	2167 Third Ave	212-876-8838	$$	12 am	Local Creole.
La Hacienda	219 E 116th St	212-987-1617	$	12 am	Mexican.
Orbit East Harlem	2257 First Ave	212-348-7818	$$$	1 am	We like it—dinner, brunch, music, etc.
Patsy's Pizzeria	2287 First Ave	212-534-9783	$$*	11 pm	The original thin-crust pizza.
Rao's	455 E 114th St	212-722-6709	$$$$$	11 pm	We've heard it's an institution.
Sandy's Restaurant	2261 Second Ave	212-348-8654	$$	11 pm	Neighborhood joint.

Map 21 · Manhattanville / Hamilton Heights

Copeland's	547 W 145th St	212-234-2357	$$$	12:00 am	Fine southern cooking.
Devin's Fish & Chips	747 St Nicholas Ave	212-491-5518	$*	11:30 pm	Greasy goodness just steps from St. Nick's Pub. Recommended.
Jesus Taco	501 W 145th St	212-234-3330	$*	11 pm	Tacos and burgers.
The Jyraffe	1940 Amsterdam Ave	212-862-3330	$$	9 pm	Southern-style comfort food.
New Caporal	3772 Broadway	212-862-8986	$*	24 Hrs	A neighborhood institution.
Queen of Sheeba	317 W 141st St	212-862-6149	$*	11 pm	Middle Eastern.
Raw Soul	348 W 145th St	212-491-5859	$*	9 pm	All raw food, all the time.
Sunshine Jamaican Restaurant	695 St Nicholas Ave	212-368-4972	$*	9:45 pm	Delicious curried goat.

Map 22 · Harlem (Upper)

Charles' Southern-Style Chicken	2839 Frederick Douglass Blvd	212-926-4313	$	10 pm	The fried chicken they serve in heaven.
Flash Inn	107 Macombs Pl	212-283-8605	$$$	12 am	Old-timey New York Italian.
Londel's Supper Club	2620 Frederick Douglass Blvd	212-234-6114	$$	11 pm	Good Southern.
Margie's Red Rose	267 W 144th St	212-491-3665	$*	7:30 pm	Fried chicken heaven.
Miss Maude's	547 Lenox Ave	212-690-3100	$$	9 pm	Harlem soul food.
Sugar Shack	2611 Frederick Douglass Blvd	212-491-4422	$$		Fried chicken, shrimp, catfish.

Arts & Entertainment · **Restaurants**

Key: $: Under $10 / $$: $10–$20 / $$$: $20–$30 / $$$$: $30–$40 / $$$$$: $40+; *: Cash only / †: Accepts only American Express. / †† Accepts only Visa/Mastercard. Time refers to hour kitchen closes on weekends.

Map 23 · Washington Heights

Aqua Marina	4060 Broadway	212-928-0070	$	12 am	Uptown Italian.
Carrot Top Pastries	3931 Broadway	212-927-4800	$	9 pm	Baked goods and coffee too!
Coogan's	4015 Broadway	212-928-1234	$$	12 am	Where med students and cops go.
Dallas BBQ	3956 Broadway	212-568-3700	$$	12 am	When you can't get to Virgil's.
El Conde Steak House	4139 Broadway	212-781-1235	$$	1 am	Big slabs of MEAT.
El Malecon	4141 Broadway	212-927-3812	$	24 Hrs	Mexican—fabulous roast chicken.
El Ranchito	4129 Broadway	212-928-0866	$$*	1:30 am	Central America in New York!
Empire Szechuan	4041 Broadway	212-568-1600	$$	12 am	Chinese.
Hispaniola	839 W 181st St	212-740-5222	$$	12 am	Tapas, bridge views—everything you need.
International Food House	4073 Broadway	212-740-1616	$	24 Hrs	Buffet-style. Open 24 hours.
Jesse's Place	812 W 181st St	212-795-4168	$	12:30 am	Neighborhood diner.
Jimmy Oro Restaurant	711 W 181st St	212-795-1414	$	11 pm	Chinese/Spanish. Huge variety.
Parrilla	3920 Broadway	212-543-9500	$$*	4am	Argentinean with cool-ass grill.
Reme Restaurant	4021 Broadway	212-923-5452	*	8:30 pm	Comfort food.
Restaurant Tenares	2306 Amsterdam Ave	212-927-4190	$$*	12 am	Jukebox. Brush up your Spanish standards.
Taino Restaurant	2228 Amsterdam Ave	212-543-9035	$$	12 am	Neighborhood Latino w/ men constantly arguing outside.
Tipico Dominicano	4177 Broadway	212-781-3900	$	24 Hrs	Family place to watch the game. Gooooooaal!
Tu Sonrisa	132 Audubon Ave	212-543-0218	$$*	11 pm	Small sweet place. Stuffed bears in window.

Map 24 · Fort George / Fort Tryon

107 West	811 W 187th St	212-923-3311	$$	11 pm	Salads, burgers, etc.
Bleu Evolution	808 W 187th St	212-928-6006	$$	2 am	Uptown bohemian. Calm.
Caridad Restaurant	4311 Broadway	212-781-0431	$	12 am	Caribbean.
Frank's Pizzeria	94 Nagle Ave	212-567-3122	$	12 am	Pizza.
New Leaf Café	1 Margaret Corbin Dr	212-568-5323	$$$$	10 pm	Uptown haven.
Rancho Jubilee	1 Nagle Ave	212-304-0100	$$	24 hrs	Great Dominican destination. on weekends

Map 25 · Inwood

Bobby's Fish and Seafood Market and Restaurant	3842 Ninth Ave	212-304-9440	$$	24 Hrs	Fish! Fresh! Open late!
Capitol Restaurant	4933 Broadway	212-942-5090	$$*	10:00 pm	Nice neighborhood diner.
Hoppin' Jalapenos Bar & Grill	597 W 207th St	212-569-6059	$$††	11 pm	Mexican bar and restaurant, good burrrrritos!
Tacos Puebla	5-22 W 207th St	212-942-1881	$*	12 am	Large portions of succulent and inexpensive Mexican favorites.

Battery Park City

Cove Restaurant	2 South End Ave	212-964-1500	$$$	9:30 pm	New American cuisine.
Foxhounds	320 South End Ave	212-385-6199	$$	10 pm	English pub; food, "American."
Gigino at Wagner Park	20 Battery Pl	212-528-2228	$$$$		Lady Liberty is your companion as you dine Italian.
Grill Room	WFC, 225 Liberty St	212-945-9400	$$$$$	9 pm	Enter viewing palm trees; dine viewing the Hudson.
Picasso Pizza	303 South End Ave	212-321-2616	$$	10 pm	Good thin crust pizza.
PJ Clarke's	4 World Financial Ctr	212-285-1500	$$$$	11 pm	New Lower Manhattan location of 120-year old burger institution.
Samantha's Fine Foods	235 South End Ave	212-945-5555	$$	9 pm	Italian take-out and catering.
Steamer's Landing	375 South End Ave	212-432-1451	$$$	10 pm	Food from Italy, from the sea, and from the farms.
Wave Japanese Restaurant	21 South End Ave	212-240-9100	$$	10 pm	Good Japanese.
Zen	311 South End Ave	212-432-3634	$$	9 pm	Chinese and Thai.

Roosevelt Island

Trellis	549 Main St	212-752-1517	$$	12 am	Local hang out.

Map 26 · Astoria

Agnanti	19-06 Ditmars Blvd	718-545-4554	$$	12 am	Wonderful Greek/Cypriot cuisine just across from Astoria Park.
Aliada	29-19 Broadway	718-932-2240	$$	12 am	Excellent Cypriot with deservedly famous lamb chops.
Bel Aire Diner	31-91 21st St	718-721-3160	$$	24 Hrs	Voted best diner in Queens by the Daily News.
Bosna Express	31-29 12th St	718-932-5577	$*	9 pm	Addictive Balkan-style grilled meat sandwiches.

Christos Hasapo-Taverna	41-08 23rd Ave	718-777-8400	$$$$	11 pm	Excellent Greek-inflected steakhouse.
Churrascaria Girassol	33-18 28th Ave	718-545-8250	$$	11 pm	Authentic Brazilian meals, including rodizio.
Djardan	34-04 31st Ave	718-721-2694	$$*	11 pm	Bureks and other Eastern European delights.
Jour et Nuit	28-04 Steinway St	718-204-2511	$$	1 am	Exceptional Moroccan food, very friendly staff.
Kabab Café	25-12 Steinway St	718-728-9858	$$*		Kebabs and more cooked to order by friendly chef-owner, Ali.
Mombar	25-22 Steinway St	718-726-2356	$$*	11 pm	Egyptian food in a beautiful setting.
Neptune Diner	31-05 Astoria Blvd	718-278-4853	$$	24 Hrs	Rivals Bel Aire as the best diner in Queens.
Roti Rani's	33-10 21st St	718-956-7888	$$		Indian food to go.
S'Agapo	34-21 34th St	718-626-0303	$$$		Popular Greek restaurant with outdoor dining for the warmer months.
Sabor Tropical	36-18 30th Ave	718-777-8506	$$$		Hearty Brazilian—brilliant steak.
Sal, Chris, and Charlie Deli	33-12 23rd Ave	718-278-9240	$$*	8 pm	They don't call them the "sandwich kings of Astoria" for nothing.
Stamatis	29-12 23rd Ave	718-932-8596	$$	1 am	Top Astoria Greek, octopus and other grilled fish recommended.
Tokyo Japanese Restaurant	31-05 24th Ave	718-777-1880	$$	11 pm	Try the Jimmy roll.
Trattoria L'Incontro	21-76 31st St	718-721-3532	$$$$	11 pm	One of Queens's best Italian restaurants.
Watawa	33-10 Ditmars Blvd	718-545-9596	$$	12 am	Fresh, fresh sushi in a cozy Japanese setting.
Zenon	34-10 31st Ave	718-956-0133	$$*	11 pm	Cypriot taverna with the best meze in town.
Zlata Praha	28-48 31st St	718-721-6422	$$	11 pm	Hearty, cheap Czech food.
Zygos Tavern	22-55 31st St	718-728-7070	$$	12 am	Fairly priced Greek dining. Great homemade tzaziki sauce with dill and diced cucumbers.

Map 27 · Long Island City

5 Stars Punjabi	13-15 43rd Ave	718-784-7444	$$	24 Hrs	Indian diner/cabbie hangout.
Bella Via	47-46 Vernon Blvd	718-361-7510	$$	10:30 pm	Wonderful modern Italian dishes and brick oven pizza.
Brooks 1890 Restaurant	24-28 Jackson Ave	718-937-1890	$$	8 pm	Classic American fare in historic setting.
Café Henri	10-10 50th Ave	718-383-9315	$$	12 am	BYOB French bistro.
Court Square Diner	45-30 23rd St	718-392-1222	$*	24 Hrs	Reliable grub available 24 hrs.
Cup Diner	35-01 36th St	718-937-2322	$$	2 am	Trendy diner open 24 hrs.
Jackson Ave Steakhouse	12-23 Jackson Ave	718-784-1412	$$$$	11 pm	Wood-paneled steakhouse with a busy happy hour.
Lil Bistro 33	33-04 36th Ave	718-609-1367		11 pm	Neighborhood café serving Asian-French cuisine.
Lounge 47	47-10 Vernon Blvd	718-937-2044	$$	11 pm	70s décor, solid bar food, nice garden.
Manducatis	13-27 Jackson Ave	718-729-4602	$$$	10 pm	Classic Italian cuisine expertly prepared; a beloved neighborhood institution.
Masso	47-25 Vernon Blvd	718-482-8151	$$	12 am	Simple Italian food in a cozy space.
Tournesol	50-12 Vernon Blvd	718-472-4355	$$$	11:30 pm	Cozy French bistro with a great brunch menu.
Tuk Tuk	49-06 Vernon Blvd	718-472-5598	$$††	11 pm	Thai for beginners.
Water's Edge	44th Dr & East River	718-482-0033	$$$$	11 pm	Upscale American and continental cuisine with views of the skyline.

Map 28 · Greenpoint

Acapulco Deli & Restaurant	1116 Manhattan Ave	718-349-8429	$	10 pm	Authentic Mexican food with some American standards.
Amarin Café	617 Manhattan Ave	718-349-2788	$	10 pm	Good, cheap Thai food.
Baldo's Pizza	175 Nassau Ave	718-349-7770	$$*	10 pm	Pizza; best when delivered.
Bleu Drawes Café	97 Commercial St	718-349-8501	$$		Jamaican home cookin'.
Casanova	338 McGuinness Blvd	718-389-0990	$$	10:30 pm	Italian fare.
Christina's	853 Manhattan Ave	718-383-4382	$*	10 pm	Traditional Polish food, cheap breakfasts!
Dami's	931 Manhattan Ave	718-349-7501	$$	10 pm	Brand new Polish-American joint.
Divine Follie Café	929 Manhattan Ave	718-389-6770	$$	10 pm	Large selection of meats, pastas, and pizza. Small selection of sandwiches.
Enid's	560 Manhattan Ave	718-349-3859	$$††	10 pm	Popular brunch on weekends; just started serving dinners on weeknights.
Erb	681 Manhattan Ave	718-349-8215	$$††	11:30 pm	Try the curry noodles.
Fresca Tortilla	620 Manhattan Ave	718-389-8818	$$	11 pm	Cheap Mexican take-out.
God Bless Deli	818 Manhattan Ave	718-349-0605	$*	24 Hrs	The only 24-hour joint in the 'hood. Cheap sandwiches and burgers.
Imperial Palace	748 Manhattan Ave	718-389-9100	$$	11 pm	Indian food + banquet hall.
Johnny's Café	632 Manhattan Ave	n/a	$$		Home-cooked Polish standards.
Kam Loon	975 Manhattan Ave	718-383-6008	$*	11 pm	Chinese take-out and buffet.
Lamb & Jaffey	1073 Manhattan Ave	718-389-3638	$$	10 pm	Classy date spot.
Lomzynianka	646 Manhattan Ave	718-389-9439	$*	9 pm	Get your kitschy Polish fix dirt cheap.
Manhattan 3 Decker Restaurant	695 Manhattan Ave	718-389-6664	$$	9:30 pm	Greek and American fare.
Monsignor's	905 Lorimer St	718-963-3399	$$	11 pm	Cheap Italian.
Moon Shadow	643 Manhattan Ave	718-6091841	$$*	11 pm	Thai food. Cat Stevens would dig it.
Nassau Pizza	253 Nassau Ave	718-389-2190	$	12 am	Standard pizza and Italian take-out.

Arts & Entertainment · **Restaurants**

Key: $: Under $10 / $$: $10–$20 / $$$: $20–$30 / $$$$: $30–$40 / $$$$$: $40+; * : Cash only / † : Accepts only American Express. / †† Accepts only Visa/Mastercard. Time refers to hour kitchen closes on weekends.

Old Poland Restaurant	190 Nassau Ave	718-349-7775	$*	9:00 pm	Polish/American.
OTT	970 Manhattan Ave	718-609-2416	$	11 pm	Thai.
Relax	68 Newell St	718-389-1665	$*	9:30 pm	Polish diner with good prices and excellent soups—a neighborhood favorite.
San Diego	999 Manhattan Ave	718-389-7747	$$*	11 pm	Mexican kitchen.
Sapporo Haru	622 Manhattan Ave	718-389-9697	$$††	12 am	Fresh sushi, friendly service.
SunView Luncheonette	221 Nassau Ave	718-383-8121	$*	11 pm	Supercheap lunches.
Taco Bite	905 Lorimer St	718-963-3399	$$	11 pm	Walk-up window and delivery.
Thai Café	925 Manhattan Ave	718-383-3562	$*	11 pm	Vast menu, veg options, eat in or take out.
Valdiano	659 Manhattan Ave	718-383-1707	$$*	8:45 pm	Southern Italian.
Wasabi	638 Manhattan Ave	718-609-9368	$$	11:30 pm	Japanese fare.

Map 29 · Williamsburg

Acqua Santa	556 Driggs Ave	718-384-9695	$$	12 am	Bistro Italian—amazing patio.
Allioli	291 Grand St	718-218-7338	$$*	1 am	Tapas heavy on the seafood, w/ live mariachi.
Anna Maria Pizza	179 Bedford Ave	718-599-4550	$	4 am	A must after late-night drinking.
Anytime	93 N 6th St	718-218-7272	$††	4 am	Greasy but good anytime, really.
Aurora	70 Grand St	718-388-5100	$$$*	11 pm	Solid Italian bistro with a great garden.
Bamonte's	32 Withers St	718-384-8831	$$$	11 pm	Historic Italian joint.
Bliss	191 Bedford Ave	718-599-2547	$$*	11 pm	Bland vegetarian with all-vegan options.
Bonita	338 Bedford Ave	718-384-9500	$	12 am	Inexpensive Americanized Mexican in a nice atmosphere. Bring your hot sauce.
Bozu	296 Grand St	718-384-7770	$$††		Japanese tapas and weekend DJs.
Brick Oven Gallery	33 Havemeyer St	718-963-0200	$$	4 am	Gourmet individual pizzas.
Buffalo Cantina	149 Havemeyer St	718-218-7788	$	11 pm	Ameri-Mexican. Anything with carne asada tastes good here.
Café Mexicano	513 Grand St	718-599-7378	$$*		Guacamole to die for.
Diner	86 Broadway	718-486-3077	$$	12 am	Amazing simple food like you've never tasted—never disappoints.
Du Mont	432 Union Ave	718-486-7717	$$††	11 pm	Continually changing market-fresh menu and weekly desserts.
East 88	212 Bedford Ave	718-218-8828	$	12:30 am	Best Chinese food ever.
Fanny	425 Graham Ave	718-389-2060	$$*	11 pm	Cozy French bistro.
Foodswings	295 Grand St	718-388-1919	$$††	2 am	Vegan fast-food joint. For those who like their tofu to taste like meat.
Gottlieb's Restaurant	352 Roebling St	718-384-6612	$$	3 pm	Authentic Kosher deli.
Grand Café	167 Grand St	718-599-7775	$$*	8 pm	Excellent Middle Eastern.
Kellogg's Diner	518 Metropolitan Ave	718-782-4502	$$	24 Hrs	The ultimate diner/deli.
Lodge	318 Grand St	718-486-9400	$$$	1 am	The Adirondacks in Brooklyn; great space, service needs work.
Lola's	454 Graham Ave	718-389-7497	$$	10 pm	Mexican brunch.
Miss Williamsburg Diner	206 Kent Ave	718-963-0802	$$*	4 am	Creative Italian with pannacotta "to die for"!
My Moon	184 N 10th St	718-599-7007	$$	12 am	Turkish delight.
Park Luncheonette	334 Driggs Ave	718-383-3571	$$		Newly remodeled.
Peter Luger Steak House	178 Broadway	718-387-7400	$$$$$*	10:45 pm	Best steak, potatoes, and spinach in this solar system.
Planet Thailand	133 N 7th St	718-599-5758	$$*	2 am	Hyped-up Thai/Japanese in a trendy locale.
Raymund's Place	124 Bedford Ave	718-388-4200	$$*	10 pm	The Polish "Hooters."
Relish	225 Wythe St	718-963-4546	$$	1 am	Comfort food gone eclectic with a touch of class.
Roebling Tea Room	143 Roebling St	718-963-0760	$$$	1 am	Fancy tea eatery.
Sea	114 N 6th St	718-384-8850	$$	1:30 am	Outshines its Manhattan counterpart.
Snacky	187 Grand St	718-486-4848	$$*		Kitschy.
Sparky's/Egg	135A N 5th St	718-302-5151	$$*	12 am	Organic breakfast and free range burgers.
Supercore Café	305 Bedford Ave	718-302-1629	$$$*	12 am	Japanese cuisine, free wireless, no sushi.
Taco Chulo	318 Grand St	718-302-2485	$$††	2 am	"Handmade, decadently pimped out" tacos. Gotta love that!
Teddy's Bar and Grill	96 Berry St	718-384-9787	$††	1 am	Best bar food ever, good beers on tap, hipster and Polish locals unite.
Uncle Mina	436 Union Ave	718-387-0303	$$*	4 am	Fresh Middle Eastern, fast delivery.
Union Picnic	577 Union Ave	718-387-3800	$$	12 am	Southern fried comfort food.
Vera Cruz	195 Bedford Ave	718-599-7914	$$*		Authentic Mexican. Great outdoor garden, fabulous frozen margaritas.
Williamsburg Café	170 Wythe Ave	718-387-5855	$$	12 am	Hearty, unhip food.
Yola's Café	542 Metropolitan Ave	718-486-0757	*		Terrific, authentic Mexican in a claustrophobic atmosphere.

Map 30 · Brooklyn Heights / DUMBO / Downtown

Bubby's	1 Main St	718-222-0666	$$††	11 pm	It's all about the pie.
Chipotle	185 Montague St	718-243-9109	$$††	10 pm	Chain Mexican.
Curry Leaf	151 Remsen St	718-222-3900	$$	10 pm	Terrific Indian food.

DUMBO General Store	111 Front St	718-855-5288	$$*	6 pm	Food and drink for artists.
Fascati Pizzeria	80 Henry St	718-237-1278	$*	11 pm	Inexpensive pizza.
Five Front	5 Front St	718-625-5559	$$	12 am	Tasty newcomer with a beautiful garden.
Grimaldi's	19 Old Fulton St	718-858-4300	$*	11:45 pm	Excellent, though not the best, NY pizza.
Hale & Hearty Soup	32 Court St	718-596-5600	$*	7 pm	Super soups.
Heights Café	84 Montague St	718-625-5555	$$$†	11:30 pm	Decent dining near the Promenade.
Henry's End	44 Henry St	718-834-1776	$$$	11 pm	Inventive, game-oriented menu.
Miso	40 Main St	718-858-8388	$$$	11 pm	Japanese fusion cuisine.
Noodle Pudding	38 Henry St	718-625-3737	$$	11 pm	Excellent Northern Italian fare.
Pete's Downtown	2 Water St	718-858-3510	$$	11 pm	Italian food and a view.
Pig'n Out Barbeque	60 Henry St	718-522-5547	$$	10:30 pm	Perfect pulled pork.
The Plant	25 Jay St	718-722-7541	$$	5 pm	Raw and organic foods.
Rice	81 Washington St	718-222-9880	$$*	11 pm	Tasty Asian for less.
River Café	1 Water St	718-522-5200	$$$$$	11 pm	Great view, but overrated.
Siggy's Good Food	76 Henry St	718-237-3199	$$††	10 pm	Vegan and café.
Superfine	126 Front St	718-243-9005	$$	11 pm	Mediterranean-inspired menu, bi-level bar, local art and music. NFT picks.
Sushi California	71 Clark St	718-222-0308	$$	11 pm	Sushi Express, reasonable prices.
Taco Madre	118 Montague St	718-858-6363	$$	10 pm	Mexican munchies.
Thai 101	101 Montague St	718-237-2594	$$	10:30 pm	Die for this Thai.
Toro Restaurant	1 Front St	718-625-0300	$$	12 am	Spanish-Asian fusion.

Map 31 · Fort Greene / Clinton Hill

1 Greene Sushi and Sashimi	1 Greene Ave	718-422-1000	$$	11 pm	Fresh sushi, familiar standardized setting.
Academy Restaurant	69 Lafayette Ave	718-237-9326	$*	5 pm	Neighborhood diner.
Barncafé, Bam	30 Lafayette Ave	718-636-4100	$$	12 am	Café with live music weekend evenings.
Black Iris	228 DeKalb Ave	718-852-9800	$$*	11:30 pm	Middle Eastern.
Boca Soul	919 Fulton St	718-398-6444	$$*	11 pm	Midpriced Caribbean dining.
Brooklyn Moon Café	745 Fulton St	718-855-7149	*		Food and performance space.
Buff Patty	376 Myrtle Ave	718-855-3266	$$	10 pm	For those in search of curried goat.
Cake Man Raven	708 Fulton St	718-694-2253	$$		Elaborate cakes and confections.
Cambodian Cuisine	87 S Elliot Pl	718-858-3262	$$*	11 pm	Deliciously messy alternative to default Chinese.
Castro's Restaurant	511 Myrtle Ave	718-398-1459	$$	12 am	Burritos delivered con cervesas, if you like.
Chez Oskar	211 DeKalb Ave	718-852-6250	$$$	1 am	French cuisine in a good neighborhood bistro.
Dakar Restaurant	285 Grand Ave	718-398-8900	$$$		Delicious Afro-European food.
Farmer in the Deli	357 Myrtle Ave	718-875-9067	$$*	24 Hrs	Sandwiches well worth scary corner vibe outside.
Gia	68 Lafayette Ave	718-246-1755	$$*		Stylish two-level bistro.
Good Joy Chinese Takeout	216 DeKalb Ave	718-858-8899	$*	12 am	Best Chinese takeout.
Habana Outpost	755 Fulton St	718-230-8238	*		Grilled corn and free movies in a solar-powered restaurant.
Ici	246 DeKalb Ave	718-789-2778	$$$	11 pm	Beautiful new addition to FG restaurant scene, and worth the splurge.
Joloff Restaurant	930 Fulton St	718-636-4011	$$*	10:30 pm	Plain rice splendorized by West African sauces.
Kush	17 Putnam Ave	718-230-3471	$$	12 am	West African café and restaurant.
Locanda Vini & Olii	129 Gates Ave	718-622-9202	$$		Rustic Italian, a neighborhood favorite.
LouLou	222 DeKalb Ave	718-246-0633	$$$		Rustic Breton/French gem where seafood rules.
Luz	177 Vanderbilt Ave	718-246-4000	$$$	12 am	Yuppie interior with requisite brunch.
Madiba	195 DeKalb Ave	718-855-9190	$$$	12 am	South African—Bunny Chow, need we say more? Shebeen with live music.
Maggie Brown	455 Myrtle Ave	718-643-7001	$$	12 am	Food by the fireplace.
Mario's Pizzeria	224 DeKalb Ave	718-260-9520	$*	11 pm	The place to go for a slice.
Mo-Bay	112 DeKalb Ave	718-246-2800	$	11 pm	Caribbean/soul/bakery.
Mojito Restaurant	82 Washington St	718-797-3100	$$	12 am	Classy Cuban cuisine.
New Orleans	747 Fulton St	718-596-6333	$$$	12 am	Southern creole—a menu named desire.
Night of the Cookers	767 Fulton St	718-797-1197	$$$	12 am	Hip bistro with southern accents.
Olea	171 Lafayette Ave	718-643-7003	$$	12 am	Retooled Mediterranean.
Pequena	86 S Portland Ave	718-643-0000	$$*	12 am	Killer quesadillas.
Pratt Coffee Shop	274 Hall St	718-622-0185	$*	7:30 pm	Not just for students anymore.
Rice	166 DeKalb Ave	718-858-2700	$$*	11 pm	Tasty Asian for less.
Ruthie's Restaurant	96 DeKalb Ave	718-246-5189	$$*	11 pm	Soul food in mega portions.
Scopello	63 Lafayette Ave	718-852-1100	$$		Sicilian chic in stylish surroundings.
Thai 101	455 Myrtle Ave	718-855-4615	$$		Die for this Thai.
Thomas Beisl	25 Lafayette Ave	718-222-5800	$$$†	12 am	Excellent pre-Bam complement. Recently expanded with glassed-in dining annex.
Veliis	773 Fulton St	718-596-9070	$$††	12 am	Dainty Viennese vittles good for a date night.

Map 32 · BoCoCa / Red Hook

360	360 Van Brunt St	718-246-0360	$$$$*	11:30 pm	Nouveaux French; excellent and pricey.
Alma	187 Columbia St	718-643-5400	$$$	11 pm	Top NYC Mexican with great views of lower Manhattan.
Atlantic Chip Shop	129 Atlantic Ave	718-855-7775	$$	11 pm	Heart attack on a plate.
Bar Tabac	128 Smith St	718-923-0918	$$$†	3 am	Open late; fabulous frites.
Bouillabaisse 126	126 Union St	718-855-4405	$$$	11 pm	Outstanding crab cakes!
Café Luluc	214 Smith St	718-625-3815	$$$*	1 am	Friendly French bistro.

389

Key: $: Under $10 / $$: $10–$20 / $$$: $20–$30 / $$$$: $30–$40 / $$$$$: $40+; *: Cash only / †: Accepts only American Express. / †† Accepts only Visa/Mastercard. Time refers to hour kitchen closes on weekends.

Map 32 · BoCoCa / Red Hook—continued

Café on Clinton	268 Clinton St	718-625-5908	$$	11 pm	Excellent neighborhood spot—great vibe, food, and service.
Chance	223 Smith St	718-242-1515	$$$$	12 am	Upscale Asian fusion—recommended.
Chicory	243 DeGraw St	718-797-2121	$	10 pm	Gavin McAleer kicks major ass. Everything here is awesome!
Cobble Grill	212 DeGraw St	718-422-0099	$*	10 pm	Tasty sandwiches and salads for takeout.
Cubana Café	272 Smith St	718-858-3980	$$*	11 pm	Colorful, authentic Cuban—lively staff.
Cube 63	234 Court St	718-243-2208	$$$††		Manhattan sushi arrives on Cobble Hill.
Damascus Bread & Pastry	195 Atlantic Ave	718-625-7070	$	7 pm	Family bakery since 1930.
Delicatessen	264 Clinton St	718-852-1991	$$*	8 pm	Ready to go dinners @ 3pm, Euro deli.
Donut House	314 Court St	718-852-1162	$*		A classic greasy spoon. Don't get the donuts.
El Portal	297 Smith St	718-246-1416	$*	11 pm	Killer breaded steak.
Faan	209 Smith St	718-694-2277	$†	11:30 pm	Pan-Asian in a chic setting.
Fatoosh	330 Hicks St	718-243-0500	$*	7:00 pm	Nicely priced Middle Eastern Food.
Ferdinando's	151 Union St	718-855-1545	$*	10 pm	Sicilian specialties you won't find anywhere else! Get the panelle special.
Fragole	394 Court St	718-522-7133	$$	11:30 pm	Fresh and cozy Italian. An absolute gem.
Frankie's 457	457 Court St	718-403-0033	$$*	12 am	Fantastic meatballs. Cool space.
Gravy	100 Smith St	n/a	$*	12 am	Southern-style diner, open late, not good yet.
The Grocery	288 Smith St	718-596-3335	$$$$$††	11 pm	Magnificent. Reservations recommended.
Hill Diner	231 Court St	718-522-2220	$$††		We liked it better before the renovations, but the breakfast still rocks.
Hope & Anchor	347 Van Brunt St	718-237-0276	$$	12 am	Great upscale diner.
Joya	215 Court St	718-222-3484	$$*	12 am	Excellent, inexpensive, but super-noisy Thai.
Le Petite Café	502 Court St	718-596-7060	$$*		Great Bistro food—check out the garden.
Liberty Heights Tap Room	34 Van Dyke St	718-246-8050	$$	12 am	Brick oven restaurant and bar.
Osaka	272 Court St	718-643-0044	$$	12 am	Best sushi in BoCoCa.
Panino'teca 275	275 Smith St	718-237-2728	$$	12 am	Great paninis and fab cheese lasagna.
Patois	255 Smith St	718-855-1535	$$$$	11:30 pm	French bistro. Killer brunch.
Royal's Downtown	215 Union St	718-923-9866	$$*	11 pm	Upscale dining with a fireplace. NFT pick.
Savoia	277 Smith St	718-797-2727	$$†		Cozy Italian. Great individual pizzas.
Schnack	122 Union St	718-855-2879	$*	2 am	Greasy goodness.
Sherwood Café	195 Smith St	718-596-1609	$$*	1 am	Mellow French vibe—best croque in town.
Siam Garden	172 Court St	718-596-9338	$	10:30 pm	Good Brooklyn Thai.
Soul Spot	302 Atlantic Ave	718-596-9933	$$††	11 pm	American and Afro-Caribbean soul food.
Tuk Tuk	204 Smith St	718-222-5598	$$*	12 am	Authentic Thai—excellent curries.
Zaytoons	283 Smith St	718-875-1880	$$	12 am	Excellent Middle Eastern pizzas and kebabs.

Map 33 · Park Slope / Prospect Heights / Windsor Terrace

12th Street Bar and Grill	1123 Eighth Ave	718-965-9526	$$$	12 am	Outstanding gourmet comfort fare.
16th St Gourmet	21 Prospect Park W	718-369-6196	$$*	10 pm	Tiny stand for cheap falafel.
2nd Street Café	189 Seventh Ave	718-369-6928	$$	10:30 pm	Clamoring brunch crowd.
Al Di La Trattoria	248 Fifth Ave	718-783-4565	$$$	11 pm	Chandelier, brick-walled Italian.
Anthony's	426 Seventh Ave	718-369-8315	$$	12 am	New neighborhood fave for brick-oven 'za.
Applewood	501 11th St	718-768-2044	$$$	11 pm	Elegant, cheerful slow food.
Beast	638 Bergen St	718-399-6855	$$$	11:30 pm	American tapas.
Beet	344 Seventh Ave	718-832-2338	$$$	11 pm	Romantic ambiance for sumptuous Thai.
Beso	210 Fifth Ave	718-783-4902	$	11 pm	Great South American, good breakfast too.
Black Pearl	883 Union St	718-857-2004	$$$	12 am	Gourmet Italian.
Blue Ribbon Brooklyn	280 Fifth Ave	718-840-0404	$$$$$	4 am	The one and only!
Bogota Latin Bistro	141 Fifth Ave	718-230-3805	$$$	1 am	Stylish South- and Central-American restaurant.
Bonnie's Grill	278 Fifth Ave	718-369-9527	$$		Habit-forming contemporary diner.
Brooklyn Fish Camp	162 Fifth Ave	718-783-3264	$$$	11 pm	Mary's Fish Camp redux.
Café Steinhof	422 Seventh Ave	718-369-7776	$$	11 pm	Goulash Mondays: $5! German beers.
ChipShop	383 Fifth Ave	718-832-7701	$*	11 pm	Brit boys dish fish, chips, and The Beatles.
Christie's Jamaican Patties	334 Flatbush Ave	718-636-9746	$*	10 pm	Jamaican destination.
Coco Roco	392 Fifth Ave	718-965-3376	$$	11:30 pm	Inexpensive Peruvian.
Convivium Osteria	68 Fifth Ave	718-857-1833	$$$$†	11 pm	Fabulous Portuguese; rustic, warm setting.
Cousin John's Café and Bakery	70 Seventh Ave	718-622-7333	$	11 pm	Delicious Italian with a Portugese influence.
Dizzy's	511 Ninth St	718-499-1966	$$*	10 pm	Excellent brunch.
Elora's	272 Prospect Park W	718-788-6190	$$	11:45 pm	Spanish, Mexican, and Margaritas, oh my!
Franny's	295 Flatbush Ave	718-230-0221	$$$††	11:30 pm	Brilliant pizza, drop-dead fresh, NFT fave.
Garden Café	620 Vanderbilt Ave	718-857-8863	$$$		Small, semi-formal, intimate, delicious.
Gourmet Grill	291 Fifth Ave	718-369-3456	$$†		Health food made the unhealthy way.
Jack's	519 Fifth Ave	718-965-8675	$$	11 pm	Meatloaf by day, bluegrass by night.
Java Indonesian Rijsttafel	455 Seventh Ave	718-832-4583	$$	11 pm	Mom-and-Pop Indonesian, natch!
Johnny Mack's	1114 Eighth Ave	718-832-7961	$$	11 pm	Neighborhood bar and grill with sidewalk seating.
Junior's Restaurant	386 Flatbush Ave	718-852-5257	$	2 am	American with huge portions.
Kinara	473 Fifth Ave	718-499-3777	$$*	11 pm	Vegetarian and meat friendly meals.
La Taqueria	72 Seventh Ave	718-398-4300	$	10 pm	Popular, penny-wise burritos.

Long Tan	196 Fifth Ave	718-622-8444	$$		Spartan Vietnamese goes mod.
Los Pollitos II	148 Fifth Ave	718-623-9152	$	11 pm	Chicken that dreams are made of.
Maria's Mexican Bistro	669 Union St	718-638-2344	$$	11:30 pm	Well worth the trek down to Fourth Ave.
Mitchell's Soul Food	617 Vanderbilt Ave	718-789-3212	$*		Seedy, cheap soul food.
The Minnow	442 9th St	718-832-5500	$$	11 pm	Excellent surf, not so good on the turf.
Nana	155 Fifth Ave	718-230-3749	$$*	12 am	Absolutely delicious Pan-Asian.
New Prospect Café	393 Flatbush Ave	718-638-2148	$$		Try the corn and shrimp chowder.
Olive Vine Café	362 15th St	718-499-0555	$*		Tasty Middle Eastern fare.
Olive Vine Café	54 Seventh Ave	718-636-4333	$*	11 pm	Crispy Mediterranean pizzas.
Parkside Restaurant	355 Flatbush Ave	718-636-1190	$$	11:30 pm	Standard diner fare.
Red Hot	349 Seventh Ave	718-369-0700	$$	11 pm	Fake meat for vegetarians who like to pretend.
Rice	311 Seventh Ave	718-832-9512	$$††	12 am	Yummy Thai; great lunch specials.
Rose Water	787 Union St	718-783-3800	$$$	11 pm	Intimate, airy Mediterranean.
Santa Fe Grill	62 Seventh Ave	718-636-0279	$$††		Dinner? Chips, salsa, and icy pi–as!
Seventh Avenue Donut Shop	324 Seventh Ave	718-768-0748	$$*	24 Hrs	Dirt-cheap diner goodness.
Sotto Voce	225 Seventh Ave	718-369-9322	$$††	12 am	Italian cuisine with better brunch options.
Stone Park Café	324 Fifth Ave	718-369-0082	$$$$	11 pm	A contender for best Park Slope dining. NFT pick.
Sushi Tatsu	347 Flatbush Ave	718-622-8688	$$	11:30 pm	A breath of Japan on busy Flatbush.
Tom's	782 Washington Ave	718-636-9738	$$*	4 am	Old-school mom-and-pop diner since 1936. A cholesterol love affair.
Tost	427 Seventh Ave	718-965-1075	$$††		Sophisticated winebar with perfect paninis.
Tutta Pasta	160 Seventh Ave	718-788-9500	$$	12 am	Sidewalk seating, dependable penne.
Two Boots	514 2nd St	718-499-3253	$$	11 pm	Kid-friendly pizza and Cajun. Live music.
Windsor Café	220 Prospect Park W	718-788-9700	$$	11 pm	American diner with something for everyone.

Map 34 · Hoboken

Amanda's	908 Washington St	201-798-0101	$$$$$	11 pm	New American. Brunch.
Arthur's Tavern	237 Washington St	201-656-5009	$$$*	12 am	The best steak for the price.
Baja	104 14th St	201-653-0610	$$	11:30 pm	Good Mexican food, great sangria.
Bangkok City	335 Washington St	201-792-6613	$$*	11:30 pm	A taste of Thai.
Biggies Clam Bar	318 Madison St	201-656-2161	$*		Boardwalk fare and perfect raw clams.
Brass Rail	135 Washington St	201-659-7074	$$$	11 pm	You can't beat the brunch deal.
Cucharamama	233 Clinton St	201-420-1700	$$$		Great Cuban and South American.
Delfino's	500 Jefferson St	201-792-7457	$$*	10:30 pm	Pizza joint. Plus red speckled table cloths. BYO Chianti. The real thing.
East LA	508 Washington St	201-798-0052	$$	11 pm	Knock-your-socks-off margaritas.
Far Side Bar & Grill	531 Washington St	201-963-7677	$$	3:00 am	Hoboken's best pub food. Try the steak salad.
Frankie & Johnnie's	163 14th St	201-659-6202	$$$$$	11 pm	Power steakhouse. Look out for Tony Soprano.
Gaslight	400 Adams St	201-217-1400	$$*		Off the main drag, neighborhood Italian, cozy and cute. Quiz nights and comedy.
Hoboken Gourmet Company	423 Washington St	201-795-0110	$$*	8:30 pm	Hoboken's one true café. Rustic, yummy, quirky.
Karma Kafe	505 Washington St	201-610-0900	$$*	11:30 pm	Ultra-friendly Tibetan staff, hip Indian food with a wild mix of flavors.
La Isla	104 Washington St	201-659-8197	$$	10 pm	A genuine taste of Havana.
La Tarturtería	1405 Grand St	201-792-2300	$$$	11 pm	Modern, imaginative, Northern Italian fare, specializing in truffle dishes.
Robongi	520 Washington St	201-222-8388	$$	11:30 pm	Good sushi, friendly chefs, fun specials.
Sushi Lounge	200 Hudson St	201-386-1117	$$$	12 am	Popular, upscale sushi spot.
Trattoria Saporito	328 Washington St	201-533-1801	$$$	10:30 pm	Lacks the old world Italian charm but has the old world taste and service. BYOB.
Zafra	301 Willow Ave	201-610-9801	$$	11 pm	BYO wine—they'll magically turn it into sangria.

Map 35 · Jersey City

Amelia's Bistro	187 Warren St	201-332-2200	$$	11 pm	Try the crab cakes.
Casablanca Grill	354 Grove St	201-420-4072	$$*	11 pm	Moroccan.
Ibby's Falafel	303 Grove St	201-432-2400	$	12 am	One of the few JC restaurants open after 11pm.
Iron Monkey	97 Greene St	201-435-5756	$$$	3 am	Quiet and romantic with great rooftop terrace.
Kitchen Café	60 Sussex St	201-332-1010	$$*	9 pm	The Great American breakfast.
Komegashi	103 Montgomery St	201-433-4567	$$$	10:30 pm	Authentic Japanese restaurant and sushi bar.
Komegashi Too	99 Pavonia Ave	201-533-8888	$$$	10:30 pm	The other Komegashi.
Light Horse Tavern	199 Washington St	201-946-2028	$$$	11 pm	New American for brunch, lunch, and dinner.
Madame Claude	364 4th St	201-876-8800	$$$	11 pm	French café.
Marco and Pepe	289 Grove St	201-860-9688	$$$	11 pm	Small, painfully hip French restaurant.
Miss Saigon	249 Newark Ave	201-239-1988	$††	10:30 pm	Authentic and cheap Vietnamese fare.
Oddfellows Restaurant	111 Montgomery St	201-433-6999	$$	11 pm	Authentic Cajun. Good happy hour specials.
Presto's Restaurant	199 Warren St	201-433-6639	$$	9:30 pm	Italian BYOB.
Pronto Cena	87 Sussex St	201-435-0004	$$$	11 pm	Italian.
Rosie Radigans	10 Exchange Pl , Lobby	201-451-5566	$	11 pm	Excellent after work venue—terrific food, friendly bar crowd.
Saigon Café	188 Newark St	201-332-8711	$$	11 pm	Serves quality Southeast Asian cuisine.
Tania's	348 Grove St	201-451-6189	$$	10 pm	Home cooked Eastern European food.
Uno Chicago Bar & Grill	286 Washington St	201-395-9500	$$	1 am	All-American eatery with family atmosphere.

391

In New York City, why does it seem impossible to return to your apartment without carrying some kind of bag…something you've inevitably purchased while you were out? Because New York's longstanding reputation as a fabulous place to shop is well deserved. From haute couture to vintage clothing, from house and garden to cars and sporting goods, you would be hard pressed to name something you couldn't purchase in this town. But, unlike shopping at a boring, generic shopping mall with nothing but mass-market retailers and cold marble floors, New York is an exciting, sometimes even unpredictable place to shop. Where else can you buy live eel, a Victorian tea gown, and a Sopranos-style tracksuit jacket with the words "Bada Bing" emblazoned on the back—all within the same neighborhood? Yeah, we know some folks groan that there are more Ann Taylors and Banana Republics on the street corners than there used to be, but if we combine the convenience of the mass-market retailers with the many quirky, über-hip, independent retailers we have, the broad range of choices that we New Yorkers often take for granted is what makes our city arguably the best shopping destination in the world.

Clothing

For the best of the haute couture labels, head for the area around Madison Avenue and Fifth Avenue in the 50s, 60s, and 70s. There you will find the likes of **Chanel (Map 12)**, **Donna Karan (Map 15)**, **Yves St. Laurent (Map 15)**, **Armani (Map 16)**, and **Gucci (Map 12)**. For department store shopping, try **Bloomingdale's (Map 3, Map 15)**, **Macy's (Map 9)**, **Lord & Taylor (Map 9)**, and (for those with a little extra cash) **Saks Fifth Avenue (Map 12)**, **Bergdorf Goodman (Map 12)**, **Henri Bendel (Map 12)**, and **Barneys (Map 15)**. If you have the patience to deal with the crowds and to sift through the merchandise to find the real bargains, **Century 21 (Map 1)** could yield great rewards of name brand clothing, shoes, make-up, accessories, and home wares at significantly discounted prices. For wonderfully cheap and trendy duds, **H&M (Map 19)** can't be beat. This Swedish department store chain offers unbelievably hip fashion (like bubble skirts and mini-kilts) at almost throwaway prices. (In some cases, it might cost you more to get an item dry cleaned than it would to just buy a new one!) Choose from several Manhattan locations including SoHo, Harlem, and Midtown.

In SoHo, the past several years have seen the area transformed from what was once populated with nothing but small clothing boutiques and art galleries to an incredibly popular tourist destination that is home to the shops of several big name designers such as **Prada (Map 6)**, **DKNY (Map 6, Map 15)**, **Tommy Hilfiger (Map 6)**, **BCBG (Map 6)**, and **Ralph Lauren (Map 6, Map 15)**, as well as specialists like **Coach (Map 6)**. To get a gander at many designers under one roof, be sure to visit the fairly new SoHo branch of **Bloomingdale's (Map 3)**, which carries an exclusive, decidedly "downtown" collection. If your wallet is a little lighter, you'll also find a good cross-section of "middle of the road" stores such as **Banana Republic (Map 16)**, **Benetton (Map 16)** and **French Connection (Map 6)**, as well as many street vendors selling everything from handmade jewelry to floppy-eared children's hats. SoHo is a great area

for browsing and strolling, with Sullivan and Thompson Streets offering a glimpse of the smaller boutiques that once occupied the area.

The West Village is another great area for shopping. Hip purveyors of cool "downtown" style, like **Marc Jacobs (Map 5)**, **Stella McCartney (Map 5)**, and **Lulu Guinness (Map 9)** have stores here. Some say that they're part of the reason the area became such a happening hotspot. By venturing a tad northwest to the Meatpacking District, you can check out the punk rock-inspired styles of **Alexander McQueen (Map 5)**, as well as the deliciously avant-garde (but wildly expensive) department store **Jeffrey (Map 5)**. For fashions from up-and-coming designers and lots of cool independent boutiques, check out: NoHo (the area north of Houston and east of Broadway), NoLita (north of Little Italy), and the East Village (just don't expect any cheap finds—their prices compare with those at the fancier label stores).

The Upper East Side (particularly along Madison Avenue in the late 80s) has a notable amount of designer consignment stores. These shops sell gently worn items from top tier designers like Chanel and Armani at a fraction of their original cost. A few worth checking out include: **Michael's The Consignment Shop for Women (Map 15)**, **Encore (Map 15)**, and **Bis Designer Resale (Map 15)**. It is also worth meandering along "Thrift Row," a string of Upper East Side thrift shops on and near Third Avenue in the East 70s and 80s. Many of these shops, such as **Memorial Sloan-Kettering Thrift Shop (Map 15)** and the **Spence-Chapin Thrift Shop (Map 15, Map 17)**, carry a nice selection of designer clothing—not to mention the added bonus that the proceeds from your purchases go toward a good cause, like AIDS-related charities, cancer research, and adoption programs.

Vintage Shopping

It's probably no shock to read that New York City has lots of vintage clothing shops—but did you know that there are more than 60 of them? For anyone who's been bitten by the vintage bug, New York is a veritable candyland when it comes to seeking out the threads and accessories of yesteryear. Most New Yorkers (even those who know very little about vintage shopping) know that there is a dense population of vintage shops in areas like the East Village (**The Hanger Bar & Boutique (Map 7)**, **Fabulous Fanny's (Map 6)**), the West Village (**Cherry (Map 5)**), the Lower East Side (**Frock (Map 7)**, **Peggy Pardon (Map 7)**), NoHo (**Screaming Mimi's (Map 6)**, **Eye Candy (Map 6)**), NoLita (**Resurrection Vintage (Map 6)**), SoHo (**What Comes Around Goes Around (Map 2)**, **Chelsea Girl (Map 6)**), Chelsea (**Family Jewels (Map 9)**, **Jim Smiley Vintage (Map 9)**), as well as in the hip Brooklyn 'hoods of Williamsburg (**Beacon's Closet**, **Calliope**, **Amarcord Vintage Fashion**) and Park Slope (**Beacon's Closet**, **Hootie Couture**). But those aren't the only areas where vintage clothing boutiques can be found. Contrary to the common belief that the Upper East and Upper West Sides are completely lacking when it comes to cool shopping options, there are a number of vintage clothing shops uptown—some of which have only recently opened their doors (which usually means that they have fresh merchandise and aren't too "picked over"). On the Upper East Side, check out **New York Vintage Club (Map 13)**, **Vintage Collections (Map 15)**, and **M.A.D. Vintage Couture & Designer Resale (Map 17)**—and don't forget the twice-yearly vintage couture and textiles auction at Doyle New York **(Map 17)**. On the Upper West Side, longtime vintage purveyor **Allan & Suzi (Map 14)** still holds court at the corner of Amsterdam and 80th Street. For those who still can't get enough vintage, be sure to attend the thrice-yearly **Manhattan Vintage Clothing Show** at the Metropolitan Pavilion, where over 75 dealers sell their vintage finery during 2-day stints. And for die-hards, there's always the **Triple Pier Antiques Show** on the far West Side of Manhattan. The prices at all of the above-mentioned shops and venues run quite a bit higher than if you were to go out to the sticks of North Carolina or Texas to buy the same items. Of course, the convenience of being able to buy vintage in the city makes the heftier price tag well worth it.

Flea Markets, Street Fairs & Bazaars

New Yorkers who once spent weekends perusing the eclectic finds scattered atop the asphalt lot at 26th Street and Sixth Avenue are still mourning the loss of the internationally known **Annex Antique Fair & Flea Market**. It turns out that a residential building will be going up in its place. The good news is that many of the same vendors from Annex now sell their wares at the **Hell's Kitchen Flea Market** on 39th Street between Ninth and Tenth Avenues. There are, of course, many other (albeit smaller) flea markets throughout the city, as well as numerous street fairs in various neighborhoods during warmer months. The best way to find them is to accidentally stumble upon them during one of those lovely long walks when you're exploring the city—whether it be an area you've never been to before or four blocks from your apartment. A fantastic indoor flea market to add to your must-see list is **The Market NYC (Map 6)**, a refreshingly offbeat collection from young, local designers who aren't afraid to be truly creative. In fact, some of the same designers selling at The Market also have booths at the relatively new **Edge*ny NOHO (Map 6)**, a Bleecker Street boutique showcasing local designers' creations. These places are great cure-alls for retail boredom and/or the unfortunate, but inevitable "H&M sale effect" when every third person is wearing the same shirt as you.

Sports

Paragon Sporting Goods (Map 9) in Union Square is hard to beat as a one-stop shop for all things sporting. The challenge is to find a recreation *not* listed on the store directory! For outdoor gear, try **Eastern Mountain Sports (Map 6, Map 14)**, **Sports Authority (Map 9, Map 13)**, **Foot Locker (Map 21, Map 25)**, and **Modell's (Map 1, Map 3, Map 13, Map 23)** provide a broad range of affordable sports clothing, shoes, and athletic equipment. **Blades Board & Skate (Map 6, Map 17)** features groovy

gear for boarding (both the wheeled and snow varieties) as well as a good selection of the latest equipment for these activities.

Housewares and Home Design

You can lose hours in **ABC Carpet & Home (Map 9)** just off of Union Square. Their exotic array of furniture and other furnishings (much of it antique and imported from Asia and Europe) is fun to look at, even if you can't afford the steep prices. **Crate and Barrel (Map 12)**, **Fish's Eddy (Map 9, Map 14, Map 15)**, **Pottery Barn (Map 13)**, and **Bed Bath & Beyond (Map 9, Map 14, Map 15)** all are good housewares stores with a wide selection of styles and prices. For cheap kitchen outfits, try some of the restaurant supply places on Bowery. For paint, window dressings, and other home decorating supplies, try Janovic **(Map 2, Map 5, Map 9, Map 11, Map 14, Map 15, Map 16)**. Experience the sensory overload of home design after wandering through over 200,000 square feet of commercial and residential furnishings at the **A&D Building (Map 13)**. While most folks shopping there are likely interior designers, the showrooms are open to the public. So why wait to plan how you would fix up the home of your dreams? After all, the only thing standing in your way is a winning lottery ticket!

Electronics

J&R (Map 3) provides most things electronic, including computers and accessories, iPods, games, cameras, music equipment, CDs, DVDs, and household appliances. **B&H (Map 8)** is another great place for photographic, audio, and video equipment. It's worth a visit just to witness the pure spectacle of this well-coordinated operation, as well as the outstanding selection of gear. Top-end audiophiles are wonderfully served by **Stereo Exchange (Map 6)** and the jaw-dropping, price-busting **Sound by Singer (Map 9)**. Other places to shop for electronics include the SoHo **Apple (Map 6)** store, **Circuit City (Map 6)**, **Radio Shack (many locations)**, **DataVision (Map 9)**, and **Best Buy (Map 17)**.

Food

If the way to a person's heart is through their stomach, then no wonder we all love New York! Try the tasty British delights at **Myers of Keswick (Map 5)** in the West Village, **East Village Cheese (Map 6)** in the East Village, **Sullivan Street Bakery (Map 6)** in SoHo, **Zabar's (Map 14)**, **Beard Papa Sweets**, and **Dale and Thomas Popcorn** on the Upper West Side, **Dylan's Candy Bar (Map 15)**, **Eli's Vinegar Factory (Map 17)**, and **Schaller & Weber (Map 17)** on the Upper East Side, and **Settepani (Map 19)** for delicious baked goods in Harlem. The gigantic **Whole Foods (Map 14)** in the AOL/Time Warner Center would even please Martha Stewart. The introduction of online ordering and home delivery from **Fresh Direct** has brought New Yorker's a whole new level of convenience, with the highest quality fresh food delivered right to their doors. You can even specify a two-hour time frame for delivery. It doesn't get a great deal better than that!

Art Supplies

Running low on Cadmium Red? Use your last stick of charcoal drawing a nude? The best art stores in NYC are scattered loosely around the SoHo area, with **Pearl Paint (Map 3, Map 10)** being the most well known. Located where Mercer and Canal Streets meet, the store occupies a full six-story building with every type of art supply you can imagine, including a great separate frame shop out back on Lispenard. Closer to NYU and Cooper Union, you can find the best selection of paper at both **New York Central Art Supply (Map 6)** on Third Avenue. Farther north on Fourth Ave is **Utrecht (Map 6)**, selling more than just the products with their name. **SoHo Art Materials (Map 3)** on Grand Street is a small, traditional shop that sells super premium paints and brushes for fine artists. Don't forget to check out both **Sam Flax (Map 9, Map 13)** and **A.I. Friedman (Map 9)** in the Flatiron area—both great for graphic design supplies, portfolios, and gifts. Should you find yourself on the Upper East Side needing art supplies in a pinch, the fairly decent selection at **Blacker & Kooby (Map 17)** will do just fine.

As the art scene has made its way to Williamsburg, having an art supply store close by is as important as a good supermarket (something folks in the 'burg are still waiting for). **Artist & Craftsman (Map 29)** on North 8th is a good bet for supplies.

*Remember to flash that student ID card if you've got it, as most art stores offer a decent discount!

Music Equipment & Instruments

There are as many starving musicians as there are artists in NYC, but that doesn't keep them from finding ways to fulfill their equipment needs. New York's large and vibrant music scene supports a thriving instrument trade. To buy a new tuba or get that banjo tuned, head over to 48th Street. You'll find the largest, most well-known stores, from generalist shops such as **Manny's (Map 12)** and **Sam Ash (Map 12)**, to more specialized shops like **Roberto's Woodwind Repair (Map 12)**. Just two blocks away, on 46th, you can delight in two shops dedicated solely to drummers—**Manhattan Drum Shop (Map 9)** and **Drummer's World (Map 12)**.

If you can't take the bustle of the Times Square area and are looking for used, vintage, or just plain cool, then you'll want to shop elsewhere. Some of our favorites include: **East Village Music (Map 6)**, **First Flight (Map 7)**, **30th Street Guitars (Map 9)**, **Rogue Music (Map 9)**, and **Ludlow Guitars (Map 7)**. We're also surprisingly impressed with the nice salespeople at the **Guitar Center (Map 6)** on 14th Street.

For an exquisite purchase where money is no object, pick up a grand piano at **Klavierhaus (Map 12)** or a Strat at **Matt Umanov (Map 5)**.

The best remaining place for sheet music is still the **Joseph Patelson Music House (Map 12)**.

Music for Listening

NYC is a hotbed for music lovers, and its record stores house the best and the worst of what the world has to offer. Whether you're shopping for that Top Ten hit or a rare piece of '70s vinyl, your options for finding it are expansive. For those who like to dig, there's **Kim's Mediapolis (Map 18)**, where you're sure to find something to fill that void in your record collection. If you're not up for the smaller indie shops, head to **J&R Music World (Map 3)**, **Tower (Map 6, Map 14)**, or the **Virgin Megastore (Map 6)**, and be prepared to spend at least a good chunk of your paycheck.

The smaller stores carry more eclectic selections and, more often than not, the staff can help you out with musical queries. Head to **Footlight** in the East Village and you'll see what we're talking about. If you're not convinced, try **Other Music (Map 6)** and **Earwax (Brooklyn)**—two stores with unique vibes.

If all else fails, stroll down Bleecker Street to **Rebel Rebel (Map 5)**, **Kim's Underground (Map 6)**, and **Bleecker Street Records (Map 5)**.

Shopping "Districts"

Manhattan is famous for its shopping districts—a conglomeration of shops in one area where you go to find what you're looking for. Hit up the **Garment District** (25th to 40th Sts, Fifth to Ninth Aves) for buttons and zippers, rickrack and ribbons; all the ingredients you'll need to fashion your own frocks. Attention men: The **Diamond and Jewelry District** (W 47th between Fifth and Sixth Aves), the world's largest market for diamonds, the **Flower District** (26th to 29th Sts, along and off Sixth Ave), and the **Perfume District** (along and off Broadway in the West 20s and 30s) are where to go to make her swoon. **Music Row** (48th St between Sixth & Seventh Aves) is where to buy that accordion you've been meaning to try. The Bowery south of Houston is another well-known strip where you'll find the **Kitchenware District** for all your culinary endeavors, the **Lighting District** (past Delancey St) for all your illuminating needs, and the **Downtown Jewelry District** (turn the corner of Bowery to Canal St) for the more exotic baubles you can't get uptown. The **Flatiron District** (from 14th to 34th Sts, Sixth & Park Aves) is a home furnishing mecca. Book Row (between 9th and 14th Sts) is sadly no more. What was once an assemblage of over 25 bookstores, now houses only the famous Strand Book Store and Alabaster Used Books, both tome troves unto themselves.

Map 1 • Financial District

Barclay Rex	75 Broad St	212-962-3355	For all your smoking needs.
Century 21	22 Cortlandt St	212-227-9092	Where most New Yorkers buy their underwear.
Christopher Norman Chocolates	60 New St	212-402-1243	Sweet chocolate shop.
Flowers of the World	80 Pine St	212-425-2234, 800-770-3125	Fulfill any feeling, mood, budget, or setting.
Godiva Chocolatier	33 Maiden Ln	212-809-8990	Everyone needs a fix now and then.
Modell's	200 Broadway	212-566-3711	Generic sporting goods.
Radio Shack	114 Fulton St	212-732-1904	Kenneth, what is the frequency?
Radio Shack	9 Broadway	212-482-8138	Kenneth, what is the frequency?
South Street Seaport	19 Fulton St		Mall with historic ships as backdrop.
The World of Golf	189 Broadway	212-385-1246	Stop here on your way to Briar Cliff Manor.
Yankees Clubhouse Shop	8 Fulton St	212-514-7182	25 and counting…

Map 2 • TriBeCa

Assets London	152 Franklin St	212-219-8777	Ultra-Mod British fashions for her.
Babylonica	51 Hudson St	212-406-7440	Children's store with clothing and educational toys.
Balloon Saloon	133 West Broadway	212-227-3838	We love the name.
Bazzini	339 Greenwich St	212-334-1280	Nuts to you!
Bell Bates Natural Food	97 Reade St	212-267-4300	No MSG?
Boffi SoHo	31 1/2 Greene St	212-431-8282	Hi-end kitchen and bath design.
Canal Street Bicycles	417 Canal St	212-334-8000	Bike messenger mecca.
Duane Park Patisserie	179 Duane St	212-274-8447	Yummy!
Gotham Bikes	112 West Broadway	212-732-2453	Super helpful staff, good stuff.
Issey Miyake	119 Hudson St	212-226-0100	Flagship store of this designer.
Jack Spade	56 Greene St	212-625-1820	Barbie's got Ken, Kate's got Jack. Men's bags.
Janovic	136 Church St	212-349-0001	Top NYC paint store.
Kings Pharmacy	5 Hudson St	212-791-3100	Notary Public - discount days!
Korin Japanese Trading	57 Warren St	212-587-7021	Supplier to Japanese chefs and restaurants.
Let There Be Neon	38 White St	212-226-4883	Neon gallery and store.
Lucky Brand Dungarees	38 Greene St	212-625-0707	Lucky you.
MarieBelle's Fine Treats & Chocolates	484 Broome St	212-925-6999	Top NYC chocolatier.
New York Nautical	158 Duane	212-962-4522	Armchair sailing.
Oliver Peoples	366 West Broadway	212-925-5400	Look as good as you see.
Shoofly	42 Hudson St	212-406-3270	Dressing your child for social success.
Steven Alan	103 Franklin St	212-343-0692	Trendy designer clothing and accessories. One-of-a-kind stuff.
Urban Archaeology	143 Franklin St	212-431-4646	Retro fixtures.
We Are Nuts About Nuts	165 Church St	212-227-4695	They're nuts.
What Comes Around Goes Around	351 W Broadway	212-343-9303	LARGE, excellent collection of men's, women's, and children's vintage.
Willner Chemists	253 Broadway	212-791-0505	Free nutritional consultations for customers.

Map 3 • City Hall / Chinatown

Aji Ichiban	167 Hester St	212-925-1133	Japanese chain of Chinese candy.
Bangkok Center Grocery	104 Mosco St	212-349-1979	Curries, fish sauce, and other Thai products.
Bloomingdale's	504 Broadway	212-729-5900	Modern Bloomingdale's. Hottest young designers and exclusive collections.
Bowery Lighting	132 Bowery	212-941-8244	Got a match, anyone?
Catherine Street Meat Market	21 Catherine St	212-693-0494	Fresh pig deliveries every Tuesday!
Chinatown Ice Cream Factory	65 Bayard St	212-608-4170	Mango and redbean milkshakes.
Dipalo Dairy	200 Grand St	212-226-1033	Saying cheese since 1925.
Fay Da Bakery	83 Mott St	212-791-3884	Chinese pastry and boba like nobody's business.
Fountain Pen Hospital	10 Warren St	212-964-0580	They don't take Medicaid!
GS Food Market	250 Grand St	212-274-0990	Cantonese market with fresh fish and veggies.
Hong Keung Seafood & Meat Market	75 Mulberry St	212-571-1445	Fresh seafood that you must eat today.
Industrial Plastic Supply	309 Canal St	212-226-2010	Plastic fantastic.
J&R Music & Computer World	33 Park Row	212-732-8600	Stereo, computer, and electronic equipment. Good prices.
Kate Spade	454 Broome St	212-274-1991	Downtown design mecca.
Lung Moon Bakery	83 Mulberry St	212-349-4945	Chinese bakery.
Mitchell's Place	15 Park Pl	212-267-8156	Ca-ching for bling bling.
Modell's	55 Chambers St	212-732-8484	Generic sporting goods.
New Age Designer	38 Mott St	212-349-0818	Chinese emporium.
Pearl Paint	308 Canal St	212-431-7932	Mecca for artists, designers, and people who just like art supplies.
Pearl River Mart	477 Broadway	212-431-4770	Chinese housewares and more.

395

Map 2 · TriBeCa—*continued*

Radio Shack	280 Broadway	212-233-1080	Kenneth, what is the frequency?
SoHo Art Materials	127 Grand St	212-431-3938	A painter's candy store.
Tan My My Market	253 Grand St	212-966-7837	Fresh fish—some still moving.
The New York City Store	1 Centre St	212-669-8246	Fun NYC-themed stuff—subway token cufflinks, manhole cover pins, etc.
Ting's Gift Shop	18 Doyers St	212-962-1081	Chinese emporium.
Unimax	269 Canal St	212-925-1051	It's like 47th Street for the tattoo and piercing set.
Vespa	13 Crosby St	212-226-4410	Rossellini! Fellini! Spaghettini!
Yellow Rat Bastard	478 Broadway	877-YELL-RAT	Filled with young street clothes and skate gear.

Map 4 · Lower East Side

Baby Cakes	248 Broome St	212-677-5047	A bakery dedicated solely to vegan, gluten-free goodies.
Doughnut Plant	379 Grand St	212-505-3700	Great, weird, recommended.
Gertel's Bake Shop	53 Hester St	212-982-3250	Great chocolate babka.
Guss' Lower East Side Pickles	85 Orchard St	516-569-0909	Old school purveyor of perfect pickles.
Hong Kong Supermarket	109 East Broadway	212-227-3388	A chance to see just how amazing food packaging can look.
Il Laboratorio del Gelato	95 Orchard St	212-343-9922	Mind-bogglingly incredible artisanal gelato.
Joe's Fabric Warehouse	102 Orchard St	212-674-7089	Designer fabrics and trimmings.
Kossar's Bagels and Bialys	367 Grand St	212-473-4810	Oldest bialy bakery in the US.
Mendel Goldberg Fabrics	72 Hester St	212-925-9110	Small store and selection of great fabrics.
Moishe's Kosher Bake Shop	504 Grand St	212-673-5832	Best babka, challah, hamantaschen, and rugalach.
Pippin	72 Orchard St	212-505-5159	Oodles of sparkling vintage costume jewelry.
Sweet Life	63 Hester St	212-598-0092	Gimme some CAN-DAY!

Map 5 · West Village

Alexander McQueen	417 W 14th St	212-645-1797	Brit bad boy designs.
Alphabets	47 Greenwich Ave	212-229-2966	Fun miscellany store.
American Apparel	373 Sixth Ave	646-336-6515	Sweatshop-free clothing for liberal New Yorkers.
Bleecker Street Records	239 Bleecker St	212-255-7899	Great selection.
Carry on Tea & Sympathy	110 Greenwich Ave	212-989-9735	A little bit of home for the Union Jack set.
Cherry	19 Eighth Ave	212-924-1410	Among NYC's top shops for high-end, vintage designer garb.
Cherry Men	17 Eighth Ave	212-924-5188	Men's source for high-end, vintage designer duds.
Chocolate Bar	48 Eighth Ave	212-366-1541	A chocoholic's fantasy/undoing.
CO Bigelow Chemists	414 Sixth Ave	212-533-2700	Classic village pharmacy.
Cynthia Rowley	376 Bleecker St	212-242-0847	Party dresses galore.
Faicco's Pork Store	260 Bleecker St	212-243-1974	Pork! Just for you!
Flight 001	96 Greenwich Ave	212-989-0001	Cute hipster travel shop.
Geppetto's Toy Box	10 Christopher St	212-620-7511	Excellent toys and puppets.
Health & Harmony	470 Hudson St	212-691-3036	Small health food store with good selection and decent prices.
Integral Yoga Natural Foods	229 W 13th St	212-243-2642	Shop in the lotus position.
Jacques Torres Chocolate Haven	350 Hudson St	212-414-2462	Tastebud bliss brought to you by the Master of Chocolate.
Janovic	161 Sixth Ave	212-627-1100	Top NYC paint store.
Jeffrey	449 W 14th St	212-206-1272	Avant-garde (and wildly expensive) mini-department store.
The Leather Man	111 Christopher St	212-243-5339	No, you won't look like James Dean. But it'll help.
Little Pie Company	407 W 14th St	212-414-2324	A home-made dessert equals happiness.
Magnolia Bakery	401 Bleecker St	212-462-2572	Wait in a line for mediocre cupcakes.
Marc Jacobs	385 Bleecker St	212-924-6126	Hip purveyor of the cool... see Lulu Guinness.
Matt Umanov Guitars	273 Bleecker St	212-675-2157	Guitars. Guitars. Guitars.
Murray's Cheese Shop	254 Bleecker St	212-243-3289	We love cheese.
Mxyplyzyk	125 Greenwich Ave	212-989-4300	Great, quirky, mid-range tchochkes and home décor.
Myers of Keswick	634 Hudson St	212-691-4194	Killer English sausages, pasties, etc.
O Ottomanelli's & Sons	285 Bleecker St	212-675-4217	Butcher shop.
Otte	121 Greenwich Ave	212-229-9424	Threads from Ella Moss to Ulla Johnson. Also in Williamsburg.
The Porcelain Room	13 Christopher St	212-367-8206	A find for china lovers.
Porto Rico Importing Company	201 Bleecker St	212-477-5421	Sacks of coffee beans everywhere.
Radio Shack	360 Sixth Ave	212-473-2113	Kenneth, what is the frequency?
Radio Shack	49 Seventh Ave	212-727-7641	Kenneth, what is the frequency?
Rebel Rebel Records	319 Bleecker St	212-989-0770	Small CD and LP shop with knowledgeable staff.
Reserva Dominica Cigars	37A Seventh Ave	212-647-7026	Cigars hand rolled and sold on location.
Scott Jordan Furniture	137 Varick St	212-620-4682	Solid hardwood furniture.
Stella McCartney	429 W 14th St	212-255-1556	Hip purveyor of... see Marc Jacobs.
Urban Outfitters	374 Sixth Ave	212-677-9350	College cool.
Vitra	29 Ninth Ave	212-929-3626	Sleek and modern home furnishings.

Map 6 · Washington Square / NYU / NoHo / SoHo

Academy Records & CDs	77 E 10th St	212-780-9166	Top jazz/classical mecca.
AG Adriano Goldschmied	111 Greene St	212-819-0980	Boutique for best butt-flattering jeans (offers in-store alterations).
American Apparel	121 Spring St	212-226-4880	Sweatshop-free clothing for liberal New Yorkers.
American Apparel	712 Broadway	646-383-2257	Sweatshop-free clothing for liberal New Yorkers.
Apple Store SoHo	103 Prince St	212-226-3126	Don't come looking for produce.
Aveda Environmental Lifestyle Store	456 West Broadway	212-473-0280	Expensive well-being.
BCBG by Max Azria	120 Wooster St	212-625-2723	Omnipresent retailer with creative, but practical clothing.
Black Hound New York	170 Second Ave	212-979-9505	Killer desserts. NFT Favorite.
Blades Board & Skate	659 Broadway	212-477-7350	One-stop shop for skateboarding and inline skating gear.
Block Drug Store	101 Second Ave	212-473-1587	Old school drug store, limited selection but personal service.
Chelsea Girl	63 Thompson St	212-343-1658	Women's vintage finery from the 1920s through 1970s.
Circuit City	52 E 14th St	212-387-0730	Electronics superstore.
Coach	143 Prince St	212-473-6925	Leather goods.
Crembebe	68 Second Ave	212-979-6848	Outrageously hip kid's clothes.
Daily 235	235 Elizabeth St	212-334-9728	A little tchotchke store; has great journals.
DKNY	420 West Broadway	646-613-1100	Sharp, wearable fashions by Donna.
Duncan Quinn	8 Spring St	212-226-7030	Bold striped shirts, whimsical ties, and bespoke suits for gents.
East Village Cheese	40 Third Ave	212-477-2601	Great soy cheeses, laughably bad service.
East Village Music Store	85 E 4th St	212-979-8222	Excellent wares and repairs service. NFT top pick!
EDGE°ny NOHO	65 Bleecker St	212-358-0255	Cutting edge fashions by local designers—divided into booths.
EMS	591 Broadway	212-966-8730	Excellent outdoor/hiking equipment and clothing.
Eye Candy	329 Lafayette St	212-343-4275	Specializing in vintage jewelry, shoes, and handbags.
Fabulous Fanny's	335 E 9th St	212-533-0637	Where fly, four-eyed fashionistas score their vintage eyewear.
Global Table	107 Sullivan St	212-431-5839	Quietly elegant tableware.
Guitar Center	25 W 14th St	212-463-7500	Guitar department store.
healthfully organic market	98 E 4th St	212-598-0777	Vast array of organic cleaning products.
Highway	238 Mott St	212-966-4388	Cool bags and purses.
JackRabbit Sports	42 W 14th St	212-727-2980	Mecca for runners, swimmers, and cyclists.
Intermix	98 Prince St	212-966-5303	Pretty and tres expensive. Five NYC locations.
Jam Paper & Envelope	135 Third Ave	212-473-6666	And… the envelope, please.
Kar'ikter	19 Prince St	212-274-1966	Toys for kids and adults.
Kate's Paperie	561 Broadway	212-941-9816	Excellent stationery. NYC favorite.
Kiehl's	109 Third Ave	212-677-3171	Great creams, lotions, and unguents; laughably good service.
Kim's Video	6 St Marks Pl	212-505-0311	Where to blow $100 quickly.
Kinnu	43 Spring St	212-334-4775	Exquisite, pricey Indian inspired silk clothing.
Knit New York	307 E 14th St	212-387-0707	Coffeehouse and knitting store with knitting and crochet lessons.
Leekan Designs	93 Mercer St	212-226-7226	Bead shop for aspiring jewelry-makers.
Lighting by Gregory	158 Bowery	212-226-1276	Bowery lighting mecca. Good ceiling fans.
Lord Willy's	223 Mott St	212-680-8888	Fab gentlemen's garb including shirts with matching pocket squares and boxers.
Lucky Wang	799 Broadway	212-353-2850	Lucky baby who gets to wear these clothes.
Meg	312 E 9th St	212-260-6329	Creative funnel-neck coats and French-y frocks.
Michael Anchin Glass	245 Elizabeth St	212-925-1470	The city's premier glassblower, still with good prices.
Mixona	262 Mott St	646-613-0100	Makes Victoria's Secret look like a bargain basement.
Mogu	258 Elizabeth St	212-625-2444	Throw cushions galore.
MOMA Design Store	81 Spring St	646-613-1367	Cutting-edge, minimalist, ergonomic, offbeat, and funky everything.
Moss	146 Greene St	212-204-7100	Awesome cool stuff you can't afford! Ever!
Nancy Koltes at Home	31 Spring St	212-219-2271	What's the thread-count?
National Wholesale Liquidators	632 Broadway	212-979-2400	They're not kidding.
New York Adorned	47 Second Ave	212-473-0007	Tattoos: It won't kill you to commit to SOMETHING permanent.
New York Central Art Supply	62 Third Ave	212-473-7705	Great selection of art, papers, and supplies.
Other Music	15 E 4th St	212-477-8150	Underground, experimental CD's, LP's, imports, and out-of-print obscurities.
Otto Tootsi Plohound	273 Lafayette St	212-431-7299	Funny name for really cool, interesting, refreshingly offbeat shoes.
Otto Tootsi Plohound	413 W Broadway	212-925-8931	Funny name for really cool, interesting, refreshingly offbeat shoes.

Arts & Entertainment • **Shopping**

Map 6 • Washington Square / NYU / NoHo / SoHo—*continued*

Paul Frank Store	195 Mulberry St	212-965-5079	Whimsical characters (including that monkey) on everything.
Prada	575 Broadway	212-334-8888	Big pretentious Rem Koolhaas-designed store!
Pylones	69 Spring St	212-431-3244	Colorful gifty things.
Radio Shack	781 Broadway	212-228-6810	Kenneth, what is the frequency?
Raffetto's	144 W Houston St	212-777-1261	Take home Italian foods. Lasagna like mamma used to make.
Resurrection Vintage	217 Mott St	212-625-1374	Top-drawer source for designer vintage duds.
Saint Mark's Comics	11 St Marks Pl	212-598-9439	Important comic book store.
Screaming Mimi's	382 Lafayette St	212-677-6464	Sex and the City's Carrie got her vintage here.
Stereo Exchange	627 Broadway	212-505-1111	Just-under-obscenely-priced audiophile equipment. Good for male depression.
Stuart Moore	128 Prince St	212-941-1023	Elegant, modern jewelry, $1,000-$10,000 range.
Sullivan Street Bakery	73 Sullivan St	212-334-9435	The best bakery, period.
Surprise, Surprise	91 Third Ave	212-777-0990	Good just-moved-to-the-neighborhood store.
The Market NYC	268 Mulberry St	212-580-8995	Hip, unique designs by young, local designers.
The Stork Club	142 Sullivan St	212-505-1927	Comfy kids clothes with French flare.
Tory by TRB	257 Elizabeth St	212-334-3000	Op-art tunics, luxe resort wear, and effortlessly chic garb.
Tower Records	692 Broadway	212-505-1500	Like a department store for music and film. Great jazz section!
Trash & Vaudeville	4 St Marks Pl	212-982-3590	Decades-old NYC HQ for punk and goth gear.
Uncle Sam's	37 W 8th St	212-674-2222	Dress your militia in fatigues con fiore.
Utrecht Art and Drafting Supplies	111 Fourth Ave	212-777-5353	Another fine downtown art store.
Veniero's	342 E 11th St	212-674-7070	Another cookie, my dear?
Virgin Megastore	52 E 14th St	212-598-4666	Massive music store for the masses.
White Trash	304 E 5th St	212-598-5956	Retro home furnishings.

Map 7 • East Village / Lower East Side

A Cheng	443 E 9th St	212-979-7324	Modern classic women's clothing.
A-One Record Shop	439 E 6th St	212-473-2970	Tons of vinyl, from old 'n rare to new 'n hip.
Alphabets	115 Ave A	212-475-7250	Fun miscellany store.
Altman Luggage	135 Orchard St	212-254-7275	It's just you and that Samsonite gorilla, baby.
Amarcord Vintage Fashion	84 E 7th St	212-614-7133	Well-edited vintage goodies, many pieces direct from Europe.
American Apparel	183 E Houston St	212-598-4600	Sweatshop-free clothing for liberal New Yorkers.
Babeland	94 Rivington St	212-375-1701	Sex toys and more.
De La Vega	102 St Marks Pl	212-876-8649	NYC-inspired street art.
Dowel Quality Products	91 First Ave	212-979-6045	Super-cool Indian grocery. Great beer selection, too.
Earthmatters	177 Ludlow St	212-475-4180	Organic groceries with a garden out back.
Economy Candy	108 Rivington St	212-254-1531	Candy brands from your childhood still being made and sold here!
Essex Street Retail Market	120 Essex St	212-312-0449	Everything, simply. Even if vegan see the butcher.
Etherea	66 Ave A	212-358-1126	Cool East Village record store.
Exit 9	64 Ave A	212-228-0145	Always fun and changeable hipster gift shop (The first place to sell NFT!).
First Flight Music	174 First Ave	212-539-1383	Good guitars and amps, spotty service.
Frock	148 Orchard St	212-594-5380	Their specialty: well-preserved, Studio 54-glam designer vintage.
Gracefully	28 Ave A	212-677-8181	Overpriced gourmet groceries.
Gringer & Sons	29 First Ave	212-475-0600	Kitchen appliances for every price range.
The Hanger Bar & Boutique	217 E 3rd St	212-228-1030	The ultimate drinking and shopping experience—vintage clothing and booze.
Happy Happy Happy	157 Allen St	212-254-4088	Baked treats minus gluten, yeast, dairy, wheat and trans-fat.
Lancelotti	66 Ave A	212-475-6851	Fun designer housewares, not too expensive.
Ludlow Guitars	164 Ludlow St	212-353-1775	New and used vintage guitars, accessories, and amps.
Masturbakers	511 E 12th St	212-475-0476	Erotic and custom cakes.
The Paris Apartment	70 E 1st St	917-749-5089	Romantic "Parisian" décor and stunning European flea market finds.
Peggy Pardon	153 Ludlow St	212-529-3686	Exquisite vintage clothing from Edwardian times to the 1940s.
R&S Strauss Auto Store	644 E 14th St	212-995-8000	Sideview mirrors, tail lights, touch up paint—mecca for the urban car owner.
Russ & Daughters	179 E Houston St	212-475-4880	Fab Jewish Soul Food—Lox, herring, sable, etc.
Tahir	412 E 9th St	212-253-2121	Vintage fashion with a personal touch.
TG170	170 Ludlow St	212-995-8660	Fun funky fresh women's clothing.
Tiny Living	125 E 7th St	212-228-2748	Boutique catering to the tight squeeze of NYC living.
Yonah Schimmel's Knishery	137 E Houston St	212-477-2858	Dishing delish knish since 1910.

Map 8 • Chelsea

B&H Photo	420 Ninth Ave	212-444-5040	Where everyone in North America buys their cameras and film. Closed Saturdays.
Buon Italia	Chelsea Market, 75 Ninth Ave	212-633-9090	Imported Italian food.
Chelsea Garden Center	499 Tenth Ave	212-929-2477	Urban gardener's delight.
Chelsea Market Baskets	75 Ninth Ave	212-727-1484	Gift baskets for all occasions.
Chelsea Wholesale Flower Market, Chelsea Market	75 Ninth Ave	212-620-7500	Remember, you're in Manhattan, not Westchester.
Eleni's	Chelsea Market, 75 Ninth Ave	888-4-ELENIS	When a card won't do, iced cookies in every shape will.
Fat Witch Bakery	Chelsea Market, 75 Ninth Ave	212-807-1335	Excellent chocolate brownies.
Find Outlet	361 W 17th St	212-243-3177	Find cheap(er) designer duds.
Kitchen Market	218 Eighth Ave	212-243-4433	Chiles, herbs, spices, hot sauces, salsas, and more.
New Museum Store	556 W 22nd	212-343-0460	One of our favorite stores on the planet Earth.

Map 9 • Flatiron / Lower Midtown

17 at 17 Thrift Shop	17 W 17th St	212-727-7516	Proceeds go to Gilda's Club.
30th Street Guitars	236 W 30th St	212-868-2660	Ax heaven.
ABC Carpet & Home	888 Broadway	212-473-3000	A NYC institution for chic, even exotic, home décor and design.
Abracadabra	19 W 21st St	212-627-5194	Magic, masks, costumes—presto!
Academy Records & CDs	12 W 18th St	212-242-3000	Top Jazz/classical mecca.
Adorama Camera	42 W 18th St	212-741-0052	Good camera alternative to B&H.
Al Friedman	44 W 18th St	212-243-9000	Art supplies, frames, office furniture, and more.
Angel Street Thrift Shop	118 W 17th St	212-229-0546	Recommended thrift store.
Anthropologie	85 Fifth Ave	212-627-5885	Urban Outfitters' more sophisticated sibling.
Ariston	69 Fifth Ave	212-929-4226, 800-422-2747	Excellent florist with orchids as well.
Aveda Environmental Lifestyle Store	140 Fifth Ave	212-645-4797	Plant & flower-infused hair and body care that smells wonderful.
Bed Bath & Beyond	620 Sixth Ave	212-255-3550	De rigeur destination when moving to a new apartment.
buybuy Baby	270 Seventh Ave	917-344-1555	Baby superstore.
Capitol Fishing Tackle	218 W 23rd St	212-929-6132	100+ year-old fishing institution.
Chelsea Flea Market	112 W 25th St		Antiquing in the outdoors, the way God intended.
The City Quilter	133 W 25th St	212-807-0390	Quilt for success!
CompUSA	420 Fifth Ave	212-764-6224	The Kmart of computer stores.
The Container Store	629 Sixth Ave	212-366-4200	Organize your closet…and your life!
Cupcake Café	18 W 18th St	646-307-5878	Pretty cupcakes.
DataVision	445 Fifth Ave	212-689-1111	Computers, printers, projectors.
The Family Jewels	130 W 23rd St	212-633-6020	Tightly-packed shop stocking yesteryear's threads for guys and gals.
Fish's Eddy	889 Broadway	212-420-9020	They do dishes.
Housing Works Thrift Shop	143 W 17th St	212-366-0820	Our favorite thrift store.
Jam Paper & Envelope	611 Sixth Ave	212-255-4593	And…the envelope, please.
Janovic	215 Seventh Ave	212-645-5454	Top NYC paint store.
Jazz Record Center	236 W 26th St	212-675-4480	All that Jazz!
Jensen-Lewis	89 Seventh Ave	212-929-4880	Upgrade from Ikea!
Jim Smiley Vintage	128 W 23rd St	212-741-1195	Lovely pre-'70s collection of Jackie-O elegance and Dietrich glamour.
Just Bulbs	5 E 16th St	212-228-7820	Do you have any lamps? How about shades?
Krups Kitchen and Bath	11 W 18th St	212-243-5787	Good prices for top appliances.
Loehmann's	101 Seventh Ave	212-352-0856	Join the other thousands of bargain hunters sifting through clothing piles.
Lord & Taylor	424 Fifth Ave	212-391-3344	Classic NYC department store.
Lucky Wang	82 Seventh Ave	212-229-2900	Lucky baby who gets to wear these clothes.
Lulu Guiness	260 W 39th St	212-302-4564	Hip purveyor of the cool "downtown" style.
M&J Trimmings	1008 Sixth Ave	212-391-6200	For your DIY sewing projects.
Macy's	151 W 34th St	212-695-4400	Love the wooden escalators.
Mandler, The Original Sausage Co	26 E 17th St	212-255-8999	Sausage emporium.
Manhattan Drum Shop & Music Studio	203 W 38th St	212-768-4892	Repairs and sells custom-made and vintage drums.
Otto Tootsi Plohound	137 Fifth Ave	212-460-8650	Funny name for really cool, interesting, refreshingly offbeat shoes.
Paper Presentations	23 W 18th St	212-463-7035	Relatively cheap paper and such.
Paragon Sporting Goods	867 Broadway	212-255-8036	Good all-purpose sporting goods store.
Phoenix	64 W 37th St	212-564-5656	Bead shop for aspiring jewelry-makers.

Map 9 • Flatiron / Lower Midtown—*continued*

Pleasure Chest	156 Seventh Ave	212-242-2158	Always a great window display.
Radio Shack	36 E 23rd St	212-673-3670	Kenneth, what is the frequency?
Rogue Music	251 W 30th St	212-629-5073	Used equipment you probably still can't afford.
Sam Flax	12 W 20th St	212-620-3038	Portfolios, frames, furniture, and designer gifts. NFT fave.
Space Kiddets	46 E 21st St	212-420-9878	Bruce Lee and CBGBs onesies.
Sports Authority	636 Sixth Ave	212-929-8971	Sporting goods for the masses.
Tekserve	119 W 23rd St	212-929-3645	Apple computer sales and repairs.
Toho Shoji	990 Sixth Ave	212-868-7465	You made this necklace yourself? Just for me? (swoon).

Map 10 • Murray Hill / Gramercy

Alkit Pro Camera	222 Park Ave S	212-674-1515	Good camera shop; developing; rentals.
City Opera Thrift Shop	222 E 23rd St	212-684-5344	They always have something or other.
Foods of India	121 Lexington Ave	212-683-4419	Large selection of Indian ingredients including harder to find spices.
Housing Works Thrift Shop	157 E 23rd St	212-529-5955	Our favorite thrift store.
Kalustyan's	123 Lexington Ave	212-685-3451	Specialty foods.
Ligne Roset	250 Park Ave S	212-375-1036	Modern, sleek furniture.
Nemo Tile Company	48 E 21st St	212-505-0009	Good tile shop for small projects.
Pastrami Factory	333 E 23rd St	212-689-8090	Pastrami, chopped liver, knishes, chicken soup and other kosher-style foods.
Pearl Paint	207 E 23rd St	212-592-2179	Not as big as the Canal St. store, but still very useful.
Poggenpohl US	230 Park Ave	212-228-3334	By appointment only. $100,000 kitchens for all you grad students!
Pookie & Sebastian	541 Third Ave	212-951-7110	Murray Hill outpost for fun, flirty, girly garb.
Quark Spy	240 E 29th St	212-683-9100	Spy shops are cool.
Urban Angler	206 Fifth Ave	212-689-6400,	We think it's for fishermen.

Map 11 • Hell's Kitchen

Amy's Bread	672 Ninth Ave	212-977-2670	Providing the heavenly smells that wake up Hell's Kitchen.
Delphinium	358 W 47th St	212-333-7732	For the "too lazy to make my own card" set.
Delphinium Home	653 Ninth Ave	212-333-3213	Everything from rubber duckies to WASP cookbooks.
Janovic	771 Ninth Ave	212-245-3241	Top NYC paint store.
Little Pie Company	424 W 43rd St	212-736-4780	A homemade dessert equals happiness.
Metro Bicycles	360 W 47th St	212-581-4500	New York's bicycle source.
Ninth Avenue International	543 Ninth Ave	212-279-1000	Mediterranean/Greek specialty store.
Pan Aqua Diving	460 W 43rd St	212-736-3483	SCUBA equipment and courses.
Poseidon Bakery	629 Ninth Ave	212-757-6173	Greek bakery.
Radio Shack	333 W 57th St	212-586-1909	Kenneth, what is the frequency?
Sea Breeze	541 Ninth Ave	212-563-7537	Bargains on fresh seafood.

Map 12 • Midtown

Alkit Pro Camera	830 Seventh Ave	212-262-2424	Good camera shop; developing; rentals.
Baccarat	625 Madison Ave	212-826-4100	Top glass/crystal you can't afford.
Bergdorf Goodman	754 Fifth Ave	212-753-7300	Hands down—the best windows in the business.
Brooks Brothers	346 Madison Ave	212-682-8800	Official outfitter of the corporate world.
Burberry	9 E 57th St	212-371-5010	How to dress well without having to think about it.
Chanel	15 E 57th St	212-355-5050	Official outfitter of "ladies who lunch."
Colony Music	1619 Broadway	212-265-2050	Great sheet music store.
CompUSA	1775 Broadway	212-262-9711	The Kmart of computer stores.
Crate & Barrel	650 Madison Ave	212-308-0011	Great selection of stylish, but affordable kitchen gear.
Drummer's World	151 W 46th St	212-840-3057	All-encompassing stop for drummers—from beginning to pro.
Ermenegildo Zegna	663 Fifth Ave	212-421-4488	A truly stylish and classic Italian designer.
FAO Schwarz	767 Fifth Ave	212-644-9400	Noisy, crowded, overrated, awesome.
Felissimo	10 W 56th St	212-247-5656	Cool design store, great townhouse.
Gucci	685 Fifth Ave	212-826-2600	Largest Gucci store in the world.
Henri Bendel	712 Fifth Ave	212-247-1100	Offbeat department store specializing in the unusual and harder-to-find.
Joseph Patelson Music House	160 W 56th St	212-582-5840	Where Beethoven would shop, if he weren't dead.
Kate's Paperie	140 W 57th St	212-459-0700	Excellent stationery. NYC favorite.
Klavierhaus	211 W 58th St	212-245-4535	Unique pianos from the 19th, 20th, and 21st centuries.
Manny's Music	156 W 48th St	212-819-0576	Uptown musical instruments mecca.
Mets Clubhouse Shop	11 W 42nd St	212-768-9534	For Amazin' stuff!
Mikimoto	730 Fifth Ave	212-457-4600	Beautiful jewelry, mostly pearls.
Modell's	51 E 42nd St	212-661-4242	Generic sporting goods.

MoMA Design Store	44 W 53rd St	212-767-1050	Cutting-edge, minimalist, ergonomic, offbeat, and funky everything.
Museum of Arts and Design Shop	40 W 53rd St	212-956-3535	Not your average museum store.
NBA Store	666 Fifth Ave	212-515-6221	Brand experience for basketball junkies.
Niketown	6 E 57th St	212-891-6453	Just do it brand experience.
Orvis Company	522 Fifth Ave	212-827-0698	For the angler in all of us. Or, for Halloween.
Paul Stuart	Madison Ave & 45th St	212-682-0320	Shop of choice for fancy lawyers and Wall Streeters. Great suspenders.
Petrossian Boutique	911 Seventh Ave	212-245-2217	Caviar and other delectables.
Radio Shack	50 E 42nd St	212-953-6050	Kenneth, what is the frequency?
Roberto's Woodwind Repair Shop	146 W 46th St	212-391-1315	Saxophones, horns, clarinets, and flutes. If it blows, bring it here.
Saks Fifth Avenue	611 Fifth Ave	212-753-4000	Fifth Avenue mainstay with lovely holiday windows and bathrooms.
Sam Ash	160 W 48th St	212-719-2299	Musical instrument superstore.
Smythson of Bond Street	4 W 57th St	212-265-4573	High quality stationery.
Steinway and Sons	109 W 57th St	212-246-1100	Cheap knockoff pianos. Just kidding.
Takashimaya	693 Fifth Ave	212-350-0100	Elegant tea, furniture, accessory store. Highly recommended.
Tiffany & Co	727 Fifth Ave	212-755-8000	Grande dame of the little blue box.

Map 13 · East Midtown

A&D Building	150 E 58th St		Over 200,000 sq. ft. of commercial and residential furnishings. Wow.
Adriana's Caravan	Grand Central Station	212-972-8804	Number 1 rated herb and spice shop.
Bridge Kitchenware	711 Third Ave	212-688-4220	For your inner-chef.
Buttercup Bake Shop	973 Second Ave	212-350-4144	Move over Magnolia. Buttercup's all grown up.
Godiva Chocolatier	560 Lexington Ave	212-980-9810	Everyone needs a fix now and then.
Ideal Cheese	942 First Ave	212-688-7579	All cheese is ideal.
Innovative Audio	150 E 58th St	212-634-4444	Quality music systems and home theaters.
Mets Clubhouse Shop	143 E 54th St	212-888-7508	For Amazin' stuff!
New York Transit Museum	Grand Central, Main Concourse	212-878-0106	Great subway fun.
New York Vintage Club	346 E 59th St	212-207-9007	Fab vintage clothing on unexpected block.
Pottery Barn	127 E 59th St	917-369-0050	Mainstream, quality home goods.
Radio Shack	940 Third Ave	212-750-8409	Kenneth, what's the frequency?
Sam Flax	900 Third Ave	212-935-5353	Portfolios, frames, furniture, and designer gifts.
Sports Authority	845 Third Ave	212-355-9725	Sporting goods for the masses.
Terence Conran Shop	407 E 59th St	212-755-9079	Awe-inspiring modern designs for the home. Can we live here?
The World of Golf	147 E 47th St	212-775-9398	Stop here on your way to Briar Cliff Manor.
Yankee Clubhouse Shop	110 E 59th St	212-758-7844	Any Yankee fan's paradise.
Zaro's Bread Basket	89 E 42nd St	212-292-0160	They've got bread. In baskets.

Map 14 · Upper West Side (Lower)

Allan & Suzi	416 Amsterdam Ave	212-724-7445	UWS vintage clothing and designer resale mainstay.
Alphabets	2284 Broadway	212-579-5702	Fun miscellany store.
Balducci's	155 W 66th St	212-653-8320	One third of the gourmet "holy trinity."
Bed Bath & Beyond	1932 Broadway	917-441-9391	De rigeur destination when moving to a new apartment.
Bonne Nuit	30 Lincoln Plz	212-677-8487	Pretty, feminine underthings and sleepwear.
Bruce Frank	215 W 83rd St	212-595-3746	Great bead shop.
Bruno the King of Ravioli	2204 Broadway	212-580-8150	Gourmet market with a shocking specialty.
Claire's Accessories	2267 Broadway	212-877-2655	Fun for the young.
EMS	20 W 61st St	212-397-4860	For all of your outdoor sporting needs.
Ethan Allen	103 West End Ave	212-201-9840	Furniture for your dead grandparents.
Fish's Eddy	2176 Broadway	212-873-8819	They do dishes.
Godiva Chocolatier	245 Columbus Ave	212-787-5804	Everyone needs a fix now and then.
Gracious Home	1992 Broadway	212-231-7800	The definition of the word "emporium."
Harry's Shoes	2299 Broadway	212-874-2035	Mecca for reasonably priced footwear.
Housing Works Thrift Shop	306 Columbus Ave	212-579-7566	Our favorite thrift store.
Janovic	159 W 72nd St	212-595-2500	Top NYC paint store.
Laytner's Linens	2270 Broadway	212-724-0180	Things that'll make you want to stay home more.
Patagonia	426 Columbus Ave	917-441-0011	Environmentally conscious store selling outstanding outdoor clothing.

Map 14 • Upper West Side (Lower)—*continued*

Pookie & Sebastian	322 Columbus Ave	212-580-5844	Flirty tops, girly dresses, and fly jeans—for UWS chicks.
Tower Records/Video	1961 Broadway	212-799-2500	Lincoln Center location with emphasis on classical, show tunes (ugh,) and jazz.
Townshop	2273 Broadway	212-787-2762	Where experts will fit you for the perfect bra.
Tumi	10 Columbus Cir	212-823-9390	When your luggage gets lost and insurance is paying.
West Side Records	233 W 72nd St	212-874-1588	Cool record store.
Whole Foods Market	10 Columbus Cir	212-823-9600	Natural and organic food superstore—giant prepared foods department.
Yarn Co	2274 Broadway	212-787-7878	The nitty gritty for knitters in the city.
Zabar's	2245 Broadway	212-787-2000	The third gourmet shop in the "holy trinity."

Map 15 • Upper East Side (Lower)

A Bear's Place	789 Lexington Ave	212-826-6465	Excellent toys and children's furniture.
American Apparel	1090 Third Ave	212-772-7462	Sweatshop-free clothing for liberal New Yorkers.
Anika Inez	243 E 78th St	212-717-9644	Unique jewelry by Parsons grad from Sweden, ranging $40-$100.
Arthritis Thrift Shop	1383 Third Ave	212-772-8816	Most eye-catching window displays on "Thrift Row."
Aveda Environmental Lifestyle Store	1122 Third Ave	212-744-3113	Pamper yourself.
Bang & Olufsen	952 Madison Ave	212-879-6161	Sleek, expensive home entertainment products.
Barneys New York	660 Madison Ave	212-826-8900	Museum-quality fashion (with prices to match). Recommended.
Bed Bath & Beyond	410 E 61st St	646-215-4702	De rigeur destination when moving to a new apartment.
Beneath	265 E 78th St	212-288-3800	New, tiny shop with hipster brands and girly lingerie.
Bis Designer Resale	1134 Madison Ave, 2nd Fl	212-396-2760	Where you can actually afford Gucci and Prada.
Black Orchid Bookshop	303 E 81st St	212-734-5980	Mysteries are their specialty—old, new, and out-of-print.
Bloomingdale's	1000 Third Ave	212-705-2000	An upscale version of Macy's.
Bra Smyth	905 Madison Ave	212-772-9400	Need a new bra?
Butterfield Market	1114 Lexington Ave	212-288-7800	UES gourmet grocer circa 1915.
Cancer Care Thrift Shop	1480 Third Ave	212-879-9868	Small, crowded thrift shop that always has great stuff in the window.
Cantaloup	1036 Lexington Ave	212-249-3566	Uptown outpost for glam, decidedly "downtown" duds.
Cantaloup Destination Denim	1359 Second Ave	212-288-3569	Ditto, but focusing more on "downtown" denim.
Caviarteria	1012 Lexington Ave	212-772-7314	One stop shopping for caviar, foie gras, salmon, and blinis.
Chuckies	1073 Third Ave	212-593-9898	Department store-quality shoe collection sans the perfume sprayers.
Chuckies	1169 Madison Ave	212-249-2254	Department store-quality shoe collection sans the perfume sprayers.
CK Bradley	146 E 74th St	212-988-7999	UES "preppy-a-porter" specializing in colorful ribbon-trimmed garb.
Council Thrift Shop	246 E 84th St	212-439-8373	Thrift shop benefiting the National Council of Jewish Women, NY.
Designer Resale	324 E 81st St	212-734-3639	Armani, Chanel, Hermes and more at bargain prices.
Designer Resale Too	311 E 81st St	212-734-3639	Armani, Chanel, Hermes and more at bargain prices.
Diesel	770 Lexington Ave	212-308-0055	Why spend $60 on a pair of jeans when you can spend $150?
DKNY	655 Madison Ave	212-223-3569	Sharp, wearable fashions by Donna.
Dolce & Gabbana	825 Madison Ave	212-249-4100	Jeans, sunglasses, suits, and known for their animal prints.
Donna Karan	819 Madison Ave	212-861-1001	Sophisticated clothing for sophisticated people.
Dylan's Candy Bar	1011 Third Ave	646-735-0078	Keeping NYC pediatric dentists in business since 2001.
EAT Gifts	1062 Madison Ave	212-861-2544	Fun gift shop—part of the Eli Zabar empire.
Eli's Manhattan	1411 Third Ave	212-717-8100	Blissful gourmet shopping experience for all the senses.
Elk Candy	1628 Second Ave	212-650-1177	Store-made marzipan and chocolates.
Encore	1132 Madison Ave, 2nd Fl	212-879-2850	Where ladies who lunch consign their worn-only-once Chanels.
Fishs Eddy	1388 Third Ave	212-517-6300	They do dishes.
French Sole	985 Lexington Ave	212-737-2859	Fabulously fashionable flats from floor to ceiling.
Fresh	1367 Third Ave	212-585-3400	Bright, cheery, and stocked with cutely-packaged beauty products.
Garnet Wines & Liquors	929 Lexington Ave	212-772-3211	Top NYC wine store.
Gentlemen's Resale	322 E 81st St	212-734-2739	Zegna, Hermes, and Hugo Boss at bargain prices.
Giorgio Armani	760 Madison Ave	212-988-9191	Fantastic store, fantastic clothes, fantasti(cally high) prices.
Gracious Home	1217 Third Ave	212-517-6300	The definition of the word "emporium."
Health Nuts	1208 Second Ave	212-593-0116	Health foods, vitamins and more.
Hermes	691 Madison Ave	212-751-3181	Get on the waiting list for the uber-expensive Birkin Bag.

Housing Works Thrift Shop	202 E 77th St	212-772-8461	Our favorite thrift store.
Janovic	1150 Third Ave	212-772-1400	Top NYC paint store.
Jump	220 E 60th St	212-644-3744	A place to get Heatherette on the UES—need we say more?
Kate's Paperie	1282 Third Ave	212-396-3670	Excellent stationery. NYC favorite.
La Maison du Chocolat	1018 Madison Ave	212-744-7117	Parisian house of chocolate.
La Terrine	1024 Lexington Ave	212-988-3366	Hand-painted French, Italian, and Portuguese ceramics.
Lascoff Apothecary	1209 Lexington Ave	212-288-9500	Delightfully well-preserved apothecary circa 1899.
Logos Bookstore	1575 York Ave	212-517-7292	Children's books, spiritual lit, and beyond.
Lyric Hi-Fi	1221 Lexington Ave	212-439-1900	Friendly, high-end stereo shop.
Marimekko	1262 Third Ave	212-628-8400	Technicolor Finnish fashions and housewares.
Martine's Chocolates too	400 E 82nd St	212-744-6289	Cute-as-a-bonbon chocolatier where decadence reigns.
Memorial Sloan-Kettering Thrift Shop	1440 Third Ave	212-535-1250	Large, upscale thrift shop with Uptown feel.
Michael's The Consignment Shop for Women	1041 Madison Ave	212-737-7273	Gently-worn Gucci and Galliano at a deep discount.
Morgane Le Fay	746 Madison Ave	212-879-9700	Princess gowns for modern-day Cinderellas.
Myla	20 E 69th St	212-570-1590	UES spot for sleek, incognito vibrators.
Oldies, Goldies & Moldies	1609 Second Ave	212-737-3935	Deliciously Deco antiques and collectibles.
Orwasher's	308 E 78th St	212-288-6569	Handmade breads. Best challah on the east side.
Ottomanelli Brothers	1549 York Ave	212-772-7900	Meat chain.
Pomegranate	201 E 74th St	212-288-4409	Sliver of a space selling soap, incense, and monogrammed towels.
Pookie & Sebastian	1488 Second Ave	212-861-0550	Flirty tops, girly dresses, and fun garb for UES chicks.
Pookie & Sebastian	249 E 77th St	212-717-1076	Outlet location—fun, flirty, girly garb on sale.
Pylones	842 Lexington Ave	212-317-9822	Colorful gifty things.
Radio Shack	1267 Lexington Ave	212-831-2765	Kenneth, what is the frequency?
Radio Shack	1477 Third Ave	212-327-0979	Kenneth, what is the frequency?
Radio Shack	782 Lexington Ave	212-421-0543	Kenneth, what is the frequency?
Radio Shack	925 Lexington Ave	212-249-3028	Kenneth, what is the frequency?
Ralph Lauren	888 Madison Ave	212-434-8000	Flagship luxury store in old Rhinelander mansion.
Ropal Stationary	1504 Second Ave	212-988-3548	Great spot for stationery and office supplies.
Scoop	1275 Third Ave	212-535-5577	Trendy threads for label-conscious fashionistas.
Sherry-Lehmann	679 Madison Ave	212-838-7500	Top-notch, comprehensive selection of international wines.
The Shoe Box	1349 Third Ave	212-535-9615	UES oasis for designer shoes—great department store alternative!
Spence-Chapin Thrift Shop	1473 Third Ave	212-737-8448	Upscale thrift benefiting adoption programs.
Steuben	667 Madison Ave	212-752-1441	Glass you can't afford.
Sylvia Pines Uniquities	1102 Lexington Ave	212-744-5141	Vintage jewelry and silver-framed purses fit for a flapper.
Tender Buttons	143 E 62nd St	212-758-7004	Ginormis button collection spanning old to new.
Venture Stationers	1156 Lexington Ave	212-288-7235	Great neighborhood stationers.
Vintage Collections	147 E 72nd St, 2nd Fl	212-717-7702	Lovely 2nd floor shop specializing in upscale vintage fashions.
The Wooglathering	318 E 84th St	212-734-4747	The place to shop for knitters in-the-know.
William Poll	1051 Lexington Ave	212-288-0501	Homemade potato chips and dips with a cult following.
Yorkville Meat Emporium	1560 Second Ave	212-628-5147	Hungarian specialties, fresh meat, cured pork, etc.
Yves St Laurent	855 Madison Ave	212-988-3821	Designer clothing from some French guy.
Zitomer	969 Madison Ave	212-737-4480	Department store with great pet gear, toy, and beauty choices.

Map 16 · Upper West Side (Upper)

Ann Taylor	2380 Broadway	212-721-3130	For the businesswoman. Conservative, classic and clean.
Banana Republic	2360 Broadway	212-787-2064	What everyone else is wearing.
Ben & Jerry's	2722 Broadway	212-866-6237	Cherry Garcia, Phish Food, and Half Baked.
Gothic Cabinet Craft	2652 Broadway	212-678-4368	Real wood furniture!
Gourmet Garage	2567 Broadway	212-663-0656	Less greasy food than in most garages.
Health Nuts	2611 Broadway	212-678-0054	Standard health food store.
Janovic	2680 Broadway	212-769-1440	Top NYC paint store.
Joon's Fine Seafood	774 Amsterdam Ave	212-932-2942	Fresh fish market.
Metro Bicycles	231 W 96th St	212-663-7531	New York's bicycle source.
Mugi Pottery	993 Amsterdam Ave	212-866-6202	Handcrafted pottery.
New York Flowers & Plant Shed	209 W 96th St	800-753-9595	Makes you wish you had more (or any) garden space.
Planet Kids	2688 Broadway	212-864-8705	Outfitter of newborns to teens.

Map 17 • Upper East Side / East Harlem

Best Buy	1280 Lexington Ave	917-492-8870	Test the electronics before you buy.
Blacker & Kooby	1204 Madison Ave	212-369-8308	Good selection of stationery, pens, and art supplies.
Blades Board & Skate	120 W 72nd St	212-996-1644	One-stop shop for skateboarding and inline skating gear.
Blue Tree	1283 Madison Ave	212-369-BLUE	Truly unique clothing and gifts for folks who think they've seen it all.
Capezio	1651 Third Ave	212-348-7210	Dance apparel and shoes.
Ciao Bella Gelato	27 E 92nd St	212-831-5555	Try the malted milk ball gelato.
The Children's General Store	168 E 91st St	212-426-4479	Toys, games, crafts, and all things kids love.
Cooper-Hewitt National Design Museum Shop	2 E 91st St	212-849-8355	Cool design stuff.
Coup de Coeur	1628 Third Ave	212-410-9720	Stylish boutique on not-so-stylish stretch of Third Avenue.
Doyle New York	175 E 87th St	212-427-2730	Auctioneers and appraisers, anything from jewelry and art to coins and china.
Eli's Vinegar Factory	431 E 91st St	212-987-0885	Gourmet market with prepared foods, cheeses, meats, seafood, and produce.
Face Stockholm	1263 Madison Ave	212-987-1411	Skincare and makeup.
Glaser's Bake Shop	1670 First Ave	212-289-2562	Best black-and-white cookies for more than a century.
Housing Works Thrift Shop	1730 Second Ave	212-722-8306	Latest Uptown outpost of our favorite thrift shop.
Kessie & Co	163 E 87th St	212-987-1732	Vintage bric-a-brac, housewares, and clothing.
La Tropezienne	2131 First Ave	212-860-5324	Bakery.
MAD Vintage Couture & Designer Resale	167 E 87th St	212-427-4333	Former art gallery turned boutique.
Marsha DD	1574 Third Ave	212-831-2422	Paul Frank gear and cheeky tees for UES tweens.
Martha Frances Mississippi Cheesecake	1707 Second Ave	212-360-0900	Southern-style bakery with big selection of cheesecakes.
Nellie M Boutique	1309 Lexington Ave	212-996-4410	Fun things for ladies to wear on dates.
New York Replacement Parts Corp	1456 Lexington Ave	212-534-0818	Plumbing supplies and bath fixtures.
Orva	155 E 86th St	212-369-3448	Ladies' discount department store.
Pickles, Olives Etc	1647 First Ave	212-717-8966	Pickle barrel-sized shop selling pickles, olives, stuffed grape leaves, etc.
Schaller & Weber	1654 Second Ave	212-879-3047	A relic of old Yorkville with great German meats.
Schatzie's Prime Meats	1200 Madison Ave	212-410-1555	Butcher with good prime meat and poultry.
Seraphim's Ark	100 E 96th St	212-996-1725	Darling gifts for friends who invite you over for dinner.
Service Hardware	1338 Lexington Ave	212-289-7270	Like a mini 'Bed, Bath & Beyond" where it's needed.
Shatzi The Shop	243 E 86th St	212-289-1830	The saving grace of strip mall-ish, chain-hogged 86th Street.
Soccer Sport Supply	1745 First Ave	212-427-6050	Omni soccer.
Spence-Chapin Thrift Shop	1850 Second Ave	212-426-7643	Like the other Spence-Chapin location, but with more furniture.
Steve Madden	150 E 86th St	212-426-0538	Trendy and modern, though not the highest quality.
Super Runners Shop	1337 Lexington Ave	212-369-6010	Brand name sneakers, apparel, and gadgets.
Temptations	1737 York Ave	212-426-6204	Wonderful homemade ice cream. Mint Oreo and Pumpkin are standouts.
Two Little Red Hens	1652 Second Ave	212-452-0476	Lovely cases of cakes and pies flanked by kitschy hen memorabilia.
Williams-Sonoma	1175 Madison Ave	212-289-6832	Fine cookware.

Map 18 • Columbia / Morningside Heights

El Mundo	3300 Broadway	646-548-3970	Cheap homegoods and discounted brand name apparel.
JAS Mart	2847 Broadway	212-866-4780	Japanese Asian Specialty. Japanese imports.
Kim's Mediapolis	2906 Broadway	212-864-5321	Audiovisual heaven.
Labyrinth Books	536 W 112th St	212-865-1588	NFT favorite.
Mondel Chocolates	2913 Broadway	212-864-2111	Mom-and-pop candy shop with great chocolates.

Map 19 • Harlem (Lower)

The Body Shop	1 E 125th St	212-348-4900	Naturally inspired skin and hair care products.
Champs	208 W 125th St	212-280-0296	Sports and street shoes and wear.
Dr Jay's Harlem NYC	256 W 125th St	212-665-7795	Inner-city urban fashions.
H&M	125 W 125th St	212-665-8300	Disposable fashion.
Harlem Underground Clothing Co	2027 Fifth Ave	212-987-9385	Embroidered Harlem t-shirts.
Harlemade	174 Lenox Ave	212-987-2500	Clothes/gifts/art.
Jimmy Jazz	132 W 125th St	212-665-4198	Urban designers with a range of sizes.
MAC Cosmetics	202 W 125th St	212-665-0676	Beauty products in many colors and shades.
Malcolm Shabazz Harlem Market	58 W 116th St		An open-air market for all your daishiki needs.
Settepani	196 Lenox Ave	917-492-4806	Lovely baked goods.
Studio Museum of Harlem Gift Shop	144 W 125th St	212-864-0014	Art produced by African Americans.
Wimp's Southern Style Bakery	29 W 125th St	212-410-2296	What it says.
Xukuma	183 Lenox Ave	212-222-0490	Capitalize Harlem.

Map 20 • El Barrio

Capri Bakery	186 E 116th St	212-410-1876	Italian El Barrio bakery.
Casa Latina	151 E 116th St	212-427-6062	El Barrio's oldest record store.
The Children's Place	163 E 125th St	212-348-3607	Cute clothes for little ones.
Don Paco Lopez Panaderia	2129 Third Ave	212-876-0700	Spanish El Barrio bakery.
Gothic Cabinet Craft	2268 Third Ave	212-410-3508	Real wood furniture.
La Marqueta	Park Ave & 114th St	212-534-4900	Mainly Puerto Rican foodstuffs.
Morrone Bakery	324 E 116th St	212-722-2972	Italian bakery with prosciutto bread, whole wheat loaves, and baguettes.
Motherhood Maternity	163 E 125th St	212-987-8808	Casual maternity wear.
Payless Shoe Source	2143 Third Ave	212-289-2251	Inexpensive shoes.
R&S Strauss Auto	2005 Third Ave	212-410-6688	Power steering fluid and windshield wipers 'till 9pm!
VIM	2239 Third Ave	212-369-5033	Street wear—jeans, sneakers, tops—for all.

Map 21 • Manhattanville / Hamilton Heights

The Adventist Care Center	528 W 145th St	212-926-1203	Thrift store with a great selection of hats.
B-Jays USA	540 W 143rd St	212-694-3160	Every sneaker under the sun.
El Mundo	3791 Broadway	212-368-3648	Cheap homegoods and discounted brand name apparel.
Foot Locker	3549 Broadway	212-491-0927	Get your sneakers here.
SOH-Straight Out of Harlem Creative Outlet	704 St Nicholas Ave	212-234-5944	Unique gifts and crafts.
VIM	508 W 145th St	212-491-1143	Street wear—jeans, sneakers, tops—for all.

Map 22 • Harlem (Upper)

Baskin-Robbins	2730 Frederick Douglass Blvd	212-862-0635	31 flavors and other frozen treats.
New York Public Library Shop	Schomburg Ctr, 515 Lenox Ave	212-491-2206	Shop specializing in Black history and culture.

Map 23 • Washington Heights

Baskin-Robbins	728 W 181st St	212-923-9239	31 flavors and other frozen treats.
Carrot Top Pastries	3931 Broadway	212-927-4800	Top carrot cake, muffins, chocolate cake, rugalach, and more.
The Children's Place	600 W 181st St	212-923-7244	Cute clothes for little ones.
Fever	1387 St Nicholas Ave	212-781-6232	For ladies, at night.
Footco	599 W 181st St	212-928-3330	Sneakers galore.
Foot Locker	621 W 181st St	212-568-6091	Get your sneakers here.
Goodwill Industries	512 W 181st St	212-923-7910	Jeans, business attire, baby and children's clothing, housewares and appliances, furniture, and more.
Modell's	606 W 181st St	212-568-3000	Generic sporting goods.
Payless Shoe Source	617 W 181st St	212-795-9183	Inexpensive shoes.
Planet Girls	3923 Broadway	212-927-0542	Cute clothes. Plants all over the store.
Santana Banana	661 W 181st St	212-568-4096	Leather shoes for men and women who are in to leather.
Tribeca	655 W 181st St	212-543-3600	Trendy store for women. Good soundtrack.
VIM	561 W 181st St	212-781-8801	Street wear—jeans, sneakers, tops—for all.

Map 25 · Inwood

Carrot Top Pastries	5025 Broadway	212-569-1532	Top carrot cake, muffins, chocolate cake, rugalach, and more.
The Cloisters	Ft Tryon Park	212-650-2277	Dark Age trinkets.
Foot Locker	146 Dyckman St	212-544-8613	There's a lot of shoe stores around here.
K&R Florist	4955 Broadway	212-942-2222	The best flower shop in the area.
Payless Shoe Source	560 W 207th St	212-544-9328	Inexpensive shoes.
Radio Shack	180 Dyckman St	212-304-0364	Official post-nuclear-war survivor, w/ Keith Richards and cockroaches.
Radio Shack	576 W 207th St	212-544-2180	Official post-nuclear-war survivor, w/ Keith Richards and cockroaches.
Tread Bike Shop	225 Dyckman St	212-544-7055	Where to fix your bike after riding through Inwood Hill Park.
VIM	565 W 207th St	212-942-7478	Street wear—jeans, sneakers, tops—for all.

Battery Park City

DSW Shoe Warehouse	102 North End Ave	212-945-7419	Fabulous choices for men's and women's shoes.
Shop Caravan	Various locations	917-415-4658	Hip, fashion boutique-on-wheels that parks all over town.

Map 26 · Astoria

El Manara	25-95 Steinway St	718-267-9495	Middle Eastern groceries and sundry items, great olive bar.
Emack & Boilio's	21-50 31st St	718-278-5380	Excellent ice cream from the Boston chain.
The Furniture Market	22-08 Astoria Blvd	718-545-3935	Antiques and thrift home goods at all price points.
Jolson's Wines & Liquors	22-24 31st St	718-728-2020	Friendly, knowledgeable staff and a great wine selection.
Laziza of New York Pastries	25-78 Steinway St	718-777-7676	City's best Middle Eastern baked treats.
Loveday 31	33-06 31st Ave	718-728-4057	Hip new and vintage clothes.
Martha's Country Bakery	36-21 Ditmars Blvd	718-545-9737	Best pound cake around, and everything else is good too.
Mediterranean Foods	23-18 31st St	718-721-0221	Greek groceries and prepared foods.
Rose & Joe's Italian Bakery	22-40 31st St	718-721-9422	Fresh cannolis made to order.
The Second Best	30-07 Astoria Blvd	718-204-8844	Great source for cheap secondhand furniture and knick-knacks.
Thessalikon Pastry Shop	33-21 31st Ave	718-545-8249	Famous source for takeaway trays of fabulous spanako-pita.

Map 27 · Long Island City

Celtic Art	24-15 Jackson Ave	718-482-7624	Irish and Scottish art and gifts.
City Dog Lounge	49-02 Vernon Blvd	718-707-3027	Pet accessories and services.
Greenmarket	48th Ave b/w 5th St & Vernon Blvd	212-788-7476	Local farmers and bakers, every Saturday except in winter.
Next Level Floral Design	47-30 Vernon Blvd	718-937-1155	Innovative designs that grace some of the cities' best tables.
Slovak-Czech Varieties	10-59 Jackson Ave	718-752-2093	Everything you forgot to bring back from Prague.
Subdivision	48-18 Vernon Blvd	718-482-1899	Trendy clothing boutique and art gallery.
Vine Wine	12-09 Jackson Ave	718-433-2611	Expertly selected wines, almost all under $20.

Map 28 · Greenpoint

Chopin Chemists	911 Manhattan Ave	718-383-7822	Polish-speaking; useful location.
The City Mouse	1015 Manhattan Ave	718-361-5832	Toy shop.
Dee & Dee	777 Manhattan Ave	718-389-0181	Mega dollar store; cheap stuff.
The Garden	921 Manhattan Ave	718-389-6448	Organic groceries and Polish goth chicks!
Mini Me	123 Nassau Ave	718-349-0333	Baby and kid's clothing.
Polam	952 Manhattan Ave	718-383-2763	Quality Polish meat market with cheap bulk pickles.
Pop's Popular Clothing	7 Franklin St	718-349-7677	Great second-hand clothing, especially jeans.
Syrena Bakery	207 Norman Ave	718-349-0560	Very nice Polish bakery with an espresso bar and bagels.
The Thing	1001 Manhattan Ave	718-349-8234	Unusual second-hand store offers thousands of used LPs.
Uncle Louie G's	172 Greenpoint Ave	718-349-1199	So many flavors, so little time.
The Vortex	1084 Manhattan Ave	718-609-6066	Interesting junk shop full of collectable and vintage items.
Wizard Electroland	863 Manhattan Ave	718-349-6889	Electronics store.

Map 29 · Williamsburg

Amarcord Vintage Fashion	223 Bedford Ave	718-963-4001	Well edited vintage goodies, many pieces directly from Europe.
American Apparel	104 N 6th St	718-218-0002	Sweatshop-free clothing for liberal New Yorkers.
Artist & Craftsman	761 Metropolitan Ave	718-782-7765	Art supplies.
Beacon's Closet	88 N 11th St	718-486-0816	Rad resale with lots of gems.
Bedford Cheese Shop	Mini Mall, 218 Bedford Ave	718-599-7588	Best cheese selection in the borough.
Brooklyn Industries	162 Bedford Ave	718-486-6464	Brooklyn-centric t-shirts, sweaters, coats, bags.
Buffalo Exchange	504 Driggs Ave	718-384-6901	Recycled clothing chain's first NYC store.
Calliope	135 Grand St	718-486-0697	Locally designed goods, and hip high end accessories.
Catbird	390 Metropolitan Ave	718-388-7688	Unique clothing and jewelry from up-and-coming designers.
Domsey's Warehouse	431 Broadway	718-384-6000	Ready to dig? Picked over by hipsters, but bargains still abound.
Earwax Records	Mini Mall, 218 Bedford Ave	718-486-3771	Record store with all the indie classics.
Emily's Pork Store	426 Graham Ave	718-383-7216	Broccoli rabe sausage is their specialty.
Flores Antiques Clothing	529 Grand St	718-387-3369	Vintage western and sequins.
Flowers By Marisol	568 Grand St	718-782-7917	Classic arrangements and gifts.
Flying Squirrel	96 N 6th St	718-218-7775	Cute baby clothes.
Golden Calf	86 N 6th St	718-302-8800	Eclectic retro and modern housewares.
Joe's Busy Corner	552 Driggs Ave	718-388-6372	Deli with cold cuts and pasta.
Mario and Sons Meat Market	662 Metropolitan Ave	718-486-9317	Reliable neighborhood butcher.
Marlow and Sons	81 Broadway	718-384-1441	Fancy bodega for new loft owners.
Matamoros Puebla Gorcery	193 Bedford Ave	718-782-5044	Mexican grocery and taqueria.
The Mini-Market	Mini Mall, 218 Bedford Ave	718-302-9337	Hodge-podge of tchotchkes and fun clothes.
Metropolitan Fish	635 Metropolitan Ave	718-387-6835	Good selection of fresh fish.
Model T Meats	404 Graham Ave	718-389-1553	Italian butcher with sawdust floors.
Napoli Bakery	616 Metropolitan Ave	718-384-6945	Plain old Italian bakery.
NY Design Room	339 Bedford Ave	718-302-4981	Design services with something for everyone.
PS 9 Pet Supplies	169 N 9th St	718-486-6465	Excellent pet supply store.
Roulette	188 Havemeyer St	718-218-7104	Choice vintage housewares at affordable prices.
Savino's	111 Conselyea St	718-388-2038	Homemade ravioli.
Spacial Etc	199 Bedford Ave	718-599-7962	Overpriced housewares, baby clothes, and knitted goods.
Spoonbill & Sugartown	Mini Mall, 218 Bedford Ave	718-387-7322	Excellent indie bookstore.
Tedone Dairy Products	597 Metropolitan Ave	718-387-5830	The finest mozzarella, since 1928.
Two Jakes	320 Wythe Ave	718-782-7780	Furniture: Mod, metal, misc.
Yarn Tree	347 Bedford Ave	718-384-8030	Knitting trend hit you yet? Visit and it will!

Map 30 · Brooklyn Heights / DUMBO / Downtown

Almondine Bakery	85 Water St	718-797-5026	Pastry smells waft to the street.
City Barn Antiques	145 Front St	718-855-8566	Heywood-Wakefield experts.
Design Within Reach	76 Montague St	718-643-1015	Not really, but the stuff IS cool.
Halcyon	57 Pearl St	718-260-9299	Vinyl for DJ fanatics.
Half Pint	55 Washington St	718-875-4007	Ditch Gap Kids!
Heights Prime Meats	59 Clark St	718-237-0133	Butcher.
Jacques Torres Chocolate	66 Water St	718-875-9772	The Platonic ideal of chocolate.
Lassen & Hennigs	114 Montague St	718-875-6272	Specialty foods and deli.
Recycle-A-Bicycle	55 Washington St	718-858-2972	Bikes to the ceiling.
Tapestry the Salon	107 Montague St	718-522-1202	Spa.
West Elm	75 Front St	718-875-7757	Cool home décor at reasonable prices.
Wonk	68 Jay St	718-596-8026	Furnish your penthouse.

Map 31 · Fort Greene / Clinton Hill

Cake Man Raven Confectionary	708 Fulton St	718-694-2253	Get the red velvet cake!
Carol's Daughter	1 S Elliot Pl	718-596-1862	Skincare.
Frosted Moon	154 Vanderbilt Ave	718-858-3161	Full of pretty things.
The Greene Grape	765 Fulton St	718-797-WINE	Nice new wine shop.
Kiki's Pet Spa	239 DeKalb Ave	718-857-7272	For pet-worshippers.
L'Epicerie	270 Vanderbilt Ave	718-636-0360	French gourmet.
Malchijah Hats	225 DeKalb Ave	718-643-3269	Beautiful and unique hats.
The Midtown Greenhouse Garden Center	115 Flatbush Ave	718-636-0020	Fully stocked with plants and gardening supplies.
My Little India	96 S Elliot Pl	718-855-5220	Furniture, candles, textiles.
Nubian Heritage	560 Fulton St	718-797-4400	Oils, oils, and more scented oils.
Owa African Market	434 Myrtle Ave	718-643-8487	Beads galore.

Planet Pleasure	527 Myrtle Ave	718-230-3737	Frightening array of sex toys and related items.
Sodafine	246 DeKalb Ave	718-230-3060	Hot little numbers with big price tags.
Target	Atlantic Terminal, 139 Flatbush Ave	718-290-1109	Bulls eye!
White Elephant Gallery	572 Myrtle Ave	718-789-9423	Mindset is key. It could be treasure.
Yu Interiors	15 Greene Ave	718-237-5878	Modern furniture, bags, and candles.

Map 32 • BoCoCa / Red Hook

American Apparel	112 Court St	718-855-4627	Sweatshop-free clothing for liberal New Yorkers.
American Beer Distributors	256 Court St	718-875-0226	International beer merchant. NFT pick.
Baked	359 Van Brunt St	718-222-0345	Death by dessert.
Book Court	163 Court St	718-875-3677	The neighborhood spot for books.
Brooklyn Industries	100 Smith St	718-596-3986	Represent!
Butter	389 Atlantic Ave	718-260-9033	Very cool and very expensive boutique.
Caputo's Fine Foods	460 Court St	718-855-8852	Italian gourmet specialties.
D'Amico Foods	309 Court St	718-875-5403	The best coffee in the 'hood, if not the city.
Environment337	337 Smith St	718-522-1767	Another Smith Street hit.
Frida's Closet	296 Smith St	718-855-0911	Women's skirts, shirts, and sweaters with a Frida Kahlo-feel.
The Green Onion	274 Smith St	718-246-2804	Fine children's clothing, but service with an attitude.
Hats &	266 President St	718-643-1214	Custom made chapeaus designed directly on your head.
Kimera	366 Atlantic Ave	718-422-1147	Great pillows.
Lowe's	118 Second Ave	718-249-1154	For all your home improvement needs.
Marquet	221 Court St	718-855-1289	Top NYC croissants and quiches.
Mazzola Bakery	192 Union St	718-643-1719	Top bakery in CG.
Nova Zembla	117 Atlantic Ave	718-222-5705	Furniture and housewares, every which way.
Refinery	254 Smith St	718-643-7861	Great bags and accessories.
Rocketship	208 Smith St	718-797-1348	Comic Books and Graphic Novels.
Sahadi Importing Company	187 Atlantic Ave	718-624-4550	Middle Eastern specialty and fine foods since 1948.
Staubitz Meat Market	222 Court St	718-624-0014	Top NYC butcher.
Swallow	361 Smith St	718-222-8201	Fabulous glass, excellent jewelry, great books. An exquisite store.
Sweet Melissa	276 Court St	718-855-3410	Good desserts, tea, and coffee.
Tuller	199 Court St	718-222-9933	Delectable and expensive gourmet shop. Great cheese.
Zipper	333 Smith St	718-596-0333	Excellent home accessories and great books.

Map 33 • Park Slope / Prospect Heights / Windsor Terrace

3R Living	276 Fifth Ave	718-832-0951	Eco-friendly and organic products and gifts.
Artesana Home	170 Seventh Ave	718-369-9881	Housewares better traveled than you.
Baby Bird	428 Seventh Ave	718-788-4506	Near boutique Bird's, you know, baby.
Barnes & Noble	267 Seventh Ave	718-832-9066	Books and such.
Beacon's Closet	220 Fifth Ave	718-230-1630	Rad resale with lots of gems.
Bird	430 Seventh Ave	718-768-4940	Unique women's clothes and accessories.
Blue Apron Foods	812 Union St	718-230-3180	Purveyors of cheese and other fine foods.
Bob and Judi's Collectibles	217 Fifth Ave	718-638-5770	Antiques, vintage novelties.
Boing Boing	204 Sixth Ave	718-398-0251	Boutique for mother and child.
Brooklyn Industries	206 Fifth Ave	718-789-2764	Brooklyn-centric t-shirts, sweatshirts, coats, bags.
Brooklyn Superhero Supply	372 Fifth Ave	718-499-9884	Capes, treasure maps, and bottled special powers. Also, McSweeney's publications.
Castor & Pollux	76 Sixth Ave	718-398-4141	Schmancy boutique for fashion and accessories.
Clay Pot	162 Seventh Ave	718-788-6564	Hand-crafted gifts, jewelry.
Cog and Pearl	190 Fifth Ave	718-623-8200	World's coolest crafts, jewelry, art.
Community Book Store	143 Seventh Ave	718-783-3075	Books, coffee, garden.
Ecco Home Design	232 Seventh Ave	718-788-1088	Elegant, modern.
Eidolon	233 Fifth Ave	718-638-8194	Local designer labels.

Fabrica	619 Vanderbilt Ave	718-398-3831	Elegantly designed home furnishings.
Fifth Avenue Record and Tape Center	439 Fifth Ave	718-499-8483	Unassuming locale for surprising finds.
Greenjeans	449 Seventh Ave	718-907-5835	Handcrafted jewelry and such.
Hibiscus	564A Vandebilt Ave	718-638-6850	Flowers, plants and arrangements for all occasions.
Hooti Couture	321 Flatbush Ave	718-857-1977	Girlie Vintage.
JackRabbit Sports	151 Seventh Ave	718-636-9000	Mecca for runners, swimmers, and cyclists.
Leaf and Bean	83 Seventh Ave	718-638-5791	Coffees and teas.
Loom	115 Seventh Ave	718-789-0061	Irresistible gifts and housewares.
Mandee	509 Fifth Ave	718-768-2521	Mandee girl, you are my world.
Mostly Modern	383 Seventh Ave	718-499-9867	Winsome wares for space-age bachelor pads.
Nancy Nancy	244 Fifth Ave	718-789-5262	Cards, gifts, novelties.
Orange Blossom	180 Lincoln Pl	347-247-5917	Stuff to buy for someone else's kid.
Park Slope Food Co-op	782 Union St	718-622-0560	Best spot for food shopping in Brooklyn.
Pieces	671 Vanderbilt Ave	718-857-7211	Urban clothes for sleek hip-hop crowd.
PS 321 Flea Market	Seventh Ave & 1st St	718-421-6763	Flea market in a playground setting, open weekends.
Premium Goods	347 Fifth Ave	718-369-7477	Limited-edition and rare sneakers.
Rare Device	453 Seventh Ave	718-301-6375	Cool design shop.
RedLipstick	560 Vanderbilt Ave	718-857-9534	Luxurious hand-knitted originals. Sign up for a class.
Reverse	176 Fifth Ave	718-638-2252	Tiny, eclectic vintage shop.
Shoe Mine	463 Seventh Ave	718-369-2624	Too far out to be so upscale.
Somethin' Else	294 Fifth Ave	718-768-5131	Meticulously cool music and clothes.
Sound Track	119 Seventh Ave	718-622-1888	CDs and LPs.
Stitch Therapy	176 Lincoln Pl	718-398-2020	Luxurious yarns. Plus knitting classes.
Traditions	465 Fifth Ave	718-768-1430	Organic food heaven for those who are choosy about protein power.
Trailer Park	77 Sterling Pl	718-623-2170	Unique and handcrafted furnishings.
Uncle Louie G's	741 Union St	718-623-6668	So many flavors, so little time.

Map 34 · Hoboken

Air Studio	55 2nd St	201-239-1511	Cutting edge women's clothing boutique, featuring the hot designers of tomorrow.
Basic Foods	204 Washington St	201-610-1100	Not all that personable, but a good selection.
Battaglia's	319 Washington St	201-798-1122	Interesting gifts and housewares.
Big Fun Toys	602 Washington St	201-714-9575	What it says.
City Paint & Hardware	130 Washington St	201-659-0061	Everything, including kitchen sinks.
Galatea	1224 Washington St	201-963-1522	Elegantly luscious lingerie, chosen with an expert eye.
Hand Mad	86 Park Ave	201-653-7276	Folk, Funk, Fine Art. Plus groovy gift-wrapping.
Hoboken Farmboy	127 Washington St	201-656-0581	It doesn't come much healthier. Good advice for your health needs.
Kings Fresh Ideas-333 River	333 River Rd	201-386-2300	Yuppie groceries for high-rise dwellers.
Kings Fresh Ideas-Shipyard	1212 Shipyard Ln	201-239-4060	Yuppie groceries for high-rise dwellers.
Lisa's Italian Deli	901 Park Ave	201-795-3204	Delicious heroes, large selection of Italian groceries.
Makeovers	302 Washington St	201-420-1444	Every hair care product known to womankind. A fantasy for your follicles.
Peper	1028 Washington St	201-217-1911	Hoboken's exclusive clothing. A must for your next high school reunion.
Sobsey's Produce	92 Bloomfield St	201-795-9398	Expert greengrocer. Exotic produce and gourmet foods.
Sparrow Wine and Liquor	1224 Shipyard Ln	201-659-1501	Good selection of local and imported products. Staff are helpful with selections.
Sparrow Wine and Liquor	126 Washington St	201-659-1500	Good selection of local and imported products. Staff are helpful with selections.
Tunes New & Used CDs	225 Washington St	201-653-3355	Support your local indie music store. They'll order stuff for you.
Yes I Do	312 Washington St	201-659-3300	Elegant cards, stationery, invitations, printing, and gifts.

Map 35 · Jersey City

| Harborside Shopping Complex | | | Mall. Isn't life just grand, Martha? |
| Newport Center Mall | 30 Mall Dr W | 201-626-2025 | Mall. Ah, the Jersey aesthetic… |

So long as there are adventurous artists putting on plays in abandoned storefronts and opportunistic real estate developers knocking down beautiful old theatres to put up hotels, the New York theatre scene will always be adding a few venues here and deleting a few venues there. What remains constant is that on any given night there are at least dozens, and more often hundreds, of live theatre performances to be seen. And the best ones are not always the most expensive.

Broadway (theatres in the Times Square vicinity that hold at least 500 people) still has the reputation of being the place to see American theatre at its finest, but the peculiar fact of the matter is that there is more much money to be gained by appealing to the infrequent theatregoer than there is by trying to please the connoisseur. As a result, shows that are looked down on, if not despised, by many lovers of the theatre wind up selling out for years (Mamma Mia, anyone?), while more ambitious, artistically admired plays and musicals struggle to find an audience. Check out theatre chat boards like **BroadwayWorld.com** and **TalkinBroadway.com** to see what the people who see everything have to say.

Nobody gets famous doing live theatre anymore, so if you've never heard of the actor whose name is twinkling in lights (Cherry Jones, Brian Stokes Mitchell, Raul Esparza, Christine Ebersole...) chances are that person has the stage experience and acting chops to keep you enthralled for two and a half hours, unlike the mega celebrities (P. Diddy, Melanie Griffith) who make their stage acting debuts in starring roles they're not prepared for. Of course, there are also actors with extensive stage credits who come back to Broadway regularly after becoming famous. That's why we love John Lithgow, Cynthia Nixon and Phylicia Rashad.

Many great performers work Off-Broadway (Manhattan theatres seating 100-499 people) where the writing and directing is actually more important than spectacle and scores made up of classic pop songs. Off-Off Broadway (fewer than 100 seats) is a terrific grab bag of both beginners and seasoned pros doing material that is often unlikely to draw in masses. And tickets are pretty cheap, too.

TheatreMania.com keeps an extensive list of just about every show in New York, with direct links to the web sites that sell tickets. Many shows offer a limited number of inexpensive standing room and/or same-day rush tickets. A detailed directory of such offers can be found at **TalkinBroadway.com**.

Thousands of same-day tickets for Broadway and Off-Broadway shows are sold for 25%-50% off at the **TKTS** booths in Times Square (long lines) and at the South Street Seaport (short lines). They take cash and traveler's checks only. Check for hours and to see what's been recently available at **www.tdf.org**. Don't expect to get a bargain for the top-selling hits, but most shows use this booth at some

time or another. You can also download discount coupons at Playbill.com that you can use to get seats in advance.

Keep an eye out for shows by these lesser-known companies:

The young **Classical Theatre of Harlem** (www.classicaltheatreofharlem.org) has quickly earned a reputation for mounting exciting, edgy revivals of classics from Shakespeare, Ionesco and Brecht, as well as solid productions from more recent greats such as August Wilson and Melvin Van Peebles. A multicultural company that frequently casts against racial type; they draw a youthful audience with imaginative interpretations.

The **Mint Theatre Company** (www.minttheater.org) specializes in reviving Broadway plays from the past they call "worthy, but neglected". In their tiny space you'll see interesting comedies and dramas from the likes of A.A. Milne, Edith Wharton and Thomas Wolfe played traditionally with sets and costumes that really make you feel like you're watching a production from over 50 years ago.

Musicals Tonight! does the same kind of thing with forgotten musicals, only presenting them in low budgeted, but highly energized staged readings. Nowadays most musicals revived on Broadway are revised and updated to the point where they lose their authenticity. But if you're in the mood to see what an Irving Berlin ragtime show from 1915 was really like, or if you want to see a Cole Porter turner from the 30s with all of the dated topical references that confused audiences even back then, Musicals Tonight! serves up the past as it really was written. And check for their special concerts where Broadway understudies sing songs from the roles they are currently covering.

Broadway insiders know that Monday nights, when most shows are dark, is often the hottest night of the week for entertainment. That's when performers use their night off to partake in benefits and special events. Consistently among the best are shows from Scott Siegel's **Broadway By The Year** series at Town Hall (www.the-townhall-nyc.org). Each one-night concert is packed with theatre and cabaret stars singing hits and obscurities introduced on Broadway in one selected year. Siegel also produces **Broadway Unplugged** at Town Hall, a concert of theatre performers singing showtunes without amplification. The atmosphere is like a sports event, with the audience wildly cheering each naturally-voiced solo.

Pearl Theatre Company (Map 6), presently located at 80 St. Mark's Place, is one of the 15 or so largest institutional theaters in New York City. 2004 marked their 20th anniversary, and they continue to grow as a resident company and a classical repertory, offering delights from Sheridan, Shakespeare, Aeschylus, Marivaux, and Ibsen. www.pearl-theatre.org

Now in its seventh season, Horse Trade continues its commitment to producing a varied program of performance series, readings, workshops, and fully-realized productions. Most events are performed at **The Kraine Theater** (**Map 6**), which also houses the Red Room (**Map 6**) on its third floor. The theaters are also available to rent for rehearsals and performances. www.httheater.org

HERE (**Map 5**) not only houses two small theaters, but it also has an amazing gallery space and a cozy café/bar—perfect for pre- or post-show drinks. www.here.org

In Chelsea, **The Kitchen** (**Map 8**) literally began in the unused kitchen of the Mercer Arts Center, housed in the Broadway Central Hotel in Greenwich Village. In 1985, **The Kitchen** moved into its new and permanent home at 512 W 19th Street. The venue plays host to new performance artists blending music, dance, video, art, and spoken word. www.thekitchen.org

Located in a former public school on First Avenue and 9th Street in the East Village, **P.S. 122** (**Map 7**) is a not-for-profit arts center serving New York City's dance and performance community. Shows rotate through on a regular basis, so check the website for the latest schedule. www.ps122.org

The outdoor **Delacorte Theater** (**Map 15**) in Central Park hosts performances only during the summer months. Tickets to the ridiculously popular and free Shakespeare in the Park performances are given away at 1 pm at the Delacorte and also at the **Public Theater** (**Map 6**) (425 Lafayette St) on the day of each performance. Hopefully, you enjoy camping because people line up for days in their tents and sleeping bags just to secure a ticket!

Just on the other side of the Manhattan Bridge in Brooklyn is the world famous **Brooklyn Academy of Music**. A thriving urban arts center, **BAM** brings domestic and international performances and film to Brooklyn. The center includes two theaters (**Harvey Lichtenstein Theater** and **Howard Gilman Opera House**), the Bam Rose Cinemas, and the **BAMcafé**, a restaurant and live music venue. Our favorite season is the **Next Wave**, an annual three-month celebration of cutting-edge dance, theater, music, and opera. www.bam.org

Broadway

			Map
Al Hirschfeld Theatre	302 W 45th St	212-239-6200	12
Ambassador Theatre	219 W 49th St	212-239-6200	12
American Airlines Theatre	227 W 42nd St	212-719-1300	12
August Wilson Theatre	245 W 52nd St	212-239-6200	12
Belasco Theatre	111 W 44th St	212-239-6200	12
Bernard B Jacobs Theatre	242 W 45th St	212-239-6200	12
Biltmore Theatre	261 W 47th St	212-239-6200	12
Booth Theatre	222 W 45th St	212-239-6200	12
Broadhurst Theatre	235 W 44th St	212-239-6200	12
Broadway Theatre	1681 Broadway	212-239-6200	12
Brooks Atkinson Theatre	256 W 47th St	212-307-4100	12
Cadillac Winter Garden Theatre	1634 Broadway	212-239-6200	12
Circle in the Square Theatre	1633 Broadway	212-239-6200	12
Cort Theatre	138 W 48th St	212-239-6200	12
Ethel Barrymore Theatre	243 W 47th St	212-239-6200	12
Eugene O'Neill Theatre	230 W 49th St	212-239-6200	12
Gershwin Theatre	222 W 51st St	212-307-4100	12
Helen Hayes Theatre	240 W 44th St	212-239-6200	12
Hilton Theater	213 W 42nd St	212-556-4750	12
Imperial Theater	249 W 45th St	212-239-6200	12
John Golden Theatre	252 W 45th St	212-239-6200	12
Longacre Theatre	220 W 48th St	212-239-6200	12
Lunt-Fontanne Theatre	205 W 46th St	212-307-4100	12
Lyceum Theatre	149 W 45th St	212-239-6200	12
Majestic Theater	245 W 44th St	212-239-6200	12
Marquis Theatre	1535 Broadway	212-382-0100	12
Minskoff Theatre	200 W 45th St	212-869-0550	12
Music Box Theatre	239 W 45th St	212-239-6200	12
Nederlander Theatre	208 W 41st St	212-307-4100	12
Neil Simon Theatre	250 W 52nd St	212-307-4100	12
New Amsterdam Theatre	214 W 42nd St	212-307-4100	12
Palace Theatre	1564 Broadway	212-307-4100	12
Richard Rodgers Theatre	226 W 46th St	212-221-1211	12
Roundabout/Laura Pels Theatre	111 W 46th St	212-719-1300	12
Schoenfeld Theatre	236 W 45th St	212-239-6200	12
Shubert Theatre	225 W 44th St	212-239-6200	12
St James Theatre	246 W 44th St	212-239-6200	12
Studio 54	254 W 54th St	212-719-1300	12
Vivian Beaumont Theatre Lincoln Center	W 65th St & Amsterdam Ave	212-362-7600	14
Walter Kerr Theatre	219 W 48th St	212-239-6200	12

Off Broadway

			Map
45 Bleecker Theater	45 Bleecker St	212-253-7017	6
47th Street Theater	304 W 47th St	212-239-6200	12
59E59 Theaters	59 E 59th St	212-279-4200	13
Acorn Theatre	410 W 42nd St	212-279-4200	11
Actor's Playhouse	100 Seventh Ave	212-239-6200	9
American Theatre of Actors	314 W 54th St	212-239-6200	
Astor Place Theatre	434 Lafayette St	212-254-4370	6
Atlantic Theater Company	336 W 20th St	212-645-8015	8
Barrow Street Theater	27 Barrow St	212-239-6200	5
Bouwerie Lane Theatre	330 Bowery	212-677-0060	6
Century Center for the Performing Arts	111 E 15th St	212-239-6200	10
Cherry Lane Theater	38 Commerce St	212-989-2020	5
City Center	131 W 55th St	212-581-7907	12
Classic Stage Co	136 E 13th St	212-677-4210	6
Daryl Roth Theatre	20 Union Sq E	212-239-6200	10
Delacorte Theater W 81st St	Central Park,	212-539-8750	15
Dodger Stages	340 W 50th St	212-239-6200	11
Harold Clurman Theatre	412 W 42nd St	212-279-4200	11
HSA Theater	645 St Nicholas Ave	212-868-4444	21
Irish Repertory Theatre	132 W 22nd St	212-727-2737	9
June Havoc Theater	312 W 36th St	212-868-4444	8
Kirk Theatre	410 W 42nd St	212-279-4200	11
Lambs Theater	130 W 44th St	212-239-6200	12
Lion Theatre	410 W 42nd St	212-279-4200	11
Little Shubert Theatre	422 W 42nd St	212-239-6200	11
Lucille Lortel Theatre	121 Christopher St	212-279-4200	5
Manhattan Ensemble Theatre	55 Mercer St	212-925-1900	3
Mazer Theater	197 East Broadway	212-239-6200	4

Arts & Entertainment • **Theaters**

Off Broadway—*continued*

			Map
Minetta Lane Theatre	18 Minetta Ln	212-307-4100	6
Mitzi E Newhouse Theater	W 65th &	212-239-6200	14
Lincoln Center	Amsterdam Ave		
New York Theatre	79 E 4th St	212-460-5475	6
Workshop			
Orpheum Theater	126 Second Ave	212-477-2477	6
Pearl Theatre Co	80 St Marks Pl	212-598-9802	6
Perry St Theatre	31 Perry St	212-868-4444	5
Players Theatre	115 MacDougal St		6
Playhouse 91	316 E 91st St	212-831-2000	17
Playwrights Horizons	416 W 42nd St	212-279-4200	11
Theatre			
Promenade Theatre	2162 Broadway	212-239-6200	14
Samuel Beckett Theatre	412 W 42nd St	212-307-4100	11
Second Stage Theatre	307 W 43rd St	212-246-4422	12
Signature Theatre: Peter	555 W 42nd St	212-244-7529	11
Norton Space			
Snapple Theatre Center	1627 Broadway	212-695-3401	12
St Lukes Church	308 W 46th St	212-239-6200	12
The Duke on 42nd Street	229 W 42nd St	212-239-6200	12
The Public Theater	425 Lafayette St	212-539-8500	6
The Zipper Theatre	336 W 37th St	212-563-0480	8
Theater at St Clement's	423 W 46th St	212-868-4444	11
TriBeCa Performing Arts	199 Chambers St	212-220-1460	2
Center			
Union Square Theater	100 E 17th St	212-307-4100	10
Upstairs at Studio 54	254 W 54th St	212-719-1300	12
Village Theatre	158 Bleecker St	212-307-4100	6
Vineyard Theatre	108 E 15th St	212-353-0303	10
Vinnie Black's Coliseum	221 W 46th St	212-352-3101	12
at the Edison Hotel			
Westside Theatre	407 W 43rd St	212-239-6200	11
York Theatre at St Peter's	619 Lexington	212-935-5820	13
Church	Ave		

Off-Off Broadway

			Map
13th Street Theatre	50 W 13th St	212-675-6677	6
29th Street Repertory	212 W 29th St	212-465-0575	9
Theatre			
45th St Theatre	354 W 45th St	212-279-4200	11
59E59 Theaters	59 E 59th St	212-279-4200	13
78th Street Theatre Lab	236 W 78th St	212-873-9050	14
Abingdon Mainstage	312 W 36th St	212-868-4444	8
Theatre			
Access Theatre	380 Broadway,	212-966-1047	3
Actor's Theater Workshop	145 W 28th St	212-947-1386	8
American Place Theatre	266 W 37th St	212-594-4482	8
American Theatre of	314 W 54th St	212-239-6200	11
Actors			
American Theatre of	314 W 54th St	212-239-6200	11
Actors			
ArcLight Theatre	152 W 71st St	212-595-0355	14
Ars Nova Theatre	511 W 54th St	212-868-4444	15
Axis Theater	1 Sheridan Sq	212-807-9300	5
Barrow Group Arts Center	312 W 36th St	212-868-4444	8
Belt Theater	336 W 37th St	212-563-0480	8
Blue Heron Arts Center	123 E 24th St	212-979-5000	10
Cedar Lake	547 W 26th St	212-868-4444	8
Center Stage, NY	48 W 21st St	212-929-2228	9
Collective: Unconscious	279 Church St	212-254-5277	1

Creative Artists	303 W 42nd St,	212-316-0400	12
Laboratory	3rd Fl		
Dominion Theatre	428 Lafayette St	212-868-4444	6
DR2 Theatre	103 E 15th St	212-239-6200	10
Duo Theatre	62 E 4th St	212-598-4320	6
Flea Theatre	41 White St	212-226-0051	3
Gene Frankel Theatre	24 Bond St	212-777-1767	6
Gertrude Stein Repertory	15 W 26th St	212-725-7254	
Theater			
Greenwich Street Theatre	547 Greenwich St		n/a
HERE	145 Sixth Ave	212-647-0202	5
Hudson Guild	119 Ninth Ave	212-760-9800	8
Irish Arts Center	553 W 51st St	212-757-3318	11
Jewish Community	334 Amsterdam	646-505-5708	14
Center	Ave		
Julia Miles Theater	424 W 55th St	212-765-1706	11
La Mama ETC	74A E 4th St	212-475-7710	6
Lambs Theater	130 W 44th St	212-239-6200	12
Manhattan Theatre	177 MacDougal	212-260-4698	6
Source	St		
McGinn/Cazale Theatre	2162 Broadway	212-579-0528	14
Medicine Show Theatre	549 W 52nd St	212-262-4216	11
Metropolitan Playhouse	220a E 4th St,	212-995-5302	7
	2nd Fl		
Mint Theatre	311 W 43rd St,	212-315-0231	11
	5th Fl		
National Black Theatre	2031 Fifth Ave	212-722-3800	19
Nuyorican Poets Café	236 E 3rd St	212-505-8183	7
Ohio Theater	66 Wooster St	800-965-4827	6
People's Improv Theatre	154 W 29th St,	212-563-7488	9
	2nd Fl		
Phil Bosakowski Theatre	354 W 45th St	212-352-3101	11
Producers Club II	616 Ninth Ave	212-315-4743	11
PS 122	150 First Ave	212-477-5288	7
Rattlestick Theatre	224 Waverly Pl	212-627-2556	5
Repertorio EspaÐol	138 E 27th St	212-889-2850	10
Riverside Church	490 Riverside Dr	212-870-6700	18
Sanford Meisner Theatre	164 Eleventh Ave	212-206-1764	8
Soho Playhouse	15 Vandam St	212-691-1555	5
Soho Repertory Theatre	46 Walker St	212-941-8632	3
Sol Goldman Y	344 E 14th St	212-780-0800	6
St Bart's Playhouse	Park Ave & 50th	212-378-0248	13
	St		
Stage 36 @ TBG	312 W 36th St	212-868-4444	8
Storm Theatre	145 W 46th St	212-868-4444	12
Studio at Cherry Lane	38 Commerce St	212-989-2020	5
Theatre			
T Schreiber Studio	151 W 26th St	212-741-0209	9
TADA! Theatre	15 W 28th St	212-252-1619	9
Tenement Theater	97 Orchard St	212-431-0233	4
The Kitchen	512 W 19th St	212-255-5793	8
The Kraine Theater	85 E 4th St	212-868-4444	6
The Looking Glass	422 W 57th St	212-307-9467	11
Theatre			
The Ontological Theater	131 E 10th St	212-420-1916	6
at St Mark's Church-in-the-Bowery			
The Producers Club	358 W 44th St	212-315-4743	11
The Red Room	85 E 4th St		6
Theater for the New City	155 First Ave	212-979-6570	7
Theater Ten Ten	1010 Park Ave	212-288-3246	15
Urban Stages	259 W 30th St	212-868-4444	9
West End Theatre	263 W 86th St	212-352-3101	16
Wings Theater	154 Christopher St	212-627-2961	5
WOW Café	59 E 4th St	212-777-4280	6

Perfoming Arts

92nd Street Y Theatre	1395 Lexington Ave	212-996-1100	17
Alice Tully Hall	Lincoln Center 65th & Broadway	212-875-5050	14
Amato Opera	319 Bowery	212-228-8200	6
Apollo Theater	253 W 125th St	212-531-5300	19
Baruch Performing Arts Center	55 Lexington Ave	646-312-4085	10
Beacon Theater	2124 Broadway	212-496-7070	14
Bernie West Theatre at Baruch College	17 Lexington Ave	646-312-4085	10
Carnegie Hall	154 W 57th St	212-247-7800	12
Chicago City Limits Theatre	318 W 53rd St	212-888-5233	12
City Center	131 W 55th St	212-581-7907	12
Dance Theatre Workshop	219 W 19th St	212-924-0077	9
Dicapo Opera Theatre	184 E 76th St	212-288-9438	15
French Institute Florence Gould Hall	55 E 59th St	212-355-6160	13
Harry DeJur Playhouse	466 Grand St	212-598-0400	4
Joyce Theater	175 Eighth Ave Chelsea	212-242-0800	8
Lincoln Center for the Performing Arts	Broadway & 64th St	212-875-5456	14
Manhattan School of Music	120 Claremont Ave	212-749-2802	18
Merkin Concert Hall	129 W 67th St	212-501-3330	14
Miller Theater Columbia University	200 Dodge Hall 2960 Broadway	212-854-7799	18
New Victory Theatre	209 W 42nd St	212-239-6200	12
New York State Theatre	Lincoln Ctr,	212-870-5570	14
Radio City Music Hall	1260 Sixth Ave	212-247-4777	12
Sylvia and Danny Kaye Playhouse	695 Park Ave	212-772-5207	15
Symphony Space	2537 Broadway	212-864-5400	16
The Gerald W Lynch Theater at John Jay College	899 Tenth Ave	212-237-8005	11
The Theater at Madison Square Garden	2 Penn Plz	212-307-4111	9
Town Hall	123 W 43rd St	212-840-2824	12

Brooklyn

651 Arts	BAM 651 Fulton St	718-636-4181	31
Bargemusic	Fulton Ferry Landing near Brooklyn Bridge	718-624-2083	30
BRIC Studio	57 Rockwell Pl	718-855-7882	30
Brick Theatre	575 Metropolitan Ave	718-907-6189	29
Brooklyn Arts Council	55 Washington St	718-625-0080	30
Brooklyn Arts Exchange	421 Fifth Ave	718-832-0018	33
Brooklyn Family Theatre	1012 Eighth Ave	718-670-7205	33
Brooklyn Lyceum	227 Fourth Ave	718-857-4816	33
Brooklyn Queens Conservatory of Music	58 Seventh Ave	718-622-3300	33
Charlie's Pineapple Theater Company	208 N 8th St	718-907-0577	29
Galapagos Arts Space	70 N 6th St	718-782-5188	29
Gallery Players Theater	199 14th St	718-595-0547	33
Gilman Opera House	BAM 30 Lafayette Ave	718-636-4100	31
Harvey Lichtenstein Theater	BAM 651 Fulton St	718-636-4100	31
Paul Robeson Theatre	54 Greene Ave	718-783-9794	31
Puppetworks	338 Sixth Ave	718-965-3391	33
St Ann's Warehouse	38 Water St	718-254-8779	30
The Heights Players	26 Willow Pl	718-237-2752	30

Queens

Astoria Performing Arts Center	31-30 33rd St	718-393-7505	26
The Chocolate Factory	5-49 49th Ave	718-482-7069	27

News.
Culture.
Life.

WNYC ®

93.9FM AM820

New York Public Radio®

Look at Art From Every Angle.

14-19 Purves Street, Long Island City, NY
Thursday-Monday 11am-6pm
E/V to 23rd St/Ely Ave
to 45 Rd/Courthouse Square
to Court Square

SculptureCenter

Exhibiting new work by artists from New York and around the world, SculptureCenter is one of New York's most exciting destinations for contemporary art.

For current exhibit information call 718.361.1750 or go to www.sculpture-center.org

WHEN IT COMES TO

MORTGAGE FINANCING

NOBODY GETS A
BETTER **DEAL** THAN ME!

CALL *the*
NEW GENERATION *of*
MORTGAGE PROFESSIONALS
TODAY!

1.888.79.TRUMP

40 Wall Street, 25th Floor
New York, NY 10005

www.TrumpMortgage.com

TRUMP

TRUMP MORTGAGE, LLC

RESIDENTIAL AND COMMERCIAL MORTGAGE

As of 5/19/06 Trump Mortgage, LLC is: • Registered Mortgage Broker with NY and MA Banking Departments and licensed in AK and CO. • Registered as Mortgage Banker/Broker in FL, •
ME, MN, NM, NH, CT, CA, SD, & IA • If acting as a Mortgage Broker, Trump Mortgage, LLC arranges mortgage loans with third-party providers • Registration as Mortgage Banker/Brok
in all 50 States is in process. Visit us at www.trumpmortgage.com and click on "Licensing Information" for our updated list of state licenses.

THE BROOKLYN TOURISM & VISITORS CENTER

Historic Brooklyn Borough Hall, Ground Floor
209 Joralemon St. (btw Court/Adams), Brooklyn, NY 11201
Tel: (718) 802-3846
Subway: M R 2 3 4 5 A C F
Open Monday-Friday 10am-6pm
Visit our Gift Shop for authentic Brooklyn apparel,
books, postcards, and other souvenirs

www.visitbrooklyn.org

Brooklyn Tourism is an initiative of
Borough President Marty Markowitz
& Best of Brooklyn, Inc.
All profits to
Best of Brooklyn, Inc. a 501(c)3

NEW, WEST VILLAGE
500 Hudson St.
New York, NY

NEW, CHELSEA
161 8th Ave.
New York, NY

SOHO 212.219.0862
286 Lafayette St.
New York, NY

BOERUM HILL 718.596.3986
100 Smith St.
Brooklyn, NY

WILLIAMSBURG 718.486.6464
162 Bedford Ave.
Brooklyn, NY

SOUTHBURG 718.218.9166
184 Broadway
Brooklyn, NY

PARK SLOPE 718.789.2764
206 5th Ave.
Brooklyn, NY

SEVENTH AVENUE 718.788.5250
328 7th Ave.
Brooklyn, NY

BROOKLYN INDUSTRIES

THE BIG APPLE
(worms and all)

**New York's ONLY
Alternative Newsweekly**

www.nypress.com

ake the subway to 1904.

You'll feel like you've traveled back in time. The New York Transit Museum is oused in a historic subway station where you can board our vintage collection f subway and elevated trains and check out all the antique treasures from the world's greatest subway system.

If you have children, there are free kids' workshops every weekend. And be ure to visit the Museum Store for all kinds of collectibles and souvenirs.

And get 2-for-1 admission with this ad.

The Museum is located at the corner of Boerum Place and Schermerhorn Street n Brooklyn Heights. Take the ❷ ❸ or ❹ train to Borough Hall, then walk blocks south.

For additional information and directions, call 718-694-1600. Or visit us at **www.mta.info**.

It'll be 1904 all over again.

NEW YORK TRANSIT MUSEUM

MTA **Metropolitan Transportation Authority** *Going your way*

www.mta.info

2006 Metropolitan Transportation Authority

INTRODUCING . . .

The BAR & LOUNGE DECK

PICK A CARD. DISCOVER A BAR. SAVE MONEY.

* 52 Nightlife Destinations

* Every Card is a $10 Gift Certificate

* Visit www.cityshuffle.com

ALSO BY CITY SHUFFLE: **THE DINER'S DECK** & THE SHOPPING DECK

EVERY CARD IS A $10 GIFT CERTIFICATE

SAVE 20% ON ANY CITY SHUFFLE PURCHASE AT WWW.CITYSHUFFLE.COM

enter "NFTFRIEND" at checkout

TEKSERVE

We have the best deals on Power Macs, MacBooks, iMacs, iPods and more!

Warranty, out of warranty, onsite repairs, data recovery and rentals.

Open weekdays 9am–8pm
Sat 10am–6pm, Sun 12pm–6pm
119 West 23rd St (bet 6th & 7th Ave)
F or R train to 23rd Street

(212) 929 3645

www.tekserve.com

Apple Specialist

Joseph G. Duffy Funeral Home

Burial and Cremation Services

ROBERT AMATO
JAMES STURGES
JAMES WHITTY

255 Ninth Street
Park Slope, Brooklyn

718.499.8700 ■ www.duffyfunerals.com
A wholly owned subsidiary of Alderwoods Group Inc.

Your ad here   **or here.**

We offer half- and full-page advertising options inside each of the **Not For Tourists**™ Guidebooks, includ
multi-city packages for national companies and organizations, as well as space on our website. Advertisin
NFT™ means that the city dwellers who rely on our indispensable guidebooks everyday will literally have
business information right at their fingertips wherever they go. Come on. Everybody's doing it.

For a media kit and space rates, call 212 965 8650 x223 or email us at advertising@notfortourists.

zipcars

live in your neighborhood

For work or play

Reserve online. Walk a block. Drive!
By the hour or day — from $10/hr.

Join at zipcar.com

zipcar.

OPEN 7 DAYS A WEEK
2-4-1 Happy Hour everyday 4-8pm
Mon-Fri 2pm-4am   Sat-Sun Noon-4am

Saturday & Sunday
Make your own Bloody Mary til 8pm
$5 pint Svedka Bloody Marys

Extensive Wine & Liquor selections

Available for private parties,
birthdays, film screenings.
6TVs w/ satellite connection.
Theatre style projection
screens. Wi-fi available.

Cattyshack
Brooklyn's Premiere Club & Bar

249 4th Avenue, between President & Carroll
R to Union, F/G to 4th Ave- 9th St   Must be 21+ with proper ID.
www. cattyshackbklyn.com for details   (718) 230-5740

FASHION MUSIC ART LIFESTYLE

YRB
MAGAZINE

www.yrb.us

Central
Parking System

$100 OFF- 1st month's parking fee when you prepay for the following month!*

Valid at the following locations:

340 East 34th Street (between 1st & 2nd Ave)
140 West 51st Street (between 6th & 7th Ave)
199 Water Street
135 East 47th Street (between Lexington & 3rd Ave)
169 William Street (Corner of Bleecker Street)
212-214 East 47th Street
109 West 56th Street (between 6th & 7th Ave)
29 West 28th Street (between Broadway & 6th Ave)
441 9th Ave (between 9th & 10th Ave)
1 Penn Plaza (between 7th & 8th Ave)
25-43 West 48th Street (between 5th & 6th Ave)
58 West 58th Street (between 5th & 6th Ave)
90 John Street
101 West 56th Street

Well-lit, secure, friendly staff!

For additional information, please contact our
Customer Service Department at:
(800) 836 - 6666

* Discount applied to new monthly accounts only. Must not have been a Central Parking System or Kinney System customer within the past 6 months. Must present NFT ad page to receive promotional discount.

pure. simple. mintwater.™

Made with pure water and real mint, Metromint relieves your thirst, relaxes your mind, freshens your breath, and revives your soul. No sweeteners. No preservatives. No calories. Nothing but all-natural ingredients and surprisingly vibrant taste. Available at Whole Foods, D'Agostino, Gourmet Garage, and other specialty retailers.

METROMINT.

BAM.ORG / 718.636.4100
Brooklyn Academy of Music / Peter Jay Sharp Building / 30 Lafayette Avenue

Photo of Sankai Juku by Jacques Denarnaud

Dance

Theater

Opera

Music

Film

Art

N·I·G·H·T AND D·A·Y

PARK SLOPE'S UNIQUE RESTAURANT * BAR * PERFORMANCE SPACE
* BREAKFAST * LUNCH * DINNER * WEEKEND BRUNCH *
JAZZ * SPOKEN WORD * FLIGHTS & PAIRINGS

*

230 FIFTH AVENUE AT PRESIDENT * BROOKLYN NY 11215
718 * 399 * 2161 * WWW * NIGHTANDDAYRESTAURANT * COM

THE NEW SCHOOL

Eight Schools, One University

www.newschool.edu

THE NEW SCHOOL **FOR GENERAL STUDIES** THE NEW SCHOOL **FOR SOCIAL RESEARCH MILAN** THE NEW SCHOOL **FOR MANAGEMENT AND URBAN POLICY PARSONS** THE NEW SCHOOL **FOR DESIGN** NE **LANG COLLEGE** THE NEW SCHOOL **FOR LIBERAL ARTS MANNES COLLEGE** THE NEW SCHOOL **F** USIC THE NEW SCHOOL **FOR DRAMA** THE NEW SCHOOL **FOR JAZZ AND CONTEMPORARY MUSIC**

We'll map your world.

Have us make you an **NFT™** map! **Not For Tourists™** can bring its award-winning graphic functionality to helping put your organization or event and put you on the map.

The same trademark design that makes our Guidebooks stunning and unique can put your information into a clear and beautiful map package.

NFT™'s team will come up with something new or put a fresh face on something you already have.

We provide custom map-making and information design services to fit your needs—whether simply showing where your organization is located on one of our existing maps, or creating a completely new visual context for the information you wish to convey. **NFT™** will help you—and your audience—make the most of the place you're in, while you're in it.

For more information, call us at 212-965-8650 or visit www.notfortourists.com.

Not For Tourists™
New York City • Brooklyn • Los Angeles • Chicago • San Francisco • Boston • Washington DC • Atlanta • Philadelphia • Que

THE MANHATTAN SKYLINE

Two detailed panoramas portraying the city prior to September 11, 2001. Drawn by John Wagner.

One of the world's most breathtaking sights is the New York City skyline, now captured as never before in two new panoramas called **The Manhattan Skyline Portraits**. Although photographic in appearance, these images are actually illustrations drawn by artist John Wagner. Using a computer as a pen and paintbrush, he carefully crafted a faithful likeness of each building based largely on thousands of photographs he took from the air as well as at ground level.

40 Months from Start to Finish

Drawing the 6.5 miles of Manhattan pictured in both portraits took Wagner more than three years to complete. He began in May 1998 and finished two weeks after the World Trade Center towers were destroyed in September 2001. More than 1,000 buildings take center stage in each drawing. Another 2,500 less-visible structures serve as the skyline's supporting cast, conveying the density of construction so characteristic of Manhattan.

The East River Portrait faithfully records the eastern side of the skyline as seen from Brooklyn and Queens across the East River. **The Hudson River Portrait** shows the west side of the city, looking across the Hudson River from the New Jersey shoreline. Each portrait is sold separately.

Drawn One Building at a Time

World Trade Center
Tower No. 2
1972-2001
110-1362'/415m
Minoru Yamasaki & Assocs.,
Emery Roth & Sons

In order to fit the entire 12 feet of city depicted in each portrait on a single sheet of poster paper, the image is presented in two decks with a pause at 29th Street. Each panorama reads like a two-line sentence, left to right and top to bottom. The size of each print is 18.5 x 75 inches (47 x 190.5 cm). All buildings in the panoramas are drawn using the same scale, which means no structure is diminished in size because of its distance from you, the viewer. All skyscrapers stand tall in these group portraits, even those in the back row. How tall? The Empire State Building measures 5.75 inches tall (15 cm). More than 500 buildings in each Manhattan Skyline portrait are identified. The stories of these buildings are told in these labels, such as the date completed, the street address and the architect. Labels for skyscrapers taller than 700 feet (213 m) also list the height in stories, feet and meters. In addition, many labels include further information of historic interest.

Available at www.notfortourists.com

Not For Tourists™

www.notfortourists.com

New York City · Brooklyn · Los Angeles · Chicago · San Francisco · Boston · Washington DC · Atlanta · Philadelphia · Queens

Street Index

Street	Page	Grid
First Ave		
(1-247)	7	A1/B1
(248-699)	10	A1–B2
(700-1090)	13	A2/B2
(1091-1644)	15	A2/B2
(1645-2128)	17	A2/B2
(2129-2499)	20	A2/B2
1st Pl	1	B1
Second Ave		
(1-239)	6	A2/B2
(231-737)	10	A1/B1
(738-1131)	13	A2/B2
(1132-1649)	15	A2/B2
(1650-2132)	17	A2/B2
(2133-2599)	20	A2/B2
2nd Pl	1	B1
Third Ave		
(1-135)	6	A2
(136-620)	10	A1/B1
(611-999)	13	A1/B1
(1000-1519)	15	A1/B1
(1520-1993)	17	A1/B1
(1994-2362)	20	A1/B1
Fourth Ave	6	A1/A2
Fifth Ave		
(1-82)	6	A1
(69-450)	9	A2/B2
(451-787)	12	A2/B2
(789-1047)	15	A2/B2
(1048-1283)	17	A1/B1
(1284-2230)	19	A2/B2
(2220-2380)	22	B2
Sixth Ave (Ave of the Americas)		
(1-118)	2	A2
(119-551)	5	A2
(552-1039)	9	A1–B2
(1040-1499)	12	A2/B2
Seventh Ave		
(1-68)	5	A2
(69-539)	9	A1/B1
(508-7876)	12	A1/B1
Seventh Ave S	5	A2/B2
Eighth Ave		
(1-66)	5	A1
(80-609)	8	A2/B2
(610-999)	12	A1/B1
(2031-2536)	19	A1/B1
(2537-2998)	22	A1/B1
(2982-3009)	23	B2
Ninth Ave		
(1-55)	5	A1
(56-532)	8	A2/B2
(533-998)	11	A2/B2
(3751-4199)	24	A2
(3785-3884)	25	B2
Tenth Ave		
(1-69)	5	A1
(70-525)	8	A2/B2
(526-998)	11	A2/B2
(3710-3777)	24	A2
(3774-4099)	25	A2/B2
Eleventh Ave		
(27-498)	8	A1/B1/B2
(499-898)	11	A1/B1
(100-699)	8	A1/B1
(467-858)	11	A1/B1
Twelfth Ave	18	A1

Street	Page	Grid
Abraham Kazan St	4	A2
Abraham Pl	4	A2
Academy St	24	A2
Academy St (500-699)	25	B1/B2
Adam Clayton Powell Jr Blvd		
(1800-2309)	19	A1/B1
(2310-2860)	22	A1/B1
Albany St	1	A1
Allen St (1-146)	4	A1
Allen St (147-209)	7	B1
Amsterdam Ave		
(1-528)	14	A2/B2
(529-1009)	16	A2/B2
(1010-1529)	18	A2/B2
(1530-1989)	21	A2/B2
(1990-2699)	23	A2/B2
Ann St	1	A1/A2
Arden St	24	A1
Asser Levy Pl	10	B2
Astor Pl	6	A2
Attorney St (1-83)	4	A1
Attorney St (80-175)	7	B1
Audubon Ave (1-329)	23	A2/B2
Audubon Ave (330-599)	24	A2/B2
Avenue A	7	A1/B1
Avenue B	7	A1/B1
Avenue C	7	A2/B2
Avenue D	7	A2/B2
Avenue of the Finest	3	B2
Bank St	5	A1/A2
Barclay St (1-41)	3	B1
Barclay St (36-139)	2	B1/B2
Barrow St	5	A2/B1/B2
Baruch Dr	7	B2
Baruch Pl	4	A2
Battery Pl	1	B1
Baxter St	3	A1
Bayard St	3	A1/A2
Beach St	2	A1/A2
Beak St	25	B1
Beaver St	1	A2/B1
Bedford St	5	B2
Beekman Pl	13	B2
Beekman St (2-50)	3	B1
Beekman St (51-155)	1	A2
Bennett Ave	24	A1/B1
Benson Pl	3	A1
Bethune St	5	A1
Bialystoker Pl	4	A2
Bishops Ln	2	B1
Bleecker St (1-206)	6	B1/B2
Bleecker St (207-425)	5	A1/A2/B2
Bogardus Pl	24	A1
Bond St	6	B1/B2
Bowery (1-165)	3	A2
Bowery (166-364)	6	B2
Bradhurst Ave	21	A2/B2
Bridge St	1	B2
Broad St	1	A1/A2/B2
Broadway		
(1-222)	1	A1/B1
(219-508)	3	A1/B1
(509-858)	6	A1/B1
(857-1422)	9	A1/A2/B2
(1423-1812)	12	A1/B1
(1819-2350)	14	A1/A2/B1
(2351-2829)	16	A1/B1

Street	Page	Grid
Broadway		
(2826-3349)	18	A1/B1
(3350-3809)	21	A1/B1
(3810-4282)	23	A1/B2
(4280-4753)	24	A1/B1
(4731-5488)	25	A2/B1/B2
Broadway Aly	10	B1
Broadway Ter	24	A1
Brooklyn Battery Tunl	1	B1
Brooklyn Brdg	3	B2
Brooklyn Bridge Appr	3	B2
Broome St (83-274)	4	A1/A2
Broome St (275-460)	3	A1/A2
Broome St (461-509)	2	A2
Broome St (501-532)	6	B1
Broome St (525-578)	5	B2
Cabrini Blvd (1-117)	23	A1
Cabrini Blvd (95-315)	24	B1
Canal St (1-77)	4	A1
Canal St (78-324)	3	A1/A2
Canal St (325-492)	2	A1/A2
Canal St (493-548)	5	B2
Cardinal Hayes Pl	3	B2
Carlisle St	1	A1
Carmine St	5	B2
Cathedral Pky (300-303)	19	B1
Cathedral Pky (303-699)	18	B1/B2
Catherine Ln	3	A1
Catherine St (9-76)	3	B2
Catherine St (68-99)	4	B1
Cedar St	1	A1/A2
Central Park N	19	B1/B2
Central Park S	12	A1/A2
Central Park W (1-255)	14	A2/B2
Central Park W (256-488)	16	A2/B2
Centre Market Pl	3	A1
Centre St	3	A1/B1
Chambers St (1-104)	3	B1
Chambers St (87-350)	2	B1/B2
Charles Ln	5	A1
Charles St	5	A1/A2
Charlton St	5	B2
Chatham Sq	3	B2
Cherokee Pl	15	A2
Cherry St	4	A1/A2/B1
Chisum Pl	22	B2
Chittenden Ave	24	B1
Christopher St	5	A2/B1
Chrystie St (43-142)	3	A2
Chrystie St (139-235)	6	B2
Church St (1-83)	1	A1
Church St (84-337)	2	A1
Claremont Ave	18	A1/B1
Clarkson St	5	B1/B2
Cleveland Pl	6	B2
Cliff St	1	A2
Clinton St (1-109)	7	B1
Clinton St (110-284)	4	A1/A2
Coenties Aly	1	B2
Coenties Slip	1	B2
Collister St	2	A1
Columbia St (21-3301)	4	A2
Columbia St (82-8799)	7	B2
Columbus Ave (1-529)	14	A2/B2
Columbus Ave (530-988)	16	A2/B2
Columbus Cir	14	B2
Commerce St	5	B2

Map 6 · Washington Sq./NYU/SoHo

Blown up and hung.

Your favorite **NFT** map as a poster. Any **Not For Tourists** map can be made into a 24"x 36" poster. These large wall maps are taken directly from the pages of the **Not For Tourists** Guidebooks.

Order at www.notfortourists.com

NOT FOR TOURISTS™ Guidebooks

Your ad here

or here.

We offer half- and full-page advertising options inside each of the **Not For Tourists™** Guidebooks, including multi-city packages for national companies and organizations, as well as space on our website. Advertising in **NFT™** means that the city dwellers who rely on our indispensable guidebooks everyday will literally have your business information right at their fingertips wherever they go. Come on. Everybody's doing it.

For a media kit and space rates, call 212 965 8650 x223 or email us at advertising@notfortourists.com

Address Locator

Streets	Riverside	West End	Broadway	Amsterdam	Columbus	C.P.W.	Central Park
110-116	370-440		2800-2950	995-1120			
102-110	290-370	850-920	2675-2800	856-995	850-1021	419-500	
96-102	240-290	737-850	2554-2675	733-856	740-850	360-419	
90-96	180-240	620-737	2440-2554	620-733	621-740	300-360	
84-90	120-180	500-619	2321-2439	500-619	501-620	241-295	
78-84	60-120	380-499	2201-2320	380-499	381-500	239-241	
72-78	1-60	262-379	2081-2200	261-379	261-380	121-239	
66-72		122-261	1961-2079	140-260	141-260	65-115	
58-66		2-121	1791-1960	1-139	2-140	0-65	

Streets	12th Ave.	11th Ave.	Broadway	10th Ave.	9th Ave.	8th Ave.	7th Ave.	6th Ave.
52-58	710-850	741-854	1674-1791	772-889	782-907	870-992	798-921	1301-1419
46-52	600-710	625-740	1551-1673	654-770	662-781	735-869	701-797	1180-1297
40-46	480-600	503-624	1440-1550	538-653	432-662	620-734	560-701	1061-1178
34-40	360-480	405-502	Macy's-1439	430-537	431-432	480-619	442-559	1060-1061
28-34	240-360	282-404	1178-1282	314-429	314-431	362-479	322-442	815-1060
22-28	0-240	162-281	940-1177	210-313	198-313	236-361	210-321	696-814
14-22		26-161	842-940	58-209	44-197	80-235	64-209	5520-695
8-14			748-842	0-58	0-44	0-80	2-64	420-520
Houston-8			610-748					244-402